THE MEDIEVAL READER

Lion, symbol of the Evangelist Mark

THE MEDIEVAL READER

Edited by

Norman F. Cantor

 HarperPerennial

A Division of HarperCollins*Publishers*

A hardcover edition of this book was published in 1994 by
HarperCollins Publishers, Inc.

Copyright acknowledgments appear on pages 366-368.

        HarperCollins books may be purchased for educational,
business, or sales promotional use. For information, please
write: Special Markets Department, HarperCollins Publishers,
Inc., 10 East 53rd Street, New York, New York 10022.

First HarperPerennial Edition published 1995.

The Library of Congress has catalogued the hardcover
edition as follows:

The Medieval reader / edited by Norman F. Cantor. —
1st ed.
        p. cm.
    Includes bibliographical references and index.
    ISBN 0-06-270102-9
    1. Middle Ages—History—Sources.
I. Cantor, Norman F.
    D113.M42   1994
    956—dc20   94-1981

                    ISBN 0-06-272055-4
            98 99 PS/RRD 10 9 8 7

CONTENTS

DYNAMIC INTERACTION OF THE THREE ELEMENTS

ALIENATED SEGMENTS AND UNRESOLVED PROBLEMS

PREFACE

I undertook this anthology, at the suggestion of Maron Waxman, former Editorial Director of HarperReference because I thought a comprehensive, up-to-date book of this nature would provide a real service to the general reader and the college and high school student. The deployment of a thematic rather than chronological organization of this *Reader* and the head notes to the selections allows comprehension of the book's content without previous knowledge of medieval history. Close reading of the material of this volume will make anyone knowledgeable in ways of medieval thought and behavior, even starting from a zero base.

For those users of the book who have or are currently taking courses in medieval history, the book will illustrate main themes they are examining and provide easy access to key writings of important people and exemplary documents. Students of medieval literature or art history or philosophy will find that this book provides a comprehensive context for their work.

In choosing and editing the selections, readability as well as intrinsic importance has conditioned the selections made and the way they have been edited.

A generous budget provided by HarperCollins for obtaining copyright permissions has allowed the consistent use of good translations.

Mr. John P. Rocco, a former undergraduate student of mine at New York University and now a doctoral candidate in art history at the University of Chicago, did the picture research under my direction.

I also wish to thank the following:

Robert A. Kaplan, the HarperCollins editor on the project.

My literary agent, Alexander Hoyt.

Nelly Fontanez, my secretary, for her invaluable assistance in putting the manuscript together.

The librarians at the Bobst Library of New York University and the Firestone Library of Princeton University for their unfailing cooperation and courtesy.

The publishers and scholars who granted copyright permission. sometimes for only modest fees.

Art Resources which allowed reproduction of the pictures from their excellent collection.

GENERAL INTRODUCTION

The Middle Ages are the era of Western European and Mediterranean history from the fourth century to the fifteenth century A.D., the intermediate time between the decline of the Roman empire and the Italian Renaissance, or from a religious perspective between the accession of the first Christian Roman Emperor in 312 and the outbreak of the Protestant Reformation in 1517.

The term **medieval civilization** embraces a group of European countries stretching from Ireland in the West to the Oder River in the east. That river approximates the dividing line between eastern Germany and the Slavic societies, although the Germans created many colonial outposts, some of which still exist, beyond the Oder and within the Slavic world. The term medieval geographically also embraces the north-south European axis from Scandinavian countries down to Spain and Sicily and the complex north-shore Mediterranean cultures.

Here in the South there was a powerful interaction with Muslim entities. Farther to the east, beyond Italy on its Adriatic side, stretched the world of Byzantium centered on Constantinople, with its separate Greek language and Greek church.

By and large, the Middle Ages examined in this book comprise the culture, society, government, and law of Latin Catholicism, looking forward to structural foundation of modern western Europe and the Americas. The Middle Ages are direct formative antecedents of the modern European and American world.

In reading the Middle Ages, in hearing its voices, recreating with our eye and mind its discourse, we are engaged not merely in an act of piety or memorializing. We are experiencing immediately and overwhelmingly a vibrant, creative, and complex civilization and accessing systems of value, ideas, and behavior that are capable of present-day appreciation. The Middle Ages are important to us not only for their time and place in the scheme of world history, or as a segment of Western Civilization in its genesis and destiny. The Middle Ages represent a set of assumptions, attitudes, hopes, and expectations that together comprise an identifiable way of comprehending the world and a shaping ethos for human behavior that is still a meaningful moral and ideological choice at the end of the twentieth century.

The Middle Ages are popular today. No one really knows why, but in approximately thirty years cycles—during the 1920's, from 1955 to 1965, and now since about 1990—there has been an upsurge in an already substantial intervening interest in the Middle Ages by the American reading public and on American campuses. The history, literature, and art of Western Europe from the fourth to the end of the fifteenth centuries, and particularly in the intensely creative and vibrant four centuries after 1100 A.D. today draw a very strong level of interest and curiosity.

But how to get access to the Middle Ages, how to encounter the actual voices of medieval people? Obviously, the best way is to read for oneself, with introductory guidance, medieval writers as they grapple with faith, hope, and love. Unless some special help is given, this is not an easy thing to do, even if the language problem is surmounted by the availibilty of reliable translations from Latin and the prolific vernacular languages of the Middle Ages—medieval forms of English, French, German, Spanish and Italian.

The biggest obstacle for the reading public's access to medieval writings is bulk. The imaginative literature and other surviving documents from the Middle Ages are enormous in volume—in published form they fill at least two thousand large volumes. Careful selection is called for on behalf of the lay reader and the college student to comprise a mosaic of the most original, persuasive, representative, and relevant expressions of the ideas, feelings, and experiences of the medieval European world.

The Medieval Reader is intended to be that highly useful anthology.

How can a one volume anthology provide access to medieval writings, so that the reader can directly experience the ethos, passions, anxieties, and triumphs of the medieval age? Here we have an anthology of ample size but it is only one book set against the huge library of medieval writing. How may this anthology communicate not only the essentials of medieval civilization but in such a way that the reader, whether from the general public or from the college student population, can tune in sufficiently to the nuances of medieval thought and feeling so as to render a personal judgment about aspects of medieval culture and society?

Two strategies of organization and exposition are necessary to achieve this goal. First we have to present medieval writings in a thematic, topical way—in a structured program—not according to conventional chronology with its haphazard assembly of events. A topical approach will bring into sharp focus the cultural formations, social patterns, and critical forces that activated medieval civilization. Fortunately, historical research and narrative on the Middle Ages has been so richly detailed that upon reflection an underlying paradigm or essential format of the medieval world can be perceived. Using that perception of the paradigmatic nature of the Middle Ages, the selections in this anthology can be organized for purposes of recognition and understanding of the constituent elements of medieval times.

Secondly, imaginative literature and reproductions of medieval art must be extensively offered in the anthology because in these media the authentic voice and vision of the Middle Ages are directly addressed to the reading audience. The selections of imaginative literature and art allow for personal immersion in medieval sense and sensibility.

These two conditions are the determining principles in the shaping of *The Medieval Reader*. The result is this unique kind of anthology of medieval writings, supplemented by medieval art-work on themes stressed in the writing. Not only does this book provide an extensive array of medieval voices communicating directly with the reader. These communications are presented in a programmed, structured way so that the reader is led step by step to understanding the fundamentals of medieval culture and society. Imaginative literature has been fully utilized, alongside more mundane, practical kinds of documentation, to give the reader the opportunity for emotional as well as intellectual communication with medieval modes of feeling and experience. The thematic, structured form of this book is designed to facilitate the drawing of personal conclusions about the meaning of the Middle Ages for the world of today.

Sit down and read this book right through, or dip into here and there at random, or focus on a particular aspect of the medieval world, and you will discover shades of meaning and reflective insights that relate our reason and sensibility directly with the Middle Ages.

A lot happened in the medieval centuries. Historical research, from the generous surviving documentation, has revealed an infinite amount of particular events that occurred then. But within this diverse congeries of churning events, bold continuing patterns are perceptible. Medieval culture and society persistently functioned along the lives of an identifiable structured model.

The format of this continuing, active medieval paradigm is threefold:

The Nobility. Aristocratic Heroism and Militarism

The Church. Hierarchic Authority and Tradition

Middle Class Ethos. Sensibility and Sentiment

The **nobility** refers to the 200–300 great families of western Europe who controlled most of the landed wealth and nearly all the state power and were committed to a code of behavior valorizing masculine heroism, extraordinary military strength, and patriarchal power.

The **Church** refers to the universal continuing institution that dominated religion, learning, and education and the visual arts and disseminated a hierarchic (laddered step) view of the world that affected social structures and political systems as well as ecclesiastical organization.

Middle Class refers not only to the urban bourgeois but also to the rural middle class, the lower nobility, called in England first the knights and later the gentry, and the wealthier and literate peasantry and urban artisans. From these **middle class** social groups came critically rational ideas and innovative moral and religious feelings that represented important change and progress in medieval culture and society toward the modern, post-medieval world.

Medieval civilization may therefore be visualized as a triangle, with the nobility's aristocratic heroism as the base and the church's hierarchic vision and middle class sensibility as the other two sides.

All three sides of the medieval structure were interactive with one another. They were functions of one another. They influenced each other. Their interaction generated the finest examples of medieval literature and art and made possible the growth of social and political institutions that remain central to our way of life—such as churches, universities, parliaments, and the common law. But the integrity and distinctiveness of each of the three sides of medieval culture and society must be appreciated because each side contained highly innovative and creative characteristics that made indispensable contributions to the ultimate melded pattern of medieval civilization.

In this book, to gain an effective reading of mind and society, the three-fold medieval essentials, each side of the basic triangle will **first** be exhibited in as pure a form as ever existed between 300 and 1500.

Then in the **second** part of the book we shall examine interactive expressions, two or three of the paradigmatic elements affecting another. This will immerse us in many of the most dynamic and attractive records of the medieval world and still famous medieval expressions.

In the **third** part of this book we shall consider the problems, adversities, and crises stemming from dysfunctions, reactions, tensions, and conflicts that the three-fold core nature of medieval civilization engendered.

Finally, we shall examine efforts at reintegration, resolution, and pacification, attempts at conflict resolution and absorption of the non-included others and incorporation of diversities into the central core.

The Medieval Reader therefore follows a functionally thematic rather than a chronological approach to layout of writings and pictures:

PART ONE. THE ESSENTIAL THREEFOLD PARADIGM.
PART TWO. DYNAMIC INTERACTION OF THE THREE ELEMENTS.
PART THREE. ALIENATED SEGMENTS AND UNRESOLVED PROBLEMS.
PART FOUR. REINTEGRATION AND INCLUSION.

This structural approach will not only make the particular texts and illustrations more meaningful but will allow each reader to make an independent judgment on the moral value and intellectual significance of the medieval heritage for our own cultural and social situation.

The more than hundred selections from exemplary and persuasive medieval writings supplemented by the sixty related pictures are thus organized in the form of articulated thematic structures. This will enable the reader to communicate with and understand medieval civilization in a wide-ranging, insightful and immediate way, and to make personal judgments on the relevance and value of the medieval heritage.

You can understand medieval world in terms of a chronological narrative. There is of course intellectual value in that. But you can also understand the medieval world in the form of a dynamic structure in which perpetual structural forces operate, constantly impinge upon one another, and generate an interaction that is represented in the literature, arts, institutions, behavior patterns, and mental images we appreciate as distinctively medieval and want to gain immediate access to and communicate with. It is this latter approach to the Middle Ages that this book employs. It has the advantage of immediate comprehension of the best that the European Middle Ages had to offer, of getting to the important things and leaving marginal detail and idiosyncratic fragments for other occasions, gaining for now immediate contact with the authentic voices of the Middle Ages. These voices expressed in imaginative literature and reflected in visual art are among the triumphs of the human spirit. This is therefore a book to be read not only once, but to be returned to many times for insight and inspiration. It is a coded library of medieval thought and feeling.

It is the ultimate intention of the editor that *The Medieval Reader* will provide not only a readily accessible overview and structural discourse. It is hoped via this anthology to transcend the historical boundaries of medieval studies and provide a design for stimulating of a revival of medievalism at the turning of the present millennium.

THE MEDIEVAL READER

Abraham (as Knight) and Melchisedek (as Priest)

THE ESSENTIAL THREEFOLD PARADIGM

NOBILITY
CHURCH
THE MIDDLE CLASS

Emperor Charlemagne enthroned holding sceptre and cross-inscribed orb, flanked by Roland and Oliver

THE NOBILITY. ARISTOCRATIC HEROISM AND MILITARISM

The strong man. The great warrior. The hero. He provides protection, sustenance, and leadership to a family, to an entourage, to a whole social group. This conviction was essential to the medieval world. The superior capacity of a strong man for fighting—this remained central to the ethos and operation of medieval culture and society.

Around this social fact developed what anthropologists call *a shame culture,* or, put more positively, we may call it a culture committed to aristocratic honor. The hero, the strong man, the robust male of noble birth, the warrior group patriarchal leader—these terms are almost, if not totally, identical—must never act so as to bring shame on himself by showing cowardice, by flinching from collective battle or individual duel. He is prepared to fight the enemy to the death—preferably the enemy's, but possibly his own—and in so doing he sustains his personal honor and transmits this aura of honor to his family, his entourage, his nation.

When the noble hero wins, good things flow to his kin, associates, and dependents—security, prosperity (in the early Middle Ages the hero is often called the "booty-giver"; joined to the possession of land, the medieval nobility's shame culture becomes "feudalism," and a very large feudal estate was indeed called an "honor"), societal continuity, and political power. But the core of military skill and physical strength always remains essential—whether the need is to fight dragons in the midst of pristine Germanic times, to fight the Moors on the Spanish frontiers, to contend against neighboring lords, or to lead elaborate knightly contingents into battle in the Hundred Years War of the fourteenth century.

The nobility are the base of the medieval triangle. By a long and complex process going back to the fifth century, out of old Roman families that had ruled the Mediterranean world for many centuries, and from among new Germanic warrior families and their commingling with the Romans, out of the stress of the political and economic turmoil that followed the collapse of the Roman Empire in Western Europe and the barbarian invasions, there had emerged by 900 A.D. between 200 and 300 great families of the higher nobility, also called the aristocracy. They owned, by one legal mechanism or another, at least eighty percent of the arable land in Europe. They ruled over millions of dependent peasants—usually serfs legally bound to the land. The nobility's sons governed the church as bishops and abbots, and their daughters staffed the nunneries. The highest stratum of the nobility held fancy political titles—emperor, king, duke, count—and slowly these magnates gathered around them a staff of bureaucrats and imposed systems of law and taxation on society. They wanted law and order but in a way that entirely favored themselves.

Whatever else the aristocracy did—in politics, religion, art, and literature—it was military valor and personal strength and courage that had originally made the great noble families powerful in society, and this physical prowess was continually necessary to sustain their position in society. Centered with their landed wealth and political authority as the basis of medieval society, the nobility could effectively and subtly interact with the other sides of the medieval triangle, the church and the middle class. But heroism and military honor had to be maintained if the nobility was to continue its fundamental role. The glamor of heroism, the training for fighting, the struggle for domination—these conditions remained essential to the life of the nobility, no matter the more peaceful and intellectual ingredients that eventually became included in their mind-set and behavior.

THE CID

The twelfth-century Spanish epic recounting the heroic exploits of Ruy Diaz of Vivar, El Cid Campeador, exhibits the noble hero in his purest form. Essentially he is loyal to no one except his followers. The Cid not only hammers away at the Muslim Moorish enemy, but he also has a falling out with the Christian King Alfonso. Thereby he is a loner. The Cid is immensely strong and unflinchingly brave, but he is also a shrewd master of tactics. He sheds blood freely, but he doesn't massacre civilians unnecessarily. He tries to avoid placing his army in a hazardous situation. He enriches his followers and takes for himself a lavishly enriching but still only reasonable proportion of military booty. The Cid is everything the noble hero is supposed to be.

When all the booty had been collected together the fortunate Cid, reflecting that King Alfonso might arrive with his army and seek to harm him and his vassals, ordered those charged with the task to distribute all this wealth, writing down every man's share. The gains were great, one hundred marks falling to the share of each knight and half that amount to each foot soldier, the Cid receiving his customary fifth share. He could not sell or give it away, and as he did not wish to take the men and women prisoners with him, he parleyed with the inhabitants of Castejón and sent word to those of Hita and Guadalajara, asking how much they would offer for his share—even with what the Moors would give they would make a great gain. The Moors calculated the value of the property at three thousand silver marks, and the Cid was satisfied with this gift, which was paid in full on the third day. The Cid reckoned that he and his men should not remain in the fortress, for though he could indeed hold it, there would be no water there. 'The

Moors' (he thought) 'are at peace, having a pact in writing, and King Alfonso might come after us with his entire army, so I shall leave Castejón.' (Then he said) 'Listen to me, my men, and Minaya Álvar Fáñez.

Do not take in bad part what I am about to say. We cannot remain in Castejón, for King Alfonso is not far off and will come in search of us. I do not wish to destroy the fortress, so I shall set free one hundred Moorish men and their women, that they may not blame me for taking it from them. You are all well provided for and no one has been left unpaid. Let us ride away tomorrow morning, for I should not like to fight against my lord, King Alfonso.' The Cid's decision pleased them all. They went away from the fortress which they had taken with a rich booty and the blessings of the Moorish men and women. They rode at full speed up the river Henares, traversed the Alcarria and went past the caves of Anguita. There they crossed the river (Tajuña) and entered Campo Taranz, riding down through those lands as quickly as they could, taking great booty as they went. At length the Cid pitched his camp between Ariza and Cetina. The Moors were at a loss to know what his plan might be. The next day the Cid, the man from Vivar, struck camp, passed Alhama and went down the river bend and past Bubierca and Ateca, which is farther on. Then he encamped near Alcocer on a great rounded height. As the river Jalón ran past it their water could not be cut off, so the Cid made up his mind to take Alcocer.

He took firm possession of the slopes, placing some of his men towards the mountain side and some by the river. The good Campeador ordered his men to make a trench round the hill quite close to the river bank to prevent attack by day or by night and to let the Moors know that he meant to settle down there.

The news spread through the countryside that the Cid, having left the land of the Christians to come among the Moors, had established his camp there, and they did not dare to cultivate their fields with him so near at hand. The Cid and his vassals were on the watch and they levied tribute from the fortress of Alcocer. The inhabitants of Alcocer, Ateca and Terrer all paid tribute to the Cid.

And you can understand that those of Calatayud felt their hearts sink. The Cid lay encamped there for fifteen weeks, and when he realised that Alcocer was unlikely to surrender he contrived a stratagem which he proceeded to put into practice at once. He left one tent standing and took the others away; he then made off down the Jalón with banner flying and the men in their coats of mail with swords at their belts. It was a wily move to draw them out by a trick. The men of Alcocer watched them go, and how delighted they were! (They thought) 'The Cid is short of bread and fodder, he has been forced to take up the tents against his will, leaving one behind. The Cid has gone off' (they thought) 'as if fleeing from defeat. Let us sally out to the attack and win great booty before the men of Terrer get at it. If they do they won't give us a penny. He shall pay us back double the tribute he has collected.' They rushed from Alcocer in

the greatest haste. When the Cid saw them come out he made off as if in flight. Down the river Jalón he went, with all his men around him. The inhabitants of Alcocer said: 'Our prey is escaping!' Great and small, out they came, thinking of nothing but the loot they might get, leaving the gates wide open and unguarded. The worthy Campeador looked round and saw that there was a good distance between them and the fortress. Then he ordered his standard to turn back, and his knights spurred their horses to full speed. 'Strike them, my good knights' (he cried), 'all of you, fearlessly! With the help of God the victory is ours.' They came to grips with the Moors on the flat ground. What great joy they felt that morning! The Cid and Álvar Fáñez spurred ahead, for they had good horses that carried them as swiftly as heart could wish. They cut right into the space between the Moors and the fortress. The Cid's vassals dealt pitiless blows and in a short time they had killed three hundred Moors. While the Moors in the trap uttered loud cries, those who had gone ahead disengaged, reached the fortress and waited at the gate with drawn swords. The rest, victorious in the fight, came up soon after. Note that it was by this trick that the Cid took Alcocer.

Pedro Bermúdez arrived, bearing the standard, and planted it on the highest point. The ever fortunate Cid spoke these words: 'Thanks be to God in Heaven and to all his saints. Now we shall have better lodging for the horses and their masters.

Listen to me, Álvar Fáñez, and all my knights. We have gained great wealth in capturing this stronghold; many Moors lie dead and few remain alive. We shall not be able to sell our captives, whether men or women. We should gain nothing by cutting off their heads. Let us allow them to return to the town, for we are masters here. We shall occupy their houses and make them serve us.'

While the Cid was arranging the disposal of the booty in Alcocer, he sent for the tent he had left standing. The inhabitants of Ateca, Terrer and Calatayud were greatly perturbed by these events, and sent a message to the King of Valencia, saying: 'Someone called Ruy Díaz of Vivar, the Cid, has incurred the anger of King Alfonso, who has banished him. He encamped before the stronghold of Alcocer and he got them out by a trick and took the fortress. If you do not come to our aid you will lose Ateca, Terrer and Calatayud, which cannot escape—all will go from bad to worse along the river Jalón and the same thing will happen at the Jiloca on the other side.' When King Mu'taman received this message he was much distressed. 'I have three Moorish leaders here at my court' (he said). 'Two of you go without delay, taking with you three thousand fully armed Moors. With the help of the frontier Moors take him alive and bring him here to me. He will have to answer for his invasion of my land.' Three thousand Moors mounted and rode off. They arrived at Segorbe to spend the night there, and next morning they set off again and reached Cella at nightfall. They decided to send for the frontier Moors, who immediately flocked in from all sides. They then left Cella, which people call Cella de Canal, rode all day without rest and arrived at Calatayud, where they lay encamped that night. Messengers were sent throughout the whole region and men assembled in vast numbers to join the two leaders, Fáriz and Galve, who then proceeded to besiege the Cid in Alcocer.

They pitched their tents and took up their positions, and their forces increased to enormous proportions. The scouts sent out by the Moors kept watch day and night under arms—they were many in number, for it was a large army. They found a way of cutting off the water from the Cid's men. His troops were eager to make a sortie, but the Cid firmly forbade it. The siege lasted three full weeks. [The Cid said to his followers]: 'Let us all go out and none remain behind but two foot soldiers to guard the gate. If we perish on the field our enemies will enter the fortress, but if we win the battle we shall be richer than ever. You, Pedro Bermúdez, take my standard; you will carry it loyally like the good soldier you are, but do not advance unless I give you the command.' Bermúdez kissed the Cid's hand and received the standard. They opened the gates and sallied out. The Moorish scouts saw this and returned to the camp to report it. What eagerness there was among the Moors to arm themselves! And they could be seen ranging themselves in battle order. The noise of the drums seemed to make the earth quake. There were two main banners on the Moorish side and they formed two battle lines of mixed infantry in countless numbers. The Moors advanced all along the line to attack the Cid and his followers. 'Stay where you are, my men' (said the Cid), 'and let none break ranks till I give the word of command.' But Pedro Bermúdez could hold out no longer; he held the standard and spurred on his horse, crying: 'God be on your side, loyal Campeador! I am going to plant your banner in the chief Moorish battle line. We shall see how all your true vassals rush to its defence.' The Cid cried, 'Stop, in Heaven's name!' Pedro Bermúdez answered: 'There is no going back now!' He set spurs to his horse and carried the standard into the main line of battle. The Moors, eager to capture the Cid's standard, dealt him mighty blows, but without piercing his armour. Then the Campeador spoke: 'To his aid, for pity's sake!'

The men clasped their shields to their hearts and lowered their lances, each with its pennon flying. With heads bent down over their saddlebows, they dashed to the attack courageously. The Cid, sure of success, shouted his battle cry: 'Attack them, my knights, for the love of God! I am Ruy Díaz of Vivar, the Cid Campeador!' They assailed the Moorish ranks, where Pedro Bermúdez was already in the thick of the fight. There were three hundred knights with lance and pennon, and with every lance-thrust a Moor fell dead. On returning to the charge they killed as many more.

Who could say how many lances rose and fell, how many shields were pierced, coats of mail torn asunder and white pennons stained red with blood, how many riderless horses ranged the field? The Moors called on Muhammad and the Christians on St James. In a short time one thousand three hundred Moors fell dead upon the field.

THE SONG OF ROLAND: SHAME AND HONOR

The French epic *Roland,* written around 1100, shows the moral tensions and difficult choices facing a noble hero arising from the ethos of a shame culture. Shaped by the poet's dramatic skill in exhibiting hard and controversial choices, *Roland* is the finest single work of medieval heroic literature. *Roland* is based on an incident in the wars of the Emperor Charlemagne against the Moslem Moors in northern Spain in the late eighth century. After deciding to withdraw from Spain—the only war Charlemagne lost—the Emperor places his nephew, Count Roland, in the charge of the rearguard as the French knights withdraw through a pass in the Pyrenees. Count Roland with his friend Oliver and a fighting bishop as leaders of the rearguard are hard-pressed by the Moorish king Marsilion and a much larger Arab army. But Roland refuses until too late to sound his horn summoning the help of Charlemagne and the main body of the French army, for that would, Roland believes, indicate he is cowardly and would bring shame on himself and the French nobility. Eventually, after most of his army has fallen in battle, Roland decides to summon help. The poet raises the difficult issue of what is the dividing line between military honor and reckless folly, a persistent life-and-death question for medieval nobility and one of course still critical for all military conduct.

The Franks began anew,
the blows strike hard, and the fighting is bitter;
there is a painful loss of Christian men.
To have seen them, Roland and Oliver,
these fighting men, striking down with their
    swords,
the Archbishop with them, striking with his
    lance!
One can recount the number these three killed:
it is written—in charters, in documents;
the Geste tells it: it was more than four thousand.
Through four assaults all went well with our men;
then comes the fifth, and that one crushes them.
They are killed, all these warriors of France,
all but sixty, whom the Lord God has spared:
they will die too, but first sell themselves dear.
    AOI.

Count Roland sees the great loss of his men
calls on his companion, on Oliver:
"Lord, Companion, in God's name, what would
    you do?
All these good men you see stretched on the
    ground.

We can mourn for sweet France, fair land of
    France!
a desert now, stripped of such great vassals.
Oh King, and friend, if only you were here!
Oliver, Brother, how shall we manage it?
What shall we do to get word to the King?"
Said Oliver: "I don't see any way.
I would rather die now than hear us shamed." AOI.

And Roland said: "I'll sound the olifant,
Charles will hear it, drawing through the passes,
I promise you, the Franks will return at once."
Said Oliver: "That would be a great disgrace,
a dishonor and reproach to all your kin,
the shame of it would last them all their lives.
When I urged it, you would not hear of it;
you will not do it now with my consent.
It is not acting bravely to sound it now—
look at your arms, they are covered with blood."
The Count replies: "I've fought here like a lord."
    AOI.

And Roland says: "We are in a rough battle.
I'll sound the olifant, Charles will hear it."

Said Oliver: "No good vassal would do it.
When I urged it, friend, you did not think it right.
If Charles were here, we'd come out with no
        losses.
Those men down there—no blame can fall on
        them. . . ."

And Roland said: "Why are you angry at me?"
Oliver answers: "Companion, it is your doing.
I will tell you what makes a vassal good:
        it is judgment, it is never madness;
restraint is worth more than the raw nerve of a
        fool.
Frenchmen are dead because of your wildness.
And what service will Charles ever have from us?
If you had trusted me, my lord would be here,
we would have fought this battle through to the
        end,
Marsilion [King the Moors, leader of the enemy]
        would be dead, or our prisoner.
Roland, your prowess—had we never seen it!
And now, dear friend, we've seen the last of it.
No more aid from us now for Charlemagne,
a man without equal till Judgment Day,
you will die here, and your death will shame
        France.
We kept faith, you and I, we were companions;
        and everything we were will end today.
We part before evening, and it will be hard." AOI.

Turpin the Archbishop hears their bitter words,
digs hard into his horse with golden spurs
and rides to them; begins to set them right:
"You, Lord Roland, and you, Lord Oliver,
I beg you in God's name do not quarrel.
To sound the horn could not help us now, true,
but still it is far better that you do it:
let the King come, he can avenge us then—
these men of Spain must not go home exulting!
Our French will come, they'll get down on their
        feet,
and find us here—we'll be dead, cut to pieces.
They will lift us into coffins on the backs of mules,
and weep for us, in rage and pain and grief,
and bury us in the courts of churches;
and we will not be eaten by wolves or pigs or
        dogs."
Roland replies, "Lord, you have spoken well." AOI.

Roland has put the olifant [horn] to his mouth,
he sets it well, sounds it with all his strength.
The hills are high, and that voice ranges far,
they heard it echo thirty great leagues away.
King Charles heard it, and all his faithful men.
And the King says: "Our men are in a battle."
And Ganelon disputed him and said:
"Had someone else said that, I'd call him liar!" AOI.

And now the mighty effort of Roland the Count:
he sounds his olifant; his pain is great,
and from his mouth the bright blood comes leap-
        ing out,
and the temple bursts in his forehead.
That horn, in Roland's hands, has a mighty voice:
King Charles hears it drawing through the passes.
Naimon heard it, the Franks listen to it.
And the King said: "I hear Count Roland's horn;
he'd never sound it unless he had a battle."
Says Ganelon: "Now no more talk of battles!
You are old now, your hair is white as snow,
the things you say make you sound like a child.
You know Roland and that wild pride of his—
what a wonder God has suffered it so long!
Remember? he took Noples without your com-
        mand:
the Saracens rode out, to break the siege;
they fought with him, the great vassal Roland.
Afterwards he used the streams to wash the blood
from the meadows: so that nothing would show.
He blasts his horn all day to catch a rabbit,
he's strutting now before his peers and
        bragging—
who under heaven would dare meet him on the
        field?
So now: ride on! Why do you keep on stopping?
The Land of Fathers lies far ahead of us." AOI.

The blood leaping from Count Roland's mouth,
the temple broken with effort in his forehead,
he sounds his horn in great travail and pain.
King Charles heard it, and his French listen hard.
And the King said: "That horn has a long breath!"
Naimon answers: "It is a baron's breath.
There is a battle there, I know there is.
He [Ganelon] betrayed him! and now asks you to
        fail him!
Put on your armor! Lord, shout your battle cry,

and save the noble barons of your house!
You hear Roland's call. He is in trouble."
The Emperor commanded the horns to sound,
the French dismount, and they put on their armor:
their hauberks, their helmets, their gold-dressed
swords,
their handsome shields; and take up their great
lances,
the gonfalons of white and red and blue.
The barons of that host mount their war horses
and spur them hard the whole length of the pass;
and every man of them says to the other:
"If only we find Roland before he's killed,
we'll stand with him, and then we'll do some
fighting!"
What does it matter what they say? They are too
late.

It is the end of day, and full of light,
arms and armor are ablaze in the sun,
and fire flashes from hauberks and helmets,
and from those shields, painted fair with flowers,
and from those lances, those gold-dressed gon-
fanons.
The Emperor rides on in rage and sorrow,
the men of France indignant and full of grief.
There is no man of them who does not weep,
they are in fear for the life of Roland.
The King commands: seize Ganelon the Count!
and gave him over to the cooks of his house;
summons the master cook, their chief, Besgun:
"Guard him for me like the traitor he is:
he has betrayed the barons of my house."
Besgun takes him, sets his kitchen comrades,
a hundred men, the best, the worst, on him;
and they tear out his beard and his mustache,
each one strikes him four good blows with his
fist;
and they lay into him with cudgels and sticks,
put an iron collar around his neck
and chain him up, as they would chain a bear;
dumped him, in dishonor, on a packhorse,
and guard him well till they give him back to
Charles.

High are the hills, and tenebrous, and vast, AOI.
the valleys deep, the raging waters swift;

to the rear, to the front, the trumpets sound:
they answer the lone voice of the olifant.
The Emperor rides on, rides on in fury,
the men of France in grief and indignation.
There is no man who does not weep and wail,
and they pray God: protect the life of Roland
till they come, one great host, into the field
and fight at Roland's side like true men all.
What does it matter what they pray? It does no
good.
They are too late, they cannot come in time. AOI.

King Charles the Great rides on, a man in wrath,
his great white beard spread out [defiantly] upon
his hauberk.
All the barons of France ride spurring hard,
there is no man who does not wail, furious
not to be with Roland, the captain count,
who stands and fights the Saracens of Spain,
so set upon, I cannot think his soul abides.
God! those sixty men who stand with him, what
men!
No king, no captain ever stood with better. AOI.

Roland looks up on the mountains and slopes,
sees the French dead, so many good men fallen,
and weeps for them, as a great warrior weeps:
"Barons, my lords, may God give you his grace,
may he grant Paradise to all your souls,
make them lie down among the holy flowers.
I never saw better vassals than you.
All the years you've served me, and all the times,
the mighty lands you conquered for Charles our
King!
The Emperor raised you for this terrible hour!
Land of France, how sweet you are, native land,
laid waste this day, ravaged, made a desert.
Barons of France, I see you die for me,
and I, your lord—I cannot protect you.
May *God* come to your aid, that God who never
failed.
Oliver, brother, now I will not fail *you*.
I will die here—of grief, if no man kills me.
Lord, Companion, let us return and fight."

Roland returned to his place on the field,
strikes—a brave man keeping faith—with Durendal [his sword],

struck through Faldrun de Pui, cut him to pieces,
and twenty-four of the men they valued most;
no man will ever want his vengeance more!
As when the deer turns tail before the dogs,
so the pagans flee before Roland the Count.
Said the Archbishop: "You! Roland! What a
    fighter!
Now that's what every knight must have in him

who carries arms and rides on a fine horse:
he must be strong, a savage, when he's in battle;
for otherwise, what's he worth? Not four cents!
Let that four-cent man be a monk in some minster,
and he can pray all day long for our sins."
Roland replies: "Attack, do not spare them!"
And with that word the Franks began again.
There was a heavy loss of Christian men.

Charlemagne mourning the loss of his knights

BEOWULF: THE DEATH OF THE HERO

Around 800 A.D. an English monk wrote the epic *Beowulf,* recounting the exploits of a
great hero in the distant heathen past of the Germanic peoples. The poem's setting
probably is around 500 A.D., during the era of the barbarian migrations into Western
Europe, and possibly the poet drew upon oral traditions that had long circulated
around English campfires. This is the third, concluding part of the poem, which describes the death of Beowulf and the dire consequences thereof for his people. Central

to epic heroism is the belief that, just as the hero's followers and people rise and prosper with his victories, so many very well fall into misery, subjection, and dispersion with his defeat and death. *Beowulf* is a work of brooding pessimism and, while some of this is characteristic of heathen Germanic culture, it is also a manifestation of the perpetual dilemma of a social system dependent on the hero's personal fate. The medievals were both thrilled and frightened by this critical and fragile ingredient of military heroism.

Beowulf spoke; for the last time he uttered boastful words: "In the days of my youth I ventured on many battles; and even now will I, the aged guardian of my people, go into the fight and do memorable deeds, if the great destroyer come forth to me out of his cavern." Then for the last time he greeted each of the men, bold helmet-wearers, his own dear companions. "I would not bear a sword or any weapon against the Serpent, if I knew how else I could maintain my boast against the monster, as I did of old against Grendel. But I look for hot battle-fire there, for the venomous blast of his nostrils; therefore I have upon me shield and byrnie. I will not fleet one foot's breadth from the keeper of that mound, but it shall be with us twain at the wall as Wyrd, lord of every man, allotteth. I am eager in spirit, so that I forbear boasting against the winged warrior. But do ye men tarry upon the mound with your armor upon you, clad in your byrnies, to see which of us twain after the strife shall survive the deadly woundings. It is no exploit for you, nor for the might of any man, save mine alone to measure strength with the monster and do heroic deeds. I will boldly win the gold, or else battle, yea an evil death, shall take away your lord."

Then the mighty warrior rose up with his shield, stern under his helmet; he bore his battle-mail beneath the stony cliffs; he trusted in his single strength. That is no coward's way! And he beheld hard by the wall,—he of noble worth, who had passed through many wars and clashing battles when armed hosts close in fight,—where stood an arch of stone and a stream breaking out thence from the mound; the surge of the stream was hot with battle-fire. The hero could not abide near the hoard anywhile unburned, because of the dragon's flame.

Then the lord of the Geats, for he was wroth, sent forth a word from his breast. The stout-hearted warrior stormed; his voice battle-clear, entered in and rang under the hoary rock. The keeper of the hoard knew the speech of men, and his hatred was stirred. There was no more time to seek for peace. First came fourth out of the rock the breath of the evil beast, the hot reek of battle. The earth resounded. The hero 'neath the mound, lord of the Geats, swung up his shield against the awful foe, and the heart of the coiled monster grew eager to go out to the strife. Already the good warrior-king had drawn his sword, that olden heirloom, undulled of edge. Each of those destroyers was struck with terror by the other. Stouthearted stood that prince of friends against his tall shield, while the dragon coiled himself quickly together; Beowulf awaited him in his armor.

Then the flaming dragon, curving like a bow, advanced upon him, hastening to his fate. A shorter time did the shield protect well the life and body of the mighty king than his hopes had looked for, if haply he were to get victory in the combat at that time, early in the day; but Wyrd did not thus appoint for him. The lord of the Geats lifted his hand and smote the hideous-gleaming foe with his weighty sword, in such wise that the brown blade weakened as it fell upon the bone, and bit less deeply than its lord had need of, when sore beset. Then, at the sword-stroke, the keeper of the mound was furious in spirit. He cast forth devouring fire. Far and wide shot the deadly flame. The lord of the Geats nowise boasted of victory, for his naked war-sword, his excellent blade, weakened in the fight, as was not meet. It was no easy course for the son of Ecgtheow to forsake this earth for ever; yet he was doomed against his will to take up his abode in a dwelling otherwhere. So every man must quit these fleeting days.

It was not long ere the fighters closed again. The keeper of the hoard plucked up his courage; his breast heaved anew with his venomous breathing. He who erewhile ruled the people was hard put to it, being encompassed by fire. In nowise did his own, companions, sons of heroes, surround him in a band with warlike valor, but they took refuge in the wood to save their lives. There was but one among them whose heart surged with sorrows. Naught can ever put aside the bond of friendship in him who thinketh aright.

He was called Wiglaf, son of Weohstan, a beloved warrior, lord of the Scylfings, kinsman of Aelfhere. He saw his lord suffering the heat under his helmet; and he remembered all the benefits which Beowulf had given him in time past, the rich dwelling-place of the Waegmundings, and every folk-right which his father possessed. And he could not forbear, but seized the shield, the yellow lined, with his hand, and drew forth his old sword. This was known among men as an heirloom of Eanmund, son of Ohthere, whom, when a friendless exile, Weohstan slew in fight with the edge of the sword; he bore to his kinsman the brown-hued helmet, the ringed byrnie, the old giant-sword that Onela had given him; they were his comrade's war-harness, his ready armor. He spoke not of the feud, though he had killed his brother's son. He held the spoils, the sword and byrnie, for many years until his son could do a hero's deeds, like his father before him. Then he gave to him, among the Geats, war-harness of all kinds without number, when, full of years, he passed forth out of life along his last way.

This was the first time that the young warrior was to engage in the storm of war with his high lord. But his heart melted not within him, nor did his kinsman's heirloom weaken in the fight. That the dragon learned after they had come together.

Wiglaf spoke many fitting words, saying to his companions,—for his soul was sad within him: "I can remember the time when, as we drank the mead in the beer-hall, we promised our lord, him who gave us these rings, that we would repay him for the war-harness, for helmets and hard swords, if need like this befell him. Of his own will he choose us from his host for this adventure, urged us to do gloriously, and gave me these treasures, since he deemed us good spearmen, keen helmbearers, albeit our lord, defender of his people, had thought to do this mighty work alone, for that he of all men hath performed most of famed exploits and daring deeds. Now the day is come when our lord needs the might of good warriors. Let us on to his help, whilst the heat is upon him, and the grim terror of the fire.

"God knows of me that I would much rather that the flame should enwrap my body with my king's. Methinks it unseemly that we should bear our shields back to our home, unless we can first strike down the foe and defend the life of the Weders' king. Full well I know that it is not according to his old deserts that he alone of all the Geatish force should endure the pain and sink in the fight. There shall be one sword and one helmet, one shield and one byrnie in common to us."

Then he sped through the noisome smoke, bearing his war-helmet to the aid of his lord; he spoke a few words: "Belovèd Beowulf, now do thou all things well, as thou of old sworest in the days of thy youth that thou wouldst not let thy glory fade while thou didst live. Now, O resolute hero, famed for the deeds, thou must defend thy life with all thy might. Lo, I will help thee."

After these words, the dragon, awful monster, flashing with blazing flames, came on all wroth a second time to meet his hated foe-men. Wiglaf's shield was burned away to the boss in the waves of fire; the byrnie could give no help to the young spear-warrior. But the youth went quickly under his kinsman's shield, since his own had been burned to ashes in the fire. Then again the warking took thought for his glory; mightily he smote with his battle-sword so that it stood in the dragon's head, driven by force. Naegling was shivered in pieces; Beowulf's sword, old and graymarked, weakened in the fight;—it was not granted that the iron blade should help him in the strife. Too strong was the hand, as I have heard, which by its blow overtaxed all swords whatsoever; so that he fared none the better for it, when he bore into the fight a weapon wondrous hard.

Then the destroyer of people, the dread fire-dragon, for the third time was mindful of the feud. He rushed on the brave hero, when ground was yielded him. Hot and fierce, he seized upon Beowulf's whole neck with his sharp teeth. He was all bloodied over with his life-blood; the gore welled forth in streams.

Then I have heard men tell how, in the king's great need, Wiglaf, the hero, showed forth unceasing courage, skill and valor, as was natural to him; he heeded not the dragon's head (though the brave hero's hand was burned as he helped his kinsman), but the armed man smote the evil beast a little lower down, insomuch that that bright and plated sword drove into him, and the fire began to wane forthwith. Then the king recovered himself once more; he drew the shortsword, keen and sharp in battle, which he wore on his byrnie. The defence of the Weders cut the Serpent asunder in the middle. They struck down the foe; their might drove forth his life, and thus they twain, noble kinsmen, destroyed him. E'en such should a man be, a thane good at need. That was the king's last hour of victory by his own great deeds, the last of his worldly work.

But the wound which the earth-dragon had given him began to burn and swell; presently he found that poison, deadly venom, was surging in his breast. Then the prince, still wise in mind, moved along so that he might seat him by the mound; he saw that work of giants, saw how the rocky arches standing firm on their pillars, upheld within the earth-hall everlasting. Then the thane, surpassing good, taking water, with his hands bathed the great king, his own dear lord, all gory and wearied with battle, and loosened his helmet.

Beowulf spoke and uttered words, despite his wound, his piteous battle-hurt; full well he knew that his life of earthly joy was spent, that the appointed number of his days was run, and Death exceeding near: "Now would I give my war-harness unto my son, had I been granted any heir, born of my body, to come after me. Fifty winters have I ruled this people; yet there was never a king of all the neighbor tribes who durst attack me with the sword or oppress me with terror. In my home I awaited what the times held in store for me, kept well mine own, sought out no wily quarrels, swore not many a false oath. In all this I can rejoice, though death-sick with my wounds, inasmuch as the Ruler of men cannot reproach me with murder of kinsmen, when my life parteth from my body. Now do thou, dear Wiglaf, lightly go and view the hoard 'neath the gray rock, now the dragon lieth low, sleepeth sore wounded, bereft of his treasure. Do thou make haste that I may behold the olden treasures, that store of gold, and look upon those bright and curious gems; and thus, having seen the treasured wealth, I may the easier quit life and the kingdom which long I have ruled."

And I have heard how the son of Weohstan, after these words, quickly obeyed his wounded lord, sick from the battle; he bore his ringèd mail-shirt, the woven battle-sark, 'neath the roof of the cave. And the brave thane, exultant victor, as he went by the seat, saw many precious jewels, much glistening gold lying upon the ground and wondrous treasures on the wall, and the den of the dragon, the old twilight-flier; bowls lay there, vessels of bygone men, with none to brighten them, their adornments fallen away. There was many a helmet old and rusty, many an arm-ring cunningly twisted. Treasure of gold found in the earth can easily puff with pride the heart of any man, hide it who will. Likewise he saw a banner all of gold standing there, high above the hoard, greatest of wonders, woven by skill of hand; from it there shone a ray of light, so that he could see the cavern floor, and examine the fair jewels. Naught was to be seen of the dragon there, for the sword had undone him!

Thus I have heard how one man alone at his own free will plundered the hoard within the cave, the old work of the giants, how he laid in his bosom beakers and dishes; he took the banner, too, that brightest of beacons. The old lord's blade, with its iron edge, had sorely injured him who long had been the owner of these treasures, who at midnight had borne about the fiery terror, dreadfully surging, hot before the hoard, until he died the death.

The messenger was in haste, eager to return, enriched with spoils. The great-hearted man was spurred with longing to know whether he would find alive the lord of the Weders, grievously sick, in the place where he had left him. And bringing the treasures, he found the great prince, his lord, bleeding, at the point of death; he began to sprinkle him again with water until the sword's point broke through the treasure of his heart, and Beowulf spoke, aged and sorrowful, as he gazed upon the gold: "I utter thanks unto the Ruler of all, King of Glory, the everlasting Lord, for these fair things, which here I look upon, inasmuch as ere my death-day I have been able to win them for my people. I have sold and paid mine aged life for the treasure-hoard. Fulfil ye now the needs of the people. Here can I be no more. Bid the brave warriors make a splendid mound at the sea-cape after my body is burned. There on Whale's Ness shall it tower high as a memorial for my people, so that seafarers, they who drive from far their great ships over the misty floods, may in aftertime call it 'Beowulf's Mound.' "

The great-hearted king took from his neck the ring of gold; gave to his thane, the youthful warrior, his helmet gold-adorned, his ring and his byrnie, bade him enjoy them well.

"Thou art the latest left of all our kin, the Waegmundings. Wyrd hath swept away all my kinsmen, heroes in their might, to the appointed doom. I must after them."

That was the old king's last word from the thoughts of his heart, ere he yielded to the bale-fire, the hotly surging flames. His soul departed from out his bosom unto the reward of the righteous.

Thus it went full hard with the young man to see his best-beloved friend lying lifeless on the ground, faring most wretchedly. His destroyer lay there too, the horrid earth-dragon, bereft of life, crushed in ruin. No longer could the coiled serpent rule over treasure-hoards, for the edge of the sword, the hard, battle-notched work of the hammer, had destroyed him, and he had fallen to the ground near his hoard-hall, stilled by the wound-

ing. No more in play did he whirl through the air at midnight, and show himself forth, proud of his treasure, for he sank to earth by the mighty hand of the battle-chief.

Indeed, as I have heard, it hath prospered few men in the world, e'en though mighty, however daring in their every deed, to rush on against the breath of a venomous foe, or to disturb his treasure-hall, if they found the keeper waking, abiding in his mound. Beowulf paid with his death for his share in the splendid riches. Both of them had reached the end of this fleeting life.

It was not long thereafter that the cowards left the wood, those faint-hearted traitors, the ten of them together, e'en they who in their lord's great need had not dared to brandish the spear. But shamefully now they bore their shields, their war-armor, to where the old man lay. They looked upon Wiglaf. The wearied warrior was sitting by his lord's shoulder; he was trying to revive him with water, but it availed him naught. He could not stay the chieftain's life on earth, though dearly he wished it, nor change the will of God in aught. The judgment of the Lord was wont to rule the deeds of every man, e'en as still it doth.

And straightway the youth had a fierce and ready answer for those whose courage had failed them. Wiglaf, son of Weohstan, spoke, sad at heart, as he looked upon those hated men: "Lo! he who is minded to speak the truth may say that the liege lord, he who gave you these treasures, e'en the battle-armor in which ye are standing, — what time at the ale-bench the king gave oft unto his thanes, sitting in the hall, helms and byrnies, the choicest far or near which he could find, — that he utterly and wretchedly wasted that war-harness. Nowise did the king need to boast of his comrades in arms when strife overtook him; yet God, the Lord of victory, granted him unaided to avenge himself with the sword, when he had need of valor. Little protection could I give him in the fight; and yet I tried what was beyond my power, — to help my kinsman. It was ever the worse for the deadly foe when I smote him with the sword, the fire less fiercely flamed from his head. Too few defenders thronged about their lord when the dread moment fell. Now, all sharing of treasure, all gifts of swords, all hope, all rights of home, shall cease from your kin. Every man of your house shall roam, bereft of tribal rights, as soon as the princes in far countries hear of your flight, your inglorious deed. Death is better for every man than a life of shame!"

Then he bade announce the issue of the fight to the stronghold up over the sea-cliff, where the sad warrior-band had been sitting by their shields the morning long, looking either for the death or the return of their dear lord. Little did he keep silence of the new tidings, he who rode up the headland, but truthfully spoke before them all: "Now the chief of the Weder people, lord of the Geats, source of all our joy, is fast in the bed of the death; he lieth low in slaughter because of the Dragon's deeds. Beside him lieth his deadly adversary, slain by the wounding of the knife; for with the sword he could nowise wound the monster. Wiglaf, the son of Weohstan, sitteth over Beowulf, the living hero by the dead; over his head with weary heart he keepth watch for friend and foe."

"Now the people may look for a season of war as soon as the fall of the king is published abroad among the Franks and the Frisians. . . ."

PHILIPPE DE COMMYNES

DEATH OF THE HERO

The terrifying consequences for a community that can follow the death in battle of its heroic leader resounds down the medieval centuries and is given prominence in this account by the contemporary court historian, Philippe de Commynes, of the downfall in 1477 of Duke Charles the Bold of Burgundy (principally what is today Belgium). There is also an echo in Commynes's story of the theme explored in the *Song of Roland*—a thin line exists between glorious heroism and rash folly.

The duke dressed and undressed with great reverence and by high-ranking persons. But at his last hour all these honors were gone. And he perished, with his house. . . . May God forgive him for his sins.

I have seen him as a great and honorable prince, and as esteemed and sought out by his neighbors, for a time, as any prince in Christendom, and perhaps more so. I have not seen any reason why he should have incurred the wrath of God, unless it was because he considered all the graces and honors which he had received in this world to have been the result of his own judgment and valor, instead of attributing them to God, as he should have. For indeed he was endowed with many good qualities and virtues. No prince ever surpassed him in eagerness to act as patron to great men and to give them a well-regulated way of life. His gifts were not verygrand, for he wanted everyone to feel the effects of his liberality. No lord ever granted audience more freely to his servants and his subjects. At the time when I knew him, he was not cruel; but he became so before his death, and this was a sign that his life would be short. He was very ostentatious in his dress and in everything else—a little too much. He was very courteous to ambassadors and foreigners; they were well received and lavishly entertained in his own places of residence. He desired great glory, and it was that more than anything else which made him engage in these wars. He would have liked to resemble those princes of antiquity who remained so famous after their death. And he was as daring as any man who ruled in his time.

But all his projects are over, and they all turned to his prejudice and shame; for those who win get all the honor. I do not know toward whom Our Lord showed the greatest anger: toward him, who died suddenly on the battlefield, without lingering for long, or toward his subjects, who have never since enjoyed prosperity or peace, but have been continually involved in wars in which they have not been able to resist sufficiently, or in civil strifes and cruel and fierce fighting among themselves. The hardest burden to bear has been the fact that their defenders have been foreigners who had formerly been their enemies—the Germans.

And indeed after the duke's death, there was not a man who wished them well, no matter who defended them. And judging from the way they acted, their sense seemed to have been as troubled as their prince's. For shortly after his death they rejected all good and sound advice and sought out all the ways that would be to their disadvantage. And they are in such a situation that their troubles are far from over, or at least they have reason to fear their return.

I tend to agree with the opinion of someone which I saw somewhere, which was that God assigns a prince to a region according to the degree of punishment or chastisement He wishes to inflict on his subjects, and He disposes the hearts of the subjects toward their prince according to how much He wishes to exalt or humiliate him. And thus, in regard to the house of Burgundy, He has made everything equal; for after one hundred and twenty years of long felicity and great wealth under three great, good, and wise princes, who preceded Duke Charles, God gave them this duke, who constantly maintained them in fierce wars, which involved much trouble and expense; and this took place in winter almost as often as in summer. Many rich and prosperous people were either killed or deprived of their possessions as a result of being captured. They began to incur great losses at the siege of Neuss, and this continued for three or four battles until his death—so much so that at the last battle, all the strength of his country was used up, and all his men, that is to say those who would have been willing and able to defend the position and honor of his house, were killed, destroyed, or taken prisoners.

And as I said before, it seems that this loss was equal to their former measure of felicity. For just as I have seen him great, rich, and honored, this was also true of his subjects; for I believe that I have seen and known the greater part of Europe. However, I have never known any territory or country, all things being equal, nor even one of still larger expanse, which was so abundant in riches, furniture, and buildings, nor so lavish in prodigality, expenses, feasts and entertainments as I have seen in Burgundy during the time when I was there. And if it seems to someone who has never been there in my time that I exaggerate, others who were there with me will perhaps say that I say too little.

But Our Lord, all of a sudden, caused the fall of this great and sumptuous edifice, this powerful house which had supported and educated so many worthy men, and which was honored far and wide in its time for its victories and glory, more than any other house in the vicinity. The Burgundians enjoyed this good fortune and the grace of God for one hundred and twenty years, while all their neighbors, such as France, England, and Spain, were suffering.

To continue with my subject, the king, who had already established a postal service in the kingdom (which had never had any before), was soon informed of the duke of Burgundy's defeat; and he awaited further news at every hour, for he had been advised earlier of the arrival of the Germans and everything that depended on this. Many people kept their ears open in order to be the first to hear the news and report it to the king, for he usually rewarded the first to bring him important news, without forgetting the messenger besides. And he liked to speak about prospective news before it arrived, and said: "I shall give so much to the first man who brings me news of this." My lord of Bouchage and I received the first message about the battle of Morat, and we went together to inform the king about it. He gave each one of us two hundred silver marks.

RAOUL DE CAMBRAI

LAND HUNGER

The noble's sense of military honor became by the eleventh century integrated with a belief among the great families that the status of the heroic warrior should be rewarded through a royal gift of a large estate (fief). Furthermore, these family estates, which were once granted by a king, were regarded as inheritable. As long as the son of a great noble was militarily capable and honorable in his behavior and loyal to his lord or to the descendant of the lord who had granted the fief, the young warrior had a right to inherit it. Aside from fighting and military valor, the central facet of the noble's life was land: its gaining, its inheritance, and its preservation in the family. This is the social and dramatic trigger of the twelfth-century French epic *Raoul de Cambrai*. The story is that the emperor impedes the inheritance of the child Raoul de Cambrai, his nephew, by giving his widowed mother in marriage to another nobleman, along with his father's lands. Raoul is promised by the emperor that, when he reaches maturity, the emperor will compensate him with another great fief. When the lord of such a great estate dies, Raoul insists that the emperor now give him the available land, and the monarch reluctantly does so. But the men of the dispossesed family in turn prepare to defend their own claim and a great feudal war breaks out, causing much death and destruction. The poet has legitimately communicated a central fact in the life of the noble hero—his insatiable desire for land regardless of social consequences, and to the point of madness.

Jousting Tournament

You shall now hear of the distress and disorder caused by the great interminable war. The King of France had a noble youth in his service whom the French called Gibouin of Mans. He served the king with his good sword, and made many an orphan in the course of his wars. He served our noble king so well and in such knightly fashion that he was entitled to a full reward. Those from beyond the Rhine counselled that he should be given the fief of Cambrai which was held by Aalais, conqueror of men's hearts, of the family of Geoffroy of Lavardin. Now, if God who turned the water into wine prevent it not, a fief is about to be given and bestowed by reason of which many a knight will lie prone in death.

Our emperor listened to the barons talking and advising him to give the fair Aalais to the baron of Mans who had served him so well. He took their counsel, for which he is to be blamed; he gave the glove to Gibouin, who thanked him for it and stooped and kissed his shoe. Then said the King of France: "Gibouin, my brother, I deserve thy thanks, for it is a great gift that I give thee here. But on one condition I grant it: I wish not to disinherit the boy Raoul. He is yet young, now protect him well until such time that he can carry arms. He shall hold Cambrai; no one can refuse it to him and I shall give you some other land." Said Gibouin: "I accept it on condition that you bid me marry the lady." But he acted like a fool in daring to expect this, for it afterwards caused the overthrow of many a valiant knight, for the fair lady would not accept him though she were cut to pieces for it.

King Louis did a very foolish thing when he took the heritage away from his nephew; and Gibouin on his side acted like a felon when he desired the land of another as his fief. It caused him afterwards to die a shameful death. Then the emperor called his messenger: "Go, saddle the Arab steed, and tell my fair sister in her heritage of Cambrai, that she take to husband the brave Gibouin of Mans. Between here and Carthage there is not such a knight to be found, and I give him all the land as a marriage portion. Tell her to come without delay to my court and bring her escort with her, and I will summon many of my kinsmen.

But if she fails me because of her pride, I will seize both the land and the inheritance."

The messenger took his leave and mounted the saddle of his horse; then he left Paris and rode straight for Cambrai. He entered the city by the main gate and halted by the church of St. Geri. He found the noble lady in the open space before the church with several knights in her company. He reined in his horse and dismounted, and greeted the lady in the king's name: "The king, our protector, prays God who created heaven and earth and all things therein to save the countess and all those she loves" — "May God the Creator protect thee, brother! Tell me the king's bidding and hide it not" — "In God's name, lady, I will tell you. The king's message is that he will give you Gibouin for a husband. Know of a truth, that is the king's command." Dame Aalais sank down to the earth, tears fell from her eyes and she gave a deep sigh. Then she called her counsellors. "Ah, God!" said she, "Here is an evil message. . . ."

"Just Emperor," said the baron Guerri, "Are you minded to disinherit your nephew because as yet he can neither walk nor ride? By the faith that I owe you, you shall see a thousand knights overturned ere this Knight of Mans can vaunt himself in court. Just Emperor, I declare to you that if he lets himself be seen in Cambrai he may be certain of losing his head. And you too, foolish king, deserve blame for this. The child is your nephew, and you should never have thought of such a thing." But the king replied: "Let all this be! The gift is given and I cannot go back on it now." So Guerri departed, for he had no desire to remain, and ill-omened was the leave that he took! The good steeds were ready at the foot of the steps and the barons mounted. And Guerri cried at the top of his voice: "Now make ready, you young warriors who desire hard knocks! For I swear by Him who allowed Himself to suffer, I would rather be cut to pieces than fail my nephew as long as I live."

Guerri the Red was full of anger. He returned to Cambrai and dismounted before the church. Dame Aalais saw the knight coming and spoke to him as you may now hear: "Sir Guerri, without fail now, will you tell me the truth?" "Lady," said he, "I wish not to lie to you. The king is determined to seize your heritage for Gibouin, God curse him! — Take him for thy husband, for only so canst thou make thy peace with Louis, the ruler of France." "God!" said the lady, "I could die of grief! I would rather be burnt alive than that the king should force a greyhound to lie with a watchdog. God will allow me to bring up my child till such time as he can carry arms." Then said Guerri: "Lady, a blessing on you for daring to say it; I will not desert you in your great need."

Guerri the stout-hearted speaks again: "Lady Aalais, I swear by God the Redeemer that I will not fail you as long as I live. Where is my nephew? Bring him here, I pray you." Up rose two young lords and brought the child to the fore-court. He was three years old, I tell you for a fact, and he was dressed in bright silk with a tunic of crimson cloth. A more beautiful child could not be found. Guerri takes him in his arms at once and sighs deeply from his heart: "Child," said he, "you are scarce grown yet, and the knight of Mans has evil intent towards you, since he deprives you of your land." "Uncle," said the child, "I shall get it back, if I live long enough to carry arms seated on my charger." "Truly," said Guerri, "you shall not lose a foot of it, unless twenty thousand warriors die for it first." Then the knights call for water and seat themselves at the table.

Dame Aalais and the vassal Guerri and the barons are seated at table. The seneschals have done their duty well, for they have been well trained to serve. After the meal the lady gives costly garments to the barons. Then the powerful Guerri takes his leave; he kisses the lady and departs. Straight to Arras he goes at full speed. After this many years and days passed and there was no sound of war or of discord in the land. When Raoul of Cambrai was fifteen years old he was an exceedingly courteous and noble youth and greatly beloved by his men and his nobles.

Fifteen years have now passed and gone and dame Aalais sees her son tall and broad and well-formed. There was a nobleman in that kingdom, Ybert by name, a man of dauntless spirit. He had a son who was christened Bernier when he was small. He was grown now and well-favoured, and

at fifteen years he too was both tall and strong. Count Raoul loved him dearly, and the dame Aalais out of goodness of heart had fostered him from an early age. Together they went to Paris to acquaint themselves with noble knighthood, and he waited on Raoul with the wine and the spiced cup. Better had it been for him, I can tell you, had his head been severed from his body, for grievously and shamefully he slew him in the end.

Count Raoul, the courteous youth, had a great affection for young Bernier. Bernier was the son of Ybert of Ribemont and there was no fairer youth in any land nor any that knew better the use of shield and spear, nor of wise speech in a king's court, albeit he was called a bastard. Raoul loved him and gladly made him his squire, but ill-mated comrades they proved to be.

Dame Aalais has watched her son grow up and now she sees that he is fit to bear arms, and thus she addressed him as you may hear: "Call the ban and summon your men, so that you may see them assembled at Cambrai, and we shall soon see who is loth to serve." Raoul summoned them and spoke his mind to them: "You must not fail me when I need you.". . .

The emperor has knighted the boy and now he calls his seneschals and says: "Bring hither arms, for so I bid you.". . . Then the emperor spoke to his nephew: "Nephew Raoul, I see that you have grown up tall and strong, thanks be to God the Father omnipotent.". . .

Then the king girded him with a strong sword. Its pommel and hilt were of gold and it was forged in a gloomy valley by Galant, who had put into it of his best. Except Durendal, which was the choicest sword of all, this sword was better than all others and no arm in the world could stand against it. Such were the arms which became him. For Raoul was fair and of noble form and, but for the immoderateness that was in him, a better vassal than he had never ruled his land. But because of his excess the outcome was grievous, for an unbridled man passes his days in sorrow. . . .

Raoul, who was full of wrath, spoke thus: "Just emperor, by St. Amant I swear that I have served you ever since I carried arms and you have never given me the amount of a farthing. Now at least give me the glove as a pledge that I may hold my own land as my valiant father held it before me." "I cannot grant it," replied the king; "I have given it to the Knight of Mans, and for all the wealth of Milan I would not take it from him." Guerri listened, then he shouted: "I will fight for it first, fully armed on my steed, against that mercenary Gibouin of Mans." And Raoul, ill-tempered now and sullen, cried: "By the apostle whom the penitents seek, if now thou dost not take possession of thy land, this very day or to-morrow ere the sun set, never again will I nor my men fight in thy defence." These are the words that Raoul kept so well and which caused the untimely death of many a baron. "Just emperor, I tell you all this first: every one knows that the land of the father ought by right to pass to the child. By St. Amant, every one, both small and great, will scorn me henceforth, if I do violence to my pride any longer when I see another man holding my land. By God who made the firmament, if ever I find that mercenary of Mans, no ordinary death shall he die by my sword." The king was heavy at heart when he heard these words.

The Knight of Mans was sitting at a table in the palace. He heard these threats and was filled with fear. He put on his cloak of ermine and came to the king: "Just emperor," said he, "now am I in a sorry plight. You gave me Cambresis by Artois; and now you cannot guarantee the possession of it to me. Here now is this arrogant Count Raoul with his fine equipment (he is your nephew as the Frenchmen know well), and Guerri the Red, his loyal friend. I have no friend so good in all this land who would be worth anything to me against these two. I have served thee long with my Viennese blade, and never have I obtained the worth of a farthing. I shall go forth on my good Norwegian steed poorer than I came, and the Alemans and the Germans, the men of Burgundy, of Normandy and France will all talk of it, and all my service will not have earned me a doit." Sorrow filled the heart of King Louis and he beckoned Raoul to him with his broidered glove and said: "Fair nephew, by God, the giver of laws, I pray you let him hold it for two or three years on such terms as I will tell you: if any count dies between here and Vermandois, or between Aix-la-Chapelle and Senlis, or from Monillon to Orleans, you shall inherit the rights and the land. You shall not lose a fraction of a penny by the exchange." Raoul listened and did not hesitate: at the advice of Guerri of Artois he accepted the pledge—it was by reason of it that he lay cold in death at last.

Count Raoul called Guerri to speak of the matter! "Uncle," said he, "I count on your support. I will accept this gift and there shall be no drawing back from it." It was a great thing that he demanded in exchange for his father's fief, and fatal to many a baron in the end. Then they demanded hostages from King Louis; and the king harkened to bad advice and allowed Raoul to choose some of the highest in the land. . . .

Hostages he had now; as many as he wanted, and for some time things remained thus—for a year and a fortnight at any rate, I know and Raoul returned to Cambrai. But during the time of which I have been speaking Herbert, a powerful count, died; he was a loyal man and wise and had a great many friends. All Vermandois was his territory, also Roie, Péronne, Origny, Ribemont, St. Quentin and Clairy. He is a fortunate man who possesses many friends! Raoul heard of his death and bestirred himself. He quickly mounted his steed and summoned his hostages; his uncle Guerri the Red of Arras accompanied him and with a hundred and forty men and much costly clothing he rode straight without stopping to demand from King Louis the fatal gift. Raoul was in his right, as I have told you; it was the king of St. Denis who was in the wrong. When the king is bad many a loyal man suffers for it. The barons arrived at the court at Paris and dismounted beneath the olive trees. Then they went up the palace steps and demanded to see the king. They found King Louis sitting upon his throne; he looked and saw all these nobles coming, headed by the eager Raoul; "Salutations to the great king Louis," said he, "on behalf of God who suffered on the cross." The emperor replied slowly: "May God, who made paradise, protect thee, nephew!"

Raoul, the noble baron, spoke: "Just emperor. I desire to speak only to you; I am your nephew and you must not act unfairly towards me. I have heard of the death of Herbert, lord and suzerain of Vermandois. Now invest me at once with his land, for thus you swore that you would do, and you pledged it to me by hostages." "I cannot, brother," said the baron Louis. "This noble count of whom thou speakest has four valiant sons, than whom no better knights can be found. If now I handed their land over to you, every right-minded person would blame me for it and I could not summon them to my court, for they would refuse to serve or honour me. Besides, I tell thee, I have no desire to disinherit them: I do not wish to vex four men on account of one." Raoul listened and thought he would go mad. He cannot think, he is so enraged, but he turns away in a fury and does not stop till he reaches his palace and finds the hostages waiting there, whereupon he calls them to him upon their oath.

Count Raoul was very angry. He called upon Droon and Geoffroy the bold of Anjou, who was much dismayed at the news, Herbert of the Maine and Gerard and Henry, Samson and the aged Bernard. "Come hither, barons, I bid you, as you have pledged and sworn to do. To-morrow at daybreak I summon you upon your oath to my tower and, by St. Geri, you will be filled with despair." Geoffroy shuddered when he heard these words and said: "Friend, why do you alarm me thus?" "I will tell you" replied Raoul. "Herbert who owned Origny and St. Quentin, Péronne and Clairy, Ham and Roie, Nesle and Falévy, is dead. Do you think that I have been invested with this rich fief? I tell you no, for the emperor has failed toward me completely." And the barons all replied: "Give us time: for we will go to Louis and learn from his own lips how he means to protect us." "I grant it, by my faith," said Raoul, and Bernier goes to the palace

and all the hostages go straightway to the king. Geoffroy speaks first and implores the mercy of the king: "Just emperor, we are in an evil plight; why has thou given us as hostages to this devil, the greatest felon that ever donned a hauberk? Herbert, the best of barons, is dead, and he wishes to be invested with the whole of his fief."

Geoffroy the bold spoke again: "Just emperor, you committed great folly when you gave your nephew such a heritage and the title deed to some one else's land. Count Herbert is dead and he ruled a large estate. Raoul is in the right; the outrage is yours. You will have to invest him with it — we are the hostages therefor." "God," said the king, "it nearly makes me mad to think that four men should lose their heritage on account of one! By the one who caused the statue to speak, I swear this gift will turn out to his undoing. Unless some pact of marriage stays his hand there will be grief in many a noble home."

The king speaks, and he is sad at heart: "Fair nephew Raoul, come hither. I give you the glove, but the land is yours on such terms as I shall tell you: to wit that neither I nor my men will help thee in any way." "I ask for nothing better," Raoul replies. But Bernier heard his words and leapt up, and he speaks out so that all can hear: "The sons of Herbert are valiant knights, rich and possessed of many friends and never will they suffer any loss through you." The Frenchmen in the palace, both old and young, talk of the matter, and they say: "The boy Raoul has the mind of a man. He is demanding a fair exchange for his father's land. The king is stirring up a great war which will bring a sad heart to many a fair lady."

FEUDAL HOMAGE

The performance of military service in exchange for land between the lord (who gives the land and demands loyalty) and the military vassal (who receives the land and must perform loyal service) was recognized by a formal act of homage and fealty witnessed by a written contract ("charter"). Here in France in 1110 the viscount of Carcassonne does homage to the abbot of St. Mary of Grasse.

In the name of the Lord, I, Bernard Atton, viscount of Carcassonne, in the presence of my sons, Roger and Trencavel, and of Peter Roger of Barbazan, and William Hugo, and Raymond Mantellini, and Peter de Vitry, nobles, and of many other honorable men, who had come to the monastery of St. Mary of Grasse in honor of the festival of the august St. Mary. Since Lord Leo, abbot of the said monastery, asked me, in the presence of all those above mentioned, to acknowledge to him the fealty and homage for the castles, manors, and places which the patrons, my ancestors, held from him and his predecessors and from the said monastery as a fief, and which I ought to hold as they held, I have made to the Lord Abbot Leo acknowledgment and done homage as I ought to do.

Therefore, let all present and to come know that I, the said Bernard Atton, lord and viscount of Carcassonne, acknowledge verily to thee, my Lord Leo, by the grace of God abbot of St. Mary of Grasse, and to thy successors, that I hold and ought to hold as a fief, in Carcassonne, the following: that is to say, the castles of Confoles, of Léocque, of Capendes (which is otherwise known as St. Martin of Sussagues); and the manors of Mairac, of Albars, and of Musso; also, in the valley of Aquitaine, Rieux, Traverina, Hérault, Archas, Servians, Villatroitoes, Tansiraus, Presler, and Cornelles.

Moreover, I acknowledge that I hold from thee and from the said monastery, as a fief, the castle of Termes in Narbonne; and in Minèrve, the castle of Ventaion, and the manors of Cassanolles, and of Ferral and Aiohars; and in Le Rogès, the little village of Longville; for each and all of which I render homage and fealty with hands and mouth to thee, my said Lord Abbot Leo and to thy successors; and I swear upon these four gospels of God that I will always be a faithful vassal to thee and to thy successors and to St. Mary of Grasse in all things in which a vassal is required to be faithful to his lord; and I will defend thee, my lord, and all thy successors, and the said monastery, and the monks present and to come, and the castles and manors and all your men and their possessions against all malefactors and invaders, of my own free will and at my own cost, and so shall my successors do after me; and I will give to thee power over all the castles and manors above described, in peace and in war, whenever they shall be claimed by thee or by thy successors.

Moreover, I acknowledge that, as a recognition of the above fiefs, I and my successors ought to come to the said monastery at our own expense, as often as a new abbot shall have been appointed, and there do homage and return to him the power over all the fiefs described above. And when the abbot shall mount his horse, I and my heirs, viscounts of Carcassonne, and our successors ought to hold the stirrup for the honor of the dominion of St. Mary of Grasse; and to him and all who come with him, to as many as two hundred beasts, we should make the abbot's purveyance in the borough of St. Michael of Carcassonne, the first time he enters Carcassonne, with the best fish and meat, and with eggs and cheese, honorably, according to his will, and pay the expense of shoeing the horses, and for straw and fodder as the season shall require.

And if I or my sons or their successors do not observe towards thee or thy successors each and all the conditions declared above, and should come against these things, we desire that all the aforesaid fiefs should by that very fact be handed over to thee and to the said monastery of St. Mary of Grasse and to thy successors.

I, therefore, the aforesaid Lord Leo, by the grace of God abbot of St. Mary of Grasse, receive the homage and fealty for all fiefs of castles and manors and places which are described above, in the way and with the agreements and understandings written above; and likewise I concede to thee and thy heirs and their successors, the viscounts of Carcassonne, all the castles and manors and places aforesaid, as a fief, along with this present charter. . . . And I promise by the religion of my order to thee and thy heirs and successors, viscounts of Carcassonne, that I will be a good and faithful lord concerning all those things described above. . . .

THE MILITARY INDENTURE

By the Hundred Years War in the early fifteenth century, the English army was mainly recruited by an indenture, or written contract, by which captains from the nobility and gentry were commissioned to raise regiments. In return, the king stipulated the per diem pay he would provide for the commissioned officer's soldiers and how the captain would share in the booty and ransoming of prisoners—the captain's rewards. This is how heroic impulse and military valor were institutionalized into the proto-modern army. But the degree of military innovation over the whole medieval era was small. Heroism in battle is still what is being sought here; that is still the supreme value for the warrior class, and the tangible reward was nothing new—El Cid had long ago been praised for his fair distribution of booty. This indenture is between John Duke of Bedford, the English Regent of western France, and a famous mercenary captain, Sir John Fastolf, who was known as both a heroic fighter in France over several decades and a successful acquirer of booty, which he shrewdly invested in lands back home.

This indenture, made between the most high, very excellent and most powerful prince, [John], duke of Bedford, regent of the kingdom of France, on the one hand, and Sir John Fastolf, councillor, grand master of the household, lieutenant of [the county of] Maine and of the marches thereabouts for my lord the regent, and governor of Alençon, on the other, witnesses that the said grand master is retained by my lord the regent as captain of eighty mounted men-at-arms, he himself being numbered among them, and of two hundred and fifty archers, for one whole year, beginning at the feast of St Michael last past, and finishing on the same said feast in the year to come, which will be the year 1425. [And they shall] be employed in the conquest of the said land and county of Maine, and of the border country thereabouts, held by the enemies and adversaries of our sovereign lord and of the said lord the regent, and anywhere else in the kingdom of France where it shall be the will of the said lord regent to ordain.

For which [services] he will have and receive wages as follows: for a knight banneret, captain of men-at-arms, four shillings sterling a day in English money; for a knight bachelor, likewise a captain, two shillings sterling; for a mounted man-

at-arms, twelve pence sterling a day, with the accustomed rewards; and for each archer, six pence a day of the said currency, the English noble being valued at six shillings and eight pence sterling, or French money at the current rate. And these wages shall be paid as from the day of the first musters, which the said grand master shall hold of the said men-at-arms and archers before the commissioners of the king, our said lord, or of the said regent. And after these musters, payment shall be made to him in advance, from the revenues of both France and Normandy, by order of my lords the treasurers and general governors of the said finances, and by the hand of the clerk of the treasurer of the war-receipts of our sovereign lord the king in Paris, or by the receiver-general of the said revenues in Normandy, or by one of them, for [the period of] six whole weeks and, at the end of the first quarter, for the remaining six whole weeks, and thence-forward quarter by quarter, in advance, according to the musters and reviews which he shall be obliged to hold before the commissioners and officers of the king, our sovereign lord, and of the said lord regent, from quarter to quarter, and as often as he shall be required to do so before the said commissioners.

And the said lord regent shall have both a third part of the profits of war of the said grand master, and a third of the thirds which the men of his retinue shall be obliged to give him from their profits of war, whether prisoners, booty or anything else taken, and also all other customary rights. Of the said thirds and rights thus owing to the said lord regent, the said grand master shall be obliged to certify every quarter to the said treasurers, general governors and clerk, and to others as may be required, when he requests his wages, and to account for them in the Chamber of Accounts through the farmer of the said grand master or the executor or executors of his testament. And the said grand master shall have any prisoners who may be taken during the said period by him or by those in his retinue: with the exception of any kings or princes, whoever they may be, or sons of kings, and especially Charles who calls himself Dauphin of Viennois, other important captains and persons of the blood royal, captains and lieutenants holding powers from the said kings and princes; and excepting, too, those who killed and murdered the late John, once duke of Burgundy, or who consented to or were accomplices in the crime, and those who consented to and participated in the treason done to the duke of Brittany by Olivier de Blois and his accomplices, each and all of whom shall belong to the said lord regent, and he shall pay a reasonable reward to him or those whose prisoners they shall be.

In return for these things the said grand master has undertaken, and undertakes, to serve the king, our sovereign lord, and the said lord regent, either in person or by means of others appointed by him, for whom he shall be answerable, and to use the said men-at-arms and archers in the conquest of the said land and county of Maine, and of the border country thereabouts, or anywhere else in the said kingdom of France, in the best manner and means known to him, or [in any way] which the said lord regent shall command him. And he shall keep, and cause to be kept and maintained, as best he may, the people and subjects obedient to the king, our said lord, [free] from all force, violence, pillages, robberies, seizure of provisions, horses and cattle, and all other exactions whatever.

In witness whereof, on that part of the present indenture which is to remain with the said grand master, the lord regent has caused his seal to be placed.

Given in Paris, on the 27th day of November, in the year of grace 1424.

Thus signed: By the lord regent of the kingdom of France, duke of Bedford.

R. Veret [Secretary]

FROISSART

THE NEVER-ENDING STORY

The institutionalization of aristocratic heroism and militarism in feudal contract and the army indenture system (the latter endured in England to a substantial degree until the late nineteenth century!) did not significantly change or suppress the essential ethos and behavior pattern of the European nobility. In the Hundred Years War of the fourteenth and fifteenth centuries between England and France, naked military valor and the physical and personal qualities of heroic leadership were central to the way the war was fought and perceived. The following is an account of the great English victory at Crecy in 1346, in which the English army was led by the king's eldest son, Edward the Black Prince. We might regard Edward as a cold-blooded thug and killer, and we might regard the English imperialist zeal for conquering France as unjustified aggres-

sion and the English devastation of the countryside as a war crime. Such a critical perception was not entirely foreign to the people in the fourteenth century, but nearly all members of the nobility, even in France, including the preponderance of bishops who came from the nobility, had nothing but admiration for the English victory and were fully in accord with the courtier historian Jean Froissart in celebrating it. However, our society is by no means immune to such celebration of heroic militarism and is given to an occasional frenzy of glorifying conquering heroes. Froissart tells an apparently never-ending story, thus far perpetuated in our civilization.

Battle of Crecy

The English, who were drawn up in three divisions, and seated on the ground, on seeing their enemies advance, rose undauntedly up, and fell into their ranks. That of the prince was the first to do so, whose archers were formed in the manner of a portcullis, or harp and the men at arms in the rear. The earls of Northampton and Arundel, who commanded the second division, had posted themselves in good order on his wing, to assist and succor the prince, if necessary.

You must know, that these kings, earls, barons and lords of France, did not advance any regular order, but one after the other, or any way most pleasing to themselves. But as soon as the king of France came in sight of the English, his blood began to boil, and cried out to his marshals, "Order the Genoese forward, and begin the battle, in the name of God and St. Denis." There were about fifteen thousand Genoese cross-bowmen; but they were quite fatigued, having marched on foot that day six leagues, completely armed, and with their cross-bows. They told the constable, they were not in a fit condition to do great things that day in battle. The earl of Alençon, hearing this, said, "This is what one gets by employing such scoundrels, who fall off when there is any need for them." During this time a heavy rain fell, accompanied by thunder and a very terrible eclipse of the sun; and before this rain a great flight of crows hovered in the air over all those battalions making a loud noise. Shortly afterwards it cleared up, and the sun shone very bright; the Frenchmen had it in their faces, and the English in their backs. When the Genoese were somewhat in order, and approached the English, they set up a loud shout, in order to frighten them; but they remained quite still, and did not seem to attend to it. They set up a second shout, and advanced a little forward; but the English never moved.

The first division, seeing the danger they were in, sent a knight in great haste to the King of England, who was posted upon an eminence, near a windmill. On the knight's arrival, he said, "Sir, the earl of Warwick, the lord Stafford, the lord Reginald Cobham, and the others who are about your son, are vigorously attacked by the French; and they entreat that you would come to their assistance with your battalion, for, if their numbers should increase, they fear he will have too much to do." The king replied, "Is my son dead, unhorsed, or so badly wounded that he cannot support himself?" "Nothing of the sort, thank God," rejoined the knight; "but he is in so hot an engagement that he has great need of your help." The king answered, "Now, sir Thomas, return back to those that sent you, and tell them from me, not to send again for me this day, or expect that I shall come, let what will happen, as long as my son has life; and say, that I command them to let the boy win his spurs; for I am determined, if it please God, that all the glory and honour of this day shall be given to him, and to those into whose care I have intrusted him." The knight returned to his lords, and related the king's answer, which mightily encouraged them, and made them repent they had ever sent such a message.

It is a certain fact, that sir Godfrey de Harcourt, who was in the prince's battalion, having been told by some of the English, that they had seen the banner of his brother engaged in the battle against him, was exceedingly anxious to save him; but he was too late, for he was left dead on the field, and so was the earl of Aumarle his nephew. On the other hand, the earls of Alençon and of Flanders were fighting lustily under their banners, and with their own people; but they could not resist the force of the English, and were there slain, as well as many other knights and squires that were attending on or accompanying them. The earl of Blois, nephew to the king of France, and the duke of Lorraine, his brother-in-law, with their troops, made a gallant defence; but they were surrounded by a troop of English and Welsh, and slain in spite of their prowess. The earl of St. Pol and the earl of Auxerre were also killed, as well as many others. Late after vespers, the king of France had not more about him than sixty men, every one included. Sir John of Hainault, who was of the number, had once remounted the king; for his horse had been killed under him by an arrow: he said to the king, "Sir, retreat whilst you have an opportunity, and do not expose yourself so simply: if you have lost this battle, another time you will be the conqueror." After he had said this, he took the bridle of the king's horse, and led him off by force; for he had before entreated of him to retire. The king rode on until he came to the castle of la Broyes, where he found the gates shut, for it was very dark. The king ordered the governor of it to be summoned: he came upon the battlements, and asked who it was that called at such an hour? The king answered, "Open, open, governor; it is the fortune of France." The governor, hearing the king's voice, immediately descended, opened the gate, and let down the bridge. The king and his company entered the castle; but he had only with him five barons, sir John of Hainault, the lord Charles of Montmorency, the lord of Beaujeu, the lord of Aubigny, and the lord of Montfort. The king would not bury himself in such a place as that, but, having taken some refreshments, set out again with his attendants about midnight, and rode on, under the direction of guides who were well acquainted with the country, until, about day-break, he came to Amiens, where he halted. This Saturday the English never quitted their ranks in pursuit of any one, but remained on the field, guarding their position, and defending themselves against all who attacked them. The battle was ended at the hour of vespers.

Christ in Majesty with the four symbols of the Evangelists

CHURCH: HIERARCHIC AUTHORITY AND TRADITION

The medieval church was a vast institution, eventually comprising hundreds of thousands of people, from the pope and cardinals and bishops and abbots on top to humble priests and friars at the bottom. They were held together by a common commitment to service society's religious, moral, and educational needs. They were also held together by an elaborate legal system that conformed to theological doctrine but usually worked only fitfully and in a fragmented way to realize an ideal of a unified international system. As individuals, medieval churchmen were as diverse as the people today who are designated "businessmen." There were idealists and martyrs; there were scholars and saints; there were corporate managers and accountants. There were also charlatans, ignoramuses, scoundrels, and materialists within the rubric of churchmen. But taken together they were a vital, indispensable, and withal integral force in Europe and, like the nobility, an active and distinct side of the medieval triangle.

At any given time in the Middle Ages at least three-quarters of the bishops and other upper echelons of the medieval clergy came from the nobility, whereas the same proportion of the parish clergy derived from peasant families. The bishops shared much of the outlook of their brothers and cousins in the lay nobility about heroism and militarism, and between the eighth and twelfth centuries fighting bishops who buckled on armor and wielded a sword were not uncommon. Yet the church officials comprised a distinctive group in medieval society with their own view of the world. Their outlook and behavior were separate from the secular aristocracy, even though bishops, abbots, and cardinals normally stemmed from families of the higher nobility.

Churchmen agreed that all animate things participated in the great chain of being that stretched from dumb animals below through humanity and then through the angels and up to the godhead. Beings on the higher rung of this cosmic ladder rule over all those below them. This is the essence of hierarchy. While the nobility's heroism and militarism derived mostly from social circumstances and was somewhat weak on the side of theoretical formulations, the church's hierarchic traditions were articulated in elaborate theoretical formulations.

These intellectual expressions of the church's social role congregate at two poles of ecclesiastical thinking: one was an aggressive, militant, confrontational, quite utopian mind-set; the other was more moderate, pragmatic, functional, accommodating in outlook. The more common ecclesiastical social doctrine was not only that lay society was properly hierarchical, thereby valorizing the feudal order of lords and knights. Not only should the church's hierarchical system be vigorously maintained and privileged for popes and bishops against ordinary priests, monks, and nuns, but also the church and especially the pope was ultimately superior to any laymen *including* kings and emperors—spirit had to rule over power.

This highly idealistic and confrontational political theory of the church that the high medieval papacy tried to implement—amid frequent bitter resistance from monarchs and their supporters—was balanced by a more utilitarian doctrine that recognized the value of the state in providing earthly peace so that the church could do its spiritual work, an attitude parallel to the church's conscious preservation of classical culture and educational institutions that communicated the liberal arts. These institutions were designed to perpetuate Roman literate culture, establishing the secular cultural context for the church's spiritual mission. Both politically and culturally, a moderate and accommodating kind of hierarchial theory was held to be legitimate. Although the revered figure of St. Augustine of Hippo could be cited to support the more confrontational political theory of the church, this ambiguously subtle theorist also could be quoted in favor of a more moderate and pragmatic doctrine of the church's relationship to the secular state and culture.

In practice, the church commonly came somewhere down the middle—rigidly hierarchic traditions were strenuously advocated, especially in Rome, while in practice hierarchical authority within the church took account of the social exigencies of everyday life. Hierarchic ideology was mediated through institutional structures and social operations that softened the severity of ecclesiastical theory. Energetic and shrewd management, personal capacity, and private ambition turned out to be as important as grandiose theory in the life of the church hierarchy.

A utopian vision of churchmen rightfully dictating to laity, and bishops and abbots dictating to ordinary priests, monks, and nuns, and the pope in Rome as the Vicar of Christ on earth dictating to everybody—this was the world order whose realization was sought in practice so as to sustain the momentum and plausibility of the core hierarchic tradition. But at any given point more frequently common was the softening, erosion, or plain ignoring in practice of the high ideals. In respect of this complex sociological condition, the medieval church resembled the communist states of the twentieth century. A consistently militant dominant utopian theory was balanced by a more pragmatic and moderate version. In practice, there was a very broad variety of ways in which theory was implemented at particular times and in specific places. Overall, orthodox theory fell far short of full implementation, but the dominant theory persistently affected group and individual behavior.

THE PAPAL RULES

There are many medieval statements of papal authority within the church and the papal-headed church's authority over emperors and kings. The theory was not hard to enunciate and rhetorically assert; the issue was whether the papal political rules could be realized in practice. Between 1050 and 1300 the degree of implementation of centralized papal authority within the church was significant—perhaps fifty percent of the Roman ideal. Papal claims to authority over kings and emperors gained a much smaller margin of success—perhaps twenty percent of the ideal of world papal monarchy was empirically realized, although at times papal claims stirred up so much smoke and noise that church lawyers and theorists plausibly exaggerated papal success. Thus, the medieval papacy might be likened to a paper tiger, or the Wizard of Oz. After 1300 everything fell apart for the medieval papacy.

The following are the classic statements of the papal rules for governance of society; their echo still responds in Rome.

POPE GREGORY VII. 1080

This is the key theoretical pronouncement of the Gregorian Reform that sought to implement a right order in the world, which was to be dominated by the papacy. This pronouncement was the single most important declaration in the history of the medieval papacy. Gregory flavors militant hierarchic doctrine with social class resentment. Not surprisingly, the German emperor sent an army to drive Gregory VII into exile.

POPE LEO THE GREAT. 450

When the effete late Roman emperors abandoned Rome, Pope Leo I the Great became its mayor and asserted vehemently the Petrine doctrine, an interpretation of *Matthew* 16: Simon suddenly became Peter, meaning the rock, the foundation of the church, and all popes share in Peter's merits and his power as (so it was claimed) the first bishop of Rome.

POPE GELASIUS I. 495

The emperor in Constantinople could not legislate on church doctrine, Gelasius claimed, because the pope had ultimate legislative authority (*auctoritas*), while the emperor had derivative executive power (*potestas*). The argument was derived from Roman law.

THE DONATION OF CONSTANTINE.
LATER EIGHTH CENTURY

This document was forged in papal circles by a clerk named John the Mangled-Fingers to help the pope countervail the power of the rising French monarchy. It tells this story (mythical): Constantine, the first Christian emperor, comes down with dreaded leprosy. Pope Sylvester I cures him, and Constantine is so grateful that he surrenders Rome and much of Western Europe to the pope and takes up residence in the East. Emperors and kings tried to ignore the document, whose authenticity was widely believed in, although not by everyone. It was proved a forgery in the fifteenth century, by which time it didn't matter.

INNOCENT III. 1215

The most ambitious of medieval popes, after Gregory VII, and politically the most skillful, reasserts the by-now conventional high papalist position. Innocent's distinctive focus was on the church's justified use of force against religious dissenters. The pope's claim to political supremacy was supplemented by assertion of his right to impose intellectual conformity within Christian society.

GREGORY VII

[The] Son, even as he is unquestioningly believed to be God and man, so is he considered the chief of priests, sitting on the right hand of the Father and always interceding for us. Yet he despised a secular kingdom, over which the men of this world swell with pride, and came of his own will to the priesthood of the cross. Whereas all know that kings and princes are descendants of men who were ignorant of God, and who, by arrogance, robbery, perfidy, murder, — in a word by almost every crime, — at the prompting of the prince of this world, the devil, strove with blind avarice and intolerable presumption to gain the mastery over their equals, that is, over mankind.

To whom, indeed, can we better compare them, when they seek to make the priests of God bend to their feet, than to him who is chief of all the sons of pride and who tempted the highest Pontiff himself, the chief of priests, the Son of the Most High, and promised to him all the kingdoms of the world, saying, "All these will I give thee, if thou wilt fall down and worship me"?

Who doubts that the priests of Christ should be regarded as the fathers and masters of kings and princes, and of all the faithful? Is it not evidently hopeless folly for a son to attempt to domineer over his father, a pupil over his master, or for any one, by iniquitous exactions, to claim power over him by whom he himself, as he acknowledges, can be bound and loosed both on earth and in heaven?. . .

In short, any good Christian whatsoever might far more properly be considered as a king than might a bad prince; for the former, seeking the glory of God, strenuously governs himself, whereas the latter, seeking the things which are his own and not the things of God, is an enemy to himself and a tyrannical oppressor of others. Faithful Christians constitute the body of the true king, Christ; evil rulers, that of the devil. The former rule themselves in the hope that they will eternally reign with the Supreme Emperor, but the sway of the latter ends in their destruction and eternal damnation with the prince of darkness, who is king over all the sons of pride.

LEO THE GREAT

The dispensation of Truth therefore abides, and the blessed Peter persevering in the strength of the Rock, which he has received, has not abandoned the helm of the Church, which he undertook. For he was ordained before the rest in such a way that from his being called the Rock, from his being pronounced the Foundation, from his being constituted the Doorkeeper of the kingdom of heaven, from his being set as the Umpire to bind and to loose, whose judgments shall retain their validity in heaven, from all these mystical titles we might know the nature of his association with Christ. And still to-day he more fully and effectually performs what is entrusted to him, and carries out every part of his duty and charge in Him and with Him, through Whom he has been glorified. And so if anything is won from the mercy of God by our daily supplications, it is of his work and merits whose power lives and whose authority prevails in his See.

GELASIUS I

Two things there are indeed, August Emperor, by which this world is principally ruled: the consecrated authority of priests and royal power. Of these, the burden of the priests is so much the heavier, because they will answer even for the kings of men at the divine judgment. Know therefore most merciful son, that, although you may take precedence over the human race with your dignity, nevertheless you obediently bow your head to the leaders of divine affairs and look to them for the means of your salvation. In partaking of the heavenly sacraments, when they are properly dispensed, you recognize that you ought to be obedient to the religious orders rather than rule them. In these matters, therefore, you ought to rely on their judgment and not wish that they be subject to your opinion.

THE DONATATION OF CONSTANTINE

And when, with the blessed Sylvester as my teacher, I had learned that I had been restored to full health through the kindness of St. Peter himself, we, together with all the people of Rome who are subject to the glory of our rule, considered it appropriate that just as Peter seems to have been constituted as the vicar of the Son of God on earth, in the same way the pontiffs, who represent the prince of the apostles, should obtain a greater power of supremacy than that which the earthly beneficence of our serenity is seen to have. We thought that this should be conceded to him from us and from our empire, and that we should choose this same prince of the apostles, or his vicars, to be our constant intercessors with God. We decreed that his sacrosanct Roman church should be honored with veneration to the extent of our power, and that the most sacred seat of St. Peter is gloriously exalted above our empire and earthly throne. We gave it imperial power, the dignity of glory, strength, and honor. . . .

We have also decreed that our most venerable father Sylvester, supreme pontiff, and all his successors, ought to wear the diadem, that is, the crown of purest gold and jewels, which we have given him from off of our own head, for the glory of God and the honor of St. Peter. The most holy pope, however, did not at all wish to use the golden crown above the clerical crown which he wore for the glory of St. Peter. But we, with our own hands, placed a miter of gleaming splendor on his head in token of the glorious resurrection of our Lord. Then, holding the bridle of his horse, we did him the office of groom out of reverence for St. Peter and decreed that all succeeding pontiffs, and they alone, could use that miter in processions.

Behold, in imitation of our power, in order that the supreme pontificate should not deteriorate, but should rather be adorned with more power and glory than the earthly empire, we do give and relinquish to the power and dominion of the oft-mentioned most blessed pontiff, our father Sylvester, the universal pope, and to his successors, our palace, as we have said before, the city of Rome, all the provinces, districts, and cities of Italy and the western regions. We make this inviolable gift, through this our sacred imperial charter, and decree that all these things shall permanently remain within the holy Roman church.

INNOCENT III

The provision of the Roman Empire pertains to us principally and finally: principally, because it was transferred from Greece through the Roman Church, especially for the defense of the Church; finally, because, although he may receive the crown of the kingdom elsewhere, nevertheless the emperor receives the final benediction and the crown of the Empire from the Apostolic See.

. . . [The Lord] set two great lamps in the firmament of heaven, one to illuminate the day, the other to shine in the darkness. In same fashion, He ordained two great dignities in temporal affairs, in the firmament of the Church, which is called by the name of heaven: the first to illuminate the day, that is, to guide spiritual men in spiritual matters and loose souls deceived by diabolical fraud from the bondage of sin, for, because of the power given to it, those whom it binds and looses on earth, God shall consider bound and loosed in heaven; the other to shine in the darkness, to punish heretics stricken by darkness of mind, the enemies of the Christian faith, whom the rising sun has not rewarded from on high, to punish injuries done to Christ and Christians, and to use the power of the earthly sword to avenge wrongdoers and praise good men.

ST. AUGUSTINE OF HIPPO 420:

CHURCH AND STATE

Augustine was a native North African Berber who was a master of Latin rhetoric and learning. While at one point denouncing the Roman state as a band of robbers and at another saying the virtues of the pagan Romans were only splendid vices, Augustine also gave the church an alternative and more moderate doctrine with respect to its role

in the world. The only things that really count are the two cities, one of God and the other (the earthly) of the devil, which are mystical, internal communities whose membership is known only to God until the end of time. Meanwhile, let the church be a Catholic (universal) institution preaching the gospel and providing the sacramental means of grace, and let the state provide earthly peace so that the church can do its work and the pilgrimage of the heavenly city continue. Augustine thereby proposed an accommodating view of the church's role in society and its relationship with kings and nobility. In practice, this was the way things more often worked than the clanging disputes arising from efforts to assert the papal rules. Church is superior to state, Augustine believed, but they are cooperating rather than conflicting social agencies. Similarly, the church should filter and adapt classical culture for its own use. A belief in the doctrine of hierarchy was combined by Augustine with a Roman sense of social cohesion and political stability. Hierarchy could be imbedded and function within a harmonious world system. Churchmen who served kings as administrators and secretaries liked Augustine's moderate version of hierarchic theory. And many bishops, who stemmed from great noble families and committed to fulfilling onerous managerial responsibilities, found Augustine's doctrine more practical than the confrontational papal rules.

THE CITY OF GOD

The earthly city, which does not live by faith, seeks an earthly peace, and the end it proposes, in the well-ordered concord of civic obedience and rule, is the combination of men's will to attain the things which are helpful to his life. The heavenly city, or rather the part of it which sojourns on earth and lives by faith, makes use of this peace only because it must, until this mortal condition which necessitates it shall pass away. Consequently, so long as it lives like a captive and a stranger in the earthly city, though it has already received the promise of redemption, and the gift of the Spirit as the earnest of it, it makes no scruple to obey the laws of the earthly city, whereby the things necessary for the maintenance of this mortal life are administered; . . . This heavenly city, then, while it sojourns on earth, calls citizens out of all nations, and gathers together a society of pilgrims of all languages, not scrupling about diversities in the manners, laws, and institutions whereby earthly peace is secured and maintained, but recognising that, however various these are, they all tend to one and the same end of earthly peace. It therefore is so far from rescinding and abolishing these diver-

sities, that it even preserves and adopts them so long only as no hindrance to the worship of the one supreme and true God is thus introduced. Even the heavenly city, therefore, while in its state of pilgrimage, avails itself of the peace of earth, and, so far as it can without injuring faith and godliness, desires and maintains a common agreement among men regarding the acquisition of the necessaries of life, and make this earthly peace bear upon the peace of heaven; for this alone can be truly called and esteemed the peace of the reasonable creatures, consisting as it does in the perfectly ordered and harmonious enjoyment of God and of one another in God. When we shall have reached that peace, this mortal life shall give place to one that is eternal, and our body shall be no more this animal body which by its corruption weighs down the soul, but a spiritual body feeling no want, and in all its members subjected to the will. In its pilgrim state the heavenly city possesses this peace by faith; and by this faith it lives righteously when it refers to the attainment of that peace every good action towards God and man; for the life of this city is a social life.

ON CHRISTIAN DOCTRINE

All branches of heathen learning have not only false and superstitious fancies and heavy burdens of unnecessary toil, which every one of us, when going out under the leadership of Christ from the fellowship of the heathen, ought to abhor and avoid; but they contain also liberal instruction which is better adapted to the use of the truth, and some most excellent precepts of morality; and some truths in regard even to the worship of the One God are found among them. Now these are, so to speak, their gold and silver, which they did not create themselves, but dug out of the mines of God's providence which are everywhere scattered abroad, and are preversely and unlawfully prostituting to the worship of devils. These, therefore, the Christian, when he separates himself in spirit from the miserable fellowship of these men, ought to take away from them, and to devote to their proper use in preaching the gospel. Their garments, also,— that is, human institutions such as are adapted to that intercourse with men which is indispensable in this life—we must take and turn to a Christian use.

ST. BENEDICT OF NURSIA

RULES FOR MONKS

St. Benedict (d. 543) was a Roman aristocrat and monastic leader who tried to make religious communities effective and durable institutions. He blended idealism and devotion with Roman common sense and keen psychological insight. The result was one of the most successful examples of all time in constitution-drafting. The Benedictine rule represents the effective pragmatic side of the hierarchic tradition. The life of the monks lived under the *Rule* at St. Benedict's abbey at Monte Cassino near Naples was so stable, happy, and productive that in the following three centuries the *Rule* became the documentary basis for nearly all Western monastic life. The *Rule* has remained influential with Catholic orders to the present day. Until as late as 1100, the Benedictine monastery was so neatly tied to its social context that the monks undertook social responsibilities far beyond their original spiritual calling: as missionaries, secretaries to kings, episcopal office, as librarians, publishers, artists, musicians, and estate managers and improvers. St. Benedict was firmly committed to the hierarchic view of the Church and society, but he made hierarchical systems work smoothly and harmoniously. The abbot has absolute authority over the community, but he is to exercise his authority in a caring and generous fashion within the context of both spiritual idealism and human nature. What is important is that monks be devout, sincere, and happy. St. Benedict is closer to Augustine's moderate functional thinking than to the militant papal rules.

INTRODUCTION

Listen, my son, to the precepts of your Master, and incline the ear of your heart unto them. Freely accept and faithfully fulfil the advice of a loving father, so that you may, by the labor of obedience, return to Him, Whom you abandoned through the sloth of disobedience. To you, therefore, whoever you are, my words are directed, who, renouncing your own will, takes up the strong and excellent arms of obedience to fight for the true King, our Lord Christ.

Monastic Cloister walkway

In the first place, beg with most earnest prayer that He may perfect whatever good work you begin, so that He Who has seen fit to count us among the number of His sons may never be grieved by our evil deeds. For we must always so serve Him with the gifts He has given us, that He will not, as an angry father, disinherit His sons, nor, as a dread lord, be provoked by our sins to consign to perpetual punishment His most wicked servants, who did not wish to follow Him to glory.

Let us, therefore, arise at last, for the Scripture arouses us, saying: "It is now the hour to arise from sleep." And with our eyes opened to the divine light, let us hear with awe-filled ears the warning which the divine voice daily calls out to us: "Today if you will hear His voice, harden not your ears"; and again: "He who has ears to hear, let him hear what the Spirit says to the Churches." And what does He say? "Come My sons, harken unto Me, and I will teach you the fear of the Lord. Run while you have the light of life, lest the darkness of death overtake you."

And our Lord, seeking His workman among the multitude of people to whom He thus calls, says again: "Who is the man who longs for life and desires to see good days?" And if you hear this and answer: "I am he"; God says to you: "If you wish to have true and everlasting life, restrain your tongue from evil, and let not your lips speak guile. Turn away from evil and do good, inquire after peace and pursue it." And when you have done these things My eyes shall be upon you and My ears shall be open to your prayers; and before you call Me, I will say unto you; "Behold, I am here." What can be sweeter to us, dearest brothers, than this voice of the Lord inviting us? Behold, in His loving kindness, the Lord shows us the way of life.

Let us, therefore, with our loins girt up by faith and the performance of good works, follow the guidance of His Gospel and walk in His path, so that we may deserve to see Him, Who has called us into His Kingdom. If we wish to dwell in the tabernacle of His Kingdom, we shall not reach it unless we run thither with good works.

But let us, with the Prophet, question the Lord, saying to Him: "Lord, who shall dwell in Your tabernacle, and who shall rest on Your holy hill?" After this question, my brothers, let us hear the Lord answer and show us the way to His tabernacle, saying: "he who walks without blemish and works justice; he who speaks truth in his heart; he who has used no guile on his tongue; he who has done no evil to his neighbor, and has believed no evil of his neighbor." He who takes the evil demon who tempts him and casts him and his temptation from the sight of his heart and brings them to naught. He who takes his evil thoughts as they arise and dashes them against the rock which is Christ. They who, fearing the Lord, do not exalt themselves because of their good works, but know that what is good in them is not performed by them but by the Lord, and magnify the Lord working in them, saying with the Prophet: "Not unto us, O Lord, not unto us, but to Your Name give glory." Thus the apostle Paul imputed nothing of his preaching to himself, saying: "By the grace of God I am what I am." And he says again: "He who glorifies, let him glory in the Lord."

Wherefore the Lord also says in the Gospel: "He who hears these My words and does them, I will make him like unto a wise man who has built his house upon a rock; the floods came and the winds blew, they beat upon that house and it did not fall, because it was founded upon a rock."

Having answered us in full, the Lord daily expects us to make our deeds correspond with these His holy instructions. Therefore the days of this life are lengthened to give us respite in which to mend our evil ways. For the Apostle says: "Do you not know that the patience of the Lord leads you to repentance?" And our merciful Lord says: "I do not desire the death of the sinner, but that he be converted and live."

So, my brothers, we have asked the Lord about the dwellers in His tabernacle, and have heard the duties of him who would dwell therein; but we can only attain our goal if we fulfil these duties.

Therefore must our hearts and bodies be prepared to fight under the holy obedience of His commands. Let us beg the Lord to grant us the aid of His grace where our own natures are powerless. And if, fleeing the pains of hell, we wish to attain to perpetual life, then we must—while there is still time, while we are in this body and can fulfil all these precepts by the light of this life— hasten to do now what will profit us in eternity.

Therefore must we establish a school for the service of the Lord, in which we hope to ordain nothing harsh or burdensome. But if, for some sound reason, for the amendment of vices or the preservation of charity, we proceed somewhat severely at times, do not immediately become frightened and flee the path of salvation, whose entrance is always narrow. But as we progress in our life and faith, our hearts shall be enlarged and we shall follow the path of God's commandments with the unspeakable sweetness of love: so that, never departing from His rule, and persevering in His teaching in the monastery until our deaths, we may participate in the sufferings of Christ by our patience, and thus deserve to be partakers of His Kingdom. Amen.

ON THE TYPES OF MONKS

It is evident that there are four types of monks. The first are the Cenobites: that is, those who live in monasteries, serving under a rule and an abbot.

The second type is that of the Anchorites, or Hermits: that is, those who, not in the first fervor of conversion, but after long probation in a monastery, having been taught by the example of many brothers, have learned to fight against the devil and are well prepared to go forth from the ranks of their brothers to solitary combat in the desert. They are now able, with God's assistance, to fight against the vices of the flesh and evil thoughts without the encouragement of a companion, using only their own strength.

The third and worst type of monks is that of the Sarabites, who have not been tested by any rule or the lessons of experience, as gold is in the furnace, but are as soft as lead. They still follow the standards of the world in their works and are known to lie to God by their tonsure. They live in twos or threes, or even singly, without a shepherd, not in the Lord's sheepfold, but in their own. Their desires are their law: whatever they think of or choose to do, they call holy, and they consider what they do not like as unlawful.

The fourth type of monks are called the Gyrovagues. These spend their whole lives moving from one province to the next, staying as guests for three or four days in different monasteries, always wandering and never stable. They obey their own wills and the entirements of gluttony, and are in all ways inferior to the Sarabites.

It is better to pass over the wretched observances of all these men in silence than to speak of them. Let us omit these, therefore, and proceed, with God's help, to provide for the Cenobites, the strongest type of monks.

WHAT KIND OF MAN THE ABBOT OUGHT TO BE

The abbot who is worthy to rule over a monastery should always remember what he is called and suit his actions to his high calling. For he is believed to take the place of Christ in the monastery, and therefore is he called by His title, in accordance with the words of the Apostle: "Ye have received the spirit of the adoption of sons, whereby we cry: Abba, Father."

Therefore the abbot ought not to teach, ordain, or command anything which is against the law of the Lord; but he should infuse the leaven of divine justice into the minds of his disciples through his commands and teaching. Let the abbot always remember that there will be an inquiry both as to his teachings and as to the obedience of his disciples at the dread Judgment of God. Let the abbot know that whatever lack of profit the Father of the family may find in His sheep will be accounted the fault of the shepherd. However, if the shepherd has used all his diligence on an unruly and disobedient flock, and has devoted all his care to amending their corrupt ways, he shall be acquitted at the Judgment of the Lord and may say to Him with the Prophet: "I have not hidden Your justice in my heart, I have declared Your truth and Your salvation; but they have scorned and despised me." And then at last, death itself shall be the penalty for the sheep who have not responded to his care.

When, therefore, any one receives the name of abbot, he ought to rule his disciples with a twofold doctrine—that is, he should display all that is good and holy by his deeds rather than by his words. To his intelligent disciples, let him expound the commands of the Lord in words, but to those of harder hearts and simpler minds, let him

demonstrate the divine precepts by his example. All things which he teaches his disciples to be contrary to God's law, let him show in his deeds that they are not to be done, lest while preaching to others he himself should become a castaway and God should some day say to him as he sins: "Why do you declare My justice and take My testament in your mouth? For you have hated My discipline and cast My words behind you"; and: "You saw the mote in your brother's eye and did not see the beam in your own."

Let him make no distinction of persons in the monastery. Let no one be loved more than another, unless it be him who is found better in good works or obedience. Let not the free-born monk be put before the man who was born in slavery unless there is some good reason for it. But if the abbot, for some reason, shall see fit to do so, he may fix anyone's rank as he will; otherwise let all keep their own places, because whether slave or freeman, we are all one in Christ and we must all alike bear the burden of service under the same Lord. "There is no respect of persons with God." In this regard alone are we distinguished in His sight, if we are found better than others in good works and humility. Therefore let him show equal love for all; and let one discipline be imposed on all in accordance with their deserts.

In his teaching, the abbot should always observe the apostolic rule which says: "Reprove, entreat, rebuke." That is, he ought to adapt himself to the circumstances and mingle encouragements with his reproofs. Let him show the sternness of a master and the devoted affection of a father. He ought to reprove the undisciplined and unruly severely, but should exhort the obedient, meek, and patient to advance in virtue. We warn him to rebuke and punish the negligent and scornful.

Let him not blind himself to the sins of offenders, but let him cut them out by the roots as soon as they begin to appear. . . . He should use words of warning to punish, for the first and second time, those who are of gentle disposition and good understanding; but he ought to use the lash and corporal punishment to check the bold, hard, proud, and disobedient even at the very beginning of their wrongdoing, in accordance with the text: "The fool is not corrected by words"; and again: "Beat your son with a rod, and you will free his soul from death."

The abbot should always remember what he is and what he is called, and he should know that from him, to whom more is entrusted, more is also required. Let him know how difficult and arduous a task he has taken upon himself, to govern the souls and cater to the different dispositions of many men. One must be encouraged, the second rebuked, the third one persuaded; in accordance with the disposition and understanding of each. He must so adapt and accommodate himself to all that not only will he endure no loss in the flock entrusted to his care, but even rejoice in the increase of his good sheep.

Above all else, let him not slight or undervalue the salvation of the souls entrusted to him by giving more attention to transitory, earthly, and perishable matters. Let him always remember the souls he has undertaken to govern, for which he will also have to render an account. Let him not complain of lack of means, but let him remember that it is written: "Seek first the Kingdom of God, and His justice, and all things shall be given unto you"; and again: "Nothing is lacking to those who fear Him."

Let him know that they who undertake to govern souls must prepare themselves to give answer for them. Let him understand that, however great the number of brothers he has under his care, on the Day of Judgment he will have to answer to God for the souls of all of them, as well as for his own. And so, fearing always the inquiry which the shepherd must face for the sheep entrusted to him, and anxious about the answers which he must give for the others, he becomes solicitous for his own sake also. Thus, while his admonitions help others to amend, he himself is freed of all his faults.

WHETHER THE MONKS OUGHT TO HAVE ANYTHING OF THEIR OWN

This vice especially ought to be cut out of the monastery by its roots. Let no one presume to give or receive anything without the permission of the abbot or to keep anything whatever for his own, neither book, nor tablets, nor pen, nor anything else, because monks should not even have their own bodies and wills at their own disposal. Let them look to the father of the monastery for whatever is necessary and let it be forbidden for them to have anything he has not given them or allowed them to possess.

Let all things be common to all, as it is written, lest anyone should say that anything is his own or arrogate it to himself. If anyone shall be found to indulge in this most wicked vice, let him be admonished for the first and second time. If he does not amend let him undergo punishment.

WHETHER ALL SHOULD RECEIVE EQUAL MEASURE OF NECESSARY THINGS

It is written: "Distribution was made to each according to his need." By this, we do not mean that there should be—which God forbid—respect of persons, but rather consideration of infirmities. Therefore, he who needs less should give thanks to God and not be discontented; but he that needs more should be humble because of his infirmity, not exalted by the pity shown him. In this way will all members be in peace.

Before all things, let not the sin of murmuring for any reason show itself in any word or sign. If anyone shall be found guilty of this, let him undergo severe punishment.

OF OLD MEN AND CHILDREN

Although human nature is drawn towards pity for these two ages, that is, for old men and children, nevertheless let them also be cared for by the authority of the Rule. Their weakness should always be taken into account, and in no way should the severity of the Rule in regard to food be applied to them. Let them receive, on the contrary, loving consideration, and let them eat before the regularly established hours.

THE AMOUNT OF FOOD

We believe it to be sufficient for the daily meal, whether it be at the sixth or ninth hour, that every table have two cooked dishes, on account of the individual weaknesses of the brothers, so that he who, by chance, cannot eat out of the one, may eat from the other. Therefore, let two cooked dishes suffice for all the brothers, and if there are fruits or young vegetables available, let a third dish be added.

THE AMOUNT OF DRINK

"Every man has his proper gift from God, one after this manner, another after that." And therefore it is with some misgiving that we determine the amount of food for someone else. Still, having regard for the weakness of some brothers, we believe that a hemina of wine per day will suffice for all. Let those, however, to whom God gives the gift of abstinence, know that they shall have their proper reward.

But if either the circumstances of the place, the work, or the heat of summer necessitates more, let it lie in the discretion of the abbot to grant it. But let him take care in all things lest satiety or drunkenness supervene. We do read that wine is not a proper drink for monks; but since in our days monks cannot at all be persuaded of this, let us at least agree to drink sparingly and not unto satiety: for "wine makes even the wise to fall away."

OF THE DAILY MANUAL LABOR

Idleness is the enemy of the soul. The brothers, therefore, ought to be engaged at certain times in manual labor, and at other hours in divine reading. Therefore do we think this arrangement should be ordained for both times: that is, from Easter until the Kalends of October [October 1] they shall begin early in the morning, from the first until about the fourth hours, to do the necessary tasks. Let the time from the fourth until about the sixth hour be spent on reading.

After the sixth hour, let them rise from the table and rest on their beds in perfect silence. If anyone may wish to read to himself, let him do so in such a way as not to disturb the others. Let None be said early, about the middle of the eighth hour, and then let them do the work which has to be done until Vespers. If the circumstances of the place or poverty forces them to gather the harvest

by themselves, let them not be saddened on this account: because then they are truly monks, if they live by the labor of their own hands like our Fathers or the Apostles. Let all things, however, be done in moderation because of the faint-hearted. . . .

THE MANNER OF THE RECEPTION OF BROTHERS

Let not anyone, newly coming to the religious life, be granted an easy entrance; but, as the Apostle says: "Test the spirits to see whether they are of God." If, therefore, anyone perseveres in his knocking at the door, and if he is seen, after four or five days, to bear patiently the harsh treatment inflicted on him and the difficulty of admission and to persist in his petition, let admittance be granted to him, and let him stay in the guest-house for a few days. Afterwards let him stay in the novitiate, where the novices study, eat, and sleep.

And let a senior, who is skilled at the winning of souls, be appointed to watch over them with the utmost care. Let him be diligent to learn whether the novice is truly seeking God, whether he is eager for the Work of God, for obedience, and for humiliations. Let the novices be told of all the hardships and difficulties through which we journey to God.

If he promises to persevere in his purpose, at the end of two months let this Rule be read to him from beginning to end, and let him be told: "Behold the law under which you wish to serve; if you can observe it enter; but if you cannot, depart freely." If he remains there still, then let him be led back into the above-mentioned room and let him again be tested in all patience.

After the lapse of six months let the Rule be read to him so that he may know upon what he is entering. If he still abides, let this same Rule be read to him again after four months. And if, after having deliberated with himself, he promises to observe all its provisions and to obey all commands given him, then let him be received into the congregation. But let him know that from that day forth he shall not be allowed to leave the monastery nor to withdraw his neck from under the yoke of the Rule, which it was open to him, during that long period of deliberation, either to reject or accept.

When the novice is ready to be received, let him, in the oratory, in the presence of all, and in the sight of God and His Saints; promise stability, the conversion of his life, and obedience. Let him know that, if he behaves otherwise, he shall be condemned by Him, Whom he mocks. . . .

If he has any property, let him either give it beforehand to the poor, or offer it to the monastery in a formal donation. Let him keep back nothing for himself, since he knows that from that day forth he will not even have power over his own body.

In the oratory, therefore, let him be immediately stripped of his own clothes, which he is wearing, and be attired in the clothes of the monastery. The garments which he had worn, however, should be stored and preserved in the clothes-room. Then, if he ever consents to any persuasion of the devil—which God forbid—and determines to leave the monastery, he may be stripped of the clothing of the monastery before being dismissed. Let him not receive, however, his petition, which the abbot placed above the altar, but let it be preserved in the monastery.

OF PRIESTS WHO MAY WISH TO DWELL IN THE MONASTERY

If anyone of the priestly order requests to be received into the monastery, let him not obtain this permission too quickly. If, nevertheless, he still perseveres in this petition, give him to understand that he will have to observe the entire discipline of the Rule and that none of it will be lightened for him. For Scripture says: "Friend, for what purpose have you come?"

Let him be allowed, however, to stand behind the abbot in rank, to say the blessing, and to celebrate masses, if the abbot permits him to do so. If not, let him not presume to do anything, knowing that he is subject to the discipline of the Rule, and that he, especially, ought to set an example for others by his humility.

If he entered the monastery in hopes of obtaining special station or privilege, let him know that he shall achieve his rank in accordance with the length of time which he has spent in the monastery and not because of the respect for his priesthood.

Likewise, if any clerics should wish to be admitted into the monastery, let them be placed in a middle rank; but only if they promise to observe the Rule and to be stable in this observance.

THE ORDER OF THE COMMUNITY

Let all keep their order in the community according to the date of their conversion, the merit of their lives, or as the abbot shall determine. Yet let not the abbot disturb the flock entrusted to him, nor ordain any thing unjustly by making arbitrary use of his power; but let him always consider that he will have to answer to God for all his decisions and deeds.

In accordance, therefore, with the order which the abbot has determined, or the one which the brothers themselves hold, let them receive the kiss of peace, go to Communion, intone the psalms, and stand in the choir. And in no place whatsoever should age distinguish or predetermine their order, since Samuel and Daniel, although boys, judged the priests.

Except for those, therefore, whom, as we have said, the abbot has promoted by a special decision, or degraded for a definite reason, let all the rest take their rank from the date of their conversion. Thus, for example, he who came at the second hour of the day should know that he is younger than he who came at the first hour—no matter what his age or dignity may be. Boys, however, are to be kept under discipline in all things and by every one.

Let the juniors, therefore, honor their seniors; let the seniors love their juniors. In addressing each other, let no one be permitted to use the bare name: let the seniors call the juniors "Brother," and let the juniors call the seniors "Nonnus," which means "Reverend Father."

The abbot, however, because he is believed to hold the place of Christ, should be called "Lord" and "Abbot," not because of his own pretensions, but out of honor and love for Christ. Let the abbot himself remember this, and so deport himself that he may be worthy of such honor.

Whenever brothers meet each other, let the younger ask the older for his blessing. When a senior passes by, let the junior rise and give him his seat; and let not the junior presume to sit unless his senior so instructs him, in order to fulfill what is written: "Outdo one another in showing honor."

Small boys and youths shall keep strictly to their order in the oratory and at the table. Outside, however, or anywhere else, let them be supervised and disciplined, until they come to the age of discretion.

THE APPOINTMENT OF THE ABBOT

In the appointment of the abbot, let this rule always be observed: he should be made abbot whom the whole community, unanimously, and in the fear of God, or even a minority, however small, acting more wisely, has chosen. Let him who is to be appointed be chosen for the merit of his life and for his wisdom, even if he is the last in order of the community.

But if the whole congregation—which God forbid—should agree to choose a person who supports them in their vices, and this depravity somehow comes to the knowledge of the bishop, to whose diocese the monastery pertains, or to the knowledge of the neighboring abbots and Christians, let them annul the choice of the wicked, and set up a worthy steward for the house of God. . . .

After he has been appointed, let the abbot always consider how weighty a burden he has undertaken, and to Whom he will have to answer for his stewardship. Let him understand that he ought to profit his brothers rather than to preside over them. He ought, therefore, to be learned in Divine Law, so that he may know whence to bring forth things both new and old; and to be chaste, sober, and merciful. Let him always exalt mercy above justice, so that he himself may obtain mercy. Let him hate vice and love the brothers.

Let him proceed prudently in the administration of correction, lest, being too anxious to remove the rust, he break the vessel. Let him always distrust his own frailty, and remember that the bruised reed must not be broken. By this we do not mean to imply that he should allow vice to thrive; but, as we have already said, that he should remove it prudently and with charity, in the way which seems best for each case. Let him study more to be loved than to be feared. Let him not be turbulent, or anxious, or too exacting, or obstinate, or jealous, or oversuspicious, for then he will never be at rest.

He should be prudent and considerate in all his commands; and whether the task he enjoins concerns God or the world, let him be discreet and temperate, remembering the discretion of holy Jacob, who said: "If I cause my flocks to be over-driven, they shall all die in one day."

Imitating, therefore, these and other examples of discretion, the mother of virtues, let him so arrange all things that the strong shall have something to strive for, and the weak shall not be put to flight.

And, especially, let him keep the present Rule in all things, so that, having administered it well, he may hear from the Lord what was heard by the good servant, who gave wheat to his fellow-servants in due season: "Amen, I say unto you, he will set him over all his goods."

SAMSON THE MANAGERIAL ABBOT

The cares, interests, and fortunes of the head of the great English abbey of Bury St. Edmunds in the late twelfth century are described by the monk Jocelyn of Brakelond, who was there and observed his chief executive officer judiciously and compassionately. A middle echelon bureaucrat evaluates the boss. Hierarchic theory and the

Benedictine rule are the context of the Abbot Samson's administration and the ground rules for the monastery's operation. But the destiny of this immensely wealthy and socially prominent landed corporation is shaped by the personality and fortune of the abbot, just as any major corporation today is affected by its chief executive officer.

SAMSON'S PERSONAL CHARACTERISTICS

The abbot Samson was of middle stature, nearly bald, having a face neither round nor yet long, a prominent nose, thick lips, clear and very piercing eyes, ears of the nicest sense of hearing, arched eyebrows, often shaved; and he soon became hoarse from a short exposure to cold. On the day of his election he was forty and seven years old, and had been a monk seventeen years. He had then a few grey hairs in a reddish beard, and a very few in a black and somewhat curly head of hair. But within fourteen years after his election it became as white as snow.

He was a man remarkably temperate, never slothful, of strong constitution, and willing to ride or walk till old age gained upon him and moderated such inclination. On hearing the news of the Cross being taken, and the loss of Jerusalem, he began to use under garments of horsehair and a horsehair shirt, and to abstain from flesh and flesh meats. Nevertheless, he desired that meats should be placed before him at table for the increase of the alms dish. Sweet milk, honey and such like sweet things he ate with greater appetite than other food.

He abhorred liars, drunkards and talkative folk; for virtue ever is consistent with itself and rejects contraries. He also much condemned persons given to murmur at their meat or drink, and particularly monks who were dissatisfied therewith, himself adhering to the uniform course he had practised when a monk. He had likewise this virtue in himself, that he never changed the mess set before him.

Once when I, then a novice, happened to be serving in the refectory, I wished to prove if this were true, and I thought I would place before him a mess which would have displeased any other than him, in a very black and broken dish. But when he looked at it, he was as one that saw it

Scriptorium of a monastery

not. Some delay took place, and I felt sorry that I had so done; and snatching away the dish, I changed the mess and the dish for a better, and brought it to him; but this substitution he took in ill part, and was angry with me for it.

An eloquent man was he, both in French and Latin, but intent more on the substance and method of what was to be said than on the style of words. He could read English books most admirably, and was wont to preach to the people in English, but in the dialect of Norfolk, where he was born and bred; and so he caused a pulpit to be set up in the church for the ease of the hearers, and for the ornament of the church. The abbot also seemed to prefer an active life to one of contemplation, and rather commended good officials than good monks. He very seldom approved of any one on account of his literary acquirements, unless he also possessed sufficient knowledge of secular matters; and whenever he chanced to hear that any prelate had resigned his pastoral care and become an anchorite, he did not praise him for it. He never applauded men of too compliant a disposition, saying, "He who endeavours to please all, ought to please none."

In the first year of his being abbot, he appeared to hate all flatterers, and especially among the monks; but in process of time it seemed that he heard them more readily, and was more familiar with them. It once happened that a certain brother of ours, skilled in this art, had bent the knee before him, and under the pretence of giving advice, had poured the oil of flattery into his ears. I, standing apart, smiled. The brother having departed, I was called and asked why I had smiled. I answered, "The world is full of flatterers." And the abbot replied, "My son, it is long that I have known flatterers; I cannot, therefore, avoid hearing them. There are many things to be passed over and taken no notice of, if the peace of the convent is to be preserved. I will hear what they have to say, but they shall not deceive me if I can help it, as they did my predecessor, who trusted so unadvisedly to their counsel that for a long time before his death he had nothing for himself or his household to eat, unless it were obtained on trust from creditors; nor was there anything to be distributed among the poor on the day of his burial, unless it were the fifty shillings which were received from Richard the farmer, of Palgrave, which very fifty shillings the same Richard on another occasion had to pay to the King's bailiffs, who demanded the entire farm-rent for the King's use." With this saying I was comforted. His study, indeed, was to have a well-regulated house, and enough wherewith to keep his household, so managing that the usual allowance for a week, which his predecessor could not make last for five days, sufficed him for eight, nine or even ten days, if so be that he was at his manors without any extraordinary arrival of guests. Every week, indeed, he audited the expenses of the house, not by deputy, but in his own person, which his predecessor had never been wont to do.

For the first seven years he had only four courses in his house, afterwards only three, except presents and game from his parks, or fish from his ponds. And if at any time he retained any one in his house at the request of a great man, or of a particular friend, or messengers, or minstrels, or any person of that description, by taking the opportunity of going beyond sea or travelling afar off, he prudently disencumbered himself of such hangers-on.

The monks with whom the abbot had been the most intimate, and whom he liked best before he became abbot, he seldom promoted to offices merely for old acquaintance' sake, unless they were fit persons. Wherefore certain of our brethren who had been favourable to his election as abbot, said that he cared less for those who had liked him before he became abbot than was proper, and particularly that those were most favoured by him who both openly and in secret had spoken evil of him, nay, had even publicly called him, in the hearing of many, a passionate unsociable man, a proud fellow, and Norfolk barrator. But on the other hand, as after he had received the abbacy he exhibited no indiscreet partiality for his old friends, so he refrained from showing anything like hatred or dislike to many others according to their deserts, returning frequently good for evil, and doing good to them that persecuted him.

He had this way also, which I have never observed in any other man, that he had an affectionate regard for many to whom he seldom or never showed a countenance of love; according to the common proverb which says, "Where love is, there is the regard of love." And another thing I wondered at in him was, that he knowingly suffered loss in his temporal matters from his own servants, and confessed that he winked at them; but this I believe to have been the reason, that he might watch a convenient opportunity when the matter could be advisedly remedied, or that by passing over these matters without notice, he might avoid a greater loss.

He loved his kinsmen indifferently, but not less tenderly than others, for he had not, or assumed not to have, any relative within the third degree. I have heard him state that he had relations who were noble and gentle, whom he never would in any wise recognize as relations; for, as he said, they would be more a burden than an honour to him, if they should happen to find out their relationship. But he always acknowledged those as kinsmen who had treated him as such when he was a poor monk. Some of these relations (that is, those whom he found useful and suitable) he appointed to various offices in his own house, others he made keepers of manors. But those whom he found unworthy, he irrevocably dismissed from his presence.

A certain man of lowly station, who had managed his patrimony faithfully, and had served him devotedly in his youth, he looked upon as his dearest kinsman, and gave to his son, who was a clerk, the first church that fell vacant after he came to the charge of the abbey, and also advanced all the other sons of this man.

He invited to him a certain chaplain who had maintained him in the schools of Paris by the sale of holy water, and bestowed upon him an ecclesiastical benefice sufficient for his maintenance by way of vicarage. He granted to a certain servant of his predecessor food and clothing all the days of his life, he being the very man who put the fetters upon him at his lord's command when he was cast into prison. To the son of Elias, the cupbearer of Hugh the abbot, when he came to do homage for his father's land, he said, in full court, "I have for these seven years deferred taking your homage for the land which the abbot Hugh gave your father, because that gift was to the damage of the manor of Elmswell. Now I am overcome when I call to my mind what your father did for me when I was in fetters, for he sent to me a portion of the very wine whereof his lord had been drinking, and bade me be strong in God." To Master Walter, the son of Master William of Diss, suing at his grace for the vicarage of the church of Chevington, he replied, "Your father was master of the schools, and at the time when I was a poor clerk he granted me freely and in charity an entrance to his school, and the means of learning; now I, for the sake of God, do grant you what you ask."

He addressed two knights of Risby, William and Norman, at the time when they were adjudged to be in his mercy, publicly in this wise: "When I was a cloister monk, sent to Durham upon business of our church, and thence returning through Risby, being benighted, I sought a night's lodging from Norman, and I received a blank refusal; but going to the house of William, and seeking shelter, I was honourably entertained by him. Now, therefore, those twenty shillings, which are 'the mercy,' I will without mercy exact from Norman; but contrariwise, to William I give thanks, and the amerciament of twenty shillings that is due from him I do with pleasure remit."

A certain young girl, seeking her food from door to door, complained to the abbot that one of the sons of Richard, the son of Drogo, had forced her; and at length, by the suggestion of the abbot, for the sake of peace, she took one mark in satisfaction. The abbot, moreover, took from the same Richard four marks for licence to agree; but all those five marks he ordered forthwith to be given to a certain chapman, upon the condition that he should take this poor woman to wife.

In the town of St. Edmund, the abbot purchased stone houses, and assigned them for the use of the schools, so that thereby the poor clerks should be for ever free from house-rent, towards payment whereof all the scholars, whether rich or poor, were compelled twice in the year to subscribe a penny or a halfpenny.

The recovery of the manor of Mildenhall for one thousand and one hundred marks of silver, and the expulsion of the Jews from the town of St. Edmund, and the founding of the new hospital at Babwell, are proofs of great virtue.

The lord abbot sought from the King letters enjoining that the Jews should be driven away from the town of St. Edmund, he stating that whatsoever is within the town of St. Edmund, or within the banlieue thereof, of right belongs to St. Edmund: therefore the Jews ought to become the men of St. Edmund, otherwise they should be expelled from the town. Licence was accordingly given that he might put them forth, saving, nevertheless, that they had all their chattels and the value of their houses and lands. And when they were expelled, and with an armed force conducted to divers towns, the abbot gave order that all those that from henceforth should harbour or entertain Jews in the town of St. Edmund should be solemnly excommunicated in every church and at every altar. Howbeit it was afterwards conceded by the King's justices that if the Jews should come to the great pleas of the abbot to demand their debts from their debtors, on such occasion they might for two days and two nights lodge within the town, and on the third day be permitted to depart freely.

The abbot offered King Richard five hundred marks for the manor of Mildenhall, stating that the manor was worthy sixty and ten pounds by the year, and for so much had been recorded in the great roll of Winchester. And when he had conceived hopes of success in his application, the matter rested till the morrow. In the meanwhile there came a certain person to the King, telling him that this manor was well worth yearly a hundred pounds. On the morrow, therefore, when the abbot urged his suit, the King said, "It is of no avail my lord abbot, what you ask me; you shall either give a thousand marks, or you shall not have the manor." And whereas the Queen Eleanor, according to the custom of the realm, ought to have one hundred marks where the King receives a thousand, she took of us a great gold cup of the value of a hundred marks, and gave us back the same cup for the soul of her lord, King Henry, who first gave the same cup to St. Edmund. On another occasion, when the treasure of our church was carried to London for the ransom of King Richard, the same Queen redeemed that cup for one hundred marks, and restored it to us, taking in return our charter from us as an evidence of our most solemn promise, that we should never again alienate that cup from our church upon any occasion whatever.

Now, when all this money, which was got together with great difficulty, had been paid, the abbot held a chapter, and said he ought to have some portion of the great advantage derivable from so valuable a manor. And the convent answered that it was just, and "Let it be according to your wish." The abbot replied that he could well

claim the half part as his own right, demonstrating that he had paid towards this purchase more than four hundred marks, with much inconvenience to himself. But he said that he would be content with a certain allotment of that manor called Icklingham, which was most freely granted him by the convent. When the abbot heard this, he said, "And I do accept this part of the land to my own use, but not that I intend to keep the same in my own hand, or that I shall give it to my relations, but for the good of my soul and for all your souls in common, I give the same to the new hospital at Babwell, for the relief of the poor, and the maintenance of hospitality." As he said, so it was done, and afterwards confirmed by the King's Charter.

These and all other like things worthy to be written down and lauded for ever did the abbot Samson. But he said he had done nothing, unless he could have our church dedicated in his lifetime; which done, he said he wished to die. For the solemnization of this act, he said he was ready to pay two thousand marks of silver, so that the King should be present, and the affair be completed with the reverence it demanded. . . .

SAMSON AS AN ADMINISTRATOR

In that manor of the monks of Canterbury which is called Eleigh, and is within the hundred of the abbot, a case of homicide occurred; but the men of the archbishop would not permit that those manslayers should stand their trial in the court of St. Edmund. Thereupon the abbot made his plaint to King Henry, stating that Baldwin the archbishop was claiming for himself the liberties of our church, under authority of a new charter, which the King had given to the church of Canterbury after the death of St. Thomas. The King to this made answer, that he had never made any grant in derogation of the rights of our church, nor did he wish to take away from St. Edmund anything that had ever belonged to him.

On this intelligence, the abbot said to his most intimate advisers, "It is the better counsel that the archbishop should have to complain of me than I of the archbishop. I will put myself in seisin of this liberty, and afterwards will defend myself thereupon by the help of St. Edmund, whose right our charters testify it to be." Therefore suddenly and at daybreak, by the assistance of Robert of Cockfield, there were dispatched about four-score men to the town of Eleigh, who took by surprise those three manslayers, and led them bound to St. Edmund, and cast them into the body of the gaol there.

Now, the archbishop complaining of this, Ranulf de Glanville, the justiciary, commanded that those men be put by gage and pledges to stand their trial in that court wherein they ought to stand trial; and the abbot was summoned to come before the King's court to answer touching the violence and injury which he was said to have done to the archbishop. The abbot thereupon offered himself several times without any essoin.

At length, upon Ash Wednesday, they stood before the King in the chapter house of Canterbury, and the charters of the King on one side and the other were read in court. And our lord the King said: "These charters are of the same age, and emanate from the same King, Edward. I know not what I can say, unless it be that these charters contradict each other." To whom the abbot said: "Whatever observations may apply to the charters, we are seised, and hitherto have been; and of this I am willing to put myself upon the verdict of the two counties of Norfolk and Suffolk, if they do allow this to be the case."

But Archbishop Baldwin, having first conferred with his advisers, said that the men of Norfolk and Suffolk greatly loved St. Edmund, and that great part of those counties was under the control of the abbot, and therefore he was unwilling to stand by their decision. The King at this waxed wroth, and in indignation got up, and in departing said, "He that is able to receive it, let him receive it." And so the matter was put off, and the case is yet undecided.

However, I observed that some of the men of the monks of Canterbury were wounded even to death by the country folk of the town of Milden, which is situate in the hundred of St. Edmund; and because they knew that the prosecutor ought to make suit to the jurisdiction wherein the culprit is, they chose to be silent and to put up with

it, rather than make complaint thereupon to the abbot or his bailiffs, because in no wise would they come into the court of St. Edmund to plead there.

After this the men of Eleigh set up a certain cucking-stool, whereat justice was to be done in respect of deceits in the measuring of bread or corn; whereof the abbot complained to the Lord Bishop of Ely, then justiciary and chancellor. But he was anything but desirous to hear the abbot, because it was said that he was smelling after the archbishopric, which at that time was vacant. Some time afterwards, when he had come on a visitation, being entertained as legate, before he departed he made a speech at the shrine of the holy martyr. The abbot, seizing the opportunity, said to all present, "My lord bishop, the liberty which the monks of Canterbury claim for themselves is the right of St. Edmund, whose body is here present; and because you do not choose to render me assistance to protect the privileges of his church, I place that plaint between him and you. Let him from henceforth get justice done to himself." The chancellor deigned not to answer a single word; but within a year from that time was driven from England, and experienced divine vengeance.

THE ABBOT'S FOIBLES

The wise man hath said, "No one is in every respect perfect"; nor was the abbot Samson. For this reason let me say this, that according to my judgment the abbot was not to be commended when he caused a deed to be made and ordered the same to be delivered to a certain servant of his, for him to have the sergeanty of John Ruffus, after the decease of the same John. Ten marks, as it was said, "did blind the eyes of the wise." Wherefore, upon Master Dennis, the monk, saying that such an act was unheard of, the abbot replied: "I shall not cease from doing as I like a whit the more for you than I would for that youngster." The abbot also did the like thing in respect of the sergeanty of Adam the infirmarer, upon payment of one hundred shillings. Of such an act it may be said, "A little leaven leaveneth the whole lump."

There is, also, another stain of evil doing, which I trust in the Lord he will wash away with tears, in order that a single excess may not disfigure the sum total of so many good deeds. He built up the bank of the fish-pond at Babwell so high, for the service of a new mill, that by the keeping back of the water there is not a man, rich or poor, who has land near the water, from the gate of the town to Eastgate, but has lost his garden and his orchards. The pasture of the cellarer, upon the other side of the bank, is spoilt. The arable land, also, of the neighbouring folk has been much deteriorated. The meadow of the cellarer is ruined, the orchard of the infirmarer has been flooded by the great flow of water, and all the neighbouring folk are complaining thereof. Once, indeed, the cellarer argued with him in full chapter, upon this excessive damage; but he, quickly moved to anger, made answer, that his fish-pond was not to be spoilt on account of our meadows.

The Dean of London writes thus in his chronicles: "King Henry the Second, having conferred with the archbishop and bishops concerning the vacant abbacies, so far observed the rule of the canons in appointing abbots, that it was the custom to appoint them upon votes solicited from other houses; thinking, perhaps, that if pastors were set up in every place from their own body," a previously contracted familiarity would afford impunity to vice, and old acquaintanceship would give indulgence to wickedness, and thereby too great remissness would obtain in cloisters. Another has said: "It does not seem fit that a pastor should be elected from his own house, but rather from some other house; because, if he is taken from elsewhere he will always believe, according to the greatness of the monastery which he has undertaken to rule, that many are good men and true, whose advice he will seek if he is a good man, and whose honesty he will fear if he is a bad one. But a servant of the house, better knowing the ignorance, inability and incompetence of every one, will the more carelessly serve therein, mixing square with round."

The monks of Ramsey followed this line of reasoning; for in those days, when they were able to choose one of their own body, on two occasions they chose an abbot from other houses.

In the year of grace one thousand two hundred and one there came to us the abbot of Flay, and through his preaching caused the open buying and selling which took place in the market on Sundays to be done away with, and it was ordained that the market should be held on the Monday. The like the abbot brought to pass in many cities and boroughs of England.

In the same year the monks of Ely set up a market at Lakenheath, having the permission, as well as the charter, of the King. Now, we in the first place, dealing peaceably with our friends and neighbours, sent our messengers to the chapter of Ely, and, first of all, to the lord Bishop of Ely, letters of request that he should forbear his intentions; adding that we could, in a friendly way, for the sake of peace and preserving our mutual regard, pay the fifteen marks that were given as a fine for obtaining the King's charter. Why make a long story of it? They would not give way, and then upon all sides arose threatening speeches, and "spears threatening spears."

We therefore procured a writ of inquest to ascertain whether that market was established to our prejudice, and to the damage of the market of the town of St. Edmund. The oath was made, and it was testified that this had been done to our damage. Of all which, when the King was informed, he caused it to be inquired, by his registrar, what sort of charter he had granted to the monks of Ely; and it was made to appear that he had given to them the aforesaid market, under such conditions that it should not be to the injury of the neighbouring markets. The King, therefore, forty marks being offered, granted us his charter that from thenceforward there should be no market within the liberty of St. Edmund, unless by the assent of the abbot. And he wrote to Geoffrey Fitz-Peter, his justiciary, that the market of Lakenheath should be abolished. The justiciary wrote the same to the sheriff of Suffolk.

The sheriff, being well aware that he could not enter upon the liberties of St. Edmund, or exercise any authority there, gave it in charge to the abbot, by his writ, that this should be performed according to the form of the royal command. The steward of the hundred, therefore, coming thither upon the market day, with the witnessing of freemen, in the King's name openly prohibited that market, showing the letters of the King and the sheriff; but being treated with great abuse and violence, he departed, without having accomplished his object.

The abbot, on the other hand, deferring this matter for awhile, being at London, and consulting the learned thereupon, commanded his bailiffs, that taking with them the men of St. Edmund with horse and arms, they should abolish the market, and that they should bring along with them in custody the buyers and sellers therein, if they should find any. So at dead of night, there went forth nearly six hundred men well armed, proceeding towards Lakenheath. But when the scouts gave intelligence of their arrival, all who were in the market ran hither and thither, and not one of them could be found.

Now, the prior of Ely on that same night had come thither, with his bailiffs, expecting the arrival of our men, in order that, to the best of his ability, he might defend the buyers and sellers; but he would not stir out of his inn. When our bailiffs had required from him gage and pledge to stand trial in the court of St. Edmund for the wrong committed by him, and he had refused, upon consultation, they overturned the butchers' shambles and the tables of the stalls in the market, and carried them away with them. Moreover, they led away with them all the cattle, "all sheep and oxen; yea, and the beasts of the field," and set off towards Icklingham. The bailiffs of the prior following them made suit for their cattle, by replevin within fifteen days: and their suit was allowed. Within the fifteen days there came a writ, whereby the abbot was summoned to come before the court of exchequer to answer for such act, and that the cattle taken should in the meantime be delivered up without charge. For the Bishop of Ely, who was an eloquent and well-spoken man, in his own person had made complaint thereof to the justiciary and the nobles of England, saying that a most unheard-of piece of arrogance had been committed in the land of St.

Etheldreda in time of peace; wherefore many were highly indignant with the abbot.

In the meanwhile another cause of disagreement arose between the bishop and the abbot. A certain young man of Glemsford had been summoned to the court of St. Edmund, for a breach of the King's peace, and had been sought for a long while. At length the steward of the bishop brought forth that young man in the county court, claiming the jurisdiction of the court of St. Etheldreda, and exhibiting the charters and privileges of his lord; but our bailiffs, claiming the jurisdiction of the plaint and the seisin of such liberty, could not be heard. The county court, indeed, put that plaint in respite until the justices in eyre should arrive, wherefore St. Edmund was ousted of his jurisdiction. The abbot, on hearing this, proposed to go over to the King; but because he was sick, he decided to defer the matter till the Purification.

And, behold! on St. Agnes day there came the King's messenger, bearing the writ of our lord the Pope, wherein it was contained, that the bishop of Ely and the abbot of St. Edmund should make inquisition concerning Geoffrey Fitz-Peter and William de Stutville, and certain other lords of England who had taken the cross, for whom the King required discharge, alleging their personal infirmity, and the necessity for their advice in the government of his kingdom. The same messenger also brought letters from our lord the King, commanding that he, upon the sight thereof, should come to him to confer upon the message of our lord the Pope. The abbot was troubled in his mind, and said, "I am straitened on every side; I must either offend God or the King: by the very God, whatsoever may be the consequence to me, I will not wittingly lie."

Therefore, returning home with all speed, somewhat weakened by infirmity of body and humbled, and (as was not his wont) timid, by the intervention of the prior, he sought advice of us (a thing he heretofore had seldom done), as to what course he was to pursue in respect of the liberties of the church which were in jeopardy, and whence the money was to come if he took his journey, and to whom the keeping of the abbey was to be committed, and what should be done for his poor servants who had a long time served him. And the answer was, that he might go, and that he was at liberty to take up at interest sufficient money, to be payable out of our sacristy and from our pittances, and from our other rents at his pleasure; and that he should give the abbey in charge to the prior, and some other clerk whom he had enriched, and who could, in the interval, live upon his own means, that thereby a saving might take place in the expenses of the abbot, and that he might give to each of his servants money proportioned to his length of service.

He, hearing such counsel, was pleased therewith, and so it was done. The abbot, therefore, coming into chapter the day before he took his departure, caused to be brought with him all his books, and these he presented to the church and convent, and commended our counsel which we had signified to him through the prior.

In the meantime we heard certain persons murmuring, saying that the abbot is careful and solicitous for the liberties of his own barony, but he keeps silence respecting the liberties of the convent which we have lost in his time; namely, concerning the lost court and liberties of the cellarer, and the liberty of the sacrist, as regards the appointment of the bailiffs of the town by the convent. Therefore, the Lord raised up the spirit of three brethren of but indifferent knowledge, who, having got many others to join them, conferred with the prior thereupon, in order that he should speak with the abbot respecting these matters. On our behalf the prior was to ask him, at his departure, to provide for the security of his church in respect of those liberties. On hearing this, the abbot answered that no more was to be said upon the subject, swearing that so long as he lived he would be the master; but towards evening he talked more mildly thereupon with the prior.

On the morrow, indeed, sitting in chapter, as he was about to depart and ask licence so to do, he said he had satisfied all his servants, and had made his will just as if he was now to die; and beginning to speak concerning those liberties, he

Initial page of the Gospel of Matthew

justified himself, saying that he had changed the ancient customs in order that there should not be a default in the administration of the King's justice, and threw the blame upon the sacrist, and said that if Durand, the town bailiff, who was now sick, should die, the sacrist might hold the bailiwick in his own hand, and present a bailiff to the chapter for approval, as the custom had been of old, so nevertheless that this be done with the assent of the abbot; but the gifts and offerings to be made yearly by the bailiff he would in no wise remit.

Now, when we asked him what was to be done in respect of the cellarer's court which was lost, and especially of the halfpence which the cellarer was accustomed to receive for renewing pledges, he became angry, and asked us in his turn by what authority we demanded the exercise of regal jurisdiction, and those things which appertain to regalities.

To this it was replied that we had possessed it from the foundation of the church, and even three years after he had come to the abbacy, and this liberty of renewing pledges we possessed in every one of our manors. We stated that we ought not to lose our right in consideration of a hundred shillings, which he received privately from the town bailiff every year; and we boldly required of him to give us such seisin thereof as we had had even in his time.

The abbot, being as it were at a loss for an answer, and willing enough to leave us all in peace and to depart quietly, ordered that those halfpence and the other matters which the cellarer demanded should be sequestrated until his return; and he promised that upon his return he would cooperate with us in everything, and make just order and disposition, and render to each what was justly his. On his saying this, all was quiet again; but the calm was not very great, for "In promises any man may wealthy be."

 ARCHBISHOP ODO OF ROUEN

DIOCESAN VISITATION

Instituted universally in the Latin Church by Pope Innocent III in 1215 and continuing on a grand scale for about a century, until the collapse of papal power and rigorous ecclesiastical discipline, was the papal requirement that a bishop inspect all operations in the diocese, down to the smallest nunnery and the most remote parish. This was logistically very difficult in a large diocese such as Rouen in Normandy. Archbishop Odo nevertheless tried his best. It is as if the president of a large American state university decided to inspect all freshmen classes being conducted by teaching assistants. The encounter between hierarchic power and bottom rungs of the clergy was a chastening experience for both parties and largely a waste of time and money. Even more than the dramatic conflicts with monarchs that the papal political doctrines precipitated, the visitation system shows how dysfunctional Roman theory could be when faced with complex social reality. The visitation records are often amusing to read. Hierarchic doctrine made the bishop personally responsible for drinking and fornication among the lower clergy. How he was to correct this conduct and still conduct the complex business of his huge archdiocese, nobody knew.

January 25.

We visited at Ste-Catherine, where there are thirty monks. Caleboche and another monk, who are now in prison, sing dissolute songs; we ordered that they be corrected by cutting off their food and subjecting them to flagellation. We decreed that the monastery should bring the number of its monks up to the statutory number.

October 3.

We visited the chapter at Les Andelys. Master Robert is a drunkard. Dom Peter, the sacristan, is also a toper, and quarrelsome withal. Dom Miles is too hasty of temper.

July 23.

We visited the priory at St. Aubig where there are fifteen nuns. We forbade the relatives of the nuns to sleep at the priory or to eat or drink with the nuns therein. Item, we forbade them to receive anyone as a nun without our special permission; if they do receive such a one, she is not to be regarded as a nun.

We, at the time, took the veil away from Alice of Rouen and from Eustasia of Etrépagny because of their fornications. We sent Agnes of Pont to the leper house at Rouen, because she had connived at Eustasia's fornication, and indeed had even arranged it, as the rumor goes; further, she gave the said Eustasia, as report has it, some herbs to drink in order to kill the child already conceived within the said Eustasia. We removed the prioress from her office. Until a new prioress shall be instituted, we have suspended punishment of Anastasia, the subprioress, who is ill famed of incontinence.

January 21.

We visited the priests of the deanery of Foucarmont in the same church. We found that the priest at Mesnil-David was ill famed of a certain woman from La Boissière, and because, when brought into our presence he would not admit the truth of this, we ordered the dean to make an investigation to determine whether the said woman from La Boissière was in the habit of being with the said priest, whether any other woman had been with him in a suspicious manner during the past year and more, and whether there was any scandal about these things or any one of them.

CHRISTIAN IDEALISM: ALCUIN OF YORK AND JACOB DE VORAGINE

The church's theory of hierarchic authority aimed at a system for governing human society. Some of this government was uncontroversial and socially valuable. Some was persistently controversial and difficult and expensive to implement. There was plenty of criticism of the papal rules in the Middle Ages, particularly from kings and emperors whose own self-interest and corporate ambitions clashed with those of the papacy. In the later medieval centuries the papal rules for government of humanity also encountered sharp criticism from some intellectuals, of course usually not disinterested or nonpartisan, but still sharp in their critiques. Yet the hierarchic tradition of the Catholic Church continued, and indeed still persists, in only moderately less challenging form, to the present day. What kept the hierarchic idea vigorous and persuasive was the pure stream of Christian idealism at its center. The example of personal commitment to their calling by many churchmen and their enthusiastic vision of the church as a sacramental instrument of salvation rather than, or at least more than, as a power center and bureaucracy—this kind of deep spiritual feeling enriched the hierarchic tradition generation after generation and preserved its thrust and viability. Here are two excellent examples of the spiritual idealism encased at the center of the medieval hierarchic tradition. In the late eighth century the Englishman Alcuin of York, the chief educationalist and publisher in the French realm, celebrated the idealism of his kinsmen, the Anglo-Saxon missionaries and martyrs on the continent. In the mid-thirteenth century, Jacob de Voragine—a professional author of devotional literature—wrote a little treatise on the dedication and concentration of churches. What could easily have been a dry piece of bureaucratic information became in Voragine's hand an inspired discourse, a lyrical work of spiritual uplift. If the Roman Catholic Church has sometimes been ill-served by its hyperpolitical advocates, it has also benefited from religious rhetoric that has sustained its vision of itself as a company of pilgrims.

ALCUIN OF YORK: MISSIONARIES AND MARTYRS

This race of ours, mother of famous men,
did not keep her children for herself,
nor held them within the confines of her own
     kingdom,
but sent many of them afar across the seas,
bearing the seeds of life to other peoples.
One of them was a holy bishop
called Egbert who, early in life, had left
his native country for love of his heavenly home-
     land
and, travelling abroad, set the Irish an example
of how to live; a shining light in his teaching,
he instructed all manner of men by his words and
     deeds.
Generous to the poor, but stinting himself,
this goodly man led an excellent life
brilliant with outstanding piety until the day of
     his death.
His fitting companion by character and achieve-
     ments
and comrade in exile was Wihtberht, a figure of
     high renown
for his godliness. Later he separated from Egbert
to lead in strict solitude a life of contemplation.
Then he built an excellent shelter for the monks
     of his race,
and was a credit to it through his upright and
     moral life.
Zealous to feed the sheep of Christ,
he led them devoutly, by the straight and narrow,
to the pastures of the eternal kingdom.
So he became famous for his miracles and,
     prophet-like,
saw much of the future, his fame remaining wide-
     spread,
and afterwards entered the joys of eternal life.
     Others travelled in ships across the eastern
          seas
in quest of pagan lands, where they attempted to
     spread
the word of salvation by sowing it in barbarian
     hearts.
Thus was the excellent bishop Willibrord,
who had won many thousands of the Frisian peo-
     ple for Christ

through God's instruction and for many years
had brought glory to his episcopal office,
he built there many a church to God
and set in them priests and ministers of the
     Word.
After completing all this labour, he ended his life
     in peace.
Two priests followed his example,
burning with intense fervour for the Faith,
and both of them were called by the same name
     of Hewald.
Their mission in life was the same; identical were
     their deaths.
One was fair, the other dark, the only difference
     being the
colour of their hair; but dark Hewald was keener
     on learning
than the fair Hewald. They entered the land of the
     pagan
Saxons, attempting to win some of them over to
     Christ.
But when the wretches saw the new morals and
     customs of
the Faith, they were afraid that the cult of their
     ancient gods
might be subverted rapidly and completely. Sud-
     denly they
laid hold of the monks and put them to a cruel
     death:
fair Hewald was immediately murderously
     slaughtered
but rugged dark Hewald, poor wretch, they long
     tortured,
and tossed the corpses of both into the waters of
     the Rhine.
The bodies were carried off in a wondrous way
against that river's powerful current,
floating eleven miles back to their compan-
     ions.
Wherever the bodies touched at night-time,
a brilliant ray of light shone more brightly than
     the stars
and the murderers of these holy men saw
it gleaming on throughout the night.
One of them appeared at night to a comrade of
     his,
and said: 'You can find our bodies without delay,

where you see the light streaming from the heavens.'

Nor did this vision deceive the Hewalds' comrades,

for they found the corpses in that very place

and buried them with the honour that is due to holy martyrs.

JACOB DE VORAGINE: THE DEDICATION AND CONSECRATION OF A CHURCH

The dedication of a church is celebrated by the Church among the other festivities of the year; and since a church or temple is not only a material thing but a spiritual one, we must here briefly treat of the dedication of this twofold temple. With regard to the dedication of the material temple, three things are to be seen, namely, why it is dedicated or consecrated, how it is consecrated, and by whom it is profaned. And since in the church two things are consecrated, namely the altar and the temple itself, we must first see why the altar is consecrated.

The altar is consecrated unto three purposes. The first is the offering of the Sacrament of the Lord, as we read in *Genesis:* 'Noe built an altar unto the Lord: and taking of all cattle and fowls that were clean, offered holocausts upon the altar.' This Sacrament is the Body and Blood of Christ, which we offer in memory of His Passion, as He Himself commanded, saying: 'Do this for a commemoration of Me.' Indeed, we have a threefold memorial of the Lord's Passion. The first is written or depicted, as in the images of the Passion of Christ, and this is directed to the eye. Thus the Crucifix and the other images in the church are intended to awaken our memories and our devotion, and to instruct us, they being as the layman's book. The second memorial is the spoken word, namely the preaching of the Passion of Christ, and this is addressed to the ear. The third is in the Sacrament, which so distinctly expresses the Passion, since it really contains and offers to us the Body and Blood of Christ; and this memorial is directed to the taste. Hence if the depiction of Christ's Passion inflames our love strongly, and

Facade of Reims Cathedral from the northwest

its preaching more strongly, we should be moved more strongly still by this Sacrament, which expresses it so clearly.

The second purpose for which the altar is consecrated is the invocation of the Lord's name, as we read in *Genesis:* 'Abram built there an altar to the Lord, Who had appeared to him . . . and called upon his name.' The Lord's name is to be invoked, according to the apostle in the *First Epistle to Timothy,* either by supplications, which are entreaties for the removal of evils, or by intercessions, which are offered for blessings to be acquired, or by thanksgivings, which are made for the preservation of goods already possessed. The invocation which is performed upon the altar is properly called the Mass, from the Latin *missa,* a thing sent, because Christ is sent from Heaven by the Father, through him who consecrates the Host, and through the same is sent by us to the Father to intercede for us. Hence Hugh says: 'The sacred Host itself may be called the Mass, *missa,* because it is transmitted, first by the Father, through the Incarnation, and then by us to the Father, through the Passion.' Similarly Christ is sent in this Sacrament, first by the Father to us, in the Sacrament itself, through which He begins to be with us, and then by us to the Father in the sacrifice, by which He intercedes for us.

We may note here that the Mass is sung in three languages, namely the Greek, the Hebrew, and the Latin, to represent the title of Our Lord's Passion, which was written in these three languages, and also to signify that every tongue should give praise to God. Hence the Gospels, the Epistles, the orations, and the chants are in Latin; the *Kyrie eleison* and *Christe eleison* are in Greek, and are repeated nine times, to signify that we are to enter the company of the nine orders of angels; and *amen, alleluia, sabaoth,* and *hosanna,* are Hebrew words.

Thirdly, the altar is consecrated for the singing of the chant, as is indicated in *Ecclesiasticus:* 'He gave him power against his enemies; and he set singers before the altar, and by their voices he made sweet melody.' According to Hugh of Saint Victor, this melody is of three kinds, for there are three kinds of musical sounds, namely those that are produced by striking, by wind, and by singing. The first pertains to the harp, the second to the organ, and the third to the voice. This harmony of sound may be applied not only to the offices of the Church, but to the harmony of virtue, if the works of the hands are compared to the striking of the harp, the devotion of the mind to the blowing of the organ, and vocal prayer to the singing of the voice. Hence Hugh says: 'What profiteth the sweetness of the mouth without the sweetness of the heart? Thou subduest thy voice, subdue thy will also; thou preservest harmony of voices, preserve also the harmony of virtues, so as to be in accord with thy neighbour by example, with the Lord by thy will, with the governor by obedience.'

The church itself is consecrated for a fivefold reason. The first is to drive out the Devil and his power. In one of his *Dialogues,* Gregory relates that when a certain church, which had belonged to the Arians and had been restored by the faithful, was consecrated, and the relics of Saint Sebastian and Saint Agatha were borne into it, the congregation heard a pig running hither and thither between their feet, and seeking the door; but none could see the pig, and all were moved to wonder. By this the Lord showed, as was clear to all, that an unclean dweller was departing from the place. The following night, a loud noise was heard in the church, as if someone were running about in the roofs. The second night this noise was still louder, and the third night it was as terrifying as if the whole church were about to be overturned. Then it ceased, and the Devil disturbed that church no more; but by this hubbub he made known with what reluctance he quit a place which he had so long held. Thus says Gregory.

Secondly, the church is consecrated in order that those who take refuge therein may be saved. Whence the Canon says: 'The church shall defend those who are guilty of blood, lest they lose life or limb.' Hence Joab fled into a certain tabernacle of the Lord, and laid hold on the horn of the altar.

Thirdly, it is consecrated in order that the prayers offered therein may be granted, whence Solomon, at the dedication of the Temple, said: 'So when he shall come, and shall pray in this place, then hear thou in heaven, in the firmament of thy dwelling place, and do all those things, for which that stranger shall call upon thee.' We turn toward the East when praying in the churches, and this, according to Damascenus, is for three reasons. God planted paradise in Eden in the East, and we exiles thus turn our faces toward our true country; Christ, when He was crucified, faced the West, and we look back to Him; and when He ascended, He was taken up toward the East, and we turn to Him as waiting for His coming as the Judge.

Fourthly, the church is consecrated in order that God's praises may be sung within it. This is done in the seven canonical Hours, namely Matins, Prime, Terce, Sext, Nones, Vespers, and Compline. For although God is to be praised at every hour of the day, yet, because our weakness could not suffice thereto, it was ordained that we should praise Him especially at these hours, forasmuch as they are more privileged than the others. For at midnight, when Matins are sung, Christ was born, taken captive, and mocked by the Jews, and in that hour he harrowed Hell. Moreover, He rose from the dead before dawn, and appeared at the first hour of the day; and it is said that He will come to the judgement in the middle of the night. Hence we praise God at midnight, in the office of Matins, in order to thank Him for His birth, for His capture, and for His setting free the fathers, and to await His coming watchfully. And Lauds, the Psalms of praise, are added to Matins, because it was in the morning that God drowned the Egyptians in the sea, created the world, and rose from the dead. Hence we sing Lauds at that hour, in order not to be submerged with the Egyptians in the sea of this world, and to thank God for our creation and for His Resurrection. At the first hour Christ came most often to the Temple, and the people came to meet Him there; He was presented before Pilate as soon as it was day; and at that selfsame hour He appeared to the women after His Resurrection. Hence at this first hour of the day we praise God in the office of Prime, in order to imitate Christ, to thank Him arising and appearing, and to give the first fruits of the day to God, the Principle of all things. At the third hour, Christ was crucified by the tongues of the Jews, was scourged at the pillar by Pilate (and it is said that the pillar to which He was bound still shows traces of His blood), and at this same hour the Holy Ghost was sent. At the sixth hour Christ was nailed to the Cross, and darkness came over the whole earth, that the sun, mourning for the death of its Lord, might be covered with sombre weeds, and might not give light to them that were crucifying the Lord. Likewise at this hour, on the day of His Ascension, He sat down with His disciples. At the ninth hour, Christ gave up the ghost, the soldier opened His side, the apostles were wont to come together for prayer, and Christ ascended into Heaven. On account of these prerogatives, we praise God at these hours. At eventide Christ instituted the Sacrament of His Body and Blood at the Last Supper, washed the feet of His disciples, was taken down from the Cross and laid in the sepulchre, and manifested Himself to the two disciples in the garb of a pilgrim; and for all these things the Church gives thanks in the office of Vespers. In the hour after sunset He sweated drops of blood, was entrusted to the tomb and reposed there, and brought the message of peace to His disciples after His Resurrection; and for these things we give thanks in the office of Compline.

Fifthly, the church is consecrated in order that in it the Sacraments of the Church may be administered. Thus the church becomes, as it were, the very hostel of God, wherein the Sacraments are contained and administered. Some are administered and given to them that come in, namely Baptism; some, to those that go out, namely Extreme Unction; and some to those that dwell within. Of these latter, some are ministers, and to them Order is given. Some are fighters, and of the fighters some fall, and to them Penance is given; some withstand, and to them strength and boldness of spirit is given, through Confirmation. To all, food is given to sustain them, and this by the receiving of the Eucharist; and finally, stumbling blocks are removed lest anyone stumble, and this by the union of matrimony.

Next we must see how the consecration is done, and firstly, the consecration of the altar. In this ceremony several things are included. First, four crosses are traced with blessed water upon the corners of the altar, second, the consecrator walks around it seven times, third, it is seven times sprinkled with holy water with a hyssop, fourth, incense is burnt upon it, fifth, it is anointed with chrism, and sixth, it is covered with clean cloths. These things signify the virtues which they should have who approach the altar. First, they should have the fourfold charity which comes from the Cross, namely the love of God, of self, of friends, and of enemies; and these four loves are symbolized by the four crosses traced upon the horns of the altar. Of these four horns of charity it is written in *Genesis:* 'Thou shalt spread abroad to the west, and to the east, and to the north, and to the south.' Again, the four crosses signify that Christ, by the Cross, brought salvation to the four quarters of the world: or again, that we should bear Our Lord's Cross in four ways, namely in our heart by meditation, in our mouth by open profession, in our body by mortification, and upon our face by continually signing it with the cross.

Second, those that mount the altar should watch over their flocks with vigilance and care, as is signified by the sevenfold circuit of the altar. Hence Gilbert places the negligence of a prelate in the number of ridiculous things, for he says: 'A ridiculous, or rather perilous thing is a blind spectator, a lame runner, a negligent prelate, an ignorant teacher, or a dumb herald.' Or these seven circuits represent the seven meditations or considerations concerning the sevenfold humility of Christ, which we should ofttimes turn over in our minds. This sevenfold virtue consisted first, in that being rich, He was made poor; second, in that He was placed in the crib; third, in that He was subject to His parents; fourth, in that He bowed His head beneath the hand of a slave; fifth, in that He bore with a thieving and traitorous disciple; sixth, in that He meekly held His peace before a wicked judge; seventh, in that He mercifully prayed for those that crucified Him.

Third, those that go to the altar should be mindful of Our Lord's Passion, which is signified by the sprinkling with water; for the seven aspersions stand for the seven sheddings of Christ's blood, of which the first was in the circumcision, the second in the prayer in the garden, the third in the scourging, the fourth in the crowning with thorns, the fifth in the piercing of His hands, the sixth in the nailing of His feet, and the seventh in the opening of His side. Or again, the seven aspersions signify that in baptism the seven gifts of the Holy Ghost are given.

Fourth, those who approach the altar should be fervent and devout in prayer, as is symbolized in the burning of the incense. For incense has the power of mounting upward by the lightness of its smoke, of healing by its medicinal properties, of holding firmly by its stickiness, and of giving strength by its aromatic odour. Thus prayer ascends unto the memory of God; and it heals the soul of past sins by obtaining their redress, holds it firmly against future falls by obtaining caution,

and gives strength against present temptation by obtaining God's protection.

Fifth, the ministers of the altar should have cleanness of conscience and good renown, as is signified by the chrism, which is composed of oil and balsam. They should have a pure conscience that they may say, with the apostle: 'For our glory is this, the testimony of our conscience'; and a fair repute: 'He must have a good testimony of them who are without.' And Chrysostom says: 'Clerks should be without stain either in word or in thought or in deed or in renown, because they are the beauty and the power of the Church; and if they be evil, they bring shame upon the whole Church.'

Sixth, they should have the cleanness of good conduct, which is symbolized by the clean white cloths wherewith the altar is covered. For clothing is used to cover, to warm, and to adorn; and in like manner, good works clothe the soul's nakedness, adorn the soul with righteousness, and warm it unto charity. And little would it avail him who mounted the altar, if he had the highest dignity and the lowest life.

Having seen how the altar is consecrated, we must now treat of the manner of consecrating the church; and in this, too, several things are included. The bishop first goes around the church three times, and each time, when he comes to the door, he strikes it with his pastoral staff, and says: *Attollite portas principes vestras,* 'lift up your gates, O ye princes, and be ye lifted up, O eternal gates; and the King of Glory shall enter in!' The church is sprinkled within and without with blessed water. A cross of ashes and sand is made upon the floor, from one corner at the eastern end to the transverse corner at the western end, and in this cross the letters of the Greek and Latin alphabets are inscribed. Crosses are painted on the walls of the church, and these are anointed with chrism, and candles are lighted before them. The triple circuit of the church symbolizes the triple circuit which Christ made for the sanctification of the Church; for first, He came from Heaven to earth, second He descended from earth to Limbo, and third, He returned from Limbo, arose, and ascended to Heaven. Or it shows that the church is consecrated to the honour of the Blessed Trinity. Or again, it denotes the three states of those who are to be saved in the Church, namely the virgins, the continent, and the married. These three states are also signified in the arrangement of the church building, as Richard of Saint Victor shows; for the sanctuary denotes the order of the virgins, the choir the order of the continent, and the body of the church, the order of the married. The sanctuary is narrower than the choir, and the choir narrower than the body of the church, because the virgins are fewer in number than the continent, and they than the married. In like manner the sanctuary is holier than the choir, and the choir than the body of the church. Thus Richard.

The thrice-repeated knocking at the door of the church signifies the threefold right which Christ has in the church, by reason of which it must be opened unto Him. The Church belongs to Him by right of creation, of redemption, and of the promise of glory. Of this threefold right Anselm says: 'Certes, Lord, because Thou didst make me, I owe myself wholly to Thy love; because Thou didst redeem me, I owe myself wholly to Thy love; because Thou dost promise me such great things, I owe myself wholly to Thy love. And indeed, I owe more than myself to Thy love, inasmuch as Thou art greater than I, for whom Thou didst give Thyself, and to whom Thou dost promise Thyself.'

The triple proclamation, 'Lift up your gates, O ye princes,' denotes the threefold power of Christ, namely in Heaven, in earth, and in Hell.

The church is sprinkled within and without with blessed water for a triple purpose. The first is to drive out the Devil; for the blessed water has this power. The second is to purify the church; for all earthly things are corrupted and stained by sin, and therefore the place itself must be freed, purged, and purified of all foulness and uncleanness. The third is to remove every malediction; for the earth with its fruit was cursed from the beginning, because deception was wrought with its fruit. But water lay under no malediction, and therefore the church, which is of the earth, is sprinkled with blessed water, in order to remove every curse, and to bring blessings upon it.

The double alphabet which is written upon the floor signifies the joining together of the two peoples, namely the Jews and the Gentiles; or it denotes a page of each Testament, or the articles of our faith. The union of the Jews and the Gentiles in the faith was accomplished by Christ's Cross, which likewise fulfilled both the Old and the New Testaments. The articles of the faith are denoted, because the floor of the church is as the groundwork of our faith, and the letters inscribed thereon are as the elements of the faith in which the simple and the neophytes are instructed.

There are three reasons for painting twelve crosses upon the church walls. The first is to terrify the demons, who, being driven out of the church, and seeing the sign of the cross upon the walls, dare not enter it again, for they fear this sign mightily. The second is to show forth the triumph of the Cross; for the crosses are the banners of Christ and the signs of His victory, and thus they signify that the church is subjugated to Christ's dominion. Thirdly, these crosses represent the apostles; the twelve candles which are lighted before the crosses denote the light which the apostles brought to the world by the faith of the Crucified; and the crosses are anointed with chrism as a symbol of the cleanness of conscience and the odour of good renown with which they anointed the world.

We now come to the third question, namely, by whom the church is profaned. We read that the House of God was profaned by three men, namely Jeroboam, Nabuzardan, and Antiochus. Jeroboam, as we find in the third book of *Kings,* made two golden calves, and set the one in Bethel, and the other in Dan, which means the house of God; and this he did for avarice, for he feared lest the kingdom return to Roboam. By this is signified that the avarice of clerks much pollutes the house of God, which avarice is common among the clergy. Hence Bernard says: 'Show me one among the prelates, who is not more concerned with emptying the purses of his subjects than with wiping out their vices!' And the golden calves are the little nephews whom they place in

Bethel, that is, in the house of God. The church is likewise profaned if it is built out of the avarice of usurers and thieves. We read that when a certain usurer had built a church out of his booty and his usuries, he instantly besought the bishop to come and consecrate it. And when the bishop with his clergy was about to begin the office of consecration, he saw the Devil standing at the throne behind the altar, dressed in the robes of a bishop. The Devil said to him: 'Why dost thou consecrate my church? Begone, for the jurisdiction thereof belongs to me, since the church was built of the profits of usury!' And when the bishop and the clerks had fled in terror, the Devil tore down the church with much tumult.

Similarly, we read in the fourth book of *Kings* that Nabuzardan burnt the house of the Lord. Nabuzardan was the prince of cooks, and stands for those who are addicted to gluttony and pleasure, and make their belly their god. Hugh of Saint Victor shows how the belly can be called a god, when he says: 'It is of wont to build temples to the gods, and erect altars, and ordain ministers unto their service, and immolate victims, and burn incense. Thus, for the god of the belly, the temple is the kitchen, the altar the table, the ministers the cooks, the victims the roast meats, and the smoke of incense the odour of the foods.

King Antiochus, a proud and ambitious man, defiled and profaned the house of God, as we read in the first book of *Machabees;* and he stands for the pride and self-seeking which are rife among clerks, who give honour and service but to gain the same for themselves.

As the church was profaned by three men, so it was dedicated and consecrated by another three, namely by Moses, Solomon, and Judas Machabeus. Hereby it is suggested that in the dedication of the church we should have the humility of Moses, the wisdom and discretion of Solomon, and the zeal for the defense of the faith which was shown by Machabeus.

Now at last we speak of the consecration or dedication of the spiritual temple, which is ourselves, namely the congregation of all the faithful, built up of living and polished stones. The four sides of these spiritual stones are faith, hope, charity, and good works, and these four sides are equal, as Gregory says: 'As much as thou believest, so much wilt thou hope, and as much as thou believest and hopest, so much wilt thou love; as much as thou believest, hopest, and lovest, so much wilt thou work.' In this temple, the altar is our heart, upon which three things should be offered to God. The first is the fire of everlasting love, the second is the incense of sweet-smelling prayer, and the third is the sacrifice of justice. And this spiritual temple, which we are, is consecrated in like wise as the material temple. Christ, the High Priest, finding the door of our heart shut, goes around three times, when He makes us mindful of our sins of thought and word and deed. He knocks thrice upon this door, with the blows of His gifts, His warnings, and His punishments. Likewise, the spiritual temple must be thrice sprinkled with water within and without; and this watering is the shedding of inward, and sometimes of outward tears. For, as Gregory says, the soul of the just man is afflicted at considering where he was, where he will be, where he is, and where he is not; where he was, namely in sin, where he will be, namely in the judgement, where he is, namely in misery, and where he is not, namely in glory. And when he weeps inwardly and outwardly at the thought of his sins and the judgement thereof, the spiritual temple is sprinkled once with water. When he weeps for his present misery, it is watered a second time; and a third time, when he sheds tears for the glory in which he is not.

Again, in this temple of the heart a spiritual alphabet or scripture is written, consisting of the commandments of things to be done, the testimonies of the gifts of God, and the acknowledgment of sins committed. Crosses are depicted there, these being the austerities of penance; and they are anointed and illumined, for they are to be borne not only with patience but with gladness, which is signified by anointing, and with fervour, which is signified by fire.

St. Francis preaching to the birds

THE MIDDLE CLASS: SENSIBILITY AND SENTIMENT

Demography is destiny. The expansion of population, particularly but not exclusively in pre-modern, pre-industrial, medieval "Third World" societies, has revolutionary consequences. In the late tenth century, the population of Western Europe, which had been static for several centuries, began a slow increase because of improved nutrition. By the middle of the twelfth century, this increase had become a significant demographic growth, and in the first three-quarters of the thirteenth century there was a veritable population explosion and a severe land shortage in many areas. The population of England, for example, was 1.5 million in 1100. In 1280 it was approaching 6 million, a level it would not reach again until 1760. The population boom had many consequences—among them the expansion of the frontiers of Latin Christendom towards the Slavic world to the east, against the Moslems in Spain and *Outremer*, overseas as the French said, first toward Sicily and then the eastern Mediterranean. Travelers and missionaries pushed on into central and east Asia. The population explosion stimulated economic change, particularly the growth of commercial cities and agricultural improvement (better ploughs, more systematic use of fertilizer, and crop rotation). It made much more prosperous and visible social groups now economically, intellectually, and politically active—the "burghers" (bourgeois, those who lived in a *burg*, a fortified town); the "knights," the lesser nobility, the "gentry" as they came to be called in England after 1300; and entrepreneurial peasants, the "yeomen," as they were called in fifteenth-century England.

The nobility from the great landed families exploited this advantageous major economic and social change that can be termed "the rise of the medieval middle class." As population pressed on land, the value of the aristocracy's feudal estates skyrocketed, and with it the fortunes of the great landed families and their lavish consumption of goods and services, including visual art.

At the same time, the nobility were not entirely happy with some of the cultural and political consequences of middle class expansion. Usually the nobility ignored these consequences, but, when pressed, they sometimes tried to resist. The constituted and more conservative church leaders had difficulty adjusting the church's hierarchic system to the ethos and needs of the middle class, which often had a leveling quality. But major changes came anyway, often pressed on the popes and bishops by spontaneous spiritual movements from within the middle class and by alteration of religious discourse to suit the bourgeois worldview.

In the thirteenth century, this religious and cultural upheaval integrated with middle class expansion became centered on the Franciscan order and the figure of the Little Poor Man of Assisi. Just as *The Cid* and *The Song of Roland* evoked the medieval nobility's mind-set in its purest form, and the papal rules proclaimed the centrality of the church's hierarchic tradition, Franciscanism was the purest form of middle class discourse, focusing expressively on the outcome of complex structural changes in economy and society.

By 1200, the middle class, consisting of the burghers in the cities and the gentry (lower nobility) and yeomen (wealthy peasants) in the countryside, comprised at least a quarter of the medieval population. They were hardworking, enterprising, ambitious people. They did not inherit great estates and fancy titles like the aristocracy. They did not live off official positions like churchmen. Even though occasionally a fortunate gentry family would rise into the aristocracy, and even though the middle class provided most of the personnel of the church below the top rank of the hierarchy, the middle class had a distinct consciousness that they—burghers, gentry, yeomen—were fundamentally separate from both the aristocracy and the churchmen. They were a distinctive force in medieval Europe, an identifiable unique side to the medieval triangle.

The middle class were anxious people, having neither great lands nor comfortable offices to fall back on. They had to make it by their labor, thrift, and ingenuity in the face of the ravages of nature and the vicissitudes of politics, war, and economics, or lose everything, to sink down into the ranks of the working class—the miserable common peasantry and the day-laborers in the towns. The middle class fought every day for security and status, and were often frustrated by the conservatism of power and insolence of office. They could be roused to noisy anger and rebellion. Normally they avoided violent collective action. They stayed within the bosom of their families. They went about their daily struggles and sought solace in emotional kinds of religion that would give them both spiritual solace and assurance of their moral worth in the eyes of Christ and their intensely beloved Virgin Mary and universally adored St. Francis.

THE LITTLE FLOWERS OF ST. FRANCIS

St. Francis of Assisi (1180–1223) was the favorite saint of the medieval middle class. The Order of the Friars Minor (Little Brothers) that developed out of his life and teaching, with considerable guidance from a wary papacy, not only received phenomenal support from the bourgeois and the gentry, but middle class sons (and to a more limited degree daughters) also flocked to join the Franciscan Order, which thereby drew to it a large number of academic intellectuals, even though Francis himself despised university learning as much as wealth. Francis came from the upper middle class in a dry hill town between Rome and Florence. He preached a life of poverty, humility, social service, and love of dumb animals and the environment. To the greedy, ambitious, materialistic middle class, guilt-ridden and anxious about the fitting of their life-styles into the parameters of traditional Christianity, St. Francis showed the way to peace and security: charity, civility, generosity, and, above all, sentimentality would compensate for their obscure status, lust for wealth and pleasures, and entrepreneurial rationalism. The Franciscan friars also sermonized in the vernacular and superseded the austere, formalistic Latin discourse of the old clergy with vivid storytelling that intrigued and inspired the middle class audiences who gathered in town squares or rural hills to listen to them. Franciscanism represented not only the rise of bourgeois religiosity but also the advent of a protomodern middle class culture. *The Little Flowers,* biographical anecdotes about Francis and his companions, were the all-time bestselling work of Franciscan piety voraciously consumed by the new middle class. In the form that we have them, the *Flowers* were written down around 1290, but they incorporate earlier materials—how much is uncertain. Some of the stories go back to Francis' earliest companions and carry biographical authenticity; some are much elaborated versions of earlier stories. Some were probably invented in the late thirteenth century by one or other parties during a period of intense conflict within the Franciscan order.

St Francis, the devoted servant of the crucified Jesus, through constant weeping and penance, had become nearly blind, so that he could scarcely see. Wishing one day to speak with Brother Bernard on things divine, he left the place where he was and went to join him. Being told, upon arrival, that he was in the forest praying, St Francis proceeded thither, and, calling out, said; "Come, O Brother Bernard, and speak with this blind man." But Brother Bernard did not make answer; for, his soul being rapt in divine contemplation, he did not hear him call; one of the special graces of Brother Bernard being that of holding converse with God Almighty, of which St Francis had often been a witness. The saint, therefore, since he wished specially to speak with him at that hour, called him again a second time and a third. Brother Bernard, not having heard him, neither answered nor went to him; at which St Francis went away somewhat saddened, and wondering in himself how it was that, having called him three times, Brother Bernard had not come to him. With this thought on his mind, when he had proceeded a little way, he bade his companion wait for him, and retiring to a solitary spot, fell on his knees, praying that God would reveal to him why Brother Bernard had not answered his call. As he prayed, a voice came from God, which said, "O poor little man, why art thou troubled? Is it meet for man to leave God for the creature? When thou didst call Brother Bernard he was with me, and could neither hear thee, nor go to thee; be not then surprised if he answered thee not, for he was rapt out of himself, nor did he hear aught of all thou saidst." St Francis, having received this answer from God, went back with great haste to Brother Bernard, to accuse himself humbly of the thought he had allowed to enter his mind against him. Brother Bernard, seeing St Francis coming towards him, went to meet him, and threw himself at his feet. Then St Francis bade him rise, confessing most humbly what his thoughts had been and the answer which God had made him; and with these words he concluded: "I command thee, by virtue of holy obedience, to do whatsoever I shall order thee." Brother Bernard, fearing St Francis would oblige him to inflict upon him some great punishment, as was his custom, would most willingly have avoided obeying him. "I am ready," he answered, "to obey thee, father, if thou also wilt promise me to do whatsoever I shall command thee." To this St Francis consented; and Brother Bernard then asked him what he wished him to do. "I command thee," said St Francis, "under holy obedience, in order to punish my presumption and the evil thought of my heart, when I lie down on the ground to place one of thy feet on my neck, and the other on my mouth. And this shalt thou do three times, saying each time, 'Shame upon thee, shame upon thee! Be humbled, thou son of Peter Bernardoni, for thou art but a vile wretch; how camest thou to be so proud, thou miserable servant of sin!' " On hearing this Brother Bernard was much grieved, but out of holy obedience he did what St Francis had ordered him, striving withal to acquit himself thereof as lightly as possible. Then St Francis, having promised obedience to Brother Bernard, asked what he wished him to do, whereto the latter answered: "I command thee, in virtue of holy obedience, that whenever we are together thou reprove and correct with great severity all my defects." This order much surprised St Francis, for Brother Bernard was so holy that he held him in great reverence, and did not believe it possible to find in him any fault. From that time, therefore, the saint avoided being much with Brother Bernard, fearing lest, out of holy obedience, he might be obliged to reprove him; and when he was obliged to see or to speak with him, he parted from him as soon as possible. Most edifying it was to hear with what charity, what admiration and humility, St Francis, who was his superior, spoke of Brother Bernard, who was his first son in God — to the praise and glory of Jesus Christ and his poor servant Francis. Amen. . . .

One day in winter, as St Francis was going with Brother Leo from Perugia to St Mary of the Angels, and was suffering greatly from the cold, he called to Brother Leo, who was walking on before him, and said to him: "Brother Leo, if it were to please God that the Friars Minor should give, in all lands, a great example of holiness and edification, write down, and note carefully, that this would not be perfect joy." A little farther on, St Francis called to him a second time: "O Brother Leo, if the Friars Minor were to make the lame to walk, if they should make straight the crooked, chase away demons, give sight to the blind, hearing to the deaf, speech to the dumb, and, what is even a far greater work, if they should raise the dead after four days, write that this would not be perfect joy." Shortly after, he cried out again: "O Brother Leo, if the Friars Minor knew all languages; if they were versed in all science; if they could explain all Scripture; if they had the gift of prophecy, and could reveal, not only all future things, but likewise the secrets of all consciences and all souls, write that this would not be perfect joy." After proceeding a few steps farther, he cried out again with a loud voice: "O Brother Leo, thou little lamb of God! if the Friars Minor could speak with the tongues of angels; if they could explain the course of the stars; if they knew the virtues of all plants; if all the treasures of the earth were revealed to them; if they were acquainted with the various qualities of all birds, of all fish, of all animals, of men, of trees, of stones, of roots, and of waters — write that this would not be perfect joy." Shortly after, he cried out again: "O Brother Leo, if the Friars Minor had the gift of preaching so as to convert all infidels to the faith of Christ, write that this would not be perfect joy." Now when this manner of discourse had lasted for the space of two miles, Brother Leo wondered much within himself; and, questioning the saint, he said: "Father, I pray thee teach me wherein is perfect joy." St Francis answered: "If, when we shall arrive at St Mary of the Angels, all drenched with rain and trembling with cold, all covered with mud and exhausted from hunger; if, when we knock at the convent-gate, the porter should come angrily and ask us who we are; if, after we have told him, 'We are two of the brethren', he should answer angrily, 'What ye say is not the truth; ye are but two impostors going about to deceive the world, and take away the alms of the poor; begone I say'; if then he refuse to open to us, and leave us outside, exposed to the snow and rain, suffering from cold and hunger till nightfall — then, if we accept such injustice, such cruelty and such contempt with patience, without being ruffled and without murmuring, believing with humility and charity that the porter really knows us, and that it is God who maketh him to speak thus against us, write down, O Brother Leo, that this is perfect joy. And if we knock again, and the porter come out in anger to drive us away with oaths and blows, as if we were vile impostors, saying, 'Begone, miserable robbers! go to the hospital, for here you shall neither eat nor sleep!' — and if we accept all this with patience, with joy, and with charity, O Brother Leo, write that this indeed is perfect joy. And if, urged by cold and hunger, we knock again, calling to the porter and entreating him with many tears to open to us and give us shelter, for the love of God, and if he come out more angry than before, exclaiming, 'These are but importunate rascals, I will deal with them as they deserve'; and taking a knotted stick, he seize us by the hood, throwing us on the ground, rolling us in the snow, and shall beat and wound us with the knots in the stick — if we bear all these injuries with patience and joy, thinking of the sufferings of our Blessed Lord, which we would share out of love for him, write, O Brother Leo, that here, finally, is perfect joy. And now, brother, listen to the conclusion. Above all the graces and all the gifts of the Holy Spirit which Christ grants to his friends, is the grace of overcoming oneself, and accepting willingly, out of love for Christ, all suffering, injury, discomfort and contempt; for in all other gifts of God we cannot glory, seeing they proceed not from ourselves but from God, according to the words of the Apostle, 'What hast thou that thou hast not received from God? and if thou hast received it, why dost thou glory as if thou hadst not received it?' But in the cross of tribulation and affliction we may glory, because, as the Apostle says again, 'I will not glory save in the cross of our Lord Jesus Christ.' Amen.". . .

In the beginning of the Order, St Francis, having assembled his companions to speak to them of Christ, in a moment of great fervour of spirit commanded one of them, in the name of God, to open his mouth and speak as the Holy Spirit should inspire him. The brother, doing as he was ordered, spoke most wonderfully of God. Then St Francis bade him to be silent, and ordered another brother to speak in the same way, which having done with much penetration, St Francis ordered him likewise to be silent, and commanded a third brother to do the same. This one began to speak so deeply of the things of God, that St Francis was convinced that both he and his companions had spoken through the Holy Spirit. Of which also he received a manifest proof; for whilst they were thus speaking together, our Blessed Lord appeared in the midst of them, under the form of a beautiful young man, and blessed them all. And they, being ravished out of themselves, fell to the ground as if they had been dead, and were all unconscious of things external. And when they recovered from their trance, St Francis said to them: "My beloved brothers, let us thank God, who has deigned to reveal to the world, through his humble servants, the treasures of divine wisdom. For the Lord it is who openeth the mouth of the dumb, and maketh the tongues of the simple to speak wisdom.". . .

St Francis, when residing at Assisi, often visited St Clare, to give her holy counsel. And she, having a great desire to eat once with him, often begged him to grant her this request; but the saint would never allow her this consolation. His companions, therefore, being aware of the refusal of St Francis, and knowing how great was the wish of Sister Clare to eat with him, went to seek him, and thus addressed him: "Father, it seems to us that this severity on thy part in not granting so small a thing to Sister Clare, a virgin so holy and so dear to God, who merely asks for once to eat with thee, is not according to holy charity, especially if we consider how it was at thy preaching that she abandoned the riches and pomps of this world. Of a truth, if she were to ask of thee even a greater grace than this, thou shouldst grant it to thy spiritual daughter." St Francis answered: "It seems to you, then, that I ought to grant her this request?" His companions made answer: "Yea, father, it is meet that thou grant her this favour and this consolation." St Francis answered: "As you think so, let it be so, then; but, in order that she may be the more consoled, I will that the meal do take place in front of St Mary of the Angels, because, having been for so long time shut up in San Damiano, it will do her good to see the church of St Mary, wherein she took the veil, and was made a spouse of Christ. There, then, we will eat together in the name of God." When the appointed day arrived, St Clare left her convent with great joy, taking with her one of her sisters, and followed by the companions of St Francis. She arrived at St Mary of the Angels, and having devoutly saluted the Virgin Mary, before whose altar her hair had been cut off, and she had received the veil, they conducted her to the convent, and showed her all over it. In the meantime St Francis prepared the meal on the bare ground, as was his custom. The hour of dinner being arrived, St Francis and St Clare, with one of the brethren of St Francis and the sister who had accompanied the saint, sat down together, all the other companions of St Francis seated humbly round them. When the first dish was served, St Francis began to speak of God so sweetly, so sublimely, and in a manner so wonderful, that the grace of God visited them abundantly, and all were rapt in Christ. Whilst they were thus rapt, with eyes and hearts raised to heaven, the people of Assisi and of Bettona, and of all the country round about, saw St Mary of the Angels as it were on fire, with the convent and the woods adjoining. It seemed to them as if the church, the convent, and the woods were all enveloped in flames; and the inhabitants of Assisi hastened with great speed to put out the fire. On arriving at the convent, they found no fire; and entering within the gates they saw St Francis, St Clare, with all their companions, sitting round their humble meal, absorbed in contemplation; then knew they of a certainty, that what they had seen was a celestial fire, not a material one, which God miraculously had sent to bear witness to the divine flame of love which consumed the souls of those holy brethren and nuns; and they returned home with great consolation in their hearts, and much holy edification. After a long lapse of time, St Francis, St Clare, and their companions came back to themselves; and, being fully restored by the spiritual food, cared not to eat that which had been prepared for them; so that, the holy meal being finished, St Clare, well accompanied, returned to San Damiano, where the sisters received her with great joy, as they had feared that St Francis might have sent her to rule some other convent, as he had already sent St Agnes, the sister of the saint, to be Abbess of the Convent of Monticelli, at Florence. For St Francis had often said to St Clare, "Be ready, in case I send thee to some other convent"; and she, like a daughter of holy obedience, had answered, "Father, I am always ready to go whithersoever thou shalt send me." For which reason the sisters greatly rejoiced when she returned to them, and St Clare was from that time much consoled. . . .

The humble servant of Christ, St Francis, a short time after his conversion, having already assembled and received many brothers into the Order, was much troubled and perplexed in mind as to what he ought to do; whether to give himself entirely to prayer, or now and then to preach the Word. Through his great humility, he had no opinion of himself or of the virtue of his prayers; and, wishing to know the will of God, he sought to learn it through the prayers of others. Wherefore he called to him Brother Masseo, and thus addressed him: "Go to Sister Clare, and bid her from me to set herself with some of the holiest of her sisters to pray the Lord that he may show me clearly whether he wills that I should preach or only keep to prayer. Then go to Brother Silvester, and ask of him the same favour." Now Brother Silvester had been in the world, and was the same who had seen in vision a golden cross come out of St Francis's mouth. St Francis began to preach, first ordering the swallows, who were calling, to keep silence until he had finished; and the swallows obeyed his voice. He preached with such fervour, that the inhabitants of the town wished to follow him out of devotion; but St Francis would not allow them, saying: "Be not in such haste, and leave not your homes. I will tell you what you must do to save your souls." Thereupon he founded the Third Order for the salvation of all; and leaving them much consoled and well disposed to do penance, he departed thence, and reached a spot between Cannaio and Bevagno. And as he went on his way, with great fervour, St Francis lifted up his eyes, and saw on some trees by the wayside a great multitude of birds; and being much surprised, he said to his companions, "Wait for me here by the way, whilst I go and preach to my little sisters the birds"; and entering into the field, he began to preach to the birds which were on the ground, and suddenly all those also on the trees came round him, and all listened while St Francis preached to them, and did not fly away until he had given them his blessing. And Brother Masseo related afterwards to Brother James of Massa how St Francis went among them and even touched them with his garments, and how none of them moved. Now the substance of the sermon was this: "My little sisters the birds, ye owe much to God, your Creator, and ye ought to sing his praise at all times and in all places, because he has given you liberty to fly about into all places; and though ye neither spin nor sew, he has given you a twofold and a threefold clothing for yourselves and for your offspring. Two of all your species he sent into the Ark with Noe that you might not be lost to the world; besides which, he feeds you, though ye neither sow nor reap. He has given you fountains and rivers to quench your thirst, mountains and valleys in which to take refuge, and trees in which to build your nests; so that your Creator loves you much, having thus favoured you with such bounties. Beware, my little sisters, of the sin of ingratitude, and study always to give praise to God." As he said these words, all the birds began to open their beaks, to stretch their necks, to spread their wings, and reverently to bow their heads to the ground, endeavouring by their motions and by their songs to manifest their joy to St Francis. And the saint rejoiced with them. He wondered to see such a multitude of birds, and was charmed with their beautiful variety, with their attention and familiarity, for all which he devoutly gave thanks to the Creator. Having finished his sermon, St Francis made the sign of the cross, and gave them leave to fly away. Then all those birds rose up into the air, singing most sweetly; and, following the sign of the cross, which St Francis had made, they divided themselves into four companies. One company flew towards the east, another towards the west, one towards the south, and one towards the north; each company as it went singing most wonderfully; signifying thereby, that as St Francis, the bearer of the Cross of Christ, had preached to them and made upon them the sign of the cross, after which they had divided among themselves the four parts of the world, so the preaching of the Cross of Christ, renewed by St Francis, would be carried by him and by his brethren over all the world, and that the humble friars, like little birds, should possess nothing in this world, but should cast all the care of their lives on the providence of God. . . .

At the time when St Francis was living in the city of Gubbio, a large wolf appeared in the neighbourhood, so terrible and so fierce, that he not only devoured other animals, but made a prey of men also; and since he often approached the town, all the people were in great alarm, and used to go about armed, as if going to battle. Notwithstanding these precautions, if any of the inhabitants ever met him alone, he was sure to be devoured, as all defence was useless: and,

through fear of the wolf, they dared not go beyond the city walls. St Francis, feeling great compassion for the people of Gubbio, resolved to go and meet the wolf, though all advised him not to do so. Making the sign of the holy cross, and putting all his confidence in God, he went forth from the city, taking his brethren with him; but these fearing to go any farther, St Francis bent his steps alone toward the spot where the wolf was known to be, while many people followed at a distance, and witnessed the miracle. The wolf, seeing all this multitude, ran towards St Francis with his jaws wide open. As he approached, the saint, making the sign of the cross, cried out: "Come hither, brother wolf; I command thee, in the name of Christ, neither to harm me nor anybody else." Marvellous to tell, no sooner had St Francis made the sign of the cross, than the terrible wolf, closing his jaws, stopped running, and coming up to St Francis, lay down at his feet as meekly as a lamb. And the saint thus addressed him: "Brother wolf, thou hast done much evil in this land, destroying and killing the creatures of God without his permission; yea, not animals only hast thou destroyed, but thou hast even dared to devour men, made after the image of God; for which thing thou art worthy of being hanged like a robber and a murderer. All men cry out against thee, the dogs pursue thee, and all the inhabitants of this city are thy enemies; but I will make peace between them and thee, O brother wolf, if so be thou no more offend them, and they shall forgive thee all thy past offences, and neither men nor dogs shall pursue thee any more." Having listened to these words, the wolf bowed his head, and, by the movements of his body, his tail, and his eyes, made signs that he agreed to what St Francis said. On this St Francis added: "As thou art willing to make this peace, I promise thee that thou shalt be fed every day by the inhabitants of this land so long as thou shalt live among them; thou shalt no longer suffer hunger, as it is hunger which has made thee do so much evil; but if I obtain all this for thee, thou must promise, on thy side, never again to attack any animal or any human being: dost thou make this promise?" Then the wolf, bowing his head, made a sign that he consented. Said St Francis again: "Brother wolf, wilt thou pledge thy faith that I may trust to this thy promise?" and putting out his hand he received the pledge of the wolf; for the latter lifted up his paw and placed it familiarly in the hand of St Francis, giving him thereby the only pledge which was in his power. Then said St Francis, addressing him again: "Brother wolf, I command thee, in the name of Christ, to follow me immediately, without hesitation or doubting, that we may go together to ratify this peace which we have concluded in the name of God"; and the wolf, obeying him, walked by his side as meekly as a lamb, to the great astonishment of all the people. Now, the news of this most wonderful miracle spreading quickly through the town, all the inhabitants, both men and women, small and great, young and old, flocked to the market-place to see St Francis and the wolf. All the people being assembled, the saint got up to preach, saying, amongst other things, how for our sins God permits such calamities, and how much greater and more dangerous are the flames of hell, which last for ever, than the rage of a wolf, which can kill the body only; and how much we ought to dread the jaws of hell, if the jaws of so small an animal as a wolf can make a whole city tremble through fear. The sermon being ended, St Francis added these words: "Listen, my brethren: the wolf who is here before you has promised and pledged his faith that he consents to make peace with you all, and no more to offend you in aught, and you must promise to give him each day his necessary food; to which, if you consent, I promise in his name that he will most

faithfully observe the compact." Then all the people promised with one voice to feed the wolf to the end of his days; and St Francis, addressing the latter, said again: "And thou, brother wolf, dost thou promise to keep the compact, and never again to offend either man or beast, or any other creature?" And the wolf knelt down, bowing his head, and, by the motions of his tail and of his ears, endeavoured to show that he was willing, as far as was in his power, to hold to the compact. Then St Francis continued: "Brother wolf, as thou gavest me a pledge of this thy promise when we were outside the town, so now I will that thou renew it in the sight of all this people, and assure me that I have done well to promise in thy name"; and the wolf lifting up his paw placed it in the hand of St Francis. Now this event caused great joy in all the people, and a great devotion towards St Francis, both because of the novelty of the miracle, and because of the peace which had been concluded with the wolf; and they lifted up their voices to heaven, praising and blessing God, who had sent them St Francis, through whose merits they had been delivered from such a savage beast. The wolf lived two years at Gubbio; he went familiarly from door to door without harming anyone, and all the people received him courteously, feeding him with great pleasure, and no dog barked at him as he went about. At last, after two years, he died of old age, and the people of Gubbio mourned his loss greatly; for when they saw him going about so gently amongst them all, he reminded them of the virtue and sanctity of St Francis.

BEAUTIFUL CITIES

In 1100 only five percent of Western Europe's population lived in towns, and in 1500 the urban population was still less than twenty percent. Yet certain key areas—southern England, the Loire and Rhone valleys in France, some stretches along the Rhine in Germany, and northern Italy—were much more heavily urbanized. Generally, bourgeois impact on commerce, industry, finance, religion, and culture far exceeded the urban middle class' minority status, even though in 1500 no city's population was greater than 150,000. The burghers' descriptions of their own cities invariably are written in boosterish, chamber-of-commerce prose, stressing the dynamic behavior and urban amenities central to city life. The downside of urban life—the violent politics, cyclic economy, overcrowding, expensive and inadequate housing, bad sanitation, and constant threat of fires and epidemics—gets less play. Yet burghers' pride in their city was itself very important. It was the seedbed for an ideological demand for a large measure of autonomy and freedom within landed and hierarchical society. It stimulated bourgeois patronage of the arts and efforts to beautify the urban environment. It influenced their sons, who, with suitable university education, could rise to high places in church and state. Here are two contemporary accounts of medieval urban existence—William Fitz-Stephen describing London in the twelfth century and Giovanni Vilani describing Florence in the mid-fourteenth century.

Cathedral of Florence

WILLIAM FITZ-STEPHEN: LONDON

Among the noble cities of the world that Fame celebrates the City of London of the Kingdom of the English, is the one seat that pours out its fame more widely, sends to farther lands its wealth and trade, lifts its head higher than the rest. It is happy in the healthiness of its air, in the Christian religion, in the strength of its defences, the nature of its site, the honour of its citizens, the modesty of its matrons; pleasant in sports; fruitful of noble men. Let us look into these things separately. . . .

Those engaged in the several kinds of business, sellers of several things, contractors for several kinds of work, are distributed every morning into their several localities and shops. Besides, there is in London on the river bank, among the wines in ships and cellars sold by the vintners, a public cook shop; there eatables are to be found every day, according to the season, dishes of meat, roast, fried and boiled, great and small fish, coarser meats for the poor, more delicate for the rich, of game, fowls, and small birds. If there should come suddenly to any of the citizens friends, weary from a journey and too hungry to like waiting till fresh food is bought and cooked, with water to their hands comes bread, while one runs to the river bank, and there is all that can be wanted. However great the multitude of soldiers or travellers entering the city, or preparing to go out of it, at any hour of the day or night,—that these may not fast too long and those may not go supperless,—they turn hither, if they please, where every man can refresh himself in his own way. . . . Outside one of the gates there, immediately in the suburb, is a certain field, smooth (Smith) field in fact and name. Every Friday, unless it be a higher day of appointed solemnity, there is in it a famous show of noble horses for sale. Earls, barons, knights, and many citizens who are in town, come to see or buy. . . . In another part of the field stand by themselves the goods proper to rustics, implements of husbandry, swine with long flanks, cows with full udders, oxen of bulk immense, and wooly flocks. . . . To this city from every nation under heaven merchants delight to bring their trade by sea. . . .

Four general fairs are held in the city every year, that is, on the day of the ordination of the Blessed Ambrose, on the feast of the Blessed Lawrence, on the Ascension of the Blessed Mother of God, and on the feast of the Blessed Bartholomew. It is amazing to see almost innumerable merchants with their variety of wares and buyers flocking to all these fairs. Furthermore, ordinary markets are held in different parts of the city two days a week, that is, on Fridays and Saturdays. Indeed—and this is more [amazing]—practically anything that man may need is brought daily not only into special places but even into the [open] squares, and all that can be sold is loudly advertised for sale. Also, there are many fairs in the towns and villages of our county, being held every year on certain days. In many of them, indeed, there is a market every week, and merchants and buyers hasten to all of them in large numbers. It is evident, after [all] that has been said, that in our city it is a wonderful life for those who have money enough. Every convenience for human pleasure is known to be at hand here.

Also it is obvious that here any man, if he is healthy and not a good-for-nothing, may earn his living expenses and esteem according to his station. And it is worth noting that here the fecundity in offspring is just as prolific as the abundance of temporal goods. In fact, when on festive days one looks at the merry crowds of dignified men, both of the nobility and of the people, also at the bustling throngs of children incessantly scurrying here and there, and at the comely gatherings, comely groups of ladies and virgins going back and forth or standing on the doorsteps [of their homes], as dignified as if they were daughters of kings, who would say that he has ever met such a wonderful show of people this side or the other side of the sea? . . .

Nowhere else is a city with more commendable customs of church attendance, honour to God's ordinances, keeping sacred festivals, almsgiving, hospitality, confirming betrothals, contracting marriages, celebration of nuptials, preparing feasts, cheering the guests, and also in care for funerals and the interment of the dead. The only pests of London are the immoderate drinking of fools and the frequency of fires. To this may be added that nearly all the bishops, abbots, and magnates of England are, as it were, citizens and freemen of London; having there their own splendid houses, to which they resort, where they spend largely when summoned to great councils by the king or by their metropolitan, or drawn thither by their own private affairs.

Let us now come to the sports and pastimes, seeing it is fit that a city should not only be commodious and serious, but also merry and sportful; ... But London ... hath holy plays, representations of miracles which holy confessors have wrought, or representations of torments wherein the constancy of martyrs appeared. Every year also at Shrove Tuesday, that we may begin with children's sports, seeing we all have been children, the schoolboys do bring cocks of the game to their master, and all the forenoon they delight themselves in cock-fighting: after dinner, all the youths go into the fields to play at the ball.

The scholars of every school have their ball, or baton, in their hands; the ancient and wealthy men of the city come forth on horseback to see the sport of the young men, and to take part of the pleasure in beholding their agility. Every Friday in Lent a fresh company of young men comes into the field on horseback, and the best horseman conducteth the rest. Then march forth the citizens' sons, and other young men, with disarmed lances and shields, and there they practise feats of war. Many courtiers likewise, when the king lieth near, and attendants of noblemen, do repair to these exercises; and while the hope of victory doth inflame their minds, do show good proof how serviceable they would be in martial affairs.

In Easter holidays they fight battles on the water; a shield is hung upon a pole, fixed in the midst of the stream, a boat is prepared without oars, to be carried by violence of the water, and in the fore part thereof standeth a young man, ready to give charge upon the shield with his lance; if so be he breaketh his lance against the shield, and doth not fall, he is thought to have performed a worthy deed; if so be, without breaking his lance, he runneth strongly against the shield, down he falleth into the water, for the boat is violently forced with the tide; but on each side of the shield ride two boats, furnished with young men, which recover him that falleth as soon as they may. Upon the bridge, wharfs, and houses, by the river's side, stand great numbers to see and laugh thereat.

In the holidays all the summer the youths are exercised in leaping, dancing, shooting, wrestling, casting the stone, and practising their shields; the maidens trip in their timbrels, and dance as long as they can well see. In winter, every holiday before dinner, the boats prepared for brawn are set to fight, or else bulls and bears are baited.

When the great fen, or moor, which watereth the walls of the city on the north side, is frozen, many young men play upon the ice; some, striding as wide as they may, do slide swiftly; others make themselves seats of ice, as great as millstones; one sits down, many hand in hand to draw him, and one slipping on a sudden, all fall together; some tie bones to their feet and under their heels; and shoving themselves by a little picked staff, do slide as swiftly as a bird flieth in the air, or an arrow out of a cross-bow. Sometime two run together with poles, and hitting one the other, either one or both do fall, not without hurt; some break their arms, some their legs, but youth desirous of glory in this sort exerciseth itself against the time of war. Many of the citizens do delight themselves in hawks and hounds; for they have liberty of hunting in Middlesex, Hertfordshire, all Chiltern, and in Kent to the water of Cray. . . .

GIOVANNI VILANI: FLORENCE

Now that we have spoken of the revenues and expenses of the commune of Florence in these times, I think it appropriate to mention this and the other great things about our city. Thus, our successors, who in times to come shall follow us, may become aware of the rise and decline of the wealth and power which our city achieved. Thus they may also, through the wise and courageous citizens who at various times shall govern her, see to it that she advances in wealth and great power, through the memory and example of this our chronicle.

We have diligently discovered that in these times there were in Florence about 25,000 men able to bear arms, from 15 years up to 70, all citizens. Among them there were 1500 noble and powerful citizens who as magnates posted bond with the commune. There were then in Florence upwards of 75 liveried knights. We have diligently discovered that before the popular regime, which rules at present, was established, there were more than 250 knights. Since the popular government was created, the magnates have not had the possessions or the power as before, and therefore few become knights.

It has been estimated that there are in Florence upwards of 90,000 mouths, including men, women and children, from the evidence of the bread which is continuously needed in the city, as one can well understand. It has been guessed that there were continuously in the city more than 1500 foreigners, transients and soldiers, not counting in the total religious, friars and cloistered nuns, of whom we shall make mention soon. It has been estimated that there were in these times in the countryside and district of Florence upwards of 80,000 men. We have discovered from the priest who baptized the babies that they numbered every year in these times from 5500 to 6000, with the masculine sex larger than the feminine by up to 500 per year. (The priest sets aside a black bean for every male baptized in San Giovanni and a white bean for every female, in order to know their number). We have discovered, that the boys and girls who are learning to read number from 8000 to 10,000. The boys who are learning the abacus and calculation in six schools number from 1000 to 1200. And those who are learning Latin

and logic in four large schools number from 550 to 600.

The churches which were then in Florence and in her suburbs, including the abbeys and the churches of the religious friars, have been found to be 110. Among them are 57 parishes with congregations, five abbeys with two priors and upwards of 80 monks, 24 convents of nuns with upwards of 500 women, 10 houses of friars, 30 hospitals with more than 1000 beds to serve the poor and infirm, and from 250 to 300 ordained chaplains.

The shops of the wool craft were 200 or more, and produced from 70,000 to 80,000 cloths, which were worth upwards of 1,200,000 gold florins. A third of this value remained in the country to pay for labor, without regarding the profit which the wool merchants made from that labor. More than 30,000 persons were supported by it. We have accurately discovered, that thirty years ago there were 300 shops or thereabouts, and that they made every year more than 100,000 cloths. But these cloths were cruder and worth half the present value, since wool from England was not then imported, nor was it known how to work it, as has subsequently been done. The shops of the guild of Calimala, which deals with cloth brought from France and beyond the mountains, number upwards of twenty, and import every year more than 10,000 cloths worth 300,000 gold florins. These they sell entirely in Florence, and we do not include those cloths which are shipped outside of Florence. The tables of money-changers were upwards of eighty. The gold money which was coined was upwards of 350,000 gold florins and sometimes 400,000; and of pennies worth four *piccioli* each, there were coined every year about 20,000 pounds.

The college of judges was upwards of 80. The notaries were more than 600. The pharmacists, physicians and surgeons numbered upwards of 60. The drug stores were more than 100. Merchants and dealers in dry goods were of great number. One cannot estimate the shops of the makers of shoes, slippers and boots. Those who went outside of Florence to trade numbered 300 or more, and many other masters of many crafts, and masters of stone and wood, did likewise. There were then in Florence 146 furnaces. We have discovered by the tax of milling and for the furnaces, that every day the city needed for internal consumption 140 moggia of grain. From this one can estimate what was needed every year. And we do not consider that the greater part of the rich, noble and affluent citizens spent with their families four months every year in the countryside, and some even more. We have discovered that in the year 1280, when the city was in happy and good circumstances, that it needed every week upward of 800 moggia. We have discovered by the tax at the gates that every year Florence imported upwards of 55,000 cogna of wine, and when it was plentiful about 10,000 cogna more. The city required every year about 400 cows and calves; 60,000 muttons and sheep; 20,000 she-goats and he-goats; and 30,000 pigs. In the month of July through the gate of San Frediano there entered 4000 loads of melons, which were all distributed in the city.

In these times there were in Florence the following magistracies held by foreign officials. Each held court and had the authority to torture. They were the podestà, the captain, the defender of the people and the guilds; the executor of the Ordinances of Justice; the captain of the guard, or defender of the people, who had more authority than the others. All these four [sic] magistrates had the option of inflicting personal punishment: the judge of auditing and appeals; the judge of taxes; the official supervising women's ornaments; the official over commerce; the official over the wool guild; the ecclesiastical officials; the court of the bishop of Florence; the court of the bishop of Fiesole; the inquisitor concerning heretical depravity. And other high and magnificent offices of our city of Florence ought not to be omitted, but remembered, in order to provide information to those who shall follow us.

The city was well laid out within, and constructed with many beautiful houses. Construction was going on continually in these times. Buildings were improved, to make them comfortable and elegant, and fine examples of all sorts of improvements were sought from outside the city. There were cathedral churches, and churches of brothers of every discipline, and magnificent monasteries. Besides that, there was not a citizen, of popular or magnate status, who had not built or would not build in the countryside great and rich estates, and very rich habitations, with beautiful buildings, much better than in the city. And in this they all sinned, and were considered insane for their extravagant expenditures.

And it was such a magnificent thing to behold, that foreigners coming from afar, not familiar with Florence, believed (or most of them) that the rich buildings and beautiful palaces which were outside the city about three miles were part of the city, as they are at Rome. We do not speak of the rich palaces, towers, courts and walled gardens even farther from the city, which in other regions would be called castles. In conclusion, it has been estimated, that around the city for a distance of six miles there are so many rich and noble habitations that two Florences would not contain as many.

URBAN CONFLICT: GUIBERT OF LAON

The underside of urban life was bitter conflict, leading to street-fighting and murder. Nothing produced more bitterness and mayhem on the urban scene than the struggle of the burghers to gain their independence from the king, aristocrat, or bishop who exerted old rights of lordship over the town. As a result, the burghers formed sworn associations, called communes, and sought their independence by negotiation, by purchase, and by violence if necessary. The situation could be especially bitter in cities dominated by bishops and cathedral priests (called canons), who overwhelmingly came from the nobility. Here is an account, written in the early twelfth century by Guibert, a cathedral canon of Laon in northern France, of the lethal confrontation between the commune and the bishop in his city. As might be expected, Guibert is no friend of the burghers. His hatred and contempt for them and his lack of respect for their demands for communal autonomy were widespread feelings toward the urban middle class among the nobility and the episcopate, an attitude that moderated over time but never disappeared.

Payment of the salary of the Commune

Since ancient times it had. . . . been the misfortune of the city of Laon that neither God nor any lord was feared there, but, according to each man's power and desire, the public authority was involved in rapine and murder. . . . The next day—that is, on Thursday—when the bishop and Archdeacon Gautier were engaged after the noon offices in collecting money, suddenly there arose throughout the city the tumult of men shouting, "Commune!" Then through the nave of the cathedral of Notre-Dame. . . .

A great crowd of burghers attacked the episcopal palace, armed with rapiers, double-edged swords, bows, and axes, and carrying clubs and lances. As soon as this sudden attack was discovered, the nobles rallied from all sides to the bishop, having sworn to give him aid against such an assault if it should occur. In this rally Guimar the castellan, an older nobleman of handsome presence and guiltless character, armed only with a shield and spear, ran through the church. Just as he entered the bishop's hall, he was the first to fall, struck on the back of the head with a sword by a man named Raimbert, who had been his close friend. Immediately afterward that Renier of whom I spoke before as married to my cousin, rushing to enter the palace, was struck from behind with a spear when he tried to duck under it while poised on the porch of the bishop's chapel. Struck to the ground there, he was soon consumed by the fire of the palace from his groin downward. Adon the *vidame*, sharp in small matters and even keener in important ones, separated from the rest and able to do little by himself among so many, encountered the full force of the attack as he was striving to reach the bishop's palace. With his spear and sword he made such a stand that in a moment he struck down three of those who rushed at him. Then he mounted the dining table in the hall, where he was wounded in the knees and other parts of the body. At last, falling on his knees and striking at his assailants all round him, he kept them off for a long time, until someone pierced his exhausted body with a javelin. After a little he was burned to ashes by the fire in that house.

While the insolent mob was attacking the bishop and howling before the walls of his palace, the bishop and the people who were aiding him fought them off as best they could by hurling stones and shooting arrows. Now, as at all times, he showed great spirit as a fighter; but because he had wrongly and in vain taken up that other sword, he perished by the sword. Unable to resist the reckless assaults of the people, he put on the clothes of one of his servants and fled into the warehouse of the church, where he hid himself in a container. When the cover had been fastened on by a faithful follower, he thought himself safely hidden. As those looking for him ran hither and thither, they did not call out for the bishop but for a felon. They seized one of his pages, but he remained faithful and they could get nothing out of him. Laying hands on another, they learned from the traitor's nod where to look for him . . . anyone could count, the unrestrained wickedness of his heart was displayed in his hideous face. When he ran afoul of Enguerrand, he committed himself completely to the commune at Laon. He who had before not spared monks or clerks or pilgrims, or, in fact, women, was finally to be the slayer of the bishop. As the leader and instigator of this abominable attack, he searched diligently for the bishop, whom he hated more bitterly than did the rest.

As they sought for him in every vessel, Thiégaud halted in front of the cask where the man was hiding, and after breaking in the head he asked again and again who was there. Hardly able to move his frozen lips under the blows, the bishop said, "A prisoner." Now, as a joke, the bishop used to call this man Isengrin, because

he had the look of a wolf and that is what some people commonly call wolves. So the scoundrel said to the bishop, "Is this my Lord Isengrin stored away here?" Sinner though he was and yet the Lord's anointed, he was dragged out of the cask by the hair, beaten with many blows, and brought out in the open air in the narrow lane of the cloister before the house of the chaplain Godfrey. As he implored them piteously, ready to swear that he would cease to be their bishop, that he would give them unlimited riches, that he would leave the country, with hardened hearts they jeered at him. Then a man named Bernard of Bruyères raised his sword and brutally dashed out that sinner's brains from his holy head. Slipping between the hands of those who held him, before he died he was struck by someone else with a blow running under his eye sockets and across the middle of his nose. Brought to his end there, his legs were hacked off and many other wounds inflicted. Seeing the ring on the finger of the former bishop and not being able to draw it off easily, Thiégaud cut off the dead man's finger with his sword and took the ring. Stripped naked, he was thrown into a corner in front of his chaplain's house. My God, who shall recount the mocking words that were thrown at him by passers-by as he lay there, and with what clods and stones and dirt his corpse was pelted. . . .

Since hardly anyone passed the bishop's corpse without casting at him some insult or curse and no one thought of burying him, the next day Master Anselm, who had hidden carefully when the rebellion broke out the day before, poured out his prayers to the authors of this tragedy to allow the man to be buried, if only because he had the name and rank of a bishop. They reluctantly consented. Because he had lain naked on the ground from vespers on Thursday to the third hour of the following day, treated as if he were a filthy dog, the Master ordered him to be taken up with a cloth thrown over him to be carried away at last to Saint-Vincent's. One cannot describe the threats and abuse that were showered upon those who cared for his burial or count the curses with which the dead man was pelted. Once he was carried to the church, he had at his burial none of the offices that are provided for any Christian, much less a bishop. The earth was only half scraped out to receive him and the body was so tightly packed in the tiny coffin that his breast and belly were crushed near bursting. Since he had such bad undertakers to lay him out, as I said, those who were present have argued from this that they clearly did their job as wickedly as they could. That day there was no divine service by the monks in that church. But why do I say that day? Indeed, there was none for several days, since they were fearful for the safety of those who fled to them and dreaded death for themselves, too. . . .

When the wicked citizens had duly weighed the enormity of the crime they had committed, they were consumed with dread, greatly fearing the king's judgment. Consequently, when they ought to have sought a remedy, they only added one wound to another. For they decided to call in Thomas, who held the castle of Marle, the reputed son of Enguerrand of Coucy, to defend them against a royal attack. From the beginning of his adolescence, this man seemed to attain great power for the destruction of many men by preying on poor people and pilgrims going to Jerusalem and by adding to his lands through his incestuous marriages. So unheard-of in our times was his cruelty that men who are considered cruel seem more humane in killing cattle than he in killing men. For he did not merely kill them outright with the sword and for definite offenses, as is usual, but by butchery after horrible tortures.

THE GENTRY TEMPERAMENT: SIR WALTER OF HENLEY

Although the gentry were not as innovative an element in medieval life as the bourgeois, the huge expansion in numbers among these landlords of the lower nobility, their intense cultivation of the land, their commitment to hard work and family enterprise in a circumscribed rural area, their love of the land and their devotion to it and the comfortable middle class life they derived from it, is also of central importance in medieval society. Some historians attribute the origins of the capitalist mentality in England to the mind-set of the late medieval gentry. Sir Walter of Henley's treatise on effective estate management, or good husbandry, as the English called it, reveals the gentry's interests and attitudes, and there is indeed in it a theme of not only persistent effort but of postponed gratification and maximal use of resources that presage the early modern capitalist ethos.

GOOD HUSBANDRY

The father having fallen into old age said to his son, Dear Son, live prudently towards God and the world. With regard to God, think often of the passion and death that Jesus Christ suffered for us, and love Him above all things and fear Him and lay hold of and keep His commandments; with regard to the world, think of the wheel of fortune, how man mounts little by little to wealth, and when he is at the top of the wheel, then by mishap he falls little by little into poverty, and then into wretchedness. Wherefore, I pray you, order your life according as your lands are valued yearly by the extent, and nothing beyond that. If you can improve your lands by tillage or cattle or other means beyond the extent, put the surplus in reserve, for if corn fail, or cattle die, or fire befall you, or other mishap, then what you have saved will help you. If you spend in a year the value of your lands and the profit, and one of these chances befall you, you have no recovery except by borrowing, and he who borrows from another robs himself; or by making bargains, as some who make themselves merchants, buying at twenty shillings and selling at ten. It is said in the proverb, "Who provides for the future enjoys himself in the present." You see some who have lands and tenements and know not how to live. Why? I will tell you. Because they live without rule and forethought and spend and waste more than their lands are worth yearly, and when they have wasted their goods can only live from hand to mouth and are in want, and can make no bargain that shall be for their good. The English proverb says, "He that stretches farther than his whittle will reach, in the straw his feet he must stretch." Dear son, be prudent in your doings and be on your guard against the world, which is so wicked and deceitful.

To Sow Your Lands

Sow your lands in time, so that the ground may be settled and the corn rooted before great cold. If by chance it happens that a heavy rain comes or falls on the earth within eight days of the sowing, and then a sharp frost should come and last two or three days, if the earth is full of holes and the frost will penetrate through the earth as deep as the water entered, and so the corn, which has sprouted and is very tender, will perish. There are two kinds of land for spring seed which you must sow early, clay land and stony land. Why? I will tell you. If the weather in March should be dry, then the ground will harden too much and the stony ground become more dry and open, so it is necessary that such ground be sown early, that the corn may be nourished by winter moisture.

To Free Lands from Too Much Water

Chalky ground and sandy ground need not be sown so early, for these are two evils escaped to be overturned in great moisture, but at sowing let the ground be a little sprinkled. And when your lands are sown let the marshy ground and damp ground be well ridged, and the water made to run, so that the ground may be freed from water. Let your land be cleaned and weeded after St. John's Day; before that is not a good time. If you cut thistles fifteen days or eight before St. John's Day, for each one will come two or three. Let your corn be carefully cut and led into the grange.

To Make the Issue of the Grange

When the stock of the grange is taken, place there a true man in whom you trust, who can direct the provost rightly, for one often sees that the grange-keeper and barn-keeper join together to do mischief. Make your provost and barn-keepers fill the measures, so that for every eight bushels a cantle shall be left for the waste which takes place at the putting in and taking from the barn, for in the comble is fraud. How? I will tell you. When the provost has rendered account for the return of the grange, then cause the bushel which he filled with grain to be proved. If the bushel be large then four heaped up will make five, more or less; if it be smaller five will make six; if smaller six will make seven; if still smaller eight will make nine, and so on for each, more or less. Now some of these provosts will only render account for eight in the seam, whether the bushel be large or small, and if the bushel be large there is great deceit. If the return of your grange only yields three times the seed sown you will gain nothing unless corn sells well.

For How Much You Shall Sow an Acre

You know surely that an acre sown with wheat takes three ploughings, except lands which are sown yearly; and that, one with the other, each ploughing is worth sixpence, and harrowing a penny, and on the acre it is necessary to sow at least two bushels. Now two bushels at Michaelmas are worth at least twelvepence, and weeding a halfpenny, and reaping fivepence, and carrying in

August a penny; the straw will pay for the threshing. At three times your sowing you ought to have six bushels, worth three shillings, and the cost amounts to three shillings and three halfpence, and the ground is yours and not reckoned.

How You Ought to Change Your Seed

Change your seed every year at Michaelmas, for seed grown on other ground will bring more profit than that which is grown on your own. Will you see this? Plough two selions at the same time, and sow the one with seed which is bought and the other with corn which you have grown: in August you will see that I speak truly.

How You Ought to Keep and Prepare Manure

Do not sell your stubble or take it from the ground if you do not want it for thatching; if you take away the least you will lose much. Good son, cause manure to be gathered in heaps and mixed with earth, and cause your sheepfold to be marled every fortnight with clay land or with good earth, as the cleansing out of ditches, and then strew it over. And if fodder be left beyond that estimated to keep your cattle cause it to be strewed within the court and without in wet places. And your sheep-house and folds also cause to be strewed. And before the drought of March comes let your manure, which has been scattered within the court and without, be gathered together. And when you must cart marl or manure have a man in whom you trust to be over the carters the first day, that he may see that they do their work well without cheating, and at the end of the day's work see how much they have done, and for so much must they answer daily unless they are able to show a definite hindrance. Put your manure which has been mixed with earth on sandy ground if you have it. Why? I will tell you. The weather in summer is hot, and the sand hot and the manure hot; and when these three heats are united after St. John's Day the barley that grows in the sand is withered, as you can see in several places as you go through the country. In the evening the earth mixed with manure cools the sand and keeps the dew, and thereby is the corn much spared. Manure your lands, and do not plough them too deeply, because manure wastes in descending. Now I will tell you what advantage you will have from manure mixed with earth. If the manure was quite by itself it would last two or three years, according as the ground is cold or hot; manure mixed with earth will last twice as long, but it will not be so sharp. Know for certain that marl lasts longer than manure. Why? Because manure wastes in descending and marl in ascending. And why will manure mixed last longer than pure manure? I will tell you. Of manure and the earth which are harrowed together the earth shall keep the manure, so that it cannot waste by descending as much as it would naturally. I tell you why, that you may gather manure according to your power. And when your manure has been spread and watered a little, then it is time that it should be turned over; then the earth and the manure will profit much together. And if you spread your manure at fallowing it shall be all the more turned over at a second ploughing, and at sowing shall come up again be mixed with earth. And if it is spread at second ploughing at sowing it is all the more under the earth and little mixed with it, and that is not profitable. And the nearer the fold is to the sowing the more shall it be worth. At the first feast of our Lady enlarge your fold according as you have sheep, either more or less, for in that time there is much manure.

How You Ought to Inspect Your Cattle

Sort out your cattle once a year between Easter and Whitsuntide — that is to say, oxen, cows, and herds — and let those that are not to be kept put to fatten; if you lay out money to fatten them with grass you will gain. And know for truth that bad beasts cost more than good. Why? I will tell you. If it be a draught beast he must be more thought of than the other and more spared, and because he is spared the others are burdened for his lack. And if you must buy cattle buy them between Easter and Whitsuntide, for then beasts are spare and cheap. And change your horses before they are too old and worn out or maimed, for with little money you can rear good and young ones, if you sell and buy in season. It is well to know how one ought to keep cattle, to teach your people, for when they see that you understand it they will take the more pains to do well.

How You Ought to Keep Beasts for the Plough

You must keep your plough beasts so that they have enough food to do their work, and that they be not too much overwrought when they come from the plough, for you shall be put to too great an expense to replace them; besides, your tillage shall be behindhand. Do not put them in houses in wet weather, for inflammation arises between the skin and the hair and between the skin and the wool, which will turn to the harm of the beasts. And if your cattle are accustomed to have food, let it be given at midday by one of the messers or the provost, and mixed with little barley, because it is too bearded and hurts the horses' mouths. And why shall you give it them before some one and with chaff? I will tell you. Because it often happens that the ox-herds steal the provender, and horses will eat more chaff for food and grow fat and drink more. And do not let the fodder for oxen be given them in a great quantity at a time, but little and often, and then they will eat and waste little. And when there is a great quantity before them they eat their fill and then lie down and ruminate, and by the blowing of their breath they begin to dislike the fodder and it is wasted. And let the cattle be bathed, and when they are dry curry them, for that will do them much good. And let your cows have enough food that the milk may not be lessened. And when the male calf is calved let it have all the milk for a month; at the end of the month take away a teat, and from week to week a teat, and then it will have sucked eight weeks, and put food before it, that it may learn to eat. And the female calf shall have all the milk for three weeks, and take from it the teats as with the male. And let them have water in dry weather within the houses and without, for many die on the ground of a disease of the lungs for lack of water. Further, if there be any beast which begins to fall ill, lay out money to better it, for it is said in the proverb, "Blessed is the penny that saves two.". . .

To Sell in Season

Buy and sell in season through the inspection of a true man or two who can witness the business, for often it happens that those who render account increase the purchases and diminish the sales. If you must sell by weight, be careful there, for there is great deceit for those who do not know to be on their guard.

View of Account

Have an inspection of account, or cause it to be made by some one in whom you trust, once a year, and final account at the end of the year. View of account is made to know the state of things as well as the issues, receipts, sales, purchases, and other expenses, and for raising money. If there is any let it be raised and taken from the hands of the servants. For often it happens that servants and provosts by themselves or by others make merchandise with their lord's money to their own profit and not to the profit of their lord, and that is not lawful. And if arrears appear in the final account let them be speedily raised, and if they name certain persons who owe arrears, take the names, for often it happens that servants and provosts are debtors themselves, and make others debtors whom they can and ought not, and this they do to conceal their disloyalty.

How Servants and Estate Managers Ought to Behave

Those who have the goods of others in their keeping ought to keep well four things: To love their lord and respect him, and as to making profit, they ought to look on the business as their own, and as to outlays, they ought to think that the business is another's, but there are few servants and estate managers who keep these four things altogether, as I think, but there are many who have omitted the three and kept the fourth, and have interpreted that contrary to the right way.

LEARNING FROM TRAVEL: MARCO POLO

The medieval middle class was surprisingly mobile, considering the difficulty of land transportation and the virtual absence of road maps. Merchants carried goods long distances within Europe and the Mediterranean area. Pilgrims visited shrines far away, and missionaries sought conversion at alien courts, hundreds or even thousands of miles from home. Knights traveled long distances to obtain employment as mercenaries, and peasant families and whole villages moved to distant frontier areas in search of economic opportunity. Merchants also intrepidly journeyed beyond the frontiers of Western Europe in search of new commodities and markets. East Asia, with its much desired spices and its exotic silks, perfumes, and jewels, became a target for long-distance commercial travel. When these merchants reached distant climes, middle class curiosity beyond the trading possibilities stimulated efforts to learn about the different culture and society. Marco Polo, one of a family of Venetian merchants who made a lengthy visit to China in the late fifteenth century, described what he found there closely and sympathetically. Some historians see a profound social significance in such travel writings, as they made Europeans aware of alternative ways of behavior and made them more prone to scrutinize their own institutions and behavior patterns more closely. In other words, here is the foundation of a more relativistic social attitude that led eventually to radical criticism of traditional European systems.

Kublai, who is styled the Great Khan, or Lord of Lords, is of middle stature, that is, neither tall nor short. His limbs are well formed, and in his whole figure there is a just proportion. His complexion is fair, and occasionally suffused with red, like the bright tint of the rose, which adds much grace to his countenance. His eyes are black and handsome, his nose is well shaped and prominent.

He has four wives of the first rank, who are esteemed legitimate, and the eldest born son of any one of these succeeds to the empire, upon the decease of the Great Khan. They bear equally the title of empress, and have their separate courts. None of them have fewer than three hundred young female attendants of great beauty, together with a multitude of youths as pages, and other eunuchs, as well as ladies of the bedchamber; so that the number of persons belonging to each of their respective courts amounts to ten thousand.

When his majesty is desirous of the company of one of his empresses, he either sends for her, or goes himself to her palace. Besides these, he has many concubines provided for his use, from a province of Tartary named Ungut, the inhabitants of which are distinguished for beauty of features and fairness of complexion. Every second year, or oftener, as it may happen to be his pleasure, the Great Khan sends thither his officers, who collect for him, one hundred or more, of the handsomest of the young women, according to the estimation of beauty communicated to them in their instructions.

The mode of their appreciation is as follows. Upon the arrival of these commissioners, they give orders for assembling all the young women of the province, and appoint qualified persons to examine them, who, upon careful inspection of each of them separately, that is to say, of the hair, the countenance, the eyebrows, the mouth, the

Departure of Matteo and Nicolo Polo

certain elderly ladies of the palace, whose duty it is to observe them attentively during the course of the night, in order to ascertain that they have not any concealed imperfections, that they sleep tranquilly, do not snore, have sweet breath, and are free from unpleasant scent in any part of the body. Having undergone this rigorous scrutiny, they are divided into parties of five, each taking turn for three days and three nights, in his majesty's interior apartment, where they are to perform every service that is required of them, and he does with them as he likes.

When this term is completed, they are relieved by another party, and in this manner successively, until the whole number have taken their turn; when the first five recommence their attendance. But while one party officiates in the inner chamber, another is stationed in the outer apartment adjoining. If his majesty should have occasion for anything, such as drink or victuals, the former may signify his commands to the latter, by whom the article required is immediately procured. In this way the duty of waiting upon his majesty's person is exclusively performed by these young females. The remainder of them, whose value had been estimated at an inferior rate, are assigned to the different lords of the household; under whom they are instructed in cookery, in dressmaking, and other suitable works; and upon any person belonging to the court expressing an inclination to take a wife, the Great Khan bestows upon him one of these damsels, with a handsome portion. In this manner he provides for them all amongst his nobility.

It may be asked whether the people of the province do not feel themselves aggrieved in having their daughters thus forcibly taken from them by the sovereign? Certainly not; but, on the contrary, they regard it as a favour and an honour done to them; and those who are the fathers of handsome children feel highly gratified by his condescending to make choice of their daughters. "If," say they, "my daughter is born under an auspicious planet and to good fortune, his majesty can best fulfill her destinies, by matching her nobly; which it would not be in my power to do."

lips, and other features, as well as the symmetry of these with each other, estimate their value at sixteen, seventeen, eighteen, or twenty, or more carats, according to the greater or less degree of beauty. The number required by the Great Khan, at the rates, perhaps, of twenty or twenty-one carats, to which their commission was limited, is then selected from the rest, and they are conveyed to his court.

Upon their arrival in his presence, he causes a new examination to be made by a different set of inspectors, and from amongst them a further selection takes place, when thirty or forty are retained for his own chamber at a higher valuation. These are committed separately to the care of

If, on the other hand, the daughter misconducts herself, or any mischance befalls her, by which she becomes disqualified, the father attributes the disappointment to the evil influence of her stars. . . .

The Great Khan usually resides during three months of the year, namely December, January, and February, in the great city of Kanbalu [Peking], situated towards the north-eastern extremity of the province of Cathay. Here, on the southern side of the new city, is the site of his vast palace, the form and dimensions of which are as follows.

In the first place is a square enclosed with a wall and deep ditch; each side of the square being eight miles in length, and having at an equal distance from each extremity an entrance-gate, for the concourse of people resorting thither from all quarters. Within this enclosure there is, on the four sides, an open space one mile in breadth, where the troops are stationed. This is bounded by a second wall, enclosing a square of six miles, having three gates on the south side, and three on the north, the middle portal of each being larger than the other two, and always kept shut, excepting on the occasions of the emperor's entrance or departure. Those on each side always remain open for the use of common passengers.

In the middle of each division of these walls is a handsome and spacious building, and consequently within the enclosure there are eight such buildings, in which are deposited the royal military stores; one building being appropriated to the reception of each class of stores. Thus, for instance, the bridles, saddles, stirrups, and other furniture serving for the equipment of cavalry, occupy one storehouse; the bows, strings, quivers, arrows, and other articles belonging to archery, occupy another; cuirasses, corselets, and other armour formed of leather, a third storehouse; and so of the rest.

Within this walled enclosure there is still another, of great thickness, and its height is full twenty-five feet. The battlements or notched parapets are all white. This also forms a square four miles in extent, each side being one mile, and

it has six gates, disposed like those of the former enclosure. It contains in like manner eight large buildings, similarly arranged, which are appropriated to the wardrobe of the emperor. The spaces between the one wall and the other are ornamented with many handsome trees, and contain meadows in which are kept various kinds of beasts, such as stags, the animals that yield the musk, roe-bucks, fallow-deer, and others of the same class. Every interval between the walls, not occupied by buildings, is stocked in this manner. The pastures have abundant herbage. The roads across them being raised three feet above their level, and paved, no mud collects upon them, nor rain-water settles, but on the contrary runs off, and contributes to improve the vegetation.

Within these walls, which constitute the boundary of four miles, stands the palace of the Great Khan, the most extensive that has ever yet been known. It reaches from the northern to the southern wall, leaving only a vacant court, where persons of rank and the military guards pass and repass. It has no upper floor, but the roof is very lofty. The paved foundation or platform on which it stands is raised ten spans above the level of the ground, and a wall of marble, two paces wide, is built on all sides. This wall serves as a terrace, where those who walk on it are visible from without. Along the exterior edge of the wall is a handsome balustrade, with pillars, which the people are allowed to approach. The sides of the great halls and the apartments are ornamented with dragons in carved work and gilt, figures of warriors, of birds, and of beasts, with representations of battles. The inside of the roof is contrived in such a manner that nothing besides gilding and painting presents itself to the eye.

On each of the four sides of the palace there is a grand flight of marble steps, by which you ascend from the level of the ground to the wall of marble which surrounds the building, and which constitute the approach to the palace itself.

The grand hall is extremely long and wide, and admits of dinners being there served to great multitudes of people. The palace contains a number of separate chambers, all highly beautiful, and so admirably disposed that it seems impossible to suggest any improvement to the system of their arrangement. The exterior of the roof is adorned with a variety of colours, red, green, azure, and violet, and the sort of covering is so strong as to last for many years. The glazing of the windows is so well wrought and so delicate as to have the transparency of crystal.

In the rear of the body of the palace there are large buildings containing several apartments, where is deposited the private property of the monarch, or his treasure in gold and silver bullion, precious stones, and pearls, and also his vessels of gold and silver plate. Here are likewise the apartments of his wives and concubines; and in this retired situation he dispatches business with convenience, being free from every kind of interruption.

On the other side of the grand palace, and opposite to that in which the emperor resides, is another palace, in every respect similar, appropriated to the residence of Chinghis, his eldest son, at whose court are observed all the ceremonials belonging to that of his father, as the prince who is to succeed to the government of the empire. Not far from the palace, on the northern side, and about a bow-shot distance from the surrounding wall, is an artificial mount of earth, the height of which is full a hundred paces, and the circuit at the base about a mile. It is covered with the most beautiful evergreen trees; for whenever his Majesty receives information of a handsome tree growing in any place, he causes it to be dug up, with all its roots and the earth about them, and however large and heavy it may be, he has it transported by means of elephants to this mount, and adds it to the verdant collection. Because the trees on this hill are always green it has acquired the name of the Green Mount.

On its summit is erected an ornamental pavilion, which is likewise entirely green. The view of this altogether,—the mount itself, the trees, and the building, form a delightful and at the same time a wonderful scene. In the northern quarter also, and equally within the precincts of the city, there is a large and deep excavation, judiciously

formed, the earth from which supplied the material for raising the mount. It is furnished with water by a small rivulet, and has the appearance of a fish-pond, but its use is for watering the cattle. The stream passing from thence along an aqueduct, at the foot of the Green Mount, proceeds to fill another great and very deep excavation formed between the private palace of the emperor and that of his son Chingis; and the earth from hence equally served to increase the elevation of the mount. In this latter basin there is great store and variety of fish, from which the table of his Majesty is supplied with any quantity that may be wanted.

The stream discharges itself at the opposite extremity of the piece of water, and precautions are taken to prevent the escape of the fish by placing gratings of copper or iron at the places of its entrance and exit. It is stocked also with swans and other water birds. From the one palace to the other there is a communication by means of a bridge thrown across the water. Such is the description of this great palace. . . .

The city of Kanbalu is situated near a large river in the province of Cathay, and was in ancient times eminently magnificent and royal. The name itself implies "the city of the Emperor"; but his Majesty was informed by the astrologers, that it was destined to become rebellious to his authority and resolved upon the measure of building another capital, upon the opposite side of the river, where stand the palaces just described. The new and the old cities are separated from each other only by the stream that runs between them. . . .

It is strictly forbidden to every tradesman, mechanic, or husbandman throughout his Majesty's dominions, to keep a vulture, hawk, or any other bird used for the pursuit of game, or any sporting dog; nor is a nobleman or cavalier to presume to chase beast or bird in the neighbourhood of the place where his Majesty takes up his residence, the distance being limited to five miles, for example, on one side, ten on another, and perhaps fifteen in a third direction, unless his name be inscribed in a list kept by the grand falconer, or he has a special privilege to that effect. Beyond those limits it is permitted. There is an order, however, which prohibits every person throughout all the countries subject to the Great Khan, from daring to kill hares, roebucks, fallow deer, stags, or other animals of that kind, or any large birds, between the months of March and October. This is that they may increase and multiply; and as the breach of this order is attended with punishment, game of every description increases prodigiously.

When the usual time is elapsed, his Majesty returns to the capital by the road he went; continuing his sport during the whole of the journey.

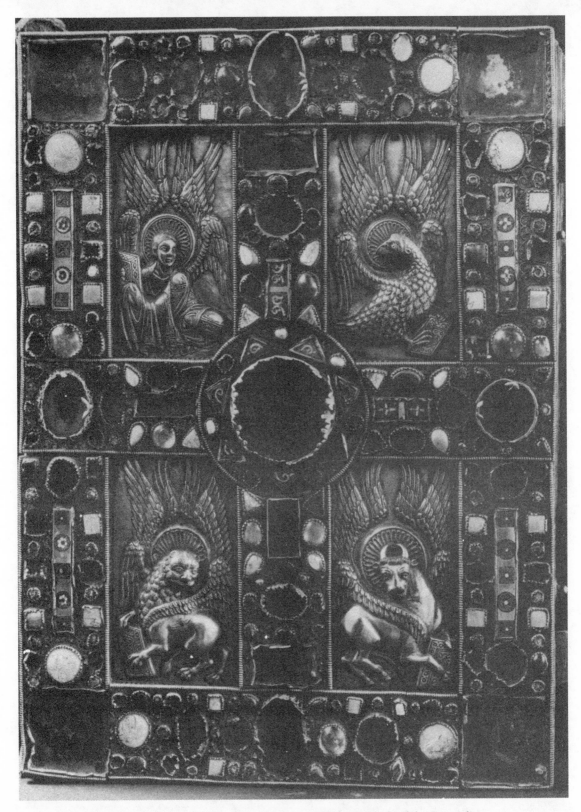

Cover of Roger of Helmarshausen Gospel Book, with four symbols of the Evangelists

DYNAMIC INTERACTION OF THE THREE ELEMENTS

THE GOOD AND BEAUTIFUL MIDDLE AGES

Nobility, with its aristocratic heroism and militarism; church, with its hierarchic authority and tradition; and the middle class, with its sensibility and sentiment, while intrinsically independently functional, powerfully and creatively interacted with each other. Out of this interaction emerged most of the original and distinctive aspects of medieval civilization. What is especially treasured today as the good things the Middle Ages have contributed to our well-being, particularly in religion, literature, art, and philosophy, were mainly products of this dynamic interaction. Such creative impact was particularly evident in the period loosely called the twelfth century, which more accurately extended from about 1080 to 1230. A very great part of what we value in the Middle Ages, what we regard benignly and enthusiastically as the good Middle Ages, most worthy of our civilization and possibly deserving active recovery, stems from these 150 years that have inevitably received such historical labels as "The Twelfth Century Renaissance," "The Making of the Middle Ages," "The Rise of Europe," "The Flowering of Medieval Civilization," and "The Intellectual Expansion of Europe." However we may judge the three elements of the medieval world, their interaction generated much that resonates with unusual insight into humanity, nature, and divinity. Two special factors contributed to the interaction of the three elements and the creative outcomes. One was the population explosion, mild weather, economic boom, and relative good public health of the period 1080–1230—in other words, a fortunate ambience. Another was the rapid transition from a mainly oral to a heavily literate culture, a moment of anthropological transition that seems to have augmented the functional impact of one element upon another.

We have here in this dynamic interaction of the three elements of nobility, church, and middle class within a very positive context of fortunate material environment and stimulating transition from oral to literate society, a pushing outward of medieval sense and sensibility. We have reason, learning, and feeling engaged in a process of discovery of the nature of things. What is the human personality and what is its relation to the Divine Being? What is this experience called love and how can its benefits be maximized in human life? What is a Christian society and how may it be achieved? How can state power be made to function so that in a particular community and in the lives of individuals there is a positive outcome from political authority and legal systems? How may learning and art—libraries, schoolrooms, and architectural and painterly ateliers—be harnessed for the celebration of faith and cultivation of humanity?

These are the kinds of questions dynamic triangular interaction pursues with optimism, confidence, and curiosity. Intellectual limits have not been run up against. It is discovery and revelation that are the modes of consciousness and perception now. When there is a steady economic growth, bellies are full of good food, and the ever-expanding population is still gainfully employed with no difficulty, the nature of self, society, state, and cosmos can be sought and a final limit never expected—only the quest itself needs to be exploited.

When mostly oral communication is being heavily supplemented and in some ways replaced by the written text, there is further buoyant feeling about human capacity for creativity and growth. The carefully laid out page of the medieval manuscript, its straight lines, elegant, clean script, and wide margins comes to represent that work of exposure and definition that the culture as a whole has become engaged in.

The open character of oral culture runs down after awhile into rigidifying repetition and loses its plastic vitality and creative capacity. The linear quality of the written text now stimulates convention-breaking, an escape from repetitive memory into new ideas that rationality provides. The linear quality of the text seems at this point a radical departure, an inspiration, and a vehicle of truth determination beside which orality seems to stand for numbing recycling and mindless chorusing. The closing of mind that linear rationality can over time foster, and its service to power, is not clearly encountered during the efflorescence of dynamic interaction into good and beautiful modes of thought and feeling.

FULBERT OF CHARTRES

CHRISTIAN MILITARISM

By the early eleventh century, bishops like Fulbert of Chartres were valorizing the nobility's social relationships built on feudal vassalage by absorbing them into the hierarchic tradition of society organized along the lines of moral principles. This sanctioning of Christian militarism not only closed the gap between nobility and church; it probably made feudalism a more rigidly hierarchic social and political system than it had been before. Historians today believe that feudalism—lordships and vassalage—was grounded in and shaped at least partly by the hierarchal ideology advocated by the church. The nobility's social behavior and organization were significantly transformed by contact with ecclesiastical theory.

To William, most glorious duke of the Aquitanians, Bishop Fulbert, the favor of his prayers:

Asked to write something concerning the forms of fealty, I have noted briefly for you, on the authority of the books, the things which follow. He who swears fealty to his lord ought always to have these six things in memory: what is harmless, safe, honorable, useful, easy, practicable. *Harmless,* that is to say, that he should not injure his lord in his body; *safe,* that he should not injure him by betraying his secrets or the defenses upon which he relies for safety; *honorable,* that he should not injure him in his justice or in other matters that pertain to his honor; *useful,* that he should not injure him in his possessions; *easy* and *practicable,* that that good which his lord is able to do easily he make not difficult, nor that which is practicable he make not impossible to him.

That the faithful vassal should avoid these injuries is certainly proper, but not for this alone does he deserve his holding; for it is not sufficient to abstain from evil, unless what is good is done also. It remains, therefore, that in the same six things mentioned above he should faithfully counsel and aid his lord, if he wishes to be looked upon as worthy of his benefice and to be safe concerning the fealty which he has sworn.

The lord also ought to act toward his faithful vassal reciprocally in all these things. And if he does not do this, he will be justly considered guilty of bad faith, just as the former, if he should be detected in avoiding or consenting to the avoidance of his duties, would be perfidious and perjured.

THE TRUCE OF GOD

One thing bishops demanded of the nobility (in addition to generous endowment grants for churches and monasteries)—that the nobility's fighting be constrained, organized, and regulated, and that the warrior class refrain from indiscriminate violence. A prime effort in this direction was the Truce of God movement, which tried to get the nobility to swear they would not fight on certain days and in certain places and would recognize the ecclesiastics as umpires of legitimate violence. Here is a proclamation of the Truce of God by the bishop of Cologne in the late eleventh century.

Inasmuch as in our own times the church, through its members, has been extraordinarily afflicted by tribulations and difficulties, so that tranquillity and peace were wholly despaired of, we have endeavored by God's help to aid it, suffering so many burdens and perils. And by the advice of our faithful subjects we have at length provided this remedy, so that we might to some extent re-establish, on certain days at least, the peace which, because of our sins, we could not make enduring. Accordingly we have enacted and set forth the following: Having called together our parishioners to a legally summoned council, which was held at Cologne, the chief city of our province, in the Church of St. Peter, in the 1083rd year of our Lord's Incarnation, in the sixth indiction, on the XII day before the Kalends of May [April 20], after arranging other business, we have caused to be read in public what we proposed to do in this matter. After this had been for some time fully discussed "pro and con" by all, it was unanimously agreed upon, both the clergy and the people consenting, and we declared in what manner and during what parts of the year it ought to be observed:

Namely, that from the first day of the Advent of our Lord through Epiphany, and from the beginning of Septuagesima to the eighth day after Pentecost and through that whole day, and throughout the year on every Sunday, Friday and Saturday, and on the fast days of the four seasons, and on the eve and the day of all the apostles, and on all days canonically set apart—or which shall in the future be set apart—for fasts or feasts, this decree of peace shall be observed; so that both those who travel and those who remain at home may enjoy security and the most entire peace, so that no one may commit murder, arson, robbery or assault, no one may injure another with a sword, club or any kind of weapon, and so that no one irritated by any wrong, from the Advent of our Lord to the eighth day after Epiphany, and from Septuagesima to the eighth day after Pentecost, may presume to carry arms, shields, sword or lance, or moreover any kind of armor. On the remaining days indeed, viz., on Sundays, Fridays, apostles' days and the vigils of the apostles, and on every day set aside, or to be set aside, for fasts or feasts, bearing arms shall be legal, but on this condition that no injury shall be done in any way to anyone. If it shall be necessary for anyone in the time of the decreed peace—*i.e.,* from the Advent of our Lord to the eighth day after Epiphany, and from Septuagesima to the eighth day after Pentecost—to go from one bishopric into another in which the peace is not observed, he may bear arms, but on the condition that he shall not injure anyone, except in self-defence if he is attacked; and when he returns into our diocese he shall immediately lay aside his arms. If it shall happen that any castle is besieged during the days which are included within the peace the besiegers shall cease from attack unless they are set upon by the besieged and compelled to beat the latter back.

It is not an infringement of the peace, if anyone orders his delinquent slave, pupil, or anyone in any way under his charge to be chastised with rods or cudgels. It is also an exception to this constitution of peace, if the Lord King publicly orders an expedition to attack the enemies of the kingdom or is pleased to hold a council to judge the enemies of justice. The peace is not violated if, during the time, the duke or other counts, advocates or their substitutes hold courts and

inflict punishment legally on thieves, robbers and other criminals.

The statute of this imperial peace is especially enacted for the security of those engaged in feuds; but after the end of the peace, they are not to dare to rob and plunder in the villages and houses, because the laws and penalties enacted before the institution of the peace are still legally valid to restrain them from crime, moreover because robbers and highwaymen are excluded from this divine peace and indeed from any peace.

If anyone attempts to oppose this pious institution and is unwilling to promise peace to God with the others or to observe it, no priest in our diocese shall presume to say a mass for him or shall take any care for his salvation; if he is sick, no Christian shall dare to visit him; on his death-bed he shall not receive the Eucharist, unless he repents. The supreme authority of the peace promised to God and commonly extolled by all will be so great that it will be observed not only in our time, but forever among our posterity, because if anyone shall presume to infringe, destroy or violate it, either now or ages hence, at the end of the world, he is irrevocably excommunicated by us.

THE CRUSADES

The church's effort to regulate and valorize military heroism resulted in the First Crusade of 1095–1096, in which a substantial part of the French nobility was persuaded by Pope Urban II to invade the Middle East and capture Jerusalem for the cross. Mostly because the Arabs were disunited at the time, the crusade succeeded. The French crusaders held Jerusalem for nearly a century against the resurgent Arabs and lost their last fortress in the Holy Land, Acre, two centuries later. The First Crusade was followed in the next 150 years by another six Latin Christian collective military adventures in the Middle East. None resulted in victory. Slowly during the thirteenth century the crusading impetus declined, because recognition spread that a successful European attack upon the Arabs involved a staggeringly large commitment of resources, which scarcely any king or lord was willing to make. Here are two records of the crusading spirit at its fervent and naked best. First, the speech that Pope Urban II gave at Claremont in France, inaugurating the First Crusade. Second, a description of how the crusaders behaved when they took Jerusalem in 1096 from the historical account by William of Tyre, a leading Christian Levantine bishop. William of Tyre was not an eyewitness to these events—he wrote several decades later—but drawing upon earlier accounts, William of Tyre expresses the memory of it as retained by the crusaders, the way they wanted the event to be remembered. It is not gentle in tone. The ingredient of religious and moral hatred within the crusading movement was substantial.

Crusading Knights embarking overseas

SPEECH OF POPE URBAN II AT THE COUNCIL OF CLERMONT 1095

O, race of the Franks, race from across the mountains, race beloved and chosen by God! As is clear from your many works you are a race set apart from all other nations by the situation of your country as well as by your catholic faith and the honor which you render to the holy church. To you our discourse is addressed and for you our exhortations are intended. . . .

From the confines of Jerusalem and from the city of Constantinople has gone forth a horrible tale which has very frequently been brought to our ears. It has been reported that a race from the kingdom of the Persians, an accursed race, a race wholly alienated from God . . . has violently invaded the lands of those Christians and has depopulated them by pillage and fire. They have led away a part of the captives into their own country, and a part they have destroyed by cruel tortures. They have either destroyed the churches of God or appropriated them for the rites of their own religion. They destroy the altars, after having defiled them with their uncleanness. They circumcise the Christians, and the blood of the circumcision they either spread upon the altars or pour into the baptismal vases.

When they wish to torture anyone by a base death, they perforate his navel and dragging forth the extremity of the intestines, bind it to a stake; then by blows they compel the victim to run around the stake, until the viscera gush forth and the victim falls prostrate on the ground. Others they bind to a post and pierce with arrows. Others they compel to extend their necks and then, attacking them with naked swords, attempt to cut through the neck with a single blow. What shall I say of the abominable rape of the women? To speak of it is worse than to be silent. The kingdom of the Greeks is now dismembered by them and deprived of territory so vast in extent that it could not be traversed in two month's time.

On whom therefore is the labor of avenging these wrongs and of recovering this territory incumbent, if not upon you? You, upon whom above all other nations God has conferred remarkable glory in arms, great courage, bodily activity, and strength to humble the heads of those who resist you. Let the deeds of your ancestors encourage you and incite your minds to manly achievements; the glory and greatness of king Charlemagne, and of his son Louis, and of your other monarchs, who have destroyed the kingdoms of the Turks and have extended the sway of the holy church over the lands of the pagans. Let the holy sepulchre of our Lord and Saviour, which is possessed by the unclean nations, especially incite you, and the holy places which are now treated with ignominy and irreverently polluted with the filth of the unclean. O, most valiant soldiers and descendants of invincible ancestors, be not degenerate, but recall the valor of your progenitors.

But if you are hindered by love of children, parents or wife, remember what the Lord says in the Gospel, "He that loveth father or mother more than me, is not worthy of me." "Everyone that hath forsaken houses, or brethren, or sisters, or father, or mother, or wife, or children, or lands for my name's sake shall receive an hundred-fold and shall inherit everlasting life." Let none of your possessions retain you nor solicitude for your family affairs. For this land which you inhabit, shut in on all sides by the seas and surrounded by mountain peaks, is too narrow for your large population; nor does it abound in wealth; and it furnishes scarcely food enough for its cultivators. Hence it is that you murder and devour one another, that you wage war, and that very many among you perish in intestine strife.

Let therefore hatred depart from among you, let your quarrels end, let wars cease, and let all dissensions and controversies slumber. Enter upon the road to the Holy Sepulchre; wrest that land from the wicked race, and subject it to yourselves. That land which as the Scripture says "floweth with milk and honey," was given by God into the power of the children of Israel. Jerusalem is the centre of the earth; the land is fruitful above all others, like another paradise of delights. This the Redeemer of mankind has made illustrious by His advent, has beautified by His residence, has consecrated by His passion, has redeemed by His death, has glorified by His burial.

This royal city, however, situated at the centre of the earth, is now held captive by the enemies of Christ, and is subjected by those who do not know God, to the worship of the heathens. She seeks therefore and desires to be liberated and does not cease to implore you to come to her aid. From you especially she asks succor, because, as we have already said, God has conferred upon you above all other nations great glory in arms. Accordingly undertake this journey for the remission of your sins, with the assurance of the imperishable glory of the kingdom of heaven.

When Pope Urban had said these and very many similar things in his urbane discourse, he so influenced to one purpose the desires of all who were present, that all cried out, "It is the will of God! It is the will of God!" When the venerable Roman pontiff heard that, with eyes uplifted to heaven he gave thanks to God and, with his hand commanding silence, said:

Most beloved brethren, to-day is manifest in you what the Lord says in the Gospel, "Where two or three are gathered together in my name there am I in the midst of them." For unless God had been present in your spirits, all of you would not have uttered the same cry. For, although the cry issued from numerous mouths, yet the origin of the cry was one. Therefore I say to you that God, who implanted this in your breasts, has drawn it forth from you. Let that then be your war-cry in combats, because it is given to you by God. When an armed attack is made upon the enemy, let this one cry be raised by all the soldiers of God: it is the will of God! It is the will of God!

And we do not command or advise that the old or feeble, or those incapable of bearing arms, undertake this journey. . . .

Whoever, therefore, shall determine upon this holy pilgrimage and shall make his vow to God to tnat effect and shall offer himself to Him for sacrifice, as a living victim, holy and acceptable to God, shall wear the sign of the cross of the Lord on his forehead or on his breast. When, truly, in fulfillment of his vow he wishes to enter upon his journey, let him place the cross on his back between his shoulders. This two-fold action will fulfill the precept of the Lord, as He commands in the Gospel, "He that taketh not his cross and followeth after me, is not worthy of me."

WILLIAM OF TYRE: THE CAPTURE OF JERUSALEM BY THE FRENCH CRUSADERS

The legions of the duke and the two counts, who. . . . were attacking the city on the north, had, by the aid of God, succeeded in shattering the outworks and filling up the moat. The enemy, now utterly exhausted, could resist no longer. Accordingly, the Christian troops were able to approach the wall without danger, for only here and there were found adversaries bold enough to try to attack them through the loopholes.

At the duke's command, the fighters in the siege engines had set on fire sacks of straw and cushions stuffed with cotton. Fanned into a blaze by the north wind, these poured forth such dense smoke into the city that those who were trying to defend the wall could scarcely open their mouths or eyes. Bewildered and dazed by the torrent of black smoke, they abandoned the defense of the ramparts. As soon as this situation became apparent, the duke ordered the beams which had been rescued from the enemy to be brought aloft at once and so placed that one end rested on the machine and the other on the wall. He then caused the movable side of the siege tower to be lowered. This, supported by the heavy beams which had been placed beneath it, formed a bridge of sufficient strength. Thus material which the enemy had brought in for their own benefit was turned to their injury.

When the bridge had been adjusted in this manner, the noble and illustrious Duke Godfrey, accompanied by his brother Eustace, led the way into the city and encouraged the rest to follow. They were followed immediately by the two noble brothers Ludolf and Gislebert, natives of the city of Tournai, who well deserve to be remembered forever. Then a host of cavalry and infantry crossed, so many in number that neither the engine nor the bridge could support more. When the enemy perceived that the Christians were in possession of the wall and that the duke had already raised his standard, they abandoned the ramparts and towers and betook themselves to the narrow streets.

As soon as our people observed that the duke and a majority of the leaders had seized the towers, they did not wait to ascend the machine, but vied with one another in raising to the walls the scaling ladders with which they were well supplied. For, in obedience to a public proclamation, each pair of knights had prepared a ladder to be used in common. By means of these, without waiting for the duke's command, they now joined the others on the wall.

Immediately following Godfrey came the count of Flanders, the duke of Normandy, and the gallant Tancred, a warrior praiseworthy in every respect.

As soon as the duke saw that all these knights

had entered safely, he sent some of their number with an honorable escort to open the north gate, now the gate of St. Stephen, that the people who were waiting outside might enter. This was unbarred without delay, and the entire army rushed in pell-mell without order or discipline.

It was a Friday at the ninth hour. Verily, it seemed divinely ordained that the faithful who were fighting for the glory of the Saviour should have obtained the consummation of their desires at the same hour and on the very day on which the Lord had suffered in that city for the salvation of the world. It was on that day, as we read, that the first man was created and the second was delivered over to death for the salvation of the first. It was fitting, therefore, that, at that very hour, those who were members of His body and imitators of Him should triumph in His name over His enemies.

The duke and those who were with him then united their forces and, protected by their shields and helmets, swept hither and thither through the streets and squares of the city with drawn swords. Regardless of age and condition, they laid low, without distinction, every enemy encountered. Everywhere was frightful carnage, everywhere lay heaps of severed heads, so that soon it was impossible to pass or to go from one place to another except over the bodies of the slain. Already the leaders had forced their way by various routes almost to the center of the city and wrought unspeakable slaughter as they advanced. A host of people followed in their train, athirst for the blood of the enemy and wholly intent upon destruction.

Meanwhile, the count of Toulouse and the leaders who were fighting with him in the vicinity of Mt. Sion were entirely ignorant that the city had been taken and that the victory was ours. But the loud shouts of the Christians as they entered Jerusalem and the fearful cries which arose as the massacre of the infidels proceeded brought consternation to the defenders in that section of the city. They were at a loss to account for the unusual clamor and the ominous uproar. All too soon they discovered that the city had been entered by force and the legions of the Christians

introduced. Without delay they abandoned the towers and fortifications and fled in different directions, intent on safety alone. The majority took refuge in the citadel, because that was close at hand.

The army let down the bridge unopposed, raised their ladders to the walls, and entered the city without the slightest hindrance on the part of the enemy. As soon as they themselves were admitted, they threw open the south gate which was the nearest to them and let in the rest of the people. It was here that the illustrious and valiant count of Toulouse entered, accompanied by Isoard, count of Die, Raymond Pilet, William de Sabran, the bishop of Albara, and many other nobles whose names and number no history has preserved for us. In one united body these forces, armed to the teeth, swarmed everywhere through the midst of the city, and, with a common purpose, wrought fearful havoc. For when those who had escaped the ravages of the duke and his people fled to other parts of the city and believed that in some way they had avoided death, they encountered this company. Thus, while they were trying to avoid Scylla, they fell into the more serious peril of Charybdis. So frightful was the massacre throughout the city, so terrible the shedding of blood, that even the victors experienced sensations of horror and loathing.

The greater part of the people had taken refuge in the court of the Temple because it lay in a retired part of the city and was very strongly defended by a wall, towers, and gates. But their flight thither did not save them, for Tancred immediately followed with the largest portion of the whole army. He forced his way into the Temple and, after terrible carnage, carried off with him, according to report, a vast amount of gold, silver, and jewels. It is believed, however, that later, after the tumult had quieted down, he restored these treasures untouched.

After the other leaders had slain all whom they encountered in the various parts of the city, they learned that many had fled for refuge to the sacred precincts of the Temple. Thereupon as with one accord they hurried thither. A crowd of knights and foot soldiers was introduced, who massacred all those who had taken refuge there. No mercy was shown to anyone, and the whole place was flooded with the blood of the victims.

It was indeed the righteous judgment of God which ordained that those who had profaned the sanctuary of the Lord by their superstitious rites and had caused it to be an alien place to His faithful people should expiate their sin by death and, by pouring out their own blood, purify the sacred precincts.

It was impossible to look upon the vast numbers of the slain without horror; everywhere lay fragments of human bodies, and the very ground was covered with the blood of the slain. It was not alone the spectacle of headless bodies and mutilated limbs strewn in all directions that roused horror in all who looked upon them. Still more dreadful was it to gaze upon the victors themselves, dripping with blood from head to foot, an ominous sight which brought terror to all who met them. It is reported that within the Temple enclosure alone about ten thousand infidels perished, in addition to those who lay slain everywhere throughout the city in the streets and squares, the number of whom was estimated as no less.

The rest of the soldiers roved through the city in search of wretched survivors who might be hiding in the narrow portals and byways to escape death. These were dragged out into public view and slain like sheep. Some formed into bands and broke into houses where they laid violent hands on the heads of families, on their wives, children, and their entire households. These victims were either put to the sword or dashed headlong to the ground from some elevated place so that they perished miserably. Each marauder claimed as his own in perpetuity the particular house which he had entered, together with all it contained. For before the capture of the city the pilgrims had agreed that, after it had been taken by force, whatever each man might win for himself should be his forever by right of possession, without molestation. Consequently the pilgrims searched the city most carefully and boldly killed the citizens. They penetrated into the most retired and out-of-the-way places and broke open the most private apartments of the foe. At the entrance of each house, as it was taken, the victor hung up his shield and his arms, as a sign to all who approached not to pause there but to pass by that place as already in possession of another.

HELMHOLD

THE PUSH TO THE EAST

Religious militarism supported the German princes in their push to the east against the Slavs in the twelfth and thirteenth centuries. Insofar as the Slavs were heathens, massacring them was justified. Then new settlers could be brought in from what is today Belgium and the Low Countries. A leader in this transformation of East Central Europe was the margrave Albert the Bear, whose work of ethnic cleansing in what is today western Poland is here enthusiastically described by the priest Helmhold, who wrote a history of German eastward expansion. Helmhold was favorite reading in German schools and universities in the century before 1945.

At that time Albert, the margrave whose by-name is the Bear, held eastern Slavia. By the favor of God he also prospered splendidly in the portion of his lot; for he brought under his sway all the country of the Brizani, the Stoderani, and the many tribes dwelling along the Havel and the Elbe, and he curbed the rebellious ones among them. In the end, as the Slavs gradually decreased in number, he sent to Utrecht and to places lying on the Rhine, to those, moreover, who live by the ocean and suffer the violence of the sea—to wit, Hollanders, Zeelanders, Flemings—and he brought large numbers of them and had them live in the strongholds and villages of the Slavs. The bishopric of Brandenburg, and likewise that of Havelberg, was greatly strengthened by the coming of the foreigners, because the churches multiplied and the income from the tithes grew enormously. At the same time foreigners from Holland also began to settle on the southern bank of the Elbe; the Hollanders received all the swamp and open country, the land which is called Balsamerlande and Marscinerlande, together with very many cities and villages from the city of Salzwedel clear to the Bohemian woodland. These lands, indeed, the Saxons are said to have occupied of old—namely in the time of the Ottos—as can be seen from the ancient levees which had been constructed in the lowlands of the Balsami along the banks of the Elbe. But afterwards, when the Slavs got the upper hand, the Saxons were killed and the land has been held by the Slavs down to our own times. Now, however, because God gave plentiful aid and victory to our duke and to the other princes, the Slavs have been everywhere crushed and driven out. A people strong and without number have come from the bounds of the ocean, and taken possession of the territories of the Slavs. They have built cities and churches and have grown in riches beyond all estimation.

THEOCRATIC MONARCHY: EUSEBIUS ON CONSTANTINE

No medieval symbiosis had a more powerful and long-range effect than the integration of ecclesiastical ideas with kingship, the most important form of medieval government. The tradition was established not by St. Augustine, for whom the state was a purely instrumental agency confined to being a big policeman, but by Eusebius, bishop of Caesarea in the 320s and 330s and the chief adviser to the first Christian Emperor Constantine I the Great on ecclesiastical matters. Eusebius' incessant proclamation that Constantine's rule was God-ordained was the foundation for the medieval doctrine of theocratic monarchy or divinely ordained kingship. God rules in heaven; his representative the emperor rules the earth. This political doctrine has various names and guises—political monotheism, divine right of kings, royal absolutism. It was the predominant political doctrine until the eighteenth century.

This is He who holds a supreme dominion over this whole world, Who is over and in all things, and pervades all things visible and invisible: the Word of God. From Whom and by Whom our divinely favored emperor, receiving, as it were, a transcript of the Divine sovereignty, directs, in imitation of God himself, the administration of this world's affairs. . . . Invested as he [the Emperor Constantine] is with a semblance of heavenly sovereignty, he directs his gaze above, and frames his earthly government according to the pattern of that Divine original, feeling strength in its conformity to the monarchy of God. And this conformity is granted by the universal Sovereign to man alone of the creatures of this earth: for He only is the author of sovereign power, who decrees that all should be subject to the rule of one. And surely monarchy far transcends every other constitution and form of government. . . . Hence there is one God, and not two, or three or more. . . .

... Such were the dealings of the Supreme Sovereign, who ordained an invincible champion to be the minister of his heaven-sent vengeance (for our emperor's surpassing piety delights in the title of Servant of God) and him He has proved victorious over all that opposed him. . . . Our emperor is one, appointed by, and representative of, the one Almighty Sovereign. . . . As truly worthy of the name of VICTOR, he has subdued the twofold race of barbarians: soothing the savage tribes of men by prudent embassies, compelling them to know and acknowledge their superiors, and reclaiming them from a lawless and brutal life to the governance of reason and humanity; at the same time that he proved by the facts themselves that the fierce and ruthless race of unseen spirits had long ago been vanquished by a higher power. . . .

. . . Our emperor as the one ruler on earth, . . . as a skillful pilot, sits on high at the helm of state, and directs the vessel with unerring course. . . . Meanwhile God himself, the great Sovereign, extends the right hand of his power from above for his protection, giving him victory over every foe, and establishing his empire by a lengthened period of years: and He will bestow on him yet higher blessings. . . .

CHARLEMAGNE THE ONE AND ONLY

Charlemagne ruled what is today France, much of western Germany, northern Italy, and a slice of northern Spain from 774 to 814. He was a great warrior, a conservative but attentive governor, a lavish supporter of learning and the arts, and an enthusiastic advocate of the Benedictine order of monks. How he was viewed by churchmen can be seen from the following two selections. Einhard was a cleric who was Charlemagne's secretary. Here is an account of the emperor as a giant but quite human personality, exhibiting many of the traits of a Germanic chieftain. On the other hand, Alcuin of York, the English cleric who became the emperor's minister of education and the head of the Palace School in Aachen, devoted to publishing the Bible and classical texts, accords the emperor an aura similar to Eusebius on Constantine. Charlemagne is addressed as King David, the prototype of the anointed king; Alcuin uses classical names for himself. Alcuin's image of Charlemagne became the standard one by which clerics perceived strong kings.

EINHARD: LIFE OF CHARLEMAGNE

Chapter 4

I pass by the birth, infancy, and childhood of Charles, because there is no written record concerning them, nor is any one now known to survive who can speak from personal knowledge. I have therefore thought it foolish to write about them, and have given my attention to relating and explaining those actions, habits, and other portions of his life which are not matters of uncertainty; first narrating his military exploits at home and abroad, then his domestic habits and occupations, then his administration of the kingdom, and lastly, about his death, omitting nothing that is worthy and necessary to be narrated.

Chapter 5

Charles was engaged in many wars. The first he undertook was the Aquitanian, because there seemed to be good hope of quickly bringing it to an end. It had been begun by his father, but not finished. . . .

Chapter 6

When the war was finished and affairs settled in Aquitaine—his partner in the government being now dead—Charles was induced by the prayer and entreaty of Adrian, Bishop of the city of Rome, to undertake a war against the Lombards. . . .

Chapter 7

The Lombard war being thus finished, the Saxon war, which seemed for the time to have been neglected, was again renewed. No war undertaken by the Franks was so protracted or so fierce, or so full of toil and hardship, since the Saxons, like most of the nations inhabiting Germany, were naturally brave, and being addicted to heathenism, were hostile to our religion, and thought it no disgrace to dishonour divine laws or violate human ones.

Causes, too, daily arose which contributed to disturb the peace. The boundaries of their country and ours were in the open and almost everywhere contiguous. It was only in a few places that large forests, or ranges of mountains coming between, formed a well-defined and natural boundary line to both countries. On the borders therefore, plundering, burning, and bloodshed never ceased.

The Franks were so enraged at this that they judged it now to be no longer a matter of making reprisals, but so important that it warranted them in undertaking an avowed war against them. War therefore was declared, and was carried on continuously during thirty-three years, with much bitterness on both sides, but with greater loss to the Saxons than to the Franks. It was the bad faith of the Saxons which prevented a more speedy termination. It is hard to say how often they were beaten, and humbly surrendered to the king, promising to obey his orders, giving up at once the hostages he asked, and acknowledging the ambassadors sent to them; how sometimes they were so tamed and compliant as even to promise to give up their idolatry, declaring they wished to

embrace Christianity. But ready as they were at times to undertake all these things, they were always far readier to renounce them. It is difficult to state correctly to which failing they were more prone, since it is certainly the fact that, after the war was begun, scarcely a single year passed in which they did not pursue this shifty course.

But the magnanimity of the King, and the unwavering firmness of his disposition, alike in adversity and prosperity, could not be shaken by any faithlessness on their part, nor could they divert him from his purpose by tiring him out.

He never allowed any act of insincerity to be done with impunity; either taking the command in person, or despatching an army under his counts, he took vengeance on their perfidy and exacted from them a commensurate penalty.

He pursued this course until all who continued to resist him were overcome and brought into submission. He then transported ten thousand men, taken from both banks of the Elbe, together with their wives and children, and distributed them here and there, in very small groups, in Gaul and Germany.

It was on the following terms, offered by the King and accepted by the Saxons, that this war, which had lasted so many years, was brought to a close. The Saxons were to put away their heathen worship and the religious ceremonies of their fathers; were to accept the articles of the Christian faith and practice; and, being united to the Franks, were to form with them one people.

Chapter 8

. . . During those years many great wars sprang up against the Franks in different parts, which were, by the skill of the King, so well managed that it was not without reason that men were perplexed whether to admire more the patience with which the King pursued his undertakings, or the good fortune which attended them.

This war was begun two years before the Italian war, and although it was carried on at the same time without any intermission, there was no relaxation anywhere. In both places the campaign was equally carried on without diminution of effort, for all contemporary sovereigns, King

Karl took the highest rank for his good administration, and was most distinguished for his ability. In all his undertakings and enterprises there was nothing he shrank from because of the toil, and nothing he feared because of the danger; but, skilful in weighing everything at its true value, he was neither yielding in adversity nor deceived by the smiles of fortune in prosperity.

Chapter 9

It was during the time that the Saxon war was being vigorously and incessantly carried on, garrisons having been placed in all the most suitable places on the borders, that Charles marched into Spain with the best-appointed army possible. Having crossed the Pyrenean mountains, he reduced all the fortified towns and castles he came to, and was on his march home with his army safe and sound, when in the very pass of the Pyrenees on his way back, he had a slight experience of Gascon treachery.

The army was moving in column, and its formation was much extended, as the narrowness of the pass required, when the Gascons, who had placed ambuscades on the highest ledges of the mountains—the abundant thick cover of wood making the place most suitable for the disposal of an ambush—rushed down from their vantage ground into the valley below, and threw themselves upon the extreme section of the baggage, and on those who were marching with it for its protection. The Gascons attacked them in a hand-to-hand fight, killed them all to a man, and destroyed the baggage; and being protected by the darkness of the night, which was then coming on, they quickly dispersed in all directions.

In this exploit the Gascons were much favoured by the lightness of their weapons and the nature of the place where the attack was made, while the Franks, impeded by their heavy arms and the unevenness of the ground, were at a great disadvantage.

There were killed in this fight, Eggihard the King's Sewer; Anselm, the Pfalsgraf; Roland, Count of the British March, and many others. No revenge could be taken at the time for this defeat, for the enemy immediately dispersed, and so

secretly that no trace was left by which they could be followed. . . .

Chapter 13

The greatest of all the wars waged by the King, except the Saxon, was that which now followed, against the Avars or Huns. He set about it with far more ardour and preparation than was bestowed upon any of the others. The King himself only made one expedition into Pannonia—it was that province which the Avar race then inhabited; the others he entrusted to the direction of his son Pippin, and to the prefects of the provinces, and to the counts and lieutenants. Although these commanders used the greatest exertions, it was not until the eighth year that the war was finished. . . .

In this war the whole nobility of the Avars perished, and the glory of their nation was destroyed. All their riches and treasures, which they had long been accumulating, were carried away, nor can memory recall any war of the Franks in which they have gained greater booty or by which they have been more enriched. Indeed, we may confess that, up to this time, the Franks appeared to be a poor nation; but so much gold and silver was found in the palace, and such a quantity of valuable spoil was taken in the battles, as can scarcely be believed.

The Franks justly spoiled the Huns (Avars) of this booty, for the Huns themselves had no right to it, it being the plunder they had carried off from other nations. . . .

The war was almost a bloodless one for the Franks, and although it lasted longer than its magnitude seemed to warrant, its result was most successful.

Chapter 14

. . . The last war undertaken was against the Northmen who are called Danes, who, at first as pirates, and afterwards with a larger fleet, were ravaging the coasts of Gaul and Germany. . . .

Chapter 15

Such were the wars waged by the most potent prince with the greatest skill and success in different countries during the forty-seven years of his reign. Great and powerful as was the realm of the Franks, which Karl had received from his father Pippin, he nevertheless so splendidly enlarged it by these wars that he almost doubled it. . . .

Chapter 16

The renown of his Kingdom was also much increased by the friendly alliances he cultivated with different kings and nations. . . .

Haroun, king of the Persians, who, with the exception of India, ruled over nearly all the East, was held by the King in such hearty friendship, that he valued Karl's esteem above that of all other Kings and princes of the world, and thought that he alone was worthy to be honoured by his regard and munificence. When the officers sent by King Karl with offerings to the most sacred sepulchre and place of the resurrection of our Lord and Saviour came to Haroun and announced the pleasure of their master, he not only gave them permission to do as they desired, but granted that that revered and sacred spot should be considered as belonging to King Karl. When the ambassadors set out on their return, he sent with them his own envoys, who conveyed to the King strange and curious gifts, with garments and spices and other rich products of the East, just as he had sent him a few years before, upon his request, the only elephant he then possessed.

The Constantinopolitan Emperors, Nicephorus, Michael, and Leo, of their own accord, also sought his friendship and alliance, and sent to him several embassies; and since by assuming the Imperial title he had laid himself open to the grave suspicion of wishing to deprive them of Empire, he made with them the most binding treaty possible, that there might be no occasion of offence between them. But the Romans and Greeks always viewed with distrust the power of the Franks; hence arose the Greek proverb, "Have a Frank for a friend but not for a neighbour."

Chapter 17

Illustrious as the King was in the work of enlarging his Kingdom and in conquering foreign nations, and though so constantly occupied with such affairs, he nevertheless began in several places very many works for the advantage and beautifying of his Kingdom. Some of these he was able to finish. Chief among them may be mentioned, as deserving of notice, the Basilica of the Holy Mother of God, built at Aachen, a marvel of workmanship; and the bridge over the Rhine at Mainz, five hundred paces in length, so broad is the river at that place. . . .

Chapter 19

The King thought so much about the education of his children that he caused both sons and daughters to be early instructed in those liberal studies which attracted his own attention. As soon as his sons were old enough he caused them to ride on horseback, as was the Frankish custom, and to practice themselves in arms and hunting. He bade his daughters should learn wool-spinning and the use of the distaff and spindle, and be taught to employ themselves industriously in every virtuous occupation, that they might not be enervated by idleness.

Of this large family, two sons and one daughter died before him—Karl, the eldest, and Pippin, whom he had made King of Italy, and Hruodrud, his eldest girl, who had been betrothed to Constantine VI, the Emperor of the Greeks. Pippin left surviving one son, Bernhard, and five daughters, Adalhaid, Atula, Guntrada, Berthaid, and Theodorada. The King showed marked tokens of his affection toward them, allowing his grandson to succeed to his father's Kingdom, and bringing up his grand-daughters with his own daughters. He bore the deaths of his sons and daughters with that greatness of soul for which he was known.

Charles was so careful in the bringing up of his sons and daughters that when at home he never dined without them, and they always accompanied him on his journeys, his sons riding by his side, and his daughters following close behind, attended by a train of servants appointed for that purpose. His daughters were very fair, and he loved them passionately. Strange to say, he would never consent to give them in marriage, either to any of his own nation or to foreigners; but he kept them all at home and near his person at all times until his death, for he used to say that he could not deprive himself of their society. On account of this, although happy in all else, he here experienced the malignity of fortune; but he concealed his vexation, and conducted himself as if they had never given rise to injurious suspicions, and as if no reports had ever gone abroad concerning them.

The person of Charles was large and robust, and of commanding stature, though not exceeding good proportions, for it appears that he measured seven feet in height. The top of his head was round, his eyes large and animated, his nose somewhat long, his hair white, and his face bright and pleasant; so that, whether standing or sitting, he showed very great presence and dignity. Although his neck was thick and rather short, and his belly too prominent, still the fair proportions of his limbs concealed these defects. His walk was firm, and the whole carriage of his body was manly. His voice was clear, but not so strong as his frame would have led one to expect. His health was good until the last four years of his life, when he was attacked with frequent fevers, and latterly walked lame on one foot. Even in illness he leaned more on his own judgment than on the advice of physicians, whom he greatly disliked, because they used to recommend him to leave off roasted meats, which he preferred, and to accustom himself to boiled.

He took constant exercise in riding and hunting, which was natural for a Frank, since scarcely any nation can be found to equal them in these pursuits. He also delighted in the natural warm baths, frequently exercising himself by swimming, in which he was very skilful, no one being able to outstrip him. It was on account of the warm baths that he built the palace at Aachen, living there constantly during the last years of his life and until his death. He not only invited his sons to bathe with him, but also his chief men and friends, and occasionally even a crowd of his attendants and guards, so that at times one hundred men or more would be bathing together.

He wore the dress of his native country—that is, the Frankish; on his body a linen shirt and linen drawers; then a tunic with a silver border, and stockings. He bound his legs with garters and wore shoes on his feet. In the winter he protected his shoulders and chest with a vest made of the skins of otters and sable. He wore a blue cloak, and was always girt with his sword, the hilt and belt being of gold and silver. Sometimes he wore a jewelled sword, but only on great festivals, or when receiving foreign ambassadors. He thoroughly disliked the dress of foreigners, however fine, and he never put it on except at Rome—once at the request of Pope Hadrian, and again a second time, to please his successor, Pope Leo. He then wore a long tunic, chlamys, and shoes made after the Roman fashion. On festivals he used to walk in processions clad in a garment woven with gold, and shoes studded with jewels, his cloak fastened with a golden clasp, and wearing a crown of gold set with precious stones. At other times his dress differed little from that of a private person.

In his eating and drinking Charles was temperate; more particularly so in his drinking, since he had the greatest abhorrence of drunkenness in anybody, but more especially in himself and his companions. He was unable to abstain from food for any length of time, and often complained that fasting was injurious to him. He very rarely feasted, only on great festive occasions, when there were very large gatherings. The daily service of his table was only furnished with four dishes, in addition to the roast meat, which the hunters used to bring in on spits, and of which he partook more freely than of any other food.

While he was dining he listened to music or reading. History and the deeds of men of old used to be read. He derived much pleasure from the works of St. Augustine, especially from his book called "The City of God." He took very sparingly of wine and other drinks, rarely taking at meals more than two or three draughts. In summer, after the mid-day repast, he would take some fruit and one draught, and then, throwing aside his clothes and shoes as at night, he would repose for two or three hours. He slept at night so lightly that he would break his rest four or five times, not merely by awaking, but even getting up.

While he was dressing and binding on his sandals, he would receive his friends; and also, if the Count of the palace announced that there was any cause which could only be settled by his decree, the suitors were immediately ordered into his presence, and, as if sitting in court, he heard the case and gave judgment. And this was not the only business that used to be arranged at that time, for orders were then given for whatever had to be done on that day by any officer or servant.

He was ready and fluent in speaking, and able to express himself with great clearness. He did not confine himself to his native tongue, but took pains to learn foreign languages, acquiring such knowledge of Latin that he used to repeat his prayers in that language as well as in his own. Greek he could better understand than pronounce. In speaking he was so voluble that he almost gave one the impression of a chatterer. He was an ardent admirer of the liberal arts, and greatly revered their professors, whom he promoted to high honours. In order to learn grammar, he attended the lectures of the aged Peter of Pisa, a deacon; and for other instruction he chose as his preceptor Albinus, otherwise called Alcuin, also a deacon—a Saxon by race, from Britain, the most learned man of the day, with whom the King spent much time in learning rhetoric and logic, and more especially astronomy. He learned the art of computation, and with deep thought and skill very carefully calculated the courses of the planets.

Charles also tried to write, and used to keep his tablets and writing-book under the pillow of his couch, that when he had leisure he might practice his hand in forming letters; but he made little progress in a task too long deferred, and begun too late in life.

The Christian religion, in which he had been brought up from infancy, was held by Charles as most sacred, and he worshipped in it with the greatest piety. For this reason he built at Aachen a most beautiful church, which he enriched with gold and silver, and candlesticks, and also with lattices and doors of solid brass. When columns and marbles for the building could not be obtained from elsewhere, he had them brought from Rome and Ravenna.

As long as his health permitted, he was most regular in attending the church at matins and evensong, and also during the night, and at the time of the Sacrifice; and took especial care that all the services of the church should be performed in the most fitting manner possible, frequently cautioning the sacristans not to allow anything improper or unseemly to be brought into, or left in, the building.

He provided for the church an abundance of sacred vessels of gold and silver, and priestly vestments, so that when service was celebrated it was not necessary even for the doorkeepers, who are the lowest order of ecclesiastics, to perform their duties in private dress. He carefully revised the order of reading and singing, being well skilled in both, though he did not read in public, nor sing, except in a low voice and only in the chorus.

He was most devoted in providing for the poor, and in charitable gifts, which the Greeks call almsgiving. In this matter he took thought not only for those of his own country and kingdom, but also for those whom he heard were living in poverty beyond the seas, in Africa, Egypt, and Syria, at Carthage, Alexandria, and Jerusalem, to whom he used to send money in compassion for their wants. It was on this account especially that he courted the friendship of foreign princes, that he might be able to become a solace and comfort to those Christians who were living under their rule.

He held the church of the blessed Peter the Apostle, at Rome, in far higher regard than any other place of sanctity and veneration, and he enriched its treasury with a great quantity of gold, silver, and precious stones.

To the Pope he made many and rich presents; and nothing lay nearer his heart during his whole reign than that the city of Rome should attain to its ancient importance by his zeal and patronage, and that the church of St. Peter should, through him, not only be in safe keeping and protection, but should also by his wealth be ennobled and enriched beyond all other churches. Although he thought so much of this, it was only four times, during the forty-seven years of his reign, that he had leisure to go to Rome for prayer and supplication.

The last visit he paid to Rome was not only for the above reasons, but also because the Romans had driven Pope Leo to ask his assistance—for they had grievously ill-treated him; indeed, his eyes had been plucked out and his tongue cut off.

Charles therefore went to Rome, and stayed there the whole winter in order to reform and quiet the Church, which was in a most disturbed state. It was at this time that he received the title of Emperor and Augustus, to which at first he was so averse that he remarked that had he known the intention of the Pope, he would not have entered the church on that day, great festival though it was.

He bore very quietly the displeasure of the Roman Emperors, who were exceedingly indignant at his assumption of the Imperial title, and overcame their sullenness by his great magnanimity, in which, without doubt, he greatly excelled them, sending them frequent embassies, and styling them his brothers in his letters to them.

Interior of the Palace Chapel of Charlemagne

ALCUIN OF YORK: TO CHARLEMAGNE

What signifies the purchase of a sword? What signifies the bag, the purse, and the mantle? Why were two swords later said to be enough?. . . The purchase of this sword symbolized the renunciation of the world. On this subject the Lord said: "He who does not renounce all that he has cannot be My disciple"; that is: he who seeks to satisfy his avarice cannot be a preacher, since he destroys in his deeds what he preaches with his mouth. In the bag, hidden riches can be understood; in the purse, public riches. Carnal pleasure is symbolized in the mantle. All these must be sold, that is, utterly cast away, so that the soldier may become worthy to accept the sword of the word of Christ the God. But when the disciples said: "behold, here are two swords," and the Lord replied: "It is enough," the two swords meant the body and the soul, armed with which each one of us, in accordance with the grace given to him by God, ought to do battle for the will of the Lord God. And it will be enough for the will of God if His instructions are fulfilled by the body and the soul. . . .

If this sword is, as we said, the word of God, why did it cut off the ear of the adversary, since the word of God is wont to go from the hearing to the secret chambers of the heart so that there it may bring forth increase, a hundredfold, sixtyfold, or thirtyfold? What can this cutting off signify, I ask, unless it be that the ear of infidelity shall be cut off, so that it may be healed by a new touch of divine grace? Therefore that slave was called Malchus. In the Latin language Malchus may mean either king or prince. How could a man be both king and slave, unless in our old selves we were the slaves of sin, and in our new selves, healed by the grace of the Lord God, we shall be kings and princes with Christ? Why is it that the Lord Himself healed His persecutor, if not to show that every preacher in the Church of Christ should not stop healing his enemies with the word of piety?. . .

We have said that the two swords signify the

body and soul. Both of these ought to work with one faith, so that the faith, which lies hidden in the soul, may be shown to the world outside in the deeds of the body. "Out of the abundance of the heart the mouth speaks." The disciples, therefore, when they had received the gifts of the Holy Spirit in their fiery tongues, are said to have spoken of the great works of God. And it is for this reason: when holy love burns deep within the soul, it will soon, through the gift of the Holy Spirit, become well-known outside in the words of preaching. The two swords can also, without much inconvenience, be understood to mean faith and good works: the former lying hidden within the heart, the latter manifesting itself publicly in deeds. This explanation can also be discovered if one diligently examines the earlier meaning, since faith is of the soul, and good works of the body. Let each and every man, therefore, search out the depths of his heart to learn how much he loves God. . . .

And let the ministers of the Church of Christ, especially, show the charity of our Redeemer to the people through the words of their earnest sermons. Let them be burning lamps in the house of God. Let them be strong cities founded on mountains of virtue. Let them be wise shepherds, leading the flock of Christ to the pastures of life everlasting; so that, along with their great flock of souls, they may deserve to enter into the pleasures of their Lord God. Let your most excellent dignity and your will, most holy in its love of Christ, always encourage these things; nay rather, urge them to the ranks of priests with your most loving exhortation. Thus, on the great day of our Lord Jesus Christ, you also will be worthy to hear the loving words: "Well done, good and faithful servant, since you have been faithful over little, I will set you over much; enter into the joy of your Lord God." For do not imagine that this shall be heard only by priests and clerks. Know that it will also be said to good laymen, who labor hard in the work of God, especially to those who have been placed in the more sublime ranks of this world: those whose good observance, sanctity of life, and instructive words about eternal life can be as a sermon to their subjects. For each and every man shall have to answer for the property which he has received from his Lord on the Day of Judgment; and he who labors more shall receive a greater reward. Therefore, most beloved and honorable defender and ruler of the churches of Christ, let the venerable zeal of your most holy wisdom encourage some with admonitions, chastise others with punishment, and instruct others with the learning of life. Thus, when all has been done, you, among the rest, shall deserve to have a perpetual reward; and thus you, along with the great and praiseworthy multitude of peoples, shall appear glorious in the sight of your Lord God. . . .

Behold, on you alone rests the entire safety of the churches of Christ. You are the avenger of crimes, you are the guide of the erring, you are the consoler of the grieving, you are the exaltation of good men. . . .

Nothing can be concealed from your wisdom: for we know that you are exceedingly well-learned both in the holy Scriptures and in secular histories. In all these things you have been given full knowledge by God, so that through you the holy Church of God might be ruled, exalted, and preserved for the Christian people. Who can describe the magnitude of the reward which God will give you for your greatest devotion?

SACRED KINGSHIP

The doctrine and ritual of theocratic monarchy was attacked by Pope Gregory VII in the 1070s. He claimed that the pope was superior to any king, who was said by the papal reformers to be after all only a layman, not a priest. In polemical response came the treatise of the so-called Anonymous of York (either the archbishop of York or the archbishop of Rouen or one of their secretaries) setting forth in extravagant terms the idea of sacred kingship.

The Coronation of Clovis

By divine authority and the institution of the holy fathers, kings are consecrated in God's Church before the sacred altar and are anointed with holy oil and sacred benediction to exercise the ruling power over Christians, the Lord's people, . . . the Holy Church of God. . . . The power of the king is the power of God, but it is God's through nature, the king's through grace, and whatever he does is not simply as a man, but as one who has been made God and Christ through grace. . . . No one by right ought to take precedence over the king, who is blessed with so many and such great benedictions, who is consecrated and deified by so many and such great sacraments. No one receives greater or better blessings or is consecrated and dedicated to God with greater or higher sacraments, not even indeed with as many and equal sacraments, and because of this no one is the king's equal. Wherefore he is not to be called a layman, since he is the anointed of the Lord [Christus Domini] and through grace he is God. He is the supreme ruler, the chief shepherd, master, defender and instructor of the Holy Church, lord over his brethren and worthy to be "adored" by all, since he is chief and supreme prelate. Nor is he to be spoken of as inferior to the bishop, because the bishop consecrates him, since it often happens that superiors are consecrated by their inferiors. . . .

It is manifest that kings have the sacred power of ecclesiastical rule over the bishops of God and power over them. . . . Therefore it is not against the rule of sanctity, if kings confer on bishops the signs of holy rule, that is the staff and ring of honor. . . .

ST. LOUIS OF FRANCE

After the Gregorian reform's onslaught upon the doctrine of theocratic monarchy, it was played down by clerics serving kings. Instead, emphasis was placed on the king's sovereign authority in law and also the king's charismatic personal qualities that made him the national leader. The classic work by Joinville on the wonderful personality of a medieval king is the *Life of St. Louis* (Louis IX) of France, who ruled for four decades in the thirteenth century. Joinville was seneschal of Champagne, a very highly honored position among the French nobility. Joinville held a high position at Louis' court; he also was a personal friend and fought alongside Louis during Louis' audacious but vain invasion of Muslim Egypt. Joinville was in a position to know all sides of the most admired and successful king of the thirteenth century. But Joinville, in addition to some intriguing circumstantial details, imports into his royal biography a heavy ethical glaze patterned by the church. Once again there is a conjuncture of heroism and hierarchic values, but now laid on more subtly than in the more ideological doctrine of theocratic kingship. Joinville's book was written in support of the effort by the French government of Louis IX's grandson to get the popular ruler canonized by the papacy as a saint, a successful breakthrough of great political use to the mean and aggressive French royal administration after 1300. Joinville's *Life* was among the campaign documents presented to Rome on behalf of the claim to Louis' sanctity. It worked.

In the name of God Almighty, I, Jean, Lord of Joinville, Seneschal of Champagne, dictate the life of our good King, Saint Louis, in which I shall record what I saw and heard both in the course of the six years in which I was on pilgrimage in his company oversea, and after we returned to France. But before I speak to you of his great-deeds and his outstanding valour, I will tell you what I myself observed of his good teaching and his saintly conversation, so that it may be set down in due order for the edification of those to whom this book is read.

This saintly man loved our Lord with all his heart, and in all his actions followed His example. This is apparent from the fact that as our Lord died for the love he bore His people, even so King Louis put his own life in danger, and that several times, for the very same reason. It was danger too that he might well have avoided, as I shall show you later.

The great love King Louis bore his people is shown by what he said, as he lay dangerously ill at Fontainebleau, to his eldest son, my Lord Louis. 'My dear son,' he said, 'I earnestly beg you to make yourself loved by all your people. For I would rather have a Scot come from Scotland to govern the people of this kingdom well and justly than that you should govern them ill in the sight of all the world.' This upright king, moreover, loved truth so well that, as I shall show you later, he would never consent to lie to the Saracens with regard to any convenant he made with them.

He was so temperate in his appetite that I never heard him, on any day of my life, order a special dish for himself, as many men of wealth and standing do. On the contrary, he would always eat with good grace whatever his cooks had prepared to set before him. He was equally temperate in his speech. I never, on any single occasion, heard him speak evil of any man; nor did I ever hear him utter the name of the Devil—a name in very common use throughout the

Reliquary bust of St. Louis

kingdom—which practice, so I believe, is not pleasing to God.

He used to add water to his wine, but did so reasonably, according as the strength of the wine allowed it. While we were in Cyprus he asked me why I did not mix my wine with water. I replied that this was on the advice of my doctors, who had told me that I had a strong head and a cold stomach, so that I could not get drunk. He answered that they had deceived me; for if I did not learn to mix my wine with water while I was still young, and wished to do so in my old age, gout and stomach troubles would take hold on me, and I should never be in good health. Moreover, if I went on drinking undiluted wine when I was old, I should get drunk every night, and it was too revolting a thing for any brave man to be in such a state.

The king once asked me if I wished to be honoured in this world, and to enter paradise when I died. I told him I did. 'If so,' said he, 'you should avoid deliberately saying or doing anything which, if it became generally known, you would be ashamed to acknowledge by saying "I did this," or "I said that." ' He also told me not to contradict or call in question anything said in my presence—unless indeed silence would imply approval of something wrong, or damaging to myself, because harsh words often lead to quarrelling, which has ended in the death of countless numbers of men.

He often said that people ought to clothe and arm themselves in such a way that men of riper age would never say they had spent too much on dress, or young men say they had spent too little. I repeated this remark to our present king when speaking of the elaborately embroidered tabards that are in vogue today. I told him that, during the whole of our voyage oversea, I had never seen such embroidered tabards, either on the king or on any one else. He said to me that he had several such garments, with his own arms embroidered on them, and they had cost him eight hundred *livres parisis.* I told him that he would have put his money to better use if he had given it to God, and had his clothes made of good plain taffeta bearing his arms, as his father had done.

King Louis once sent for me and said: 'You have such a shrewd and subtle mind that I hardly dare speak to you of things concerning God. So I have summoned these two monks to come here, because I want to ask you a question.' Then he said: 'Tell me, seneschal, what is your idea of God?' 'Your Majesty,' I replied, 'He is something so good that there cannot be anything better.' 'Indeed,' said he, 'you've given me a very good answer; for it's precisely the same as the definition given in this book I have here in my hand.'

'Now I ask you,' he continued, 'which you would prefer: to be a leper or to have committed some mortal sin?' And I, who had never lied to him, replied that I would rather have committed thirty mortal sins than become a leper. The next day, when the monks were no longer there, he called me to him, and making me sit at his feet said to me: 'Why did you say that to me yesterday?' I told him I would still say it. 'You spoke without thinking, and like a fool,' he said. 'You ought to know there is no leprosy so foul as being in a state of mortal sin; for the soul in that condition is like the Devil; therefore no leprosy can be so vile. Besides, when a man dies his body is healed of its leprosy; but if he dies after committing a mortal sin, he can never be sure that, during his lifetime, he has repented of it sufficiently for God to forgive him. In consequence, he must be greatly afraid lest that leprosy of sin should last as long as God dwells in paradise. So I beg you,' he added, 'as earnestly as I can, for the love of God, and for love of me, to train your heart to prefer any evil that can happen to the body, whether it be leprosy or any other disease, rather than let mortal sin take possession of your soul.'

At another time King Louis asked me if I washed the feet of the poor on Maundy Thursday. 'Your Majesty,' I exclaimed, 'what a terrible idea! I will never wash the feet of such low fellows.' 'Really,' said he, 'that is a very wrong thing to say; for you should never scorn to do what our Lord Himself did as an example for us. So I beg you, first for the love of God and then for love of me, to accustom yourself to washing the feet of the poor.'

This good king so loved all manner of people who believed in God and loved Him that he appointed Gilles le Brun, who was not a native of his realm, as High Constable of France, because he was held in such high repute for his faith in God and devotion to His service. For my part, I believe he well deserved that reputation. Another man, Maître Robert de Sorbon, who was famed for his goodness and his learning, was invited, on that account, to dine at the royal table.

It happened one day that this worthy priest was sitting beside me at dinner, and we were talking to each other rather quietly. The king reproved us and said: 'Speak up, or your companions may think you are speaking ill of them. If at table you talk of things that may give us pleasure, say them aloud, or else be silent.'

When the king was feeling in a mood for fun, he would fire questions at me, as for instance: 'Seneschal, can you give me reasons why a wise and upright layman is better than a friar?' Thereupon a discussion would begin between Maître Robert and myself. When we had disputed for some length of time the king would pronounce judgement. 'Maître Robert,' he would say, 'I would willingly be known as a wise and upright man, provided I were so in reality—and you can have all the rest. For wisdom and goodness are such fine qualities that even to name them leaves a pleasant taste in the mouth.'

On the other hand, he always said that it was a wicked thing to take other people's property. 'To "restore",' he would say, 'is such a hard thing to do that even in speaking of it the word itself rasps one's throat because of the *r*'s that are in it. These *r*'s are, so to speak, like the rakes of the Devil, with which he would draw to himself all those who wish to "restore" what they have taken from others. The Devil, moreover, does this very subtly; for he works on great usurers and great robbers in such a way that they give to God what they ought to *restore* to men.'

On one occasion the king gave me a message to take to King Thibaut, in which he warned his son-in-law to beware lest he should lay too heavy a burden on his soul by spending an excessive amount of money on the house he was building for the Predicants of Provins. 'Wise men,' said the king, 'deal with their possessions as executors ought to do. Now the first thing a good executor does is to settle all debts incurred by the deceased and restore any property belonging to others, and only then is he free to apply what money remains to charitable purposes.' . . .

King Louis also spoke to me of a great assembly of clergy and Jews which had taken place at the monastery of Cluny. There was a poor knight there at the time to whom the abbot had often given bread for the love of God. This knight asked the abbot if he could speak first, and his request was granted, though somewhat grudgingly. So he rose to his feet, and leaning on his crutch, asked to have the most important and most learned rabbi among the Jews brought before him. As soon as the Jew had come, the knight asked him a question. 'May I know, sir,' he said, 'if you believe that the Virgin Mary, who bore our Lord in her body and cradled Him in her arms, was a virgin at the time of His birth, and is in truth the Mother of God?'

The Jew replied that he had no belief in any of those things. Thereupon the knight told the Jew that he had acted like a fool when—neither believing in the Virgin, nor loving her—he had set foot in that monastery which was her house. 'And by heaven,' exclaimed the knight, 'I'll make you pay for it!' So he lifted his crutch and struck the Jew such a blow with it near the ear that he knocked him down. Then all the Jews took to flight, and carried their sorely wounded rabbi away with them. Thus the conference ended.

The abbot went up to the knight and told him he had acted most unwisely. The knight retorted that the abbot had been guilty of even greater folly in calling people together for such a conference, because there were many good Christians there who, before the discussion ended, would have gone away with doubts about their own religion through not fully understanding the Jews. 'So I tell you,' said the king, 'that no one, unless he is an expert theologian, should venture to argue with these people. But a layman, whenever he hears the Christian religion abused, should not attempt to defend its tenets, except with his sword, and that he should thrust into the scoundrel's belly, and as far as it will enter.' . . .

In the midst of attending to the affairs of his realm King Louis so arranged his day that he had time to hear the Hours sung by a full choir and a Requiem mass without music. In addition, if it was convenient, he would hear low mass for the day, or high mass on Saints' days. Every day after dinner he rested on his bed, and when he had slept and was refreshed, he and one of his chaplains would say the Office for the Dead privately in his room. Later in the day he attended vespers, and compline at night.

A Franciscan friar once came to see him at the castle of Hyères, where we had disembarked on our return to France. In his sermon, intended for the king's instruction, he said that in his reading of the Bible and other books that speak of non-Christian princes he had never found, in the history of either heathen or Christian peoples, that a kingdom had been lost or had changed its ruler, except where justice had been ignored. 'Therefore,' said he, 'let the king who is now returning to France take good care to see that he administers justice well and promptly to his people, so that our Lord may allow him to rule his kingdom in peace to the end of his days.' I have been told that the worthy man who taught the king this lesson lies buried at Marseilles, where our Lord, for his sake, still performs many a fine miracle. He would never consent to remain with the king for more than a single day, however strongly his Majesty pressed him to stay. All the same, the king never forgot the good friar's teaching, but governed his kingdom well and faithfully according to God's law.

In dealing with each day's business, the king's usual plan was to send for Jean de Nesles, the good Comte de Soissons, and the rest of us, as soon as we had heard mass, and tell us to go and hear the pleadings at the gate of the city which is now called the Gate of Requests.

After he had returned from church the king would send for us, and sitting at the foot of his bed would make us all sit round him, and ask us if there were any cases that could not be settled except by his personal intervention. After we had told him which they were, he would send for the interested parties and ask them: 'Why did you not accept what our people offer?' 'Your Majesty,' they would reply, 'because they offer us too little.' Then he would say: 'You would do well to accept whatever they are willing to give you.' Our saintly king would thus do his utmost to bring them round to a right and reasonable way of thinking.

In summer, after hearing mass, the king often went to the wood of Vincennes, where he would sit down with his back against an oak, and make us all sit round him. Those who had any suit to present could come to speak to him without hindrance from an usher or any other person. The king would address them directly, and ask: 'Is there anyone here who has a case to be settled?' Those who had one would stand up. Then he would say: 'Keep silent all of you, and you shall be heard in turn, one after the other.' Then he would call Pierre de Fontaines and Geoffroi de Villette, and say to one or other of them: 'Settle this case for me.' If he saw anything needing correction in what was said by those who spoke on his behalf or on behalf of any other person, he would himself intervene to make the necessary adjustment.

I have sometimes seen him, in summer, go to administer justice to his people in the public gardens in Paris, dressed in a plain woollen tunic, a sleeveless surcoat of linsey-woolsey, and a black taffeta cape round his shoulders, with his hair neatly combed, but no cap to cover it, and only a hat of white peacock's feathers on his head. He would have a carpet laid down so that we might sit round him, while all those who had any case to bring before him stood round about. Then he would pass judgement on each case, as I have told you he often used to do in the wood of Vincennes.

I saw the king on another occasion, at a time when all the French prelates had said they wished to speak with him, and he had gone to his palace to hear what they had to say. Bishop Guy of Auxerre, the son of Guillaume de Mello, was among those present, and he addressed the king on behalf of all the prelates. 'Your Majesty,' he said, 'the Lords Spiritual of this realm here present, have directed me to tell you that the cause of Christianity, which it is your duty to guard and defend, is being ruined in your hands.' On hearing these words the king crossed himself and said: 'Pray tell me how that may be.'

'Your Majesty,' said the bishop, 'it is because at the present time excommunications are so lightly regarded that people think nothing of dying without seeking absolution, and refuse to make their peace with the Church. The Lords Spiritual require you therefore, for the love of God and because it is your duty, to command your provosts and your bailiffs to seek out all those who allow themselves to remain under the ban of the Church for a year and a day, and compel them, by seizure of their possessions, to get themselves absolved.'

The king replied that he would willingly give such orders provided he himself could be shown without any doubt that the persons concerned were in the wrong. The bishop told him that the prelates would not on any account accept this condition, since they questioned his right to adjudicate in their affairs. The king replied that he would not do anything other than he had said; for it would be against God and contrary to right and justice if he compelled any man to seek absolution when the clergy were doing him wrong.

'As an example of this,' he continued, 'I will quote the case of the Comte de Bretagne, who for seven whole years, while under sentence of excommunication, pleaded his cause against the bishops of his province, and carried his case so far that in the end the Pope condemned all his adversaries. Now, if at the end of the first year I had forced the count to seek absolution, I should have sinned against God and against the man himself.' So the prelates resigned themselves to accepting things as they were; and I have never heard tell that any further demand was made in relation to this matter.

In making peace with the King of England, King Louis acted against the advice of his council, who had said to him: 'It seems to us that Your Majesty is needlessly throwing away the land you are giving to the King of England; for he has no right to it, since it was justly taken from his father.' To this the king replied that he was well aware that the King of England had no right to the land, but there was a reason why he felt bound to give it to him. 'You see,' said he, 'our wives are sisters and consequently our children are first cousins. That is why it is most important for us to be at peace with each other. Besides, I gain increased honour for myself through the peace I have made with the King of England, for he is now my vassal, which he has never been before.'

The king's love for fair and open dealing may be gathered from his behaviour in the case of a certain Renaud de Trit. This man had brought the king a charter stating that he had granted the county of Dammartin in Gouelle to the heirs of the late Comtesse de Boulogne. However, the seal of the charter was broken, so that nothing remained of it except half the legs of the figure representing the king, and the stool on which his feet were resting. The king showed the seal to all of us who were members of his council, and asked us to help him come to a decision. We all unanimously expressed the opinion that he was not bound to put the charter into effect. Then he told Jean Sarrasin, his chamberlain, to hand him a charter he had asked him to get. As soon as this was in his hands the king said to us: 'My lords, here is the seal I used before I went oversea, and you can clearly tell from looking at it that the impression on the broken seal corresponds exactly with that of the one that is whole. Therefore I could not, with a clear conscience, keep back this land.' So the king sent for Renaud de Trit and said to him: 'I restore your county to you.'

 ST. AUGUSTINE

JESUS LOVES ME

Self-consciousness, whose literary expression is autobiography, is a middle class phenomenon. Intrinsically, the nobility's temperament is not one of consciousness of a distinct and free self. The aristocratic individual sees himself as part of a family. What counts is the story of the family, not the individual, who achieves a life course through the instrument of the noble family and service to it. The church's hierarchic tradition is also hostile to self-consciousness. It is sinful arrogance. We must see ourselves, said the medieval church, as dependent on divine grace, not as individuals pursuing a private purpose. Furthermore, the church liked elaborate structures and immersion of the individual in these complex structures, whether episcopal or monastic organizations. Self-consciousness and its literary genre, autobiography, are therefore a middle class affect. The strong and ambitious middle class person has neither the nobility's great family nor the church's institutional means of grace to be absorbed within, and develops a sense of making it as a person, as an individual. Middle class people rise because they have lots of room to do so; they start at a modest level of achievement and security. The scion of the great family and the holder of high ecclesiastical office can only fulfill the prescribed opportunities of their order. The middle class person can see a long avenue of transformation open to him or her and develops a strong ego in challenge to the environment. Autobiographical egoism existed in ancient literature. Augustine of Hippo (354–430), by origin an obscure, dark North African who opened up a career for himself by his excellence in Latin rhetoric, drew upon this classical genre and the psychological tendencies of his class to write an account of his life up to his mid-30s, when he became a Christian and a priest. Formally, it is antiegoistic because all the time he was allegedly making choices and experiencing upheavals of one sort or another, his Christian God was, he maintained, leading him through an edifying obstacle course to his predestined conversion. The *Confessions* therefore accords with the hierarchic doctrine of the church, and St. Augustine in his maturity played an important role in elaborating that doctrine. But in this book he manages to tell one of the great personal stories in literature while superficially at least giving full recognition to the ecclesiastical doctrine of salvation by divine grace (gift). It is an interesting question why Augustine felt justified in writing or at least publishing this book some ten years after his conversion. He has a ready answer: He is Everyman and his story is an anthropological case study in which his road to salvation represents mankind's. Yet more simply the book reads as though Augustine thought his life was an exciting experience to read about if it was artistically written, and it was. In Augustine, conversion means the capacity to become "continent," to suppress his sexual desires. He helped to establish an antierotic tradition in the Catholic Church.

THE INNER CONFLICT

So sick was I and in agony of mind, accusing myself much more sharply than my habit was, writhing and twisting in my chain until that should be broken which bound me. It still held me though its grip was weakening. Yet, Lord, you pressed upon my inner person, in severe mercy doubling the lashes of fear and shame, lest I should slip back again, and that small, thin fetter which remained should not be snapped, but should gather strength again and bind me more firmly. And I was murmuring to myself: 'Look, let it be done now, done now.' As I said the word I almost did it—almost did it, yet did it not. Yet I did not quite go back to that which was, but stood nearer and gathered breath. I tried again, and little by little got nearer and all but touched and

Portrait of St. Augustine in his study

laid hold of it. Yet I was not quite there to touch and hold, hesitating to die to death and live to life, and the ingrained worse was more powerful in me than the unaccustomed better. And that very instant of time on which I was to be something different, the nearer it drew to me, the greater dread did it beat into me, though it did not beat me back nor turn me aside. It only held me in suspense.

The trifles of trifles, the worthless amid the worthless, past objects of my affections, were what was holding me, pulling at the garment of my flesh and whispering: 'Are you sending us away? From this moment we shall not be with you for eternity? And from this moment you will not be permitted to do this and that for ever?' And what did they suggest by my 'this and that,' my God? Let your mercy turn it away from your servant's soul. What impurities, what acts of shame they suggested. But by now I was much less than half hearing them, and they were not so openly meeting me on the path and contradicting me, but rather muttering behind my back, and furtively tugging at my cloak to make me look back, as I made away from them. Yet they did hold me back from tearing myself away and shaking them off, and leaping over to the place to which I was called, while a violent habit cried: 'Do you think you can live without them?'

It was speaking very faintly by now. For on that side to which I had set my face and which I trembled to approach appeared clear the chaste dignity of Continence. Serene was she, not carelessly merry, honourably alluring me to come and not to doubt, and stretching out to receive and to embrace me, holy hands, full of hosts of good examples. With her were so many boys and girls, a multitude of youth and every age, grave widows, aged virgins, and Continence herself in every one of them, by no means childless, but the fertile mother of children and of joys from you her husband, Lord. And she was smiling at me with an encouraging smile saying as it were: 'Will you not be able to do what these youths and maidens have done? And are any of these or those able so to do save it be in the Lord, their God? The Lord their God gave me to them. Why do you

stand in your own strength, and so fail to stand? Cast yourself fearlessly on him. He will not pull back and let you fall. Cast yourself on him without a care. He will receive and heal you.' I was blushing the more for I still could hear the whisperings of those trifles, and I was hanging back. And again she seemed to say: 'Make yourself deaf to those unclean members of yours, and let them die. They tell you of delights but not according to the law of the Lord your God.' Such was the controversy in my heart, nothing but myself against myself. Alypius, sitting by my side, was silently awaiting the outcome of my extraordinary agitation.

CLIMAX

A strong surge of thought dredged from my secret depths and cast up all my misery in a heap before my inner eye. A mighty tempest arose bearing a great storm of tears. To shed it with befitting speech, for to be alone seemed the better state for weeping, I rose from Alypius' side, and withdrew some distance, so that even his presence should not be an embarrassment to me. Thus I thought, and he was sensitive. I think I had earlier said something in which the sound of my voice made it clear that I was heavy with tears. I thus arose, while he stayed where we had been sitting, greatly amazed. I flung myself carelessly down under some fig tree, and let the reins of weeping go. The streams of my eyes broke forth, a sacrifice acceptable to you. I said to you, in words something like these: 'And you, O Lord, how long, how long? Will you be angry for ever? Remember not past iniquities.' For I felt I was in their grip and I cried out in lamentation: 'How long, how long, tomorrow and tomorrow? Why not now? Why not an end to my vileness in this hour?'

Such were my words and I wept in the bitter contrition of my heart. And, see, I heard a voice from a neighbouring house chanting repeatedly, whether a boy's or a girl's voice I do not know: 'Pick it up and read it, pick it up and read it.' My countenance changed, and with the utmost concentration I began to wonder whether there was any sort of game in which children commonly used such a chant, but I could not remember having heard one anywhere. Restraining a rush of tears, I got up, concluding that I was bidden of heaven to open the book and read the first chapter I should come upon. I had heard of Antonius that from a public reading of the gospel he had chanced upon, he had been commanded as if what was read was said especially to him: 'Go, sell all that which you have, give it to the poor, and you shall have treasure in heaven, and come and follow me', and that by such a word from God, he had been immediately converted to you. Excitedly then I went back to the place where Alypius was sitting, for there I had put down the apostle's book when I got up. I seized it, opened it and immediately read in silence the paragraph on which my eyes first fell: '. . . not in the ways of banqueting and drunkenness, in immoral living and sensualities, passion and rivalry, but clothe yourself in the Lord Jesus Christ, and make no plans to glut the body's lusts. . .' I did not want to read on. There was no need. Instantly at the end of this sentence, as if a light of confidence had been poured into my heart, all the darkness of my doubt fled away.

Putting my finger or some other mark in the page, I shut the book and with a calm face now I told Alypius, and he thus made known to me what had taken place in his heart unknown to me. He asked to see what I had read. I showed him. He read on, and I did not know what followed. It was this: 'Let the weak in faith receive.' He took it to himself and showed it to me, and by such admonition he was given strength, and to that resolution and purpose without any stormy hesitation he applied himself along with me. This was most like him, for his was a character which had long been much, much better than mine. Then we went inside to my mother, and told her to her joy. We told her the course of events. She rejoiced triumphantly, and blessed your name, 'who are able to do above all that we ask or think.' She saw that you had given her so much more concerning me than she had sought with her pitiful and tearful lamentations. You converted me to yourself, so that I no longer sought a wife nor any hope in this world, standing on that rule of faith in which so many years before you had shown me to her. You changed her grief to joy, more richly than she had desired of you, and a joy more cherished and chaster than she sought from grandchildren of my body.

PETER ABELARD

THE RADICAL PROFESSOR

Peter Abelard's *History of My Calamities* is the finest medieval autobiography after Augustine's *Confessions.* Abelard was a bourgeois phenomenon of the early twelfth century. The son and heir of one of the lower nobility in the frontier regime of Brittany, he abandoned his patrimony and became a brilliant philosophy student and then professor at the emerging university in Paris. He depicts himself as a particular bourgeois personality: the superstar libidinous professor. Abelard's punishment and fall accord with ecclesiastical doctrine, but there is plenty of ambiguity about how deeply he recognizes the justice of his public abnegation.

Scholars debate whether Abelard's account of the behavior and ideas of his beloved Heloise is plausible and probably true, or whether she becomes merely a literary device for his self-dramatization.

Music, Pythagoras (left), Mucis, Donatus (right)

OF THE BIRTHPLACE OF PETER ABELARD AND OF HIS PARENTS

Know, then, that I am come from a certain town which was built on the way into lesser Brittany, distant some eight miles, as I think, eastward from the city of Nantes, and in its own tongue called Palets. Such is the nature of that country, or, it may be, of them who dwell there—for in truth they are quick in fancy—that my mind bent itself easily to the study of letters. Yet more, I had a father who had won some smattering of letters before he had girded on the soldier's belt. And so it came about that long afterwards his love thereof was so strong that he saw to it that each son of his should be taught in letters even earlier than in the management of arms. Thus indeed did it come to pass. And because I was his first born, and for that reason the more dear to him, he sought with double diligence to have me wisely taught. For my part, the more I went forward in the study of letters, and ever more easily, the greater became the ardour of my devotion to them, until in truth I was so enthralled by my passion for learning that, gladly leaving my brothers the pomp of glory in arms, the right of heritage and all the honours that should have been mine as the eldest born, I fled utterly from the court of Mars that I might win learning in the bosom of Minerva. And since I found the armory of logical reasoning more to my liking than the other forms of philosophy, I exchanged all other weapons for these, and to the prize of victory in war I preferred the battle of minds in disputation. Thenceforth, journeying through many provinces, and debating as I went, going withersoever I heard that the study of my chosen art most flourished, I became such an one as the Peripatetics.

OF THE PERSECUTION HE HAD FROM HIS TEACHER ANSELM [OF LAON]

Now this venerable man of whom I have spoken was acutely smitten with envy, and straightway incited, as I have already mentioned, by the insinuation of sundry persons, began to persecute me from my lecturing on the Scriptures no less bitterly than my former master, William, had done for my work in philosophy. At that time there were in this old man's school two who were considered far to excel all the others: Alberic of Rheims and Lotulphe the Lombard. The better opinion these two held of themselves, the more they were incensed against me. Chiefly at their suggestion, as it afterwards transpired, yonder venerable coward had the impudence to forbid me to carry on any further in his school the work of preparing glosses which I had thus begun. The pretext he alleged was that if by chance in the course of this work I should write anything containing blunders—as was likely enough in view of my lack of training—the thing might be imputed to him. When this came to the ears of his scholars, they were filled with indignation at so undiguised a manifestation of spite, the like of which had never been directed against any one before. The more obvious this rancour became, the more it redounded to my honour, and his persecution did nought save to make me more famous.

OF HOW HE RETURNED TO PARIS AND FINISHED THE GLOSSES WHICH HE HAD BEGUN AT LAON

And so, after a few days, I returned to Paris, and there for several years I peacefully directed the school which formerly had been destined for me, nay even offered to me, but from which I had been driven out. At the very outset of my work there, I set about completing the glosses on Ezekiel which I had begun at Laon. These proved so satisfactory to all who read them that they came to believe me no less adept in lecturing on theology than I had proved myself to be in the field of philosophy. Thus my school was notably increased in size by reason of my lectures on subjects of both these kinds, and the amount of financial profit as well as glory which it brought to me cannot be concealed from you, for the matter was widely talked of. But prosperity always puffs up the foolish, and worldly comfort enervates the soul, rendering it an easy prey to carnal temptations. Thus I, who by this time had come to regard myself as the only philosopher remaining in the whole world, and had ceased to fear any further disturbance of my peace, began to loosen the rein on my desires, although hitherto I had always lived in the utmost continence. And the greater progress I made in my lecturing on philosophy or theology, the more I departed alike from the practice of the philosophers and the spirit of the divines in the uncleanness of my life. For it is well known, methinks, that philosophers, and still more those who have devoted their lives to arousing the love of sacred study, have been strong above all else in the beauty of chastity.

Thus did it come to pass that while I was utterly absorbed in pride and sensuality, divine grace, the cure for both diseases, was forced upon me, even though I, forsooth, would fain have shunned it. First was I punished for my sensuality, and then for my pride. For my sensu-

ality I lost those things whereby I practiced it; for my pride, engendered in me by my knowledge of letters—and it is even as the Apostle said: "Knowledge puffeth itself up" (I Cor. viii, 1)—I knew the humiliation of seeing burned the very book in which I most gloried. And now it is my desire that you should know the stories of these two happenings, understanding them more truly from learning the very facts than from hearing what is spoken of them, and in the order in which they came about. Because I had ever held in abhorrence the foulness of prostitutes, because I had diligently kept myself from all excesses and from association with the women of noble birth who attended the school, because I knew so little of the common talk of ordinary people, perverse and subtly flattering chance gave birth to an occasion for casting me lightly down from the heights of my own exaltation. Nay, in such case not even divine goodness could redeem one who, having been so proud, was brought to such shame, were it not for the blessed gift of grace.

OF HOW, BROUGHT LOW BY HIS LOVE FOR HÉLOÏSE, HE WAS WOUNDED IN BODY AND SOUL

Now there dwelt in that same city of Paris a certain young girl named Héloïse, the niece of a canon who was called Fulbert. Her uncle's love for her was equalled only by his desire that she should have the best education which he could possibly procure for her. Of no mean beauty, she stood out above all by reason of her abundant knowledge of letters. Now this virtue is rare among women, and for that very reason it doubly graced the maiden, and made her the most worthy of renown in the entire kingdom. It was this young girl whom I, after carefully considering all those qualities which are wont to attract lovers, determined to unite with myself in the bonds of love, and indeed the thing seemed to me very easy to be done. So distinguished was my name, and I possessed the advantages of youth and comeliness, that no matter what woman I might favour with my love, I dreaded rejection of none.

Then, too, I believed that I could win the maiden's consent all the more easily by reason of her knowledge of letters and her zeal therefor; so, even if we were parted, we might yet be together in thought with the aid of written messages. Perchance, too, we might be able to write more boldly than we could speak, and thus at all times could we live in joyous intimacy.

Thus, utterly aflame with my passion for this maiden, I sought to discover means whereby I might have daily and familiar speech with her, thereby the more easily to win her consent. For this purpose I persuaded the girl's uncle, with the aid of some of his friends, to take me into his household—for he dwelt hard by my school—in return for the payment of a small sum. My pretext for this was that the care of my own household was a serious handicap to my studies, and likewise burdened me with an expense far greater than I could afford. Now, he was a man keen in avarice, and likewise he was most desirous for his niece that her study of letters should ever go forward, so, for these two reasons, I easily won his consent to the fulfillment of my wish, for he was fairly agape for my money, and at the same time believed that his niece would vastly benefit by my teaching. More even than this, by his own earnest entreaties he fell in with my desires beyond anything I had dared to hope, opening the way for my love; for he entrusted her wholly to my guidance, begging me to give her instruction whensoever I might be free from the duties of my school, no matter whether by day or by night, and to punish her sternly if ever I should find her negligent of her tasks. In all this the man's simplicity was nothing short of astounding to me; I should not have been more smitten with wonder if he had entrusted a tender lamb to the care of a ravenous wolf. When he had thus given her into my charge, not alone to be taught but even to be disciplined, what had he done save to give free scope to my desires, and to offer me every opportunity, even if I had not sought it, to bend her to my will with threats and blows if I failed to do so with caresses? There were, however, two things which particularly served to allay any foul suspicion: his own love for his niece, and my former reputation for continence.

Why should I say more? We were united first in the dwelling that sheltered our love, and then in the hearts that burned with it. Under the pretext of study we spent our hours in the happiness of love, and learning held out to us the secret opportunities that our passion craved. Our speech was more of love than of the books which lay open before us; our kisses far outnumbered our reasoned words. Our hands sought less the book than each other's bosoms; love drew our eyes together far more than the lesson drew them to the pages of our text. In order that there might be no suspicion, there were, indeed, sometimes blows, but love gave them, not anger; they were the marks, not of wrath, but of a tenderness surpassing the most fragrant balm in sweetness. What followed? No degree in love's progress was left untried by our passion, and if love itself could imagine any wonder as yet unknown, we discovered it. And our inexperience of such delights made us all the more ardent in our pursuit of them, so that our thirst for one another was still unquenched.

In measure as this passionate rapture absorbed me more and more, I devoted ever less time to philosophy and to the work of the school. Indeed, it became loathsome to me to go to the school or to linger there; the labour, moreover was very burdensome, since my nights were vigils of love and my days of study. My lecturing became utterly careless and lukewarm; I did nothing because of inspiration, but everything merely as a matter of habit. I had become nothing more than a reciter of my former discoveries, and though I still wrote poems, they dealt with love, not with the secrets of philosophy. Of these songs you yourself well know how some have become widely known and have been sung in many lands, chiefly, methinks, by those who delighted in the things of this world. As for the sorrow, the groans, the lamentations of my students when they perceived the preoccupation, nay, rather the chaos, of my mind, it is hard even to imagine them.

A thing so manifest could deceive only a few, no one, methinks, save him whose shame it chiefly bespoke, the girl's uncle, Fulbert. The truth was often enough hinted to him, and by many persons, but he could not believe it, partly, as I have said, by reason of his boundless love for his niece, and partly because of the well-known continence of my previous life. Indeed we do not easily suspect shame in those whom we most cherish, nor can there be the blot of foul suspicion on devoted love. Of this St. Jerome in his epistle to Sabinianus (Epist. 48) says: "We are wont to be the last to know the evils of our own households, and to be ignorant of the sins of our children and our wives, though our neighbours sing them aloud." But no matter how slow a matter may be in disclosing itself, it is sure to come forth at last, nor is it easy to hide from one what is known to all. So, after the lapse of several months, did it happen with us. Oh, how great was the uncle's grief when he learned the truth, and how bitter was the sorrow of the lovers when we were forced to part! With what shame was I overwhelmed, with what contrition smitten because of the blow which had fallen on her I loved, and what a tempest of misery burst over her by reason of my disgrace! Each grieved most, not for himself, but for the other. Each sought to allay, not his own sufferings, but those of the one he loved. The very sundering of our bodies served but to link our souls closer together; the plenitude of the love which was denied to us inflamed us more than ever. Once the wildness of shame had passed, it left us more shameless than before, as shame died within us the cause of it seemed to us ever more desirable. And so it chanced with us, as in the stories that the poets tell, it once happened with Mars and Venus when they were caught together.

It was not long after this that Héloïse found that she was pregnant, and of this she wrote to me in the utmost exaltation, at the same time asking me to consider what had best be done. Accordingly, on a night when her uncle was absent, we carried out the plan we had determined on, and I stole her secretly away from her uncle's house, sending her without delay to my own country. She remained there with my sister until she gave birth to a son, whom she named Astrolabe. Meanwhile her uncle, after his return, was almost mad with grief; only one who had then seen him could rightly guess the burning agony of his sorrow and the bitterness of his shame. What steps to take against me, or what snares to set for me, he did not know. If he should kill me or do me some bodily hurt, he feared greatly lest his dear-loved niece should be made to suffer for it among my kinsfolk. He had no power to seize me and imprison me somewhere against my will, though I make no doubt he would have done so quickly enough had he been able or dared, for I had taken measures to guard against any such attempt.

At length, however, in pity for his boundless grief, and bitterly blaming myself for the suffering which my love had brought upon him through the baseness of the deception I had practiced, I went to him to entreat his forgiveness, promising to make any amends that he himself might decree. I pointed out that what had happened could not seem incredible to any one who had ever felt the power of love, or who remembered how, from the very beginning of the human race, women had cast down even the noblest men to utter ruin. And in order to make amends even beyond his extremest hope, I offered to marry her whom I had seduced, provided only the thing could be kept secret, so that I might suffer no loss of reputation thereby. To this he gladly assented, pledging his own faith and that of his kindred, and sealing with kisses the pact which I had sought of him—and all this that he might the more easily betray me.

OF THE ARGUMENTS OF HÉLOÏSE AGAINST WEDLOCK—OF HOW NONE THE LESS HE MADE HER HIS WIFE

. . . After our little son was born, we left him in my sister's care, and secretly returned to Paris. A few days later, in the early morning, having kept our nocturnal vigil of prayer unknown to all in a certain church, we were united there in the benediction of wedlock, her uncle and a few friends of his and mine being present. We departed forthwith stealthily and by separate ways, nor thereafter did we see each other save rarely and in private, thus striving our utmost to conceal what we had done. But her uncle and those of his household, seeking solace for their disgrace, began to divulge the story of our marriage, and thereby to violate the pledge they had given me on this point. Héloïse, on the contrary, denounced her own kin and swore that they were speaking the most absolute lies. Her uncle, aroused to fury thereby, visited her repeatedly with punishments. No sooner had I learned this than I sent her to a convent of nuns at Argenteuil, not far from Paris, where she herself had been brought up and educated as a young girl. I had them make ready for her all the garments of a nun, suitable for the life of a convent, excepting only the veil. . . .

When her uncle and his kinsmen heard of this, they were convinced that now I had completely played them false and had rid myself forever of Héloïse by forcing her to become a nun. Violently incensed, they laid a plot against me, and one night, while I, all unsuspecting, was asleep in a secret room in my lodgings, they broke in with the help of one of my servants, whom they had bribed. There they had vengeance on me with a most cruel and most shameful punishment, such as astounded the whole world, for they cut off those parts of my body with which I had done that which was the cause of their sorrow. This done, straightway they fled, but two of them were captured, and suffered the loss of their eyes and their genital organs. One of these two was the aforesaid servant, who, even while he was still in my service, had been led by his avarice to betray me.

OF THE SUFFERING OF HIS BODY— OF HOW HE BECAME A MONK IN THE MONASTERY OF ST. DENIS AND HÉLOÏSE A NUN AT ARGENTEUIL

. . . The abbey, however, to which I had betaken myself was utterly worldly and in its life quite scandalous. The abbot himself was as far below his fellows in his way of living and in the foulness of his reputation as he was above them in priestly rank. This intolerable state of things I often and vehemently denounced, sometimes in private talk and sometimes publicly, but the only result was that I made myself detested of them all. They gladly laid hold of the daily eagerness of my students to hear me as an excuse whereby they might be rid of me; and finally, at the insistent urging of the students themselves, and with the hearty consent of the abbot and the rest of the brotherhood, I departed thence to a certain hut, there to teach in my wonted way. To this place such a throng of students flocked that the neighbourhood could not afford shelter for them nor the earth sufficient sustenance.

Here, as befitted my profession, I devoted myself chiefly to lectures on theology, but I did not wholly abandon the teaching of the secular arts, to which I was more accustomed, and which was particularly demanded of me. I used the latter, however, as a hook, luring my students by the bait of learning to the study of the true philosophy, even as the Ecclesiastical History tells of Origen, the greatest of all Christian philosophers. Since apparently the Lord had gifted me with no less persuasiveness in expounding the Scriptures than in lecturing on secular subjects, the number of my students in these two courses began to increase greatly, and the attendance at all the other schools was correspondingly diminished. Thus I aroused the envy and hatred of the other teachers.

MARGERY KEMPE

AUTOBIOGRAPHY OF A VICTIMIZED WOMAN

Kempe was a fifteenth-century Englishwoman of lower middle class background who experienced conversions, saw visions, went on pilgrimages incessantly, endured nasty illnesses, and got into repeated trouble with the church authorities—exactly why, by her account, is not clear. She seems a harmless if outspoken crank. In other words, she was a perfect lower middle class female victim, with an unquenchable conviction in her own righteousness and sanctity, a perfect fit for the TV talk shows today. Kempe appears to have been illiterate and to have dictated her whole book, but that too may be a put-on, another manufactured victimizing quality.

The said creature, lying in her bed on the following night, heard with her bodily ears a loud voice calling, 'Margery.' With that voice she awoke, greatly frightened, and, lying still in silence, she said her prayers as devoutly as she could at that time. And soon our merciful Lord, everywhere present, comforting his unworthy servant, said to her, 'Daughter, it is more pleasing to me that you suffer scorn and humiliation, shame and rebukes, wrongs and distress, than if your head were struck off three times a day every day for seven years. And therefore, daughter, do not fear what any man can say to you. But in my goodness, and in your sorrows that you have suffered, you have great cause to rejoice, for when you come home to heaven, then shall every sorrow be turned into joy for you.'

On the next day she was brought into the Chapterhouse of Beverley, and there was the Archbishop of York, and many great clerics with him, priests, canons, and secular men. Then the Archbishop said to this creature, 'What, woman, have you come back again? I would gladly be rid of you.'

And then a priest brought her before him, and the Archbishop said, in the hearing of all present, 'Sirs, I had this woman before me at Cawood, and there I with my clerics examined her in her faith and found no fault in her. Furthermore, sirs, I

have since that time spoken with good men who hold her to be a perfect woman and a good woman. Notwithstanding all this, I gave one of my men five shillings to lead her out of this part of the country, in order to quieten the people down. And as they were going on their journey they were taken and arrested, my man put in prison because of her; also her gold and her silver was taken away from her, together with her beads and her ring, and she is brought before me again here. Is there any man here who can say anything against her?'

Then other men said, 'Here is a friar who knows many things against her.'

The friar came forward and said that she disparaged all men of Holy Church—and he uttered much evil talk about her that time. He also said that she would have been burnt at Lynn, had his order—that was the Preaching Friars—not been there. 'And, sir, she says that she may weep and have contrition when she will.'

Then came the two men who had arrested her, saying with the friar that she was Cobham's daughter, and was sent to carry letters about the country. And they said she had not been to Jerusalem, nor in the Holy Land, nor on other pilgrimage, as she had been in truth. They denied all truth, and maintained what was wrong, as many others had done before. When they had said enough for a long while, they held their peace.

Then the Archbishop said to her, 'Woman, what do you say to all this?'

She said, 'My lord, saving your reverence, all the words that they say are lies.'

Then the Archbishop said to the friar, 'Friar, the words are not heresy; they are slanderous words and erroneous.'

'My lord,' said the friar, 'she knows her faith well enough. Nevertheless, my lord of Bedford is angry with her, and he will have her.'

'Well, friar,' said the Archbishop, 'and you shall escort her to him.'

'No, sir,' said the friar, 'it is not a friar's job to escort a woman about.'

'And I will not have it,' said the Archbishop, 'that the Duke of Bedford be angry with me because of her.'

Then the Archbishop said to his men, 'Watch the friar until I want to see him again,' and commanded another man to guard the said creature as well, until he wanted to see her another time, when he pleased. The said creature begged his lordship that she not be put amongst men, for she was a man's wife. And the Archbishop said, 'No, you shall come to no harm.'

Then he who was charged with her took her by the hand and led her home to his house, and made her sit with him to eat and drink, making her very welcome. Many priests and other men came there to see her and talk to her, and many people were very sorry that she was being so badly treated.

A short time afterwards the Archbishop sent for her, and she was led into his chamber, and even up to his bedside. Then she, bowing, thanked him for his gracious favour that he had shown her before.

'Yes, yes,' said the Archbishop, 'I am told worse things of you than I ever was before.'

She said, 'My lord, if you care to examine me, I shall avow the truth, and if I be found guilty, I will be obedient to your correction.'

Then a Preaching Friar came forward, who was Suffragan to the Archbishop, to whom the Archbishop said, 'Now, sir, as you said to me when she was not present, say now while she is present.'

'Shall I do so?' said the Suffragan.

'Yes,' said the Archbishop.

Then the Suffragan said to this creature, 'Woman, you were at my Lady Westmorland's.'

'When, sir?' said she.

'At Easter,' said the Suffragan.

She, not replying, said, 'Well, sir?'

Then he said, 'My Lady herself was well pleased with you and liked your talk, but you advised my Lady Greystoke to leave her husband, and she is a baron's wife, and daughter to my Lady of Westmorland. And now you have said enough to be burned for.' And so he multiplied many sharp words in front of the Archbishop—it is not fitting to repeat them.

At last she said to the Archbishop, 'My lord, if it be your will, I have not seen my Lady Westmorland these two years and more. Sir, she sent for me before I went to Jerusalem and, if you like, I will go to her again for a testimonial that I prompted no such matter.'

'No,' said those who stood round about, 'let her be put in prison, and we will send a letter to the noble lady, and, if it be the truth that she is saying, let her go free, without any grudging.'

And she said she was quite satisfied that it should be so.

Then a great cleric who stood a little to one side of the Archbishop said, 'Put her in prison forty days, and she will love God the better for the rest of her life.'

The Archbishop asked her what tale it was that she told the Lady of Westmorland when she spoke with her.

She said, 'I told her a good tale of a lady who was damned because she would not love her enemies, and of a bailiff who was saved because he loved his enemies and forgave them their trespasses against him, and yet he was held to be an evil man.'

The Archbishop said it was a good tale. Then his steward said, and many others with him, crying with a loud voice to the Archbishop, 'My lord, we pray you, let her go from here this time, and if she ever comes back again, we will burn her ourselves.'

The Archbishop said, 'I believe there was never woman in England so treated as she is, and has been.'

Then he said to this creature, 'I do not know what I shall do with you.'

She said, 'My lord, I pray you, let me have your letter and your seal as a record that I have vindicated myself against my enemies, and that nothing admissible is charged against me, neither error nor heresy that may be proved against me, our Lord be thanked. And let me have John, your man, again to bring me over the water.'

And the Archbishop very kindly granted her all she desired—our Lord grant him his reward—and delivered to her her purse with her ring and beads, which the Duke of Bedford's men had taken from her before. The Archbishop was amazed at where she got the money to travel about the country with, and she said good men gave it her so that she would pray for them.

Then she, kneeling down, received his blessing and took her leave with a very glad heart, going out of his chamber. And the Archbishop's household asked her to pray for them, but the Steward was angry because she laughed and was so cheerful, saying to her, 'Holy folk should not laugh.'

She said, 'Sir, I have great cause to laugh, for the more shame and scorn I suffer, the merrier I may be in our Lord Jesus Christ.'

Then she came down into the hall, and there stood the Preaching Friar who had caused her all that unhappiness. And so she passed on with a man of the Archbishop's, bearing the letter which the Archbishop had granted her for a record, and he brought her to the River Humber, and there he took his leave of her, returning to his lord and bearing the said letter with him again, and so she was left alone, without any knowledge of the people.

All the aforesaid trouble befell her on a Friday, God be thanked for everything. . . .

When she had crossed the River Humber, she was immediately arrested as a Lollard [Heritic] and led towards prison. There happened to be a person there who had seen her before the Archbishop of York, and he got her leave to go where she wanted, and excused her to the bailiff, and undertook for her that she was no Lollard. And so she escaped away in the name of Jesus.

Then she met a man from London, and his wife who was with him. And so she went on with them until she came to Lincoln, and there she suffered much scorn and many annoying words, answering back in God's cause without any hindrance, wisely and discreetly, so that people were amazed at her knowledge.

There were men of law who said to her, 'We have gone to school many years, and yet we are not sufficient to answer as you do. From whom do you get this knowledge?'

And she said, 'From the Holy Ghost.'

Then they asked, 'Do you have the Holy Ghost?'

'Yes, sirs,' said she, 'no one may say a good word without the gift of the Holy Ghost, for our Lord Jesus Christ said to his disciples, "Do not study what you shall say, for it shall not be your spirit that shall speak in you, but it shall be the spirit of the Holy Ghost." '

And thus our Lord gave her grace to answer them, worshipped may he be.

Another time there came a great lord's men to her, and they swore many great oaths, saying, 'We've been given to understand that you can tell us whether we shall be saved or damned.'

She said, 'Yes, truly I can, for as long as you swear such horrible oaths, and break God's commandment as knowingly as you do, and will not leave your sin, I dare well say you shall be damned. And if you will be contrite, and shriven of your sin, willingly do penance and leave sin while you may, with a will to turn back to it no more, I dare well say you shall be saved.'

'What! Can't you tell us anything other than this?'

'Sirs,' she said, 'this is very good, I think.'

And then they went away from her.

After this she went on homewards again, until she came to West Lynn. When she was there, she sent into Bishop's Lynn for her husband, for Master Robert, her confessor, and for Master Aleyn, a doctor of divinity, and told them in part of her tribulations. And afterwards she told them that she could not come home to Bishop's Lynn until such time as she had been to the Archbishop of Canterbury for his letter and his seal.

'For when I was before the Archbishop of York,' she said, 'he would give no credence to my words, inasmuch as I didn't have my Lord of Canterbury's letter and seal. And so I promised him that I would not come to Bishop's Lynn until I had my Lord of Canterbury's letter and seal.'

And then she took her leave of the said clerks, asking their blessing, and went on with her husband to London. When she got there, she was soon successful over her letter from the Archbishop of Canterbury. And so she stayed in the city of London a long time, and was very well received by many worthy men.

Afterwards, she was coming towards Ely on her way home to Lynn, and she was three miles from Ely, when a man came riding after them at a great speed, and arrested her husband and her also, intending to take them both to prison. He cruelly rebuked them and utterly reviled them, repeating many reproving words. And at last she asked her husband to show him my Lord of Canterbury's letter. When the man had read the letter he spoke handsomely and kindly to them, saying, 'Why didn't you show me your letter before?'

And so they parted from him, and then came to Ely, and from there home to Lynn, where she suffered much humiliation, much reproof, many a scorn, many a slander and many a curse.

And on one occasion a reckless man, caring little for his own shame, deliberately and on purpose threw a bowlful of water on her head as she was coming along the street. She, not at all disturbed by it, said, 'God make you a good man,' highly thanking God for it, as she did of many other things at different times. Afterwards God punished her with many great and various illnesses. She had dysentery for a long time, until she was anointed, expecting to be dead. She was so weak that she could not hold a spoon in her hand. Then our Lord Jesus Christ spoke to her in her soul and said that she should not die yet. Then she recovered again for a little while.

And shortly afterwards she had a great sickness in her head, and later in her back, so that she feared to lose her wits because of it. Afterwards, when she was recovered from all these illnesses, another illness followed within a short time, which settled in her right side, lasting over a period of eight years, all but eight weeks, at different times. Sometimes she had it once in a week, lasting sometimes thirty hours, sometimes twenty, sometimes ten, sometimes eight, sometimes four, sometimes two, so hard and so sharp that she must discharge everything that was in her stomach, as bitter as if it had been gall, neither eating nor drinking while the sickness lasted, but always groaning until it was gone.

Then she would say to our Lord, 'Ah, blissful Lord, why would you become man and suffer so much pain for my sins and for all men's sins that shall be saved, and we are so unkind, Lord, to you; and I, most unworthy, cannot suffer this little pain? Ah, Lord, because of your great pain, have mercy on my little pain; for the great pain that you suffered, do not give me as much as I am worthy of, for I may not bear as much as I am worthy of. And if you wish, Lord, that I should bear it, send me patience, for otherwise I may not endure it.

'Ah, blissful Lord, I would rather suffer all the cutting words that people might say about me, and all clerics to preach against me for your love (provided it were no hindrance to any man's soul), than this pain that I have. For to suffer cruel words for your love hurts me not at all, Lord, and the world may take nothing from me but respect and worldly goods, and on the respect of the world I set no value at all.

'And all manner of worldly goods and dignities, and all manner of loves on earth, I pray you, Lord, forbid me, especially all those loves and possessions of any earthly thing which would decrease my love towards you, or lessen my merit in heaven. And all manner of loves and goods which you know in your Godhead should increase my love towards you, I pray you, grant me for your mercy to your everlasting worship.'

Sometimes, notwithstanding that the said creature had great bodily sickness, the Passion of our merciful Lord Christ Jesus still so worked in her soul that at that time she did not feel her own illness, but wept and sobbed at the memory of our Lord's Passion, as though she saw him with her bodily eye suffering pain and Passion before her.

Afterwards, when eight years were passed, her sickness abated, so that it did not come week by week as it did before, but then her cries and weeping increased so much that priests did not dare to give her communion openly in the church, but privately, in the Prior's chapel at Lynn, out of people's hearing.

And in that chapel she had such high contemplation and so much confabulation with our Lord, inasmuch as she was put out of church for his love, that she cried at the time when she should receive communion as if her soul and her body were going to be parted, so that two men held her in their arms till her crying ceased, for she could not bear the abundance of love that she felt in the precious sacrament, which she steadfastly believed was very God and man in the form of bread.

Then our blessed Lord said to her mind, 'Daughter, I will not have my grace hidden that I give you, for the busier people are to hinder it and prevent it, the more I shall spread it abroad and make it known to all the world.'

 ST. ANSELM OF CANTERBURY

THE MEANING OF THE INCARNATION

The combination of aristocratic heroism, in which culture the hero is the exemplary figure, with religious idealism involved in the church's hierarchic tradition and middle class sentimentality inspired a new interpretation of the significance of the Incarnation. In addition to the traditional sacramental purpose, there will now be a deeply human meaning. This major change in theology, with vast implication for popular piety, literature, art, and everyday human behavior, was first clearly enunciated by the prominent theologian St. Anselm of Canterbury (d. 1109) in *Why God Became Man*, one of the few truly innovative, breakthrough books in the history of Christian thought. Anselm was a northern Italian nobleman who became a Benedictine monk and abbot in Normandy and a controversial archbishop of Canterbury. He surrounded himself at Canterbury with young monks for whom he had strong but probably chaste personal feelings, and he expanded the old Anglo-Saxon cult of the Virgin Mary into an elaborate movement in mass devotion. Here is the key passage of *Why God Became Man*, in which Anselm argues that a key purpose of the Incarnation of the Son as a human being was educational—Christ is the exemplary man who by the perfection of his life shows us experientially what a Christian life ought to be. He further argues for the complete freedom of the Son to undertake this exemplary role, an emotionally correct but intellectually problematic theological principle.

A. But tell me now what you think must still be resolved regarding the problem you set forth at the beginning—because of which problem many other topics intruded themselves.

B. The crux of the problem was why God became a man in order to save mankind through His death, although He was apparently able to accomplish man's salvation in some other way. Responding to this problem, you showed by many compelling reasons that the restoration of human nature ought not to be left undone, and yet could not be done unless man paid what he owed to God for his sin. This debt was so great that only God was able to pay it, although only a

Souls being saved and entering Heaven during the Last Judgment

man ought to pay it; and, thus, the same [individual] who was divine was also human. Hence, it was necessary for God to assume a human nature into a unity of person, so that the one who with respect to his nature ought to make payment, but was unable to, would be the one who with respect to his person was able to. Next, you showed that that man who was God had to be taken from a virgin by the person of the Son of God; and you showed how He could be taken sinless from the sinful mass. You proved very clearly that the life of this man was so sublime and so precious that it can suffice to make payment for what is owed for the sins of the whole world—and even for infinitely more [sins than these]. Therefore, it now remains to show how His life is paid to God for the sins of men.

A. If He allowed Himself to be killed for the sake of justice, did He not give His life for the honor of God?

B. Even though I do not see how He could reasonably have done this—since He was able to keep justice unwaveringly and His life eternally—nevertheless, if I can understand a thing which I do not doubt, I will admit that He freely gave to God, for God's honor, some such gift to which whatever is not God is not comparable in value, and which can make recompense for all the debts of all men.

A. Do you not realize that when He endured with patient kindness the injuries, the abuses, the crucifixion among thieves—which were all inflicted upon Him (as I said above) for the sake of the justice which He obediently kept—He gave men an example, in order that they would not, on account of any detriments they can experience, turn aside from the justice they owe to God? He would not at all have given this example if, as He was able to do, He had turned aside from the death that was inflicted upon Him for such a reason. . . .

Since He Himself is God—viz., the Son of God—He offered Himself to Himself (just as to the Father and the Holy Spirit) for His own honor. That is, [He offered] His humanity to His divinity, which is one and the same divinity common to the three persons. Nevertheless, in order to say

more clearly what we mean, while still abiding within this truth, let us say (as is the custom) that the Son freely offered Himself to the Father. For in this way we speak most fittingly. For by reference to one person [viz., the Father] we understand it to be God as a whole to whom the Son offered Himself according to His humanity: and through the name "Father" and the name "Son," an enormous devotion is felt in the hearts of those listening when the Son is said to entreat the Father for us in this way.

B. I accept this most gladly.

ST. BERNARD OF CLAIRVAUX

MARIOLOGY

The French Cistercian monk, itinerant preacher, ecclesiastical politician, and counselor to kings, St. Bernard of Clairvaux (d.1154), was more responsible than any other single churchman for the definition and expansion of the Marian cult. The Virgin became the Mother of God and in effect another person in the Christian Godhead, one to whom prayer was especially efficacious. She, like her Son, was a supreme exemplar of good humanity, especially for women. What is happening here, in Bernard's sermons on the Virgin Mary, is a cultural as well as religious change of great importance. Feminine qualities of compassion, caring, and domesticity were given high valorization as a model mainly but not exclusively for women. The feminization of medieval culture and Catholic piety had begun in a most forceful and explicit manner. Bernard does not hesitate to speak of Mary in quite human terms and make his audience conscious of her body, pure and sacrosanct as it may be, as well as her soul. Thereby he is legitimating the use of sexual imagery for defining the relationship between God and mankind and at the same time increasing the legitimacy of heterosexual love. Whether this latter change was intended by him or was an indirect consequence of his propensity to quasi-erotic discourse is uncertain. Bernard came from the middle ranks of the French nobility; he was an incessant traveler and an anxious and voluble preacher. There are identifiable noble, ecclesiastical, and middle class strands in his thinking. But above all he was driven by his own strong personality and his image of himself as a homiletic superstar.

Prepare thyself now, O Virgin, expand thy breast and open thy bosom, "because He That is mighty" is going to do great things for thee, so that, instead of being accursed in Israel, "all generations shall call thee blessed." And fear not, O prudent Virgin, the fruitfulness offered thee, because it shall leave thy virginity inviolate. Thou shalt conceive, yet without concupiscence; thou shall be pregnant, yet not burdened; thou shalt bring forth, yet not with sadness; thou shalt be a mother, yet know not man. But of whom shalt thou be mother? Thou shalt be the Mother of Him

The Virgin adored by the devoted

Who has God for His Father. The Son of the Father's glory shall be the Crown of thy virginity. The Wisdom of the Father's Heart shall be the Fruit of thy virginal womb. In a word, thou shalt bring forth God and conceive by God. Be of good cheer, therefore, fruitful Virgin, chaste childbearer, Mother undefiled, because thou shalt no longer be accursed in Israel, or reputed with the barren. And if thou shalt continue to be cursed by those who are Israelites according to the flesh, not because they judge thee sterile, but from envy of thy fruitfulness, remember that Christ also endured the curse of the cross, and has blessed thee, His Mother, in the glory of heaven. Yea, even on earth thou art declared blessed by the Angel, and all generations of men shall justly call thee blessed.

Then the Angel, looking upon the Virgin, and easily perceiving that she is revolving anxious thoughts in her mind, consoles her timidity, dissipates her doubts, and familiarly addressing her by her name, tells her kindly not to be afraid. "Fear not, Mary," he says, "for thou hast found grace with God. There is here no guile and no deception. Do not suspect any artifice or treachery in me, because I am not a man but a spirit, and an angel not of Satan but of God. Fear not, Mary, for thou hast found grace with God. Oh, if thou knewest how pleasing thy humility is to the Most High and what a sublime throne of glory awaits thee in His kingdom! Then thou wouldst no longer deem thyself unworthy to be saluted and served by angels. For how canst thou regard as undue to thee the love and devotion of the angels, seeing that thou hast found grace with God? Thou hast found what thou hast been seeking, thou hast found what no one before thee has been able to find: 'thou hast found grace with God.' And what is this grace which thou hast found? It is the reconciliation of men with God, the destruction of death, and the restoration of life."

Learn also from the Lord's mother how to have much faith in miracles but to preserve modesty in such faith. Learn to adorn faith with modesty, to repress audacity. *They have no wine,* she says. With what few, what reverent words she suggested what she was anxious about. And that you might learn to utter a grievous groan rather than a presumptuous prayer in such a case, she tempered the warmth of love with the shade of shame and modestly suppressed the trust she had in prayer. She did not step up boldly and speak openly, saying before all, Please, son, the wine has run short, the guests are inconvenienced, the bridegroom is embarrassed, show what you can do. Though a warm heart, a glowing sympathy might have said this or much more, yet the loving mother came privately to her omnipotent son, not to test his omnipotence but to discover his will. *They have no wine,* she says. What could be more modest, more trustful? Her love did not lack faith, nor her words dignity, nor her prayer efficacy.

. . . From all this it is clear, what is the stem proceeding from the root of Jesse, what is the Flower

Flower upon which rests the Holy Spirit. The Virgin, the *Genetrix Dei,* is the stem, her Son the Flower. Yes, the Son of the Virgin is that Flower "white and glowing red, chiefest among ten thousand"; the Flower upon which the Angels come to gaze, of which the perfume restores life to the dead; and as He Himself declares, a flower of the field, not of the garden. For the field blooms with flowers without human help; it is not sown nor tilled, nor enriched with nourishment. Thus it was with the womb of the Virgin: inviolate, untouched, it brought forth, as a prairie of living green, this Flower of immortal fairness, whose glory shall never fade. O Virgin, lofty stem, to what an exalted height dost thou attain! even to Him who sitteth upon the throne, unto the Lord of Glory. Nor is this strange, since thou sendest deeply into the ground the roots of humility.

O plant truly heavenly, more precious and pure than all others, truly the tree of life, which was found worthy to bear the fruit of salvation! Thy cunning, O malignant serpent, has overreached itself; thy falseness is made evident. Two charges thou hadst brought against the Creator; of untruth, and of envy: and in each thou hast been shown to have lied. He, to whom thou didst say, "Thou shalt by no means die," dies from the beginning; and the truth of the Lord endurest for ever. Tell me, if thou canst, what tree there is whose fruit can be an object of envy to him, to whom God has not denied this chosen stem and its lofty fruit? "He who spared not His own Son, how shall He not with Him also freely give us all things?"

You have now understood, I think, that the Virgin is that royal way, by which the Saviour came to us; proceeding from her womb, as a bridegroom from his chamber.

ST. BERNARD OF CLAIRVAUX

PRACTICAL MYSTICISM

Bernard's other main contribution to medieval religious culture was his insistence that a mystical experience which brings the individual in direct communication with the Son and the Mother, resulting in a blessed state of beatific exaltation, was possible for and to be desired by any devout member of the Church. How this popular mysticism was compatible with hierarchic authority and ecclesiastical discipline and stability, he did not explain. While Bernard hammered away at Peter Abelard as a wise-guy rationalist dangerous to the church, and while he also condemned conservative bishops and abbots for lavish displays of art in their buildings, his own mystical teachings were also controversial. They inspired a kind of religious individualism that eroded ecclesiastical control and encouraged sectarianism and dissent—developments more dangerous to the church's place in society than academic radicalism and elaborate and expensive church architecture and interior decoration. While Bernard's mystical doctrine is not new—it is in fact philosophically pure Platonism—his expression of it was rhetorically effective and remains persuasive. That a churchman of such elite status as Bernard should advocate individualized mystical experience gave it an aura of high legitimacy.

. . . If, then, any of us finds it, with the Psalmist, good for him to draw near to God, and to speak more plainly, if any among us is so filled with an earnest longing [for those things that are above] that he desires to be dissolved and be with Christ; but desires it vehemently, thirsts for it ardently, and, without ceasing, dwells upon the hope of it: he shall, without doubt, receive the

Word, and in no other form than that of the Bridegroom in the time of the visitation; that is to say, in the hour when he shall feel himself inwardly embraced, as it were, by the arms of wisdom, and shall receive a sweet inpouring of the Divine Love. For the desire of his heart shall be granted unto him, though he is still in the body as in a place of pilgrimage, and though only in part for a time, and that a short time. For when [the Lord] has been sought in watching and prayers, with strenuous effort, with showers of tears, He will at length present Himself to the soul; but suddenly, when it supposes that it has gained His Presence, He will glide away. Again He comes to the soul that follows after Him with tears; He allows Himself to be regained, but not to be retained, and anon He passes away out of its very hands. Yet if the devout soul shall persist in prayers and tears, He will at length return to it; He will not deprive it of the desire of its lips, but will speedily disappear again, and not return unless He be sought again with the whole desire of the heart. Thus, then, even in this body the joy of the Presence of the Bridegroom is frequently felt; but not the fulness of His Presence, because though His appearance renders the heart glad, the alternation of His absence affects it with sadness. And this the Beloved must of necessity endure, until, having laid down the burden of an earthly body, she shall be borne up upon the pinions, so to speak, of her earnest desires, and fly away, passing freely over the plains of contemplation as a bird through the air, and following in spirit her Beloved, whithersoever He goeth, without anything to hinder or retard. . . .

For to be, while still living, delivered from the power of desires for things material is a degree of human virtue; but to be brought out of the sphere of material forms and ideas is a privilege of angelic purity. Yet each of these two is a Divine gift—each of them consists in coming out of yourself, in rising above yourself; but the one carries you only a little way, while the other carries you far indeed. Blessed is he who can say: "Lo, I have fled far away, and abode in solitude." He was not content to go forth unless he could go far away, so as to obtain repose. Have you overpassed the pleasures of the flesh, so that you no longer obey its lusts, nor are subject to its allurements? Then you have made progress; you have separated yourself [from the world]; but you have not the power to banish, by the mere purity of your spirit, and to rise entirely out of the reach of, the inrushing and thronging crowd of material images and ideas. Do not, at the point which you have thus far attained, promise yourself rest of soul. You mistake if you think that the place of repose, the secret of solitude, the habitation of peace, the stillness of serene light, is to be found on this side of your earthly existence. But show me the soul who has attained that point of freedom of which I speak, who can justly say: "Return unto thy rest, O my soul; for the Lord hath dealt bountifully with thee," and I will at once confess that he has found the rest desired. And this place is truly in a solitude, this dwelling is truly in the light, according to the prophet; a tabernacle for a shadow in the day-time from the heat, and for a place of refuge, and for a covert from storm and from rain; and of it holy David also says: "In the time of trouble He shall hide me in His pavilion: in the secret of His tabernacle shall He hide me. . . ."

HILDEGARD OF BINGEN

SALVATION

Bernard of Clairvaux approved of the writings of Abbess Hildegard of Bingen (d.1178) in western Germany, and he persuaded the pope to give an official stamp of approval to one of her books. Hildegard was a brilliant musician, and there are many recordings of her choral work available today. She achieved renown as a physician and

pharmacologist and she currently is regarded as perhaps the leading feminist theorist of the Middle Ages. But to contemporaries it was Hildegard's expression of a message of spiritual uplift and practical mysticism in the Bernardine mode that gained wide attention. Her visions, of which this is typical, written down after severe and long bouts of migraine, take an optimistic view of the human capacity to rise to the level of angels.

The spirit of believers spreads as swiftly as the clouds. The longing of the soul by which blissful persons seek God's work in order to carry it out—that longing can never be put to rest. Thus streams that originate in the sea never cease to flow. And because that holy longing, which is the source of all good, is rooted to such a degree in those persons, God adorns them with the heavenly host. For such persons cling to God in such a way that they cannot be separated from God.

God's order of creation foresaw from the beginning that we were to be renewed in our spiritual life. And if God permitted animals to be bound, slaughtered, and burnt under the Law so that their blood might flow, this was a sign that those persons who hasten like clouds and look up to the divine would be tortured and killed and then offered up for the love of God. Since such persons nurse in this way at the breast of virtue by avoiding lust and other vices, they already bear in their hands the palm of victory. Indeed, they shed their blood before they might have the misfortune to fall out of the net of justice through the faithless acts.

In this way they are crucified in two ways: by fighting against their body and by shedding their blood in accord with God's command. Hence, they resemble the angels who constantly stand before God. But persons who carry out their tasks in life by teaching others according to the command of almighty God resound, so to speak, on flutes of sanctity. For by the voice of reason they chant justice right.

And we human beings have our existence like a deed carried out by the right side of almighty God—a deed of God's right hand. We shall complete the choir of the fallen angels. And thus we serve also to defend the good angels. God has great joy in these two systems of order: the angels' order of creation and that of human beings. God has joy in the angels' hymn of praise and in the holy deeds of human beings. By them God has accomplished in accord with the divine will everything foreseen from all eternity. But angels are constant before God's countenance while human beings are inconstant (*homo instabilis*). Therefore, our actions so often fail while nothing is lacking in the angels' hymn of praise.

Heaven and Earth concern God so because they were created by God for the divine honor. But because we humans are mortal, the divine revelations, which at times were made known to the prophets and sages, have often been veiled as if by a shadow. But if in days to come we will be relieved of our inconstancy and become unchangeable (*homo immutabilis*), we shall behold through our understanding God's splendor and may be permitted to abide forever with God.

SIR THOMAS MALORY

THE DEATH OF ARTHUR

Literature is shaped as much by its audience as by its author. The poem or story has to meet the demands of readers and listeners. Literature is a consumer product, and the makeup and attitude of the consumers (the writer's patron or cash-bearing buyers) play a major role in what the poet or narrator writes. On the other hand, there are indeed writers of such transcendent insight, power, and self-assurance that they go beyond the prevailing bounds of audience taste and create new horizons for readers and listeners. These basic facts of literary history might be borne in mind as we now examine significant examples of the romantic literature of the later Middle Ages, from the twelfth to the fifteenth century. This literature, written in the emerging European vernaculars, reflects the dynamic interaction of aristocratic heroism (which had already produced the epics) with ideas about love (now brought down from spiritual and angelic to a human level), and middle class sentimentality (which focused on and validated human feelings). In spite of these general factors at work in the molding of the marvelous body of European romantic literature of the later Middle Ages, recognition must be given to the individual writers, about whose lives we unfortunately know only the vaguest minimum and whose personal feelings we have to gauge from the writings themselves. First there was the great body of literature called by medievals the "Affair of Britain," the Arthurian legend involving King Arthur, Queen Guinevere, Camelot and the round table, Sir Lancelot, the Queen's lover and betrayer of Arthur, sundry other chivalric heroes like Parsifal and Gawain, and Modred, Arthur's kinsman, the black heart who eventually defeats the glorious king and, in most versions, brings about his death in battle. These sentimental and dramatic stories of life among royalty and nobility, spiced with a lot of heroism and sex, were staple entertainment in noble and upper middle class households. In the mid-fifteenth century the Camelot stories were given definitive form for the soon-to-be introduced printing press by an English mercenary captain (and possibly highwayman), Sir Thomas Malory. His *Death of Arthur* was heavily used by both nineteenth-century (Tennyson) and twentieth-century (Lerner and Loewe) elaborators of the Camelot stories. It is not very important, but historians now believe that the *historical* Arthur was a British (Welsh) Christian prince who led a resistance against the invading heathen Anglo-Saxons around 500 A.D., finally falling in battle. The earliest version of the Arthurian story was written down in 1136 by Geoffrey of Monmouth, a Welsh cleric and graduate student at Oxford. The significance of the Arthurian cycle lies not in Arthur's marginal historicity, but in the values and idealized behavior that the stories communicate. Aristocratic heroism was blended with the church's moralizing and with middle class sentimentality. This was the combination, plus a strong narrative line, that shaped medieval romance as a literary genre.

During the absence of King Arthur from Britain, Sir Modred, already vested with sovereign powers, had decided to usurp the throne. Accordingly, he had false letters written—announcing the death of King Arthur in battle—and delivered to himself. Then, calling a parliament, he ordered the letters to be read and persuaded the nobility to elect him king. The coronation took place at Canterbury and was celebrated with a fifteen-day feast.

Sir Modred then settled in Camelot and made overtures to Queen Gwynevere to marry him.

The queen seemingly acquiesced, but as soon as she had won his confidence, begged leave to make a journey to London in order to prepare her trousseau. Sir Modred consented, and the queen rode straight to the Tower which, with the aid of her loyal nobles, she manned and provisioned for her defense.

Sir Modred, outraged, at once marched against her, and laid siege to the Tower, but despite his large army, siege engines, and guns, was unable to effect a breach. He then tried to entice the queen from the Tower, first by guile and then by threats,

King Arthur and the Knights of the Round Table—
Vision of the Holy Grail

"Away, false priest, or I shall behead you!"

The Archbishop withdrew, and after excommunicating Sir Modred, abandoned his office and fled to Glastonbury. There he took up his abode as a simple hermit, and by fasting and prayer sought divine intercession in the troubled affairs of his country.

Sir Modred tried to assassinate the Archbishop, but was too late. He continued to assail the queen with entreaties and threats, both of which failed, and then the news reached him that King Arthur was returning with his army from France in order to seek revenge.

Sir Modred now appealed to the barony to support him, and it has to be told that they came forward in large numbers to do so. Why? it will be asked. Was not King Arthur, the noblest sovereign Christendom had seen, now leading his armies in a righteous cause? The answer lies in the people of Britain, who, then as now, were fickle. Those who so readily transferred their allegiance to Sir Modred did so with the excuse that whereas King Arthur's reign had led them into war and strife, Sir Modred promised them peace and festivity.

Hence it was with an army of a hundred thousand that Sir Modred marched to Dover to battle against his own father, and to withhold from him his rightful crown.

As King Arthur with his fleet drew into the harbor, Sir Modred and his army launched forth in every available craft, and a bloody battle ensued in the ships and on the beach. If King Arthur's army were the smaller, their courage was the higher, confident as they were of the righteousness of their cause. Without stint they battled through the burning ships, the screaming wounded, and the corpses floating on the blood-stained waters. Once ashore they put Sir Modred's entire army to flight.

The battle over, King Arthur began a search for his casualties, and on peering into one of the ships found Sir Gawain, mortally wounded. Sir Gawain fainted when King Arthur lifted him in his arms; and when he came to, the king spoke:

"Alas! dear nephew, that you lie here thus, mortally wounded! What joy is now left to me on this earth? You must know it was you and Sir

but she would listen to neither. Finally the Archbishop of Canterbury came forward to protest:

"Sir Modred, do you not fear God's displeasure? First you have falsely made yourself king; now you, who were begotten by King Arthur on his aunt, try to marry your father's wife! If you do not revoke your evil deeds I shall curse you with bell, book, and candle."

"Fie on you! Do your worst!" Sir Modred replied.

"Sir Modred, I warn you take heed! or the wrath of the Lord will descend upon you."

Launcelot I loved above all others, and it seems that I have lost you both."

"My good uncle, it was my pride and my stubbornness that brought all this about, for had I not urged you to war with Sir Launcelot your subjects would not now be in revolt. Alas, that Sir Launcelot is not here, for he would soon drive them out! And it is at Sir Launcelot's hands that I suffer my own death: the wound which he dealt me has reopened. I would not wish it otherwise, because is he not the greatest and gentlest of knights?

"I know that by noon I shall be dead, and I repent bitterly that I may not be reconciled to Sir Launcelot; therefore I pray you, good uncle, give me pen, paper, and ink so that I may write to him."

A priest was summoned and Sir Gawain confessed; then a clerk brought ink, pen, and paper, and Sir Gawain wrote to Sir Launcelot as follows:

"Sir Launcelot, flower of the knighthood: I, Sir Gawain, son of King Lot of Orkney and of King Arthur's sister, send you my greetings!

"I am about to die; the cause of my death is the wound I received from you outside the city of Benwick; and I would make it known that my death was of my own seeking, that I was moved by the spirit of revenge and spite to provoke you to battle.

"Therefore, Sir Launcelot, I beseech you to visit my tomb and offer what prayers you will on my behalf; and for myself, I am content to die at the hands of the noblest knight living.

"One more request: that you hasten with your armies across the sea and give succor to our noble king. Sir Modred, his bastard son, has usurped the throne and now holds against him with an army of a hundred thousand. He would have won the queen, too, but she fled to the Tower of London and there charged her loyal supporters with her defense.

"Today is the tenth of May, and at noon I shall give up the ghost; this letter is written partly with my blood. This morning we fought our way ashore, against the armies of Sir Modred, and that is how my wound came to be reopened. We won the day, but my lord King Arthur needs you, and I too, that on my tomb you may bestow your blessing."

Sir Gawain fainted when he had finished, and the king wept. When he came to he was given extreme unction, and died, as he had anticipated, at the hour of noon. The king buried him in the chapel at Dover Castle, and there many came to see him, and all noticed the wound on his head which he had received from Sir Launcelot.

Then the news reached Arthur that Sir Modred offered him battle on the field at Baron Down. Arthur hastened there with his army, they fought, and Sir Modred fled once more, this time to Canterbury.

When King Arthur had begun the search for his wounded and dead, many volunteers from all parts of the country came to fight under his flag, convinced now of the rightness of his cause. Arthur marched westward, and Sir Modred once more offered him battle. It was assigned for the Monday following Trinity Sunday, on Salisbury Down.

Sir Modred levied fresh troops from East Anglia and the places about London, and fresh volunteers came forward to help Arthur. Then, on the night of Trinity Sunday, Arthur was vouchsafed a strange dream:

He was appareled in gold cloth and seated in a chair which stood on a pivoted scaffold. Below him, many fathoms deep, was a dark well, and in the water swam serpents, dragons, and wild beasts. Suddenly the scaffold tilted and Arthur was flung into the water, where all the creatures struggled toward him and began tearing him limb from limb.

Arthur cried out in his sleep and his squires hastened to waken him. Later, as he lay between waking and sleeping, he thought he saw Sir Gawain, and with him a host of beautiful noblewomen. Arthur spoke:

"My sister's son! I thought you had died; but now I see you live, and I thank the lord Jesu! I pray you, tell me, who are these ladies?"

"My lord, these are the ladies I championed in righteous quarrels when I was on earth. Our lord God has vouchsafed that we visit you and plead with you not to give battle to Sir Modred tomorrow, for if you do, not only will you yourself be killed, but all your noble followers too. We beg you to be warned, and to make a treaty with Sir Modred, calling a truce for a month, and granting him whatever terms he may demand. In a month Sir Launcelot will be here, and he will defeat Sir Modred."

Thereupon Sir Gawain and the ladies vanished, and King Arthur once more summoned his squires and his counselors and told them his vision. Sir Lucas and Sir Bedivere were commissioned to make a treaty with Sir Modred. They were to be accompanied by two bishops and to grant, within reason, whatever terms he demanded.

The ambassadors found Sir Modred in command of an army of a hundred thousand and unwilling to listen to overtures of peace. However, the ambassadors eventually prevailed on him, and in return for the truce granted him suzerainty of Cornwall and Kent, and succession to the British throne when King Arthur died. The treaty was to be signed by King Arthur and Sir Modred the next day. They were to meet between the two armies, and each was to be accompanied by no more than fourteen knights.

Both King Arthur and Sir Modred suspected the other of treachery, and gave orders for their armies to attack at the sight of a naked sword. When they met at the appointed place the treaty was signed and both drank a glass of wine.

Then, by chance, one of the soldiers was bitten in the foot by an adder which had lain concealed in the brush. The soldier unthinkingly drew his sword to kill it, and at once, as the sword flashed in the light, the alarums were given, trumpets sounded, and both armies galloped into the attack.

"Alas for this fateful day!" exclaimed King Arthur, as both he and Sir Modred hastily mounted and galloped back to their armies. There followed one of those rare and heartless battles in which both armies fought until they were destroyed. King Arthur, with his customary valor, led squadron after squadron of cavalry into the attack, and Sir Modred encountered him unflinchingly. As the number of dead and wounded mounted on both sides, the active combatants continued dauntless until nightfall, when four men alone survived.

King Arthur wept with dismay to see his beloved followers fallen; then, struggling toward him, unhorsed and badly wounded, he saw Sir Lucas the Butler and his brother, Sir Bedivere.

"Alas!" said the king, "that the day should come when I see all my noble knights destroyed! I would prefer that I myself had fallen. But what has become of the traitor Sir Modred, whose evil ambition was responsible for this carnage?"

Looking about him King Arthur then noticed Sir Modred leaning with his sword on a heap of the dead.

"Sir Lucas, I pray you give me my spear, for I have seen Sir Modred."

"Sire, I entreat you, remember your vision— how Sir Gawain appeared with a heaven-sent message to dissuade you from fighting Sir Modred. Allow this fateful day to pass; it is ours, for we three hold the field, while the enemy is broken."

"My lords, I care nothing for my life now! And while Sir Modred is at large I must kill him: there may not be another chance."

"God speed you, then!" said Sir Bedivere.

When Sir Modred saw King Arthur advance with his spear, he rushed to meet him with drawn sword. Arthur caught Sir Modred below the shield and drove his spear through his body; Sir Modred, knowing that the wound was mortal, thrust himself up to the handle of the spear, and then, brandishing his sword in both hands, struck Arthur on the side of the helmet, cutting through it and into the skull beneath; then he crashed to the ground, gruesome and dead.

King Arthur fainted many times as Sir Lucas and Sir Bedivere struggled with him to a small chapel nearby, where they managed to ease his wounds a little. When Arthur came to, he thought he heard cries coming from the battlefield.

"Sir Lucas, I pray you, find out who cries on the battlefield," he said.

Wounded as he was, Sir Lucas hobbled painfully to the field, and there in the moonlight saw the camp followers stealing gold and jewels from the dead, and murdering the wounded. He returned to the king and reported to him what he had seen, and then added:

"My lord, it surely would be better to move you to the nearest town?"

"My wounds forbid it. But alas for the good Sir Launcelot! How sadly I have missed him today! And now I must die—as Sir Gawain warned me I would—repenting our quarrel with my last breath."

Sir Lucas and Sir Bedivere made one further attempt to lift the king. He fainted as they did so. Then Sir Lucas fainted as part of his intestines broke through a wound in the stomach. When the king came to, he saw Sir Lucas lying dead with foam at his mouth.

"Sweet Jesu, give him succor!" he said. "This noble knight has died trying to save my life—alas that this was so!"

Sir Bedivere wept for his brother.

"Sir Bedivere, weep no more," said King Arthur, "for you can save neither your brother nor me; and I would ask you to take my sword Excalibur to the shore of the lake and throw it in the water. Then return to me and tell me what you have seen."

"My lord, as you command, it shall be done."

Sir Bedivere took the sword, but when he came to the water's edge, it appeared so beautiful that he could not bring himself to throw it in, so instead he hid it by a tree, and then returned to the king.

"Sir Bedivere, what did you see?"

"My lord, I saw nothing but the wind upon the waves."

"Then you did not obey me; I pray you, go swiftly again, and this time fulfill my command."

Sir Bedivere went and returned again, but this time too he had failed to fulfill the king's command.

"Sir Bedivere, what did you see?"

"My lord, nothing but the lapping of the waves."

"Sir Bedivere, twice you have betrayed me! And for the sake only of my sword: it is unworthy of you! Now I pray you, do as I command, for I have not long to live."

This time Sir Bedivere wrapped the girdle around the sheath and hurled it as far as he could into the water. A hand appeared from below the surface, took the sword, waved it thrice, and disappeared again. Sir Bedivere returned to the king and told him what he had seen.

"Sir Bedivere, I pray you now help me hence, or I fear it will be too late."

Sir Bedivere carried the king to the water's edge, and there found a barge in which sat many beautiful ladies with their queen. All were wearing black hoods, and when they saw the king, they raised their voices in a piteous lament.

"I pray you, set me in the barge," said the king.

Sir Bedivere did so, and one of the ladies laid the king's head in her lap; then the queen spoke to him:

"My dear brother, you have stayed too long: I fear that the wound on your head is already cold."

Thereupon they rowed away from the land and Sir Bedivere wept to see them go.

"My lord King Arthur, you have deserted me! I am alone now, and among enemies."

"Sir Bedivere, take what comfort you may, for my time is passed, and now I must be taken to Avalon for my wound to be healed. If you hear of me no more, I beg you pray for my soul."

The barge slowly crossed the water and out of sight while the ladies wept. Sir Bedivere walked alone into the forest and there remained for the night.

In the morning he saw beyond the trees of a copse a small hermitage. He entered and found a hermit kneeling down by a fresh tomb. The hermit was weeping as he prayed, and then Sir Bedivere recognized him as the Archbishop of Canterbury, who had been banished by Sir Modred.

"Father, I pray you, tell me, whose tomb is this?"

"My son, I do not know. At midnight the body was brought here by a company of ladies. We buried it, they lit a hundred candles for the service, and rewarded me with a thousand bezants."

"Father, King Arthur lies buried in this tomb."

Sir Bedivere fainted when he had spoken, and when he came to he begged the Archbishop to allow him to remain at the hermitage and end his days in fasting and prayer.

"Father, I wish only to be near to my true liege."

"My son, you are welcome; and do I not recognize you as Sir Bedivere the Bold, brother to Sir Lucas the Butler?"

Thus the Archbishop and Sir Bedivere remained at the hermitage, wearing the habits of hermits and devoting themselves to the tomb with fasting and prayers of contrition.

Such was the death of King Arthur as written down by Sir Bedivere. By some it is told that there were three queens on the barge: Queen Morgan le Fay, the Queen of North Galys, and the Queen of the Waste Lands; and others include the name of Nyneve, the Lady of the Lake who had served King Arthur well in the past, and had married the good knight Sir Pelleas.

In many parts of Britain it is believed that King Arthur did not die and that he will return to us and win fresh glory and the Holy Cross of our Lord Jesu Christ; but for myself I do not believe this, and would leave him buried peacefully in his tomb at Glastonbury, where the Archbishop of Canterbury and Sir Bedivere humbled themselves, and with prayers and fasting honored his memory. And inscribed on his tomb, men say, is this legend:

HIC IACET ARTHURUS, REX QUONDAM REXQUE FUTURUS. [Here lies Arthur, once and future King]

ANDREAS CAPELLANUS

COURTLY LOVE

By itself, the Arthurian cycle is just a popularized and sentimentalized heroic epic. The Arthurian stories were however rewritten, often to the point of great subtlety, with high symbolism and often nonchalantly eroding the simple narrative thrust of the original story, by writers of deep imagination and elaborate literary skill who infused the conventional stories with disquisitions on the meaning of human love (invariably heterosexual, the church by this time having come to condemn homoerotic love, although it was practiced in monasteries quite commonly). This eroticism—this focusing on the realities of human love—has come to be called *courtly love* because nearly all of the love poetry was written in aristocratic courts, usually under the patronage of a queen or duchess or countess, particularly in northern France, the Rhineland, or southern England in the twelfth and thirteenth centuries, spreading to northern Italy in the late thirteenth century. Historians give much credit for getting this intellectual and literary movement going to Eleanor, Duchess of Aquitaine and queen first of France and then of England. In turn, some scholars believe that eroticism came up from Moslem Spain into southwest France (Aquitaine) in the late eleventh and twelfth centuries and was then carried by Eleanor and her daughter, the Countess Marie de Champagne, to northern France and England. The writers, at least in Champagne, were "young men," ambitious university graduates and underemployed clerics working under the patronage of Countess Marie de Champagne and such like. One scholar examined all the legal and administrative records of the county of Champagne and found no evidence of anyone practicing courtly love there, which is like trying to find the weekend amours of Wall Street lawyers and bankers in the business records of their law firms and investment houses. The actual impact of courtly love on aristocratic behavior was likely important although inconsistent and intermittent. Courtly love literature itself is among the great imaginative constructions of the human mind, so subtle and complex as often to be difficult to translate. A key work that shows the rise of eroticism and general interest in the subtleties of human love is a prose treatise in dialogue form on courtly love produced by Andreas Capellanus (Andrew the Chaplain) at the court of Champagne around 1175. It is partly tongue-in-cheek dialogue about how lovers should and do behave, whether there can be love within marriage or only in adulterous relationships, and so forth. But underneath there is a keen sense that aristocratic women were being pressured to make difficult choices. Andreas had certainly read *The Art of Love* by the Roman poet Ovid, who was very popular in the late twelfth century, but this is not a work of literary adaptation. It is a slick, original dramatization of some beautiful people's problems.

Man offering his heart to a Woman (courtly romance)

THE MAN SAYS: 'It would be quite pleasant for you to grant me this, unless perhaps you find your will opposed to mine. In short, it is your love which I seek as salve to my health, and which I am zealous to obtain by pursuing you.'

THE WOMAN SAYS: 'It seems to me that you are wandering from love's true path and sinning against the best convention of suitors in demand-

ing love with such haste. The wise and informed suitor, on addressing a lady previously unknown to him at their first meeting, should not demand the gifts of love in explicit terms. Rather by his energy he should make himself known to the loved one, and by all he says show himself amiable and complaisant. Next, he should ensure that his deeds can of full right speak well of him to his loved one, even when he is away. And then at the third stage he may approach her more boldly to ask for her love. You, however, have clearly erred, and turned this order upside down; and I imagine you have done this because you thought I was all too ready to grant your requests, or because you are a novice in the art of love. So your love deserves to be regarded with suspicion.'

THE MAN SAYS: 'If it is true that I have reversed the stages of courtship, I think your approval countenanced this. For though my intention might have been obvious to you from the careful and oblique language which I used, you pretended that you wholly failed to understand my request, and demanded that I speak in more explicit terms. It was not that I believed in your compliance, or was asking that you immediately confer your love when I agreed to explain my request; I wished to reveal my purpose in answer to your question.

'Again, though the order you mention should be observed, it can be reversed if a proper reason obtrudes. If I am constrained by deep emotion, and wounded by an inner shaft of love, justified necessity defends me from this charge of unworthiness. Insistent necessity cannot be confined by any rule of law. Then, too, if I am deficient in the labour love demands, I must inevitably request the love of one of great wisdom or resource, for thus my lack of experience can be remedied and I can learn thoroughly the lore of love. Obviously if a novice seeks the love of a novice, the love of such partners could not experience the appropriate growth, nor could an apposite relationship last any time. When a ship is exposed to the hazards of the sea and is at the mercy of stormy waters, the wind which gets up may be pleasant, but if the ship has no experienced helmsman or oarsman it is sunk and goes to the bottom, though the wind is favourable and its force slight. So both arguments advanced by you are disarmed by effective replies, and can in no way disqualify the proposal I have made.'

Love, we live apart from each other, separated by a tract of country too extensive and hard to cross for occasion to devise a suitable time and place for affording each other the consolations of love. Lovers who are close at hand can reciprocally assuage the torments springing from love. They can aid each other in their sufferings, and nourish their love because of the fortunes and afflictions they share. But lovers living apart cannot recognise that their pains are mutual, so that each must nurse his own labours and heal his own pains. It therefore seems that we must not consummate our love, for Love's rule shows us that the daily sight of each other makes the love of lovers grow. So I conclude that the opposite is true, that love diminishes and fades through distance. Accordingly each individual should be sure to win a love close at hand.'

THE MAN SAYS: 'You strive to maintain a position contrary to all reason. It is clear to all mankind that to obtain what one desires without difficulty breeds a cheap relationship at the start, and converts into an object of contempt what the whole mind's emotion earlier desired. On the other hand we take up with greater eagerness and preserve with more watchful zeal the good which is deferred because of the difficulty of

bestowing it. So the lover's embrace which is infrequent and hard to achieve induces the lovers to be bound with a warmer bond of mutual love, and their minds to be tied with a readier and closer affection. Constancy is perfected in a sea of troubles, and perseverance is clearly recognised in adversity. Rest has a sweeter taste for the man exhausted by many toils than for him who loiters in continuous idleness. Fresh shade seems to offer more to the man troubled by heat than to him who lives in a climate constantly temperate. Accordingly the rule you cited, that when lovers rarely meet it diminishes the power of love, is not Love's rule, for it is seen to be false and deceitful. This is why you cannot rightly debar me from your love because of the long and extensive distance separating us; on the contrary, you ought to be more interested in me than in one who dwells near by, for love between people apart is more easily concealed than is that between lovers joined in regular association.'

THE WOMAN SAYS: 'So far as concealing one's love is concerned, I think there should never be discrimination between an absent lover and one present. If a lover is established as wise and resourceful, it does not matter whether he is far from or close to his loved one; he will control his actions and desire in such a way that no one will be able to plumb the secrets of his love. On the other side, a lover who is a fool will never be able to hide the secrets of his love, whether he is distant or on the spot. So your argument comes off worst for it most clearly clashes with reason.

'There is an additional powerful reason forbidding me to pledge my love. I have a husband renowned for his universal nobility, civility and moral worth, and it would be wicked to pollute his bed or to be joined in any man's embraces. For I know that he loves me with all the heart's affection, and I am bound to him with all my heart's devotion. Since I am adorned with the reward of this great love, Love's laws command me to refrain from loving another.'

THE MAN SAYS: 'I admit the truth that your husband rejoices in a character universally worthy, and is endowed with blessed joys more than all men alive, since he has deserved to savour in his embraces the joys of your exalted person. But I am mightly surprised that you consent to allow marital affection, which any couple is allowed to have after being joined in matrimony, to appropriate the name of love, for it is clearly known that love cannot claim a place between husband and wife. Although they may be united in great and boundless affection, their feelings cannot attain the status of love because they cannot be gathered under the heading of any true definition of love.

'Love is nothing other than an uncontrolled desire to obtain the sensual gratification of a stealthy and secret embrace. Now I ask you: what stealthy embrace could take place between a married couple, since they are acknowledged to possess each other, and can fulfil all the desires that they will from each other without fear of opposition? The most outstanding teaching of princes shows that no one can obtain the use of his own possessions by secret enjoyment of them.

'Do not think absurd my statement that the relationship of a married couple, though joined in universal feelings of affection, cannot obtain the title of love, for we see the same outcome in the matter of friendship. A father and son can have regard for each other in all matters, but true friendship does not exist between them; for as the teaching of Cicero attests, it is merely blood-descent which preserves the affectionate regard between them.

'So there is obviously as much difference between the all-embracing affection of a married couple and the obligation between lovers as there is between the mutual regard of father and son and the most constant friendship between two men. In the first case, love is not considered to exist, and likewise in the second there is said to be no friendship. You see clearly, therefore, that Love can in no sense play his role between married people, but has desired his privileges to be wholly withdrawn.

'Then there is a further argument opposing mutual love between husband and wife. Jealousy, which is of the nature of love itself and without

which true love cannot exist, is wholly rejected between husband and wife, and must be always expelled by them as a harmful bane. But lovers must embrace it always as the mother, so to say, and nurse of love.

'Hence it is clear to you that love can in no way flourish between your husband and yourself. So since it is appropriate for any honest woman to be a prudent lover, you can accept a suitor's prayers without harm to yourself and enrich with your love him that asks for it.'

THE WOMAN SAYS: 'You are striving to lend your support to what all men even from ancient times are agreed is generally reckoned blameworthy and condemned as loathsome. Who could with justice praise grudging jealousy, or defend it with his words? It is nothing other than a base and malevolent suspicion about a woman. So God forbid that any honest man should be possessed with jealousy for someone, for it is recognised to be every wise man's enemy and loathsome to all good men throughout the world.

'Then you seek to condemn love between married people under the cloak of a definition of love. You say that they cannot have secret embraces because they can satisfy their desires towards one another without fear of opposition. But if only you understand the definition correctly, love between married people cannot be hindered by it. For the expression "secret embrace" explains the preceding term in its metaphorical extension. The argument from impossibility does not appear to prevent married persons from offering secret embraces to each other, nor can the unlimited opportunity of consummating love without fear of opposition obstruct all love's working. In fact all should choose the love nurtured in continual embraces in the confidence that one can serve it; or more important, all should choose the love which can be practised daily without reproach. Such is the man whom I must choose to take joy in my embraces, who in my company can attain the role of both husband and lover; for whatever the definition of love lays down, love seems to be nothing other than an uncontrolled desire of physical affection for someone, and there is no obstacle to a married couple experiencing this.'

THE MAN SAYS: 'If Love's teaching was more fully clear to you, and if Love's pursuing darts had ever pricked you, your opinion would in truth have maintained that true love cannot exist without jealousy. As I recounted more fully to you earlier, jealousy between lovers is praised by all with experience of love, and is censured throughout the world when it exists between husband and wife. The reason for this will become clear to you with the clarity of truth once you understand the definition of jealousy.

'Jealousy, then, is a genuine mental emotion which provokes sharp fear in us that the substance of our love is being diminished through a failure to serve the wishes of the loved one. There is anxiety that love is not evenly poised, and suspicion against a lover is aroused, but this is unaccompanied by base thoughts. So it is quite clear that jealousy has three aspects. The truly jealous man is perpetually afraid that his services cannot be adequate to preserve his love: he fears that his love is not reciprocated to the same degree: and he reflects on the harsh pains he would have to suffer if his partner took another lover, though he believes that this could not possibly happen.

'It is quite obvious and clear that this third contingency could not happen to married couples. A husband cannot suspect his wife without having unworthy thoughts about her. Jealousy in its pure form, if applied to a husband, is defiled through the defect in the substance in which it has its place, and ceases to be what it was. It is like water renowned for being perfectly clear, which on beginning to flow into a sandy channel is seen to take on the dark colour of the sand, and its natural limpidity leaves it. Or again, take almsgiving; though of its nature it deserves the rewards of eternal blessedness, if expended on the poor by a hypocrite or a glutton for vainglory it loses its natural function and causes the extinction of both virtue and reward.

'So it is quite obviously clearly established that jealousy cannot claim a natural role between husband and wife, and consequently love must have no place there, for jealousy and love are constant companions. But jealousy is said to preserve love between lovers, for all three roles earlier allotted to jealousy are judged necessary to the lover, and so jealousy between lovers themselves is not condemned. However, many people are plainly deceived in this matter. They mistakenly maintain that base suspicions are jealousy, and accordingly a considerable number who know nothing of its source and description are very often misled and drawn into intractable error. Even between an unmarried couple this false jealousy can claim a place; and subsequently they are termed not lovers but male friend and lady friend.

'The contention in your reply that the love which can be practised without sin is certainly to be preferred, seemingly cannot stand. Whatever consolation is afforded each other by the married couple beyond affection for their offspring or discharge of obligations, cannot but involve sin. The punishment is all the keener if abuse disfigures the use of something sacred than if we follow an abuse which is customary. The sin is more serious in a wife than in another woman, for as we are taught by apostolic law a lover who shows eagerness towards his own wife is accounted an adulterer.

'Now your interpretation, which went beyond the definition of love, seems worthy of no man's praise, for it is certainly recorded by the witness of the ancients that explanatory glosses are not to be joined to actual definitions of things. So it is crystal clear to all that your interpretation is void of the truth of reason because it seems to have been introduced contrary to the intention of the definition.

'Moreover your definition, which you are seen to have applied to love, cannot rest on any rational basis. For according to it the blind and the mad are included, whereas the teaching of the lover Andreas, chaplain to the royal court, shows us beyond doubt that they are utterly debarred from the court of Love. Since then you cannot oppose my purpose with any rational reply, no man will consider it honourable on your part if you make me languish for love of you and undergo such great tortures on your behalf.'

THE WOMAN SAYS: 'You have not, I think, shown any reason such as can invalidate my opinion, or compel me rightly to assent to your wish. However, since in places the laws you propound seem persuasive, and in order that you may be deprived of any chance of accusing me, I accept the arbitration of any lady or honourable man you wish on the subjects discussed by us—namely, whether love can claim a place in marriage, and whether envy between lovers can be justly praised. For the disagreement in the argument seems impossible for us to resolve or to be laid to rest by a right decision.'

THE MAN SAYS: 'I do not wish to seek anyone's arbitration in this dispute, as long as you are willing to subject your statements to just investigation.'

THE WOMAN SAYS: 'It is unheard of since the world began that anyone should preside as judge over his own case, and so I refuse to intrude on this matter, which I leave to be entrusted to another.'

THE MAN SAYS: 'You may have the full right to name an arbiter for our disagreement. But I should like to abide by the judgment of a woman, not a man.'

THE WOMAN SAYS: 'If you are agreeable, I think the Countess of Champagne should be given the honour of deciding this problem and of lulling the dispute.'

THE MAN SAYS: 'I promise to maintain her judgment in its full import wholly and for ever, and to preserve it without spot or stain, for no man can ever rightly doubt her wisdom or balance of judgment. So a letter must be composed with the agreement and desire of both of us, expressing the main lines of the dispute and revealing the promise contained in it.

CHRÉTIEN DE TROYES

THE PSYCHOLOGY OF LOVE

Of the French romantic poets, by far the most original and subtle was Chrétien de Troyes, another member of Countess Marie de Champagne's productive entourage. What Chrétien is mainly interested in is not the heroics of Arthur and all that, but in the joys and pains of human relationships, how men and women feel about each other, how they talk to one another, how they join together or don't, how they imagine each other, how they react to these conjunctures. Here is an example from *Lancelot,* one of Chrétien's four lengthy romances that have survived. If we join with his audience in expecting to hear about Lancelot and Gueneviere again, we find that is only the vague casing for the work. Most of it doesn't deal with that at all. Nowadays a publisher would call this work "how men talk to women and vice versa." Here in this selection is a typical example: a potentially tempestuous physical relationship between a knight and young woman he meets that doesn't come off, with suggestions of why not and how they feel about it. Chrétien is the poet of difficult and failed relationships, and he has marvelous perceptions of the psychology of the sadomasochistic and power facets of heterosexual behavior. The splendid verse translation by William W. Kibler should be noted.

Beside the table, on the end of a bench,
They found two basins brimming
With hot water to wash their hands.
On the other end they saw
A finely embroidered
White towel to dry them.
They neither saw nor found
Valet, servant, or squire therein.
The knight lifted his shield
From his neck and hung it
On a hook; he took his lance
And laid it upon a rack.
Then he jumped down from his horse
And the girl from hers.
The knight was pleased
That she did not wish to wait
For his help to dismount.
As soon as she had dismounted,
Without hesitation or delay
She hastened to a room
From which she brought forth a short mantle
Of rich material to place upon him.
The hall was not at all dark
Though the stars were already shining;
A great light from the many large,
Twisted wax candles banished
All darkness from the hall.
After placing over his shoulders
The mantle, she said: "My friend,
Here is the water and the towel.
No one else offers or gives them to you,
For here you see no one but myself.
Wash your hands and be seated
When it pleases you to do so;
The hour and the food require it,
As you can see.
Now wash, then take your place."
"Most willingly."—Then he sat down
With her beside him, which pleased him.
They ate and drank together
Until it was time to leave the table.
When they had risen from eating,
The girl said to the knight:
"Sir, go out and entertain yourself a while,
If you do not object;
But only remain without,

If you please, until you think
That I am in bed.
Do not be displeased or troubled,
For then you may come to me at once
If you will keep the promise you have made."
He replied: "I will keep
My promise to you and return
When I believe the time is come."
Then he went out and tarried
A long while in the courtyard,
Until he had to return—
For he could not break his promise.
He came back into the hall
But could not find his would-be love,
For she was not there.
Unable to see or discover her,
He said: "Wherever she might be
I'll seek until I have her."
He set off at once to find her
On account of the promise he had given.
Upon entering the first room, he heard
A girl scream out loudly:
It was that very one
With whom he was to lie.
Then he saw before him the open door
Of another room; he came in that direction
And right before his eyes he saw
That a knight had attacked her
And was holding her
Quite naked across the bed.
The girl, who thought surely
That he would help her,
Screamed out: "Help! Help!
Sir knight—you who are my guest—
If you do not pull this other knight from off me,
I'll not find anyone to pull him away;
And if you do not help me at once
He will shame me before your eyes!
You are the one to share my bed,
As you have sworn to me!
Will this man forcibly have his will
With me before your eyes?
Gentle knight, take strength
And aid me quickly!"
He saw that the other villainously
Held down the girl

Uncovered to the waist,
And he was embarrassed and troubled
To see that naked body touching hers.
Yet this sight evoked no desire in our knight,
And he felt not the least bit of jealousy.
Furthermore, doormen guarded the entrance:
Two well-armed knights
With drawn swords;
Behind them four men-at-arms,
Each holding an axe—
The kind with which one could split
A cow's spine
As easily as a root
Of juniper or broom.
The knight stopped at the doorway
And said: "My God, what can I do?
I am engaged in pursuit
Of no one less than the queen, Guinevere.
I must not have a hare's heart
Since I am in quest of her.
If Cowardice lends me its heart
And I follow its command,
I'll never attain what I pursue.
I am disgraced if I remain here.
Indeed, I am greatly shamed
Even to have considered holding back—
My heart is black with sadness.
I am so shamed and filled with despair
That I feel I should die
For having delayed here so long.
May God never have mercy on me
If there is a word of pride in all I say
And if I would not rather die
Honorably than live shamed.
If the way to her were clear,
What honor would there be
Were these enemies to give me leave
To cross unchallenged?
In truth, the basest man alive
Could save her then;
Yet still I hear this poor victim
Who beseeches my aid constantly,
Reminding me of my promise
And reproaching me most bitterly!"
He came at once to the doorway
And thrust his head and neck through;

Looking up toward the gable
He saw swords flashing toward him
And swiftly drew back.
The knights could not
Check their strokes
And both swords shattered
As they struck the ground.
After they were shattered,
He was less concerned about the axes,
And feared and dreaded them less.
He leapt among them and jabbed one man down
With his elbows and another after him.
The two he found nearest
He struck with his elbows and forearms
And beat them both to the ground;
The third missed his stroke,
But the fourth, attacking,
Struck him a blow which ripped his mantle
And his chemise and tore open
The white flesh of his shoulder,
Causing blood to flow from the wound.
Yet he took no respite,
And without complaining of his hurt
He went and redoubled his efforts
Until he had grabbed the head
Of the one who was raping his hostess.
(Before he leaves, our knight
Will be able to keep his pledge and promise to
    her.)
He stood him up in spite of his resistance.
But the man who had missed his blow
Came after him as fast as he could
And prepared to strike another—
He meant to hack the knight's skull
Through to the teeth with his axe.
Yet our knight, skilled in defense,
Held the other knight in front of himself
And the axeman's blow struck him
Where the shoulder joins the neck,
Splitting the two asunder.
The knight seized the axe
And wrested it free from his grip.
He dropped the man he'd been holding
To look once more to his own defense,
For the two knights were upon him,
And the three remaining axemen

Were again most cruelly assailing him.
He leapt to safety
Between the bed and the wall
And challenged them: "Come on all of you!
Even if there were twenty-seven of you,
You would find your match
As long as I hold this position.
You will never have the better of me!"
The girl, who was watching him,
Said: "By my eyes, you need not worry
From now on, as long as I am with you."
She immediately dismissed
The knights and men-at-arms,
And they all left their presence
At once without objection.
Then the girl continued:
"You have defended me well, sir,
Against my entire household.
Now come along with me."
Hand in hand they entered the hall;
Yet he was not pleased,
For he would gladly have been free of her.
A bed had been set up in the middle of the hall.
Nothing had soiled
Its fine broad, white sheets.
The bedding was neither of cut straw
Nor rough-quilted padding.
A covering of two silk clothes of floral design
Was stretched over the mattress.
The girl lay down,
But without removing her chemise.
The knight was at great pain
To remove his leggings and take off his clothes.
He was sweating from the effort,
But in the midst of his sufferings
His promise overpowered him and urged him on.
Is this duress? As good as such,
For because of it he had to go
To lie with the girl.
His promise summoned and beckoned to him.
He lay down hesitatingly;
Like her, he did not
Remove his chemise.
He carefully kept from touching her,
Moving away and turning his back.
Nor did he say any more than would a lay brother

To whom speech was forbidden
When lying in bed.
Not once did he look toward her,
Nor anywhere but straight before him.
He could show her no favor.
But why? Because his heart felt nothing for her
Since it was focused on another—
Not everyone desires or is pleased
By what is beautiful and fair.
The knight had but one heart,
And it no longer belonged to him.
Rather, it was promised to another,
So he could not bestow it elsewhere.
His heart was kept fixed on a single object
By Love, which rules all hearts.
All hearts? Not really, only those it esteems.
And whomever Love deigns to rule
Should esteem himself the more.
Love esteemed this knight's heart
And ruled it more than any other
And gave it such sovereign pride
That I would not wish to find fault with him
For refusing what Love forbids him
And for setting his purpose by Love's commands.
The girl saw clearly and understood
That he disliked her company
And would gladly be rid of her,
And that he would never seek her favors,
For he had no wish to touch her.
Said she: "If it does not displease you,
Sir, I will depart from here
And go to bed in my own room
So you might be more at ease.
I hardly think that the comfort
Of my presence is pleasing to you.
Do not think me ill-bred
For telling you what I believe.
Now rest well this night,
For you have kept so faithfully
Your promise that I have no right
To ask even the least thing more of you.
Now I wish to commend you to God,
Then I'll leave."—With these words she arose.
This did not upset the knight;
On the contrary he willingly let her go,
For his heart was wholly given

To another. Having perceived
This clearly, the girl
Went into her room,
Disrobed completely, and lay in bed
Saying to herself:
"Of all the knights I have ever known,
There is not one except this knight
That I would esteem

The third part of an angevin.
For as I surmise and believe,
He is intent upon a quest
More dangerous and painful
Than any ever undertaken by a knight.
May God grant that he succeed in it!"
Thereupon she fell asleep and lay abed
Until the light of day appeared.

WOLFRAM VON ESCHENBACH

IN SEARCH OF THE GRAIL

The need for new subject matter in the late twelfth century led to the romantic poets developing a whole new subset of the Arthurian cycle—the search for the Grail, in which one or other members of the Camelot Round Table goes off in a perilous quest for the Grail (or Gral). Eventually it is Parsifal who finds it because he is the purest of the knights. The Grail was originally either the cup from which Jesus drank at the Last Supper, or the cup that received the blood of the Lord when his side was pierced as he hung on the Cross and he was stabbed by a well-meaning Roman soldier who wanted to shorten His suffering. But the Grail became a magical or sacred Stone, a blinding illumination of Truth, the ineffable goal of perilous quest in life. The Grail poem *Parzival*, written by Wolfram von Eschenbach, an obscure knight in the German Rhineland in the early thirteenth century, defines the chivalric life in terms of heroism and spirituality, a combined search for both earthly and divine paradise. There is a heavy dose of Bernard's and Hildegard's practical mysticism in this work. Furthermore, Parzival affirms again and again his love for his wife and how much he longs for her, a clear negation of adulterous sexuality. What the poem is supposed to signify is variously perceived. On one hand, it can be regarded as a neoconservative reaffirmation of traditional values against eroticism. On the other hand, it can be regarded as subversive, at least politically. At right angles to the vertical hierarchic structure of church and lay society is the horizontal plane of the good knight going out on his own and winning the Stone—a praise of individualism against institutions and traditions. The early years of the thirteenth century, when the poem was written, were a time of tremendous political turmoil in Germany, featuring ugly behavior by both lay and ecclesiastical leaders, including the pope, so the poet may be saying the only thing left with secure moral grounding is the good will and effort of a high-minded individual. The latter interpretation would explain why the poem was so revered in Germany during the Nazi era—there is a bit of the *fuhrer-prinzip*, the transcendent man of destiny, the pure personal incarnation of the German people, about it.

'**O**pen!'

'To whom? Who is there?'

'I wish to enter your heart.'

'Then you want too narrow a space.'

'How is that? Can't I just squeeze in? I promise not to jostle you. I want to tell you marvels.'

'Can it be you, Lady Adventure? How do matters stand with that fine fellow?—I mean with noble Parzival, whom with harsh words Cundrie drove out to seek the Gral, a quest from which there was no deterring him, despite the weeping of many ladies. He left Arthur the Briton then: but how is he faring now? Take up the tale and tell us whether he has renounced all thought of happiness or has covered himself with glory, whether his fame has spread far and wide or has shrivelled and shrunk. Recount his achievements in detail. Has he seen Munsalvæsche again and gentle Anfortas, whose heart was so fraught with sighs? Please tell us—how it would console us!—whether *he* has been released from suffering? Let us hear whether Parzival has been there, he who is your lord as much as mine. Enlighten me as to the life he has been leading. How has sweet Herzeloyde's child, Gahmuret's son, been faring? Tell us whether he has won joy or bitter sorrow in his battles. Does he hold to the pursuit of distant goals? Or has he been lolling in sloth and idleness? Tell me his whole style of living.'

Now the adventure tells us that Parzival has ranged through many lands on horseback and over the waves in ships. None who measured his charge against him kept his seat, unless he were compatriot or kinsman—in such fashion does he down the scales for his opponents and, whilst making others fall, raise his own renown! He has defended himself from discomfiture in many fierce wars and so far spent himself in battle that any man who wished to lease fame from him had to do so in fear and trembling.

The sword which Anfortas gave Parzival when he was with the Gral was shattered in a duel. But the virtues of the well near Karnant and known by the name of Lac made it whole again. That sword helped him in winning fame. He sins who does not believe it.

The story makes it known to us that Parzival,

brave knight, came riding to a forest—I cannot say at what hour—where his eyes fell on a new-built cell through which ran a fast-flowing stream. It was reared with one end above the water. The fearless young knight was riding in search of adventure—and God was graciously disposed towards him! He found an anchoress who for the love of God had dedicated her maidenhood and given up all joy. The seed of woman's sorrow blossomed from her heart ever-anew, though fed by love that was old. Schionatulander and Sigune!—These two did he find there. The young warrior lay buried inside, while above his tomb she led a life of pain. Duchess Sigune never heard Mass: her life was one long prayer on bended knee. Her full, hot, red lips were withered and blenched now that joy of this world had deserted her. No maiden ever endured such affliction. For her laments she needed solitude.

For the sake of the love that had died with this prince without his having enjoyed her, she now loved him dead as he was. Had she become his wife, Lady Lunete would have been slow to offer her the rash advice she gave to her own mistress. Even today one can often see a Lady Lunete ride in to give counsel out of season. When a woman shuns amorous ties outside the marriage-bond during her husband's life-time both for the sake of their partnership and her own decency, he has been blessed with treasure beyond price, as I see it. No restraint becomes her so well, and I am ready to testify, if wanted. If he dies, let her do as her circumstances guide her. Then if she still maintains their honour she would not wear so fair a garland were she to seek pleasure at the dance.

But why do I speak of pleasure in face of the suffering to which Sigune's love condemned her? I had better drop the subject.

Parzival rode up to the window over fallen trees—there was no path—nearer than he would have wished, since he merely wanted to discover his bearings in the forest. He asked for an answer there.

'Is anyone inside?'

'Yes!' answered Sigune.

Hearing a woman's voice he promptly threw his mount round on to the untrodden grass. He reproached himself and felt a stab of shame, not to have dismounted at once. He tethered his horse firmly to the branch of a fallen tree and hung his pierced and battered shield on it, too. Then the bold yet modest man ungirt his sword and laid it aside as courtesy required and went to the window in the wall to ask what he wanted to know.

That cell was empty of joy, bare of all light-heartedness. Great sorrow was all he found there. He asked her to come to the window. The pallid young lady courteously left her prayers and rose to her feet. And still he had no inkling who she was or might be. Under her grey cloak next her skin she was wearing a hair-shirt. Her lover was Great Sorrow, who laid her Gaiety down and roused many sighs from her heart.

The maiden came politely to the window and received him with a gentle greeting. She was holding a psalter in her hand, on which the warrior Parzival espied a little ring she had kept, despite her rigours, for true love's sake. Its gemstone was a garnet that darted its rays through the window like fiery sparks. Her wimple showed bereavement.

'There is a bench by the wall outside, sir,' she said. 'Pray be seated, if you have leisure and inclination. May God who rewards honest greetings reward you for bestowing yours on me!'

The knight accepted her suggestion and went and sat down at the window, with the request that she, too, be seated within.

'I have never before sat here in the presence of a man,' said she.

The knight began to question her about her régime and sustenance. 'It is inconceivable to me, madam, how you can lodge here in this wilderness so far from any road, and how you nourish yourself, since there is no cultivation anywhere around you.'

'My nourishment is brought to me from the Gral by Cundrie la surziere punctually every Saturday evening, this is how she has arranged it. Well provided for with food as I am, I have little anxiety on that score—would that I were as content in others ways!'

Parzival fancied she was lying and might well deceive him further. 'For whose sake are you wearing your ring?' he asked banteringly through the window. 'I have always heard it said that anchoresses and anchorites should refrain from having love-affairs!'

'If your words had power to do so you would make me an imposter. If ever I learn fraud, point it out, if you happen to be there! Please God, I am free of all deceit. It is not in me to thwart truth! I wear this engagement-ring for the sake of a dear man,' she went on, 'of whose love I never took possession by any human deed: yet my maiden's heart impels me to love him. Here inside, I have the man whose jewel I have worn ever since Orilus slew him in joust, and I shall give him love through the joyless days that remain to me. It is true love that I shall bestow on him, for he strove to win it in chivalric style with shield and lance till he died in my service. I am a virgin and unwed: yet before God he is my husband. If thoughts could produce deeds, then I have no hidden reservation that could impede my marriage. His death wounded my life. And so this ring, token of true wedlock, shall assure my safe passage to God. The torrent welling up from my heart and through my eyes guards my steadfast love. There are two of us in here. Schionatulander is one, I am the other.'

Hearing this, Parzival realized she was Sigune and was deeply affected by her sorrow. In haste he bared his head from his coif before addressing her again. The young lady then glimpsed the fair skin gleaming through the rust and recognized the gallant knight.

'You are Parzival! Tell me, how have you fared with regard to the Gral? Have you at last got to know its nature? Or what turn has your quest now taken?'

'I have forfeited much happiness in that endeavour,' he told the well-born maiden. 'The Gral gives me no few cares. I left a land over which I wore a crown, and a most lovable wife, too, than whom no fairer person was ever born of human kind. I long for her modest, courteous ways, and often pine for her love—yet even more for that high goal as to how to see Munsalvæsche and the Gral! For this has not yet come to pass. Cousin

Sigune, unacquainted with all my many sorrows as you are, it is very unjust of you to treat me as your enemy.'

'All cause I had to censure you, cousin, shall be forgiven,' said the girl, 'for you have indeed forfeited much happiness after neglecting to ask the Question that would have brought you high honour, when gentle Anfortas was your host and your good fortune. A Question would have won you all the heart can wish for: but now perforce your happiness turns tail on you, and your high spirits limp behind. Your heart has made Care its familiar that would have remained a stranger had you asked to be told.'

'I acted as an ill-starred man,' he said. 'Dear cousin, give me your advice. Remember that we are blood-relations and tell me for your part how matters stand with you. I should mourn your sorrows, did I not bear a greater load of suffering than ever any man bore. My burden threatens to crush me.'

'May the hand of Him to Whom all suffering is known succour you!—What if you should prove so lucky that a track should lead you to where you can see Munsalvæsche, with which, so you tell me, your whole happiness is bound up! Cundrie la surziere rode away from here quite recently. I am sorry I did not ask her whether she was going to Munsalvæsche or to some other place. When she comes here her mule always stands over there, where the spring gushes from the rock. I advise you to ride after her. Most likely she will not be riding ahead of you so fast that you could not soon catch up with her.'

The warrior at once took his leave and set out along the fresh track. Cundrie's mule had gone that way: but tangled undergrowth baulked him of the path which he had chosen, and so the Gral was lost a second time, and his happiness utterly dashed. Had he arrived at Munsalvæsche, he would assuredly have done better with the Question than on the earlier occasion you know of.

Now let him ride on. Where is he to go?

A man came riding towards him, bare-headed but wearing a sumptuous tabard above his shining armour. Indeed, but for his head, he was fully caparisoned. He advanced against Parzival at speed.

'Sir,' he said, 'it displeases me that you beat a track through my lord's forest in this fashion. I shall give you a reminder such as you will regret. Munsalvæsche is unaccustomed to having anyone ride so near without fighting a desperate battle or offering such amends as those beyond our forest call "death".'

In one hand he carried a helmet whose attachment was of silver cords and a keen lance-head helved on a new shaft. In high dudgeon the warrior laced his helmet level on to his head. His threats and his bellicosity were soon to cost him dear, yet all unaware he made ready for the joust.

Parzival, too, had shattered many lances no less fine. 'Were I to ride over this man's crops nothing could save me, how should I escape his wrath? As it is, I am only trampling his wild bracken. Unless my arms and hands fail me, I shall ransom my passage without his binding me.'

On both sides they gave free rein for the gallop, then drove with the spur and pulled their mounts into full tilt—and of neither did the thrust miss its mark! Parzival's high chest had braved many lance-thrusts, while, guided with zest and skill, his went cleanly and accurately to where the other's helmet-lace was knotted. He struck his man at the spot where you hang your shield at tournaments, with the result that the Templar from Munsalvæsche rolled from his saddle down a deep gulley in the mountain-side so far that his couch knew no rest. Parzival followed his joust through with his horse racing ahead so that it pitched down and smashed its bones. He himself gripped a bough of a cedar with both hands—now do not account it a disgrace in him that he hanged himself without an executioner!—then caught firm rock beneath him with his feet. Down below him his charger lay dead in the thick undergrowth. The other knight was making all speed to safety up the farther side of the gulley. Had he been intending to share any gain won from Parzival, as matters turned out, the Gral back home had more to offer!

Parzival climbed back again. The reins of the horse which the other had left behind were dangling down, and it had stepped through them and was waiting as though told to do so. When Parzival had taken his seat in the saddle he had lost nothing but his lance; but in view of what he had found he was reconciled to the loss. If you ask me, neither the mighty Làhelin, nor proud Kingrisin, nor King Gramoflanz, nor Count Lascoyt fiz Gurnemanz ever rode a better joust than that in which this war-horse was won.

Parzival then rode on with no notion of where he was going, but in such direction that the Company of Munsalvæsche did not come into conflict with him. It grieved him that the Gral kept so aloof from him. . . .

'My deepest distress is for the Gral,' said Parzival. 'After that it is for my wife, than whom no fairer creature was ever given suck by mother. I languish and pine for them both.'

'You are right, sir,' said his host. 'The distress you suffer is as it should be, since the anguish you give yourself comes from longing for the wife that is yours. If you are found in holy wedlock, however you may suffer in Purgatory, your torment shall soon end, and you will be loosed from your bonds immediately through God's help. You say you long for the Gral? You foolish man—this I must deplore! For no man can win the Gral other than one who is acknowledged in Heaven as destined for it. This much I have to say about the Gral, for I know it and have seen it with my own eyes.'

'Were you there?' asked Parzival.

'Indeed, sir,' was his host's reply.

Parzival did not reveal to him that he, too, had been there, but asked to be told about the Gral.

'It is well known to me,' said his host, 'that many formidable fighting-men dwell at Munsalvæsche with the Gral. They are continually riding out on sorties in quest of adventure. Whether these same Templars reap trouble or renown, they bear it for their sins. A warlike company lives there. I will tell you how they are nourished. They live from a Stone whose essence is most pure. If you have never heard of it I shall name it for you here. It is called "Lapsit exillis". By virtue of this Stone the Phoenix is burned to ashes, in which he is reborn.—Thus does the Phoenix moult its feathers! Which done, it shines dazzling bright and lovely as before! Further:

however ill a mortal may be, from the day on which he sees the Stone he cannot die for that week, nor does he lose his colour. For if anyone, maid or man, were to look at the Gral for two hundred years, you would have to admit that his colour was as fresh as in his early prime, except that his hair would grey!—Such powers does the Stone confer on mortal men that their flesh and bones are soon made young again. This Stone is also called "The Gral".

'Today a Message alights upon the Gral governing its highest virtue, for today is Good Friday, when one can infallibly see a Dove wing its way down from Heaven. It brings a small white Wafer to the Stone and leaves it there. The Dove, all dazzling white, then flies up to Heaven again. Every Good Friday, as I say, the Dove brings it to the Stone, from which the Stone receives all that is good on earth of food and drink, of paradisal excellence—I mean whatever the earth yields. The Stone, furthermore, has to give them the flesh of all the wild things that live below the aether, whether they fly, run or swim—such prebend does the Gral, thanks to its indwelling powers, bestow on the chivalric Brotherhood.

'As to those who are appointed to the Gral, hear how they are made known. Under the top edge of the Stone an Inscription announces the name and lineage of the one summoned to make the glad journey. Whether it concern girls or boys, there is no need to erase their names, for as soon as a name has been read it vanishes from sight! Those who are now full-grown all came here as children. Happy the mother of any child destined to serve there! Rich and poor alike rejoice if a child of theirs is summoned and they are bidden to send it to that Company! Such children are fetched from many countries and forever after are immune from the shame of sin and have a rich reward in Heaven. When they die here in this world, Paradise is theirs in the next.

'When Lucifer and the Trinity began to war with each other, those who did not take sides, worthy, noble angels, had to descend to earth to that Stone which is forever incorruptible. I do not know whether God forgave them or damned them in the end: if it was His due He took them back. Since that time the Stone has been in the care of those whom God appointed to it and to whom He sent his angel. This, sir, is how matters stand regarding the Gral.'

'If knightly deeds with shield and lance can win fame for one's earthly self, yet also Paradise for one's soul, then the chivalric life has been my one desire!' said Parzival. 'I fought wherever fighting was to be had, so that my warlike hand has glory within its grasp. If God is any judge of fighting He will appoint me to that place so that the Company there know me as a knight who will never shun battle.'

GOTTFRIED OF STRASBOURG

LOVE'S PERILS

What is impressive about the erotic writers of medieval Europe is not their discovery of romantic love—the Romans and the Iberian Arabs both had had a go at it—but how deeply they explored the dimensions and implications of eroticism, its perils as well as its glories. The most telling criticism of eroticism and surrender to the sexual drive came from a contemporary of Wolfram von Eschenbach, another middle class writer in western Germany, Gottfried von Strasbourg, in *Tristan and Isolde*. In Gottfried's telling of this familiar plot offshoot of the Arthurian cycle, about how Queen Isolde and her lover Tristan betrayed her husband, good King Mark, the ugly side of eroticism is graphically presented—how the sex drive, if not repressed and socialized, makes fine people corrupt and evil and destructive of those who love them and of themselves. The narrative power of the work is exceptional.

Embarkation of Tristan and Isolde

Mark, meanwhile, was burdened with a double sorrow. He was harassed by the doubt and suspicion which he had and could not fail to have. He deeply suspected his darling Isolde; he had doubts about Tristan, in whom he could find no sign either of deceit or of treachery. His friend Tristan, his joy Isolde—these two were his chief affliction. They pressed sorely on him, heart and soul. He suspected both her and him, and had doubts about them both. He bore with this double pain after the common fashion and desert, for when he wished to have his pleasure with Isolde, suspicion thwarted him, and then he wished to investigate and track down the truth of the matter. But since this was denied him, doubt racked him once more, and all was again as before.

What harms love more than doubt and suspicion? What constricts a lover's heart so much as doubt? In its grip he does not for one moment know where to go. From some offense that he sees or hears he could now swear that he had got to the bottom of it: but before you can lift a finger things are back to where they were, and he sees something else that arouses his doubts, as a result of which he gets lost again! Except that it is the way of the world, it is a very imprudent attitude and great folly to harbor suspicion in love: for none is at ease with a love of which he must needs be suspicious.

Yet it is far more remiss in a man to reduce doubt and surmise to certainty; since when he has gained his object and knows that his doubts are justified, the fact which he was at pains to track down becomes a grief surpassing all others. The two ills which troubled him before would now be welcome to him. If only he could have them back, he would now accept doubt and surmise, if only he need never know the truth. Thus it happens that evil brings about evil till something worse arrives: when this works greater ill, what once was bad seems good. However distressing suspicion is in love, its presence is not so irksome but that one would endure it far better than proven animosity. There is no help for it — love must breed doubt. Doubt *should* have part in love. Love must find her salvation with it. So long as Love has doubt there is some hope for her; but when she sees the truth, she is suddenly past all remedy.

Furthermore, Love has a way which has entangled her more than all else, namely, that when things are to her liking she refuses to remain steadfast and very easily lets go; and as soon as she sights suspicion she will not be parted from it. She is all impatient to join it and, stealthily pursuing it, goes to greater pains to discover her mortal sorrow than she will take for the joy that she can find and possess there.

Mark persevered in this same senseless habit. Day and night he bent his whole mind to ridding himself of doubt and suspicion, and was most eager to arrive through proof positive at his own mortal sorrow. Such was his set intention.

It happened again one night that Mark spread his toils before Isolde as he and Marjodoc had plotted it, in the hope of sounding her further by such subtleties. But things took the opposite turn: following Brangane's instructions, the Queen caught her royal master in the snare which he had laid for her and contrived for her downfall. Here Brangane was most efficacious. It stood them both in good stead that cunning had been met with cunning.

The King drew the Queen to his heart and kissed her eyes and mouth many times. 'Lovely woman,' he said, 'I hold nothing so dear as you, and my having to leave you soon is robbing me of my reason, may God in Heaven be witness!'

The well-tutored Queen parried cunning with cunning. Fetching a deep sigh, she addressed him: 'Alas, poor wretched me. I have been thinking the whole time that this hateful news was a joke, but now I see you really mean it!' And she gave vent to her distress with tears and laments, and fell to weeping so piteously that she forced the simple man to yield up all his doubt, and he could have sworn she did it from her heart. For (to take one's words from their own lips) the ladies have no greater harm or guile or duplicity in them of any description than that they can weep for no reason at all, as often as they please. Isolde wept copiously.

'Tell me, lovely woman,' asked Mark in his credulity, 'what is the matter, why do you cry?'

'I have good cause to cry,' answered Isolde. 'I have every reason to give way to my unhappiness. I am a woman in a strange land and have but one life and the wits that I possess, and have so abandoned them to you and your love that I am unable to cherish anything in my thoughts but you alone. There is nothing so truly dear to me as you, and I know that you do not love me as much as you say and pretend. From the fact that you ever conceived the wish to go away and leave me in such strange surroundings, I can see that you heartily dislike me, so that I shall never feel happy again!'

'But why, lovely woman? You will have the land and the people at your command. They are yours as much as mine. Rule them, they are yours to dispose of. Whatever your bidding, it shall be done. While I am on my travels, my nephew, courtly Tristan, shall take care of you—he well knows how to do so. He is prudent and circumspect, he will make every effort to see that you are happy and to enhance your reputation. I trust him, as I have every reason to do. He has the same affection for you as for me; he will do it for the sake of both of us.'

'Lord Tristan?' asked fair Isolde. 'Indeed, I would rather be dead and buried than consent to be in his keeping! That sycophant is always toadying at my side with his flattery, and protesting how much he esteems me! But God can read his thoughts and knows with what sincerity he does so. And I know well enough myself, for he killed my uncle and fears my hatred. It is in dread of this that he is always fawning, beguiling, and flattering in his false way, imagining all the time that he will gain my friendship by it. But it is all to no purpose, his wheedling will not serve him. And God knows, were it not for you, for whose sake more than for my own honor I make a show of friendship towards him, I would never look at him with friendly eyes. And since I cannot avoid hearing and seeing him, it will have to happen without sincere affection on my part. I have, there is no denying it, occupied myself with him time and again with eyes devoid of warmth and with lies on my lips, merely to avoid censure. Women are said to hate their husband's friends. Thus I have beguiled the time for him with many a false look and with words lacking in affection, so that he would have sworn I did it from my heart. Sire, do not be deceived by it. Your nephew lord Tristan shall not have me in his keeping for so much as a day, if I can win your consent. You yourself must take charge of me on your travels, if you will. Wherever you wish to go, I wish to go there too, unless you alone should prevent me, or death should cheat me of it.'

Thus wily Isolde dissembled towards her lord and husband till she had won him from his suspicion and anger with her tricks, and he would have sworn she meant it. Mark, the waverer, had found the right path again. His companion had rid him of his doubts. All that she said and did was now well done. The King at once told the Steward what she had answered in all detail, as precisely as he could, asserting that she was free of all deceit. This displeased the Steward and mortified his heart: nevertheless he instructed Mark farther as to how he could test Isolde once more.

At night, when Mark lay abed again conversing with the Queen, he once more spread his snares and traps by means of questions, and decoyed her into them.

'Listen,' he said. 'As I see it, we must bow to necessity. Show me how women guard the realm! My lady, I must go abroad and you must remain with my friends. My kinsmen and vassals and all who wish me well must afford you honor and resources whenever you please to ask them. And if there are knights and ladies whose company irks you or whom you do not care to see about you, send them all away! You shall neither see nor hear anything that annoys you, whether it concerns people or property, if it goes against the grain. Nor shall I love anyone whom you regard with disfavor: this is the truth. Be merry and gay, and live as you think fit—you have my blessing on it! And since you cannot abide my nephew Tristan, I will shortly dismiss him from court on some convenient pretext. He must sail to Parmenie and see to his own affairs—both he and his country need it.'

'Thank you, my lord,' answered Isolde. 'You speak loyally and wisely. Since you now assure me that you are quick to take offense at whatever vexes me, it seems only right in return that I should defer to you to the utmost of my power in whatever suits your whim or finds favor in your eyes, and that I should help and advise, morning and night, in all that may serve your reputation. Now listen, Sire, to what you must do. I shall never wish or advise, now or at any time, that you should remove your nephew from court. For it would reflect on me if you did so. People would be quick to spread the rumor, here at court and in the country, that it was I who had put you up to it in order to settle an old score that rankles with me—namely, that he killed my uncle! There would be a good deal said on this topic that would be degrading for me and no great honor for you. I shall never consent to your humiliating your friend for love of me, or to your offending for my sake anyone to whom you owe favor. You should also consider this. If you go away, who is to guard your two territories? They will rest neither well nor peacefully in a woman's hands. Whoever is to maintain two kingdoms justly and honorably needs courage and intelligence, and, apart from my lord Tristan, there is not a baron in them who would do them any good if you permitted him to govern. Apart from Tristan, no one could take office whose commands would be respected. If the misfortune of war should come, for which we must be ready any day, it might easily happen that we should come off worst. Then, in their malice, they would twit and taunt me with Tristan. "Had Tristan been here" they would go on repeating "we should not have come to grief like this!" And then by common report they would all put the blame on me for having lost him your favor, to your injury and theirs. Sire, it would be better to refrain. Reconsider the matter. Weigh these two things: either let me accompany you, or place him in charge of your lands. Whatever my feelings for him are, I would rather he were on the scene than someone else should fail us and ruin us.'

The King realized in a flash that her whole heart was bent on Tristan's advancement, and immediately veered round to his former doubts and suspicions. As a result, he was more than ever immersed in angry resentment. Isolde for her part acquainted Brangane with their conversation in all detail and recounted one thing and the next without forgetting a word. Brangane was very sorry indeed that she had spoken as she had, and that the conversation had taken such a turn. She lectured her once more as to what she was to say.

At night, when the Queen went to bed with her lord, she took him in her arms and, kissing and embracing him and pressing him close to her soft smooth breasts, resumed her verbal stalking by means of question and answer.

'Sire,' she said, 'tell me as you love me: have you seriously arranged matters in accordance with what you told me about my lord Tristan— that for my sake you mean to send him home? Could I be sure of that I would thank you now and for the rest of my life. Sire, I have great trust in you, as well I may and should, but at the same time I fear that this may be some test. Yet if I knew for certain (as you explained to me) that you meant to banish from my sight whatever was hateful to me, I would know from this that you loved me. I would gladly have made this request long ago, but that I was reluctant; for I am well aware what I shall have to expect from Tristan if I am to have long acquaintance of him. Now, Sire, make up your mind to it—yet not because of ill-feeling on my part! If he is to administer these kingdoms while you are on your travels and some accident befalls you, as may easily happen on a journey, he will deprive me of my lands and honor. Now you have learned in full the harm that I can suffer at his hands. Think it over sympathetically, as a friend should, and rid me of lord Tristan. You would be acting wisely. Send him home again, or arrange for him to travel with you and for Steward Marjodoc to care for me meanwhile. But if you felt inclined to let me travel with you, I would leave our lands to be governed and protected by whoever was willing, if only I might go with you! But despite all this, dispose of your territories and of me entirely as you please, that is my wish and intention. I am mindful to do what will please you. The realm and the people are all the same to me.'

She worked on her lord with her frauds till she forced him to relinquish his doubts for the second time, and once more to abandon his suspicions concerning her thoughts and affections. He judged the Queen in every way innocent of any misdemeanor; but the Steward Marjodoc he judged in every way a liar, though Marjodoc had informed him correctly and told him the truth about the Queen. . . .

Once more Tristan and Isolde had surmounted their cares and perils, once more they were happy at court, which again overflowed with their honors. Never had they enjoyed such esteem. They were as intimate again as ever with Mark their common lord. They also hid their feelings very thoroughly; for, when it was not propitious for them to seize their chance together, they deemed the will sufficient, which often consoles a pair of lovers. Hope and expectation of how to accomplish the desire on which the heart is set never fail to give it a blossoming vigor and a living joy. Here is true attachment, such are the best instincts in matters of love and affection—that where one cannot have the deed in a way that is serviceable to Love, one gladly foregoes it, and takes the will for the deed. Wherever there is a sure will but no good opportunity, lovers should assuage their longing with that same sure will. Companions in love should never want what opportunity denies them, or they will want their sorrow. To desire when the means are lacking is a very useless game. Whatever one can [have], one should desire. This game is rich in opportunities, it is not fraught with sorrow. When these partners Isolde and Tristan were unable to seize their opportunity, they let the occasion pass, content in their common will, which, never tiring, stole tenderly and lovingly from one to the other. A common desire and affection seemed sweet and good to them.

The lovers hid their love at all times from the court and from Mark, as much and as well as they were allowed to do by the blind passion that would not leave them. But the seed of suspicion in love is of a nature so accursed that it takes root wherever it is cast. It is so fertile, so fecund, and so sturdy, as long as it finds just a little moisture it does not die and it can never die entirely.

Busy suspicion shot up luxuriantly and began once more to play about Tristan and Isolde. Here was excess of moisture, of their tender looks and signs in which Love's proofs were ever visible. How right he was who said that however one guards against it, the eye longs for the heart, the finger for the pain. The eyes, those lodestars of the heart, long to go raiding to where the heart is turned: the finger and the hand time and time again go towards the pain. So it was always with these lovers. However great their fears, they had not the power to refrain from nourishing suspicion with many a tender look, often and all too often. For alas, as I have just said, that friend of the heart, the eye, was ever turned towards the heart, the hand would go to the pain. Many a time did they enmesh their eyes and hearts with looks that passed between them, so intimately that they often failed to disengage them before Mark had found Love's balm in them, for he was always watching them. His eye was always on them. He secretly read the truth in their eyes many, many times, and indeed in nothing but their glances—it was so very lovely, so tender, and so wistful that it pierced him to the heart, and he conceived such anger, such envy and hatred from it that doubt and suspicion were the same to him; for now pain and anger had robbed him of measure and reason. It was death to his reason that his darling Isolde should love any man but himself, he valued nothing above Isolde, and in this he never wavered. For all his anger, his beloved wife was as dear and dearer to him than life. Yet however dear she was to him, this vexation and maddening pain brought him to such a frenzy that he was rid of his affection and wholly taken up by his anger—he was past all caring whether his suspicions were true or false.

In his blind agony Mark summoned them both to court in the Palace before the household. Addressing Isolde publicly in full sight and hearing of the court, he said: 'My lady Isolde of Ireland, it is well known to my land and people under what dire suspicion you have long stood with regard to my nephew Tristan. Now I have subjected you to tests and trials of many kinds to discover whether, for my sake, you would restrain yourself from this folly; but I see that you will not leave it. I am not such a fool as not to know or see from your behavior in public and in private that your heart and eyes are for ever fixed on my nephew. You show him a kinder face than ever you show me, from which I conclude that he is dearer to you than I am. Whatever watch I set on you or him, it is of no avail. It is all to no purpose, whatever lengths I go to. I have put a distance between you so often that I never cease to marvel that you remain so one at heart all this long while. I have severed your tender glances so many times, yet I fail to sunder your affections. In this I have overindulged you. But now I will tell you how it is to end. I will bear with you no longer the shame and grief that you have caused me, with all its suffering. From now on I will not endure this dishonor! But neither shall I revenge myself on you for this state of affairs to the extent that I am entitled, did I wish to be revenged. Nephew Tristan, and my lady Isolde, I love you too much to put you to death or harm you in any way, loath as I am to confess it. But since I can read it in the pair of you that, in defiance of my will, you love and have loved each other more than me, then be with one another as you please—do not hold back from any fear of me! Since your love is so great, from this hour I shall not vex or molest you in any of your concerns. Take each other by the hand and leave my court and country. If I am to have grief because of you I wish neither to see nor hear it. This fellowship between the three of us can hold no longer; I will leave you two together, and I alone shall quit it, however I succeed in freeing myself. Such fellowship is vile—I mean to be rid of it! For a King to be partnered in love with open eyes is beneath contempt! Go, the two of you, with God's protection. Live and love as you please: this companionship in love is ended!'

It duly happened as Mark commanded. With moderate distress and cool regret, Tristan and his lady Isolde bowed to their common lord, the King, and then to the royal retainers. Then these steadfast companions took each other by the hand and crossed the court. They told their friend Brangane to keep well, and asked her to remain and pass the time at court until she should hear how they were faring—this they urgently commended to her. Of Isolde's store of gold, Tristan took twenty marks for Isolde and himself for their needs and sustenance. They also brought him his harp, his sword, his hunting-bow, and his horn, which he had asked them to fetch for his journey. In addition he had chosen one of his hounds, a handsome, slender animal called Hiudan, and he took charge of it himself. He commended his followers to God, telling them to return home to his father Rual, all except for Curvenal, whom he retained in his own party. He gave Curvenal his harp to carry, but took his crossbow himself, and his horn and hound too—Hiudan, not Petitcreiu. And so the three of them rode from the court.

Comely Brangane remained in grief and sadness, utterly alone. This sorrowful event and most hateful parting from her two dear friends wrung her heart so cruelly that it was a marvel she did not die of grief. They, too, took their leave of her in great sorrow, except that they left her with Mark and told her to stay for a while, so that she might bring about a reconciliation between themselves and him. . . .

The king at once summoned his councillors and kinsmen, at court and in the country, to ask them for their advice. He told them how he had found the lovers (as I have just narrated) and declared himself no longer willing to believe that Tristan and Isolde had misconducted themselves. His councillors realized immediately which way his wishes were tending, and that he had made his declaration with a mind to having Tristan and Isolde back. Like the wise men they were, they advised him according to his own desires and inclinations, namely, that since he knew of nothing contrary to his honor, he should recall his wife and his nephew and take no further notice of slanderous talk concerning them.

Curvenal was summoned, and since he was conversant with the lovers' affairs, was appointed ambassador to them. Through him the King informed them of his good will and favor, and asked them to return and harbor no malice towards him.

Curvenal repaired there and told them what Mark had in mind. This met with the lovers' approval, and they were glad of it in their hearts. But they were happy far more for the sake of God and their place in society than for any other reason. They returned by the way they had come to the splendor that had been theirs. But never again in all their days were they so close and familiar as they had been, nor did opportunity ever again so favor their amors. On the other hand Mark, his court, and his household were devoted to their honor. Yet Tristan and Isolde were never free and open again. Mark, the waverer, commanded them and urged them for God's sake and his own to keep within the bounds of propriety and to refrain from entangling their ardent looks so tenderly, and no longer to be so intimate or talk with such familiarity as they had been accustomed to do. This command gave the lovers much pain.

Mark was happy once more. For his happiness

he again had in his wife Isolde all that his heart desired—not in honor, but materially. He possessed in his wife neither love nor affection, nor any of the splendid things which God ever brought to pass, except that in virtue of his name she was called 'Queen' and 'Lady' where he by right was King. He accepted it all and invariably treated her with affection as if he were very dear to her.

Here was a case of that foolish, insensate blindness of which a proverb says 'Love's blindness blinds outside and in'. It blinds a man's eyes and mind so that they do not wish to see what they see very well between them. So it had come to be with Mark. He knew it as sure as death and saw full well that his wife Isolde was utterly absorbed in her passion for Tristan, heart and soul, yet he did not wish to know it.

And who is to blame for the life so bare of honor that Mark led with Isolde?—for, believe me, it would be very wrong of anyone to accuse Isolde of deception! Neither she nor Tristan deceived him. He saw it with his own eyes, and knew well enough, without seeing it, that she bore him no affection, yet he cherished her in spite of it! But, you ask, why did he harbor tender feelings towards her? For the reason that many do today: lust and appetite pain that one most obstinately whose lot it is to suffer.

Ah, how many Marks and Isoldes you can see today, if one may broach the topic, who are as blind or blinder in their hearts and eyes! Far from there being none, there are very many who are so possessed by their blindness that they do not wish to know what stands before their eyes, and regard as a delusion the thing they see and know. Who is to blame for their blindness? If we look at it fairly we cannot take the ladies to task for it. When they let their husbands see with open eyes what they are about, they are innocent of any offense towards them. It cannot be said that one is deceived or outwitted by one's wife where the fault is manifest.—In such a case lust has obstructed a man's vision; appetite is the delusion that lies all the time in men's clear-seeing eyes. Whatever is said about blindness, no blindness blinds so utterly as lust and appetite. However

much we pass over it in silence, it is a true word that says: 'In beauty there lurks danger.' Mark was blinded outside and in, in his eyes and in his senses, by the marvellous beauty of Isolde in her prime. He could see nothing in her that he would account a fault, and all that he knew of her was the very best! But to make an end of this. He desired so much to be with her that he overlooked the wrong that he suffered at her hands.

How hard it is to ignore what lies locked and sealed in our hearts! How we long to do what keeps nagging at our thoughts! Our eyes cleave to their quarry. Hearts and eyes often go ranging along the path that has always brought them joy. And if anyone tries to spoil their sport, God knows, he will make them more enamored of it. The more firmly you take it from them, the more they like the game and the closer they will cling.

So it was with Tristan and Isolde. As soon as they were debarred from their pleasures by watchers and guardians and denied them by prohibitions, they began to suffer acutely. Seductive Desire now tormented them in earnest, many times worse than before. Their need of one another was more painful and urgent than it had ever been. The ponderous load of cursed Surveillance weighed on their spirits like a mountain of lead. This devilish machination, Surveillance, enemy of Love, drove them to distraction, especially Isolde. She was in a desperate plight. Tristan's avoidance was death to her. The more her master forbade her any familiarity with him, the more deeply her thoughts were embedded in him.

This must be said of surveillance: those who practise it raise nothing but briars and thorns. This is the maddening fetter that galls reputation and robs many a woman of her honor who would otherwise gladly have kept it, had she received just treatment. But when in fact she is treated unjustly, her desire for honor begins to flag; so far as this is concerned, close-keeping spoils her character. Yet, when all is said, to whatever lengths you take it, surveillance is wasted on a woman in that no man has the power to guard a vicious one. A virtuous woman does not need to be guarded; she will guard herself, as they say. But if a man nevertheless sets a watch on her, believe me, she will hate him. Such a man is bent on his wife's ruin, in body and honor, and, most likely, to such an extent that she will not mend her ways so far that something of what her hedge of thorns has borne will not cling to her ever after. For once having struck root in such kindly soil, the bitter thorn-bush is harder to destroy there than in parched and other places. I am convinced that if one wrongs a willing heart so long that ill-treatment robs it of its fruitfulness it will yield worse ills than one that was always evil. This is true, for I have read it.

A wise man, therefore, that is, one who grants woman her esteem, should keep no watch over her privacy in defiance of her own good will other than by counsel and instruction, and by tenderness and kindness. Let him guard her with that, and may he know this for a fact: he will never keep better watch. For whether she be vicious or good, if a man wrongs a woman too often she may well conceive a whim that he would rather be without. Every worthy man, and whoever aspires to be one, should trust in his wife and himself, so that for love of him she may shun all wantonness.

However much he tries, a man will never extort love from a woman by wrong means—that is how to extinguish it. In matters of love, surveillance is an evil practice. It awakens ruinous anger and leads to a woman's downfall. In my opinion, he who does without prohibitions acts wisely and well. They give rise to much scandal among women. Women do many things, just because they are forbidden, from which they would refrain were it not forbidden. God knows, these same thistles and thorns are inborn in them! Women of this kind are children of mother Eve, who flouted the first prohibition. Our Lord God gave Eve the freedom to do as she pleased with fruits, flowers, and grasses, and with all that there was in Paradise—excepting one thing, which he forbade her on pain of death. Priests tell us that it was the fig-tree. She broke off its fruit and broke God's commandment, losing herself and God. But indeed it is my firm belief today that Eve would never have done so, had it never been forbidden her. In the first thing she ever did, she proved true

to her nature and did what was forbidden! But if one considers the matter, Eve could certainly have done without that one fruit. When all is said and done, she had all the rest at her pleasure without exception, yet she wanted none but that one thing in which she devoured her honor! Thus they are all daughters of Eve who are formed in Eve's image after her. Oh for the man who could forbid all the Eves he might find today, who would abandon themselves and God because they were told not to do something!

And since women are heirs to it, and nature promotes it in them, all honor and praise to the woman who nevertheless succeeds in abstaining! For when a woman grows in virtue despite her inherited instincts and gladly keeps her honor, reputation, and person intact, she is only a woman in name, but in spirit she is a man! One should judge well of all her doings, and honor and esteem them. When a woman lays aside her woman's nature and assumes the heart of a man, it is then the fir drips with honey, the hemlock yields balm, and the roots of the nettles bear roses above ground! What can ever be so perfect in a woman as when, in alliance with honor at her side, she does battle with her body for the rights of both body and honor? She must so direct the combat that she does justice to them both and so attends to each that the other is not neglected. She is no worthy woman who forsakes her honor for her body, or her body for her honor, when circumstance so favors her that she may vindicate them both. Let her deny neither the one nor the other, let her sustain the two, through joy and through sorrow, however she sets about it. Heaven knows, all will be able to gain dignity and respect through great effort. Let her commend her ways to seemly moderation, let her restrain her instincts and adorn herself and her conduct with it! Noble moderation will enhance her honor, person, and reputation.

Of all the things on which the sun ever shone, none is so truly blessed as a woman who has given herself and her life in trust to Moderation, and holds herself in right esteem. For so long as she esteems herself, by the innate fitness of things everyone else will esteem her. When a woman acts against herself and so directs her thoughts that she becomes her own enemy—who, in face of this, is going to love her? When a woman treats herself with contempt and gives proof of this in public, what honor or affection can one accord her? One quenches desire as soon as one feels the urge and yet wishes to bestow the exalted name on such meaningless behavior! No, no, it is not Love, but her deadly enemy, the vile and shameful one, base Lechery! She brings no honor to the name of woman, as a true proverb says: 'She who thinks to love many, by many is unloved!' Let the woman who desires to be loved by all first love herself and then show us all her love-tracks. If they are Love's true traces, all will love her.

People should laud and extol a woman who, in order to please them, shows tender concern for her womanhood. They should crown her with garlands and fête her every day, and enhance their glory in her company. And on whomever she takes courage to bestow her love and person, that man was born most fortunate! He was altogether destined for present bliss, he has the living paradise implanted within his heart! He need have no fear that the thorns will vex him when he reaches for the flowers, or that the prickles will pierce him when he gathers the roses. There are no thorns or prickles there: thistly anger has no business there at all. Rose-like Conciliation has uprooted them all—prickles, thistles, and thorns! In such a paradise nothing buds on the twig or puts on green or grows but what the eye delights in—it all blossoms there by grace of a woman's virtue. There is no other fruit there but love and devotion, honor and worldly esteem. Ah me, in such a paradise, so fecund of joy and so vernal, the man on whom Fortune smiles might find his heart's desire and see his eyes' delight. In what would he be worse off than Tristan and Isolde? If only he would take my word for it, he would not need to exchange his life for Tristan's! For, truly, to whomever a virtuous woman resigns and surrenders her honor and her person, oh, with what deep love she will foster him, how tenderly she will cherish him! How she will clear all his

paths of thorns and thistles and of all the vexations of love! How well she will free him from his sufferings, as no Isolde ever freed her Tristan better! And I firmly believe that, were one to seek as one ought, there would still be living Isoldes in whom one would find in plenty whatever one was able to seek.

Now let us return to Surveillance. As you have heard, the watch that was set on Tristan and Isolde was torment to those lovers, the royal command that they were to avoid each other so afflicted them that never before did they give such thought to their chances of a meeting, until, after all their pangs, they at last accomplished it. But they both reaped suffering from it, and mortal sorrow, too.

It was noon, and the sun was shining strongly, alas, upon their honor. Two kinds of sunshine, the sun and love, shone into the Queen's heart and soul. Her languor and the noonday heat vied with each other to distress her. She therefore intended by some means or other to elude this dissension between her mood and the hour—and was soon deep in trouble.

Tristan was in two minds about whether he wanted Isolde or not. Indeed, her tender treatment disquieted him exceedingly. 'Do I desire her or don't I?' he was constantly asking himself. 'I think I do not, and then I think I do.' But Constancy was always at hand. 'No, lord Tristan, consider your pledge to Isolde, hold fast to faithful Isolde who never swerved an inch from you!' He was at once reclaimed from these thoughts and returned to his mourning for the love of Isolde, the queen of his heart, with the result that his looks and his manner were so changed that, wherever he was, he did nothing but pine, and whenever he joined Isolde and began to converse with her, he grew oblivious of himself and sat sighing endlessly beside her. The signs of his secret sorrow were so plain to see that the whole court declared that his melancholy and suffering were all because of Isolde. Indeed, they were right. The source of Tristan's pining and distress was no other than Isolde. Isolde was his misfortune, yet she was by no means the one whom they believed—she of the White Hands. It was Isolde the Fair, not the Maid of Arundel.

But they all imagined the contrary, and Isolde thought so, too, and was utterly misled by it. For at no time was Tristan consumed with longing for Isolde when the girl was not consumed with a greater longing for him. And so these two passed their time with suffering in which the other had no part. They were both filled with longing and grief, but their grief did not coincide. Their love and affection were unshared. Tristan and the girl Isolde did not keep step with one another in mutual affection. For his sole source of suffering Tristan desired another Isolde, but Isolde desired no other Tristan—she of the White Hands loved and had her thoughts on him alone, her heart and mind were centered upon him. His sorrow was her distress. And when she saw how the color left his face, and that he then began to sigh most tenderly, she looked at him tenderly, too, and sighed with him in company. She bore his suffering with him most companionably, though it did not in the least concern her. His sufferings tor-

mented her so much that they affected him more because of her than on his own account. He was filled with regret for the kindness and affection which she so faithfully entertained for him. It filled him with pity that she had abandoned her thoughts so far to loving him for nothing at all, and had bestowed her heart on him with such vain hopes. Yet he did as courtesy required and devoted himself with all the charm of manner and conversation he could summon to freeing her from her oppression, as he dearly would have done. But she was too far gone in it, and the greater the pains he went to the more he inflamed the girl, from hour to hour, till at last she reached the point where Love won the victory over her, so that she regaled him time out of number with looks and words and glances of such melting tenderness that for the third time he fell into the stress of indecision and the bark that was his heart once more came afloat to toss on the tide of dark thoughts. And little wonder, for, heaven knows, delight that lies laughing up at a man all the time blinds his eyes and thoughts and keeps tugging at his heart.

DANTE ALIGHIERI

IMAGINED LOVE

The difficulties involved in a real erotic relationship, which the medieval poets well understood, were resolved to his own satisfaction by the Italian poet Dante around 1300 in *The New Life*. Here is his account of his love for Beatrice, a woman whom he saw only once in his life when they were both very young. She became for him his erotic ideal and something of a spiritual force as well. Here is the erotic relationship so internalized that it is only a one-person, inward experience. In other words, Dante's approach to romanticism is intellectualized autoerotism. A love fixation stimulates and inspires but avoids tensions, conflicts, and corruption through the transforming experience of love without peril. Not only is the physical side of love eliminated, but its social side as well. Dante is in love with a chimera which is enough to center his life. This is a pretty sophisticated, if highly neurotic approach. It is essentially humanistic— only the personal vibrations are real.

How short this life is, even in health, I began to weep about our wretched state. Sighing deeply, I said to myself: 'One day, inevitably, even your most gracious Beatrice must die.' This thought threw me into such a state of bewilderment that I closed my eyes, and I began, like a person who is delirious, to be tormented by these fantasies. First, as my mind began to wander, I saw faces of dishevelled women, who said: 'You too will die.' And then, after these women, other faces appeared, strange and horrible to look at, saying: 'You are dead.' Then, my imagination still wandering, I came to some place I did not know, where I saw women going about the street, weeping and in disarray, in terrible distress. I seemed to see the sun grow dark and stars turn to such a colour that I thought they were weeping; birds flying in the air fell dead, and the earth trembled with great violence. As I marvelled in my fantasy, growing very much afraid, I thought that a friend came to me and said: 'Do you not know? Your wonderful lady has departed from this world.' Then I began to weep most piteously, and I wept not only in my dreams but with my eyes, which were wet with real tears. I thought I was looking up into the heavens, where I seemed to see a multitude of angels returning to their realm, and before them floated a little cloud of purest white. The angels were singing to the glory of God and the words I seemed to hear were: *Osanna in excelsis,* and that was all I could make out. Then my heart, which was so full of love, said to me: 'It is true that our lady is lying dead.' And when I heard this, I seemed to go to see the body in which that most noble and blessed soul had been; and the illusion was so powerful that I saw my lady lying dead, and women seemed to be covering her, that is, her head, with a white veil. On her face was such an expression of serenity that she seemed to say: 'I now behold the fountainhead of peace.' In my dream I was filled with such serenity at the sight of her that I called on Death and said: 'Sweet Death, come to me; do not be cruel to me, for you must now have grown gracious after being in such a presence! Come now to me, for I greatly desire you; see, I already wear your colour!' When I had seen all the sorrowful necessities completed which it is customary to perform for the bodies of the dead, I thought that I returned to my room; there I looked up towards Heaven and so vivid was my fantasy that as I wept I began to say in my real voice: 'O most beautiful soul, how blessed is he who beholds you!' As I was sobbing out these words and calling on Death to come to me, a kind and gentle young woman who was standing beside my bed, thinking my tears and cries were caused solely by the pain of my illness, began to weep herself, in great alarm. Whereupon, other women who were present in the bedroom noticed that I was weeping by the distress which it was causing her. Sending away from my bedside this young woman, who was closely related to me, they drew near to arouse me, thinking I was dreaming, and said: 'Sleep no longer' and 'Do not be distressed.' And as they spoke, my vivid dream was broken just at the moment when I was about to say: 'O Beatrice, blessed are you!' I had already uttered the words 'O Beatrice' when I opened my eyes with a start and realized I had been dreaming. And though I did utter her name, my voice was so broken by my sobs that I had the impression that no one understood. I felt very much abashed, but in response to Love's prompting, I turned my face towards the women. When they saw me, they began to say: 'He looks as if he were dead.' And they said to each other: 'Let us see if we can rally him.' So they said many things to reassure me and kept asking what had frightened me. When I felt a little comforted, realizing it had all been a dream, I answered: 'I will tell you what happened to me,' and so I told them what I had seen from beginning to end, keeping back only the name of my most gracious lady. Later, when I had recovered from my illness, I decided to write some verses about what I had experienced, as it seemed appropriate as a love-theme. So I wrote this *canzone* which begins: *A lady, youthful . . . ,* the arrangement of which is made clear in the analysis which follows.

A lady, youthful and compassionate,
Much graced with qualities of gentleness,
Who where I called on Death was standing near,
Beholding in my eyes my grievous state,

And hearing babbled words of emptiness,
Began to weep aloud in sudden fear.
And other women, being made aware
Of my condition by the one who cried,
Dismissed her from my side,

And drew, to rally me, about my bed.
'Wake from your sleep,' one said;
And one: 'What has bereft you of all cheer?'
My strange illusion then I put aside,
Calling the name of her for whom I sighed.

THE LEGAL FRAMEWORK: THE JUSTINIAN CODE

How shall society be governed and disputes between individuals and groups be resolved? The aristocratic approach said: leave it to the hero and great landed families. The church said: we will do it in God's name. The middle class didn't know the answer, but they were not inclined to entrust government and law mainly to either the nobility or the church. Between 1050 and 1350, a different solution was developed, that of a legal continuum in which the public law courts resolved problems and a judicially endorsed political authority managed the administration. This is the modern or—shall we say—medieval solution. The continent of Europe and England went different ways in implementing this juristic solution. Each developed its own distinctive legal system and a political and administrative mechanism tied to it. The split in the judicial life of Europe between England and the continent endures to this day, between common law and Roman law countries. As the name implies, continental Roman law is derived from the law of ancient Rome as developed and codified under Byzantine Emperor Justinian I (527–565). His code began to be intensively studied in European law schools in the mid-eleventh century, first at Bologna (the law school there is still in existence) in northern Italy and then in many other places, especially in France. The *Corpus of the Civil Law*—the official title of the Justinian Code—is the last product of east Roman or Byzantine culture to be written in Latin. After the Islamic expansion of the seventh century, Byzantium was cut off from the west and became more and more an oriental civilization outside the ambience of Western civilization. The Justinian Code is the most remarkable single legal achievement of the Western world. In a dozen or so volumes it sums up, along principles of reason, equity, and absolutism, the legal doctrines and practices of a whole complex society. The rediscovery and application of Roman law in medieval Europe was enthusiastically favored by kings, who claimed, often successfully, the power of the Roman emperor; by churchmen, whose own canon law was based on Roman law doctrines and language and who found in the Justinian Code a common judicial culture; and by the bourgeoisie, who welcomed a legal system from a society that recognized the legitimacy and needs of commercial agencies (e.g., contracts, laws of incorporation). The nobility and gentry were less enthusiastic about the introduction of Roman law, and one reason England resisted it was the political strength of the landed classes in that country. Another reason was that Roman law was much more expensive to operate than English common law, because it needed a large number of university-trained judges and attorneys.

University of Bologna (Law) Professor's Lecture to students

THE CORPUS OF THE CIVIL LAW

The Making of the Corpus Iuris Civilis

THE EMPEROR CAESAR, FLAVIUS, JUSTINIANUS, PIOUS, FORTUNATE, RENOWNED, CONQUEROR AND TRIUMPHER, EVER AUGUSTUS, TO TRIBONIANUS HIS QUAESTOR: GREETING. With the aid of God governing Our Empire which was delivered to Us by His Celestial Majesty, We carry on war successfully. We adorn peace and maintain the Constitution of the State, and have such confidence in the Protection of Almighty God that We do not depend upon Our arms, or upon Our soldiers, or upon those who conduct Our Wars, or upon Our own genius, but We solely place Our reliance upon the providence of the Holy Trinity, from which are derived the elements of the entire world and their disposition throughout the globe.

1. Therefore, since there is nothing to be found in all things so worthy of attention as the authority of the law, which properly regulates all affairs both divine and human, and expels all injustice; We have found the entire arrangement of the law which has come down to Us from the foundation of the City of Rome and the times of Romulus, to be so confused that it is extended to an infinite length and is not within the grasp of human capacity; and hence We were first induced to begin by exam-

ining what had been enacted by former most venerated princes, to correct their constitutions, and make them more easily understood; to the end that being included in a single Code, and having had removed all that is superfluous in resemblance and all iniquitous discord, they may afford to all men the ready assistance of their true meaning.

2. After having concluded this work and collected it all in a single volume under Our illustrious name, raising Ourself above small and comparatively insignificant matters, We have hastened to attempt the most complete and thorough amendment of the entire law, to collect and revise the whole body of Roman jurisprudence, and to assemble in one book the scattered treatises of so many authors; which no one else has herebefore ventured to hope for or to expect, and it has indeed been considered by Ourselves a most difficult undertaking, nay, one that was almost impossible; but with Our hands raised to heaven and having invoked the Divine aid, We have kept this object in Our mind, confiding in God who can grant the accomplishment of things which are almost desperate, and can Himself carry them into effect by virtue of the greatness of His power.

3. We have also taken into consideration your marked integrity as disclosed by your labors, and have committed this work to you, after having already received the evidence of your talents in the preparation of Our Code; and We have ordered you in the prosecution of your task, to select as your assistants whomever you might approve of from among the most eloquent professors of law, as well as from the most learned men belonging to the bar of this great city. These, therefore, having been collected and introduced into Our palace, and accepted by Us upon your statements, We have permitted the entire work to be accomplished; it being provided, however, that it should be conducted under the supervision of your most vigilant mind.

4. Therefore We order you to read and revise the books relating to the Roman law drawn up by the jurists of antiquity, upon whom the most venerated princes conferred authority to write and interpret the same; so that from these all the substance may be collected, and, as far as may be possible, there shall remain no laws either similar to or inconsistent with one another, but that there may be compiled from them a summary which will take the place of all. And while others have written books relating to the law, for the reason that their writings have not been adopted by any authorities, or made use of in practice, We do not deem their treatises worthy of Our consideration.

5. Since this compilation is to be ascribed to the extraordinary liberality of Our Imperial will, it ought to constitute a most excellent work and, as it were, be revered as a peculiar and most holy temple of justice. You shall divide the entire law into fifty books, and into a certain number of titles following, as far as may be convenient for you, the arrangement of Our Code, as well as that of the Perpetual Edict, so that nothing may be omitted from the above mentioned collection; and that all the ancient law which has been in a confused condition for almost fourteen hundred years shall be embraced in the said fifty books, and this ancient law, purified by Us, shall be, so to speak, surrounded by a wall, and shall have nothing beyond it. All legal authors shall possess equal authority, and no preference shall be given to any, because all of them are neither superior nor inferior to one another in every respect, but some are of greater or less weight as far as certain subjects are concerned. . . .

6. We desire you to be careful with regard to the following: if you find in the old books anything that is not suitably arranged, superfluous, or incomplete, you must remove all superfluities, supply what is lacking, and present the entire work in regular form, and with as excellent an appearance as possible. You must also observe the following, namely: if you find anything which the ancients have inserted in their old laws or constitutions that is incorrectly worded, you must correct this, and place it in its proper order, so that it may appear to be

true, expressed in the best language, and written in this way in the first place; so that by comparing it with the original text, no one can venture to call in question as defective what you have selected and arranged. Since by an ancient law, which is styled the *Lex Regia,* all the rights and power of the Roman people were transferred to the Emperor, We do not derive Our authority from that of other different compilations, but wish that it shall all be entirely Ours, for how can antiquity abrogate Our laws?

We wish that all these matters after they have been arranged in place shall be observed to such an extent that, although they may have been written by the ancients in a different way than appears in Our collection, no blame shall be imputed the text, but it shall be ascribed to our selection. . . .

7. However, by no means do We allow you to insert into your treatise laws that appearing in ancient works have now fallen into desuetude; since We only desire that legal procedure to prevail which has been most frequently employed, or which long custom has established in this benign City; in accordance with the work of Salvius Julianus which declares that all states should follow the custom of Rome, which is the head of the world, and not that Rome should follow the example of other states; and by Rome is to be understood not only the ancient city, but Our own royal metropolis also, which by the grace of God was founded under the best auguries.

8. Therefore We order that everything shall be governed by these two works, one that of the Imperial Constitutions, the other, that of the law to be interpreted and compiled in a future Code; so that if anything else should be promulgated by Us in the form of an elementary treatise, the uninstructed mind of the student, being nourished by simple matters, may the more readily be conducted to a knowledge of the higher principles of jurisprudence. . . .

9. Let it be your earnest desire, therefore, to do all these things, God willing, by the aid of your own wisdom and that of those other most eloquent men, and bring the work to as excel-

lent and rapid a conclusion as possible; so that it having been completed and digested into fifty books may remain a monument to the great and eternal memory of the undertaking, a proof of the wisdom of Almighty God, to the glory of Our Empire and of your service. Given on the eighteenth day before the *Kalends* of January [December 15], during the Consulship of those most illustrious men Lampadius and Orestes, 530.

General Legal Conceptions

CONCERNING JUSTICE AND LAW. Justice is the constant and perpetual desire to give to each one that to which he is entitled.

1. Jurisprudence is the knowledge of matters divine and human, and the comprehension of what is just and what is unjust.

2. These divisions being generally understood, and We being about to explain the laws of the Roman people, it appears that this may be most conveniently done if separate subjects are at first treated in a clear and simple manner, and afterwards with greater care and exactness; for if We, at once, in the beginning, load the still uncultivated and inexperienced mind of the student with a multitude and variety of details, We shall bring about one of two things; that is, We shall either cause him to abandon his studies, or, by means of excessive labor—and also with the distrust which very frequently discourages young men—conduct him to that point to which, if led by an easier route, he might have been brought more speedily without much exertion and without misgiving.

3. The following are the precepts of the Law: to live honestly, not to injure another, and to give to each one that which belongs to him.

4. There are two branches of this study, namely: public and private. The Public Law is that which concerns the administration of the Roman government; Private Law relates to the interests of individuals. Thus Private Law is said to be threefold in its nature, for it is composed of precepts of Natural Law, of those of the Law of Nations, and of those of the Civil Law.

CONCERNING NATURAL LAW, THE LAW OF NA-TIONS, AND THE CIVIL LAW. Natural Law is that which nature has taught to all animals, for this law is not peculiar to the human race, but applies to all creatures which originate in the air, on the earth, and in the sea. Hence arises the union of the male and the female which we designate marriage; and hence are derived the procreation and the education of children; for we see that other animals also act as though endowed with knowledge of this law.

1. The Civil Law and the Law of Nations are divided as follows. All peoples that are governed by laws and customs make use of the law which is partly peculiar to themselves and partly pertaining to all men; for what each people has established for itself is peculiar to that State, and is styled the Civil Law; being, as it were, the especial law of that individual commonwealth. But the law which natural reason has established among all mankind and which is equally observed among all peoples, is called the Law of Nations, as being that which all nations make use of. . . .

2. Whatever is approved by the sovereign has also the force of law, because by the *Lex Regia,* from whence his power is derived, the people have delegated to him all their jurisdiction and authority. Therefore, whatever the Emperor establishes by means of a Rescript or decrees as a magistrate, or commands by an Edict, stands as law, and these are called Constitutions. Some of these are personal and are not considered as precedents, because the sovereign does not wish them to be such; for any favor he grants on account of merit, or where he inflicts punishment upon anyone or affords him unusual assistance, this affects only the individual concerned; the others, however, as they are of general application unquestionably are binding upon all.

IMPERIAL AUTHORITY. THE EMPEROR JUSTINIAN TO DEMOSTHENES, PRAETORIAN PREFECT. When His Imperial Majesty examines a case for the purpose of deciding it, and renders an opinion in the pres-

ence of the parties in interest, let all the judges in Our Empire know that this law will apply, not only to the care with reference to which it was promulgated, but also to all that are similar. For what is greater or more sacred than the Imperial Majesty? Or who is swollen with so much pride that he can despise the royal decisions, when the founders of the ancient law have decided that the constitutions which have emanated from the Imperial Throne have plainly and clearly the force of law?

1. Therefore, as We have found that a doubt existed in the ancient laws as to whether a decision of the Emperor should be considered a law, We have come to the conclusion that this vain subtlety is not only contemptible, but should be suppressed.

    For this reason We hold that every interpretation of the laws by the Emperor, whether in answer to requests made to him, or whether given in judgment, or in any other way whatsoever, shall be considered valid, and free from all ambiguity; for if, by the present enactment, the Emperor alone can make laws, it should also be the province of the Imperial Dignity alone to interpret them. For when any doubt arises in Litigation on account of the conflicting opinions of the legal authorities, and they do not think that they are either qualified or able to decide the question, why should they have recourse to Us? And wherefore should all the ambiguities which may exist with reference to the laws be brought to Our ears, if the right to interpret them does not belong to Us? Or who appears to be capable of solving legal enigmas, and explaining them to all persons, unless he who alone is permitted to be legislator? Therefore, these ridiculous doubts having been cast aside, the Emperor shall justly be regarded as the sole maker and interpreter of the laws; and this provision shall in no way prejudice the founders of ancient jurisprudence, because the Imperial Majesty conferred this privilege upon them.

Given on the sixth day before the *Kalends* of November [October 27], during the Consulate of Decius, 529.

WALTER MAP

THE LAWYER-KING, HENRY II

The distinctive English common law system was largely the creation of the reign of the first Angevin (or Plantagenet) king, Henry II (1154–1189), the second husband of Eleanor of Aquitaine (she was eleven years older than him, leading eventually to marital discord). It was during this reign that the use of the unpaid jury of gentry became the central institution in English law. Henry personally played a major role in the Angevin legal revolution. Here is a portrait of him by Walter Map, a royal courtier and minor government official who had the opportunity to observe Henry closely for several decades. Henry's personality is that of a successful lawyer today in one of the major American law firms.

I saw the beginning of his reign and his subsequent life, which in many respects was commendable. He was a little taller than the tallest men of middle height, and was blessed with soundness of limb and comeliness of face, one, in fact, whom men flocked to gaze upon, though they had scrutinized him a thousand times already. In agility of limb he was second to none, failing in no feat which anyone else could perform; with no polite accomplishment was he unacquainted; he had skill of letters as far as was fitting or practically useful, and had a knowledge of all the tongues used from the French sea to the Jordan, but spoke only Latin and French. He had discretion in the making of laws and the ordering of all his government, and was a clever deviser of decisions in unusual and dark cases: affable, sober, and modest: tolerant of the discomforts of dust and mud; when oppressed by importunate complaints or provoked by abuse, bearing it all in silence. On the other hand, he was always on the move, travelling in unbearably long stages, like a post, and in this respect merciless beyond measure to the household that accompanied him: a great connoisseur of hounds and hawks, and most greedy of that vain sport: perpetually wakeful and at work. When troubled by erotic dreams he would curse his body which neither toil nor abstinence could avail to tame or reduce. Further, we used to ascribe his exertions, not to fickleness, but to his fear of growing too fat. . . .

Now the aforesaid King Henry II was distinguished by many good traits and blemished by some few faults. There is a fault which, as I have already said, he contracted from his mother's teaching: he is wasteful of time over the affairs of his people, and so it comes about that many die before they get their matters settled, or leave the court depressed and thwarted, driven by hunger. Another fault is that when he makes a stay anywhere (away from home), which rarely occurs, he does not allow himself to be seen as honest men would have him do, but shuts himself up within, and is only accessible to those who seem unworthy of such ready access. There is a third fault, that he is intolerant of quiet and does not in pity refrain from troubling almost the half of Christendom. In these three ways he goes wrong: in other respects he is very good, and in all amiable. There does not seem to be anyone beside him possessed of such good temper and affability. Whatever way he goes out he is seized upon by the crowds and pulled hither and thither, pushed whither he would not, and, surprising to say, listens to each man with patience, and though assaulted by all with shouts and pullings and rough pushings, does not challenge anyone for it, nor show any appearance of anger, and when he is hustled beyond bearing silently retreats to some place of quiet. He does nothing in a proud or overbearing fashion, is sober, modest, pious, trustworthy and careful, generous and successful, and ready to honour the deserving.

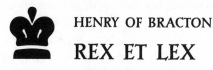

HENRY OF BRACTON

REX ET LEX

In his treatise on *The Laws and Customs of England,* written in the 1240s, Henry of Bracton, Chief Justice of the Common Pleas, takes pains to interpret the Justinian Code's dictum that what pleases the prince has the force of law in such a way that he actually affirms a very different proposition: in England law rules, not the personal will of the king. The king's power to make law extends only in so far as the king furthers the public good. This is an early statement of the English common law doctrine of juristic liberalism, or what the English called the doctrine of the king's two bodies—the king has two personalities, and his political personality (the king in parliament, the king under the law) is superior to his natural personality (his private will).

What has pleased the prince is law [Justinian Code]. This is not what has been rashly presumed to be the personal will of the king, but what has been rightly defined by the counsel and council of the king's magnates, and after deliberation and council concerning it.

The king's power refers to making law and not injury. And since the king is the author of law, an opportunity to injury and lawlessness should not be nascent at the very place where the laws are born.

The king has no other power, since he is the vicar of God and his minister on earth, except this alone which he derives from the law.

The king himself must be, not under Man but under God and the law, because the law makes the king. . . . For there is no king where arbitrary will dominates, and not the law. And that he should be under the law because he is God's vicar, becomes evident through the similitude with Jesus Christ in whose stead he governs on earth. For He, God's true Mercy, though having at His disposal many means to recuperate ineffably the human race, chose before all other expedients the one which applied for the destruction of the devil's work; that is, not the strength of power, but the maxim of Justice, and therefore he wished to be under the law in order to redeem those under the law. For he did not wish to apply force, but reason and judgement.

MAGNA CARTA

Behind Bracton's doctrine that in England the law is superior to the personal will of the king was the Angevin legal revolution and its making of the jury the central institution in English law. Behind Bracton's doctrine was also Magna Carta, the Great Charter of 1215, in which Stephen Langton, the Archbishop of Canterbury, and a majority of the higher nobility, the king's barons, forced King John to approve a document limiting his power. Nearly all of the provisions of Magna Carta deal with specific grievances against the royal government in matters of taxation and other administrative matters. But two of the clauses of Magna Carta are general in nature and make the king promise to observe the law of the land and its due process, and to provide fair and equal justice to all. Although John soon repudiated Magna Carta, precipitating a war with his barons that was cut short by his early death, the government of his son Henry III reissued and confirmed the document in 1225, omitting some of the more radical tax and administrative provisions. But the two general clauses remained in the document, which came to be recognized anachronistically by 1300 as the first official parliamentary statute in England and therefore as a sort of fundamental constitutional law. Here is a description of the making of Magna Carta in 1215 by a well-informed contemporary historian, Roger Wendover, and the two general clauses of the document.

A.D. 1215; which was the seventeenth year of the reign of king John; he held his court at Winchester at Christmas for one day, after which he hurried to London, and took up his abode at the New Temple; and at that place the above-mentioned nobles came to him in gay military array, and demanded the confirmation of the liberties and laws of king Edward, with other liberties granted to them and to the kingdom and church of England, as were contained in the charter, and above-mentioned laws of Henry the First; they also asserted that, at the time of his absolution at Winchester, he had promised to restore those laws and ancient liberties, and was bound by his own oath to observe them. The king, hearing the bold tone of the barons in making this demand, much feared an attack from them, as he saw that they were prepared for battle; he however made answer that their demands were a matter of importance and difficulty, and he therefore asked a truce till the end of Easter, that he might, after due deliberation, be able to satisfy them as well as the dignity of his crown. After much discussion on both sides, the king at length, although unwillingly, procured the archbishop of Canterbury, the bishop of Ely, and William Marshal, as his sureties, that on the day pre-agreed on he would, in all reason, satisfy them all, on which the nobles returned to their homes. The king however, wishing to take precautions against the future, caused all the nobles throughout England to swear fealty to him alone against all men, and to renew their homage to him; and, the better to take care of himself, he, on the day of St. Mary's purification, assumed the cross of our Lord, being induced to this more by fear than devotion . . .

In Easter week of this same year, the above-mentioned nobles assembled at Stamford, with horses and arms; for they had now induced almost all the nobility of the whole kingdom to join them, and constituted a very large army; for in their army there were computed to be two thousand knights, besides horse soldiers, attendants, and foot soldiers, who were variously equipped . . . all of these being united by oath, were supported by the concurrence of Stephen archbishop of Canterbury, who was at their head. The king at this time was awaiting the arrival of his nobles at Oxford. On the Monday next after the octaves of Easter, the said barons assembled in the town of Brackley; and when the king learned this, he sent the archbishop of Canterbury, and William Marshal earl of Pembroke, with some other prudent men, to them to inquire what the laws and liberties were which they demanded. The barons then delivered to the messengers a paper, containing in great measure the laws and ancient customs of the kingdom, and declared that, unless the king immediately granted them and confirmed them under his own seal, they would, by taking possession of his fortresses, force him to give them sufficient satisfaction as to their before-named demands. The archbishop with his fellow messengers then carried the paper to the king, and read to him the heads of the paper one by one throughout. The king when he heard the purport of these heads, derisively said, with the greatest indignation, "Why, amongst these unjust demands, did not the barons ask for my kingdom also? Their demands are vain and visionary, and are unsupported by any plea of reason whatever." And at length he angrily declared with an oath, that he would never grant them such liberties as would render him their slave. . . .

As the archbishop and William Marshal could

not by any persuasions induce the king to agree to their demands, they returned by the king's order to the barons, and duly reported all they had heard from the king to them; and when the nobles heard what John said, they appointed Robert Fitz-Walter commander of their soldiers, giving him title of "Marshal of the army of God and the holy church," and then, one and all flying to arms, they directed their forces toward Northampton. . . .

King John, when he saw that he was deserted by almost all, so that out of his regal superabundance of followers he scarcely retained seven knights, was much alarmed lest the barons would attack his castles and reduce them without difficulty, as they would find no obstacle to their so doing; and he deceitfully pretended to make peace for a time with the aforesaid barons, and sent William Marshal earl of Pembroke, with other trustworthy messengers, to them, and told them that, for the sake of peace, and for the exaltation and honour of the kingdom, he would willingly grant them the laws and liberties they required; he also sent word to the barons by these same messengers, to appoint a fitting day and

place to meet and carry all these matters into effect. The king's messengers then came in all haste to London, and without deceit reported to the barons all that had been deceitfully imposed on them; they in their great joy appointed the fifteenth of June for the king to meet them, at a field lying between Staines and Windsor. Accordingly, at the time and place pre-agreed on, the king and nobles came to the appointed conference, and when each party had stationed themselves apart from the other, they began a long discussion about terms of peace and the aforesaid liberties. . . . At length, after various points on both sides had been discussed, king John, seeing that he was inferior in strength to the barons, without raising any difficulty, granted the underwritten laws and liberties, and confirmed them by his charter. . . .

No free man shall be taken or imprisoned or dispossessed, or outlawed, or banished, or in any way destroyed, nor will we go upon him, nor send upon him, except by the legal judgment of his peers or by the law of the land.

To no one will we sell, to no one will we deny, or delay right or justice.

ST. THOMAS AQUINAS
JURISTIC LIBERALISM

The idea of the rule of law enshrined in Magna Carta and Bracton's legal theory was also advocated, in a more philosophical fashion, by St. Thomas Aquinas (d. 1274), the Neapolitan nobleman turned Dominican friar who was professor of theology at the University of Paris, founder of one of the two leading philosophical schools of the later Middle Ages, and, since the sixteenth century, the official philosopher of the Catholic Church. Similar to Archbishop Stephen Langton and Justice Henry of Bracton in England, Aquinas argues for a theory of juristic liberalism: The purpose of law is the common good and universal happiness, and all positive law of the state must conform to natural law (the universal law of reason) and eternal (divine) law. Aquinas is here advocating an ethical or formalistic approach to law as against the voluntarist or pragmatic view, which regards law as the dictate of sovereign power. Aquinas therefore stands at the head of a long list of liberal juristic philosophers that culminates in John Locke and Thomas Jefferson. It is significant that Stephen Langton had been a professor at the University of Paris some years before becoming archbishop of Canterbury, and that Henry of Bracton also studied there. It is therefore likely that Aquinas,

Langton, and Bracton are, in their legal ideas, products of an intellectual movement of juristic liberalism in the theology and philosophy faculty at Paris in the first half of the thirteenth century. That this ideology of juristic liberalism took practical root in England and not on the continent is due to its conformity with the institutional results of Henry II's legal revolution and with Magna Carta, and on the other side the domination of continental legal systems by Roman law with its antiliberal juristic absolutism.

The Trial of Robert III of Artois, Count of Beaumont, with Philip VI presiding over the court of peers

Law is a rule and measure of acts whereby man is induced to act or is restrained from acting: for *lex* (law) is derived from *ligare* (to bind), because it binds one to act. Now the rule and measure of human acts is the reason, which is the first principle of human acts, as is evident from what has been stated above, since it belongs to the reason to direct to the end, which is the first principle in all matters of action. . . .

The law belongs to that which is a principle of human acts, because it is their rule and measure. Now as reason is a principle of human acts, so in reason itself there is something which is the principle in respect of all the rest: wherefore to this principle chiefly and mainly law must needs be referred. Now the first principle in practical matters, which are the object of the practical reason, is the last end: and the last end of human life is bliss or happiness. . . .

Consequently the law must needs regard principally the relationship to happiness. Moreover, since every part is ordained to the whole, as imperfect to perfect; and since one man is a part of the perfect community, the law must needs regard properly the relationship to universal happiness. . . .

A command denotes an application of a law to matters regulated by the law. Now the order to the common good, at which the law aims, is applicable to particular ends. And in this way commands are given even concerning particular matters.

Actions are indeed concerned with particular matters: but those particular matters are referable to the common good, not as to a common genus or species, but as to a common final cause, according as the common good is said to be the common end.

Just as nothing stands firm with regard to the speculative reason except that which is traced back to the first indemonstrable principles, so nothing stands firm with regard to the practical reason, unless it be directed to the last end which is the common good: and whatever stands to reason in this sense, has run on the nature of a law. . . .

Law is nothing else but a dictate of practical reason emanating from the ruler who governs a perfect community. Now it is evident, granted that the world is ruled by divine providence, as was stated in the first part, that the whole community of the universe is governed by divine reason. Wherefore the very idea of the government of things in God the Ruler of the universe, has the nature of a law. And since the divine reason's conception of things is not subject to time but is eternal . . . therefore it is that this kind of law must be called eternal. . . .

Law, being a rule and measure, can be in a person in two ways: in one way, as in him that rules and measures; in another way, as in that which is ruled and measured, since a thing is ruled and measured, in so far as it partakes of the rule or measure. Wherefore, since all things subject to divine providence are ruled and measured by the eternal law, as was stated above; it is evident that all things partake somewhat of the eternal law, in so far as, namely, from its being imprinted on them, they derive their respective inclinations to their proper acts and ends. . . . Now among all others, the rational creature is subject to divine

providence in the most excellent way, in so far as it partakes of a share of providence, by being provident both for itself and for others. Wherefore it has a share of the eternal reason, whereby it has a natural inclination to its proper act and end: and this participation of the eternal law in the rational creature is called the natural law. Hence the Psalmist, after saying, *Offer up the sacrifice of justice*, as though someone asked what the works of justice are, adds: *Many say, Who showeth us good things?* In answer to which question he says: *The light of Thy countenance, O Lord, is signed upon us;* thus implying that the light of natural reason, whereby we discern what is good and what is evil, which is the function of the natural law, is nothing else than an imprint on us of the divine light. It is therefore evident that the natural law is nothing else than the rational creature's participation of the eternal law.

GERVASE OF CANTERBURY

ARCHITECTS AT WORK

Around the year 1000, ecclesiastical leaders and communities began to erect large stone churches. The purpose was not only to celebrate the glory of God and the piety of a particular saint to whom the church was customarily dedicated. These stone churches had a very practical purpose: They were intended to be the amphitheaters where the liturgical ritual of Catholic Christianity could be celebrated using song, brilliant displays of light and jewels at the altar, and even perfumed smell (incense). These multimedia exhibitions, to which preaching of sermons was added, were intended to impress the laity with the incomparable grandeur of church manifestations of Christian faith. The stone churches of the eleventh century were low, flat structures that emphasized the horizontal plane—this has been called the Romanesque style. The architectural engineering of the period did not allow for buildings that rose high off the ground. After the conquest of England by the Norman French in 1066, the vigorous and wealthy French bishops and abbots brought over by the Norman kings employed architects from northern France who elevated the roof of the large stone churches that these bishops commissioned. They also placed high-pillared towers at the corners of the churches. This innovative style, emphasizing the vertical rather than the horizontal plane, is called Norman Perpendicular by art historians. In 1140, there was dedicated at St. Denis, the royal abbey of France just outside Paris (today well within the city), an extensive renovation of an old church that now provided a raised clerestory so that light could bathe the alter. Another feature of this new Parisian style, eventually called Gothic by unfriendly fifteenth-century art critics, was a large rose window over the front door.

The Abbot of St. Denis, Suger, was also the principal architect of this new style that became standard in northern France and western Germany over the next century. But the Norman Perpendicular style in early twelfth-century England had begun the shift to emphasize the vertical plane and high windows.

In 1174, the great Norman French edifice of Christ Church, Canterbury, where the monastic community that the archbishop headed conducted their services, suffered a severe fire, requiring extensive reconstruction. In this account by Gervase of Canterbury, a member of the Christ Church community, a brilliant and courageous French architect, William of Sens, was brought in to direct the reconstruction. The account reveals that good architects were hard to find, were well paid, and that the architect personally supervised the construction work, taking physical risks that could have resulted in severe injury. William of Sens became a fabled figure and is the subject of a modern novel. He is a kind of romantic hero.

T hen the people and the monks assemble in haste, they draw water, they brandish their hatchets, they run up the stairs, full of eagerness to save the church, already, alas! beyond their help. But when they reach the roof and perceive the black smoke and scorching flames that pervade it throughout, they abandon the attempt in despair, and thinking only of their own safety, make all haste to descend.

And now that the fire had loosened the beams from the pegs that bound them together, the half-burnt timbers fell into the choir below upon the seats of the monks; the seats, consisting of a great mass of wood-work, caught fire, and thus the mischief grew worse and worse. And it was marvellous, though sad, to behold how that glorious choir itself fed and assisted the fire that was destroying it. For the flames multiplied by this mass of timber, and extending upwards full fifteen cubits [25 feet] scorched and burnt the walls, and more especially injured the columns of the church. . . .

The people were astonished that the Almighty should suffer such things, and maddened with excess of grief and perplexity, they tore their hair and beat the walls and pavement of the church with their heads and hands, blaspheming the Lord and His saints, the patrons of the church; and many, both of laity and monks, would rather have laid down their lives than that the church should have so miserably perished.

For not only was the choir consumed in the

Abbot Suger Kneeling

fire, but also the infirmary, with the chapel of St. Mary, and several other offices in the court; moreover many ornaments and goods of the church were reduced to ashes. . . .

The brotherhood sought counsel as to how and in what manner the burnt church might be repaired, but without success; for the columns of the church, commonly termed the *pillars,* were exceedingly weakened by the heat of the fire, and were scaling in pieces and hardly able to stand, so that they frightened even the wisest out of their wits.

French and English artificers were therefore summoned, but even these differed in opinion. On the one hand, some undertook to repair the aforesaid columns without mischief to the walls above. On the other hand, there were some who asserted that the whole church must be pulled down if the monks wished to exist in safety. This opinion, true as it was, excruciated the monks with grief, and no wonder, for how could they hope that so great a work should be completed in their days by any human ingenuity.

However, amongst the other workmen there had come a certain William of Sens, a man active and ready, and as a workman most skilful both in wood and stone. Him, therefore, they retained, on account of his lively genius and good reputation, and dismissed the others. And to him, and to the providence of God was the execution of the work committed.

And he, residing many days with the monks and carefully surveying the burnt walls in their upper and lower parts, within and without, did yet for some time conceal what he found necessary to be done, lest the truth should kill them in their present state of pusillanimity.

But he went on preparing all things that were needful for the work, either of himself or by the agency of others. And when he found that the monks began to be somewhat comforted, he ventured to confess that the pillars rent with the fire and all that they supported must be destroyed if the monks wished to have a safe and excellent building. At length they agreed, being convinced by reason and wishing to have the work as good as he promised, and above all things to live in

security; thus they consented patiently, if not willingly, to the destruction of the choir.

And now he addressed himself to the procuring of stone from beyond sea. He constructed ingenious machines for loading and unloading ships, and for drawing cement and stones. He delivered molds for shaping the stones to the sculptors who were assembled, and diligently prepared other things of the same kind. The choir thus condemned to destruction was pulled down, and nothing else was done in this year. . . .

[A.D. 1177] In the third year he placed two pillars on each side, the two extreme ones of which he decorated with marble columns placed around them, and because at that place the choir and crosses were to meet, he constituted these principal pillars. To which, having added the keystones and vault, he intermingled the lower triforium from the great tower to the aforesaid pillars, that is, as far as the cross, with many marble columns. Over which he adjusted another triforium of other materials, and also the upper windows. And in the next place, three *claves* [bosses] of the great vault, from the tower, namely, as far as the crosses. All which things appeared to us and to all who saw them, incomparable and most worthy of praise. And at so glorious a beginning we rejoiced and conceived good hopes of the end, and provided for the acceleration of the work with diligence and spirit. Thus was the third year occupied and the beginning of the fourth.

[A.D. 1178] In the summer of which, commencing from the cross, he erected ten pillars, that is, on each side five. Of which the two first were ornamented with marble columns to correspond with the other two pinicipal one. Upon these ten he placed the arches and vaults. And having, in the next place, completed on both sides the triforia and upper windows, he was, at the beginning of the fifth year, in the act of preparing with machines for the turning of the great vault, when suddenly the beams broke under his feet, and he fell to the ground, stones and timbers accompanying his fall, from the height of the capitals of the upper vault, that is to say, of fifty feet. Thus sorely bruised by the blows from the beams and stones, he was rendered helpless alike to himself and for the work, but no other person than himself was in the least injured. Against the master only was this vengeance of God or spite of the devil directed.

The master, thus hurt, remained in his bed for some time under medical care in expectation of recovering, but was deceived in this hope, for his health amended not. Nevertheless, as the winter approached, and it was necessary to finish the upper vault, he gave charge of the work to a certain ingenious and industrious monk, who was the overseer of the masons; an appointment whence much envy and malice arose, because it made this young man appear more skilful than richer and more powerful ones. But the master reclining in bed commanded all things that should be done in order. And thus was completed the ciborium [canopy] between the four principal pillars. In the keystone of this ciborium the choir and crosses seem as it were to meet. Two ciboria on each side were formed before the winter; when heavy rains beginning stopped the work. In these operations the fourth year was occupied and the beginning of the fifth. But on the eighth day from the said fourth year, on the idus of September, there happened an eclipse of the sun at about the sixth hour, and before the master's accident.

And the master, perceiving that he derived no benefit from the physicians, gave up the work, and crossing the sea, returned to his home in France. And another succeeded him in the charge of the works; William by name, English by nation, small in body, but in workmanship of many kinds acute and honest.

[A.D. 1179] He in the summer of the fifth year finished the cross on each side, that is, the south and the north, and turned the ciborium which is above the great Altar, which the rains of the previous year had hindered, although all was prepared. Moreover, he laid the foundation for the enlargement of the church at the eastern part, because a chapel of St. Thomas [Becket] was to be built there.

For this was the place assigned to him; namely, the chapel of the Holy Trinity, where he celebrated his first mass, where he was wont to prostrate himself with tears and prayers, under whose crypt for so many years he was buried, where God for his merits had performed so many miracles, where poor and rich, kings and princes, had worshipped him, and whence the sound of his praises had gone forth into all lands.

The master William began, on account of these foundations, to dig in the cemetery of the monks, from whence he was compelled to disturb the bones of many holy monks. These were carefully collected and deposited in a large trench, in that corner which is between the chapel and the south side of the infirmary house. Having, therefore, formed a most substantial foundation for the exterior wall with stone and cement, he erected the wall of the crypt as high as the bases of the windows.

Thus was the fifth year employed and the beginning of the sixth.

[A.D. 1180] In the beginning of the sixth year from the fire, and at the time when the works were resumed, the monks were seized with a violent longing to prepare the choir, so that they might enter it at the coming Easter. And the master, perceiving their desires, set himself manfully to work, to satisfy the wishes of the convent. He constructed, with all diligence, the wall which encloses the choir and presbytery. He erected the three altars of the presbytery. He carefully prepared a resting-place for St. Dunstan and St. Elfege. A wooden wall to keep out the weather was set up transversely between the penultimate pillars at the eastern part, and had three glass windows in it.

The choir, thus hardly completed even with the greatest labour and diligence, the monks were resolved to enter on Easter Eve with the new fire. As all that was required could not be fully performed on the Saturday because of the solemnities of that sacred day, it became necessary that our holy fathers and patrons, St. Dunstan and St. Elfege, the co-exiles of the monks, should be transferred to the new choir beforehand. Prior Alan, therefore, taking with him nine of the brethren of the church in whom he could trust, went by night to the tombs of the saints, that he might not be incommoded by a crowd, and having locked the doors of the church, he commanded the stonework that enclosed them to be taken down.

The monks and servants of the church, therefore, in obedience to the Prior's commands, took the structure to pieces, opened the stone coffins of the saints, and bore their relics to the *vestiarium*. Then, having removed the cloths in which they had been wrapped, and which were half consumed from age and rottenness, they covered them with other and more handsome palls, and bound them with linen bands. They bore the saints, thus prepared, to their altars, and deposited them in wooden chests, covered within and without with lead; which chests, thus lead-covered, and strongly bound with iron, were enclosed in stone-work that was consolidated with melted lead. Queen Ediva also, who had been placed under the altar of the holy cross after the fire, was similarly conveyed to the vestiarium.

[Wednesday night, April 16] These things were done on the night preceding the fifth feria before the holy Easter; that is, on the sixteenth calend of May. On the morrow, however, when this translation of the saints became known to the whole convent, they were exceedingly astonished and indignant that it should have been done without their consent, for they had intended that the translation of the fathers should have been performed with great and devout solemnity.

They cited the prior and those who were with him, before the venerable Archbishop Richard, to answer for the slight thus presumptuously cast upon themselves and the holy patrons of the church, and endeavoured to compel the prior and his assistants to renounce their offices. But by the intervention of the archbishop and other men of authority, and after due apology and repentance, the convent was appeased; and harmony being thus restored, the service of Holy Saturday was performed in the chapter-house, because the station of the monks and the altar which had been in the nave of the church, were removed to prepare for the solemnities of the following Easter Sunday. About the sixth hour the archbishop in cope and mitre, and the convent in albs, according to the custom of the church, went in procession to the new fire, and having consecrated it, proceeded

towards the new choir with the appointed hymn. At the door of the church which opens to the martyrium of St. Thomas, the archbishop reverently received from a monk the pix [vessor], with the Eucharist, which was usually suspended over the great Altar. This he carried to the great Altar of the new choir. Thus our Lord went before us into Galilee, that is, in our transmigration to the new church. The remainder of the offices that appertain to the day were devoutly celebrated. And then the pontiff, standing at the Altar and vested with the infula, began the Te Deum laudamus; and the bells ringing, the convent took up the song with great joy, and shedding sweet tears, they praised God with voice and heart for all His benefits. . . .

It has been above stated, that after the fire nearly all the old portions of the choir were destroyed and changed into somewhat new and of a more noble fashion. The differences between the two works may now be enumerated. The pillars of the old and new work are alike in form and thickness but different in length. For the new pillars were elongated by almost twelve feet. In the old capitals the work was plain, in the new ones exquisite in sculpture. There the circuit of the choir had twenty-two pillars, here are twenty-eight. There the arches and every thing else was plain, or sculptured with an axe and not with a chisel. But here almost throughout is appropriate sculpture. Not marble columns were there, but here are innumerable ones. There, in the circuit around the choir, the vaults were plain, but here they are arch-ribbed and have keystones. There a wall set upon pillars divided the crosses from the choir, but here the crosses are separated from the choir by no such partition, and converge together in one keystone, which is placed in the middle of the great vault which rests on the four principal pillars. There, there was a ceiling of wood decorated with excellent painting, but here is a vault beautifully constructed of stone and light tufa. There, was a single triforium, but here are two in the choir and a third in the aisle of the church. All which will be better understood from inspection than by any description.

This must be made known, however, that the new work is higher than the old by so much as the upper windows of the body of the choir, as well as of its aisles, are raised above the marble tabling.

And as in future ages it may be doubtful why the breadth which was given to the choir next the tower should be so much contracted at the head of the church, it may not be useless to explain the causes thereof. One reason is, that the two towers of St. Anselm and of St. Andrew, place in the circuit on each side of the old church, would not allow the breadth of the choir to proceed in the direct line. Another reason is, that it was agreed upon and necessary that the chapel of St. Thomas should be erected at the head of the church, where the chapel of the Holy Trinity stood, and this was much narrower than the choir.

The master, therefore, not choosing to pull down the said towers, and being unable to move them entire, set out the breadth of the choir in a straight line, as far as the beginning of the towers. Then, receding slightly on either side from the towers, and preserving as much as he could the breadth of the passage outside the choir on account of the processions which were there frequently passing, he gradually and obliquely drew in his work, so that from opposite the altar, it might begin to contract, and from thence, at the third pillar, might be so narrowed as to coincide with the breadth of the chapel, which was named of the Holy Trinity. Beyond these, four pillars were set on the sides at the same distance as the last, but of a different form; and beyond these other four were arranged in a circle, and upon these the superposed work (of each side) was brought together and terminated. This is the arrangement of the pillars. . . all of which may be more clearly and pleasantly seen by the eyes than taught in writing.

GOLIARDIC VERSE

The emergence of the universities in the twelfth century produced a distinctive new population, the students. By 1175 universities weren't much different from such institutions today. The liberal arts were treated as introductory programs, ill-taught by underpaid junior faculty and graduate students. Campus power and consumer student demand rested with the professional schools of law and medicine, although the Dominican and Franciscan orders of friars in the thirteenth century supported chairs for a few distinguished theologians and philosophers. The students, ill-housed, ill-fed, and exploited by the townspeople, and thereby prone to riot, were there to prepare for a career, mainly in administrative jobs in church or state. Out of this febrile atmosphere came student literature complaining about ill treatment and expressing cynicism about adult society. The best of this genre is the Goliardic poetry celebrating wine and women. "Golias" was a synonym for the devil. The following *Confessions of Golias* was actually written by a middle-aged alumnus who had a good job in the German church.

Boiling in my spirit's veins
    With fierce indignation,
From my bitterness of soul
    Springs self-revelation:
Framed am I of flimsy stuff,
    Fit for levitation,
Like a thin leaf which the wind
    Scatters from its station.

While it is the wise man's part
    With deliberation
On a rock to base his heart's
    Permanent foundation,
With a running river I
    Find my just equation,
Which beneath the self-same sky
    Hath no habitation.

Carried am I like a ship
    Left without a sailor,
Like a bird that through the air
    Flies where tempests hale her;
Chains and fetters hold me not,
    Naught avails a jailer;
Shall I find my fellows out
    Toper, gamester, railer.

To my mind all gravity
    Is a grave subjection;
Sweeter far than honey are
    Jokes and free affection.
All that Venus bids me do,
    Do I with erection,
For she ne'er in heart of man
    Dwelt with dull dejection.

Down the broad road do I run,
    As the way of youth is;
Snare myself in sin, and ne'er
    Think where faith and truth is,
Eager far for pleasure more
    Than soul's health, the sooth is
For this flesh of mine I care,
    Seek not ruth where ruth is.

Prelate, most discreet of priests,
    Grant me absolution!
Dear's the death whereof I die,
    Sweet my dissolution;
For my heart is wounded by
    Beauty's soft suffusion;
All the girls I come not nigh,
    Mine are in illusion.

'Tis most arduous to make
    Nature's self surrender;
Seeing girls, to blush and be
    Purity's defender!
We young men our longings ne'er
    Shall to stern law render,
Or preserve our fancies from
    Bodies smooth and tender.

Who, when into fire he falls,
    Keeps himself from burning?
Who within Pavia's walls
    Fame of chaste is earning?
Venus with her finger calls

Youth at every turning,
    Snares them with her eyes, and thralls
    With her amorous yearning.

If you brought Hippolitus
    To Pavia Sunday,
He'd not be Hippolitus
    On the following Monday;
Venus there keeps holiday
    Every day as one day;
'Mid these towers in no tower dwells
    Venus Verecunda.

In the second place I own
    To the vice of gaming:
Cold indeed outside I seem,
    Yet my soul is flaming:
But when once the dice-box hath
    Stripped me to my shaming,
Make I songs and verses fit
    For the world's acclaiming.

In the third place, I will speak
    Of the tavern's pleasure;
For I never found nor find
    There the least displeasure;
Nor shall find it till I greet
    Angels without measure,
Singing requiems for the souls
    In eternal leisure.

In the public-house to die
    Is my resolution;
Let wine to my lips be nigh
    At life's dissolution:
That will make the angels cry,
    With glad elocution,
"Grant this toper, God on high,
    Grace and absolution!"

With the cup the soul lights up,
    Inspirations flicker;
Nectar lifts the soul on high
    With its heavenly ichor:
To my lips a sounder taste
    Hath the tavern's liquor
Than the wine a village clerk
    Waters for the vicar.

Nature gives to every man
    Some gift serviceable;
Write I never could nor can
    Hungry at the table;
Fasting, any stripling to
    Vanquish me is able;
Hunger, thirst, I liken to
    Death that ends the fable.

Nature gives to every man
    Gifts as she is willing;
I compose my verses when
    Good wine I am swilling,
Wine the best for jolly guest
    Jolly hosts are filling;
From such wine rare fancies fine
    Flow like dews distilling.

Such my verse is wont to be
    As the wine I swallow;
No ripe thoughts enliven me
    While my stomach's hollow;
Hungry wits on hungry lips
    Like a shadow follow,
But when once I'm in my cups,
    I can beat Apollo.

Never to my spirit yet
    Flew poetic vision
Until first my belly had
    Plentiful provision;
Let but Bacchus in the brain
    Take a strong position,
Then comes Phoebus flowing in
    With a fine precision.

There are poets, worthy men,
    Shrink from public places,
And in lurking-hole or den
    Hide their pallid faces;
There they study, sweat, and woo
    Pallas and the Graces,
But bring nothing forth to view
    Worth the girls' embraces.

Fasting, thirsting, toil the bards,
    Swift years flying o'er them;
Shun the strife of open life,
    Tumults of the forum;
They, to sing some deathless thing,

Lest the world ignore them,
    Die the death, expend their breath,
    Drowned in dull decorum.

Lo! my frailties I've betrayed,
    Shown you every token,
Told you what your servitors
    Have against me spoken;
But of those men each and all
    Leave their sins unspoken,
Though they play, enjoy today,
    Scorn their pledges broken.

Now within the audience-room
    Of this blessèd prelate,
Sent to hunt out vice, and from
    Hearts of men expel it;
Let him rise, nor spare the bard,
    Cast at him a pellet:
He whose heart knows not crime's smart,
    Show my sin and tell it!

I have uttered openly
    All I knew that shamed me,
And have spewed the poison forth
    That so long defamed me;
Of my old ways I repent,
    New life hath reclaimed me;
God beholds the heart—'twas man
    Viewed the face and blamed me.

Goodness now hath won my love,
    I am wroth with vices:
Made a new man in my mind,
    Lo, my soul arises!
Like a babe new milk I drink—
    Milk for me suffices,
Lest my heart should longer be
    Filled with vain devices.

Thou Elect of fair Cologne,
    Listen to my pleading!
Spurn not thou the penitent;
    See, his heart is bleeding!
Give me penance! what is due
    For my faults exceeding
I will bear with willing cheer,
    All thy precepts heeding.

Lo, the lion, king of beasts,
    Spares the meek and lowly;
Toward submissive creatures he
    Tames his anger wholly.

Do the like, ye powers of earth,
    Temporal and holy!
Bitterness is more than's right
    When 'tis bitter solely.

THE GREAT HYMNS

Nearly all of the student cynics went on to hold important jobs in church and state and to fulfill them effectively. The later medieval church contained in its ranks thousands of well-educated university graduates who were attentive to both hierarchic traditions and middle class devotional sentiment. The outcomes of this solid cultural formation were the Latin hymns of the later medieval church, of which the most highly regarded in the twentieth century is perhaps *Dies Irae,* the Day of the Wrath.

Day of wrath, that day of burning!
Earth shall end, to ashes turning:
Thus sing saint and seer, discerning.

Ah, the dread beyond expression
When the Judge in awful session
Searcheth out the world's transgression.

Then is heard a sound of wonder:
Mighty blasts of trumpet-thunder
Rend the sepulchers asunder.

What can e'er that woe resemble,
Where even death and nature tremble
As the rising throngs assemble!

Vain, my soul, is all concealing;
For the book is brought, revealing
Every deed and thought and feeling.

On his throne the Judge is seated,
And our sins are loud repeated,
And to each is vengeance meted.

Wretched me! How gain a hearing,
When the righteous falter, fearing,
At the pomp of his appearing?

King of majesty and splendor,
Fount of pity, true and tender,
Be, thyself, my strong defender.

From thy woes my hope I borrow:
I did cause thy way of sorrow:
Do not lose me on that morrow.

Seeking me, thou weary sankest,
Nor from scourge and cross thou shrankest;
Make not vain the cup thou drankest.

Thou wert righteous even in slaying:
Yet forgive my guilty straying,
Now, before that day dismaying.

Though my sins with shame suffuse me,
Though my very moans accuse me,
Canst thou, Loving One, refuse me!

Blessed hope! I have aggrieved thee:
Yet, by grace the thief believed thee,
And the Magdalen received thee.

Though unworthy my petition,
Grant me full and free remission,
And redeem me from perdition.

Be my lot in love decreed me:
From the goats in safety lead me;
With thy sheep forever feed me.

When thy foes are all confounded,
And with bitter flames surrounded,
Call me to thy bliss unbounded.

From the dust I pray thee, hear me:
When my end shall come, be near me;
Let thy grace sustain and cheer me.

Carved capital of shackled monkeys eating fruits and baskets

ALIENATED SEGMENTS AND UNRESOLVED PROBLEMS

UNHAPPY PEOPLE

Every culture and society has its "others"—groups, large or small, that feel alienated, underprivileged, marginalized, exploited, discriminated against, or outright persecuted. The medieval world had such groups, and possibly they constituted at certain times an actual majority of the population—many, most, but never all, women; Jews; heretics—religious dissenters and separatists; witches. In Part Two we reviewed the happy, creative, and loving Middle Ages, the medieval world of our fond imagination. Now we proceed to the darker side. Here we read about unhappy, critical, querulous, discontented, angry, rebellious, and just plain miserable people. Yet the outcome of the behavior and discourse of these alienated and adversarial segments of medieval society was not only negative. Their views set up a dialogue with male nobility, the church hierarchy, and the prosperous male middle class that, while not transformative, raised important issues and generated some fruitful dialogue with intelligent and sympathetic people in the power structure who became aware of alternative perspectives. By and large, the power and privileged elite of the medieval world resisted demands for more freedom and equality, for profound change and wide reform to accommodate discontented groups, but the demands and justification for them entered into the mosaic of medieval culture and started radical and reformist traditions that extended down through the centuries into the modern world.

In addition to this debate about the status and rights of certain groups, there were two kinds of unresolved general problems of a more impersonal nature in the late medieval world. Epidemics caused high mortality and social dislocation, and the medieval world lacked the science of medicine and public health systems to respond to this biomedical challenge. In both rural and urban areas there were also expressions and images of intense class conflicts that were hard to resolve and which generated bitter feelings and endemic violence, leading to tempestuous but abortive working-class rebellion. The church seemed consistently to bear the brunt of these discontents, which is one of the prime causes for the Protestant Reformation.

Every civilization runs up against its limits eventually. Some groups cannot be incorporated into the brilliant canvas of joyful creation and comfortable exploitation of intellectual and material resources. Ideas finally reveal their twists and conundrums, feelings their ambivalences, institutions their duplicity and oppression. This was true of medieval civilization, as it was of the classical world, and is evident in our own. But these downsides never appear spontaneously—they are always ambient triggers that generate conflict and turn natural limits into menacing reactive forces.

In the medieval world the negative triggers were pandemics and class struggles. A biomedical holocaust, the Black Death, left in its wake a twisted carnage of moral anxieties and terrorized ambiguities, spilling over to reach nihilistic desperation. This devastation was never entirely healed in medieval times; it cut so deep into consciousness and confidence as to leave internal scars that remained at the center of the Christian ethos. The other problem was the incapacity of this economy (like ours in the 1930s and the 1990s) to continue to generate a sufficient expansionary margin to satisfy the ambitions of all social groups. The aristocracy used its political power to push back upon the entrepreneurial middle class groups, and these groups responded with hostility not only against aristocratic privilege, but even more corrosively against each other. In the towns and in the villages, social polarization and class conflict achieved nothing except the venting of hatred in the streets and along the byways.

THE MURDER OF THOMAS BECKET

Churchmen who took their calling too literally, who adopted too idealistic a stance and discomfited some great power broker, who seemed to be reverting to the antiroyalist views of the ill-fated Gregorian reform, who impeded the centralized course of the juristic and bureaucratic state, could find themselves removed in a crushing and even lethal manner, even if they were prominent, presumably well-connected bishops. The prime example was Thomas Becket, the Archbishop of Canterbury, cut down by four knights from Henry II's circle on the altar of his cathedral in 1170. Becket had previously been Henry's chancellor and seemingly a close personal friend of the young and ambitious ruler. But when Becket ostensibly stood in the way of the expansion of royal power and law, he was eliminated. What motivated Becket's resistance to Henry is uncertain. He was undereducated and perhaps was naively impressed by the papal rules that he came to study only after his elevation to the episcopate. He was the son of a London merchant and possibly hyperconscious about his background, making him eventually resentful of the high-flying king and his ministers. As a former chancellor he understood better than most people the ominous implications of Henry's state-building. There are indications that Becket was a severe manic-depressive, and in one of his down moods he may have suicidally decided to seek martyrdom. This account by Edward Grim, one of Becket's entourage, is of how the archbishop was killed. While vehemently partisan, it can be regarded as the report of an eyewitness. It should be noted that the penance that the pope imposed on Henry II for his ultimate responsibility for this foul deed was very modest and scarcely limited Henry's legal and political program in a significant way. Becket made the pope feel almost as uncomfortable as he did the king.

So then the aforesaid men, no knights forsooth but miserable wretches, as soon as they landed, summoned the king's officials, whom the archbishop had already excommunicated, and by falsely proclaiming that they were acting with the king's approval and in his name, they got together a band of knights and their followers. For they were easily persuaded to this crime by the knights' statement that they had come to settle the affair by order of the king. They then collected in a body, ready for any impious deed, and on the fifth day after the Nativity of Christ, that is, on the morrow of the Feast of the Holy Innocents, they gathered together against the innocent. The hour of dinner being over, the saint had already withdrawn with some of his household into an inner chamber to transact some business, leaving the crowd awaiting his return in the hall without.

The four knights with one attendant forced their way in. They were received with respect as servants of the king and well known to the archbishop's household; and those who had waited on the archbishop, being now themselves at dinner, invited them to share their table. They scorned the offer thirsting rather for blood than for food. By their order the archbishop was informed that four men had arrived who wished to speak with him on behalf of the king. On his giving consent, they were permitted to enter. For a long time they sat in silence and neither saluted the archbishop nor spoke to him. Nor did the man of wise counsel salute them immediately they came in, in order that, according to the Scriptures, "By thy words shalt thou be justified," he might discover their intentions from their questions. After a while, however, he turned to them and, carefully scanning the face of each, he greeted them in a friendly manner; but the unhappy wretches, who had made a pact with death, straightway answered his greeting with curses and ironically prayed that God might help him. At these words of bitterness and malice the man of God flushed deeply, for he now realized that they had come to work him injury. Whereupon fitz Urse, who seemed to be their leader and more prepared for the crime than the others, breathing fury, broke out in these words: "We have somewhat to say to thee by the king's command; say if thou wilt that we tell it here before all." But the archbishop knew what they were about to say and answered, "These things should not be spoken in private or in the chamber, but in public." Now these wretches so burned for the slaughter of the archbishop that if the doorkeeper had not called back the clerks—for the archbishop had ordered them all to withdraw—they would have killed him with the shaft of his cross which stood by, as they afterwards confessed. When those who had gone out returned, he, who had before reviled the archbishop, again addressed him saying, "When the king made peace with you and all disputes were settled, he sent you back to your own see, as you requested; but you, in contrary fashion, adding insult to injury, have broken the peace, and in your pride

have wrought evil in yourself against your lord. For those, by whose ministry the king's son was crowned and invested with the honours of sovereignty, you with obstinate pride have condemned with sentence of suspension. You have also bound with the chain of anathema those servants of the king by whose counsel and prudence the business of the kingdom is transacted. From this it is manifest that you would take away the crown from the king's son if you had the power. But now the plots and schemes you have hatched in order to carry out your designs against your lord the king are known to all men. Say therefore whether you are prepared to come into the king's presence and make answer to these charges." The archbishop replied, "Never was it my wish, as God is my witness, to take away the crown from my lord the king's son or to diminish his power; rather would I wish him three crowns and help him to obtain the greatest realms of the earth, so it be with right and equity. But it is unjust that my lord the king should be offended because my people accompany me through the towns and cities and come out to meet me, when for seven years now they have been deprived through my exile of the consolation of my presence. Even now I am ready to satisfy my lord wherever he pleases, if in anything I have done amiss; but he has forbidden me with threats to enter any of his cities and towns, or even villages. Moreover, it was not by me, but by the lord pope that the prelates were suspended from office." "It was through you," said the infuriated knights, "that they were suspended; do you absolve them?" "I do not deny," he answered, "that it was done through me, but it is beyond my power and utterly incompatible with my dignity to absolve those whom the lord pope has bound. Let them go to him, on whom redounds the injury and contempt they have shown towards me and their mother, the Church of Christ at Canterbury."

"Well then," said these butchers, "this is the king's command, that you depart with all your men from the kingdom and the lands which own his dominion; for from this day forth there can be no peace betwixt him and you or any of yours, for you have broken the peace." To this the archbishop answered, "Cease your threats and still your brawling. I put my trust in the King of Heaven who for his own suffered on the Cross; for from this day forth no one shall see the sea between me and my church. I have not come back to flee again; here shall he who wants me find me. It is not fitting for the king to issue such commands; sufficient are the insults received by me and mine from the king's servants, without further threats." "Such were the king's commands," they replied, "and we will make them good, for whereas you ought to have shown respect to the king's majesty and submitted your vengeance to his judgment, you have followed the impulse of your passion and basely thrust out from the Church his ministers and servants." At these words Christ's champion, rising in fervour of spirit against his accusers, exclaimed, "Whoever shall presume to violate the decrees of the holy Roman see or the laws of Christ's Church, and shall refuse to come of his own accord and make satisfaction, whosoever he be, I will not spare him, nor will I delay to inflict ecclesiastical censures upon the delinquent."

Confounded by these words, the knights sprang to their feet, for they could no longer bear the firmness of his answers. Coming close up to him they said, "We declare to you that you have spoken in peril of your head." "Are you then come to slay me?" said he. "I have committed my cause to the great Judge of all mankind; wherefore I am not moved by threats, nor are your swords more ready to strike than is my soul for martyrdom. Go, seek him who would fly from you; me you will find foot to foot in the battle of the Lord." As they retired amidst tumult and insults, he who was fitly surnamed 'the bear' brutishly cried out, "In the king's name we command you, both clerks and monks, to seize and hold that man, lest he escape by flight ere the king take full justice on his body." As they departed with these words, the man of God followed them to the door and cried out after them, "Here, here will you find me"; putting his hand on his neck, as though marking beforehand the place where they were to strike.

The archbishop then returned to the place where he had before been seated, consoled his clerks and exhorted them not to fear; and, so it seemed to us who were present, he sat there waiting as unperturbed, although his death alone was sought, as if they had come to invite him to a wedding. Ere long back came the murderers in full armour, with swords, axes and hatchets, and other implements suitable for the crime on which their minds were set. Finding the doors barred and unopened at their knocking, they turned aside by a private path through an orchard till they came to a wooden partition, which they cut and hacked and finally broke down. Terrified by the noise and uproar, almost all the clerks and the servants were scattered hither and thither like sheep before wolves. Those who remained cried out to the archbishop to flee to the church; but he, mindful of his former promise that he would not through fear of death flee from those who kill the body, rejected flight. For in such case it were not meet to flee from city to city, but rather to set an example to those subject to him, so that every one of them should choose to die by the sword rather than see the divine law set at naught and the sacred canons subverted. Moreover, he who had long since yearned for martyrdom, now saw that the occasion to embrace it had seemingly arrived, and dreaded lest it should be deferred or even altogether lost, if he took refuge in the church. But the monks still pressed him, saying that it was not becoming for him to absent himself from vespers, which were at that very moment being said in the church. He lingered for a while motionless in that less sacred spot, deliberately awaiting that happy hour of consummation which he had craved with many sighs and sought with such devotion; for he feared lest, as has been said, reverence for the sanctity of the sacred building might deter even the impious from their purpose and cheat him of his heart's desire. For, being confident that after martyrdom he would pass from this vale of misery, he is reported to have said in the hearing of many after his return from exile, "You have here a martyr, Alphege, beloved of God and a true saint; the divine compassion will provide you with yet another; he will not tarry." O pure and trustful was the conscience of that good shepherd, who in defending the cause of his flock would not delay the hour of his own death, when it was in his power to do so, nor shun the executioner, that the fury of the wolves, satiated with the blood of the shepherd, might spare the sheep. But when he would not be persuaded by argument or entreaties to take refuge in the church, the monks seized hold of him in spite of his resistance, and pulled, dragged and pushed him; without heeding his opposition and his clamour to let him go, they brought him as far as the church. But the door, which led to the monks' cloister, had been carefully barred several days before, and as the murderers were already pressing on their heels, all hope of escape seemed removed. But one of them, running forward seized hold of the bolt, and to the great surprise of them all, drew it out with as much ease as if it had been merely glued to the door.

After the monks had retreated within the precincts of the church, the four knights came following hard on their heels with rapid strides. They were accompanied by a certain subdeacon called Hugh, armed with malice like their own, appropriately named Mauclerc, being one who showed no reverence either to God or his saints, as he proved by his subsequent action. As soon as the archbishop entered the monastic buildings, the monks ceased the vespers, which they had already begun to offer to God, and ran to meet him, glorifying God for that they saw their father alive and unharmed, when they had heard he was dead. They also hastened to ward off the foe from the slaughter of their shepherd by fastening the bolts of the folding doors giving access to the church. But Christ's doughty champion turned to them and ordered the doors to be thrown open, saying, "It is not meet to make a fortress of the house of prayer, the Church of Christ, which, even if it be not closed, affords sufficient protection to its children; by suffering rather than by fighting shall we triumph over the enemy; for we are come to suffer, not to resist." Straightway these sacrilegious men, with drawn swords, entered the house of peace and reconciliation, causing no little horror to those present by the mere sight of them and the clash of their armour. All the onlookers were in tumult and consternation, for by this time those who had been singing vespers had rushed up to the scene of death.

In a spirit of mad fury the knights called out, "Where is Thomas Becket, traitor to the king and the realm?" When he returned no answer, they cried out the more loudly and insistently, "Where is the archbishop?" At this quite undaunted, as it is written, "The righteous shall be bold as a lion and without fear," he descended from the steps, whither he had been dragged by the monks through their fear of the knights, and in a perfectly clear voice answered, "Lo! here am I, no traitor to the king, but a priest. What do you seek from me?" And whereas he had already told them that he had no fear of them, he now added, "Behold, I am ready to suffer in His Name who redeemed me by His Blood. Far be it from me to flee from your swords, or to depart from righteousness." Having thus said, he turned aside to the right, under a pillar, having on one side the altar of the blessed Mother of God, Mary ever-Virgin, on the other, that of the holy confessor, Benedict, by whose example and prayers, having crucified the world and its lusts, he endured whatsoever the murderers did to him with such constancy of soul, as if he were no longer in the flesh. The murderers pursued him. "Absolve," they cried, "and restore to communion those whom you have excommunicated, and the functions of their office to the others who have been suspended." He answered, "There has been no satisfaction made, and I will not absolve them." "Then you shall die this instant," they cried, "and receive your desert." "I, too," said he, "am ready to die for my Lord, that in my blood the Church may obtain peace and liberty; but in the name of Almighty God I forbid you to harm any of my men, whether clerk or lay." Thus did the noble martyr provide piously for his followers, and prudently for himself, in that no one standing near should be hurt nor the innocent oppressed, lest any serious mishap befalling any that stood by him should dim the lustre of his glory as his soul sped up to Christ. Most fitting was it that the soldier-martyr should follow in the footsteps of his Captain and Saviour, who, when the wicked sought to take him, said, "If ye seek me, let these go their way."

Then they made a rush at him and laid sacrilegious hands upon him, pulling and dragging him roughly and violently, endeavouring to get him outside the walls of the church and there slay him, or bind him and carry him off prisoner, as they afterwards confessed was their intention. But as he could not easily be moved from the pillar, one of them seized hold of him and clung to him more closely. The archbishop shook him off vigorously, calling him a pandar [pimp] and saying, "Touch me not, Reginald; you owe me fealty and obedience; you are acting like a madman, you and your accomplices." All aflame with a terrible fury at this rebuff, the knight brandished his sword against that consecrated head. "Neither faith," he cried, "nor obedience do I owe you against my fealty to my lord the king." Then the unconquered martyr understood that the hour was approaching that should release him from the miseries of this mortal life, and that the crown of immortality prepared for him and promised by the Lord was already nigh at hand. Whereupon, inclining his head as one in prayer and joining his hands together and uplifting them, he commended his cause and that of the Church to God and St. Mary and the blessed martyr, St. Denys. Scarce had he uttered the words than the wicked knight, fearing lest he should be rescued by the people and escape alive, leapt suddenly upon him and wounded the sacrificial lamb of God in the head, cutting off the top of the crown which the unction of the sacred chrism had dedicated to God, and by the same stroke he almost cut off the arm of him who tells the story. For he, when all the others, both monks and clerks had fled, steadfastly stood by the saintly archbishop and held his arms around him, till the one he opposed to the blow was almost severed. Behold the simplicity of the dove, the wisdom of the serpent in this martyr who presented his body to the strikers that he might preserve his head, that is to say, his soul and the Church, unharmed, nor would he take any forethought or employ any stratagem against those who slay the body whereby he might escape. O worthy shepherd, who gave himself so boldly to the wolves, in order that his flock might not be torn to pieces! Because he had cast

Scribe Eadwine writing

away the world, the world in seeking to crush him unconsciously exalted him.

Next he received a second blow on the head, but still he stood firm and immovable. At the third blow he fell on his knees and elbows, offering himself a living sacrifice and saying in a low voice, "For the Name of Jesus and the protection of the Church I am ready to embrace death." But the third knight inflicted a terrible wound as he lay prostrate. By this stroke the sword was dashed against the pavement and the crown of his head, which was large, was separated from the head in such a way that the blood white with the brain and the brain no less red from the blood, dyed the floor of the cathedral with the white of the lily and the red of the rose, the colours of the Virgin and Mother and of the life and death of the martyr and confessor. The fourth knight warded off any who sought to intervene, so that the others might with greater freedom and licence perpetrate the crime. But the fifth—no knight he, but that same clerk who had entered with the knights—that a fifth blow might not be wanting to the martyr who in other things had imitated Christ, placed his foot on the neck of the holy priest and precious martyr and, horrible to relate, scattered the brains and blood about the pavement, crying out to the others, "Let us away, knights; this fellow will rise no more."

In all his sufferings the illustrious martyr displayed an incredible steadfastness. Neither with hand nor robe, as is the manner of human frailty, did he oppose the fatal stroke. Nor when smitten did he utter a single word, neither cry nor groan, nor any sound indicative of pain. But he held motionless the head which he had bent to meet the uplifted sword until, bespattered with blood and brains, as though in an attitude of prayer, his body lay prone on the pavement, while his soul rested in Abraham's bosom.

ST. AMBROSE

THE ONLY REALLY GOOD WOMAN IS A VIRGIN

A highly influential perception of woman's nature and the place of women in Christian society was expounded by the Latin church father, St. Ambrose, Bishop of Milan, around 385. Mothers are acceptable to the church, but they are not free—they are subordinate to their husbands. Only the happy virgins who have withdrawn from the world to embrace the Bridegroom of Christ are free from the decadent and meretricious use of cosmetics and jewelry, against which Ambrose was fanatical. Ambrose had taken a very hostile view of women—only those women who have sexually and socially neutered themselves are highly regarded by the church. Whence came this downside attitude to women? From St. Paul, who out of his rabbinical background was convinced that women ought to sit silently at the back of the church; from the patriarchal mind-set of Roman law; and from the intense dislike by the church fathers for any competitive practical claim by women, even holy virgins, to play a significant role in the church government and the ministration of its sacraments. The latter was to be exclusively a male preserve. Even the lavishly praised virgin nuns became vague, ethereal, marginal figures.

Let us compare, if it pleases you, the advantages of married women with that which awaits virgins. Though the noble woman boasts of her abundant offspring, yet the more she bears the more she endures. Let her count up the comforts of her children, but let her likewise count up the troubles. She marries and weeps. How many vows does she make with tears! She conceives, and her fruitfulness brings her trouble before offspring. She brings forth and is ill. How sweet a pledge which begins with danger and ends in danger, which will cause pain before pleasure! It is purchased by perils, and is not possessed at her own will.

Why speak of the troubles of nursing, training, and marrying? These are the miseries of those who are fortunate. A mother has heirs, but it increases her sorrows. . . . Why should I further speak of the painful ministrations and services due to their husbands from wives, to whom before slaves God gave the command to serve? . . . And in this position spring up those incentives to vice, in that they paint their faces with various colours, fearing not to please their husbands; and

Scene from the Life of St. Ambrose

from staining their faces, come to think of staining their chastity. What madness is here, to change the fashion of nature and seek a painting, and while fearing a husband's judgment to give up their own. . . .

And next, what expense is necessary that even a beautiful wife may not fail to please? Costly necklaces on the one hand hang on her neck, on the other a robe woven with gold is dragged along the ground. Is this display purchased, or is it a real possession? And what varied enticements of perfumes are made use of! The ears are weighed down with gems, a different colour from nature is dropped into the eyes. What is there left which is her own, when so much is changed? The married woman loves her own perceptions, and does she think that this is to live?

But you, O happy virgins, who know not such torments, rather than ornaments, whose holy modesty, beaming in your bashful cheeks, and sweet chastity are a beauty, ye do not, intent upon the eyes of men, consider as merits what is gained by the errors of others. You, too, have indeed your own beauty, furnished by the comeliness of virtue, not of the body, to which age puts not to an end, which death cannot take away, nor any sickness injure. Let God alone be sought as the judge of loveliness, Who loves even in less beautiful bodies the more beautiful souls. You know nothing of the burden and pain of childbearing, but more are the offspring of a pious soul, which esteems all as its children, which is rich in successors, barren of all bereavements, which knows no deaths, but has many heirs.

So the holy Church, ignorant of wedlock, but fertile in bearing, is in chastity a virgin, yet a mother in offspring. She, a virgin, bears us her children, not by a human father, but by the Spirit. She bears us not with pain, but with the rejoicings of the angels. She, a virgin, feeds us, not with the milk of the body, but with that of the Apostle, wherewith he fed the tender age of the people who were still children. For what bride has more children than the holy Church, who is a virgin in her sacraments and a mother to her people, whose fertility even holy Scripture attests, saying, "For many more are the children of the desolate than of her that hath an husband"? She has not an husband, but she has a Bridegroom, inasmuch as she, whether as the Church amongst nations, or as the soul in individuals, without any loss of modesty, she weds the Word of God as her eternal Spouse, free from all injury, full of reason.

EVE THE TEMPTRESS

The following selection is taken from *The Quest of the Holy Grail,* an Arthurian romance written in early thirteenth-century France. The view of woman as Eve the temptress, a view strongly held by the Church Fathers, is dogmatically stressed in this work even though it is itself a product of romantic literature. The image of the good woman is the other extreme from Eve the temptress, namely the Virgin Mary. Here is a polarized view of women–the whore or saint theme. Also, when Eve had sexual intercourse with Adam they became one flesh, so that Adam completely henceforth controlled her and spoke for her. This latter doctrine that husband and wife are one flesh and that a married woman has no freedom and autonomy was still prevalent in English common law in the middle of the nineteenth century and is still operative in the state of Israel.

Here the tale of the Holy Grail relates that when it came to pass that sinful Eve, the first woman, had taken counsel of the mortal enemy, the devil (who from that day on set about ensnaring the human race by guile), and when he had goaded her into committing mortal sin, even the sin of concupiscence, through which he himself had been cast out of Paradise and hurled down from heaven's great glory, he worked upon her criminal desire until he made her pluck the deadly fruit from the tree, breaking off as she did so a twig of the tree itself, as it often happens that the twig adheres to the gathered fruit. As soon as she had taken it to her husband, Adam, to whom she recommended and urged its eating, he took hold of it in such a way as to tear the fruit from the branch, and ate it to our hurt and his, and to his dire perdition and our own. When he had torn it from the stem as you have heard, this branch by chance stayed in the woman's hand, as one may sometimes hold an object in one's hand without remarking it. Directly they had eaten of the deadly fruit, which must rightly be termed deadly since death first came thereby to these two and to others afterwards, their former attributes were changed and they saw that they were flesh and naked, where before they had been spiritual beings, for all they had had bodies. Notwithstanding this, the story does not affirm that they were wholly spiritual; for a thing that is formed of such base stuff as clay cannot be clean in essence. But they resembled spiritual beings in that they were created to live for ever, if it so happened that they kept from sin. When, then, their eyes were opened, they knew that they were naked and knew, too, the shameful members and felt ashamed in one another's sight: thus far did they already feel the consequences of their fault. Then each one covered the basest parts of his person with his hands. Eve however, was still clutching the branch in her hand, nor did she ever let it drop, either then or later.

When He who knows all thoughts and plumbs the human heart knew that they had committed this sin He called to Adam first. And it was right that he should be held more culpable than his wife, for she was of a frailer nature, having been fashioned from the rib of man; and it was right that she should obey him, but not he her; and for this reason God called Adam first. And when He had spoken those harsh words to him: 'In the sweat of thy brow shalt thou eat bread,' He did not wish the woman to get off scot free, nor escape her share of the punishment where she had been a partner in the fault, so He said to her: 'In pain and sorrow shalt thou bring forth children.' Thereupon He drove them both from Paradise, which the Scriptures call the garden of delight. When they stood without, Eve still had hold of the little branch, but never marked its presence in her hand. But when, on taking stock of herself, she saw the twig, it caught her eye because it was still as fresh and green as if it had just been picked. She knew that the tree from which it had been broken was the cause of her exile and her misery. So she said then that, in remembrance of the cruel loss she had suffered through that tree, she would keep the branch for as long as she could, where it would often be before her eyes to remind her of her great misfortune.

Then Eve bethought herself that she had neither casket nor any other box in which to house it, for no such things as yet existed. So she thrust it into the ground, so that it stood erect, saying that in this way it would often catch her eye. And the branch that had been stuck in the earth, by the will of Him whom all created things obey, quickened and took root in the soil and grew.

This branch which the first sinner brought with her out of Paradise was charged with meaning. In that she held it in her hand it betokened a great happiness, as though she were speaking to her heirs that were to follow her (for she was still a maid), and saying to them through the medium of this twig:

'Be not dismayed if we are banished from our inheritance: it is not lost to us eternally; see here a sign of our return hereafter.'

As for him who might ask of the book why it was not the man rather than the woman who carried the branch out of Paradise, since he is her superior, the book makes answer that the bearing of the branch pertained not to the man but to the woman. For in that the woman bore it, it signified that through a woman life was lost, and through a woman life would be regained, meaning that through the Virgin Mary the inheritance that had just then been lost should one day be recovered.

With that the tale returns to the twig that was stuck in the earth and tells how it grew and shot up apace, till within a little lapse of time it had become a tree. When it had grown into a tall, shade-giving tree, its trunk and boughs and leaves were all as white as snow. This was the mark of virginity; for virginity is a virtue whereby the body is kept clean and the soul white. And the tree being white in all its parts signified that she who had planted it was still a virgin at the hour of its planting: for at the time when Adam and Eve were cast forth from Paradise they were still virgins, unspotted by the shame of lust. It must furthermore be understood that virginity and maidenhood are nowise identical, indeed there is a deep distinction to be drawn between them. Maidenhood is not to be equated with virginity for reasons I will show. The former is a virtue common to those of either sex who have not known the contact born of carnal commerce. But virginity is something infinitely higher and more worth: for none, whether man or woman, can possess it who has inclined in will to carnal intercourse. Such virginity did Eve still have when she was driven out of Paradise and the delights it held; nor had she lost this virtue at the time of the branch's planting. But after, God commanded Adam that he know his wife, which is to say that he lie with her carnally, as nature requires that a man lie with his wife and a woman with her lord. So Eve lost her virginity, and from then on the two lived as one flesh.

WOMEN OF THE NOBILITY

In theological writings and popular literature alike there was the constant reiteration that woman's febrile, untrustworthy, and oversexed nature requires her subjection to masculine authority—father, husband, bishop. But in practice what was the condition of women? What role did they play in society? Did they exhibit some degree of autonomy? More than one would expect from reading nasty St. Ambrose and misogynist *The Quest of the Holy Grail.* At least among women of the nobility, there seem to have been at all times and places very considerable autonomy. It is true that their life was circumscribed within the circle of their families. The only break from that was entering a nunnery, in which case they became part of another kind of family where control was perhaps even tighter. But within their families, the women played forceful roles. They were strong people. Churchmen may repeat the canonical view of them as necessarily being under tight discipline, but they seem to have had plenty of freedom to act and make important decisions. There is a tendency in the accounts we have to see women of the nobility acting like Eve the Temptress—they scheme, they seduce, they even kill—and a hostile, traditionally ecclesiastical view of woman's nature may be conditioning their behavior in the stories. But the women certainly don't seem meek, withdrawn, highly dependent; quite the contrary. They are if anything stronger and more determined than the men they live with. Here are four different accounts of the behavior of women in high and middling noble families between the sixth and thirteenth centuries.

Gregory of Tours, History of the Franks. Gregory was a member of a distinguished Gallo-Roman family in sixth-century France, and he was close to the ruling French Merovingian dynasty and was its chronicler.

Ordericus Vitalis was a monk of mixed English and Norman French background who wrote a five-volume history of Norman French aristocratic families. In this selection he is writing about the Normans in Sicily.

The Nibelungenlied. This epic was written in Austria in the early thirteenth century. Its selling is vaguely the Germanic peoples in earlier times. In this work, perhaps the two strongest characters are a couple of sisters-in-law whose quarrel produces family turmoil and social conflict. *The Nibelungenlied* inspired Wagner to write the scenario of his *Ring* opera. But he didn't simply borrow the poem as his libretto; he constructed his own pseudo-medieval epic. Yet *The Nibelungenlied's* feminine strength is retained in Wagner's *Ring* operas.

The Lais of Marie de France. Marie was a court poetess in the entourage of Eleanor of Aquitaine in the twelfth century. She has become popular recently in women's studies courses. But the image of an aristocratic woman in this romance seems about the same as the other examples—the woman is ambitious and devious.

Young Ladies playing Tarot

GREGORY OF TOURS

Now King Sigibert, seeing his brothers take to themselves unworthy wives and even wed serving-maids, sent an embassy to Spain with many gifts to demand in marriage Brunhild, daughter of King Athanagild. For she was a girl of graceful form, fair to look upon, honourable and comely, prudent in judgement, and amiable of address. Her father did not refuse her, but sent her with great treasures to the king, who, assembling the chief men of his kingdom, and making ready a feast, received her as his wife with boundless rejoicing and delight. And because she was subject to the Arian law, she was converted by the preaching of bishops and the admonitions of the king himself, so that she confessed the blessed Trinity in Unity, and received the holy chrism, remaining a Catholic in the name of Christ until this day.

21 (28). When King Chilperic saw this, although he already had several wives, he sent to demand her sister Galswinth, promising by the mouth of his envoys that he would forsake the others if only he were deemed worthy to receive a spouse befitting his rank and of blood royal. Her father believed his promises, and sent this daughter like the other with a rich dower to the king: Galswinth was the elder sister. When she was come to King Chilperic, he received her with great honour, and was joined to her in marriage, loving her dearly, for she had brought with her great treasures. But because of his passion for Fredegund, his former wife, a great quarrel arose between them. She had already been converted to the Catholic faith, and baptized. She soon made constant complaint to the king of the

wrongs which she had to endure, declaring that she had no part in his royalty; she craved his permission to return in freedom to her own country, leaving behind her the treasures which she had brought with her. He cleverly dissembled, and appeased her with smooth words. At last he ordered her to be strangled by a slave, so that she was found dead in her bed. After her death God showed forth a great miracle. A lamp was suspended by a cord above her tomb, and without being touched of any, this lamp fell to the paved floor. But the hardness departed from the pavement before it. It was as if the lamp sank into some soft substance; it was buried up to the middle without being broken at all. Which thing appeared a great miracle to all who saw it. The king made mourning for her death; but after a few days took Fredegund again to wife. Thereupon his brothers cast him out from the kingdom, deeming that the aforesaid queen was not slain without his prompting.

ORDERICUS VITALIS

Robert Guiscard's wife Sichelgaita was a daughter of Gaimar, duke of Salerno, and sister of Gisulf, who had been deprived of the duchy by the attack of his covetous brother-in-law. This woman conceived a hatred for her stepson Bohemond, fearing that, because he was stronger than her son Roger and excelled in judgement and valour, he might cause Roger to lose the duchy of Apulia and Calabria, which was his due by hereditary right. Therefore she brewed a deadly potion and sent it to the physicians of Salerno, amongst whom she had been brought up and from whom she had acquired great skill in the preparation of poisons. On receiving it they understood the will of their mistress and pupil, and administered the deadly poison to Bohemond, whom they should have attempted to cure. After taking it he sickened to the point of death and hastily sent a messenger to tell his father of his illness. The shrewd duke immediately recognized his wife's evil-doing and, sending for her with a heavy heart, asked her, 'Does my lord Bohemond live or not?' To which she answered, 'I do not know, my lord.' 'Bring

me,' he said, 'the text of the Gospels and a sword.' When they had been brought, he took the sword and swore on the holy books in these words, 'Listen, Sichelgaita: by this holy Gospel I swear that if my son Bohemond dies of the sickness that afflicts him I will slay you with this sword.' At this, terrified by the fearful vow, she prepared a sound antidote and dispatched it hastily to the doctors at Salerno, who had been her instruments in the intended murder, earnestly pressing the messenger with promises and entreaties to rescue her from her perilous position. When the physicians heard that the treachery was discovered and their mistress in distress, they took measures to prevent the execution of the duke's terrible threats and exerted all their arts of healing to cure the young man they had harmed. With the help of God, who intended him to be the scourge of the Turks and Saracens, the enemies of the Christian faith, the sick man recovered; but he remained pale all his life as a result of the poison that had been administered to him.

Meanwhile the shifty, cunning woman turned over many schemes in her mind; haunted day and night by terror she knew that if the messenger she had sent were delayed in crossing the sea so that the sick man died before his arrival she would not escape death by her husband's sword, as he had vowed. Consequently she devised another plot, which was cruel and utterly depraved. Terrible to relate, she administered poison to her husband. The moment his sickness began, when she was sure that he could not escape death, she sent for her dependants and the other Lombards and set out at dead of night to the coast, where she embarked in the best ships with all her partisans. To prevent the Normans from following her she burned the remaining ships.

THE NIBELUNGENLIED

Before vespers one evening there arose in the courtyard a great turmoil of warriors pursuing their pleasure at their knightly sports, and a crowd of men and women ran up to watch.

The mighty Queens had sat down together, and their thoughts were on two splendid knights.

'I have a husband of such merit that he might rule over all the kingdoms of this region,' said fair Kriemhild.

'How could that be?' asked lady Brunhild. 'If there were no others alive but you and he, all these kingdoms might well subserve him, but as long as Gunther lives it could never come about.'

'See how magnificently he bears himself, and with what splendour he stands out from the other knights, like the moon against the stars,' rejoined Kriemhild. 'It is not for nothing that I am so happy.'

'However splendid and handsome and valiant your husband may be,' replied Brunhild, 'you must nevertheless give your noble brother the advantage. Let me tell you truly: Gunther must take precedence over all kings.'

'My husband is a man of such worth,' answered lady Kriemhild, 'that I have not praised him vainly. His honour stands high on very many counts. Believe me, Brunhild, he is fully Gunther's equal.'

'Now do not misunderstand me, Kriemhild, for I did not speak without cause. When I saw them for the first time and the King subdued me to his will and won my love so gallantly, I heard them both declare—and Siegfried himself said so—that he was Gunther's vassal, and so I consider him to be my liegeman, having heard him say so.'

'It would be a sad thing for me if that were so,' retorted Kriemhild. 'How could my noble brothers have had a hand in my marrying a liegeman? I must ask you in all friendship, Brunhild, if you care for me, kindly to stop saying such things.'

'I cannot,' answered the Queen, 'for why should I renounce my claim to so many knights who owe us service through Siegfried?'

At this lovely Kriemhild lost her temper. 'You will have to renounce your claim to him and to his attending you with services of any kind! He ranks above my noble brother Gunther, and you must spare me such things as I have had to hear. I must say I find it very odd, since he is your liegeman and you have such power over us, that he has been sitting on his dues for so long! You should not bother me with your airs.'

'You are getting above yourself,' replied the Queen, 'and I should like to see whether you are held in such esteem as I.' The ladies were growing very angry.

'We shall very soon see!' said lady Kriemhild. 'Since you have declared my husband to be your liegeman, the two Kings' vassals must witness today whether I dare enter the minster before the Queen of the land. You must see visible proof this day that I am a free noblewoman, and that my husband is a better man than yours. Nor do I intend for my part to be demeaned by what you say. You shall see this evening how your liege-woman will walk in state in Burgundy in sight of the warriors. I claim to be of higher station than was ever heard of concerning any Queen that wore a crown!' And now indeed fierce hate grew up between those ladies.

'If you deny you are a vassal, you and your ladies must withdraw from my suite when we enter the cathedral.'

'We certainly shall,' answered Kriemhild. 'Now dress yourselves well, my maidens,' she said to them, 'for I must not be put to shame. Let it appear beyond all doubt whether you have fine clothes or not. We must make Brunhild eat her words.'

They needed little persuading and fetched out their sumptuous robes. And when all the ladies and maidens were beautifully attired, Queen Kriemhild, herself exquisitely gowned, set out with her train of forty-three maids-in-waiting whom she had brought with her to Worms, all dressed in dazzling cloth-of-gold from Arabia.

And so those shapely girls arrived at the minster, before which Siegfried's men were waiting, so that people were wondering why it was that the Queens appeared separately and no longer went together as before. However, in the end, many brave knights had to suffer dearly for their division.

Gunther's Queen was already standing before the cathedral and all the knights were passing the time pleasantly taking note of her lovely women, when lady Kriemhild arrived with a great and splendid company. However fine the clothes ever worn by daughters of any noble knights, they were as nothing beside those of her suite:

Kriemhild was so rich in possessions that thirty queens could not have found the wherewithal to do as she had done. Even if his wishes were to come true, no man could assert that he had ever seen such magnificent clothes paraded as Kriemhild's fair maidens were wearing, though she would not have demanded it except to spite Brunhild.

The two processions met before the minster and the lady of the land, prompted by great malice, harshly ordered Kriemhild to halt. 'A liege-woman may not enter before a Queen!'

'It would have been better for you if you could have held your tongue,' said fair Kriemhild angrily, 'for you have brought dishonour on your own pretty head. How could a vassal's paramour ever wed a King?'

'Whom are you calling a paramour?' asked the Queen.

'I call you one,' answered Kriemhild. 'My dear husband Siegfried was the first to enjoy your lovely body, since it was not my brother who took your maidenhead. Where were your poor wits?—It was a vile trick.—Seeing that he is your vassal, why did you let him love you? Your complaints have no foundation.'

'I swear I shall tell Gunther of this,' replied Brunhild.

'What is that to me? Your arrogance has got the better of you. You used words that made me your servant, and, believe me, in all sincerity I shall always be sorry you did so. I can no longer keep your secrets.'

Brunhild began to weep, and Kriemhild delayed no more but, accompanied by her train, entered the cathedral before Gunther's queen. Thus great hatred arose and bright eyes grew very moist and dim from it.

However pious the ministrations and the chanting, the service seemed to Brunhild as though it would never end, since she was troubled to the depths of her being. Many good warriors had to pay for it later. At last she went out with her ladies and took her stand before the minster thinking: 'Kriemhild must tell me more about this thing of which she accuses me so loudly, sharp-tongued woman that she is. If

Siegfried has boasted of it, it will cost him his life!'

And now noble Kriemhild appeared, attended by many brave knights. 'Halt for one moment,' said lady Brunhild. 'You declared me to be a paramour—now prove it! Let me tell you, your remarks have offended me deeply.'

'You would do better not to stand in my way! I prove it with this gold ring on my finger here which my sweetheart brought me when he first slept with you.' Never had Brunhild known a day so fraught with pain.

'This noble ring was stolen and has long been maliciously withheld from me! But now I shall get to the bottom of this affair and discover who took it.' The two ladies were now very agitated.

'You shall not make me the thief who stole it! If you cared for your honour it would have been wise to hold your tongue. As proof that I am not lying, see this girdle which I have round me—you shared my Siegfried's bed!'

She was wearing a fine silk braid from Nineveh adorned with precious stones, and Brunhild burst into tears when she saw it. She was resolved that Gunther should hear of this, together with the men of Burgundy. 'Ask the lord of the Rhenish lands to come here. I want to tell him how his sister has insulted me; for she openly declares me to be Siegfried's concubine.'

The King came with his warriors and saw his spouse in tears. 'Tell me, dear lady,' he said very tenderly, 'has anyone annoyed you?'

'I have cause enough to be unhappy. Your sister means to rob me of my honour. I accuse her before you of having said for all to hear that her husband made me his paramour!'

'She would have acted very ill if she had,' said King Gunther.

'She is wearing the girdle that I lost and my ring of red gold. I shall regret the day that I was born unless you clear me of this monstrous infamy, Sire, and earn my eternal thanks!'

'Ask Siegfried to appear. The knight from the Netherlands must either tell us that he made this boast or deny it.' And Kriemhild's beloved husband was summoned at once.

When lord Siegfried saw the Queens' distress

(he had no idea what was amiss) he quickly asked: 'Why are these ladies weeping? I should very much like to know. Or why has the King sent for me?'

'I deeply regret this neccessity,' said King Gunther, 'but my lady Brunhild tells me some tale of your having boasted you were the first to enjoy her lovely person—so your wife, lady Kriemhild, avers.'

'If she said this,' answered mighty Siegfried, 'she will regret it before I have finished with her. I am willing in the presence of your vassals to rebut with my most solemn oaths that I ever said this to her.'

'You must give us proof of that. If the oath you offer is duly sworn here I shall clear you of all treason.' And he commanded the proud Burgundians to stand in a ring. Brave Siegfried raised his hand to swear but the mighty king said: 'Your great innocence is so well known to me that I acquit you of my sister's allegation and accept that you are not guilty of the deed.'

'If my wife were to go unpunished for having distressed Brunhild I should be extremely sorry, I assure you,' rejoined Siegfried, at which the good knights exchanged meaningful glances. 'Women should be trained to avoid irresponsible chatter,' continued Siegfried. 'Forbid your wife to indulge in it, and I shall do the same with mine. I am truly ashamed at her unseemly behaviour.'

All those comely women parted in silence. But Brunhild was so dejected that Gunther's vassals could not but pity her. Then Hagen of Troneck came to his liege lady, and, finding her in tears, asked her what was vexing her. She told him what had happened, and he at once vowed that Kriemhild's man should pay for it, else Hagen, because of that insult, would never be happy again. Then Ortwin and Gernot arrived where the knights were plotting Siegfried's death and took part in their discussion. Noble Uote's son Giselher came next, and, hearing their deliberations, he asked in his loyal-hearted fashion: 'Why are you doing this, good knights? Siegfried has never in any way deserved such hatred that he should die for it. Why, it is a trifle over which the women are quarrelling!'

'Are we to rear cuckoos?' asked Hagen. 'That would bring small honour to such worthy knights. His boast that he enjoyed my dearlady shall cost him his life, or I shall die avenging it!'

'He has done us nothing but good,' interposed the King himself, 'and he has brought us honour. He must be allowed to live. To what purpose should I now turn against him?—He has always shown us heartfelt loyalty.'

'His great strength shall not avail him,' said brave Ortwin of Metz. 'If my lord will let me, I shall do him some harm!'

Thus those warriors declared themselves his enemies, though he had done them no wrong. Yet none followed Ortwin's proposal, except that Hagen kept putting it to Gunther that if Siegfried were no more, Gunther would be lord of many kingdoms, at which Gunther grew very despondent.

There they let the matter rest and went to look at the sports. And what a forest of stout shafts was shattered before the minster and all the way up to the hall for Kriemhild to see! But, for their part, many of Gunther's men nursed feelings of resentment.

'Let your murderous anger be,' said the King. 'Siegfried was born for our honour and good fortune, and moreover he is so terribly strong and so prodigiously brave that were he to get wind of it, none could dare oppose him.'

'He will not,' answered Hagen. 'You just say nothing at all, and I fancy I shall manage this so well in secret that he will repent of Brunhild's weeping. I declare that I, Hagen, shall always be his enemy!'

'How could the thing be done?' asked King Gunther.

'I will tell you,' replied Hagen. 'We shall send envoys to ourselves here in Burgundy to declare war on us publicly, men whom no one knows. Then you will announce in the hearing of your guests that you and your men plan to go campaigning, whereupon Siegfried will promise you his aid, and so he will lose his life. For in this way I shall learn the brave man's secret from his wife.'

The King followed his vassal Hagen's advice,

to evil effect, and those rare knights began to set
afoot the great betrayal before any might discover
it, so that, thanks to the wrangling of two women,
countless warriors met their doom.

MARIE DE FRANCE

Most noble barons
were those Bretons of Brittany.
In the old days they were accustomed, out of
    bravery,
courtliness, and nobility,
to create *lais* from the adventures they heard,
adventures that had befallen all sorts of people;
they did this as a memorial,
so that men should not forget them.
They made one that I heard—
it should never be forgotten—
about Equitan, a most courtly man,
the lord of Nauns, a magistrate and king.

Equitan was a man of great worth,
dearly loved in his own land.
He loved sport and lovemaking;
and so he kept a body of knights in his service.
Whoever indulges in love without sense or mod-
    eration
recklessly endangers his life;
such is the nature of love
that no one involved with it can keep his head.
Equitan had a seneschal,
a good knight, brave and loyal,
who took care of his land for him,
governed and administered it.
Unless the king was making war,
he would never, no matter what the emergency,
neglect his hunting,
his hawking, or his other amusements.

This seneschal took a wife
through whom great harm later came to the land.
She was a beautiful woman
of fine breeding,
with an attractive form and figure.
Nature took pains in putting her together:
bright eyes in a lovely face,
a pretty mouth and a well-shaped nose.
She hadn't an equal in the entire kingdom.
The king often heard her praised.

He frequently sent his greetings to her,
presents as well;
without having seen her, he wanted her,
so he spoke to her as soon as he could.

For his private amusement
he went hunting in the countryside
where the seneschal dwelt;
in the castle, where the lady also lived,
the king took lodging for the night
after he had finished the day's sport.
He now had a good chance to speak to the wife,
to reveal to her his worth, his desires.
He found her refined and clever,
with a beautiful body and face,
and a pleasing, cheerful demeanor.
Love drafted him into his service:
he shot an arrow at the king
that opened a great wound in the heart,
where Love had aimed and fixed it.
Neither good sense nor understanding were of
    use to the king now;
love for the woman so overcame him
that he became sad and depressed.
Now he has to give in to love completely;
he can't defend himself at all.
That night he can't sleep or even rest,
instead he blames and scolds himself:
"Alas," he says, "what destiny
led me to these parts?
Because I have seen this woman
pain has struck at my heart,
my whole body shivers.
I think I have no choice but to love her—
yet if I love her, I'm doing wrong;
she's the wife of my seneschal.
I owe him the same faith and love
that I want him to give me.
If, by some means, he found out about this
I know how much it would upset him.
Still, it would be a lot worse
if I went mad out of concern for him.
It would be a shame for such a beautiful woman
not to have a lover!
What would become of her finer qualities
if she didn't nourish them by a secret love?
There isn't a man in the world

who wouldn't be vastly improved if she loved
      him.
And if the seneschal should hear of the affair,
he oughtn't be too crushed by it;
he certainly can't hold her all by himself,
and I'm happy to share the burden with him!"
When he had said all that, he sighed,
and lay in bed thinking.
After a while, he spoke again: "Why
am I so distressed and frightened?
I still don't even know
if she will take me as her lover;
but I'll know soon!
If she should feel the way I do,
I'd soon be free of this agony.
God! It's still so long till morning!
I can't get any rest,
it's been forever since I went to bed."

The king stayed awake until daybreak;
he could hardly wait for it.
He rose and went hunting,
but he soon turned back
saying that he was worn out.
He returns to his room and lies down.
The seneschal is saddened by this;
he doesn't know what's bothering the king,
what's making him shiver;
in fact, his wife is the reason for it.
The king, to get some relief and some pleasure,
sends for the wife to come speak with him.
He revealed his desire to her,
letting her know that he was dying because of
      her;
that it lay in her power to comfort him
or to let him die.
"My lord," the woman said to him,
"I must have some time to think;
this is so new to me,
I have no idea what to say.
You're a king of high nobility,
and I'm not at all of such fortune
that you should single me out
to have a love affair with.
If you get what you want from me,
I have no doubt about it:
you'll soon get tired of me,

and I'll be far worse off than before.
If I should love you
and satisfy your desire,
love wouldn't be shared equally
between the two of us.
Because you're a powerful king
and my husband is your vassal,
I'm sure you believe
your rank entitles you to my love.
Love is worthless if it's not mutual.
A poor but loyal man is worth more—
if he also possesses good sense and virtue—
and his love brings greater joy
than the love of a prince or a king
who has no loyalty in him.
Anyone who aims higher in love
than his own wealth entitles him to
will be frightened by every little thing that oc-
      curs.
The rich man, however, is confident
that no one will steal a mistress away
whose favor he obtains by his authority over her."

Equitan answered her,
"Please, my lady! Don't say such things!
No one could consider himself noble
(rather, he'd be haggling like a tradesman)
who, for the sake of wealth or a big fief,
would take pains to win someone of low repute.
There's no woman in the world—if she's smart,
refined, and of noble character,
and if she places a high enough value on her love
that she isn't inconstant—
whom a rich prince in his palace
wouldn't yearn for
and love well and truly,
even if she'd nothing but the shirt on her back.
Whoever is inconstant in love
and gives himself up to treachery
is mocked and deceived in the end;
I've seen it happen many times like that.
It's no surprise when someone loses out
who deserves to because of his behavior.
My dear lady, I'm offering myself to you!
Don't think of me as your king,
but as your vassal and your lover.
I tell you, I promise you

I'll do whatever you want.
Don't let me die on your account!
You be the lord and I'll be the servant—
you be the proud one and I'll be the beggar!"

The king pleaded with her,
begged her so often for mercy,
that she promised him her love
and granted him possession of her body.
Then they exchanged rings,
and promised themselves to each other.
They kept their promises and loved each other
        well;
they died for this in the end.

Their affair lasted a long time,
without anyone hearing of it.
At the times set for their meetings,
when they were to speak together at the king's
        palace,
the king informed his followers
that he wanted to be bled privately.
The doors of his chamber were closed,
and no one was so daring,
if the king didn't summon him,
that he would ever enter there.
Meanwhile, the seneschal held court
and heard pleas and complaints.
The king loved the seneschal's wife for a long
        time,
had no desire for any other woman;
he didn't want to marry,
and never allowed the subject to be raised.
His people held this against him,
and the seneschal's wife
heard about it often; this worried her,
and she was afraid she would lose him.
So when she next had the chance to speak to
        him—
when she should have been full of joy,
kissing and embracing him
and having a good time with him—
she burst into tears, making a big scene.
The king asked
what the matter was,
and the lady answered,
"My lord, I'm crying because of our love,
which has brought me to great sorrow:

you're going to take a wife, some king's daughter,
and you will get rid of me;
I've heard all about it, I know it's true.
And—alas!—what will become of me?
On your account I must now face death,
for I have no other comfort than you."
The king spoke lovingly to her:
"Dear love, don't be afraid!
I promise I'll never take a wife,
never leave you for another.
Believe me, this is the truth:
If your husband were dead,
I'd make you my lady and my queen;
no one could stop me."
The lady thanked him,
said she was very grateful to him;
if he would assure her
that he wouldn't leave her for someone else,
she would quickly undertake
to do away with her lord.
It would be easy to arrange
if he were willing to help her.
He agreed to do so;
there was nothing she could demand of him
that he wouldn't do, if he possibly could,
whether it turned out well or badly.

"My lord," she says, "please
come hunting in the forest,
out in the country where I live.
Stay awhile at my husband's castle;
you can be bled there,
and on the third day after that, take a bath.
My lord will be bled with you
and will bathe with you as well;
make it clear to him—and don't relent—
that he must keep you company!
I'll have the baths heated
and the two tubs brought in;
his will be so boiling hot
that no man on earth
could escape being horribly scalded
as soon as he sat down in it.
When he's scalded to death,
send for his men and yours;
then you can show them exactly how
he suddenly died in his bath."

The king promised her
that he'd do just as she wished.

Less than three months later,
the king went out into the countryside to hunt.
He had himself bled to ward off illness,
and his seneschal bled with him.
On the third day, he said he wanted to bathe;
the seneschal was happy to comply.
"Bathe with me," said the king,
and the seneschal replied, "Willingly."
The wife had the baths heated,
the two tubs brought;
next to the bed, according to plan,
she had them both set down.
Then she had boiling water brought
for the seneschal's tub.
The good man got up
and went outside to relax for a moment.
His wife came to speak to the king
and he pulled her down beside him;
they lay down on her husband's bed
and began to enjoy themselves.
They lay there together.
Because the tub was right before them,
they set a guard at the bedroom door;
a maidservant was to keep watch there.
Suddenly the seneschal returned,

and knocked on the door; the girl held it closed.
He struck it so violently
that he forced it open.
There he discovered the king and his own wife
lying in each other's arms.
The king looked up and saw him coming;
to hide his villainy
he jumped into the tub feet first,
stark naked.
He didn't stop to think what he was doing.
And there he was scalded to death,
caught in his own evil trap,
while the seneschal remained safe and sound.
The seneschal could see very well
what had happened to the king.
He grabbed his wife at once
and thrust her head first into the tub.
Thus both died,
the king first, the wife after him.
Whoever wants to hear some sound advice
can profit from this example:
he who plans evil for another
may have that evil rebound back on him.

It all happened just as I've told you.
The Bretons made a *lai* about it,
about Equitan, his fate,
and the woman who loved him so much.

BOCCACCIO'S WOMEN

Giovanni Boccaccio was a mid-fourteenth-century Florentine humanist and scholar. He held a municipal chair of Dante studies. He had great success as a popular writer with the *Decameron,* a retailing of hundreds of funny stories favored by his middle class audience. The framework for the stories is that the Black Death has driven smart young men and women from the city to a country villa, and there they amuse themselves by telling these stories. Boccaccio's skill with narrative and dialogue is of a high order. Essentially, this is a work of soft-core pornography. The women in Boccaccio's story are usually nubile and dumb, highly sexed and self-indulgent, prey to frauds and tricksters, usually from the clergy. The Florentine bourgeois women seem less self-reliant, less ambitious, and softer and more passive than the women of the nobility. Here is a typical Boccaccio story.

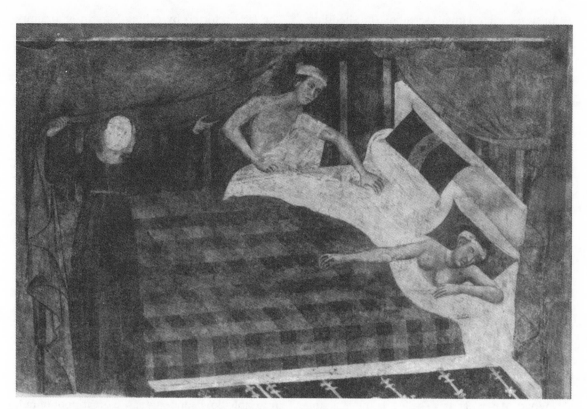
Bedroom chamber scene with male and female couple

In the town of Imola, excellent ladies, there once lived a depraved and wicked fellow by the name of Berto della Massa. The townspeople learned from experience that his dealings were crooked, and he brought himself into so much disrepute that there was not a single person in the whole of Imola who was prepared to believe a word he uttered, no matter whether he was speaking the truth or telling a lie. He therefore perceived that Imola no longer afforded him any outlet for his roguery, and as a last resort he moved to Venice, where the scum of the earth can always find a welcome. There he decided to go in for some different kind of fraud from those he had practised elsewhere, and from the moment of his arrival, as though conscience-stricken by the crimes he had committed in the past, he gave people the impression that he was a man of quite extraordinary humility. What was more, having transformed himself into the most Catho-

lic man who ever lived, he went and became a Franciscan, and styled himself Friar Alberto of Imola. Having donned the habit of his Order, he gave every appearance of leading a harsh, frugal existence, began to preach the virtues of repentance and abstinence, and never allowed a morsel of meat or a drop of wine to pass his lips unless they came up to his exacting standards.

Nobody suspected for a moment that he had been a thief, pander, swindler and murderer before suddenly blossoming into a great preacher; nor had he abandoned any of these vices, for he was simply biding his time until an opportunity arose for him to practise them in secret. His crowning achievement was to get himself ordained as a priest, and whenever he was celebrating mass in the presence of a large congregation, he would shed copious tears for the Passion of the Saviour, being the sort of man who could weep as much as he pleased at little cost to himself.

In short, what with his sermons and shedding of tears, he managed to hoodwink the Venetians so successfully that hardly anyone there made a will without depositing it with him and making him the trustee. Many people handed over their money to him for safe keeping, and he became the father-confessor and confidential adviser to the vast majority of the men and women of the city. Having thus been transformed from a wolf into a shepherd, he acquired a reputation for saintliness far greater than any St. Francis had ever enjoyed in Assisi.

Now it happened that a frivolous and scatter-brained young woman, whose name was Monna Lisetta da Ca' Quirino, the wife of a great merchant who had sailed away to Flanders aboard one of his galleys, came to be confessed by this holy friar of ours accompanied by a number of other ladies. Being a Venetian, and therefore capable of talking the hind leg off a donkey, she had only got through a fraction of her business, kneeling all the time at his feet, when Friar Alberto demanded to know whether she had a lover.

'What, Master Friar?' she exclaimed, giving him a withering look. 'Have you no eyes in your head? Does it seem to you that my charms are to be compared to those of these other women? I could have lovers to spare if I wanted them, but my charms are not at the service of every Tom, Dick or Harry who happens to fall in love with them. How often do you come across anyone as beautiful as I? Why, even if I were in Heaven itself, my charms would be thought exceptional.'

But this was only the beginning, and she droned on interminably, going into such raptures about this beauty of hers that it was painful to listen to her.

Friar Alberto had sensed immediately that she was something of a half-wit, and realizing that she was ripe for the picking, he fell passionately in love with her there and then. This was hardly the moment, however, for whispering sweet nothings in her ear, and in order to show her how godly he was, he got up on to his high horse, reproached her for being vainglorious and made her listen to a great deal more of his balderdash.

The lady retorted by calling him an ignoramus, and asserting that he was incapable of distinguishing one woman's beauty from another's. And since he did not want to irritate her unduly, Friar Alberto, having heard the rest of her confession, allowed her to proceed on her way with the others.

After biding his time for a few days, he went with a trusted companion to call upon Monna Lisetta at her own house, and, having got her to take him into a room where nobody could see what he was doing, he threw himself on his knees before her, saying:

'Madam, in God's name I beseech you to forgive me for talking to you as I did on Sunday last, when you were telling me about your beauty. That same night, I was punished so severely for my insolence that I have been laid up in bed ever since, and was only able to rise again today for the first time.'

'Who was it who punished you, then?' asked Lady Numskull.

'I will tell you about it,' said Friar Alberto. 'When I was praying in my cell that night, as I invariably do, I suddenly saw a great pool of radiant light, and before I was able to turn round and discover its source, I caught sight of an incredibly handsome young man, standing over me with a heavy stick in his hand. He grabbed me by the scruff of the neck, dragged me to the floor at his feet, and beat me so severely that my body was an aching mass of weals and bruises. When I asked him why he had done it, he replied: "Because, earlier today, you had the infernal cheek to speak ill of Monna Lisetta's celestial charms, and apart from God himself there is no one I love so dearly." I then asked him who he was, and he told me that he was the Angel Gabriel. "Oh, sir," said I, "I beg you to forgive me." "Very well," said he, "I shall forgive you, but on this sole condition, that you pay a personal call on the lady at your earliest opportunity and offer her your apologies. And should she refuse to accept them, I shall come back here again and give you such a hiding that you will never recover from it." He then went on to tell me something else, but I dare not tell you what it was unless you forgive me first.'

Being somewhat feeble in the upper storey, Lady Bighead believed every word and felt positively giddy with joy. She paused a little, then said:

'You see, Friar Alberto? I told you my charms were celestial. However, so help me God, I do feel sorry for you, and in order to spare you any further injury I shall pardon you forthwith, but only on condition that you tell me what it was that the Angel said next.'

'Since I am forgiven, madam, I will gladly tell you,' he replied. 'However, I must ask you to take great care never to repeat it to another living soul, because by so doing you will ruin everything and you will no longer be the luckiest woman alive, as you assuredly are at present.

'The Angel Gabriel asked me to tell you that he had taken such a liking to you that he would have come to spend the night with you on several occasions except for the fact that you might have been frightened. He now charges me to inform you that he would like to come to you on some night in the near future and spend a little time in your company. But since he is an angel and would not be able to touch you if he were to come in his own angelic form, he says that for your own pleasure he would prefer to come in the form of a man. He therefore desires that you should let him know when, and in whose form, you would like him to come, and he will carry out your instructions to the letter. Hence you have every reason to regard yourself as the most blessed woman on earth.'

Lady Noodle said she was delighted to hear that the Angel Gabriel was in love with her, for she herself was greatly devoted to him and never failed to light a fourpenny candle in his honour whenever she came across a painting in which he was depicted. So far as she was concerned, he would be welcome to visit her whenever he pleased, but only if he promised not to desert her for the Virgin Mary, of whom it was said that he was a great admirer, as seemed to be borne out by the fact that in all the paintings she had seen of him, he was invariably shown kneeling in front of the Virgin. As for the form in which he should visit her, she would leave the choice entirely to

him so long as he was careful not to give her a fright.

'You speak wisely, madam,' said Friar Alberto, 'and I shall certainly arrange for him to do as you suggest. But I want to ask you a great favour and one that will cost you nothing, namely, that you should instruct him to use this body of mine for the purpose of his visit. The reason is this, that when he enters my body, he will remove my soul and set it down in Heaven, where it will stay for the whole of the time he remains in your company.'

'What a good idea!' said Lady Birdbrain. 'It will make up for the blows he gave you on my account.'

'Very well, then,' said Friar Alberto. 'Now remember to leave your door unlocked for him tonight, because otherwise, since he will be arriving inside a human body, he will be unable to get in.'

The woman assured him that it would be done, and Friar Alberto took his leave of her. As soon as he had gone, she strutted up and down sticking her head so high in the air that her smock rose clear of her bottom, and thinking that the hour for the Angel Gabriel's visit would never come, so slowly did the time seem to pass.

Meanwhile, Friar Alberto, working on the assumption that his role would be that of a paladin rather than an angel during the night ahead, began to gorge himself on sweetmeats and various other delicacies so as to ensure that he would not be easily thrown from his mount. And as soon as darkness had fallen, having received permission to be absent, he departed with a companion and went to the house of a lady-friend which he had used as his base before when setting out to sow his wild oats. At what he judged a suitable hour, he made his way thence, suitably disguised, to Monna Lisetta's house; and having let himself in, he transfigured himself into an angel with the aid of certain gewgaws that he had brought along for the purpose. Then he climbed the stairs and strode into her bedroom.

When she saw this pure white object advancing towards her, the woman fell upon her knees before it. The Angel gave her his blessing, helped her to her feet, and motioned her to get into bed. This she promptly did, being only too ready to obey, and the Angel lay down at his votary's side.

Friar Alberto was a powerful, handsomely-proportioned fellow at the peak of physical fitness, and his approach to the bedding of Monna Lisetta, who was all soft and fresh, was altogether different from the one employed by her husband; hence he flew without wings several times before the night was over, causing the lady to shriek with delight at his achievements, which he supplemented with a running commentary on the glories of Heaven. Then, shortly before dawn, having made arrangements to visit her again, he collected his trappings and returned to his companion, with whom the mistress of the house had generously bedded down for the night so that he would not be afraid of the dark.

After breakfast, the lady went with her maidservant to call upon Friar Alberto and brought him tidings of the Angel Gabriel, describing what he was like, repeating all the things he had told her about the glories of the Life Eternal, and filling out her account with wondrous inventions of her own.

'Madam,' said Friar Alberto, 'I know not how you fared with him. But I do know that when he came to see me last night and I gave him your message, he immediately took my soul and set it down amid a multitude of flowers and roses, more wonderful to behold than anything that was ever seen on earth. And there I remained until matins this morning, in one of the most delectable places ever created by God. As for my actual body, I haven't the slightest idea what became of it.'

'But that's exactly what I am telling you,' said the lady. 'Your body spent the whole night in my arms with the Angel Gabriel inside it. And if you don't believe me, take a look under your left breast, where I gave the Angel such an enormous kiss that it will leave its mark there for the best part of a week.'

'In that case,' said Friar Alberto, 'I shall undress myself later today—which is a thing I have not done for a very long time—in order to see whether you are telling the truth.'

The woman chattered away for a good while longer before returning once more to her own house, which from then on Friar Alberto visited regularly without encountering let or hindrance.

One day, however, Monna Lisetta was chatting with a neighbour of hers, and their conversation happened to touch upon the subject of physical beauty. She was determined to prove that no other woman was as beautiful as herself, and, being a prize blockhead, she remarked:

'You would soon cease to prattle about the beauty of other women if I were to tell you who has fallen for mine.'

At this, her neighbour's curiosity was thoroughly aroused, and, well knowing the sort of woman with whom she was dealing, she replied:

'You may well be right, my dear, but you can hardly expect to convince me unless I know who it is that you are talking about.'

'My good woman,' retorted Monna Lisetta, who was quick to take offence, 'I should not be telling you this, but my admirer is the Angel Gabriel, who loves me more than his very self. And he informs me that it is all because I am the most beautiful woman on the face of the earth, or the face of the water for that matter.'

Her neighbour wanted to burst out laughing there and then, but being eager to draw Monna Lisetta out a little further on the subject, she continued to keep a straight face.

'God bless my soul!' she exclaimed. 'If your admirer is the Angel Gabriel, my dear, and if he tells you this, then it must be perfectly true. But I never imagined the angels did this sort of thing.'

'That is where you are mistaken,' said the lady. 'I swear to you by God's wounds that he does it better than my husband, and he informs me that they do it up there as well. But he has fallen in love with me because he thinks me more beautiful than any of the women in Heaven, and he is forever coming down to keep me company. So there!'

On leaving Monna Lisetta, her friend could scarcely contain her eagerness to repeat what she had heard, and at the earliest opportunity, whilst attending a party with a number of other ladies, she recounted the whole of the story from beginning to end. These ladies passed the tale on to their husbands and to various of their female acquaintances, and thus within forty-eight hours the news was all over Venice. Unfortunately, however, the brothers of Monna Lisetta's husband were among those to whose ears the story came, and they firmly made up their minds, without breathing a word to the lady herself, to run this angel to earth and discover whether he could fly. And for several nights running they lay in wait for his coming.

Some tiny hint of what had occurred chanced to reach the ears of Friar Alberto, who, having called upon the lady one night with the intention of giving her a scolding, had scarcely stripped off his clothes before her brothers-in-law, who had seen him arrive at the house, were hammering at the door and trying to force it open. Hearing the noise and guessing what it signified, Friar Alberto leapt out of bed, and seeing that there was nowhere to hide, he threw open a window overlooking the Grand Canal and took a flying leap into the water.

Friar Alberto was a good swimmer, and because the water was deep he came to no harm. Having swum across the canal, he dashed through the open door of a house on the other bank, and pleaded with its tenant, an honest-looking fellow, to save his life for the love of God, spinning him some yarn to account for his arrival there at such a late hour in a state of nudity.

The honest man took pity on him, and since he was in any case obliged to go and attend to certain affairs of his, he tucked the Friar up in his own bed and told him to stay there until he returned. And having locked him in, he went about his business.

On forcing their way into her room, the lady's in-laws discovered that the Angel Gabriel had flown, leaving his wings behind. They were feeling discountenanced, to say the least, and bombarded the woman with a torrent of violent abuse, after which they left her there, alone and disconsolate, and returned home with the Angel's bits and pieces.

Meanwhile, in the clear light of morning, the honest man happened to be passing through the Rialto district when he heard people talking about how the Angel Gabriel, having gone to spend the night with Monna Lisetta, had been discovered there by her in-laws, whereupon he had hurled himself into the canal in a fit of terror, thereafter vanishing without trace. The man immediately realized that the person in question was none other than the one he was sheltering under his roof, and having returned to the house, he persuaded the Friar, after turning a deaf ear to a string of tall stories, to admit that this was indeed the case. The man then insisted on being paid fifty ducats in exchange for keeping the Friar's whereabouts secret from the lady's in-laws, and the two of them devised a way for the payment to be made.

Once the money had been handed over, Friar Alberto was anxious to get away from the place, and the honest man said to him:

'There is only one way of doing it, but it won't work unless you are willing to cooperate. Today we are holding a carnival, to which everyone has to bring a partner wearing some form of disguise, so that one man will be dressed up as a bear, another as a savage, and so on and so forth. To round off the festivities, there is to be a sort of fancy-dress hunt, or *caccia,* in St. Mark's Square, after which all the people disperse, going off wherever they choose and taking their partners with them. Now if, instead of lying low here until someone gets wind of your whereabouts, you were to let me take you along in one of these disguises, after the ceremony I could leave you off wherever you wished. Apart from this, I can think of no other way for you to escape from here without being recognized, because the lady's in-laws have realized that you must have gone to ground somewhere in this part of the city, and their men are keeping watch over the whole neighbourhood, ready to seize hold of you the moment you appear.'

Although he baulked at the notion of going about the streets in a disguise of this sort, Friar Alberto was so terrified of the lady's in-laws that he allowed himself to be persuaded, and he told the fellow where he wanted to be taken, leaving him to work out the actual details.

The man applied a thick layer of honey to the Friar's body, after which he covered him with downy feathers from head to foot. He then tied a chain round his neck, put a mask over his face, and placed a club in one of his hands, whilst to the Friar's other hand he tethered two enormous dogs which he had collected earlier from the slaughterhouse. Meanwhile, he sent an accomplice to the Rialto to announce that anyone wishing to see the Angel Gabriel should hurry along to St. Mark's Square—which goes to show how far you can trust a Venetian.

Once these preparations were complete, the man waited a little longer and brought the Friar forth, getting him to lead the way whilst he held on to him from behind by means of the chain. Eventually, having stirred up a great commotion along the route and provoked the question 'Whoever is it?' from all the people he met, he drove his captive into the square. And what with all the crowds following in his wake, and those who had flocked from the Rialto after hearing the announcement, there were so many people in the square that it was impossible to count them. Upon his arrival, the man had tied his savage to a pillar in an elevated and conspicuous position, and was now pretending to wait for the mock-hunt, or *caccia,* to begin, whilst the Friar, since he was smeared with honey, was being pestered by hordes of gnats and gadflies.

When he saw that the square was more or less filled to capacity, the man stepped towards his savage as though to release him. But instead of setting him free, he tore the mask from Friar Alberto's face, proclaiming:

'Ladies and gentlemen, since the pig refuses to put in an appearance, there is not going to be any *caccia.* But so that you will not feel that your coming here was a waste of time, I want you to see the Angel Gabriel, who descends by night from Heaven to earth to amuse the women of Venice.'

As soon as his mask was removed, Friar Alberto was immediately recognized by all the onlookers, who jeered at him in unison, calling him by the foulest names and shouting the filthiest abuse ever to have been hurled at any scoundrel in history, at the same time pelting his face with all the nastiest things they could lay their hands upon. They kept this up without stopping, and would have gone on all night but for the fact that half-a-dozen or so of his fellow friars, having heard what was going on, made their way to the scene. The first thing they did on arriving was to throw a cape over his shoulders, after which they set him free and escorted him back, leaving a tremendous commotion in their wake, to their own quarters, where they placed him under lock and key. And there he is believed to have eked out the rest of his days in wretchedness and misery.

Thus it was that this arch-villain, whose wicked deeds went unnoticed because he was held to be good, had the audacity to transform himself into the Angel Gabriel. In the end, however, having been turned from an angel into a savage, he got the punishment he deserved, and repented in vain for the crimes he had committed. May it please God that a similar fate should befall each and every one of his fellows.

CHAUCER'S WOMEN

Geoffrey Chaucer, who died in 1400, is today regarded as England's greatest medieval poet. He was a cosmopolitan, a man of the world, thoroughly steeped in English ways but also deeply learned in French and Italian culture. He was a lifelong member of the distinguished and powerful entourage of John of Gaunt, Duke of Lancaster, uncle of one English king and father of another, the most visible and admired aristocratic leader of his time. Chaucer's wife was probably one of Lancaster's legions of mistresses. Chaucer served as a high-level customs official in London, as a diplomat to Italy for the royal government, and as a court poet who wrote on a variety of subjects and in many genres, borrowing much from Italy—Boccaccio was a favorite source. For edification of his Lancastrian patrons, and addressing a highly literate middle class audience as well, Chaucer's most original and ambitious work, *The Canterbury Tales* (pilgrims on the way to the shrine of St. Thomas Becket the Martyr at Canterbury are sharply described and each tells a story), is a subtle and boisterous mosaic of his society. Chaucer writes much about the middle class women, and they come out as autonomous, outspoken, highly promiscuous, earthy, greedy, demanding, and difficult. His greatest character is the many-times married wife of Bath, who manipulates the marriage market for all it is worth and is the loudest mouth in Albion.

Words between the Host and the Miller

The Miller, very drunk and rather pale,
Was straddled on his horse half-on half-off
And in no mood for manners or to doff
His hood or hat, or wait on any man,
But in a voice like Pilate's he began
To huff and swear. 'By blood and bones and belly,
I've got a noble story I can tell 'ee,
I'll pay the Knight his wages, not the Monk.'

    Our Host perceived at once that he was drunk
And said, 'Now hold on, Robin, dear old brother;
We'll get some better man to tell another;
You wait a bit. Let's have some common sense.'
'God's soul, I won't!' said he. 'At all events
I mean to talk, or else I'll go my way.'
Our Host replied, 'Well, blast you then, you may.
You fool! Your wits have gone beyond recall.'

    'Now listen,' said the Miller, 'one and all,
To what I have to say. But first I'm bound
To say I'm drunk, I know it by my sound.
And if the words get muddled in my tale
Just put it down to too much Southwark ale.
I will relate a legend and a life
Of an old carpenter and of his wife,
And how a student came and set his cap . . .'

    The Reeve looked up and shouted, 'Shut your
        trap!
Give over with your drunken harlotry.
It is a sin and foolishness,' said he,
'To slander any man or bring a scandal
On wives in general. Why can't you handle
Some other tale? There's other things beside.'

    To this the drunken Miller then replied,
'My dear old brother Oswald, such is life.
A man's no cuckold if he has no wife.
For all that, I'm not saying you are one;

There's many virtuous wives, all said and done,
Ever a thousand good for one that's bad,
As well you know yourself, unless you're mad.
Why are you angry? What is this to-do?
I have a wife, God knows, as well as you,
Yet not for all the oxen in my plough
Would I engage to take it on me now
To think myself a cuckold, just because . . .
I'm pretty sure I'm not and never was.
One shouldn't be too inquisitive in life
Either about God's secrets or one's wife.
You'll find God's plenty all you could desire;
Of the remainder, better not enquire.'

The Wife of Bath's Prologue

I am free
To wed, o' God's name, where it pleases me.
Wedding's no sin, so far as I can learn.
Better it is to marry than to burn.
    'What do I care if people choose to see
Scandal in Lamech for his bigamy?
I know that Abraham was a holy man
And Jacob too—I speak as best I can—
Yet each of them, we know, had several brides,
Like many another holy man besides.
Show me a time or text where God disparages
Or sets a prohibition upon marriages
Expressly, let me have it! Show it me!
And where did He command virginity?
I know as well as you do, never doubt it,
All the Apostle Paul has said about it;
He said that as for precepts he had none.
One may advise a woman to be one;
Advice is no commandment in my view.

He left it in our judgement what to do.
'Had God commanded maidenhood to all
Marriage would be condemned beyond recall,
And certainly if seed were never sown,
How ever could virginity be grown?
Paul did not dare pronounce, let matters rest,
His Master having given him no behest.
There's a prize offered for virginity;
Catch as catch can! Who's in for it? Let's see!

'It is not everyone who hears the call;
On whom God wills He lets His power fall.
The Apostle was a virgin, well I know;
Nevertheless, though all his writings show
He wished that everyone were such as he,
It's all mere counsel to virginity.
And as for being married, he lets me do it
Out of indulgence, so there's nothing to it
In marrying me, suppose my husband dead;
There's nothing bigamous in such a bed.
Though it were good a man should never touch
A woman (meaning here in bed and such)
And dangerous to assemble fire and tow
— What this allusion means you all must know —
He only says virginity is fresh,
More perfect than the frailty of the flesh
In married life — except when he and she
Prefer to live in married chastity.

'I grant it you. I'll never say a word
Decrying maidenhood although preferred
To frequent marriage; there are those who mean
To live in their virginity, as clean
In body as in soul, and never mate.
I'll make no boast about my own estate.
As in a noble household, we are told,
Not every dish and vessel's made of gold,
Some are of wood, yet earn their master's praise,
God calls His folk to Him in many ways.
To each of them God gave His proper gift,
Some this, some that, and left them to make shift.
Virginity is indeed a great perfection,
And married continence, for God's dilection,
But Christ, who of perfection is the well,
Bade not that everyone should go and sell
All that he had and give it to the poor
To follow in His footsteps, that is sure.
He spoke to those that would live perfectly,

And by your leave, my lords, that's not for me.
I will bestow the flower of life, the honey,
Upon the acts and fruit of matrimony.

'Tell me to what conclusion or in aid
Of what were generative organs made?
And for what profit were those creatures
    wrought?
Trust me, they cannot have been made for
    naught.
Gloze as you will and plead the explanation
That they were only made for the purgation
Of urine, little things of no avail
Except to know a female from a male,
And nothing else. Did somebody say no?
Experience knows well it isn't so.
The learned may rebuke me, or be loth
To think it so, but they were made for both,
That is to say both use and pleasure in
Engendering, except in case of sin.
Why else the proverb written down and set
In books: "A man must yield his wife her debt"?
What means of paying her can he invent
Unless he use his silly instrument?
It follows they were fashioned at creation
Both to purge urine and for propagation.

'But I'm not saying everyone is bound
Who has such harness as you heard me expound
To go and use it breeding; that would be
To show too little care for chastity.
Christ was a virgin, fashioned as a man,
And many of his saints since time began
Were ever perfect in their chastity.
I'll have no quarrel with virginity.
Let them be pure wheat loaves of maidenhead
And let us wives be known for barley-bread;
Yet Mark can tell that barley-bread sufficed
To freshen many at the hand of Christ.
In that estate to which God summoned me
I'll persevere; I'm not pernickety.
In wifehood I will use my instrument
As freely as my Maker me it sent.
If I turn difficult, God give me sorrow!
My husband, he shall have it eve and morrow
Whenever he likes to come and pay his debt,
I won't prevent him! I'll have a husband yet
Who shall be both my debtor and my slave

And bear his tribulation to the grave
Upon his flesh, as long as I'm his wife.
For mine shall be the power all his life
Over his proper body, and not he,
Thus the Apostle Paul has told it me,
And bade our husbands they should love us well;
There's a command on which I like to dwell . . .'

The Pardoner started up, and thereupon
'Madam,' he said, 'by God and by St John,
That's noble preaching no one could surpass!
I was about to take a wife; alas!
Am I to buy it on my flesh so dear?
There'll be no marrying for me this year!'

'You wait,' she said, 'my story's not begun.
You'll taste another brew before I've done;
You'll find it doesn't taste as good as ale;
And when I've finished telling you my tale
Of tribulation in the married life
In which I've been an expert as a wife,
That is to say, myself have been the whip.
So please yourself whether you want to sip
At that same cask of marriage I shall broach.
Be cautious before making the approach,
For I'll give instances, and more than ten.
And those who won't be warned by other men,
By other men shall suffer their correction,
So Ptolemy has said, in this connection.
You read his *Almagest;* you'll find it there.'

'Madam, I put it to you as a prayer,'
The Pardoner said, 'go on as you began!
Tell us your tale, spare not for any man.
Instruct us younger men in your technique.'
'Gladly,' she said, 'if you will let me speak,
But still I hope the company won't reprove me
Though I should speak as fantasy may move me,
And please don't be offended at my views;
They're really only offered to amuse.

'Now, gentlemen, I'll on and tell my tale
And as I hope to drink good wine and ale
I'll tell the truth. Those husbands that I had,
Three of them were good and two were bad.
The three that I call 'good' were rich and old.'

The Merchant's Prologue

'Weeping and wailing, care and other sorrow,
I know them well enough by eve and morrow,'

The Merchant said; 'like others I suppose
That have been married, that's the way it goes;
I know too well that's how it goes with me.
I have a wife, the worst that there could be;
For if a fiend were coupled to my wife,
She'd overmatch him, you can bet your life.
Why choose a special instance to recall
Her soaring malice? She's a shrew in all.
There's a wide difference I'm bound to say
Between Griselda's patience and the way
My wife behaves; her studied cruelty
Surpasses everything. If I were free,
Never again, never again the snare!
We married men, our life is grief and care.
Try it who will, and he will find, I promise
That I have spoken truly, by St Thomas,
For most of us — I do not say for all,
And God forbid that such a thing befall.

'Ah, my good Host, I have been wedded now
These two months past, no more than that, I vow,
Yet I believe no bachelor alive,
Not if you were to take a knife and rive
Him to the heart, could tell of so much grief
As I could tell you of; beyond belief,
The curst malignity I get from her!'

Our Host replied, 'God bless you, my dear sir!
But since you know so much about the art
Of marriage, let me beg you to impart.'
'With pleasure,' he said, 'but on the personal
    score
I'm so heart-scalded I shall say no more.'

Epilogue to the Merchant's Tale

'Ey, mercy of God!' our Host exclaimed thereat,
'May God preserve me from a wife like that!
Just look what cunning tricks and subtleties
There are in woman! Busy little bees
They are, deceiving silly men like us!
They're always sliding and evading thus,
Dodging the truth; the Merchant's tale has shown it
And it's as true as steel — I have to own it.
I have a wife myself, a poor one too,
But what a tongue! She is a blabbing shrew,
And she has other vices, plenty more.
Well, let it go! No sense to rub a sore.
But, d'you know what? In confidence, good sir,

I much regret that I am tied to her.
Were I to reckon her vices one by one,
I'd only be a fool when I had done;
And why? Because it would be sure to be
Reported back to her, by two or three

Among us here; by whom I needn't say;
In all such matters women find a way.
And anyhow my brains would hardly run
To telling you, and so my story's done.'

ABUSED WOMEN

There are a great many examples of abused women in medieval historical and literary sources. Here are two instances. The first, the *Laxdaela Saga,* a thirteenth-century Icelandic saga, describes the choosing of a concubine by a wealthy lord. Women are treated simply as commodity slaves. Unquestionably this practice was common in early medieval Europe and was still being openly conducted in a less developed area like one of the outlying Scandinavian islands in the thirteenth century. In the second selection, the fourteenth-century Italian historian Salimbene de Adam describes the extremely vicious treatment of a group of noblewomen after the men in their group have been defeated in a war and executed. The women are abused in just about every conceivable way, and the sadistic sexual ingredient in the victor's behavior is prominent. That such abuse of women frequently occurred in medieval war zones is evident. Yet, before the Middle Ages are specifically condemned for abusing women, we might remember this: The selling of women concubines was commonly practiced in China in the 1930s and is still practiced in the Middle East today. One of Thomas Hardy's novels, set in England of the 1870s, features as a plot device a man selling his wife at a country fair. The abuse of women in war zones as here described is similar to what goes on in Bosnia and in the Middle East today. That women, even of the nobility, were occasionally, one might even say frequently, abused in the Middle Ages is true, but caution should be used in following the press' tendency to describe this appalling behavior as distinctly "medieval."

LAXDAELA SAGA

It so happened early next summer that King Hakon went on a naval expedition east to the Brenn Isles for a royal assembly which, in accordance with the laws, had to be held every third summer to secure continuing peace in the realm; these meetings were convened by the Scandinavian kings to deal with matters of mutual concern. To attend them was considered a festive occasion, and people flocked to them from practically every known country.

Hoskuld Dala-Kollsson wanted to attend the assembly and launched his ship, since he had not been to see the king during the winter; and besides, it was an important trading market.

There were huge crowds at the assembly that year and there was a great deal of celebration, with drinking and games and every form of entertainment. Nothing of any great moment took place. Hoskuld met many of his kinsmen from Denmark there.

Then one day when Hoskuld was on his way out to enjoy himself with some companions, he noticed a gaily-decorated tent standing apart from the other booths. He went over to it and entered;

inside he found a man dressed in costly clothing and wearing a Russian hat. Hoskuld asked him his name.

'My name is Gilli,' he replied, 'and most people realize who I am when they hear my nickname: I am called Gilli the Russian.'

Hoskuld said he had often heard him spoken of, for he was said to be the wealthiest man the guild of merchants had ever known—'So no doubt you can offer us whatever we want to buy?'

Gilli asked them what they were looking for. Hoskuld replied that he wanted to buy a slave-girl—'if you have one for sale.'

'You're not trying to embarrass me, are you, by asking for something you don't expect me to have?' said Gilli. 'I wouldn't be too sure of that.'

Hoskuld could see a curtain drawn right across the booth. Gilli lifted it up, and Hoskuld now saw that there were twelve women sitting behind it. Gilli invited him to go through and have a look to see if he wanted to buy any of them. Hoskuld went through. The women were all sitting in a row across the booth, and he inspected them carefully. The one sitting right at the edge of the tent caught his eye; she was shabbily dressed, but Hoskuld thought her beautiful, from what he could see.

'How much would that woman cost, if I wanted to buy her?' he asked Gilli.

'You'd have to pay three marks of silver for her,' replied Gilli.

'That's rather a high price you're charging for a slave-girl, surely?' said Hoskuld. 'It's three times the normal price.'

'You're quite right,' said Gilli, 'I value her more highly than the rest. You can have any one of the eleven others for only one mark of silver, and leave this one with me.'

'Let me see first how much silver there is in this purse at my belt,' said Hoskuld, and asked Gilli to fetch the scales while he looked in his purse.

Then Gilli said, 'I don't want to cheat you over this, Hoskuld. The woman has one serious defect, and I want you to know of it before we clinch a deal.'

Hoskuld asked what it was.

'The woman is a mute,' said Gilli. 'I've tried every way of coaxing her into speech, but I've never got a word out of her. I'm quite convinced she cannot speak.'

'Bring out your scales,' said Hoskuld, 'and we'll see how much there is in this purse.'

Gilli did so; and when they weighed the silver it came to three marks precisely.

Then Hoskuld said, 'So it seems we have a deal on our hands after all. Here's the money, and I'll take the woman. I must say you've dealt most fairly over this, for you certainly didn't try to deceive me in any way.'

With that, Hoskuld went back home to his booth. And that night he slept with the woman.

Next morning when they were getting up, Hoskuld said to her, 'Gilli the Wealthy wasn't very generous with the clothes he gave you to wear; but I suppose it was harder for him to clothe twelve than for me to clothe only one.'

He opened one of his chests and took out some fine clothing and gave it to her; and everyone remarked that fine clothes certainly suited her well. . . .

Olaf was a peerless child, and Hoskuld loved him dearly.

Next summer Jorunn said that the concubine would have to do some work or else go. Hoskuld told the woman that she was to wait upon Jorunn and himself, and look after her child as well. By the time the boy was two years old he could speak perfectly and was running about on his own like a child of four.

It so happened one morning that Hoskuld was out of doors seeing to his farm; it was a fine day, and the dawn sun was shining. He heard the sound of voices and went over to the stream at the foot of the sloping homefield. There he saw two people he knew well: it was his son Olaf, and the boy's mother. He realized then that she was not speechless at all, for she was talking busily to the child. Hoskuld now went over to them and asked her what her name was, and told her there was no point in concealing it any longer. She agreed, and they sat down on the slope of the homefield.

Then she said, 'If you want to know my name, I am called Melkorka.'

Hoskuld asked her to tell him more about her family.

'My father is called Myrkjartan, and he is a king in Ireland,' she said. 'I was taken captive and enslaved when I was fifteen.'

Hoskuld said she had kept silent for far too long over such a noble lineage. Then he went back into the house and told Jorunn what he had discovered while he was out. Jorunn said she had no way of knowing whether the woman was telling the truth, and that she had little liking for mystery folk, and they discussed it no further. Jorunn was certainly no kinder to Melkorka after this, but Hoskuld was rather more friendly.

A little later, when Jorunn was going to bed, Melkorka helped her off with her shoes and stockings and laid them on the floor; Jorunn picked up the stockings and started beating her about the head with them. Melkorka flew into a rage and struck her on the nose with her fist, drawing blood. Hoskuld came in and separated them. After that he sent Melkorka away and gave her a place to live in farther up Laxriverdale; this farm has been known as Melkorkustead ever since. It is derelict now. It is on the south side of the river. Melkorka made her home there, and her son Olaf went with her; Hoskuld supplied everything that was needed for the farm.

As Olaf grew up it was quickly apparent that he would be a paragon of good looks and courtesy.

SALIMBENE DE ADAM

Alberigo had had twenty-five civic leaders of Treviso hanged on a single day, and they had neither offended nor harmed him in any way. But because he was afraid that they would perhaps do him harm, he had them removed from before his face [cf. II Kings 7.15] and shamefully hanged. And he required thirty noble women—their mothers, wives, daughters, and sisters—to come and watch the execution. He wanted also to cut off the noses of these women, but by the happy intervention of a man who was falsely said to be Alberigo's bastard son, this was not done. Furthermore, he had their clothes cut off from their breasts down so that with bodies all nude they stood before the eyes of the men who were to be hanged. Moreover, he had the men hanged very near the ground and then forced the women to walk between their legs so that the men kicked them in the face as they were dying in bitterness of spirit [cf. Job 21.25]. And the women had to endure the horror and pain of such base mockery. To see such things was the greatest kind of misery and cruelty, the like of which has never been heard. Then Alberigo had these women carried off beyond the river Sial or Sile to go wherever they could. And with the pieces of garment they had about their breasts, the women made coverings for their genitals (that is, their pudenda), and then walked the whole day for fifteen miles with bare feet and nude bodies through wild fields, bitten by flies, and torn by thorns and briars and nettles and burrs and thistles. And they went weeping, for they had cause for weeping, and they had nothing to eat:

O God, Look upon
The sorrow and pain!
These troubled ones,
These your children,
Are lost without You.
Yours it is to help.
Yours it is to help.

Fragment of a casket with runic inscription

HROSWITHA OF GANDERSHEM

SADOMASOCHISTIC DRAMA

There are extant authentic voices of medieval women. We can read their work and try to understand their consciousness. One of these was Hroswitha of Gandershem, a Benedictine nun in late-tenth-century western Germany. She wrote short dramas, mainly about virgins and martyrs, of which this is one. The dramaturgy is simple but quite effective. The dramatic form is obviously modeled on classical Roman dramas. Hroswitha is devout, and she has a strong interest in science as well as theology. But the work is surprising; there is a powerful sexual tone here, quite explicit. It is obvious that Hroswitha has a strong taste for sadomasochistic fantasies. That is not surprising in a nun, perhaps, but she makes it a central component of the drama. We remember the bodily tortures of the virgin martyrs, recounted in detail with a sort of relish through the mouths of pagan Roman persecutors, more than the Christian piety. Hroswitha uses the feminine body and its pleasures for aggressive men as a weapon against masculine power.

THE MARTYRDOM OF THE HOLY VIRGINS FIDES, SPES AND KARITAS

ANTIOCHUS: *In the hope that your Highness, Emperor Hadrian, achieve prosperity and success, according to your wish,/ and that your state may flourish/ in happiness and without disturbance, I have always desired to uproot immediately/ and destroy entirely/ whatever might harm the state, whatever might threaten its peace and tranquility./*

HADRIAN: *Rightly so, I say,/ for our* prosperity is the reason for *your* own good fortunes' sway,/ because we increase your rank and standing day by day./

ANTIOCHUS: I am grateful to Your Highness. Therefore, whenever I discover anything that appears subversive or brings contention/ I do not hide it but bring it immediately to your attention./

HADRIAN: And justly so, so that you avoid what is forbidden/ by hiding what should not be hidden./

ANTIOCHUS: I have never been guilty of committing such a crime./

HADRIAN: I know that. But tell me if you had discovered anything new this time./

ANTIOCHUS: Recently, a certain woman arrived in Rome/ not alone/ but accompanied by her three little children./

HADRIAN: What is the sex of the children?/

ANTIOCHUS: They are all girls.

HADRIAN: Could the arrival of these three little girls possibly present a danger for the state?/

ANTIOCHUS: The danger is great./

HADRIAN: Why?/

ANTIOCHUS: The peace is disturbed thereby./

HADRIAN: How can that be? Specify!/

ANTIOCHUS: What could possibly disrupt the harmony of civic peace more than religious dissent?

HADRIAN: Nothing is graver, nothing more dangerous. The Roman Empire testifies to that fact,/ infected everywhere by the mortal plague of the Christian sect./

ANTIOCHUS: This woman, whom I just mentioned, exhorts our citizens and clients/ to abandon the ancestral and ancient rites/ and to convert to Christianity.

HADRIAN: Do her exhortations succeed?/

ANTIOCHUS: They do so, indeed!/ For our wives despise us so that they refuse to eat with us,/ or even more to sleep with us./

HADRIAN: I admit that poses a danger./

ANTIOCHUS: Your Highness should take some preventative measures as concerns this stranger./

HADRIAN: You are right./ Have her arraigned and questioned in our sight/ to see whether she might change her mind./

ANTIOCHUS: Do you wish for me to bring her to you?/

HADRIAN: Certainly I do./

ANTIOCHUS: Foreign woman, what's your name?

SAPIENTIA: Sapientia.

ANTIOCHUS: Emperor Hadrian orders you to come to court and appear before him.

SAPIENTIA: I do not fear to enter the palace/ in the noble company of my daughters, nor do I fear the menace/ of looking upon the Emperor's threatening face./

ANTIOCHUS: This hateful Christian race/ is always bent on spurning our ruler's authority.

SAPIENTIA: The Ruler of the Universe, Who never can be conquered, will not permit the fiend to overcome His people.

ANTIOCHUS: Bridle your tongue/ and hurry now along./

SAPIENTIA: Go ahead, and show the way;/ we shall follow without delay./

ANTIOCHUS: Behold the Emperor seated on his throne; be careful of what you say.

SAPIENTIA: Christ's command preempts that need/ for He promised us gifts of wisdom that will always succeed./

ADRIANUS: Come hither, Antiochus.

ANTIOCHUS: Here I am, My Lord.

ADRIANUS: Are these the little women whom you denounced as Christians?

ANTIOCHUS: Yes.

HADRIAN: The beauty of every one of them stuns my senses;/ I cannot stop admiring the nobility of their bearing, their many excellences./

ANTIOCHUS: Desist from admiring them, my Lord,/ and force them to worship our gods./

HADRIAN: What if I mollify them first with flattering speech;/ perhaps, they will then give in, one and each./

ANTIOCHUS: That would be much better, for the female sex's fragility,/ makes it prone to yield to flattery./

HADRIAN: Noble lady, I invite you amiably and kindly, to worship our gods and so enjoy our friendship./

SAPIENTIA: I don't care to satisfy your wish by worshipping your gods nor do I seek your friendship./

HADRIAN: Having controlled my anger, I am not indignant but am concerned with fatherly care/ for you and your daughters' welfare./

SAPIENTIA: My children, do not open your hearts to the tricks of this devilish snake;/ scorn him like I do for Christ's sake./

FIDES: We despise him in our souls and scorn the nonsense he spoke.

HADRIAN: What are you whispering? What are you saying, not to be heard?/

SAPIENTIA: I spoke to my daughters and only a word./

HADRIAN: You appear to be of noble descent. I would like to know from where you came,/ who are your ancestors, and what is your name?/

SAPIENTIA: Even though pride in our noble descent is of little consequence to us, I do not deny to trace/ my birth from an illustrious race./

HADRIAN: I can believe that that is the case./

SAPIENTIA: My ancestors were princes of Italy of eminent acclaim,/ and Sapientia is my name./

HADRIAN: The splendor of your noble ancestry illumines your face;/ and wisdom, inherent in your name, flows in your speech's grace./

SAPIENTIA: You flatter us in vain;/ your attempt to sway us will reap no gain./

HADRIAN: Tell me why you came here, and why you incite our people, subverting our reign?/

SAPIENTIA: For no other matter/ but to be a witness to truth, to understand the faith, which you persecute, better,/ and to consecrate my daughters to Christ.

HADRIAN: Tell me their names.

SAPIENTIA: One is called Fides, the second Spes, the third Karitas.

HADRIAN: How old are they?/

SAPIENTIA: Would it please you, children, say,/ if I fatigued this fool/ with a lesson in arithmetical rule?/

FIDES: Yes, mother, it would please us, greatly,/ and we, too, will hear it gladly./

SAPIENTIA: Oh, Emperor, you wish to know my children's ages; Karitas has completed a diminished, evenly even number of years;/ Spes, on the other hand a diminished evenly uneven number, and Karitas an augmented unevenly even number of years./

HADRIAN: Your reply leaves me totally ignorant as to the answer to my question./

SAPIENTIA: That is no wonder/ since not only a single number but several fall into the categories I mentioned./. . .

HADRIAN: What a thorough, perplexing lecture has arisen from my question concerning the children's ages!

SAPIENTIA: Praise be thereof to the supreme wisdom of the Creator/ and to the marvelous science of this world's Maker,/ Who not only created the world in the beginning out of nothing and ordered everything according to number, measure and weight/ but also in the seasons and in the ages of men gave us the ability to grasp and relate/ the wondrous science of the arts.

HADRIAN: For long I bore your discourse so as to make you ready to comply now./

SAPIENTIA: How?/

HADRIAN: By worshipping the gods.

SAPIENTIA: That I will never consent to do.

HADRIAN: If you refuse, you will have to be forced with tortures.

SAPIENTIA: You may lacerate my body with the weapons you wield,/ but you will never succeed in compelling my soul to yield./

ANTIOCHUS: The day is ending, night is near./ This is no time to quarrel; dinnertime is here./

HADRIAN: Let them be placed in prison under guard. I'll grant them three days to reconsider./

ANTIOCHUS: Guard these women closely, soldiers! Don't give them an occasion to escape from hither./

SAPIENTIA: My sweet little daughters, my darling little children, hark!/ Do not be saddened by our prison's dismal dark,/ do not be afraid of the punishments at hand./

FIDES: Our bodies may tremble at the thought of tortures, yet our souls exult in the reward so grand./

SAPIENTIA: Overcome the softness of your tender years by the strength of mature reflection!/

SPES: You must support us with your prayers so that we may win perfection./

SAPIENTIA: That is what I pray for incessantly,/ that is what I ask for and request earnestly/ that you persevere in your faith which from your early childhood on I never ceased to instill in your mind./

KARITAS: To forget what we learned sucking at your breast in our cradle, we will never be inclined./

SAPIENTIA: It was for this that I nursed you, my milk flowing free;/ it was for this that I carefully reared you three;/ that I may espouse you to a heavenly, not an earthly bridegroom and may thus deserve to be called the mother-in-law of the Eternal King thereby./

FIDES: For the love of that Bridegroom we are prepared to die./

SAPIENTIA: Your decision delights me more than the sweet taste of nectar, my dears./

SPES: Lead us to the judges and you shall promptly see how our love for Him overcomes our fears./

SAPIENTIA: My only wish is this: that by your virginity I may be crowned/ and by your martyrdom, renowned./

SPES: Hand in hand, let us go and the grim tyrant confound./

SAPIENTIA: Wait, until the appointed date./

FIDES: Though weary of delay, we shall wait./

HADRIAN: Antiochus, have those Italian captives brought before us.

ANTIOCHUS: Come forth, Sapientia, you and your children are to appear before the Emperor.

SAPIENTIA: Come with me, my daughters; be firm,/ persevere in faith and yearn,/ that you may blessedly earn the palm of martyrdom.

SPES: We come with all speed/ and He will accompany us indeed,/ for Whose love we are to die.

HADRIAN: The serenity of Our Majesty granted you three days to reflect upon what's good for you; so yield to our orders and comply!/

SAPIENTIA: We reflected upon what is best for us, that is, our decision not to comply./

ANTIOCHUS: Why do you deign to exchange words with this impertinent woman who keeps insulting you with insolent glee?/

HADRIAN: Should I leave her unpunished, to go free?/

ANTIOCHUS: Of course not.

HADRIAN: Then what should be done?

ANTIOCHUS: Urge those little girls to yield and if they resist, do not spare their youth, but let them be killed so that their rebellious mother may be tormented all the more acutely by their pain./

HADRIAN: What you suggest I shall ordain./

ANTIOCHUS: So in the end, you shall prevail./

HADRIAN: Fides, look with respect upon the venerable image of great Diana and bring offerings to the holy goddess,/ so that her favor you may possess./

FIDES: Oh, what a foolish Imperial command; worthy of nothing but contempt!

HADRIAN: What are you mumbling in derision,/ whom are you mocking with your wry expression?/

FIDES: It's your foolishness I deride, and I mock your stupidity./

HADRIAN: My stupidity?/

FIDES: Yes.

ANTIOCHUS: The Emperor's?

FIDES: Yes, his!

ANTIOCHUS: This is abominable!

FIDES: For what is more foolish, what can seem more stupid than your command to show contempt for the Creator of All and venerate base metal instead./

ANTIOCHUS: Fides, you are mad!/

FIDES: Antiochus, you lie!

ANTIOCHUS: Isn't it the sign of great insanity and of severe madness when you call the ruler of the world a fool?/

FIDES: I have called him a fool,/ I now call him a fool/ and I shall call him a fool/ as long as I live.

ANTIOCHUS: You will not live long; soon you shall expire./

FIDES: To die in Christ is just what I desire./

HADRIAN: Twelve centurions shall flog her limbs each in turn./

ANTIOCHUS: She gets what she has earned./

HADRIAN: Oh brave centurions come to the fore/ and avenge the insults that I bore./

ANTIOCHUS: A just punishment./

HADRIAN: Antiochus, ask again if she is willing to repent./

ANTIOCHUS: Will you, Fides, continue to insult the Emperor,/ as you did before?/

FIDES: Why should I be less inclined to do it now?/

ANTIOCHUS: Because lashes will stop you, I trow./

FIDES: Flogging will not make me refrain/ because I will not feel the pain./

ANTIOCHUS: What wretched obstinacy;/ what insolent audacity!/

HADRIAN: Her body is ripped open by the flogging but her mind/ is still puffed up with pride./

FIDES: You are mistaken, Hadrian, if you think that you weary me with these tortures, it is not I but my torturers who are tired and weak,/ and it is they who are exhausted and with sweat reek./

HADRIAN: Have her nipples cut off, Antiochus, so that through shame at last she be coerced to relent.

ANTIOCHUS: Oh, would that she could be somehow coerced./

HADRIAN: Perhaps she can be forced . . ./

FIDES: You have wounded my chaste breast, but you have not hurt me. Look, instead of blood,/ there flows a milky flood./

HADRIAN: Have her thrown on a fiery hot grill/ so that the glowing coals will make her still./

ANTIOCHUS: She deserves to die miserably, she who did not fear to scorn your will./

FIDES: Whatever you plan for my pain,/ becomes

the calm of joyful gain;/ so I rest comfortably on the grill,/ as if I were in a tranquil ship./

HADRIAN: Prepare a pot full of wax and pitch, place it on the pyre/ and cast this rebel into the boiling mire!/

FIDES: I'll jump into it of free volition./

HADRIAN: Go ahead, with my permission./

FIDES: Where are your threats now? Behold, unhurt I frolic and swim in the boiling stew/ and I feel the cool of the early morning dew./

HADRIAN: Antiochus, what is to be done?/

ANTIOCHUS: Make sure that she doesn't escape and run./

HADRIAN: Behead her!

ANTIOCHUS: Otherwise she will not be defeated.

FIDES: My joy I must now voice;/ and in the Lord I must now rejoice./

SAPIENTIA: Christ, unconquered victor over Satan, grant my daughter Fides endurance.

FIDES: Oh, venerable mother, say your last farewell to your child, give a kiss to your firstborn,/ expel from your heart sadness' thorn/ because I am on my way to eternal rewards.

SAPIENTIA: Oh my child, my child, I am not disturbed. I feel no sadness,/ but I say farewell exalting in you and kiss your mouth and eyes with tears of gladness/ praying that you preserve the holy mystery of your name, even as you fall under the executioner's blow.

FIDES: Oh my sisters, born of the same mother, give me a kiss of peace, and prepare yourselves to bear the impending strife./

SPES: Help us with your constant prayers so that we may deserve to follow to everlasting life./

FIDES: Obey the admonitions of our saintly parent who has always exhorted us to despise this present world/ so that we may deserve to attain the other world./

KARITAS: Gladly we obey our mother's admonitions so that we may reap eternal bliss./

FIDES: Come, then, executioner, kill me! Perform your office, don't be remiss./

SAPIENTIA: I embrace the severed head of my dead daughter, and keep kissing her lips; I thank Thee Christ for granting victory/ to a little girl, still in infancy./

HADRIAN: Spes, give in to my admonition./ I counsel you in paternal affection./

SPES: What do you urge me?/ What do you counsel me?/

HADRIAN: That you don't imitate your sister's obstinacy and thus avoid suffering similar pain./

SPES: Oh, how I wish to be worthy of her, and imitate her in her pain/ so that, like her, I may achieve similar gain./

HADRIAN: Lay aside this callousness of heart and relent, bringing incense to the great Diana. Then I will adopt you as my own child/ and cherish you with all my heart./

SPES: I don't want you for my father, I have no desire for your favors; therefore, you chase after empty dreams,/ if you think that I shall yield./

HADRIAN: Watch your speech or you'll feel my ire!/

SPES: I do not care, be irate, Sire!/

ANTIOCHUS: I wonder, my Lord,/ why you let yourself be scorned/ by this worthless little girl for so long./ I myself am bursting with rage as I hear her bark at you so fearlessly.

HADRIAN: For long I spared her youth but I will not spare her any longer; I'll give her the punishment she deserves.

ANTIOCHUS: Oh, I wish you would.

HADRIAN: Lictors, come forth! Take this rebel in your grip/ and beat her to death with your heaviest whip./

ANTIOCHUS: Now she will feel the severity of your

anger because she cared so little for your kind mildness.

SPES: But *this* is the kindness I desire, *this* is the mildness I hope for./

ANTIOCHUS: Sapientia, what are you mumbling, standing there with eyes up-turned next to your dead child's corpse?/

SAPIENTIA: I pray to our eternal Father, that He may grant Spes the same perseverance and strength as He granted Fides.

SPES: Oh mother, mother, how efficacious, how useful are the prayers you say!/ Behold, even while you pray,/ my torturers are breathless, they flog me again and again,/ yet I feel not the slightest pain./

HADRIAN: If the lashes don't hurt you,/ harsher punishments will force you./

SPES: Bring on, bring on whatever cruel, whatever deadly thing you have invented;/ the more savage your punishment is the more you will be confounded when you are defeated./

HADRIAN: She is to be suspended in mid air and torn to pieces with claws so that when her bowels have been severed/ and her bones have been bared,/ cracking, limb by limb, she dies./

ANTIOCHUS: That is the Emperor's order, and his just reprisal./

SPES: You speak with the deceit of a fox, Antiochus, and, with the two-faced cunning of the were-wolf.

ANTIOCHUS: Hold your tongue, you wretch, your chatter must now end./

SPES: It will not turn out as you hope, but you and your lord humiliated will stand./

HADRIAN: What new fragrance do I smell?/ What amazing sweetness do I sense?/

SPES: The pieces of my lacerated flesh give off this fragrant heavenly scent;/ so that you'll be forced to admit against your will that I cannot be harmed by your punishment./

HADRIAN: Antiochus, what am I to do?/

ANTIOCHUS: Think of tortures anew./

HADRIAN: Place a brazen cattle over the flames full of oil, wax, fat, and pitch,/ and tied up, throw her in./

ANTIOCHUS: When she is given over to Vulcan's force/ perhaps there'll be no escape nor recourse./

SPES: Christ's mighty power has been known to change the nature of fire,/ to make its rage harmless in its entire./

HADRIAN: What is it I hear, Antiochus, it sounds like a crashing flood./

ANTIOCHUS: Alas, alas, my lord!/

HADRIAN: What is happening to us? I am alarmed./

ANTIOCHUS: That bubbling hot brew bursted the pot, destroyed the servants and that witch appears to be unharmed./

HADRIAN: I admit defeat./

ANTIOCHUS: Full and complete./

HADRIAN: Behead her!/

ANTIOCHUS: There is no other way to kill her./

SPES: Oh beloved Karitas, Oh, my only sister! Do not fear the tyrant's threats,/ and do not dread his punishments,/ follow in firm faith your sisters' example/ who precedes you to Heaven's palace./

KARITAS: I am weary of this life,/ I am weary of this earthly abode because even if it is for a very short while,/ I'll be separated from you.

SPES: Lay aside this loathing and concentrate on the prize, for even though we will be separated for short/ we shall soon be reunited in the Heavenly port./

KARITAS: Let it be done, Let it be so!/

SPES: Rejoice good mother, be glad/ and in maternal concern do not be sad,/ have hope instead of grief as you see me die for Christ.

SAPIENTIA: Now I am happy but later I'll exalt in perfect joy, when I will have sent your little sister to heaven, martyred like you,/ and when I myself will follow you too./

SPES: The eternal holy Trinity/ will restore to you all three/ of your daughters in everlasting life.

SAPIENTIA: Take comfort my child. Don't be afraid./ The henchman approaches with his naked blade./

SPES: I welcome the sword. Thou, Christ, accept my soul,/ separated from its bodily frame/ for bearing witness to Thy holy name./

SAPIENTIA: Oh Karitas, my hope, my darling child, single one left of my womb, do not disappoint your mother who expects you to win this strife./ Spurn the comfort of this life/ so that you may reach never-ending joy where your sisters already sparkle, radiant with the crowns of untouched virginity.

KARITAS: Stand by me, mother with your saintly prayers, so that I may be worthy to partake in that bliss./

SAPIENTIA: I beg you to stay firm in your faith to the very end and I have no doubt you will be rewarded with heavenly bliss./

HADRIAN: Karitas, I have had more than enough! I am fed up with your sisters' insults and I was rather exasperated with their drawn-out arguments; I will therefore not contend with you for long, but reward you richly with goods if you obey,/ and punish you if you disobey./

KARITAS: I embrace the good with all my heart, and I detest all evil that be./

HADRIAN: That's a wholesome attitude for you to take and is acceptable to me./ Therefore, by the grace of my kindness I will require very little of you./

KARITAS: What is it you wish me to do?/

HADRIAN: Simply say "Great Diana" and beyond that, I will not compel you a sacrifice to procure./

KARITAS: I will not say that, that's for sure./

HADRIAN: Why?/

KARITAS: Because I don't wish to lie./ I am born of the same parents as my sisters, imbued by the same sacraments, strengthened by the same firmness of faith. Know, therefore, that we are one and the same in what we want, what we feel and what we think. In nothing will I differ from them.

HADRIAN: How insulting to be held in contempt by a mere child.

KARITAS: I may be young in years, yet I am expert enough to confound you in argument.

HADRIAN: Take her, Antiochus, and have her hung and lashed on a rack./

ANTIOCHUS: I fear, lashes won't be of any use, alack./

HADRIAN: If they are of no use, then order a furnace to be heated for three continuous days and nights and throw her into the raging fire./

KARITAS: What an impotent judge who cannot overcome an eight year old infant without the force of fire./

HADRIAN: Go Antiochus, and carry out my desire./

KARITAS: Even though he'll try to comply with your savage decree/ he will not in the least hurt me/ because the lashes will not lacerate my flesh nor will the flames harm my garments or hair.

HADRIAN: That is to be seen./

KARITAS: I hope that it will be seen./

HADRIAN: Antiochus, why so dejected,/ why are you returning sadder than expected?/

ANTIOCHUS: As soon as you learn the cause of my gloom, you will be no less affected./

HADRIAN: Speak up, don't hide it.

ANTIOCHUS: That petulant little girl whom you gave over to me to be tortured, was flogged in my presence but the lashes didn't even scratch her tender skin. Finally, I threw her into the furnace, glowing red-hot with its heat . . ./

HADRIAN: Why do you cease to speak?/ Report the outcome.

ANTIOCHUS: The flame exploded and burned five thousand men./

HADRIAN: And what happened to her then?/

ANTIOCHUS: To Karitas?

HADRIAN: Yes.

ANTIOCHUS: Playfully she walked among the flame-spewing vapors, quite unhurt,/ and sung hymns in praise of her God. And those who watched her and were alert/ said that three men dressed in white were walking along with her.

HADRIAN: I blush to see her again,/ my efforts to harm her are all in vain./

ANTIOCHUS: By the sword let her be killed./

HADRIAN: Right away let that be filled./

ANTIOCHUS: Uncover, your stubborn neck, Karitas, and prepare for the executioner's sword./

KARITAS: In this I do not resist your wish but gladly obey your word./

SAPIENTIA: Now my child I must exalt, now I must rejoice in Christ's glory; no more worry,/ no more care, for I am sure of your victory./

KARITAS: Give me a kiss, mother, and commend my departing soul to Christ.

SAPIENTIA: He who gave you life in my womb, receive your soul which He breathed into you from Heaven.

KARITAS: Glory be to Thee oh Christ./ Thou hast called me to you elevated by the martyr's palm./

SAPIENTIA: Farewell my dearest daughter, and when you are united with Christ in heaven, remember your mother, having been made patron of her who bore you.

SAPIENTIA: Come noble ladies, come and help bury my daughters' remains.

MATRONS: We shall preserve the bodies with spice/ and celebrate the service with all honors thrice./

SAPIENTIA: Great is your kindness and wondrous your support which you show my dead children and me.

MATRONS: Whatever you wish, with devoted hearts we shall fulfill./

SAPIENTIA: I don't doubt your good will./

MATRONS: Where is the place that you chose as the burial site?/

SAPIENTIA: At the third milestone outside of town, if the long distance is all right./

MATRONS: We don't mind a long journey's strain,/ gladly we follow the funeral train./

SAPIENTIA: Here is the place./

MATRONS: It is worthy to harbor the children's remains./

SAPIENTIA: I commit to you, earth, the flowers of my womb: Guard them in your earthen lap until in glory they bloom afresh/ after the resurrection of the flesh./ And Thou Christ, imbue their souls in the meantime with splendorous bliss,/ and grant that their bones may rest in peace./

MATRONS: Amen.

SAPIENTIA: I am grateful for your kindness in my great loss and for the consolation you convey./

MATRONS: Do you wish for us to stay?/

SAPIENTIA: No.

MATRONS: Why not?

SAPIENTIA: I don't wish for you to incur any more trouble on my behalf. Go forth in peace, and return safely—enough that you stayed with me three nights long./

MATRONS: Are you not coming along?/

SAPIENTIA: No.

MATRONS: What do you plan to do?/

SAPIENTIA: To remain here. Perhaps what I desire will be fulfilled, perhaps my wish will come true./

MATRONS: What do you pray for, what do you desire?/

SAPIENTIA: Only that when my prayers are completed, in Christ I may expire./

MATRONS: We will stay until we have buried you; then we will retire./

SAPIENTIA: As you wish. Adonai Emmanuel, Whom before all times God, the Father of all, created and Whom in our own time the virgin mother bore; one Christ, of two natures but the duality of natures not dividing the unity of the one person, and the unity of the person not lessening the diversity of Thy two natures. Let the lovely angels' choir their voices raise/ and the sweet harmony of the stars exalt Thee in jubilant praise;/ let all that is knowable through science praise Thee,/ and all that is made of the material of the four elements exalt Thee,/ because Thou alone with the father and the Holy Ghost/ art made form without matter, begotten by the Father with the Holy Ghost./ Thou did not scorn to become man, capable of human suffering,/ while Thy divinity remained oblivious to suffering,/ so that all who believe in Thee should not perish in eternal strife,/ but have the joy of everlasting life;/ Thou hast not refused to taste death for us only to destroy it by rising again from the dead./ Very God and very man,/ I know that Thou hast said that Thou will reward a hundred fold/ all of those who gave up the hold/ of worldly possessions and earthly love for the worship of Thy name,/ and Thou hast promised to the same/ to bestow upon them the gift of life everlasting. Inspired by the hope for this promise, I followed Thy command, freely offering up the children I bore./ Therefore do not Thou delay any more/ to keep Thy promise and free me quickly/ from the fetters of my earthly body/ so that I may rejoice in the heavenly reception of my daughters whose sacrifice I didn't prolong/ and exalt in their glory hearing their new joyful lauding song/ as they follow the Paschal Lamb in the midst of other maidens./ And even though I cannot join them in chanting the canticles of virginal maidens, yet may I be permitted to join them in their eternal praise of Thee, Who art not the Father,/ but art of the same substance with the Father/ and the Holy Ghost, sole Lord of the Universe, sole King of the upper, mid and lower regions, Thou who reignest and are Lord forever and ever.

MATRONS: Receive her, Oh Lord, Amen.

HILDEGARD OF BINGEN
KNOW THE WAY

Abbess Hildegard, the mid-twelfth-century German Benedictine abbess, has in recent years become a focus for high attention in women's studies courses, and this is appropriate. She is probably the leading feminist theorist of the Middle Ages, and her writings can be read today as a provocative and compelling, if somewhat conservative, statement of late-*twentieth*-century Catholic feminism. Her most widely read publication in her lifetime was *Scivias* (Know the Way), a compendium of prose and verse poems presented as episodic visions, in which Christ seems to be speaking through the instrument of the abbess. The work was endorsed by St. Bernard of Clairvaux, by the pope, and by a church synod and was obviously conforming to the canonical view of women: Mary is contrasted against Eve; virginity is praised in exalted terms; a married man and woman are one flesh; androgyny is condemned. But it is hard to come away from reading this work as anything other than a claim for the full equality among the genders. Sexual love in marriage is explicitly approved, and in terms of full equality and interchange between man and wife. The concept that the church is the Bride of Christ in the traditional mode is used to give the impression that virgin nuns have a special role to play as the vanguard of the Bride. At one point, Hildegard seems to suggest, by use of an artful literary device, that some virgin nuns are equal to the church fathers, a claim that was explicitly rejected by St. Ambrose and St. Augustine. Within a rhetoric that sustains traditional views of women, there is a subtext that is not very well hidden which asserts women's full equality and indeed special visionary role in the Christian community. Hildegard's visions very likely came to her in German, and after she made notes in that language a Latin text was produced with the aid of secretaries and editors. Her Latin is difficult and elusive in meaning, perhaps in some instances intentionally so, and requires perseverance and skill to put into English.

Zodiacal-Cosmological map of the Year's Cycle

WHAT THINGS ARE TO BE OBSERVED AND AVOIDED IN MARRIAGE

Because a mature woman was given not to a little boy but to a mature man, namely Adam, so now a mature woman must be married to a man when he has reached the full age of fertility, just as due cultivation is given to a tree when it begins to put forth flowers. For Eve was formed from a rib by Adam's ingrafted heat and vigor, and therefore now it is by the strength and heat of a man that a woman receives the semen to bring a child into the world. For the man is the sower, but the woman is the recipient of the seed. Wherefore a wife is under the power of her husband because the strength of the man is to the susceptibility of the woman as the hardness of stone is to the softness of earth.

But the first woman's being formed from man means the joining of wife to husband. And thus it is to be understood: This union must not be vain or done in forgetfulness of God, because He Who brought forth the woman from the man instituted this union honorably and virtuously, forming flesh from flesh. Wherefore, as Adam and Eve were one flesh, so now also a man and woman become one flesh in a union of holy love for the multiplication of the human race. And therefore there should be perfect love in these two as there was in those first two. For Adam could have blamed his wife because by her advice she brought him death, but nonetheless he did not dismiss her as long as he lived in this world, because he knew she had been given to him by divine power. Therefore, because of perfect love, let a man not leave his wife except for the reason the faithful Church allows. And let them never separate, unless both with one mind want to contemplate My Son, and say with burning love for Him: "We want to renounce the world and follow Him Who suffered for our sake!" But if these two disagree as to whether they should renounce the world for one devotion, then let them by no means separate from each other, since, just as the blood cannot be separated from the flesh as long as the spirit remains in the flesh, so the husband and wife cannot be divided from each other but must walk together in one will.

But if either husband or wife breaks the law by fornication, and it is made public either by themselves or by their priests, they shall undergo the just censure of the spiritual magisterium. For the husband shall complain of the wife, or the wife of the husband, about the sin against their union before the Church and its prelates, according to the justice of God; but not so that the husband or wife can seek another marriage; either they shall stay together in righteous union, or they shall both abstain from such unions, as the discipline of church practice shows. And they shall not tear each other to pieces by viperous rending, but they shall love with pure love, since both man and woman could not exist without having been conceived in such a bond.

ON THE AVOIDANCE OF ILLICIT AND LUSTFUL POLLUTION

But let not a man emit his semen in excessive lust before the years of his strength; for if he tries to sow his seed in the eagerness of lust before that seed has enough heat to coagulate properly, it is proof that he is sinning at the Devil's suggestion. And when a man is already strong in his desire, let him not exercise his strength in that work as much as he can; because if he thus pays attention to the Devil, he is doing a devilish work, making his body contemptible, which is entirely unlawful. But let the man do as human nature teaches him, and seek the right way with his wife in the strength of his heat and the vigor of his seed; and let him do this with human knowledge, out of desire for children.

But I do not want this work done during the wife's menses, when she is already suffering the flow of her blood, the opening of the hidden parts of her womb, lest the flow of her blood carry with it the mature seed after its reception, and the seed, thus carried forth, perish; at this time the woman is in pain and in prison, suffering a small portion of the pain of childbirth. I do not remit this time of pain for women, because I gave it to Eve when she conceived sin in the taste of the fruit; but therefore the woman should be cherished in this time with a great and healing tenderness.

THE BRIDEGROOM

Her womb is pierced like a net with many openings, with a huge multitude of people running in and out; that is, she displays her maternal kindness, which is so clever at capturing faithful souls by diverse goads of virtue, and in which the trusting peoples devoutly lead their lives by the faith of their true belief. But He Who casts the net to capture the fishes is My Son, the Bridegroom of His beloved Church, whom He betrothed to Himself in His blood to repair the fall of lost humanity.

THOSE REGENERATED BY THE CHURCH THEIR MOTHER IN THE FAITH OF THE TRINITY

She (the church) will often, however, be bothered by the wicked, but with the help of her Bridegroom she will always most strongly defend herself, like a virgin who is often assailed by the cravings of desire through the Devil's art and the arguments of men, but pours out her prayers to God and is forcibly liberated from their temptations and her virginity preserved. So also the Church resists her wicked corrupters, the heretical errors of Christians, Jews and pagans, who infest her and try to corrupt her virginity, which is the Catholic faith. She resists them strongly, lest she be corrupted, for she was and is and will remain a virgin; the true faith which is her virginity keeps its wholeness against all error, so that her honor as a chaste virgin remains uncorrupted by any touch of lust in the modesty of her body.

And thus the Church is the virginal mother of all Christians, since by the mystery of the Holy Spirit she conceives and bears them, offering them to God so that they are called the children of God. And as the Holy Spirit overshadowed the Blessed Mother, so that she miraculously conceived and painlessly bore the Son of God and yet remained a virgin, so does the Holy Spirit illumine the Church, happy mother of believers, so that without any corruption she conceives and bears children naturally, yet remains a virgin.

WORDS OF THE GOSPEL

"Truly, truly I say to you, unless a man is born again of water and the Spirit, he cannot enter the Kingdom of Heaven" [John 3:5]. What does this mean? With firmest certainty and not with wavering doubt, I say to you who are born of filth that Man, risen out of burning heat and wrapped in a poisonous form, will be confounded by his apathy unless in the true joy of a new child he is born again from the water of sanctification and the spirit of illumination. How? Because Man, who overflows like water with the spirit of his enlivening, will not be able to enter into salvation as an heir to the Kingdom of his Creator unless he is purified by the true regeneration, as water cleans the dirty and spirit gives life to the inanimate; for he is guilty of the sin of the first parent, who was fraudulently deceived by the Devil. How?

As the thief who wishes to steal the King's most noble and precious possession sneaks in furtively, so the deceptive idea crept in by the maw of the Devil, by which he wickedly stole the beloved jewel of holy innocence and chastity in which dwelt the Holy Spirit; so it must now be cleansed by the holy ablution. For the death-bearing heat, which comes out of transgression of Almighty God's commands and is kindled by lust in the curdling of desire, must now be drowned in Him, Who never grudgingly hides His wonders, but generously shows them forth in infinite mercy.

GOD RECEIVES IN BAPTISM BOTH SEXES AT ALL AGES

For in whatever hour and of whatever sex or age a person may be, male or female, infant or decrepit, when he comes to baptism with loving devotion I will receive him with My merciful help. And I do not refuse the washing of baptism to an infant, as certain false deceivers declare who lyingly say I reject such an offering; as in the Old Testament I did not spurn the circumcision of an infant, though he did not request it with his own voice or receive it of his own will, but his parents supplied it for him.

So now in the new grace I do not reject the baptism of an infant, although he does not ask it by speech or by consent; his parents do this for him.

And as a baby is nourished in its body by milk and the food another grinds up for it, so also a baptized person must observe from his inmost heart the doctrine and the faith given to him in his baptism. But if the baby does not suck at its mother's breast or take the food ground up for it, it will die at once; and so also if a baptized person does not receive the nurturing of his most loving mother, the Church, or retain the words his faithful teachers proposed to him at baptism, he will not escape a cruel death for his soul, for he has refused his soul's salvation and the sweetness of eternal life. And as, when the baby cannot chew its bodily food with its teeth, someone else grinds it up for it to swallow lest it should die, so too in baptism, since it lacks words to confess Me, of necessity there are spiritual helpers there for it, who provide it with the food of life, namely the Catholic faith, lest it fall into the snare of perpetual death. How?

A master gives his orders to his servant in a commanding voice, and the latter carries them out in anxiety and fear; likewise a mother teaches her daughter charity, and the latter fulfils her words in obedience; and in the same way, let those who have vowed the faith offer the words of salvation at the proper time to the baptized person, that he may carry them out with faithful devotion for the love of Heaven.

ON THE IMAGE OF THE MAIDEN

In this brightness appears a most beautiful image of a maiden, with bare head and black hair. This is serene Virginity, innocent of all foulness of human lust. Her mind is unbound by any shackle of corruption, but is not yet perfectly able to bar troubled and dark thoughts from the minds of her children, as long as they are in the world; but she forcefully resists and opposes such thoughts.

Therefore *she wears a red tunic, which flows down about her feet;* for she perseveres toward the goal of widest and most blessed perfection by the sweat of her labor in virtuous works, surrounded with the variety of virtues and imitating Him Who is the plenitude of sanctity. She is also, as is shown you in this hidden and supernal light, the noble daughter of the celestial Jerusalem, the glory and honor of those who have shed their blood for love of virginity or in radiant humility preserved their virginity for the sake of Christ and died sweetly in peace. For she was betrothed to the Son of Almighty God, the King of all, and bore Him a noble brood, the elect choir of virgins, when she was strengthened in the peace of the Church.

THE THRONG THAT STANDS AROUND THAT MAIDEN

And around that maiden you see standing a great crowd of people, brighter than the sun, all wonderfully adorned with gold and gems. This is to say that noble Virginity is surrounded and ardently embraced by a wonderful crowd of virgins. They all shine before God more brightly than the sun does on the earth; for they have conquered themselves and bravely trodden death underfoot in the glorious works they have humbly performed for Christ, and so are adorned beautifully with the highest wisdom.

Among those who flourish in the honor of virginity there are some in the celestial city who ably held the rank of the ancient fathers and the glory of higher offices in the world, yet did not lose the ornament of virginity. Hence, as you hear, all those who in their desire kept their integrity for the sake of celestial love are called "daughters of Zion" in the celestial habitations; for in their love of virginity they imitated My Son, Who is the flower of virginity. Therefore the sounding echoes of the blessed spirits and the outpouring of voices and the winged decorations of happy minds and the golden vision of shining stones and jewels are all with them. How? Because the Son of God grants them this, that a sound goes forth from the Throne in which the whole choir of virgins joins in singing with great desire and harmonizing in the new song, as John, the beloved virgin, testifies, saying:

SHE WHO BREAKS THE VOW OF VIRGINITY WILL BE NOT A LADY BUT A HANDMAID

And a maiden who of her own will is betrothed in holiness to My Son is becomingly received by Him, for He wishes to have her united with Him in companionship. How? That she may embrace Him with chaste love, and He may love her in secret; for to Him she is always lovable, since she seeks Him rather than an earthly bridegroom.

MEN AND WOMEN SHOULD NOT WEAR EACH OTHER'S CLOTHES EXCEPT IN NECESSITY

A man should never put on feminine dress or a woman use male attire, so that their roles may remain distinct, the man displaying manly strength and the woman womanly weakness; for this was so ordered by Me when the human race began. Unless a man's life or a woman's chastity is in danger; in such an hour a man may change his dress for a woman's or a woman for a man's, if they do it humbly in fear of death. And when they seek My mercy for this deed they shall find it, because they did it not in boldness but in danger of their safety. But as a woman should not wear a man's clothes, she should also not approach the office of My altar, for she should not take on a masculine role either in her hair or in her attire.

CHASTITY AND HER APPEARANCE

After people have placed their hope fully in God, the perfect work increases in them, and then by Chastity they start wanting to restrain themselves from the desires of the flesh. For abstinence in the flower of the flesh feels strongly, as a young girl who does not want to look on a man nonetheless feels the fire of desire. But Chastity renounces all filth and longs with beautiful desire for her sweet Lover, the sweetest and loveliest odor of all good things.

And *in her right hand she holds a royal scepter, but she has laid her left hand on her breast.* This is to say that on the right, the side of salvation, life is shown in Chastity through the Son of God who is the King of all people. And through Him as defender, Chastity confounds the left, the side of lust, and reduces it to nought in the hearts of those who love her. How? She allows no liberty to lust; as a fierce bird snatches a rotting corpse and tears it and reduces it to naught, she rejects and crushes stinking lust in God's sight. And, defeated by her, it cannot survive, as she hints in her words, already quoted.

LEGITIMATE MARRIAGE

"But I do not reject the chaste coupling of legitimate marriage, which was set up by divine counsel when the children of Adam were fruitful and multiplied. But it is to be done for the true desire of children and not for the false pleasure of the flesh, and only by those to whom it is allowed and harmless by divine law, those allied to the world and not set apart for the Spirit. You should love the good you have from Me better than yourself. You are heavenly in spirit but earthly in flesh; and so you should love heavenly things and tread the earthly underfoot. When you do heavenly things I show you a supernal reward; but when you seek to do what is unjust by the will of your flesh, I show you My martyrdom and the pains I endured for your sakes, that you may fight your wrong desires for love of My Passion.

"You have been given great intelligence; and so great wisdom is required of you. Much has been given to you, and much will be required of you. But in all these things I am your Head and your helper. For when Heaven has touched you, if you call on Me I will answer you. If you knock at the door, I will open to you. You are given a spirit of profound knowledge, and so have in yourself all that you need. And, this being so, My eyes will search you closely and remember what they find.

"Therefore, I require of your conscience a wounded and sorrowful heart; for thus you can restrain yourself when you feel drawn toward sin and burn in it to the point of suffocation. Behold, I am watching you; what will you do? If you call upon Me in this travail, with a wounded heart and tearful eyes and fear of My judgment, and keep calling on Me to help you against the wickedness of your flesh and the attacks of evil spirits, I will do for you all that you desire, and make My dwelling-place in you.

Songs to Holy Mary

O splendid jewel, serenely infused with the Sun!
The Sun is in you as a fount from the heart of the
    Father;
It is His sole Word, by Whom He created the
    world,
The primary matter, which Eve threw into
    disorder.
He formed the Word in you as a human being;
And therefore you are the jewel that shines most
    brightly,
Through whom the Word breathed out the whole
    of the virtues,
As once from primary matter He made all
    creatures.

    O sweet green branch that flowers from the
        stem of Jesse!
O glorious thing, that God on His fairest daughter
Looked as the eagle looks on the face of the sun!
The Most High Father sought for a Virgin's
    candor,
And willed that His Word should take in her His
    body.
For the Virgin's mind was by His mystery
    illumined,
    And from her virginity sprang the glorious
        Flower.

To the Virgins

O lovely faces who look on the face of God
And build in the dawn; O noble blessed virgins!
The King took thought for you, sealing you to His
    purpose
And decking you with all ornaments of Heaven,
And so you are a garden adorned in sweetness.

    O noble verdure. which grows from the Sun
        of splendor!
Your clear serenity shines in the Wheel of
    Godhead,
Your greatness is past all earthly understanding,
And Heaven's wonders surround you in their
    embrace.
    You glow like dawn, and burn like the Sun in
        glory.

CHRISTINE DE PISAN

THE WOMAN'S ROOM

Hildegard's competitor today in women's studies courses for the role of spokesperson for medieval women would be Christine de Pisan, a prolific early-fifteenth-century French writer. She was Venetian by birth and accompanied her father to Paris when he was appointed court astrologer to the French king. Unfortunately, her father died prematurely and Christine was forced to rely on her own resources. She married and had a daughter, who became a nun, but her husband also died early. Christine made her living principally as a manuscript copyist while trying her hand at a variety of books written for the market. Today she would be a journalist writing a women's column on the op-ed page or in the "Style" section. She gained a reputation in her day also as a pioneering and controversial literary critic. At one point, she was approached by the English king to write propaganda for him, but she demurred because of her loyalty to the French monarchy, which does not, however, seem to have been particularly generous to her. Christine's major book is *The City of Women,* which provides advice on behavior for women in various classes and roles in society. The book is consistently well-informed in detail, insightful and subtle on social matters, and persistently hews to a moderately conservative line. It reads like a Victorian middle class manual. Be cautious, hardworking, agreeable, thrifty, and quiet—this about sums up what Christine has to say to all women. The issue is: What is it supposed to signify? Is Christine complaining that women's lives in all classes are circumscribed, burdensome, repressive, and boring? Or is she merely giving a journalistic description of common social practices, a dollop of practical conformist advice? Does a feminist consciousness lurk behind the text, wanting to subvert the stolid world that she describes?

THE WISE HOUSEWIFE

This wise lady or housewife ought to be very familiar with everything pertaining to the preparation of food so that she may know how best to organize it and give orders to her serving-men or women; in this way she may always be able to keep her husband contented. If he sometimes invites important people to the house, she herself (if need be) ought to go into the kitchen and supervise the serving of the food. She ought to see that her home is kept clean and everything in its place and in order. She should see that her children are well taught and disciplined, even if they are small, and that they are not heard whining or making a lot of noise. They should be kept tidy and established in their own routine. Neither the wet-nurses' swaddling clothes nor anything else that belongs to them should be left lying around the house. She ought to ensure that her husband's garments and other things are kept clean, for the good grooming of the husband is the honour of the wife. She should ensure that he is well served and his peace and quiet are uninterrupted. Before he comes home for dinner everything should be ready and in good order, with tables and sideboards according to their means.

If she wants to act prudently and have the praise of both the world and her husband, she will be cheerful to him all the time, so that if he should be in any way troubled in his thoughts, perhaps by various things that sometimes give rise to problems for a man of property, she may be able by her gracious welcome to get him to put

Christine de Pisan presenting her book

affairs or other confidential things at table or in front of the household, but only when they are alone together and in her chamber.

The wise housewife will be careful to rise early in the morning. When she has heard Mass and said her devotions and returned home, she will issue orders to her people for whatever is necessary. Then she will take up some useful work, whether spinning or sewing or something else. When her chambermaids have done their housework, she will want them to do some other work. She will not want to see either girls or women or even herself tolerate any idle hours. She will buy flax cheaply at fairs; she will have it spun in town by poor women (but she will be careful not to take advantage of them deceitfully or by her superior rank, for she would damn herself, and there would be no advantage in it for her). She will have fine wide cloth, tablecloths, napkins and other linen made. She will be most painstaking about this, for it is the natural pleasure of women and not odious or sluttish, but upright and proper. In the end she will have very fine linen—delicate, generously embroidered and well made. She will keep it white and sweet smelling, neatly folded in a chest; she will be most conscientious about this. She will use it to serve the important people that her husband brings home, by whom she will be greatly esteemed, honoured, and praised.

This wise woman will take great care that no food goes bad around her house, that nothing goes to waste that might help the poor and indigent. If she gives them to the poor, she will ensure that the leftovers are not stale and that the clothes are not moth-eaten. But if she loves the welfare of her soul and the virtue of charity, she will not give her alms only in this way, but with the wine from her own cellar and the meat from her table, to poor women in childbed, to the sick, and often to her poor neighbours. She will do this with pleasure if she is wise and has the means, for these acts are all the laid-up treasure that she will take with her, nor will she ever be the poorer for it. She ought, however, to be careful and have discretion about all her charity.

This woman will be wise and gracious, that is,

them somewhat out of his mind. It is undoubtedly a great refreshment for a man of substance when he comes into his house with some troubling thought and his wife wisely and graciously welcomes him. It is quite right that she should do this, for the man who is occupied with the burden and care of earning a living can at least be warmly welcomed in his own home. The wife ought not to quarrel with the other members of the household nor nag them nor make a fuss at the table, but if there is something that they have done wrong, she ought to correct them at the time in a few calm words, but at meals, which ought to be taken happily, this kind of thing strikes a very harsh note. If her husband is bad or quarrelsome, she ought to appease him as much as she can by soothing words. She should not ask him about his business of pleasant expression, modest, with restrained language; she will welcome and receive the friends and acquaintances of her husband. She will speak nicely to everyone. She will cultivate the friendship of her neighbours; she will offer them companionship and friendship if they need it and she will not refuse to lend little things. To her household staff she will be neither mean, sharp-tongued, nor spiteful, nor will she nag them all day about trifles, but reprimand them properly when they do something wrong and threaten to dismiss them if they do not mend their ways. But she will do this without raging or making a noisy fuss that can be heard in the next street, as some foolish women do who imagine that by being quite disagreeable and quarrelling vehemently about nothing with their husbands and their household servants, and making a lot of work out of only a small job, and finding things everywhere to complain about, and always gossiping, they will be regarded as good and wise housewives. But that kind of housewifery has nothing to do with our teaching, for we want our adherents to be wise in all their actions. There can be no sensible behaviour without moderation, which does not require malice or anger or shouting—all things that are most unseemly in a woman.

THIS DESCRIBES HOW WOMEN OF RANK OUGHT TO BE CONSERVATIVE IN THEIR CLOTHING, AND HOW THEY CAN PROTECT THEMSELVES AGAINST THOSE WHO TRY TO DECEIVE THEM

The third point that we want to tell you about—you town-dwellers and women of rank in fine towns—concerning your garments and clothing, is that in these you must not be extravagant, either in the cost or in the fashions. There are five particular reasons that ought to persuade you to guard against extravagance. The first: that it is a sin and it displeases God to be so attentive to one's own body; the second: that by making an extravagant show one is not the more esteemed for it, but less, as has already been said elsewhere; the third: that it is a waste of money, an impov-

erishment and emptying of the purse; the fourth: that you give a bad example to others. (That is, you give them reason to do likewise or worse, for it will seem to a lady who sees a young woman or a townswoman assume a grand style of dressing that by as much as she is greater so should her clothes be finer. This is what makes the pomp and luxurious clothing multiply and increase every day, because each person is always trying to outdo the other—by which many people are ruined in France and elsewhere.) The fifth: that by an inappropriate or extravagant outfit you give another woman the occasion of sinning, either in envious whispering or in a desire to dress above her station, which is a thing that displeases God very much. And so, dear ladies, as this can do you no good and a great deal of harm, please do not take too much enjoyment in such base behaviour. However, it is quite right that each woman wear such clothing as indicates her husband's and her rank, rather than if she is a middle-class townswoman and she dresses like a young noblewoman and the young noblewoman like a lady—and so on, step by step on up the scale. It is indubitably a thing contrary to good public order, in which, in any country, if it is well regulated everything ought to be within limits.

Now we come to the fourth point, which is how you will keep from rebuke and from getting a bad name, to which point the matter of your clothing may be relevant, both in the extravagance or too high a cost and in the sort of fashions. In this connection let us suppose, for example, that a woman is of excellent character and without any bad deed or thought in her head: but no one will believe it, for she is seen wearing clothing above her station. Many bad judgements will be made against her, however good she may really be. It therefore behoves any woman who wants to preserve her good reputation to be modest and conservative in her clothing. Her garments should not be too tight nor the neckline too low, nor should she take up other unchaste fashions, nor new-fangled things, especially indecent ones. Also a lady's manner and expression count for a good deal. For as has already been mentioned before, there is nothing more unseemly in a woman than a disagreeable manner and a sour expression, also nothing more pleasant than a fair countenance and a quiet demeanour. Even if she is young, she ought to be moderate and not disorderly in her games and laughter. She ought to know how to enjoy them in moderation so that they are seemly, and her speech should be without flirtatiousness, but proper and mild, orderly and comely, with a simple and decorous look, and not glancing about; she should be merry, but in moderation.

But to return to the matter that we mentioned above: that is, that besides the talk and blame that can spring up around a woman because of inappropriate clothing and a vulgar manner, there is one other drawback that is more dangerous, and that is the wrong impression given to foolish men who may think that she is doing it in order to be desired and lusted after in illicit love. She will perhaps not think of it at all, doing it only for her own pleasure and because her temperament inclines her to it. There are men of many classes who will try diligently to seduce her, pursuing her with various meaningful signs, and they will exert themselves considerably to this end. But what should the wise young woman do who does not wish to slip into error and who is well aware that nothing can come of such a love affair but all sorts of bad things, harm and dishonour, which these reckless men choose to ignore? She does not want to do as some thoughtless women do, whom it pleases very much to be pursued with great ardour. They fancy it is a fine thing to say. 'I am greatly loved by several men! It is a sign that I am beautiful and that there is much good in me. I will not fall in love with any of them, however, but I will be pleasant to all of them, to one as much as to another, and I will talk to them all.'

This is not the way to protect your honour, but rather it is impossible that this position can long be maintained by a woman, whoever she may be, without her sliding into error. For this reason as soon as the wise lady notices by any sign or indication that some man has designs on her, by her own words and gestures and manner she ought to give him every opportunity to give up the idea, and finally make him realize that she is

not interested and does not want to be. And if he speaks to her, she should reply to him along these lines: 'Sir, if you have been thinking about me, please stop it! For I promise you and swear by my faith that I have no intention of embarking on such a love affair, nor will I ever have. I can easily swear this, for I am so strongly confirmed in this conviction that there is neither a man nor any other thing that can dissuade me from it, and all my life I shall remain firm on this point. You may be certain of that! So your trouble is all for nothing as long as you waste your time on this. I beg of you most strenuously not to make any more such overtures to me nor to say these words, for in good faith I will take great displeasure in them, and I will do everything in my power to avoid going where you are. I tell you once and for all, you can be absolutely certain that you will never find me in any other opinion, and so I bid you farewell.'

In this way, briefly and without listening to him for very long, the good and wise young woman who loves her honour ought to reply to any man who importunes her. Moreover, signs and gestures with the same import as the words may be used. In other words, she should not make by either look or demeanour any sign by which he can have a glimmer of hope that he can ever succeed in his scheme. If he sends her gifts of whatever kind, she must take care not to accept any of them, for whoever accepts a gift seriously compromises herself. If any person should give her some message from him, she should say emphatically and with a frown never again to speak of him to her. And if her chambermaid or servant-boy dares to mention it again she will not keep that person in her house, for such servants are not reliable. She will find some tactful way to dismiss the servant for some other reason, without quarrel and without bad feelings.

But whatever happens, she must take great care that she does not mention it to her husband. With the best intentions she might accidentally put him into such a frenzy that she could not pacify him. It is a very great danger but also a needless one, if she takes wise precautions and keeps quiet about it. No man is so determined that he will not give up if the lady really wants him to go away and shows it by her manner. Neither should she mention it to a neighbour, man or woman, nor to anyone else, for words are reported, and men sometimes make up wicked stories about women out of spite at being refused and at knowing that the women are talking or have been talking about them. So it is no hardship to keep quiet about the thing when mentioning it would accomplish nothing. Boasting is not a pretty thing in a woman. Furthermore, women who wish to protect themselves from blame ought to avoid associating with people who are not good and respectable, nor should they attend gatherings made in gardens or in other places by prelates or lords or other people on the pretext of entertaining a group of people, when it may be for a scheme for some assignation, whether for the ladies themselves or for someone else. Let us suppose that a woman knows very well that such a gathering is not meant for her; nevertheless she ought to be very careful not to provide a means of dalliance for others, for it would be the cause of evil and of sin. She ought not to go there if she knows of such a plot or has any suspicion of it; it would be preferable that she not go out at all, anywhere. If she is wise, she ought to consider carefully how and where she goes.

Neither should she use pilgrimages as an excuse to get away from the town in order to go somewhere to play about or kick up her heels in some merry company. This is merely sin and wickedness in whoever does it, for it is offensive to God and a sad shame. 'Pilgrimages' like that are not worthy of the name. Nor should she go gadding around the town with young women, on Monday to St. Audrey, on Thursday I don't know where, on Friday to St. Catherine, and so forth on other days. Although some do it, there is no great need for it—not that we wish to prevent their doing good, but undeniably, considering the dangers and the thoughtlessness of youth and the great desire men commonly have to seduce women and the baseless talk that is soon circulating about it, the very safest course for the profit of the soul and the honour of the body is not to be in the habit of gadding all over town. For God is

everywhere, who answers the prayers of devout supplicants, whoever they may be, and who wishes all things to be done discreetly and not wilfully. Also the warm baths and the gossip sessions and other get-togethers that women frequent too much without need or good cause are only a waste of money, and no good can come of them. Therefore a woman who loves honour, if she is wise and wishes to avoid reproach, ought to guard against all such things and other similar ones.

OF THE WIVES OF MERCHANTS

Now we come to merchants, that is, the wives of men who deal with merchandise, who in Paris and elsewhere are very rich and whose wives dress expensively and with great show, and even more so in some regions and cities than in Paris, as, for example, in Venice, Genoa, Florence, Lucca, Avignon and elsewhere. But these places (although any place has its excesses) can be excused more easily than these parts of France, because there are not so many distinctions of high rank as in Paris and that area, that is, queens and duchesses, countesses and other ladies and young ladies, by which the ranks are more differentiated. And for that reason in France, which is the noblest realm in the world and where all things ought to be in the best order (according to the ancient usages of France), it is not fitting for women to do what they do in other places (as has been mentioned several times): that the wife of a country labourer enjoy the same rank as the wife of an honest artisan in Paris, nor the wife of a common artisan as a merchant's wife, nor a merchant's wife as an unmarried lady, nor the unmarried lady as a married lady, nor the lady as a countess or duchess, nor the countess as the queen. Rather, each woman ought to keep to her own station in life, and just as there is a difference in the way of life of people, so there ought to be a difference in their estates. But these rules are not kept nowadays, nor many other good ones that always used to be, and for this reason a woman loses the effect that she seeks. For beyond a doubt neither the pride nor the pomp were ever so extreme in all sorts of people from the great to the indigent as they are now; one can see this by reading the chronicles and ancient histories. For this reason we have said that although it is true that in Italy the women still wear greater finery, they do not go to such great expense as they do here, considering the retinues and all sorts of luxuries that ladies go in for. In these things as well as in their gowns they all try to outdo each other.

But now let us say something about merchants' wives. Was this not truly a great extravagance for a wife of a grocer? Even as a merchant, the husband is not like those of Venice or Genoa who go abroad and have their agents in every country, buy in large quantities and have a big turnover, and then they send their merchandise to every land in great bundles and thus earn enormous wealth. Such ones as these are called 'noble merchants'. But this one we are describing now buys in large quantities and sells in small amounts for perhaps only a few pennies, more or less, although his wife is rich and dresses like a great lady. Not long ago she had a lying-in before the birth of her child. Now, before one entered her chamber, one passed through two other very fine chambers, in each of which there was a large bed well and richly hung with curtains. In the second one there was a large dresser covered like an altar and laden with silver vessels. And then from that chamber one entered the chamber of the woman in childbed, a large and well-appointed room hung from floor to ceiling with tapestries made with her device worked very richly in fine Cyprus gold.

In this chamber was a large, highly ornamented dresser covered with golden dishes. The bed was large and handsome and hung with exquisite curtains. On the floor around the bed the carpets on which one walked were all worked with gold, and the large ornamented hangings, which extended more than a hand span below the bedspread, were of such fine linen of Rheims that they were worth three hundred francs. On top of this bedspread of tissue of gold was another large covering of linen as fine as silk, all of one piece and without a seam (made by a method only recently invented) and very expensive; it

was said to be worth two hundred francs and more. It was so wide and long that it covered all sides of this large, elaborate bed and extended beyond the edge of the bedspread, which trailed on the floor on all sides. In this bed lay the woman who was going to give birth, dressed in crimson silk cloth and propped up on big pillows of the same silk with big pearl buttons, adorned like a young lady. And God knows what money was wasted on amusements, bathing and various social gatherings, according to the customs in Paris for women in childbed (some more than others), at this lying-in! Although there are many examples of great prodigality, this extravagance exceeds all the others, and so is worth putting in a book! This thing was even reported in the queen's chamber! Some people will remark that the people of Paris have too much blood, and that the abundance of it sometimes brings on certain illnesses. In other words, a great abundance of riches can easily lead them astray. It would be better for them if the king imposed some *aide*, impost or tax on them to prevent their wives from going about comparing themselves with the queen of France, who scarcely looks any grander.

Now, such a circumstance is not in the right order of things and comes from presumption and not from good sense, for those men and women who do these things acquire from them not esteem but contempt. Although they adopt the style of great ladies or princesses, they are not really such, nor are they called that, but rather they retain the name of merchants or wives of merchants, even those who in Lombardy would be called not merchants but retailers because they sell in small quantities. It is very great folly to dress up in clothes more suitable for someone else when everyone knows very well to whom they rightfully belong; in other words, to take up the grander style that belongs to another and not to oneself. Even if those men and women who indulge in such excesses, whether in clothing or grand style, left their business and took up the fine horses and the status of princes and lords, their real social position would still dog them. It is very stupid not to be ashamed to sell their merchandise and conduct their business, but yet to be ashamed to wear the corresponding clothing. Truly the clothing is very handsome, fine and respectable for whoever has the right to wear it, and the rank of merchant is fine and honourable in France and in any other country. Such people can be called 'disguised people', and we do not say this to diminish their honour, for we have just said that the rank of a merchant is fine and good for those who deserve it. We say this with the best intentions, in order to give counsel and advice to women. We want to protect them from such unnecessary and wasteful things, which are good neither for body nor soul and can be the cause of their husbands' being assessed for some new tax. So it is to their advantage and it is their best course of action to wear their rightful clothing, each woman according to her own position. Assuming that the women are rich, they may wear handsome, fine and modest clothing without adopting others.

Good Lord, what can such people do with their wealth? Certainly if they stored up treasure in Heaven according to the counsel of the Gospels, they would be well advised, for as we have said before, this life is very brief and the next one is everlasting. It would be a good investment for them for the time to come if they shared their great riches among the poor in true charity. If many did this (and it is certainly very needful), through this good and noble virtue of charity, which God considers very desirable, they could buy the field mentioned in the parable in the Gospel where the great treasure is hidden. This treasure is the joy of Paradise. Pope Leo speaks nobly of this holy virtue in his sermon on the Apparition, where he says, 'So great is the virtue of charitable mercy that without it the other virtues cannot thrive, for however much any person may be abstinent and devout, guard himself against sin, and possess all other virtues, without this one which gives value to the others it is all for nothing. On the day of the Last Judgement it will be carrying the banner before all the other virtues for those who in this world have loved it and lived by it. It will conduct them to Paradise, and Our Lord will destroy and give his final sentence to those in whom charity is lacking. The text of the Gospels assures us of this.'

If you rich women want to be saved in this way, see that in your business dealings you do not deal fraudulently or deceitfully with your neighbours.

OF YOUNG AND ELDERLY WIDOWS

To make our work more entirely to the profit of all conditions of women, we will speak to the widowed commoners, although we have mentioned this condition above in regard to princesses.

Dear friends, you move us to pity for your fall into the state of widowhood by the death that deprives you of your husbands, whoever they were. This pitiful state usually involves much anguish and much troublesome business. But it happens in different ways—to those women who are rich in one way and to those who are not at all rich in another. Rich women often have trouble because people try to relieve them of their wealth. Trouble comes to the poor or to those who are not rich, because in their affairs they do not find pity from anyone. Besides the grief that you feel at having lost your spouses, which should be enough to have to suffer, there are three principal evils that you should know about very generally, whether you are rich or poor.

The first, which has already been mentioned, is that you commonly find hard-heartedness and little esteem or pity in anyone. Such people as were in the habit of honouring you while your husbands were alive (who were officials or of some high position) are no longer very friendly and have little regard for you. The second evil that afflicts you is the various suits and many requests to do with debts or disputes over land or pensions. The third is the abusive language of people who in the nature of things are inclined to attack you, so that you can hardly do anything without people finding something to criticize. You therefore need to be armed with good sense against these plagues and all the others that can come to you. We would also like to acquaint you with what can be valuable to you, however much we have perhaps spoken of it elsewhere, for as it is pertinent to the present matter, we will remind you of it again.

As for the hard-heartedness that you commonly find in everyone (which is the first of the above-mentioned evils), there are three remedies for it. First of all turn to God, who so wished to suffer for humankind, and if you contemplate this, it will teach you to be patient, which is a quality you will have great need for. The contemplation of God will also protect you in these circumstances if you put your heart into it, for you little realize the ways of the world, and you are about to learn how changeable are the things of this world.

The second remedy is that you must dispose your heart to be kind and gentle in speech and defer to everyone, so that in this way you may conquer and soften the hearts of evil-doers by gentle petitions and humble requests. The third remedy is to be kind and humble in speech, clothing and countenance and consider how with prudence and wise conduct you may defend and guard yourself against those who are bent on tormenting, injuring and oppressing you; in other words, strenuously avoid their company and try not to have anything to do with them. Try to keep close to your hearth and home and not engage in arguments or quarrels with a neighbour, neither man nor woman, nor even with a servant nor chambermaid. Speak softly, but always protect your rights, and by doing this and by not associating much with certain people if you do not need to, you will avoid being injured and dominated by other people.

As for those who bring lawsuits against you (which is the second evil), you ought to know that you must avoid suits and legal proceedings if you possibly can, for it is something that can greatly trouble a widowed woman for several reasons. The first is that she does not know all the ins and outs and is naive in such matters. Secondly, it necessitates her putting herself at the mercy of others in order to have her needs attended to, and people are commonly careless about women's affairs and cheat them when they see the chance and put them to so much expense that they spend eight sous to get six.

Another reason to settle the case amicably is that she cannot go to court at all hours as a man would, and for this reason the best advice is to drop the case even if she loses a little by it, as long as it is not too much. She ought to make every reasonable offer to settle out of court, considering carefully what is asked of her. If she has to be a plaintiff, she should pursue her rights courteously and see whether she can get them by some other means. If she is hounded by debts, she should look at what reason and justification her creditors have. Even if there are no letters or witnesses, if her conscience feels that something is owed, she must take good care that she does not keep what rightfully belongs to someone else, for she would be weighing down both her husband's soul and her own, and God might well send her so many corresponding losses in another quarter that in the end she would lose twice as much. But if she wisely knows how to protect herself against the charlatans who make groundless demands, she does the right thing.

But if eventually she is obliged to go to law, she ought to know that three principal things are necessary to a person who brings a suit. The first is to work through the counsel of wise lawyers and clerks who are very knowledgeable in the discipline of justice and the law. The second is to have great care and diligence in pursuing the case. And the third is to have enough money to do this, for without a doubt, if one of these three things is lacking (whatever good case the person may have), she will be in danger of losing it. So it is necessary for the sensible widow in these circumstances to go to the oldest and most experienced lawyers, the ones most used to pleading different cases (and not the younger ones), and explain her case to them and show them her letters and documents. She should attend carefully to what they say, and not conceal from them anything that can have any bearing on the case, whether in her favour or against it, for they cannot advise her except according to what she tells them. Then she should bring her suit or settle amicably according to their considered opinion. Now, if she undertakes her suit with diligence and pays well for it, her chances will be better. It will behove her to do these things, and likewise resist all her other enemies. If she wants to win, she must adopt a man's heart (in other words, constant, strong and wise) to consider and to pursue the best course of action. She must not collapse like a simple woman into tears and sobs without putting up a fight, like a poor dog who cowers in a corner while all the others attack it. For if you women did this, you would find plenty of pitiless people who would take the bread out of your hand and would consider you ignorant and simple, nor would you ever find any pity in their souls. So therefore, you must not try to go it alone nor trust only in your own intelligence, but get sound advice about everything, especially for important things that you do not know much about.

You widows ought to conduct your affairs in this way, that is, those of you who are older and who do not wish to marry again, but as for young widows, it is seemly that they be governed by their parents and friends until they remarry. They should behave kindly and simply towards those parents and friends, and in such a manner that a bad reputation cannot get started about them, for that would destroy all their advantages.

The third remedy for the three above-mentioned evils to widowed women, who are at the mercy of abusive language, is that they ought to be sure in all respects not to give occasion for defamation or slander about them in any way, whether in their expressions, conduct or clothing, which ought to be simple, modest and decent, demure and subdued. Unless they are relatives, they must not be too friendly nor intimate with any men who are seen to come and go at their houses, even though it is done discreetly. She should be careful with even priests and monks, however devout she may be, because the world is much inclined to say or think evil. Widows must avoid having a household where anyone might have any cause for suspicion; they must not indulge in intimacy or familiarity, however good they know their servants to be. Nor, although the ladies may not see anything wrong with it, should they spend money so lavishly that

people talk about it. The better to conserve what she has, a widow should not live in too grand a style, in regard to servants or cloaks or food, for the proper way of life for a widowed woman is to be sober and to do without unnecessary knick-knacks. Since there is so much hardship for women in the state of widowhood (we say it, and it is true), it could seem to some people that therefore it would be better for them all if they remarried. This assumption could be countered by saying that if in married life everything were all repose and peace, truly it would be sensible for a woman to enter it again, but because one sees quite the contrary, any woman ought to be very wary of remarriage, although for young women it may be a necessity or anyway very convenient. But for those who have already passed their youth and who are well enough off and are not constrained by poverty, it is sheer folly, although some women who wish to remarry say that it is no life for a woman on her own. So few widows trust in their own intelligence that they excuse themselves by saying that they would not know how to look after themselves. But the height of folly is an old woman taking a young man! After a while she is singing a different song! It is difficult to feel very sorry for her, because she has brought her misfortune on herself.

OF THE INSTRUCTION FOR BOTH GIRLS AND OLDER WOMEN IN THE STATE OF VIRGINITY

In the course of our lessons it would not be right to forget the women or girls who are virgins. They may be in one of two different situations: namely, those who intend to keep their virginity for life for the love of Our Lord, and those who are awaiting the time of their marriage, to be decided by their parents. Just as there is a difference in their intention, there should likewise be a difference in their clothing, circle of friends and way of life, for to those women who have firmly decided never to lose their virginity belongs a most devout and solitary life, and although it may be a seemly sort of life for all women, nevertheless for these women it is even more suitable than for others. If it is necessary for them to do any work to make a living or to be a servant anywhere, they ought to see to it that all their other work comes after they have done their necessary labour of devout prayers in the service of God. This work for God also includes fasts and abstinences, but done using some discretion; they should not be so strict that the women cannot bear them or continue them, nor so harsh that their brains can be addled by it, for nothing of too great stringency ought to be undertaken without good advice. They ought to keep themselves from all sin, especially in deed and in thought, so that the good that they do in one place they do not cancel out in another, for it does little good to be a virgin, or chaste, and make fasts and devotions, and then be a great sinner. Any person who sets out to do good ought to ensure that she offers God a pure offering, for whoever would present the King with an excellent and beautiful dish all mixed up with filth and garbage would not please the King in the least; he would be quite right to refuse it. So their speech must be good, simple, devout and not too garrulous, their clothing chaste and without any fripperies, their behaviour simple and courteous. They should display an expression of humility with the eyes lowered, and their speech should be kindly. It ought to be their joy to hear the Word of God and to go often to church. Those women who have chosen this life are fortunate, for they have taken the best course.

The other virgins who are waiting for the state of marriage ought to be in their countenances, conduct and speech moderate and chaste, and, especially in church, quiet, looking at their books or with their eyes lowered. In the street and in public they should be mild and sedate, and at home not idle but always busy with some housework. Their clothing should be well made, tasteful, tidy and clean, with no indencency. Their hair should be tidy and not dirty or straggling. Their speech should be amiable and courteous to all people; they should have a humble manner and not be too talkative. If they are at celebrations, dances or assemblies, they should be sure to have a gracious manner and excellent conduct, because more people have their eyes on them there. They should dance demurely and sing softly and not stare vacantly here and there. They should not join the men too much, but always seek the company of their mothers or the other women. These maidens ought to take care not to get into arguments or disputes with anyone, neither serving-man nor chambermaid. It is a very ugly thing in a girl to be argumentative and to answer back, and she could lose her good name because of it, thanks to the false and lying reports that household servants often make. A maiden must not be in any way forward, outspoken or loose, especially in the presence of men, whoever they may be, neither clerks in the household service, nor serving-men, nor other members of the household staff. She must not allow a man to touch her on whatever pretext, nor to touch her with his hands in a playful manner, nor to joke with her too much, for that would be very harmful to the respectability and good reputation that she ought to have.

A young girl should also especially venerate Our Lady, St. Catherine, and all virgins, and if she can read, eagerly read their biographies. She should fast on certain days and above all be moderate in drinking and eating. She should be content with a small amount of food and with weak wines, for gluttony of wine and food in a girl is above all else an odious blemish. For this reason she ought to take good care that no one should ever see her affected by having drunk too much wine, for if she had such a fault, nothing good would be said of it. So all young girls ought to be in the habit of putting generous amounts of water in their wine, and they should habitually drink very little. Also besides the good qualities and manners appropriate to her, any young girl ought to be very humble and obedient to her mother and father. She should serve them diligently as well as she can, and rely on them to arrange her marriage. She should not make the match herself without their consent, nor should she say anything about it herself nor listen to anyone else talk about it. Young girls taught and brought up in this way are much sought after by men looking for wives.

HOW ELDERLY LADIES OUGHT TO CONDUCT THEMSELVES TOWARDS YOUNG ONES, AND THE QUALITIES THAT THEY OUGHT TO HAVE

There is quite often argument and discord, as much in outlook as in conversation, between old people and young ones, to the point that they can hardly stand each other, as though they were members of two different species. The difference in age ensures a difference in their attitudes and social positions. We should like to make peace in this war between women of different ages. If they can hear our teaching, we will remind them of some things that may be good for them. We will speak first to the elderly ladies of the behaviour proper to them.

It is seemly for any older woman to be sensible in her actions, her clothing, facial expression and speech. She ought to be sensible in her actions because she ought to remember the things that she has seen happen in her lifetime; before she undertakes to do anything she ought to be guided by her experience. For if she has seen evil or good happen to anyone because of having certain habits of conduct, she may think that the same thing will happen to her if she does likewise. For this reason it is said that old people are usually wiser than the young, and it is true for two reasons.

First, because their understanding is more perfect and is to be taken more seriously; second, because they have greater experience of past events because they have seen more. So therefore, they are likely to be wiser, and if they are not, they are the more reprehensible. Inevitably nothing is more ridiculous than old people who lack good judgement or who are foolish or commit the follies that youth prompts in the young (and which are reprehensible even in them). For this reason the elderly woman ought to see to it that she does nothing that looks foolish. It is not seemly for her to dance, frolic about or to laugh uproariously. But if she is of a happy disposition, she ought always to see that she takes her pleasure sedately and not in the manner of young people, but in a more dignified way.

 MECHTHILD OF MAGDEBURG
BEGUINE SPIRITUALITY

Beginning in the thirteenth century hundreds of women in the Low Countries, western Germany, and northern France joined groups called "Beguines." Some of the Beguines took monastic vows, but most remained without permanent vows in voluntary laypeople's associations. The Beguines aroused the concern of some conservative churchmen who regarded them as heretics or potential heretics. Any organized group of women not in orders who professed piety aroused suspicion among the more conservative churchmen because women were prominent in heretical groups. Probably there was visibly little or no difference in practice between the professed piety of Beguines and most female members of heretical groups. The Beguines were self-help voluntary associations of middle class women devoted to bonding and to helping out in social services. Some of their writings, such as the following by Mechthild of Magdeburg in the late thirteenth century, have survived. There is nothing here doctrinally beyond a kind of moderate Franciscanism. What is important is that women were joining together to give each other emotional sustenance and friendship, under the rubric of a soft-core mysticism. That the traditional institutional framework of the church could not easily find a place for these well-meaning and pious women says something about the leadership of the late medieval church and its male slackness in meeting the spiritual and moral needs of middle class women.

The Wilderness has Twelve Things

You should love what is not
And flee what is.
You should stand alone
And approach no one.
You should strive always
To be free from all things.
You should free the bound
And bind the free.
You should comfort the sick
And yet possess nothing.
You should drink the water of suffering
And feed the fire of love with the fuel of virtue.
Then you shall live in the true wilderness.

FOUR KINDS OF HUMILITY

The first form of humility can be seen in the clothes that we wear, which should be of an appropriate style and clean, and in the place where we live. The second is apparent in the way that we behave towards others, whether we are loving in all circumstances and in all things. This causes the love of God to grow. The third kind of humility appears in the senses and in the way that we use and love all things rightly. The fourth form of humility lives in the soul, which is the self-effacing humility which creates so much sweet wonder in the loving soul. And it is this humility which makes us rise up to Heaven.

On the Tenfold Value of the Prayer of a Good Person

The prayer has great power
Which we pray with all our strength.
It makes an embittered heart mellow,
A sad heart joyful,

A foolish heart wise,
A timid heart bold,
A weak heart strong,
A blind heart clear-seeing,
A cold heart ardent.
It draws God who is great into a heart which is small.
It drives the hungry soul up to the fullness of God.
It unites the two lovers, God and soul, in a place of bliss,
Where they converse long of love.

How you Should Behave in Fourteen Things

When you pray, you should make yourself small in great humility,
When you confess your sins, you should do so frankly,
When you perform penances, you should do so with commitment,
When you eat, you should be restrained,
When you sleep, you should do so in an orderly way,
When you are alone, you should be faithful,
When you are in company, you should be wise,
When someone teaches you good habits, you should be attentive,
When someone rebukes you, you should be patient,
When you do something good, then you should regard yourself as poor,
When you do something that is wrong, then you should immediately seek grace,
When you are being vain, then you should feel fear,
When you are troubled, then you should have great trust in God,

When you work with your hands, you should do
   so swiftly,
So you can banish evil thoughts.

Temptation, the World and a Good End Test Us

We do not know how firmly we stand
until we feel the temptation of the body.

We do not know how strong we are
until the evil of the world attacks us.

We do not know what goodness there is in us,
until we die a holy death.

ST. BERNARD OF CLAIRVAUX

THE JEWISH PROBLEM

Although the leaders of the church had been hostile to Jews from early times, the small
Jewish population in Christian Western Europe in the early Middle Ages prospered
because the Jews' capacity in international commerce and banking was valuable to the
more intelligent rulers, particularly Charlemagne and his family. Jews were also prominent landowners in southern France. While in the late ninth century French bishops
began to complain loudly that the Jews were overprivileged and should be segregated, their situation did not deteriorate until the eleventh century. Then it went
downhill sharply because of the intensified Christian piety initially represented in the
Gregorian reform and the hostile competition from Christian bankers and money-
lenders. The requisite taking of oaths of loyalty as landholding became feudalized
drove Jews off the land, as the Jewish farmers could not take Christian oaths, and the
rise of merchant guilds decreased the scope of their operations in urban commerce.
The First Crusade of 1095 marked the outbreak of pogroms against Jews, precipitated
by the French crusaders on the way to the Holy Land. In the twelfth century, as their
economic and social position severely deteriorated, the Jews suffered from fervent
outbreaks of hostility exacerbated by the blood libel, the claim that Jews engaged in
ritual murder of Christian children. Leaders of the Church like St. Bernard of Clairvaux
confirmed the old ecclesiastical Jewish policy set down by St. Augustine in the fifth
century—the Jews were to be segregated and prevented from prospering but they
were not to suffer violence or forced to convert. They were to be left to the judgment of
Jesus at His Second Coming. But when Bernard delivered hate-mongering blowtorch
sermons against the Jews, such as the following, there was bound to be violence
against them. The Jews were a perpetual monster in the popular mind of the late
medieval society. Eve the temptress, Jew the Christ-killer, these were structural stereo-
types in the cultural mix.

Personification of Synagogue

worship God? For their actions carried them [of old] into many wars, their inclinations are all devoted to the pursuit of gain, their intelligence stopped short in the thick husk of the letter of their Law, and their worship consists in shedding the blood of sheep and cattle. . . .

O how much worse were the last than the former ones! At first they were only useless, but the last came to be hurtful and poisonous. O nature not merely crude, but touched with viperous venom, to hate that Man, who not only cures the bodies of men, but saves their souls! O intelligence, coarse, dense, and, as it were, bovine, which did not recognise God even in His own works!

Perhaps the Jew will complain, as of a deep injury, that I call his intelligence bovine. But let him read what is said by the prophet Isaiah, and he will find that it is even less than bovine. For he says: "The ox knoweth his owner, and the ass his master's crib: but Israel doth not know, My people doth not consider." You see, O Jew, that I am milder than your own prophet. I have compared you to the brute beasts; but he sets you below even these. Or, rather, it is not the Prophet who says this in his own name; but he speaks in the Name of God, who declares Himself by the very works He does to be God. "Though ye believe not Me," He says, "believe the works"; and, "If I do not the works of My Father, believe Me not"; and not even that aroused them to understand. Not the flight of demons, not the obedience of the elements, nor life restored to the dead, was able to expel from their minds that stupidity bestial, and more than bestial, which caused them, by a blindness as marvellous as it was miserable, to rush headlong into that crime, so enormous and so horrible, of laying impious hands upon the Lord of Glory. . . .

. . . What is there in that [Jewish] people which is not crude and coarse, whether we consider their actions, their inclinations, their understanding, or even the rites with which they

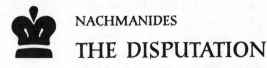

NACHMANIDES

THE DISPUTATION

The new orders of friars founded in the thirteenth century took it as one of their prime responsibilities to secure the conversion of the Jews. This aim had eschatological significance—it was believed that the conversion of the Jews would be a sign that Jesus was coming back, or even that He was waiting for this. A prime vehicle for Jewish conversion was a disputation between a friar learned in the Talmud and a rabbi whom a king was solicited to sponsor. Naturally the rabbis were not keen about entering these public debates; it was hard to defend Jewish doctrine about the Messiah without insulting the Christian faith. But disputations occurred. The best documented of these disputations took place in the Spanish Christian kingdom of Aragon in the late thirteenth century. Friar Paul, a converted Jew like a surprising number of other Dominican brothers, took the Christian side. The Jewish side was taken by the rabbinical scholar and mystic Nachmanides, and it is his detailed account of the disputation that we have here. It is partisan, but Nachmanides seems to have intended it for the king's attention as well as for other Jews, and it has a degree of plausibility even though it is a one-sided report. Nachmanides claims he won the debate.

Our lord the King commanded me to hold a Disputation with Fray Paul in his palace in his presence and in the presence of his counsellors in Barcelona. I replied, 'I will do as my lord the King commands if you will give me permission to speak as I wish.' I was seeking thereby the permission of the King and the permission of Fray Raymon of Pennaforte and his associates who were there.

Fray Ramon of Pennaforte replied, 'Provided only that you do not speak disrespectfully.'

I said to them, 'I do not wish to have to submit to your judgement on that, but to speak as I wish on the matter under dispute, just as you say all that you wish; and I have enough understanding to speak with moderation on the matters of dispute just as you do, but let it be according to my own discretion.' So they all gave me permission to speak freely.

Upon this I replied, 'There is dispute between Gentiles and Jews on many points of religious practice in the two religions which are not essential for religious belief. In this honoured court, I

wish to dispute only on matters which are fundamental to the argument.'

They all replied, 'You have spoken well.' And thus we agreed to speak first on the subject of the Messiah, whether he has already come as Christians believe, or whether he is yet to come as Jews believe. And after that, we would speak on whether the Messiah was truly divine, or entirely human, born from a man and a woman. And after that we would discuss whether the Jews still possess the true law, or whether the Christians practise it.

The Sages of the Talmud were believers in Jesus' Messiahship, and that they believed that he was not merely human, but truly divine, as Christians think? Is it not a well-known thing in truth that the affair of Jesus took place in the time of the Second Temple, and he was born and killed before the destruction of the Temple, while the Sages of the Talmud, such as Rabbi Akiva and his associates, were after the Destruction? And those who composed the Mishnah, Rabbi and Rabbi Nathan, were many years after the Destruction, and all the more so Rav Ashi, who composed the Talmud and wrote it down, for he lived about 400 years after the Destruction. And if these Sages believed in the Messiahship of Jesus and that he and his faith and religion were true, and if they wrote the things from which Fray Paul says he will prove this, if so how did they remain in the original religion and practice of Judaism? For they were Jews and remained in the Jewish religion all their lives and died as Jews, they and their sons and their pupils who listened to all their words from their own mouths. Why did they not become converted to Christianity, as Fray Paul did when he understood from their sayings that Christianity is the true faith, and he went and became converted according to their words? Yet they and their pupils who took instruction from their mouths lived and died as Jews like us today. And they were the very ones who taught us the religion of Moses and of the Jews, for everything we do today is according to the Talmud, and according to the custom and practice which we have observed in the Sages of the Talmud from the day it was composed until now. For the whole purpose of the Talmud is only to teach us the practice of the Torah, and how our Fathers practised it in the time of the Temple from the mouth of the prophets and from the mouth of Moses our teacher, on him be peace. And if they believed in Jesus and his religion, why did they not do as Fray Paul has done, who understands their words better than they did themselves?'. . .

'My lord King, hear me. The Messiah is not fundamental to our religion. Why, you are worth more to me than the Messiah! You are a king, and he is a king. You are a Gentile king, and he is a Jewish king; for the Messiah is only a king of flesh and blood like you. When I serve my Creator in your territory in exile and in affliction and servitude and reproach of the peoples who "reproach us continually", my reward is great. For I am offering a sacrifice to God from my body, by which I shall be found more and more worthy of the life of the world to come. But when there will be a king of Israel of my religion ruling over all the peoples, and there will be no choice for me but to remain in the Jewish religion, my reward will not be so great. No, the real point of difference between Jews and Christians lies in what you say about the fundamental matter of the deity; a doctrine which is distasteful indeed. You, our lord King, are a Christian and the son of a Christian, and you have listened all your life to priests who have filled your brain and the marrow of your bones with this doctrine, and it has settled with you, because of that accustomed habit. But the doctrine in which you believe, and which is the foundation of your faith, cannot be accepted by the reason, and nature affords no ground for it, nor have the prophets ever expressed it. Nor can even the miraculous stretch as far as this as I shall explain with full proofs in the right time and place, that the Creator of Heaven and earth resorted to the womb of a certain Jewess and grew there for nine months and was born as an infant, and afterwards grew up and was betrayed into the hands of his enemies who sentenced him to death and executed him, and that afterwards, as you say, he came to life and returned to his original place. The mind of a Jew, or any other person, cannot tolerate this; and you speak your words entirely in vain, for this is the root of our controversy.

MAIMONIDES

THE JEWISH RESPONSE

The large Jewish community in Spain had prospered under Moslem rule, but in the twelfth century groups of Islamic fundamentalists from North Africa took over rule in Arabic Spain and the Jewish position there deteriorated. The great rabbinical scholar and Aristotelian philosopher, Maimonides, who lived in the second half of the twelfth century, took refuge in still liberal Egypt, where he became a court physician as well as the leader of the Jewish community. In a remarkable letter to the persecuted Jewish community in Yemen, possibly not intended as a public document, Maimonides lashed out at both persecuting religions, Christianity and Islam. His tirade shows that the medieval Jews were beaten down but unbowed, and how deeply even the most learned and intellectual of medieval Jews hated the other religions. The Jews may have suffered in virtual silence, but not without ferocious hatred for the other medieval faiths.

And now, my coreligionists, it is essential for you all to give attention and consideration to that which I am going to point out to you. You should impress it upon the minds of your women and children, so that their faith which may be enfeebled and impaired may be strengthened, and that they be re-established in an unceasing belief. May the Lord deliver us and you from religious doubt!

Remember, that ours is the true and authentic divine religion, revealed to us through Moses, the master of the former as well as the later prophets, by means of which God has distinguished us from the rest of mankind. . . .

Ever since the time of Revelation, every despot or slave that has attained to power, be he violent or ignoble, has made it his first aim and his final purpose to destroy our law, and to vitiate our religion, by means of the sword, by violence, or by brute force, such as Amalek, Sisera, Sennacherib, Nebuchadnezzar, Titus, Hadrian, may their bones be ground to dust, and others like them. This is one of the two classes which attempt to foil the divine will.

The second class consists of the most intelligent and educated among the nations, such as the Syrians, Persians, and Greeks. These also endeavor to demolish our law and to vitiate it by means of arguments which they invent, and by means of controversies which they institute. They seek to render the Law ineffectual and to wipe out every trace thereof by means of their polemical writings, just as the despots plan to do it with the sword. But neither the one nor the other shall succeed. We possess the divine assurance given to Isaiah concerning any tyrant that will wish to undermine our Law and to annihilate

it by weapons of war, that the Lord will demolish them so that they will have no effect. This is only a metaphorical way of saying that his efforts will be of no avail, and that he will not accomplish his purpose. In like manner whenever a disputant shall attempt to demonstrate the falsity of our Law, the Lord will shatter his arguments and prove them absurd, untenable, and ineffective. . . .

Although the exponents of both methods persuade themselves that this is a structure which can be demolished, and they exert themselves to undermine its firmly established foundations, they only increase their pain and toil. The structure remains as firmly planted as ever, while the God of truth mocks and derides them, because they endeavor, with their feeble intelligence, to achieve a goal that is beyond the powers of mortal man. . . .

Both of these parties have harassed and afflicted us incessantly throughout the epoch of our political independence, and partly during the period of our dispersion.

After that there arose a new sect [Christians] which combined the two methods, namely, conquest and controversy, into one, because it believed that this procedure would be more effective in wiping out every trace of the Jewish nation and religion. It, therefore, resolved to lay claim to prophecy and to found a new faith, contrary to our divine religion, and to contend that it was equally God-given. Thereby it hoped to raise doubts and to create confusion, since one is opposed to the other and both supposedly emanate from a divine source, which would lead to the destruction of both religions. For such is the remarkable plan contrived by a man who is envious and querulous. He will strive to kill his enemy and to save his own life, but when he finds it impossible to attain his objective, he will devise a scheme whereby they both will be slain.

The first one to have adopted this plan was Jesus the Nazarene, may his bones be ground to dust. He was a Jew because his mother was a Jewess although his father was a Gentile. . . .

All of these men [Moslems] purposed to place their teachings on the same level with our divine religion. But only a simpleton who lacks knowledge of both would liken divine institutions to human practices. Our religion differs as much from other religions for which there are alleged resemblances as a living man endowed with the faculty of reason is unlike a statue which is ever so well carved out of marble, wood, bronze or silver.

The tenets of the other religions which resemble those of Scripture have no deeper meaning, but are superficial imitations, copied from and patterned after it. They modelled their religions upon ours in order to glorify themselves, and indulge the fancy that they are similar to so and so. However, their counterfeiting is an open secret to the learned. Consequently they became objects of derision and ridicule just as one laughs and smiles at an ape when it imitates the actions of men.

JEWISH PENIS IS BETTER THAN CHRISTIAN PENIS

Isaac ben Yedaiah, a radical follower of Maimonides in southern France around the middle of the thirteenth century, supports Maimonides' argument against the Christians by considering the sexual implications of circumcision.

[A beautiful woman] will court a man who is uncircumcised in the flesh and lie against his breast with great passion, for he thrusts inside her a long time because of the foreskin, which is a barrier against ejaculation in intercourse. Thus she feels pleasure and reaches an orgasm first. When an uncircumcised man sleeps with her and then resolves to return to his home, she brazenly grasps him, holding on to his genitals and says to him, "Come back, make love to me." This is because of the pleasure that she finds in intercourse with him, from the sinews of his testicles—sinew of iron—and from his ejaculation—that of a horse—which he shoots like an arrow into her womb. They are united without separating and he makes love twice and three times in one night, yet the appetite is not filled. And so he acts with her night after night. The sexual activity emaciates him of his bodily fat and afflicts his flesh and he devotes his brain entirely to women, an evil thing. . . .

But when a circumcised man desires the beauty of a woman, and cleaves to his wife, or to another woman comely in appearance, he will find himself performing his task quickly, emitting his seed as soon as he inserts the crown. . . . He has an orgasm first; he does not hold back his strength. As soon as he begins intercourse with her, he immediately comes to a climax. She has no pleasure from him when she lies down or when she arises and it would be better for her if he had not known her . . ., for he arouses her passion to no avail and she remains in a state of desire for her husband, ashamed and confounded, while the seed is still in her "reservoir." She does not have an orgasm once a year, except on rare occasions, because of the great heat and the fire burning within her. Thus he who says "I am the Lord's" will not empty his brain because of his wife or the wife of his friend. He will find grace and good favor; his heart will be strong to seek out God.

OTTO OF FREISING

SOFT-CORE HERESY

During the first seven centuries of its existence, the church had been racked by doctrinal disputes over theological propositions between orthodox and heretical (i.e., "erroneous") groups. The only way to make intellectual sense out of these disputes is to say that the winners became orthodox and the losers heretics. The church in Western Europe down to the twelfth century was too busy with its missionary, educational, and organizational responsibilities to devote time and energy toward defining and pursuing heretics. Occasional doctrinal disputes were settled locally and in a genteel manner. But that all changed at about the middle of the twelfth century. Church authorities became very concerned about alleged heretical leaders and groups, and devoted increasingly large resources and segments of time to combating these oppositional movements. How to account for the furor about heresy? The church now had the time, leisure, and communication skills to attend to sectarian doctrines and peoples; nothing is heretical until hierarchic authority says it is. Second, the growing urban populations, about which the conservative authorities were nervous, showed themselves prone to attend to irregular preachers, perhaps simply looking for diversion, and this was conceived as a threat to the unity and stability of the church. The medieval church, having developed in a rural society, had trouble adjusting its organization and homiletics to city people. Therefore, it was very sensitive to radical preaching within urban enclaves. Thirdly, when people separated themselves from the Catholic Church and joined a sectarian group, they stopped paying tithes and making gifts to the traditional ecclesiastical institutions—heresy therefore meant a diminution in church income, which was serious business. Essentially there were two kinds of heretics. The first we may call soft core: radical people who were obnoxious to authorities. Almost anything they said would be construed as heretical. Such a fearsome designation was a way of making these troublemakers vulnerable. A typical and also prominent example of a soft-core heretic was Arnold of Brescia, a radical in Rome and a disciple of Peter Abelard. Arnold is here described by Otto of Freising, a Cistercian monk and bishop and German court historian—Otto was the uncle of the German emperor, not one prone to be very sympathetic to radical Arnold.

A certain Arnold of Brescia ... under guise of religion and—to use the words of the Gospel—acting as a wolf in sheep's clothing, entered the City [of Rome], inflamed to violence the minds of the simple people by his exceedingly seductive doctrines, and induced—nay, rather, seduced—a countless throng to espouse that cause.

That Arnold, a native of Italy from the city of Brescia, a cleric ordained only as a lector of the church there, had once had Peter Abelard as his

teacher. He was a man not indeed dull of intellect, yet abounding rather in profusion of words than in the weight of his ideas; a lover of originality and eager for novelty. The minds of such men are inclined to devise heresies and the tumult of schisms. Returning from his studies in France to Italy, he assumed the religious habit that he might deceive the more, assailing all things, carping at everything, sparing no one—a disparager of the clergy and of bishops, a persecutor of monks, a flatterer only of the laity. For he used to say that neither clerics that owned property, nor bishops that had regalia, nor monks with possessions could in any wise be saved. All these things belong to the prince, and should be bestowed of his beneficence for the use of the laity only. Besides this, he is said to have held unreasonable views with regard to the sacrament of the altar and infant baptism. While he was keeping the church of Brescia in uproar in these and other ways, which it would take too long to enumerate, and was maliciously defaming ecclesiastical personalities to the laity of that land, who have itching ears as regards the clergy, he was accused by the bishop and pious men of that city at the great council held at Rome under Innocent. Therefore the Roman pontiff decided that silence should be imposed upon the man, that his pernicious teaching might not spread to more people. And thus it was done.

HARD-CORE HERESY: THE ALBIGENSIANS

The Albigensians (from the town of Albi in southwest France, their citadel), also known as Catharists (the purifiers), were hard-core heretics. They unquestionably held ideas contrary to traditional Catholic teaching—they were dualists. They believed in two gods, one of Good and one of Evil, and the evil in the world as substantial, that is, it was created by a god of evil, the devil. This seemed like a revival of the ancient Manichaean heresy, which originated in Persia as a separate religion and in the fourth and fifth centuries was popular in the Roman Empire. It now required strong opposition from the pope. The Albigensians gained adhesion of a significant minority, perhaps twenty percent of the population of southern France, and some support among the nobility there, and they appeared to be a powerful threat to the established church. Against the Albigensians the papacy sent in preachers, who were threatened physically and in at least one instance murdered. This required that stronger measures be taken—the setting up of special church courts, the papally licensed inquisitions, staffed heavily by Dominican friars, to attack the Catharists. A crusade was launched against the Albigensians by armies brought in to seize their enclaves. Although Catharism was still around in the Alps in the early seventeenth century, by and large these draconian methods used by the early-thirteenth-century papacy against the Albigensians were successful. Here is an extract from an Albigensian treatise, *The Book of Two Principles,* on why there must be two gods. This is followed by a selection from the *Inquisitor's Manual,* by the Dominican friar Bernard Gui, written in 1316. Bernard first suggests how the inquisition functioned (it was a Roman law court, making use of informers and seeking self-incrimination from the defendants through torture). Bernard Gui then provides his perceptions of the Catharists and their teachings. Recent liberal accounts of high medieval heresy think that Bernard was much too harsh on the Albigensians. They are held to have been for the most part hardworking, simple yet devout people. On the other hand, Bernard was there—he knew the people personally. One reason Catharism caught on was that in the thirteenth century, as in the case of some heretical movements in the early church, it seemed to accord greater equality to women in the church than rigidly sexist Catholicism. Another strength of Catharism was the unusually strong family bonding among its adherents.

Portrait of Jan Huss, burned to death the 6th of July, 1415

BOOK OF TWO PRINCIPLES

That God Cannot Make Another God. — Now, with reason and without fear I can say further that the true God himself, with all His powers, could not, cannot, and never will be able in any manner, either intentionally or unintentionally, to make another god and lord and creator, like and co-equal unto himself in all things. This I prove.

I say, indeed, that it is impossible for the good God to make another god like unto himself in all things, that is to say, eternal and everlasting, creator and maker of all things that are good, with neither beginning nor end, one who was never made, created, or born of anyone in the sense that the good God was not made, created, or born of anyone. Yet in Holy Scriptures the true Lord God is not called impotent, because of this. Hence it must firmly be believed that the reason the good God is called omnipotent is not that He can make, has made, or shall make all the evils which are, were, and shall be made hereafter, but because He is omnipotent over all things which were, are, and shall be good; and this particularly because He is wholly the cause and origin of all good, but is in no way, of himself exclusively and essentially, the cause of any evil. It follows, therefore, that among wise men the true God is called omnipotent in respect of all things that He has done, does, and shall do in the future; but among those who understand correctly He is not called omnipotent in the sense that He can do what He has not done, does not do, and never will do. And if our opponents say that He has no desire to do so, the argument carries no weight against me, because He and His will are one and the same, as was demonstrated above.

That God Is Not Mighty in Evil, but That There Is Another and Evil Potency. — Therefore, it is firmly to be believed that because there exists in God no potency for evil by which He might bring evil things into existence, there is another principle, one of evil, who is potent in evil. From that one flow all evils which were, are, and shall be. It is evidently of him that David says: "Why doest thou glory in malice, thou that art mighty in iniquity? All the day long thy tongue hath devised injustice; as a sharp razor thou hast wrought deceit. Thou hast loved malice more than goodness, and iniquity rather than to speak righteousness." And the Blessed John says in the Apocalypse, "And that great dragon was cast out, that old serpent who is called the devil and Satan, who seduceth the whole world." And Christ says in the Gospel of Luke: "The seed is the word of God. And they by the wayside are they that hear; then the devil cometh and taketh the word out of their heart, lest believing they should be saved." And the prophet Daniel says: "I beheld, and lo, that horn made war against the saints and prevailed over them, till the Ancient of Days came and gave judgment to the saints of the Most High," and so on. And again: "And another shall rise up after them; and he shall be mightier than the former, and he shall bring down three kings. And he shall speak words against the High One, and shall crush the saints of the Most High, and he shall think himself able to change times and laws." And again: "And it [the little horn] became great against the south, and against the east, and against the strength. And it was magnified even unto the strength of heaven; and it threw down of the strength, and of the stars, and trod upon them. And it was magnified even to the prince of the strength; and it took away from him the continual sacrifice, and cast down the place of his sanctuary." And the Blessed John says in the Apocalypse: "And there was seen another sign in heaven; and behold a great red dragon, having seven heads, and ten horns, and on his head seven diadems, and his tail drew the third part of the stars of heaven, and cast them to the earth." And again: "And power was given to him to do two and forty months; and he opened his mouth unto blasphemies against God, to blaspheme his name and his tabernacle and them that dwell in heaven. And it was given unto him to make war with the saints and to overcome them." So, in the view of wise men, it is deemed wholly impossible that from the true Lord God derive absolutely and directly this mighty one and his potency or power, he who daily works in the most evil fashion against God and His creation, against whom the Lord our God seeks mightily to contend. This the true God could not do if that one, in all his characteristics, were entirely from Him, as most of our opponents declare.

On the Evil Principle. — For this reason, in the opinion of the wise it is firmly to be believed that there is another principle, one of evil, who is mighty in iniquity, from whom the power of Satan and of darkness and all other powers which are inimical to the true Lord God are exclusively and essentially derived, as was demonstrated above and will appear below, God willing. Otherwise, it

would seem obvious to these same [wise] persons that this Divine Might struggles, destroys, and wars against itself.

BERNARD GUI: AN INQUISITOR'S MANUAL

On the Method, Practice, and Procedure Used in Seeking Out and Interrogating Heretics, Their Believers, and Accomplices. — Here follows the fifth and last part of the treatise, wherein are discussed the method, practice, and procedure used in searching out and interrogating heretics, their believers, and accomplices. It includes the separate frauds, devices, and wiles whereby they conceal themselves, each the more subtly to escape from the interrogations aimed especially at him. Among them are included the Manichaeans; and the Waldenses, or Poor of Lyons; as well as certain pseudo-Apostles, who falsely claim to be the apostles of Christ although they are rather apostles of Antichrist. There are also included a considerable number of others of a certain pestiferous sect which emerged in recent times, who, in simulation rather than assimilation of the poverty of evangelical perfection, call themselves the Poor of Christ, saying that theirs is the third order or third rule of St. Francis and who, in the vernacular, are commonly called Beguins and Beguines. It also includes others, who, after having been converted from the perfidy of the Jews to the faith of Christ, return to the vomit of Judaism. Lastly are given the methods of attack upon the pestilence or the pestilential error of sorcerers, diviners, invokers of demons, and others of that kind. Various special forms for abjuring heresy during the course of a hearing are also set forth.

General Advice and Remarks. — This is the procedure when anyone is to be heard or examined, whether he has come in person of his own free will, has been cited, or has been summoned as suspect, noted, defamed, or accused of the crime of heresy, of showing favor or hospitality to heretics, or of anything else which falls within the cognizance of the Inquisition of heretical depravity or has any connection with it. In the first place, after he has been quietly and unostentatiously summoned and warned by the inquisitor or the inquisitor's deputy, have him swear upon the Holy Gospels of God to tell the whole truth and nothing but the truth in regard to the matter of heresy and whatever touches thereupon or is connected in any way with the office of the Inquisition. He is to do this both in respect of himself as a principal and also as a witness in the case of other persons, living or dead.

Once the oath has been taken and registered, let the witness be urgently exhorted to tell the truth, of his own accord, in the matter of heresy, so far as he knows, has known, or has heard of it. If, however, he requests time or opportunity for deliberation in order to give a more carefully considered response, that may be granted him if it seems expedient to the inquisitor, especially if he seems to be seeking it in good faith, not guilefully. Otherwise, he is required to answer about himself without delay.

Thereupon, the date of the hearing may be entered by a notary, thus: "In such a year, on such date, one N., from such town or village, of such diocese, who came of his own free will, or was cited or summoned, was formally placed in judgment before the religious person N.—inquisitor of heretical depravity, deputed by the Apostolic See to the kingdom of France—having taken oath upon the Holy Gospels of God to speak the whole truth and nothing but the truth about the fact or the crime of heresy and everything pertaining thereto, both in respect of himself as a principal and also as a witness in the case of other persons, living or dead, has said and confessed," etc.

It should be noted further that if anyone should argue openly and obviously against the faith, adducing the arguments and the authorities upon which heretics are wont to rely, such a person may easily be proved guilty of heresy by loyal, learned sons of the Church, for one is presumed to be a heretic from the very fact of striving to defend error. But because modern heretics endeavor and seek covertly to disguise their errors rather than openly to confess them, even men versed in the Scriptures cannot prove their guilt, because they manage to escape by verbal trickery and carefully contrived subtleties. The result of this is that men of learning are rather thrown into confusion by them, and those heretics, glorying therein, are further encouraged by observing how they thus elude learned men, slipping cleverly out of their hands by the sly cunning and tortuous ambiguity of their replies.

For it is exceedingly difficult to catch heretics when they themselves do not frankly avow error but conceal it, or when sure and sufficient evidence against them is not at hand. Under such circumstances, serious problems beset the investigator from every side. For, on the one hand, his conscience torments him if an individual is punished who has neither confessed nor been proved guilty; on the other, it causes even more anguish to the mind of the inquisitor, familiar through much experience with the falsity, cunning, and malice of such persons, if by their wily astuteness they escape punishment, to the detriment of the faith, since thereby they are strengthened, multiplied, and rendered more crafty. Another consideration, too, is that the faithful laity see occasion for scandal in the fact that the proceedings of the Inquisition, once started against someone, are abandoned, as it were, in confusion, and they are to some extent weakened in the faith by observing that learned men are thus mocked by low and uncouth persons. For they believe that we have at our command in support of the faith arguments so clear and obvious that no one may oppose us in these matters without our knowing at once how to overcome him, in such wise that even laymen may clearly perceive just what these reasons are. Hence, in such a situation, it is not expedient to dispute in matters of the faith against such astute heretics in the presence of laymen.

Furthermore, a point worthy of attention is that just as no one medicine is for all diseases, but rather different and specific medicines exist for particular diseases, so neither is the same method of questioning, investigation, and examination to be employed for all heretics of the various sects, but for each, whether there be one or many, a particular and suitable method ought to be utilized. So the inquisitor, like a prudent physician of souls, will proceed cautiously in regard to the persons whom he questions or concerning whom he makes inquiry. He will weigh their quality, condition, standing, health, and local circumstances, and will act with caution on the matters upon which there is to be inquiry and examination. He should not impose or force all the following interrogatories upon everyone without distinction and in the same order; nor, in the case of some, should he be satisfied with these questions and only these. But with the bridle of discretion let him so harness the wiles of heretical persons that, with the help of God and the skill of a midwife, he may draw the writhing serpent from the sink and abyss of errors.

In these matters, no single and infallible pattern can be set, for, if that were done, the children of darkness might anticipate too far in advance the sole customary method and might too easily avoid or guard against it as a trap. Therefore, the wise inquisitor should be careful to set his course by the replies of the witnesses, the sworn statements of accusers, the counsel of men taught by experience, the shrewdness of his own natural intelligence, and the following questions or interrogatories, as God shall direct.

We shall append in order in the following pages material of use in giving some sort of idea as to how examinations may be conducted against five sects—the Manichaeans; the Waldenses, or Poor of Lyons; the pseudo-Apostles; those who are called in the vernacular Beguins; Jews who have been converted to the faith of Christ and have returned to the vomit of Judaism—and also against sorcerers, diviners, and invokers of demons, whose noxious influence is exceedingly harmful to the purity of the faith. A general outline of the error of each sect will be given first, followed by an outline of the plan and method of conducting the examination, as will appear on the following pages.

Concerning the Errors of the Manichaeans of the Present Time.—The sect and heresy of the Manichaeans and the supporters of its aberration declare and confess that there are two gods and two lords, to wit, a beneficent God and an evil one. They assert that the creation of everything visible and corporeal was wrought, not by God the Heavenly Father, whom they term the benefi-

cent God, but by the devil, or Satan, the wicked God—for him they call the evil god, the god of this age, and the prince of this world. Thus, they postulate two creators, namely, God and the devil; and two creations, that is, one invisible and incorporeal, the other visible and corporeal.

Also, they pretend that there are two churches: The beneficent one, they say, is their sect, which they declare to be the Church of Jesus Christ. But the other they call the evil church; this they hold to be the Roman Church, which they shamelessly refer to as the mother of fornication, the great Babylon, the harlot and cathedral of the devil, and the synagogue of Satan. They despise and distort all its offices, its orders, its ordinations, and its statutes. They call all who hold its faith heretics and sinners, and they declare as dogma that no one can be saved in the faith of the Roman Church.

Also, all the sacraments of the Roman Church of our Lord Jesus Christ—the Eucharist or sacrament of the altar, baptism which makes use of actual water, confirmation, ordination, extreme unction, penance, and marriage of man and woman—each and every one they declare empty and vain. And, like monkeys, they devise in imitation certain others which seem almost like them. In place of baptism by water, they concoct another baptism, a spiritual one, which they call the consolamentum of the Holy Spirit, whenever they admit anyone, in health or in sickness, into their sect and order by the imposition of hands, in accordance with their abominable rite. In place of the consecrated bread of the Eucharist, the body of Christ, they concoct a certain bread which they call "blessed bread" or "bread of holy prayer." This they hold in their hands at the beginning of their meal; and, following their ritual, they bless, break, and distribute it to those present and to their believers. As for the sacrament of penance, they say that true penance consists in entering and remaining faithful to their sect and order. They say that all sins have been forgiven 2those who enter their sect and order, whether in sickness or in health; that such persons have been absolved from all their sins without any atonement whatsoever and even without making restitution, should they possess another's property, so long as they remain true to their sect and order. They claim that they have the identical and equivalent power over these matters that Peter, Paul, and the other apostles of the Lord possessed. Confession of sins made to priests of the Roman Church they hold to be utterly without value for salvation, and they say that neither the pope nor anyone else connected with the Roman Church has the power to absolve anyone from his sins. Instead of the sacrament of carnal marriage between man and woman, they pretend that there is a spiritual marriage between the soul and God, namely, when the perfected or consoled heretics themselves receive anyone into their sect or order.

Also, they deny the incarnation of the Lord Jesus Christ through Mary, ever virgin, declaring that He did not have a true human body or true human flesh such as other men have because of their human substance, that He did not really suffer and die on the Cross, nor really rise from the dead, nor really ascend into heaven in human body and flesh, but that all these things happened only figuratively. Also, they deny that the Blessed Virgin Mary was the true mother of our Lord Jesus Christ or was a carnal woman, but say that their sect and order is the Virgin Mary, that is, the true, chaste, and virginal repentance which gives birth to sons of God on the occasion of their reception into this very sect and order. Also, they deny that there will be a resurrection of human bodies, imagining in its stead certain spiritual bodies and a sort of inner man. They say that the future resurrection is to be understood in terms of these two concepts.

They hold, believe, and teach the aforementioned errors and very many others which necessarily proceed therefrom. Nevertheless, because of misleading expressions and terms, to inexperienced persons and to laymen they seem at first sight to profess the true faith, for they say that they believe in God the Father, the Son, and the Holy Spirit, the creator of all; that they believe in the Holy Roman Church, in the Lord Jesus Christ, in the Blessed Virgin Mary, in the incarnation, passion, resurrection, and ascension of the same Lord Jesus Christ, in holy baptism, in true penance, in the true body of Christ, and in the sacrament of matrimony. Yet, when the truth is more attentively tested, sought for, and searched out, it appears that they utter all the foregoing in duplicity and falsehood, in accordance with their ideas as set forth and explained above, in order thus to deceive simple persons and even highly educated men if they happen to be inexperienced. They teach and expound to their believers all the errors mentioned above and, once they have been discovered and cannot hide, they openly defend, affirm, and profess them before inquisitors. Thenceforth, what is needful is to exhort them to conversion and, in every possible way, to show them their error, using the services of specially trained and diligent men.

Inquisitors, in normal practice, detain such perfected heretics for a rather long time for a number of reasons, first, in order more frequently to urge them to conversion, for their conversion is especially helpful. The conversion of Manichaean heretics is usually genuine and seldom feigned; when they are converted, they tell everything, reveal the truth, and betray their confederates, whence results a great harvest. Also, as long as such perfected heretics are held, their believers and accomplices more readily confess and expose themselves and others, fearing to be betrayed by the heretics if the latter are converted. However, after their conversion has been repeatedly urged and invited, if the heretics are unwilling to return to the faith and seem to be obdurate, sentence is pronounced against them and they are abandoned to the secular arm and tribunal.

Concerning the Way of Life and the Practices of These Manichaeans. — It is expedient, also, to touch on some facts in regard to the way of life, the customs, and the behavior of these heretics, since thereby they are more easily recognized and apprehended.

In the first place, it should be known that under no circumstances do they take an oath.

Also, they observe annually three forty-day fasts, namely, from the feast of St. Brice [November 13] until Christmas, from Shrove Sunday until Easter, and from the feast of Pentecost until the feasts of the apostles Peter and Paul [June 29]. The first and last week of each period they call "strict," for then they fast on bread and water, whereas, during the other weeks, they fast on bread and water for three days only. All the rest of the year they fast on bread and water three days each week, unless they are traveling or are ill. Also, they never eat meats or even touch them, or cheese, eggs, or anything which is born of the flesh by generation or coition.

Also, under no circumstances will they kill any animal or any winged creature, for they say and believe that there are in brute animals and even in birds those spirits which leave the bodies of men (if they have not been received into their sect and order through the imposition of hands according to their custom), and that these spirits pass from one body to another.

Also, they touch no woman.

Also, at the beginning of the month, when they are gathered together with their believers or by themselves, they bless a loaf or a piece of bread. Holding it in their hands, with a towel or some white cloth hanging from their necks, they say the Lord's Prayer and break the bread into small pieces. This bread they call "bread of holy prayer," and "broken bread"; their believers call it "blessed bread" or "consecrated bread" (*panem signatum*). They partake of it as communion at the beginning of a meal; they give and distribute it to their believers.

Also, they teach their believers to show them reverence in a ceremony which they call the melioramentum, although we call it adoration. The believer bends the knees and, with hands clasped, bows low before the heretics over some bench or down to the ground. He bows three times, each time saying as he rises, "Bless us," and finally concluding, "Good Christians, give us God's blessing and yours. Pray the Lord for us that God may keep us from an evil death and bring us to a good end or into the hands of faithful Christians." The heretic replies: "From God and from us you have it (that is, the benediction); and may God bless you and save your soul from an evil death, and bring you to a good end." By "evil death," the heretics mean dying in

the faith of the Roman Church, while by "a good end" and by "the hands of faithful Christians," they mean being received at the end of one's life into their own sect and order, according to their practice; this they hold to be a good end. However, they say that the reverence described above is made not to themselves but to the Holy Spirit, who, they say, is in them and by Whom they have been received into the sect and order which they claim is theirs.

Also, they teach their believers to make with them a pact, which they call "the agreement" (*la covenensa*), to the effect that the believers desire to be taken into the heretics' sect and order at the end of their life. Once that pact is sealed, the heretics may accept them during an illness, even though they should have lost the power of speech or their memory should have failed.

Concerning the Method of Heretication or the Reception of the Sick into This Sect or Order. — The following is the method of admitting persons to their sect or order during an illness or near the end of life of the suppliant. The heretic asks the individual who is to be received, if [the invalid] can speak, if he or she wishes to become a good Christian man or woman and wishes to receive holy baptism. Upon receiving an affirmative answer, accompanied by the request, "Bless us," the heretic, with his hand over the head of the sick person (but not touching her if it be a woman) and holding the Book, repeats the Gospel, "In the beginning was the Word," as far as "the Word was made flesh and dwelt among us." At the conclusion of the reading, the invalid repeats the Lord's Prayer, if he can; if not, one of those present says it for him. Thereafter, the sick man, if able, bows his head over clasped hands and says three times, "Bless us," while all the others present adore the heretic in the fashion described above. On the spot, or in a place apart, the heretic makes many prostrations, obeisances, and genuflections to the ground, repeating the Lord's Prayer several times while bowing and rising.

Concerning Their Method of Religious Instruction. — It would take long to treat in detail of the methods by which these Manichaean heretics preach and propound their doctrines to their believers, but it is well to present some of them briefly here.

In the first place, they usually say of themselves that they are good Christians who do not swear or lie or speak evil of anyone; that they kill neither man nor beast nor anything which has the breath of life; and that they hold the faith of the Lord Jesus Christ and His Gospel, as Christ and the apostles taught it. They say that they occupy the place of the apostles and that it is because of the foregoing facts that the members of the Roman Church, to wit, the prelates, the secular and regular clergy, and especially the inquisitors of heretics, persecute them and call them heretics, just as the Pharisees persecuted Christ and His apostles, although they are really good men and good Christians.

Also, they discuss with laymen at every opportunity the wicked life of clerics and prelates of the Roman Church. They give examples and speak at length about their pride, cupidity, avarice, their uncleanliness of life, and whatever other evils they know.

WITCHCRAFT

The good thing about the Inquisition is that, contrary to later Protestant myth, the papal inquisitors were not normally sadists and maniacs thirsting to turn over victims to the state for execution by burning. This extreme penalty occurred, but it was rare. What the inquisitors wanted was to bring the heretical defendants back to the Catholic fold by persuasion or, if that didn't work, by threats. Most of the punishments handed out by the papal Inquisition were relatively mild forms of penance. For those who recanted their heresy and then went back to it, there was imprisonment and loss of property. The death penalty was for repeated backsliders and persistent resisters. The bad thing about the Inquisition is that once a judicial system to control thought and deviant behavior is established at any time (including the United States in the 1950s), it inevitably goes around seeking alleged criminals and begins to pursue harmless, marginal, and thoroughly pathetic people. Thus the Inquisition took off after Jews, partly because in France there was overlap between the doctrines of the Albigensians and the Jewish Kabbalists (mystics), such as a belief in metempsychosis (transmigration of souls). Inevitably the inquisitors began to listen to accusations of witchcraft against a group of defendants who were mostly old women burdensome to their neighbors and themselves. Witchcraft had forever existed in medieval society. Now it became a big issue in the later Middle Ages. Historians are unsure whether the cult of witchcraft was really on the rise in this era or whether the same meager number of unfortunate witches as before now were subject to more active prosecution. Here is a summary of a typical witchcraft trial, from the year 1477. Note how it meanders all over the place, seeking self-incrimination and accusations against other alleged witches. There were some wise inquisitors who wouldn't give any credibility to such proceedings; unfortunately there weren't enough of such rationalists, and the witchcraft hysteria spilled over into the Protestant era and only died out after 1700. There are two things to be noted in this trial record. First, the defendant is a poor, frightened, bewildered farm woman. Second, a judicial system that tortures people to get the truth will get a lot of elaborate stories told in confession. It is the best way to get lenient treatment.

The trial of Antoine, wife of Jean Rose, of Villars-Chabod (near Annecy in Savoy) by the vice-inquisitor Étienne Hugonod in 1477 . . .

What was the evidence against her is not told. She has an audience, September 9, in which she is questioned in various ways as to her being a heretic and going to the [witches'] synagogue (*i.e.*, Sabbat), which she denies. She is then given the first monition to confess and return to the Church . . . and two other monitions on the following days, assigning September 14 as the term by which she must confess, as otherwise she will be proceeded against. The next audience is on September 15, when simply the names of five persons are mentioned whom she says she knows and that they are of good repute and she has no enmity towards them. Also the name of Massetus Garini, "submersus pro heresi" [apparently a man executed for witchcraft] who has denounced her as accomplice whom she says she knew and there was no enmity between them. She is asked also whether she had cured children or animals by charms, which she denies. . . .

She is then taken to the torture chamber and hung in the strappado for half an hour. . . .

Then, on October 20, she is brought out and asked if she will confess. Says she knows nothing of the said heresy. The prosecutor appears and demands a continuation of the torture, which is at once administered as before. . . . She bore this for a short space and then said she would confess all the truth if taken down, but when removed to the audience chamber she would not confess and was remitted to the next day . . . The next day, October 21, she is brought to the audience chamber, when she agrees to confess, imploring the grace of God and the mercy of the Church. She said that eleven years before she was coming from the chapelle du Puys full of grief, for Jacquemart of Annecy had seized three pieces of land for a debt due to him, when she met the above-named Massetus Garini and told him her trouble. He said he would find her a man to furnish money to redeem her property if she would do what he told her. She promised and in the evening between 9 and 10 P.M. he called for her and took her to the place called laz Perroy, where there was a synagogue of many men and women enjoying themselves and *dancing backwards*. She was frightened and wished to withdraw, but Massetus persuaded her to do homage to the demon, in the shape of a dark man, called Robinet, who promised her plenty of gold and silver, speaking in a hoarse, almost unintelligible voice. Under his persuasion and that of others present she renounced God and the faith, kissed him on the foot, and promised him yearly tribute . . . which she has paid since then. He marked her on the little finger of the left hand . . .

He gave her a purse full of gold and silver, but on opening it at home it was empty. He also gave her a stick 18 inches long and a pot of ointment; she would anoint the stick with it, place it between her legs and say "Go; in the name of the devil, go!" and at once she would be transported through the air to the synagogue. Then they had bread and meat to eat; what meat she knows not, for she ate bread and cheese and drank wine. Then they danced again; the demon changed to the shape of a black dog, which they all kissed under the tail. The lights went out and he called "Mechlet, Mechlet!" when the men had intercourse with the women, "in a brutal manner" she with Massetus Garini. Questioned as to whom she recognized there, she mentions three, one of whom, Antoine wife of Pierre Rose, told her she had tried to take a son of Michel Rose by night and would have done so, had not Michel wounded her in the arm. Questioned further, she mentions other synagogues she had attended in other places, with the same details. She is then sent back to her cell to think over and complete her confession, as otherwise further steps would be taken with her. On October 22 she is brought out again and confirms her confession and gives the names of thirteen others recognized in various synagogues. On October 23 she gives the names of four more and says that three days before her torture the demon appeared to her in prison and forbade her confessing, with a threat of beating her; she asked him to take her place and liberate her, which he refused, but promised to preserve her from torment and all other evil. Then he changed himself to an obscure shape and hung himself to a beam in the prison, saying that it did not hurt him. . . .

Also she confessed that she saw the flesh of infants brought to the synagogue and ate of it; the heads of infants exhumed from the cemeteries were not brought on account of the chrism of baptism. Further that the demon gave them ointments to sicken people; six years ago she touched with this ointment the hand of a four-year-old daughter of Louis Fabri of Filliez . . . the child sickened and died in a fortnight. Also they made powders of the bones and intestines of infants to work evil to men and beasts. With powders given her by the demon she had killed four cows of Pierre Jacquemont because he had beaten a goat of hers; also a cow of Pierre Girard because he had damaged her oats. The demon ordered them to do all the evil they could; that he would preserve her from all evil and she should not be arrested; also that in church they should not adore the host and when they took holy water they should sprinkle themselves backward; on days when she took holy water the demon did not appear to her; also he ordered that when they passed crosses they should adore him and not Christ, and when they received communion at Easter they should spit it out, but she could not do so. At one synagogue a consecrated host was brought, and they trampled on it. . . .

On October 25, she was examined again, and ratified all the above. She also said that after her audience of the twenty-third the demon had appeared to her in the shape of a huge man and told her that she had renounced him, to which she replied that she had and had returned to the bosom of the Church, giving herself to God and the blessed Mary and St. Bernard, offering three coins in honor of St. Bernard, so that the demon should not tempt or injure her. Then she threw herself on her knees, weeping, and with clasped hands begged for the mercy of God and grace of the Church—also that the case be concluded to sentence. Then the prosecutor appears and asks for conclusion and sentence. The vice-inquisitor concludes the case and assigns a time for pronouncing sentence.

THE TRIAL OF THE TEMPLARS

The prosecutions of heretics and witches produced a feverish atmosphere in which accusations of secret betrayal against established authority could assume plausibility. The more exalted a group was in society, the more it could be suspected of being in league with the devil. A radical fringe in the Franciscan Order accused the pope of being the Antichrist, who, a latter-day prophet had proclaimed, would sit on the Throne of Peter just before the Second Coming. In 1308 came the sensational inquisitorial trial of the Templars in Paris. The Templars were originally a crusading order who had become the official bankers for the papacy, rich and elegant corporate finance people. The accusation was pushed by officials of the French king who had their eye on seizing the Templars' huge assets in France. A former member of the Order said that the Order was secretly practicing blasphemy and sodomy that they had long ago learned in the Middle East from the Moslems. The Master and the leaders of the Order were put to torture and confessed to all sorts of salacious and peculiar details in line with this accusation. Later they repudiated their confessions and were quickly executed through public burning by the French state. Most historians believe that the whole thing was a put-up job, like Stalinist purge trials in the Soviet Union, from start to finish. However, it is just remotely possible that there was a small grain of truth in the accusations to start with, especially the part about sodomy (homoerotic behavior). Here are the Articles of Accusation against the Templars.

These are the articles on which inquiry should be made against the Order of the Knighthood of the Temple.

Firstly that, although they declared that the Order had been solemnly established and approved by the Apostolic See, nevertheless in the reception of the brothers of the said Order, and at some time after, there were preserved and performed by the brothers those things which follow:

Namely that each in his reception, or at some time after, or as soon as a fit occasion could be found for the reception, denied Christ, sometimes Christ crucified, sometimes Jesus, and sometimes God, and sometimes the Holy Virgin, and sometimes all the saints of God, led and advised by those who received him.—Item, [that] the brothers as a whole did this.—Item, that the majority [of them did this].

Item, that [they did this] also sometimes after the reception.

Item, that the receptors said and taught those whom they were receiving, that Christ, or sometimes Jesus, or sometimes Christ crucified, is not the true God.

Item, that they told those whom they received that he was a false prophet.

Item, that he had not suffered nor was he crucified for the redemption of the human race, but on account of his sins.

Item, that neither the receptors nor those being received had a hope of achieving salvation through Jesus, and they said this, or the equivalent or similar, to those whom they received.

Item, that they made those whom they received spit on a cross, or on a representation or sculpture of the cross and an image of Christ, although sometimes those who were being received spat next [to it].

Item, that they sometimes ordered that this cross be trampled underfoot.

Item, that brothers who had been received sometimes trampled on the cross.

Item, that sometimes they urinated and trampled, and caused others to urinate, on this cross, and several times they did this on Good Friday.

Item, that some of them, on that same day or another of Holy Week, were accustomed to assemble for the aforesaid trampling and urination.

Item, that they adored a certain cat, [which] sometimes appeared to them in their assembly.

Item, that they did this in contempt of Christ and the orthodox faith.

Item, that they did not believe in the sacrament of the altar.—Item, that some of them [did not believe].—Item, that the majority [of them did not believe].

Item, that nor [did they believe] in the other sacraments of the Church.

Item, that the priests of the Order by whom the body of Christ is consecrated did not speak the words in the canon of the mass.—Item, that some of them [did not].—Item, that the majority [did not].

Item, that the receptors enjoined this upon them.

Item, that they believed, and thus it was told to them, that the Grand Master could absolve them from sin.—Item, that the Visitor [could].—Item, that the preceptors [could], of whom many were laymen.

Item, that they did this de facto.—Item, that some of them [did].

Item, that the Grand Master of the aforesaid Order confessed this, in the presence of important persons, before he was arrested.

Item, that in the reception of the brothers of the said Order or at about that time, sometimes the receptor and sometimes the received were kissed on the mouth, on the navel, or on the bare stomach, and on the buttocks or the base of the spine.—Item, [that they were kissed] sometimes on the navel.—Item, [that they were kissed] sometimes on the base of the spine.—Item, [that they were kissed] sometimes on the penis.

THE TRIAL OF JOAN OF ARC

The English crown used accusations of heresy and witchcraft to get rid of a dangerous political enemy, the Maid of Orleans, Joan of Arc. In the 1420s, in the concluding stage of the Hundred Years War, the English still held the western third of France. Joan was a peasant girl who experienced saintly visions summoning her to help the French king retake the city of Orleans, so that he could benefit from an official coronation in this traditional crowning-place of French monarchs. Joan put on armor, rallied the French soldiers and people, and the French took the city. It was the turning point of the Hundred Years War; after that it was downhill all the way for the centuries-old English empire in France. When Joan was captured by French allies of the English, she was subjected to an inquisitorial trial, condemned as a heretic and a witch (among her most prominent crimes was wearing men's clothes, an androgynous threat that even Hildegard of Bingen had warned against), and "released" to the secular arm, the English government in France, for burning. Here are the key parts of the trial record.

Joan of Arc on horseback

On Monday following, the day after Holy Trinity Sunday, we the said judges repaired to Jeanne's prison to observe her state and disposition.

Now because the said Jeanne was wearing a man's dress, a short mantle, a hood, a doublet and other garments used by men (which at our order she had recently put off in favor of woman's dress), we questioned her to find out when and for what reason she had resumed man's dress and rejected woman's clothes. Jeanne said she had but recently resumed man's dress and rejected woman's clothes.

Asked why she had resumed it, and who had compelled her to wear it, she answered that she had taken it of her own will, under no compulsion, as she preferred man's to woman's dress.

She was told that she had promised and sworn not to wear man's dress again, and answered that she never meant to take such an oath.

Asked for what reason she had assumed male costume, she answered that it was more lawful and convenient for her to wear it, since she was among men, than to wear woman's dress. She said she had resumed it because the promises made to her had not been kept, which were to permit her to go to Mass and receive her Saviour, and to take off her chains.

Asked whether she had not abjured and sworn in particular not to resume this male costume, she answered that she would rather die than be in chains, but if she were allowed to go to Mass, if her chains were taken off and she were put in a gracious prison [and were given a woman as companion], she would be good and obey the Church.

As we her judges had heard from certain people that she had not yet cut herself off from her illusions and pretended revelations, which she had previously renounced, we asked her whether she had not since Thursday heard the voices of St. Catherine and St. Margaret. She answered yes.

Asked what they told her, she answered that they told her God had sent her word through St. Catherine and St. Margaret of the great pity of this treason by which she consented to abjure and recant in order to save her life; that she had damned herself to save her life. She said that before Thursday they told her what to do and say

then, which she did. Further her voices told her, when she was on the scaffold or platform before the people, to answer the preacher boldly. The said Jeanne declared that he was a false preacher, and had accused her of many things she had not done. She said that if she declared God had not sent her she would damn herself, for in truth she was sent from God. She said that her voices had since told her that she had done a great evil in declaring that what she had done was wrong. She said that what she had declared and recanted on Thursday was done only for fear of the fire.

Asked if she believed her voices to be St. Catherine and St. Margaret, she answered "Yes, and they came from God."

Asked to speak truthfully of the crown which is mentioned above, she replied: "In everything, I told you the truth about it in my trial, as well as I could."

When she was told that when she made her abjuration on the scaffold or platform before the judges and the people, she had admitted that she had falsely boasted that her voices were St. Catherine and St. Margaret, she answered that she did not mean to do or say so.

She said she did not deny or intend to deny her apparitions, that is that they were St. Catherine and St. Margaret; all that she said was from fear of the fire. She recanted nothing which was not against the truth. She said she would rather do penance once and for all, that is die, than endure any longer the suffering of her prison. She said that whatever they had made her deny she had never done anything against God or the faith: she did not understand what was in the formula of abjuration. She said she did not mean to revoke anything except at God's good pleasure. If the judges wished, she would once more wear woman's dress, but for the rest she would do no more.

After hearing these declarations we left her to proceed further according to law and reason.

JUDGMENT OF THE COURT

"Therefore before us your competent judges, namely Pierre by divine mercy bishop of Beauvais and brother Jean Le Maistre, vicar in this city and diocese of the notable master Jean Graverent,

Inquisitor of Heretical Error in the kingdom of France, and especially appointed by him to officiate in this cause, you, Jeanne, commonly called *The Maid,* have been arraigned to account for many pernicious crimes and have been charged in a matter of the faith. And having seen and examined with diligence the course of your trial and all that occurred therein, principally the answers, confessions and affirmations which you made, after having also considered the most notable decision of the masters of the Faculties of Theology and Decrees in the University of Paris, in addition to that of the general assembly of the University, and of the prelates, doctors and men learned in canon and civil law and in theology who were met together in a great multitude in this town of Rouen and elsewhere for the discussion and judgment of your statements, words and deeds; having taken counsel and mature conference with those zealots of the Christian faith, and having seen and weighed all there is to see and weigh in this matter, all that we and any man of judgment and law could and should observe: We, having Christ and the honor of the orthodox faith before our eyes, so that our judgment may seem to emanate from the face of Our Lord, have said and decreed that in the simulation of your revelations and apparitions you have been pernicious, seductive, presumptuous, of light belief, rash, superstitious, a witch, a blasphemer of God and His saints, a despiser of Him in His sacraments, a prevaricator of the divine teaching and the ecclesiastical sanctions, seditious, cruel, apostate, schismatic, erring gravely in our faith, and that by these means you have rashly trespassed against God and the Holy Church.

"Moreover, although you have very often, not by Us only but also by certain learned expert masters and doctors full of zeal for the salvation of your soul, been duly and sufficiently admonished to amend and reform yourself, and to submit to the disposition, decision and correction of Holy Mother Church, you would not, and cared not to do so, and even in the hardness of your heart stubbornly and obstinately declared that you would not, and on many occasions expressly refused to submit to Our Holy Father the Pope and the holy General Council. *Therefore,* we declare you of right excommunicate and heretic, being stubborn and obstinate in your crimes, excesses and errors; and we pronounce it meet to abandon you and do abandon you to the secular justice as a limb of Satan, infected with the leprosy of heresy, cut off from the Church, in order to prevent the infection of the other members of Christ; praying this same power on this side of death and the mutilation of your limbs to moderate its judgment towards you, and if true signs of penance appear in you to permit the sacrament of penance to be administered to you."

JOHN OF SALISBURY

ECCLESIASTICAL HYPOCRITES AND CHARLATANS

No society was more critical of itself than that of Western Europe from the twelfth through the fifteenth centuries, unless it was the United States in the last two decades of the twentieth century. A major subset of late medieval culture was the culture of complaint. The searchlight of criticism began with focus on the church and slowly spread out to cast accusations against all other social groups. Was this chorus of complaint justified? That is a very hard question to answer. It was probably excessive, but it was not just paranoia or an overused literary genre. The medieval world, at the same time as it reached its zenith of prosperity, creativity, and spirituality, did suffer remarkably from disorganization, mismanagement, and corruption in every facet of

the social and political system. Its oversight, watchdog, and corrective mechanisms were never very effective, and repeated reform movements and agencies addressing visible problems rarely had much success beyond an initial impetus (again this sounds like the United States at the end of the twentieth century). The medieval world was deficient in systems analysis and managerial capacity with regard to complex phenomena, particularly on the ecclesiastical side. On the other hand, the medievals had a propensity to be excessively critical of their society, its constituent groups, and its prime institutions. This is because their understanding of society was almost entirely based on strictly moral and religious perspectives. Until the fourteenth century, and then only with isolated and marginally influential exceptions, they lacked an amoral, secular, and sociological way of looking at their society, its institutions, and its group functionings. When your criteria of judgment is on the very high plane of Christian spirituality supplemented by the high-flown ethical criteria of classical humanism, you are going to see a lot that is wrong in your society. Whether justified or excessive, the medieval culture of complaint began to develop in the twelfth century and had become a torrent of accusation and guilt-mongering by 1300. A pioneer critic was John of Salisbury, an Englishman who was not only an experienced ecclesiastic (he served as secretary to the English Pope Adrian IV and then to Archbishop Thomas Becket and himself ended up a bishop of Chartres), but he was also the finest classical scholar of his day. He was immersed in the ethical perspectives and rhetoric of Cicero and the Stoics. John was a trenchant critic of his society, and in his major work *Policraticus* (1159) he spared no one in either church or state. Here is his brilliant and subtle attack on hypocrites and demagogues in the church, particularly among the religious orders and newly fashionable itinerant preachers of one sort or another (vulgar imitations of St. Bernard of Clairvaux) and the damage they do and confusion they bring. Criticism of deceitful and corrupt clergy became a whole literary genre in itself in the later Middle Ages. Chaucer, for one, never stopped talking about this social ill. Boccaccio constantly used it as a plot device. It is to John of Salisbury's credit that his sophisticated temperament and sharp eye saw early on the problems inherent in popular piety. On the other hand, his indictment can arguably be viewed as the response of a conservative to an emerging demotic culture. The flourishing of the literary genre of criticizing the clergy can also be regarded as the paradoxical outcome of the church's attack upon possible scapegoats for society's ills. When Jews, heretics, and witches are repressed, and the world is still replete with customary miseries, the clergy are likely to be next on the blaming list. If John of Salisbury could have seen ahead two centuries on this "overmuch blaming of the clergy," as a fifteenth-century English archbishop called it, he might not have taken up his brilliant pen against the people he regarded as hypocrites and frauds. Some probably were, but there is intellectual arrogance and elitist contempt in this critique that leaves ambivalent feelings in the reader.

Although the rashness of the people or the licence of the powerful can be restrained by legal precepts and divine instructions, still ambition cannot be controlled. For if it does not risk public attention, it spreads secretly and enters fraudulently. If it does not open up the gates of the Church with presents, if they are unbarred by neither its own violence nor that of another, it has recourse to the arts of deception. Everything which assails liberty, which disrupts the decretal statutes, and which is contrary to religion, it detests with the whole liberty of the Spirit. You might wonder if Sinon had returned in order that the simple and the naive might be fooled. He pretends and he dissimulates and he bears the cunning of the fox within his heart; he is more liberated than any Stoic, more restrained than Cato. He is also occasionally more sincere and more careful than Paul, the teacher of the Romans, and more fervent than Peter; and Christ is living to him and wealth is dying; and he does not pride himself on anything except the cross of Christ, which he continually bears upon his body in order that his spirit may be saved, desiring merely to be set free and to live with Christ. He, therefore, mortifies the vices and desires of the flesh and, although passing his life among men, behaves angelically and keeps company with the heavens, unlike other men. These sorts fast continually, they pray without interruption and 'yet clearly so that a visitor hears,' they are clothed in rough and filthy attire and they censure the people. They accuse clerics, they remonstrate about the amendment of the moral characters of princes and powerful men, acquiring evidence of their own justice when they disparage the lives of others.

In order that fraud may flourish under the appearance of honour, these men seek out the company of the praiseworthy, they submit to arduous oaths, they boast of difficult deeds and they pursue possible courses of action which are beneficial both for themselves personally and for humanity generally. They declare themselves followers of Basil, Benedict, Augustine or, if this is not enough, of the apostles and prophets; they dress in the clothes of the Carthusians, the Cistercians or the Cluniacs, and those who are deemed worthy of being canons pride themselves on their tunics of wool and lamb skin. For they come in sheep's clothing, yet inside they are predatory wolves; but, as the Lord asserts, they will be known most manifestly by their own fruits. Yet the glory of true religion is not diminished by their deceptions. For it is agreed by everyone without doubt that the causes which they profess and to which they pledge themselves are the most honourable and most faithful duties. For within these movements religious faith is so true, so excellent, that it never fears the sting of censure; indeed the Carthusians are everywhere prominent as the chief vanquishers of avarice; the Cistercians follow to precision the precepts and footprints of blessed Benedict, who is agreed by everyone to have been full of the spirit of the just; the Cluniacs have transmitted the plan of religion to many provinces. And it ought to suffice for the fullest praise of the canons that their rule should be imitated by all clerics. Moreover, hermits have as the authority for their practices the Baptiser of our Saviour and the sons of the prophets. The Brothers of the Temple lay down their lives for their fellows, on the example of the Maccabeans. The Xenodochi or Hospitallers follow the footprints of the apostles and, aspiring to the height of perfection, they obey Christ most faithfully in this: they live innocently and disperse all that they have to the poor.

Yet among all of these are found both the faithful and the reprobate, and neither religion nor the profession of truth is disfigured as a result of it. For what occupation is there, or what association has there been about which we read, upon which no blemish has insinuated itself? We read of the apostate angel, of fratricide among the earliest brothers, of the reprobate prophet, and of the wicked disciples of Christ. Yet the purity of the persevering angels is not corrupted, nor is the mutual association of loving fellows less holy, nor is prophetic grace among the elect a sin, nor is apostolic authority contemptible among the faithful, nor is Christ's teaching deformed by the various errors of the heterodox. Therefore, just as the angel of Satan transfigures himself into the angel of light and the pseudo-apostles aspire to the authority rather than to the life of the apostles, so likewise hypocrites resort to the arrogance of the Pharisees, 'enlarging their phylacteries and broadening the fringes of their clothing,' but their fingers are unable to touch those things which are written in the law of God, inasmuch as these things may be viewed by the men from whom hypocrites expect a reward of honour or other remuneration. It is as a result of this that they display the pallor of their faces, they affect by means of practice deep sighs, they are unexpectedly flooded with artificial and compliant tears; their heads are lowered, their eyes half closed, their hair short, their heads nearly shaved, their voices lowered, their lips moving in prayer, their movements serene and their steps like a sort of well-arranged harmony. They are tattered and covered with dirt, and they commend dirty clothes and contrived tawdriness—all in order that those persons may more easily raise themselves up who seem to have cast themselves down with zeal into the lowest place and that those who voluntarily diminish themselves will be compelled to become powerful against their wishes.

It is these hypocrites who, if some blemish has attached itself to the Church while it wanders the earth, expose it for public inspection, in order that they may be seen to be immune themselves from all blemishes. It is they who preach that the benefices which are granted to not yet holy men are to be withdrawn. It is they who persuade the powerful that churches are to be deprived of their rights on account of the vices of particular people. They carry off the titles and first fruits of churches and they accept for themselves churches from the hands of laymen without consulting the bishops. It is they who, carrying off the spoils of ancestral lands from those born to them, reduce villages and rural regions to solitude and who convert everything in the vicinity to their own uses; they destroy churches or they transfer them to secular uses. That which was a house of prayer is made into either a cattle barn or a workshop for craftsmen or woolmakers. They also perform with impunity greater evils and do not hold back from disturbing the Church, in whose lap they rest and under whose cover they are protected, with the twin, horn-like powers of Rome and court. For indeed they run away to the Roman Church, that pious mother of religion which has grown accustomed to providing for peace. They appeal for its assistance, they obtain the protection of its shield lest they might be molested by anyone's malice, and, in order that they can sustain themselves more fully and carry out the duties of charity, they are protected by apostolic privilege so that they do not pay tithes. They proceed further and, in order that they may allow themselves more with impunity, they release themselves from the jurisdiction of all churches and are made the special children of the Roman Church; thus, while they can bring legal action against a defendant anywhere, still they cannot be sued except at Rome or Jerusalem.

At the same time, they entreat the aid of secular powers and promise them divine favour. And they become mediators between God and man and they gather into their association those who need forgiveness. They receive confessions and, usurping or creeping up on the keys of Peter, they presume to bind and to loose, and they release their scythe upon harvests belonging to others which are forbidden to them by the Lord. Moreover, they too readily exonerate the powerful and the more wealthy upon receipt of favours or payment and, placing upon their shoulders the sins of others, they order them to go out in tunics and mourning garments as penance for whatever deeds they lamented that they had committed. They extend the mercy of the Lord, who wishes no one to perish, which they proclaim to be open and accessible just as much to penitents as it is closed only to those without hope. They meanwhile make allowance for those who are ardently and tenaciously involved in crimes to sin in hope; yet they are always paid something in advance for the redemption of such men and they boldly promise forgiveness, because just as water extinguishes fire, so alms extinguish sins.

In addition, while penitence is never too late if it is still genuine, these men assent to wicked morals and, contending for popular affection by means of flattery, they plug up the ears of men lest they hear the reproval of prelates. To this end, they investigate idle gossip, rejoice in disorders, search out the secrets of opposing groups and communicate them first to the friends, then to the enemies, favouring both and faithless to both. Yet they seem better suited to these activities because they are rendered less suspect by the pretext of religion. They alone are believed to have knowledge of what is expedient in the palace, in the market place, on the farm, and in the camp because those who are constantly interfering with everything are seen above others to be in charge of everything. If the elders convene at court, the citizens in the market place, the troops on campaign, in short, if council or synod is convoked, these retiring men of religion will occupy the principal section of seats. You might think that the bars on all the cloister doors were smashed, the poor-houses and hospices emptied out, and that a swarm of carousers had escaped from these venerable places — to so great an extent do these sorts of religious men insinuate themselves into the crowds and public displays. They usurp the best seats, the best beds, the highest salutations and, if you do not allot these things to them, they are most vehemently indignant.

If you reproach them, you are called an enemy of religion and an opponent of the truth. And so you endure it patiently, if your injuries and suffering have been caused by those who are seen to have obtained licence from all apostolic and royal authorities; for this is believed to be owed them by reason of their merits. Surely 'he who resists the powerful resists the ordinances of God'; and I do not suppose that apostolic and royal majesty is to be resisted. Speaking with due respect to the faithful, I still wonder: how is it that they are not ashamed to usurp tithes and rights that belong to others? Perhaps they might say: 'We are religious men.' Surely it is part of religion to pay tithes, and God exacts them only of a religious people. 'But those who exact them are irreligious.' And who appointed you judge over them? Or 'Who are you that you exercise judgment over the servants of another? Every person stands or falls before his own lord. Indeed, he will stand.' They say, 'We are protected by apostolic privilege, according to which we retain the benefits of physical nourishment and the tithes of our labours.' Unquestionably, the apostles are permitted all things; but everything done by the pupils of the apostles is by no means expedient. Concede that they granted this licence to you; consider whether you rightfully sought it. Unquestionably, he who desires not to do what he should do does not freely obey justice. Did not Abel have respect for the Lord in regard to his nourishment? Cain had offered his crops, and rightly so because they were owed to God, but he committed a sin in their inequitable division in so far as he subtracted some from the divided portion. Yet these presents were accepted in preference to the presents of those who divided

the offspring of their animals with the Lord. And perhaps presents of animals are more rightfully bestowed because they are obtained without our cultivation and care; for there is more labour in the fruits of planting and harvesting. They respond: 'No one is forced to sacrifice from his own goods.' Yet who is to render account of the labour of others? What more may be said? By many and extended excuses they are seen to affirm that others are not prohibited from giving tithes while they themselves are immune from giving them because they are so religious that they can for their part abrogate divine statutes and by this licence they are less thankful for the grace of God, the benefits of which they experience more fully. For those things which are obtained by grace alone, such as seed and natural offspring, are not considered to be subject to religion.

While in the beginning religion rejoiced in poverty and shared fully of the depths of its own want for the needs and uses of others, the monastic orders are favoured with privileges which, ceasing to be necessary and snubbing charity, are deemed to be instruments of avarice rather than of religion. For behold that all these privileged men occupy themselves solely with those things which are theirs and Jesus, who is commended in public, either is absent entirely or is concealed in a secret place. Thus it is that blessed [Pope] Adrian observed privileges squandered for the iniquitous profit of avarice; although not wishing to revoke them entirely, he restricted their licence with this precept of moderation: that what they may appropriate from their labours is to be construed solely with regard to fallow land. For thus they can enjoy their privileges without cost to the rights of others.

Yet there is one more thing that such a great father somehow upheld; and because it evades the canons of the Fathers, it is a wonder to our eyes. For the Knights of the Temple with the pope's approval claim for themselves the administration of the churches, they occupy them through surrogates, and they whose normal occupation it is to shed human blood in a certain way presume to administer the blood of Christ. Not of course that I would call those — almost alone among men—who wage legitimate war 'men of blood,' since even David was called a man of blood not because he engaged in wars which were legitimate but on account of Uriah, whose blood he criminally shed. For as is provided by the canons, none of the powers of the ecclesiastical sphere may be seen to be ascribed to laymen, even if they are religious men. Above all, it would be a sign of true religion if they refrained from the administration of those things which by God's prohibition it is not permitted for them to touch. And I do not believe that hospitality is to be carried out from the spoils of plunder (I mean neither that of churches nor that of any of the faithful whomsoever) because God hates the bread of sacrilege and he spurns sacrifices which are offered out of blood; and as often as He is called upon by such means, He closes His ears so that He is not open to their supplications.

It was by no means intended to speak at present about these deeds, which are committed by such men in injury to the justice of God. Still it is entirely wicked that, enticed by the love of money, they open churches which are closed by bishops. Those suspended from office celebrate the sacraments, they bury the dead whom the Church refuses, and they act once a year so that during the rest of the year the erring people are deaf to the voice of the Church; and he who cannot be coerced seems to be corrected. Therefore, they travel around to the churches, they praise the merits of their own orders, they bring absolution for crimes, and sometimes they preach a new gospel, falsifying the word of God because they preach living not by grace but by a price, by pleasure and not by truth. And in the end, when they convene in their lairs late at night, 'after speaking of virtue by day they shake their hips in nocturnal folly and exertion.' If one moves in this fashion towards Christ, then the doctrine of the Fathers which teaches that the narrow and steep path heads towards the true life of man is false and vain.

Indeed when these men disdain the Church, none are so disturbed with utter propriety as those truly religious men upon whom all of these injuries will back up. The people are roused to anger, but the religious orders are more justly stirred up against the disgrace of these hypocrites. For this blemish is said to have been caused not by the hypocrite but by the Cistercians or the Cluniacs or others in whose apparel these jugglers and ventriloquists dress and whose lives they falsify. The cloistered who are clearly religious men, in so far as they keep their vows, are exempted from this malice. No life is more faithful, none more simple, none happier than the life of those who live humbly in a cloister, rejoicing in their submission, obeying their prelates in all matters of subjection and reverence, neither desiring mastery under the pretext of obedience nor the licence to be deceptive or to roam or to be idle, possessing their vessels with holiness and honour, waiting in silence and patience to pay respects to God, unfamiliar with grumbling and defamation, receiving in tranquillity from the mouth of the Lord the words which can save their souls, participating in courteous discourse with God; like terrestrial angels, they are totally ignorant of all earthly troubles. If there is something that seems to sadden them, this is to be traced back to their fraternal charity, since even the angels in heaven feel pity in a certain measure for our errors and they rejoice together over even one sinner moved to repentance.

Although it is difficult to imitate the philosophers in our own times . . . the life of the cloistered excels incomparably the virtue of the philosophers or, what I would rather believe, it is to be a philosopher in the most correct and secure manner. Truly those who step out of the cloister humbly in order to satisfy the needs of their brothers and who are faithfully engaged in their labours are occupied with more useful, even though not more secure, lives and are deemed worthy of great praise and reverence; by no means do they resemble the faction of Epicureans or hypocrites. For you will correctly group hypocrites together with Epicureans, who teach philosophy and who serve their own private wills. When they foment disputes, abuse privileges, are slaves to passion, never exercise the duties of charity and seek their own private glory, do they not proceed according to the flesh although they style themselves as spirituals? Deservedly anticipating the annihilation of the flesh, will they not be partners in Hell with him who is a spirit and who was cast down and thrown headlong into the lake of eternal damnation because, swelling up with vain glory, he wished to be equal to and preferred before the Most High? Doubtless those who move along this path are foolish and more miserable than all the gentiles, since they are deprived both of a good life in the present world and of eternal life—the

more so since He who had suffered sin to be done for the sake of sinners and who had shown Himself an intimate of tax-collectors and prostitutes, had not been able to maintain peace with hypocrites who were not in need of His justice. This much is clear to those who attend diligently to the debates He carried out with the Pharisees. Yet they strive to possess the chief offices, on the example of the Pharisees.

JUAN RUIZ

THE POWER OF MONEY

One of the persistent myths about the Middle Ages is that it was a precapitalist era. Status and traditions remained important to the very end of the Middle Ages. But certainly by 1300 Europe was in active transition to a capitalist society in which money as well as honor and tradition were greatly valued. In a still predominantly rural and agricultural society, cash flow can yet have enormous impact and profiteering can be a common motive. Given the heroic and hierarchic traditions of the Middle Ages, and the common moral and spiritual discourse that was imbibed from education and reading, the rise of a money economy was bound to be bitterly resisted in many quarters and subject to constant criticism. The mid-fourteenth-century Spanish writer Juan Ruiz here succinctly assesses the power of money at all levels and within all groups of society. It is noticeable that he reserves his harshest criticism for the clergy because of their alleged hypocritical discrepancy between their high-flown ideals and professions and the reality of their mercenary pursuits like everyone else. This was a constant theme in late medieval literature.

The Usurer

"Money can do much; it should be held in high esteem. It turns a tramp into a respected and honorable man; it makes the lame man run and the dumb man speak. Even a man without hands reaches out and grabs for money. A man may be an idiot or an ill-bred peasant, but money will make him a noble and a sage; the more money a man has, the more worthy he becomes, while the man who is penniless cannot call himself his own master. If you have money, you can have luxury, pleasure, and joy, and benefices from the Pope; you can buy Paradise and earn salvation. Piles of money bring piles of blessings.

"Over in Rome, the seat of holiness, I myself observed them all curtseying and scraping before Money, and doing him solemn homage. They humble themselves as they do before the Crucifix. There, money created many priors, bishops and abbots, archbishops, doctors, patriarchs, and men of power. Money won dignities for many ignorant clerics; it turned truths into lies and lies into truths. Money created many clerics and priests, monks and nuns, consecrated religious, certifying that they had sufficient knowledge, while the poor were informed that they lacked learning. Money bought judgments and verdicts galore, lived with crooked lawyers, and fostered unjust suits and settlements, so that finally, thanks to money, even absolution could be obtained.

"Money snaps heavy chains, destroys irons and pillories, those feared prisons, but the man who lacks money finds himself handcuffed. All over the world, money does marvelous things. I have seen money restore to life many who deserved to die, and cut down many who were innocent. Many souls has he damned, many souls has he saved. Money can destroy a poor man's house and his orchards, his furniture and his estate. Its itch and scab infest the whole earth. Where money is involved, you will always find intrigue. Money makes knights out of stupid farmers, counts and noblemen out of peasants. The man who has money puts on the airs of a gentleman and everybody kisses his hand.

"I have observed that Money always had the best, the largest, the most costly and elegant mansions; castles, estates, turreted palaces served Money and were bought by him. Money dined on exotic delicacies, decked himself in rich and gilded clothes, wore precious jewels, all this in leisure and pleasure, with rare ornaments and noble mounts. I have often heard monks in their sermons condemn money and its temptations—and immediately afterward grant pardons, waive penances, and offer prayers—for money. These monks may scorn money in the public square, but back in the cloister they hoard it in vases and chalices. Money has more hiding places than do thrushes or magpies. And with money they indulge all their vices.

"Even while friars and priests protest that they are servants of God, if they hear a rumor that a rich man is dying and catch the sound of his silver, they begin to haggle over which of them is to attend him. Although friars will not take money, they give the nod to their bursars. Immediately afterward, their cellarers grab hold of it. (If they are supposed to be poor, what need do they have for bursars?) They stand about, waiting to see who will get the largest share. The man has barely breathed his last before they intone the paternoster—for an evil omen! They act as the crows did who were skinning the jackass: 'Tomorrow we will take it, because it is rightfully ours.'

"Every woman in the world and every noblewoman is fond of money and great wealth; I have never known a beautiful woman who cherished poverty. Piles of money proclaim high nobility. Money receives high praise as judge and governor, counselor and subtle advocate, bold and powerful, constable and royal judge; money controls every office. In sum, I tell you (don't take it amiss): Money, which is the world's axis, makes a lord out of a servant and a servant out of a lord.

. . . The world and its ways change for money; every woman, greedy for something, is honey-tongued. She will go out of her way for jewels and money; gifts can crack rocks and split hard wood. Money can tear down a thick wall and knock over a high tower. It can help in any kind of trouble. There is no slave in fetters whom money cannot free. But if you can't pay your way, you won't get your horse to run.

"Money makes hard things easy. Therefore, be generous and lavish with your old woman; do not send her off without some profit, large or small; I am not impressed by trifles that have no value. If you can give her nothing at all, at least be generous in your speech: do not offer foolish excuses. The man who has no honey in his jar must have it in his mouth; a trader of this sort does good business. If you know how to play or to temper musical instruments, if you can sing well, you must use your talent occasionally, where the woman may hear you."

RENARD THE FOX

BOURGEOIS CONTEMPT FOR THE NOBILITY

Immensely popular with the bourgeoisie in the later Middle Ages were the rhyming fables about Renard the Fox, who represents the clever, rational bourgeoisie. In this poem, a complaint is brought against Renard by Ysengrin the wolf, who stands for a typical nobleman. Ysengrin complains to the lion King that Renard has raped his wife Hersent. The satire proposes a defense for Renard mischievously derived from courtly romances—it wasn't rape because he was in love with the nobleman's wife. The fumbling King asks the papal legate camel to render judgment, and the latter complies with the pretentious multilingual ecclesiastical twaddle one might expect of a high cleric. The message is that the bourgeoisie are clever and know what they want; all other powerful groups in society are ridiculous and inept. Sexual aggression as a means of class conflict is a suggestive theme.

He can see Renard regaining his lair,
Renard who has shamed him to his face
And laughed at him in his disgrace.
He did not wait to speak his thought,
But went to help Hersent, still caught—
Her struggles had been to no avail.
Ysengrin grabs her by the tail
And pulls on it with might and main
Until Hersent is in such pain
That Ysengrin in anguish tries
To make the hole a larger size.
He thinks that she is coming unstuck,
And will soon be out, with any luck;
However, when he stands back a bit,
He sees that it's still too tight a fit,
And if his efforts aren't increased,
Hersent will never be released—
He would be sad to lose her so.
Ysengrin, neither lazy nor slow,
Digs and scratches with his claws,
Looking carefully and using his paws
To throw the loosened earth about.
The devil take him or he'll get her out!
When a great amount of dirt was pried
From above, below, and to each side,
He goes to Hersent, tries once more,
She's not stuck as tightly as before.
He pulls her—he doesn't want to fail—

So hard he'd have broken off her tail
If it hadn't been put on to stay.
He feels the tunnel's grip give way
At last, and he's saved Hersent from death,
With just about his final breath.
Then, as if drunk right out of his mind,
He kicked her. "Do you think I'm blind,
You vile, stinking, shameless whore—
You got what you were asking for!
I saw Renard as he straddled your tail
To cuckold me, and he did not fail!
Now will you say you're innocent?"
Hearing his angry words, Hersent
In her fury nearly lost her head,
But she replied with the truth instead:
"My lord, there's no doubt that I've been shamed,
But I've also been unjustly blamed.
Hear me out and you'll realize
That Renard took me by surprise
Against my will. But what's done is done.
It will do no good to anyone
If we just stay here quarreling,
Let's bring our grievance to the king!
That is what Noble's court is for—
Whatever might be cause for war,
Disputes and claims get a hearing there,
And the lion's judgment will be fair.
If we go to him and state our case

He will put an end to our disgrace—
You'll meet Renard on the jousting field."
Ysengrin's anger had to yield
When Hersent explained how she was caught.
"What a fool I was," he said, "to have thought
As I did! But now I've seen the light;
What you advise is surely right.
Renard will pay dearly for his sport
If I can bring him to Noble's court."

    They saw no reason to delay,
And stopped for nothing all the way
To King Noble's court where Ysengrin
Was sure of the vengeance he would win
If he could bring his foe to trial:
Renard the Red, despite his guile,
Would find that it was not a joke.
Lord Ysengrin, after all, spoke
Several languages; he presided
As marshal where the king resided.
Now they had reached the very place
Where they hoped the king would hear their
    case.
At that plenary session you could find
Creatures of every size and kind:
Big and little, weak and strong,
And to Noble all of them belong.
There on a rich throne sat the king
With all around him, in a ring,
The mighty lords of his retinue
Each one of whom showed that he knew
The strict decorum that was due
A royal court. Then came in view
Lord Ysengrin with his dear Hersent.
They indicated their intent
To address the king and took the floor.
No one would speak a word before
They'd finished. Ysengrin, with a sigh,
Said, "King, your vassals don't comply
With the law. The truth is rarely heard;
None can you trust though he give his word.
According to your royal command,
Marriage is sacred in this land;
No one loyal to you would dare
To interfere with a wedded pair.
But Renard doesn't care what you decree:
He has brought to shame my wife and me.
Misfortune follows where he goes.

His deference to you he shows
When he thinks that it is quite all right
To force himself on my wife despite
The fact that he's my relative.
No words of mine could ever give
A true idea of his wickedness.
But I do not speak of my distress,
My lord, to blacken his good name.
Hersent will bear out all I claim."
"Sire, every word my husband said
Is true. Long ago, before I was wed,
Renard already held me dear
And courted me, but I would not hear.
There was no promise and no plea
By which he could get me to agree.
Since I've been married to my lord,
I have rejected and ignored
More impertinent attempts to find
Some means to make me change my mind,
And never could he get his way
Until I chased him the other day
Into that hole. I'm big and fat,
So I got stuck, and that was that!
Renard came out of another door
And got what he'd been waiting for,
To my dishonor and my shame—
As long as he pleased he played his game.
Lord Ysengrin arrived in time
To witness, in despair, this crime."
Then Ysengrin spoke out again:
"Yes, Sire, that's what was happening when
I caught Sir Renard. What do you say?
Is that how your vassals should obey
The laws you make? When he found Hersent,
Was serving justice his intent?
I call the vassals of this land
To witness; my lord king, I demand
That Renard pay for this offense
And also for his insolence
When he paid a visit to my lair,
Pissed on my cubs, pulled out their hair,
Beat them and let them hear his scorn,
Saying that they were bastards born,
And that I'd be wearing horns for life
Because Renard had fucked my wife.
That's what he said, but of course he lied.
And even after that he's tried

Relentlessly to find some way
To dishonor me. The other day
I was out hunting with Hersent
And that was when, alas, she went
Down the hole that was so tight a fit,
And Renard was making the most of it
When I got there. To my words of blame
He said I was wrong: he'd support that claim
On oath, and would come to any place
I would appoint to state his case.
Now, my lord, it is up to you
To say what compensation's due;
Let it be enough so it would take
A fool to make the same mistake."
    Thus Ysengrin for justice pled.
Then King Noble raised his head,
And said, with a little smile, "Before
I speak are you sure there's nothing more?"
"No Sire!" he replied. "You cannot doubt
That I grieve to have it talked about,
To the great dishonor of my name."
"Hersent," King Noble said, "you claim
That Renard who's loved you for so long
Has done something you consider wrong,
But I think perhaps you love him too."
"Not I, my lord!" "Then why did you do
Such a foolish thing as to go alone
To visit him? That was never known
To be what you'd call a sign of hate!"
"Sire, if you'll let me set you straight,
It was not at all as you suppose.
If the marshal, my dear husband, chose—
Surely you would not doubt his word—
To speak as you and your lords have heard,
That is because he was in fact
Right there when I was foully attacked."
"Ysengrin was with you?" "Yes, of course!"
"You mean that Renard took you by force
With your husband standing there on guard?
By God, believing that comes hard!"
"Sire, if you please," said Ysengrin,
"You are much too eager to begin
Handing down judgments. Wait a while.
If Renard were only here on trial,
Like it or not, what you would hear
Would make the situation clear.
I swear by the loyalty I owe

To you, Sire, my argument would show
There's no doubt at all he raped Hersent.
What I said to you before I meant:
I was a witness to the deed—
More proof than that I do not need."
The king always took the greatest care
That his court's proceedings should be fair;
Someone who is of love accused
Should not, for that reason, be abused.
The best of evidence can cheat:
Perhaps Renard did not complete
What he began. King Noble thought
No action really should be brought.
    So when he saw that Ysengrin
Would not give up, being sure he'd win,
He tried to talk him out of it.
"Since it is clear, as you admit,
That Renard pursued Hersent with love,
I would say that he was guilty of
Something less than a mortal sin.
Love is the traitor, Ysengrin.
Renard is very brave and clever,
But for all my vassals I endeavor
To be sure that justice will prevail—
The law you appeal to shall not fail."
At Noble's side was a most respected
Camel from Lombardy, selected
By the Pope, who was his friend, to bring,
As legate, tribute sent to the king
From Constantinople. Now, to draw
On his understanding of the law,
The king said, "You've been to many places,
Counselor, perhaps you've heard of cases
Involving problems of this kind.
We would be glad, if you don't mind,
To have you, in your wisdom, decide
How justice can best be satisfied."
"*Monsignore*," he said, "*audite!*
In *Decretalibus, libro tre*,
De concordia officiales
Item matrimoniales
Quando sunt adulterante
Abscondito or in flagrante,
Primo: interrogazione!
If, to the *accusazione*
Responsio does not satisfy,
Ipso facto you reply:

Numquam criminalis sit!
And do unto him as you see fit.
Ergo ego te commendo
Sua fortuna confiscendo
Let Renard take his *paenitentia*

Mea culpa magna gratia;
Aut, pro bono, lapidation
Aut aflame him to damnation!
Res ipse loquitor,
Rex, what is a ruler for?"

JEUN DE MEUN

A CORRUPT SOCIETY

The first part of the French poem *Romance of the Rose,* apparently written in the late thirteenth century by a nobleman in Paris, was a highly symbolic and esoteric treatment of courtly love. Some years later a bourgeois, Jeun de Meun, made an addition to the poem, longer than the original segment, and taking a very different viewpoint. (Since nothing is known about the alleged aristocratic author of the first part of *Rose,* William de Lorris, it is just possible that Jeun de Meun actually wrote both parts.) The second part of *Romance of the Rose* contains the following savage indictment of a thoroughly corrupt society. All members of the elite—merchants, lawyers, physicians, clerics, kings—are only interested in money. Pursuit of riches is their only real calling; everything else, including charity, is either a cynical instrument for social gain or some kind of outright fraud against humanity. Jeun de Meun argues that the true, natural use of money is to aid the poor, and the only authentic people left in Europe are the workers and the poor. There is a strong element of class hostility in this statement. Jean de Meun was speaking for a large segment of the population. His tirade reveals how difficult it was even for middle class intellectuals to grasp the economic implications of capitalist development and how readily such intellectuals adopted a strictly ethical analysis of complex material and social structure. This moral assault by bourgeois intellectuals against capitalism, so familiar in our own day, is a prominent aspect of later medieval culture.

"And it remains true, no matter whom the idea displeases, that no merchant lives at ease. He has put his heart into such a state of war that he burns alive to acquire more, nor will he ever have acquired enough. He fears to lose the wealth that he has gained, and he pursues the remainder that he will never see himself possess, for his strongest desire is to acquire another's property. He has undertaken a wondrous task: he aspires to drink up the whole Seine, but he will never be able to drink so much that there will not remain more. This is the distress, the fire, the anguish which lasts forever; it is the pain, the battle which tears his guts and torments him in his lack: the more he acquires, the more he needs.

"Lawyers and physicians are all shackled by this bond. They sell knowledge for pennies; they all hang themselves by this rope. They find gain so sweet and pleasant that the physician wishes he had sixty patients for the one he has, and the lawyer thirty cases for one, indeed two hundred or two thousand, so much covetousness and guile burn in their hearts.

"The same is true of the divines who walk the earth: when they preach in order to acquire honors, favors, or riches, they acquire, in addition, hearts torn by such anguish. They do not live lawfully. But, above all, those who pursue vainglory buy their souls' death. Such a deceiver is himself deceived, for you know that however much such a preacher profits others, he profits himself nothing; for good preaching that comes in fact from evil intention is worth nothing to the preacher, even though it may save others. The hearers take good example by it, but the preacher is filled with vainglory.

"But let us leave such preachers and speak of those who heap up treasure. Certainly they neither love nor fear God when they purse up coins into treasure and save them beyond their need while they look upon the poor outside, trembling with cold and perishing of hunger. God will indeed know how to reward them. Three great misfortunes come to those who lead such lives: first, they acquire riches through great labor; then, as long as they do not cease guarding their treasures, fear keeps them in great distress; and, in the end, they grieve to leave their wealth. Those who pursue great riches die and live in this torment. Nor does this situation exist except through the lack of love, which is absent from the world; for, if those who heap up riches loved and were loved—if right love reigned everywhere, not seduced by wickedness, and if those who had more either gave more to those whom they knew to be needy, or loaned, not at usury, but out of charity pure and simple, as long as the recipients directed their efforts toward good and kept themselves from idleness—then there would be no poor man in the world, nor ought there to be any. But the world is so sick that they have made love a piece of merchandise; no one loves except for his profit, to obtain gifts or some service. Even women want to sell themselves. May such selling come to an evil end!

"Thus has Fraud dishonored everything by which the goods formerly common to everyone were appropriated to men. So bound by avarice are they that they have submitted their natural freedom to a base servitude; they are all slaves of the money which they lock up in their storehouses. Lock up! Indeed, they are the ones imprisoned when they have fallen into such error. These wretched earthly captives have made their possessions their masters. Wealth is profit only when spent; they do not know how to understand this proposition, but instead, when faced with it, they will all reply that wealth is profit only when hidden. Not so. But they hide it so well that they never spend it nor give it away. But no matter what happens it will be spent, even though they had all been hanged; for in the end, when they have died, they will leave it to the first chance passerby, who will spend it joyfully without returning any profit to them. They are not even sure that they will keep it that long, for there are those who could lay their hands on the treasure and carry it all off tomorrow.

"They do great evil to riches when they pervert them from their nature. Their nature is that they should fly to the aid and comfort of poor men, without being loaned at usury. God has provided them for this end, and now men have hidden them in prison. But riches, which, according to their natural destiny, should be led, revenge themselves honorably on their hosts, for they drag them ignominiously behind, they rend them and stab them repeatedly. They pierce their hearts with three blades. The first is the labor of acquisition. The second that oppresses their hearts is the fear that men may rob them and carry off their riches when they have gathered them up; this fear torments them unceasingly. The third blade is the pain of leaving the riches behind. As I have told you before, these deceivers walk the earth spreading evil.

"It is thus that Riches, like a free lady and queen, revenges herself upon the slaves who keep her locked up. She holds her peace, rests, and makes the wretches watch and care and toil. She subjugates them and keeps them so close underfoot that she has the honor while they have the shame, torment, and misery as they pine away in her service. No profit is to be made in such servitude, at least for him who keeps her. Without fail, after the death of him who dared not attack her, nor make her run and jump, she will dwell with just anyone. But valiant men assail her, bestride her and make her gallop, and so spur her that with their generous hearts, they take their pleasure and divert themselves with her. They take example from Daedalus, who made wings for Icarus, when, by artifice rather than by natural custom, they took the common way through the air. These valiant men do the same with Riches: they make wings for her so that she might fly and they gain glory and esteem rather than let themselves be tormented. They don't want to be reprimanded for the great ardor and vice of covetous Avarice. Therefore they perform acts of great courtesy, for which their good qualities are esteemed and celebrated throughout the world. Their virtues superabound from this practice; God considers them very sympathetic on account of their charitable, generous hearts. For as much as Avarice stinks to God, who nourished the world with His gifts when He had forged it—no one has taught you this except me—by that much is Generosity, with her courtesy and beneficence, pleasing to Him. God hates misers, these bound wretches, and damns them as idolaters, these captive slaves of immoderation, fearful and wretched. Of course they think, and say it as true, that they do not bind themselves to riches except to be secure and to live in happiness.

"O, sweet mortal riches, say, are you then such that you gladden men who have thus imprisoned you? The more they assemble you, the more they will tremble with fear. How can the man be happy who is not in a secure estate? Would blessings leap up at him if he lacked security?

"But no one who heard me say this could oppose me, to condemn and scorn my words, by bringing up the case of the kings who, to glorify their nobility, as the lower classes think, pridefully put their care into building up armed bodyguards of five hundred or five thousand sergeants. It is quite commonly said that this situation exists because of their great courage; but God knows quite the contrary. Fear, which constantly torments and troubles them, makes them act in this way. But a roustabout of La Grève could more easily go everywhere alone and secure, and dance before robbers without fearing them or their activities, than could the king in his squirrel cloak, even if he were to carry to his High Mass his amassed treasure of gold and precious stones. Every robber would take his share; whatever he brought they would steal from him, and perhaps they would want to kill him. And he would be killed, I think, before he had moved from the spot, for the thieves would be afraid that if they let him escape alive he would have them captured anywhere and have them led forcibly away to be hanged. Forcibly! But, of course, through the force of his retainers, for his own force isn't worth two apples beside that of a workman who goes around with such a light heart. By *his* retainers? In faith, I lie, or do not speak properly. Indeed they are not his, even though he may have dominion over them. Dominion? No, but service, in that he should keep them in freedom. Thus they are their own, for, when they wish, they withdraw their support from the king, who will then dwell alone as soon as the people wish. Their goodness, their good qualities, their bodies, power, wisdom—none are his, nor anything they have. Nature has indeed denied them to him.

"No matter how agreeable Fortune is to men, she cannot give them possession of things which Nature has made foreign to them, no matter how these things have been acquired."

PIERS PLOWMAN

PEASANT LIFE

Until the every end of the Middle Ages (and in fact until the late nineteenth century) the majority of European people were peasants. Their economic conditions and life-styles varied radically. There was a fundamental difference between the upper stratum of the peasantry who steadily acquired land, were economically secure, and enjoyed a middle class standard of living and the more numerous others who struggled as best they could to avoid the pit of poverty and misery. *Piers Plowman* is a gloomy, meandering late-fourteenth-century apocalyptic English poem by a London priest, possibly named William Langland, who previously spent many years working in rural areas and knew the poorer peasants well. Here are his realistic glimpses of their marginal and hazardous existence.

Usurious Couple, Monk, Bishop, and King being led into the fiery caldron of Hell

Rural Poverty

"I have no penny," quoth Piers, "pullets for to buy,
Neither geese nor young pigs, but two green
    cheeses,
A few curds and cream and an oaten cake,
And two loaves of beans and bran baked for my
    children.
And yet I say, by my soul I have no salt bacon,
Nor any eggs, by Christ, collops for to make.
But I have parsley and leeks, and many cabbage
    plants,
And also a cow and a calf, and a cart mare too
To draw afield the dung while the drought lasts.
And by these means we must make do until
    Lammas tide.
And by then, I hope, to have harvest in my croft,
And then may I dress your dinner, as dearly I wish."
All the poor people then fetched their peascods,
Beans and baked apples they brought in their laps,
Chibolles and chevrils and many ripe cherries,
And proffered Piers this present wherewith to
    please Hunger.
Then poor folk for fear fed Hunger eagerly
With green leeks and peas to poison Hunger they
    thought.

Until when it neared harvest new corn came to
    market.
Then folks became fain and fed Hunger with the
    best,
With good ale, as Glutton taught, and made
    Hunger to sleep.
Then would Waster not work but wandered about,
Nor no beggar eat bread that had beans within
But craved the best of white bread, or at least of
    clean white.
And no halfpenny ale in no wise would he drink
But the best and the brownest for sale in the
    borough.
Labourers that have no land to live on but their
    hands
Deign not to dine today on worts a night old.
No penny ale may please them, and no piece of
    bacon,
Unless it be fresh flesh or fish fried or baked,
And that hot or hotter against chilling of their
    maw.
And if he be not dearly hired, then will he chide,
And wail the time that he became a
    workman. . . .

The Month of October: Sowing fields, with the Chateau du Louvre in the background

The Peasant's Cottage

Three things there are that make a man by their
strength
To flee his own house, as Holy Writ shows.
The one is a wicked wife who will not be
corrected,
Her husband flees from her, for fear of her tongue.
And if his house be unroofed and rain falls on his
bed,
He seeks and he seeks until he sleeps dry.
And when smoke and smouldering smite in his
sight,
It does him worse than his wife or wet to sleep.
For smoke and smouldering smite in his eyes,
Until he is blear-eyed or blind, and hoarse in the
throat,

Coughing and cursing that Christ gives them
sorrow,
Who should bring better wood, or blow till it
burns.

The Peasant's Cares

The most needy are our neighbours, if we notice
right well,
As prisoners in pits and poor folk in cottages,
Charged with their children, and chief lord's rent,
What by spinning they save, they spend it in
house-hire,
Both in milk and in meal to make a mess of
porridge,
To cheer up their children who chafe for their
food,
And they themselves suffer surely much hunger
And woe in the winter, with waking at nights
And rising to rock an oft restless cradle,
Both to card and to comb, to clout and to wash,
To rub and to reel yarn, rushes to peel,
So 'tis pity to proclaim or in poetry to show
The woe of these women who work in such
cottages;
And of many other men who much woe suffer,
Crippled with hunger and with thirst, they keep
up appearances,
And are abashed for to beg, and will not be
blazoned
What they need from their neighbours, at noon
and at evensong.
This I know full well, for the world has taught me,
How churls are afflicted who have many children,
And have no coin but their craft to clothe and to
keep them,
And full many to feed and few pence to do it.
With bread and penny-ale that is less than a
pittance,
Cold flesh and cold fish, instead of roast venison;
And on Fridays and feast days a farthing's worth of
mussels
Would be a feast for such folk, or else a few
cockles.
'Twere a charity to help those that bear such
charges,
And comfort such cottagers, the crippled and
blind.

THE URBAN WORKERS: GUILD RESTRICTIONS

The craft guilds in medieval cities formed religious confraternities, provided dramatic presentations in the street, and supplied burial benefits. But their main purpose and activity was narrow regulation of industrial productivity in order to restrain competition and impede technological progress that threatened employment. Guild regulations were onerous and petty. Here are rules for the guild of spur-makers in London in the mid-fourteenth century.

Scenes of the Marketplace (shoe repair, cloth vending, metalwares)

Be it remembered, that on Tuesday, the morrow of St. Peter's Chains, in the nineteenth year of the reign of King Edward III, the articles underwritten were read before John Hammond, mayor, Roger de Depham, recorder, and the alderman; and seeing that the same were deemed befitting, they were accepted and enrolled in these words.

In the first place—that no one of the trade of spurriers shall work longer than from the beginning of the day until curfew rung out at the Church of St. Sepulchre, without Newgate; by reason that no man can work so neatly by night as by day. And many persons of the said trade, who

compass how to practice deception in their work, desire to work by night rather by day; and then they introduce false iron, and iron that has been cracked, for tin, and also they put gilt on false copper, and cracked. And further—many of the said trade are wandering about all day, without working at all at their trade; and then, when they have become drunk and frantic, they take to their work, to the annoyance of the sick, and all their neighborhood, as well by reason of the broils that arise between them and the strange folks who are dwelling among them. And then they blow up their fires so vigorously, that their forges begin all at once to blaze to the great peril of themselves and of all the neighborhood around. And then, too, all the neighbors are much in dread of the sparks, which so vigorously issue forth in all directions from the mouths of the chimneys in their forges. By reason thereof it seems unto them that working by night should be put an end to, in order such false work and such perils to avoid: and therefore the mayor and the aldermen do will, by the assent of the good folks of the said trade, and for the common profit, that from henceforth such time for working, and such false work made in the trade, shall be forbidden. And if any person shall be found in the said trade to do the contrary hereof, let him be amerced, the first time in 40d., one-half thereof to go to the use of the Chamber of the Guildhall of London, and the other half to the use of the said trade; the second time, in half a mark, and the third time in 10s., to the use of the same Chamber and trade; and the fourth time, let him forswear the trade forever.

Also that no one of the said trade shall hang his spurs out on Sundays, or any other days that are double feasts; but only a sign indicating his business. And such spurs as they shall so sell, they are to show and sell within their shops, without exposing them without, or opening the doors or windows of their shops, on the pain aforesaid.

Also, that no one of the said trade shall keep a house or shop to carry on his business, unless he is [a free man] of the city; and that no one shall cause to be sold, or exposed for sale, any manner of old spurs for new ones, or shall garnish them or change them for new ones.

Also, that no one of the said trade shall take an apprentice for a less term than seven years, and such apprentice shall be enrolled according to the usages of the said city.

Also, that if any one of the said trade, who is not a freeman, shall take an apprentice for a term of years, he shall be amerced as aforesaid.

Also, that no one of the said trade shall receive the apprentice, serving-man or journeyman of another in the same trade, during the term agreed upon between his master and him; on the pain aforesaid.

Also, that no alien of another country, or foreigner of this country, shall follow or use the said trade, unless he is enfranchised before the mayor, alderman and chamberlain; and that by witness and surety of the good folks of the said trade, who will undertake for him as to his loyalty and his good behavior.

Also, that no one of the said trade shall work on Saturdays, after None has been rung out in the City; and not from that hour until the Monday morning following.

THE EVIL BACILLUS

Falling it seems with equal devastation on rural and urban populations alike in the mid-fourteenth century was the pandemic of bubonic plague that medieval people called The Black Death. There had been medieval outbreaks of plague before, following its initial appearance from Africa in the late Roman Empire. But it had been quiescent for several centuries, and nothing compared before or since to the virulence of the pandemic that occurred in the 1340s. The plague appears to have entered Europe at Mediterranean ports and spread northward. England and Scandinavia were not spared. Around a third of the population of Europe disappeared in a matter of months. The economic dislocations were severe, and the impact on the European temperament was in the direction of heightening gloom and discontent. The bubonic plague was spread by parasites living on the backs of a particular species of rats. Medieval medicine did not know that (it was in fact unknown until the nineteenth century). Medieval physicians thought it was spread through the air. Consequently, there was a rush by affluent people to seek refuge in the less populated countryside. On the advice of erroneous medicine, drastic changes in life-style occurred that were not reversed for many centuries. Windows were covered with shutters and heavy hangings to keep out the allegedly bacillus–carrying air. Taking regular baths became unfashionable because of the putative danger of opening bodily pores to bacilli in the air. Here is a sober account of the Black Death in Siena followed by the blaming of the Jews (who else?) in Germany for intentionally spreading the disease through the poisoning of wells. The resultant pogroms caused thousands of Jews to flee eastward into Poland for refuge, taking their German dialect (Yiddish) with them.

The Triump of Death

THE BLACK DEATH IN SIENA

The mortality began in Siena in May [1348]. It was a cruel and horrible thing; and I do not know where to begin to tell of the cruelty and the pitiless ways. It seemed to almost everyone that one became stupified by seeing the pain. And it is impossible for the human tongue to recount the awful thing. Indeed one who did not see such horribleness can be called blessed. And the victims died almost immediately. They would swell beneath their armpits and in their groins, and fall over dead while talking. Father abandoned child, wife husband, one brother another; for this illness seemed to strike through the breath and sight. And so they died. And none could be found to bury the dead for money or friendship. Members of a household brought their dead to a ditch as best they could, without priest, without divine offices. Nor did the death bell sound. And in many places in Siena great pits were dug and piled deep with the multitude of dead. And they died by the hundreds both day and night, and all were thrown in those ditches and covered over with earth. And as soon as those ditches were filled more were dug.

And I, Agnolo di Tura, called the Fat, buried my five children with my own hands. And there were also those who were so sparsely covered with earth that the dogs dragged them forth and devoured many bodies throughout the city.

There was no one who wept for any death, for all awaited death. And so many died that all believed that it was the end of the world. And no medicine or any other defense availed. And the [Magistrates] selected three citizens who received a thousand gold florins from the commune of Siena that they were to spend on the poor sick and to bury the poor dead. And it was all so horrible that I, the writer, cannot think of it and so will not continue. This situation continued until September, and it would take too long to write of it. And it is found that at this time there died in Siena 36,000 persons twenty years of age or less, and the aged and other people [died], to a total of 52,000 in all in Siena. And in the suburbs of Siena 28,000 persons died; so that in all it is found that in the city and suburbs of Siena 80,000 persons died. Thus at this time Siena and its suburbs had more than 30,000 men [adult males]; and there remained in Siena [alone] less than 10,000 men. And those that survived were like persons distraught and almost without feeling. And many walls and other things were abandoned, and all the mines of silver and gold and copper that existed in Sienese territory were abandoned as is seen; for in the countryside . . . many more people died, many lands and villages were abandoned, and no one remained there. I

will not write of the cruelty that there was in the countryside, of the wolves and wild beasts that ate the poorly buried corpses, and of other cruelties that would be too painful to those who read of them. . . .

The city of Siena seemed almost uninhabited for almost no one was found in the city. And then, when the pestilence abated, all who survived gave themselves over to pleasures: monks, priests, nuns, and lay men and women all enjoyed themselves, and none worried about spending and gambling. And everyone thought himself rich because he had escaped and regained the world, and no one knew how to allow himself to do nothing. . . .

At this time in Siena the great and noble project of enlarging the cathedral of Siena that had been begun a few years earlier was abandoned. . . .

After the pestilence the Sienese appointed two judges and three non-Sienese notaries whose task it was to handle the wills that had been made at that time. And so they searched them out and found them. . . .

1349. After the great pestilence of the past year each person lived according to his own caprice, and everyone tended to seek pleasure in eating and drinking, hunting, catching birds, and gaming.

THE JEWS ARE TO BLAME

To the Noble and Prudent Magistrates, Council and Community of the Town of Strasbourg, from the Castellian of Chillon, Deputy of the Lord Magistrate at Chablais. With submissive and respectful greetings. As I am given to understand that you are desirous of being made acquainted with the confession of the Jews and with the evidence brought against them, I therefore inform you and all of your friends who may be desirous of knowing by this present communication that the Bernese have received a copy of inquisitions and confessions of the Jews who were recently in their territory and were accused of having placed poison in the wells and in many other places, and that these accusations have proved quite true, as many Jews have been submitted to torture and some were exempted because they confessed and were brought before another court and burnt. Also Christians, to whom the Jews had given some of the poison, were placed on the wheel and tortured. The burning of the Jews and the reported torturing of the Christians took place in the county of Savoy.

Confessions of the Jews made in the year of the Lord, 1348, on September 15th, at the castle of Chillon, who had been arrested in the New Town concerning the poisoning of which they were accused, of wells and springs here and elsewhere, also of food and other things with the purpose of killing and extermining the whole of Christendom.

1. Balavignus the Jew, a surgeon and inhabitant of Thonon, although arrested at Chillon, as he was found within the Castle, was only placed on the rack for a short time, and when he had been taken off he confessed after some considerable time that about six weeks ago Master Jacob, who since Easter had been staying at Chambéry, in accordance with orders, and who had come from Toledo, sent him to Thonon by a Jew boy poison in an eggshell; this was a powder in a thin sewn leather bag, together with a letter, in which he was ordered on pain of ban and in obedience to their law to put this same poison into the larger and smaller wells of his town, as much as was required to poison the people who fetched their water from there, and that he should reveal this to no one on pain of the above punishment. Further, in the same letter he was instructed to forward the same order to several other places by command of the Jewish Rabbis or masters of their law; and he confessed that he had secretly placed the quantity of poison or powder indicated in a well on the lake shore near Thonon one evening beneath a stone. He confessed further that the above-mentioned boy had brought him more letters dealing with the same matter which were addressed to many other Jews, and particularly some were directed to Mossoiet, Banditono and Samole to at Villeneuf, one to each, and others to Musseo Abramo and Aqueto of Montreux, to the Jews of Vevey, and others again to Benetono at St. Moritz and to his son; further, others to Viviandus

Jacobus, Aquetus and Musset, Jews at Moncheoli, and many other letters were borne by the boy, as he said, to various out-of-the-way places, but he could not say to whom they were addressed. Further, he confessed that when he had placed the poison mentioned in the well at Thonon, he expressly forbade his wife and children to make further use of the well, but refused to tell them the reason. He swore by his law and by all contained in the Pentateuch, in the presence of several reliable witnesses, that all he had confessed was entirely true.

Further, on the following day, Balavignus, in the presence of many reliable witnesses, of his own free will and without application of the rack, affirmed that the above-quoted confession was true, and repeated it word for word, and of his own free will confessed that one day coming from Thur, near Vevey, he placed a quantity of the poison wrapped in a rag of about the size of a walnut which had been given him by Aqueto of Montreux, an inhabitant of the above-mentioned Thur, in a well below Mustreuz, called the Fontaine de la Conerayde—that he had deposited this poison, he told and revealed to the Jew Mamssiono and his son Delosaz, inhabitants of Villeneuf, that they should not drink of the well; he stated that the colour of the poison was red and black.

Further, on the 19th day of the month of September, the above-mentioned Balavignus confessed, without application of the rack, that the Jew Mussus of Villeneuf had told him three weeks before Whitsuntide that he had placed poison in his own well at Villeneuf, in the tollhouse, and that he no longer drank its water, but water from the lake. He confessed, further, that this same Jew Mussus had told him that he had put poison in the tollhouse well at Chillon under the stones, of which well an examination was made and the above-mentioned poison found, of which a sample was given to a Jew, who died in consequence. He further stated that the rabbis had ordered him and other Jews to refrain from drinking of the poisoned water for the first nine days after the placing of the poison. Further, that as soon as he had placed the poison, as stated above, he immediately revealed it to the other Jews. He confessed, further, that, about two months ago, he had been at Evian and had discussed the matter with the Jew Jacob, and, among other things, asked him if he, like the others, had received a letter and poison. Jacob answered that he had. He asked him, further, if he had obeyed the order, and Jacob replied that he had not placed the poison, but had handed it to the Jew Saveto, who had placed it in the well de Morer at Evian, and he ordered him, Balavignus, that he should carry out carefully the instructions he had received. He said that Aqueto of Montreux had reported that he had placed some of the poison in the well above Thur, from which he had drunk several times at Thur. He confessed that Samolet had told him that he had placed the poison he had received in a well, but he refused to tell him which. Balavignus alleged, further, that as a surgeon he knew that if anyone was affected by this poison and anyone touched him in this condition, when overcome by weakness, he was sweating, that by this contact he might easily be infected, as also by the breath of anyone infected; and of this he was convinced, as he had heard it from experienced medical men, and he was further convinced that the Jews could not deny these charges, as they were fully conscious that they were guilty of the actions with which they were charged. The said Balavignus was taken across the lake in a boat from Chillon to Clarens to verify and point out the well into which, as he alleged, he had placed the poison. When he arrived he was made to get out of the boat, and when he saw the place and the well where he had deposited the poison he said: "That is the well in which I put the poison." This well was examined in his presence, and the linen bag in which the poison was wrapped was found in the mouth of the well by a public notary, Heinrich Gerhard, in the presence of many people and was shown to the said Jew. He then admitted and confessed that this was the linen cloth in which the poison had been, and that he had placed it in the open well, and that it was parti-coloured, black and red. This linen cloth was taken away and is preserved as evidence.

All this the above-mentioned Jews swore by their law before execution, stating that it was true, and all Jews above the age of seven were implicated, for they had all had knowledge of and were guilty of this matter.

THE PEASANTS REVOLT

The Black Death was one of the causes of the Peasants Revolt in England in 1381, the most extensive and damaging class revolution in the Middle Ages. The plague carried off forty percent of the peasants in the crowded arable regions of southern England. The resulting labor shortage caused wages of rural laborers to rise rapidly, and landlords, bringing their influence and presence to bear in Parliament, got legislation passed that restricted the market increase in wages. This made the rural workers very angry. The other causes of the Peasants Revolt were an effort to impose a new royal poll (head) tax on the peasants and leadership for the uprising provided by class-conscious, discontented egalitarian-minded country clergy, most of whom came from peasant families. Among the most vocal of these revolting clergy were Lollards, disciples of the heretical Oxford professor John Wyclif. The course of the revolt showed how disorganized a medieval government could be when faced with a crisis, how deferential the peasant rebels remained toward the king personally but not to members of his government, how endemic hatred toward the higher clergy resulted in the early fatality of the Archbishop of Canterbury, and how nothing tangible came of the whole thing. Eventually the rebellion was put down and punished with mindless brutality, and few among the ruling class thought about the social ills that could stir the desperate peasants in this astonishing manner. This following detailed and graphic account was written by an anonymous well-informed contemporary, probably a mid-level government or church official in London. Some of it seems to follow from personal observations of events and much of the rest from reports of other eyewitnesses. There is no social document in European history before the French Revolution quite like this.

In the year 1380, because the subsidies were lightly granted at the parliament of Northampton and because various lords and commons were advised that the subsidies were not duly or loyally levied, but commonly exacted from the poor and not from the rich, to the great profit and advantage of the collectors, and the deception of the king and the commons, the King's council ordained certain commissions to make inquiry in each township how they were levied. One of these commissions was sent to Essex to a certain Thomas Bampton [i.e. John Bampton] steward of a lord, who was regarded as a king or great magnate in that area because of the great estate that he kept. And one day before Whitsuntide he held a court at Brentwood in Essex to make inquisition, and showed the commission directed to him to raise the money which was in default, and to inquire how the collectors had levied the subsidy. He had summoned before him a hundred of the neighbouring townships and wished to have from them a new subsidy, commanding the people of those townships to inquire diligently and to give their replies and to pay their dues. Amongst these townships all the people of Fobbing gave answer that they would not pay a penny more because they already had a receipt from him for the said subsidy. On this Thomas menaced them strongly, and he had with him two sergeants at arms of our lord the king; and for fear of his wrath the people of Fobbing took counsel with the people of Corringham, and the folks of these two townships made levies and assemblies, and sent messages to the men of Stanford-le-Hope to urge them to rise too, for their common profit. And then the men of the three townships came together to the number of a hundred or more and with one assent went to Thomas Bampton and

roundly gave him answer that they would have nothing to do with him nor give him one penny. On this Thomas ordered the sergeants at arms to arrest these folks and put them into prison; and the commons rose against him and would not be arrested, but tried to kill Thomas and the two sergeants. On this Thomas fled towards London to the king's council and the commons fled to the woods for fear of his malice and lay there a long time, till they were almost famished; and afterwards they went from place to place to stir up other people to rise against the lords and good folk of the countryside. And because of these doings of Thomas Sir Robert Belknap, Chief Justice of the Common Pleas of our lord the king, was sent to the shire with a commission of trailbaston, and indictments against various persons were laid before him, so that the people of the countryside were in such fear that they proposed to abandon their homes. Therefore the commons rose against him and came before him and told him that he was a traitor to the king and the realm, and that it was of pure wickedness and malice that he wished to put them in default by means of the false inquests made before him. And because of this evil they caused him to swear on the Bible that he would never again hold such a session nor act as a justice in such inquiries. And they made him tell them the names of all the jurors, and they took all that they could catch and cut off their heads and cast their houses to the ground, and Sir Robert took his way home with all possible speed. And afterwards the commons assembled together before Whitsunday to the number of 50,000 and went to the manors and townships of those who did not wish to rise with them and rased their houses to the ground or set fire to them. At this time they caught three clerks of Thomas Bampton and cut off their heads, which they carried about with them for several days as an example to others; for it was their purpose to slay all lawyers and all jurors and all the servants of the king whom they could find. Meanwhile all the great lords of the countryside and other people of substance fled towards London and to other shires where they might be safe.

At the same time the high master of the hospital of St. John of Clerkenwell in London had a very beautiful and delectable manor-house in Essex, where he had ordered victuals and other necessities to hold his chapter general, and it was well furnished with wines and was suitably appointed, as befits such a lord and his brethren. And at this time the commons came to the manor and ate the victuals and drank three tuns of good wine and rased the manor-house to the ground and set it alight, to the great damage and loss of the master. And then the commons sent various letters into Kent and Suffolk and Norfolk to urge them to rise with them; and when they had assembled they went about in many bands doing great mischief in all the countryside. After this on the Monday next after the feast of Whitsuntide [3 June] a knight of the household of our lord the king, Sir Simon Burley by name, had in his company two sergeants at arms of the king, and came on the Monday abovesaid to Gravesend and there challenged a man as being his serf. And the good folks of the town came to make a bargain for the man in civil fashion, because of their respect for the king; but Sir Simon would not take less than £300, a sum which would have been the man's undoing. The good folks prayed him to lessen the sum, but they could not come to terms nor induce him to take a lesser sum, though they told Sir Simon that the man was a Christian and of good character and that therefore he ought not to be ruined for ever. But Sir Simon was very angry and irritable, and greatly despised these good folk, and for haughtiness of heart he bade his sergeants bind the said man and take him to Rochester Castle, to be kept in custody there; from which there came later great evil and mischief. And after his departure the commons began to rise, gathering to them the men of many townships of Kent.

And at this juncture a justice was assigned by the king and council to go into Kent with a commission of trailbaston, as had been done before in Essex, and with him went a sergeant at arms of our lord the king, Master John Legge by name, carrying with him a great number of indictments against various folks of that area to make the king rich. And they would have held a session at Canterbury, but they were driven away by the commons. And after this the commons of Kent gathered together in great numbers day by day, without head and without chieftain, and on Friday . . .[after] Whitsuntide came to Dartford; and they took counsel there and ordained that no one who dwelt near the sea in any place for the space of 12 leagues should come with them, but keep the coasts of the sea from the enemies, saying amongst themselves that there were more kings than one and that they would not suffer or have any king except King Richard.

At the same time the commons of Kent came to Maidstone and cut off the head of one of the best men of the town, and rased to the ground various places and tenements of people who would not rise with them, as had been done before in Essex. And on the Friday following they came to Rochester and there met a great number of the commons from Essex. And because of the man of Gravesend, they laid siege to Rochester Castle, to deliver their friend from Gravesend, whom the aforesaid Sir Simon had imprisoned. They laid siege with energy to the Castle, and the constable defended himself vigorously for half a day, but at last, for fear that he had of such a multitude of men deaf to reason from Essex and Kent, he delivered up the castle to them. And the commons entered and took their companion and all the other prisoners out of prison: and those who had come from Gravesend repaired home with their fellow with great joy, without doing any more, but the men of Maidstone took their way with the other commons through the countryside. And there they made their chief a certain Wat Teghler of Maidstone to maintain them and be their counsellor. And on the next Monday after the feast of the Holy Trinity they came to Canterbury before the hour of noon, and 4,000 of them entered into the minster church of St. Thomas and, kneeling down, they cried with one voice on the monks to elect a monk to be archbishop of Canterbury, "for he who is now archbishop is a traitor, and will be beheaded for his iniquity." And so he was five days afterwards! And when they had done this, they went into the town to their fellows, and by one assent they summoned the mayor, bailiffs and commons of the said town and examined them whether there were any traitors amongst them; and the townsfolk said that there were three and named them. These three the commons dragged out of their houses and cut off their heads. And afterwards they took 500 men of the town with them to London, and left the others to guard the town.

At this time the commons had as their counsellor a chaplain of evil character, Sir John Ball by name, who advised them to get rid of all the lords and archbishops, bishops, abbots, priors, and most of the monks and canons, saying that there should be no bishop in England except one archbishop, and that he should be that archbishop, and that there should be no monks or canons in any religious houses save two, and that their possessions should be shared out amongst the laity. For these sayings he was esteemed amongst the commons as a prophet, and laboured with them day by day to strengthen them in their malice; and a fitting reward he had afterwards, for he was drawn, hanged, disembowelled, and beheaded as a traitor.

After this the commons went to various towns and raised the people, whether they wished to do so or not, until they had gathered together fully 60,000. And as they journeyed towards London they encountered various lawyers and twelve knights of the king and the countryside, and they took them and made them swear to support them, or otherwise they would be beheaded. And they wrought much damage in Kent and especially to Thomas Haselden, a servant of the Duke of Lancaster, because of their hatred for the duke. They rased his manors to the ground and all his houses, and sold his beasts—his horses, oxen, cows, sheep, and pigs—and all his stores of corn, at cheap rates. And every day they wanted to have his head and that of Sir Thomas Orgrave, clerk of the receipt and sub-treasurer of England. And

when the king heard of their doings he sent his messengers to them on the Tuesday next after Trinity Sunday, to ask them why they were behaving in this fashion and why they were raising a rebellion in his land. And they returned answer by the messengers that they were rising to deliver him and to destroy the traitors to him and to his kingdom. The king sent again to them to bid them cease their doings, in reverence for him, until he could speak with them, and he would make reasonable amends, according to their will, of all that was amiss; and the commons begged him, by the said messengers, that he would be pleased to come and talk with them at Blackheath. And the king sent again the third time to say that he would willingly come next day at the hour of prime to hear their purpose; and then the king, who was at Windsor, removed with all speed to London. At this time the mayor and good folk of London came to meet him and conduct him safely to the Tower of London; there all the council and all the lords of the countryside round about assembled, that is, the Archbishop of Canterbury, chancellor of England, the Bishop of London, the Master of the Hospital of St. John of Clerkenwell, then treasurer of England, and the Earls of Buckingham, Kent, Arundel, Warwick, Suffolk, Oxford, Salisbury and other persons to the number of 600.

And on the vigil of Corpus Christi Day [12 June] the commons of Kent came to Blackheath, three leagues from London, to the number of 50,000, to await the king's arrival, and they displayed two banners of St. George and forty pennons and the commons of Essex came to the other side of the water to the number of 60,000 to help them and hear the king's response. And on the Wednesday the king who was at the Tower of London, thinking to settle the affair, caused his barges to be assembled and took with him in his barge the archbishop and the treasurer and others of his council and four other barges for his retinue, and went to Greenwich, three leagues from London; and there the chancellor and treasurer warned the king that it would be too great a folly to go to them, for they were men without reason, and had not the sense to behave properly. But as the king, by the advice of the chancellor and treasurer, would not come to the commons of Kent, they sent a petition to him requiring him to grant them the heads of the Duke of Lancaster and fifteen other lords, of whom fourteen [?three] were bishops present with him in the Tower of London; and these were their names—Sir Simon Sudbury, Archbishop of Canterbury and Chancellor of England, Sir Robert Hales, Prior of the Hospital, treasurer of England, the Bishop of London, Sir John Fordham, clerk of the privy seal and Bishop-elect of Durham, Sir Robert Belknap, chief justice of the common pleas, Sir Ralph Ferrers, Sir Robert Plessington, chief baron of the exchequer, John Legge, sergeant at arms of the king, and Thomas Bampton aforesaid and others. And to this the king would not agree, wherefore they sent again to him a yeoman, praying that he would come and speak with them; and he said that he would gladly do so, but the chancellor and treasurer gave him contrary advice, telling them that if they wished to come to Windsor the following Monday, they should have there a suitable answer.

And the commons had among themselves a watch word in English, "With whom hold you?" and the response was, "With king Richard and with the true commons," and those who could not or would not so answer were beheaded and put to death. And at this time there came a knight with all the haste that he could, crying to the king to wait; and the king was startled at this and awaited his arrival to hear what he had to say. And the knight came to the king to tell him that he had it from a servant who had been in the hands of the rebels that day, that if the king should come to them, all the land would be lost, for they would never let him loose for any consideration, but would take him round with them through all England, and that they would make him grant all their demands, and that their purpose was to slay all the lords and ladies of great renown, and all the archbishops, bishops, abbots, priors, monks, and canons, parsons, and vicars, by the advice and counsel of the aforesaid Sir John Ball. Therefore the king returned to London as fast as he could and arrived at the Tower at the hour of terce.

And at this time the yeoman already mentioned above hastened to Blackheath crying to his fellows that the king had gone, and that it would be well for them to press on to London to pursue their purpose. On the same day of Wednesday before the hour of vespers the commons of Kent came, as many as 60,000 of them, to Southwark, where the Marshalsea was, and they broke and threw down to the ground all the buildings of the Marshalsea, and took out of prison all the prisoners who were held captive there for debt or felony. And they levelled to the ground a fine house belonging to John Imworth, then marshal of the Marshalsea of the king's bench, and keeper of the prisoners of the said place, and all the houses of the jurors and questmongers belonging to the Marshalsea, throughout that night.

At the same time the commons of Essex reached Lambeth, near to London, a manor of the Archbishop of Canterbury, and entered the buildings there, and destroyed many goods of the archbishop, and burnt all the books of register and rolls of remembrance of the chancery which they found there. And the next day, Thursday, which was the feast of Corpus Christi, the 13th day of June, with the dominical letter F, the commons of Essex went in the morning to Highbury, two leagues north of London, a very fine manor-house of the Master of the Hospital of St. John of Clerkenwell, and they set it on fire, to the great damage and loss of the Hospitallers of St. John. Some of them then returned to London, while the others stayed in the open fields all night. And this same day of Corpus Christi, in the morning, the commons of Kent pulled down a house of ill fame near London Bridge, which was in the hands of Flemish women and they had the house to rent from the mayor of London. And then they surged on to the bridge to pass into the city, but the mayor was just before them and had the chain drawn up and the drawbridge lifted to stop their passage. And the commons of Southwark rose with them and cried to the keepers of the bridge to lower the drawbridge and let them in, or otherwise they would be undone. And for fear of their lives the keepers let them enter, though it was against their will. At this time all the religious and the parsons and the vicars of London were going devoutly in procession to pray God for peace.

And at the same time the commons took their way through London and did no harm or molestation until they came to Fleet Street. (And at the same time, as was said, the commons of London set fire to the beautiful manor-house of the Savoy before the arrival of the commons from the country.) And in Fleet Street the said commons of Kent broke open the Fleet prison and released all the prisoners and let them go whither they would. Then they stopped and threw to the ground, and set fire to, the shop of a certain chandler and another shop of a certain blacksmith, in the middle of the said street. There there shall never again be houses, it is said, to deface the beauty of the street. And after that they went to the Temple to destroy the tenants of the Temple, and they cast down the house to the ground and tore off all the tiles, so that the buildings were in a bad state, without any roofing.

And they went into the Temple Church and took all the books and rolls and remembrances which were in the cupboards of the apprentices at law in the Temple, and carried them into the highway and burnt them. And then they went towards the Savoy, destroying all the buildings belonging to the Master of the Hospital of St. John. And then they went to the house of the Bishop of Chester, near the church of St. Mary-le-Strand, where was dwelling Sir John Fordham, the elect of Durham, and clerk of the privy seal, and they rolled barrels of wine out of his cellar, and drank their fill, and departed without doing further damage. And then they went towards the Savoy and set fire to various houses of various folks and questmongers on the western side, and at last they came to the Savoy. They broke open the gates and entered the place and came to the wardrobe, and they took all the torches they could find and set fire to all the sheets and coverlets and beds and head boards of great worth, for their whole value amounted, it was said, to 1,000 marks. And all the napery and other things which they could find they carried into the hall and set it on fire with their torches. And they burnt the hall and chambers and all the buildings within the gates belonging to the said palace or manor, which the commons of London had left unburnt. And, as was said, they found three bar-rels of gunpowder which they took to be gold or silver, and they threw them on the fire, and this powder blew up high and set the hall in a greater blaze than before, to the great loss and damage of the Duke of Lancaster. The commons of Kent got the blame, but some said that the Londoners were really responsible, because of their hatred for the said duke. Then one party of them went towards Westminster and set on fire a house belonging to John Butterwick, under-sheriff of Middlesex, and other houses of various people, and broke open the prison at Westminster and brought out all the prisoners condemned by the law, and afterwards they returned to London by way of Holborn, and in front of St. Sepulchre's Church they set fire to the houses of Simon Hosteler and several other houses, and broke open Newgate prison and let loose all the prisoners, for whatever cause they had been imprisoned.

The same Thursday the commons went to St. Martin-le-Grand and tore away from the high altar a certain Roger Legett, a great "assizer" and took him to Cheapside and beheaded him there; on the same day eighteen others were beheaded in various parts of the town. At the same time a great body of commons went to the Tower to speak to the king, and could not gain speech with him, wherefore they laid siege to the Tower from the side of St. Katherine's, towards the south. And another part of the commons who were in the city went to the hospital of St. John of Clerkenwell and on the way burnt the house and buildings of Roger Legett the questmonger who had been beheaded in Cheapside and all the rented houses and tenements of the hospital of St. John that they could; and afterwards they came to the beautiful priory of the said hospital and set on fire several fine and desirable buildings in the same priory, a great and horrible piece of damage for all time to come; and then they returned to London to rest or to do more mischief.

At this time the king was in a turret of the great Tower of London, from which he could see the manor of the Savoy and the hospital of Clerkenwell, and the buildings of Simon Hosteler near Newgate, and John Butterwick's house, all on fire at once. And he called all his lords about him to his chamber and asked their advice as to what he should do in such an emergency; and none of them could or would give him any counsel. Wherefore the young king said that he would send to the mayor of the city to bid him order the sheriffs and aldermen to have it cried round their wards that all men between the ages of 15 and 60, on pain of life and members, should go on the morrow, Friday, to Mile End and meet him at seven in the morning. He did this so that all the commons who were surrounding the Tower would raise the siege and go to Mile End to see and hear him, and all those who were in the Tower could go away safely whither they would and save themselves; but it was of no avail, for the besieged did not have the good fortune to get away.

After this on the same Thursday, the feast of Corpus Christi, the king being in the Tower pensive and sorrowful, climbed up into a little turret towards St. Katherine's, where were lying a great number of the commons, and caused a proclamation to be made to them that they should all go home in a peaceful manner and that he would pardon them all manner of trespasses. But all cried with one voice that they would not leave before they had taken the traitors who were in the Tower and had been given charters to be free of all manner of serfdom and had been granted all the items which they wished to ask. And the king graciously granted all and caused a clerk to write a bill in their presence in this style: "Richard, king of England and of France, greatly thanks his good commons because they have such a great desire to see and hear their king, and pardons them for all manner of trespasses and misprisions and felonies committed until now, and wills and commands that now everyone should hasten to his own home and wishes and commands that each one should put his grievances into writing, and cause them to be sent to him, and he will provide, with the aid of his loyal lords and of his good counsel such remedy as shall be profitable for him and them and for the realm." And to this document he set his signet seal in their presence, and sent out the said bill with two of his knights to them before St. Katherine's and caused it to be read to them. And the knight who read it stood up on an old chair before the others so that all could hear. All this time the king was in the Tower in great distress of mind. And when the commons had heard the bill, they said that this was nothing but trifles and mockery; wherefore they returned to London and caused it to be cried throughout the city that all lawyers and all the officials of the chancery and exchequer and all those who could write a writ or a letter should be beheaded, wherever they could be found; and at this time they burnt several more houses in the city. And the king climbed to a high garret of the Tower and watched the fires, and then came down again and sent for the lords to have their counsel; but they did not know how to advise him and all were wondrously abashed.

Next day, the Friday, the commons of the countryside and the commons of London assembled in fearful strength to the number of 100,000 or more, besides some four score or more who stayed on Tower Hill to watch those who were in the Tower. And some went to Mile End towards Brentwood to await the coming of the king, because of the proclamation he had made, and the others came to Tower Hill. And when the king knew that they were there, he sent them orders by a messenger to join their friends at Mile End and he himself would join them soon. And at this time of the morning he advised the Archbishop of Canterbury and the others who were in the Tower to go down to the Little Water Gate and take a boat and save themselves. And the archbishop did so, but a wicked woman raised a cry against him and he had to return to the Tower, to his destruction. And by seven o'clock the king came to Mile End and with him his mother in a whirlecote [a wheeled carriage] with the Earls of Buckingham, Kent, Warwick, and Oxford, Sir Thomas Percy, Sir Robert Knolles, the mayor of London, and many knights and squires; and Sir Aubrey de Vere carried the king's sword. And when he was come the commons all knelt down to him, saying; "Welcome, our lord, King Richard, if it pleases you, and we will have no other king but you." And Wat Tyghler, their leader and chief, prayed to him in the name of the commons that he would suffer them to take and hold all the traitors who were against him and the law; and the king granted that they should take at their wish those who were traitors and could be proved traitors by the law. And Wat and the commons were carrying two banners and many pennons and pennoncelles, while they made their petition to the king. And they required that no man should be a serf, nor do homage or any manner of service to any lord, but should give fourpence rent for an acre of land, and that no one should serve any man but at his own will, and on terms of regular covenant. And at this time the king caused the commons to arrange themselves in two lines, and caused a proclamation to be made before them that he would confirm and grant them their freedom and all their wishes generally, and that they should go through the realm of England and catch all traitors and bring them to him in safety and that he would deal with them as the law required. Under colour of this grant Wat Tyghler and the commons took their way to the Tower, to seize the archbishop and the others, the king being at Mile End.

At this time the archbishop was chanting his mass devoutly in the Tower and shrove the prior of the hospital of Clerkenwell and others, and then he heard two masses or three, and chanted the *commendation* and the *placebo* and the *dirige* and the *seven psalms* and the *litany;* and when he was at the words "All saints, pray for us" the commons burst in and dragged him out of the chapel of the Tower, and struck and hustled him villainously, as they did the others who were with him and dragged them to Tower Hill. There they cut off the heads of Master Simon Sudbury, Archbishop of Canterbury, and of Sir Robert Hales, prior of the Hospital of St. John of Clerkenwell, Treasurer of England, Brother William Appleton, a great physician and surgeon, and one who had great influence with the king and the Duke of Lancaster. And some time afterwards they beheaded John Legge, the king's sergeant at arms, and with him a juror; and at the same time the commons proclaimed that anyone who could catch any Fleming or other alien of any nation might cut off his head, and so they did after this. And then they took the heads of the archbishop and the others and stuck them on wooden poles

and carried them before them in procession through the city, to the shrine of Westminster Abbey, in contempt of them and of God and of Holy Church, for vengeance descended on them not long afterwards. Then they returned to London Bridge and set the head of the archbishop above the bridge and the eight other heads of those that were murdered, so that they might be seen by all who passed over the bridge. And when this was done, they went to the church of St. Martin's in the Vintry, and found therein 35 Flemings, whom they dragged out and beheaded in the street. On that day were beheaded in all some 140 or 160 persons. And then they took their way to all the houses of the Lombards and other aliens, and broke into their dwellings and robbed them of all their goods which they could find. This went on throughout the day and the following night, with hideous cries and horrible tumult.

At this time, because the chancellor had been beheaded, the king made the Earl of Arundel chancellor for the day and delivered to him the great seal, and throughout the day caused various clerks to write charters and patents and protections granted to the commons touching the matters before mentioned, without taking any fines for sealing or description. And on the next day, Saturday, a great number of the commons came to the abbey of Westminster at the hour of terce and there they found John Imworth, Marshal of the Marshalsea and warden of the prisoners, a tormentor without pity; he was near the shrine of St. Edward, clinging to a marble pillar, as an aid and succour to save him from his enemies. And the commons wrenched his arms away from the pillar of the shrine and brought him to Cheapside and beheaded him. And at the same time they took from Bread Street a yeoman named John Greenfield because he had spoken well of Brother William Appleton and of other murdered persons, and brought him to Cheapside and beheaded him. All this time the king caused proclamation to be made round the city that everyone should go peacefully to his own country and his own house without doing any more evil; but to this the commons paid no heed.

And on this same day, at three o'clock in the

afternoon, the king came to Westminster Abbey, and some 200 persons with him. And the abbot and convent of the same abbey and the canons and vicars of the chapel of St. Stephen came in procession to meet him, dressed in their copes and with bare feet, half way to Charing Cross, and they brought him to the abbey and the church and the high altar and the king made his prayer devoutly and left an offering for the altar and the relics. And afterwards he spoke to the anchorite and confessed to him and was with him for some time. And then the king caused a proclamation to be made that all those commons of the country who were still in London should come to meet him at Smithfield, and so they did. And when the king had come with his train he turned to the eastern side, near St. Bartholomew's, a house of canons; and the commons arrayed themselves on the west side in battle formation, in great numbers. At this moment the mayor of London, William Walworth, came up, and the king bade him go to the commons and cause their chieftain to come to him. And when he was called by the mayor, Wat Tyghler by name, of Maidstone, he came to the king in a haughty fashion, mounted on a little horse so that he could be seen by the commons. And he dismounted, carrying in his hand a dagger which he had taken from another man, and when he had dismounted he half bent his knee, and took the king by the hand, and shook his arm forcibly and roughly, saying to him, "Brother, be of good comfort and joyful, for you shall have within the next fortnight 40,000 more of the commons than you have now and we shall be good companions." And the king said to Wat; "Why will you not go back to your own country?" And the other replied with a great oath that neither he nor his fellows would depart until they had their charter such as they wished to have, and such points rehearsed in their charter as they chose to demand, threatening that the lords of the realm would rue it badly if the points were not settled to their satisfaction. And the king asked him what were the points that he wanted, and he would have them freely without contradiction written down and sealed. And then Wat rehearsed points which were to be demanded; and

he asked that there should be no law except the law of Winchester, and that there should be henceforth no outlawry in any process of law, and that no lord should have any lordship, except only to be respected according to their rank among all folks, and that the only lordship should be that of the king; and that the goods of Holy Church should not remain in the hands of the religious, nor of the parsons and vicars, and other churchmen; but those who were in possession should have their sustenance from the endowments and the remainder of their goods should be divided amongst the parishioners; and no bishop should remain in England save one, nor more than one prelate, and that all the lands and tenements now held by them should be confiscated and shared amongst the commons, saving to them a reasonable substance. And he demanded that there should be no more bondmen in England, no serfdom nor villeinage, but that all should be free and of one condition. And to this the king gave an easy answer, and said that he should have all that could fairly be granted saving to himself the regality of the crown. And then he commanded him to go back to his home without further delay. And all this time that the king was speaking no lord nor any other of his council dared nor wished to give any answer to the commons in any place except the king himself.

Presently Wat Tyghler, in the king's presence, called for a flagon of water to rinse his mouth because he was in such a heat, and when it was brought he rinsed his mouth in a very rude and disgusting fashion before the king; and then he made them bring him a flagon of ale of which he drank a great deal, and in the king's presence mounted his horse. At this time a yeoman of Kent, who was among the king's retinue, asked to see Wat, the leader of the commons; and when Wat was pointed out to him, he said openly that he was the greatest thief and robber in all Kent. Wat heard these words and commanded him to come out to him, shaking his head at him in sign of malice; but the yeoman refused to go to him for fear of the mob. At last the lords made him go out to Wat, to see what he would do in the king's presence; and when Wat saw him, he ordered one of his followers, who was riding on a horse carrying his banner displayed, to dismount and cut off the yeoman's head. But the yeoman answered that he had done nothing worthy of death, for what he had said was true and he would not deny it, but in the presence of his liege lord he could not lawfully make debate without leave, except in his own defence; and that he could do without reproof, for if he was attacked he would strike back. And for these words Wat would have run him through with his dagger and killed him in the king's presence; and because of this, the mayor of London, William Walworth by name, reasoned with the said Wat for his violent behaviour and contempt done in the king's presence, and arrested him. And because he arrested him, the said Wat struck the mayor with his dagger in the stomach with great anger; but as God would have it, the mayor was wearing armour and took no harm. But like a hardy and vigorous man the said mayor drew his cutlass and struck back at the said Wat and gave him a deep cut on the neck and then a great cut on the head. And in this scuffle a yeoman of the king's household drew his sword and ran Wat two or three times through the body, mortally wounding him. And the said Wat spurred his horse, crying to the commons to avenge him, and the horse carried him some four score paces, and there he fell to the ground half dead. And when the commons saw him fall, and did not know for certain how it was, they began to bend their bows and to shoot; wherefore the king himself spurred his horse and rode out to them, commanding them that they should all come to him at the field of St. John of Clerkenwell.

Meanwhile the mayor of London rode as fast as he could back to the city commanding all those who were in charge of the 24 wards to make proclamation in their wards that every man should arm himself as quickly as he could, and go to the king in St. John's Fields, where the commons were, for he was in great need and necessity. And at this time nearly all the knights and squires of the king's household and many others, for fear that they had of this affray, left their liege lord and each went his own way. Afterwards when the king had reached the open fields he made the commons array themselves on the west side. And soon the aldermen came to him in a body, bringing with them the wardens of the wards, by various routes, with a fine company of people well armed in great strength and they enveloped the commons like sheep in a pen. And when the mayor had sent the wardens to the king, he returned to Smithfield with a fine company of lances to make an end of the captain of the commons abovesaid. And when he came to Smithfield he could not find the said captain Wat Tyghler, and at this he marvelled greatly and asked what had become of the traitor; and he was told that Tyghler had been carried by some of the commons to the hospital of the poorfolks near St. Bartholomew's and was put to bed in the chamber of the master of the hospital. And the mayor went thither and found him and had him carried to Smithfield in the presence of his fellows and there he was beheaded. And so ended his wretched life. And the mayor caused his head to be set upon a pole and carried before him to the king who still abode in the fields. And when the king saw the head he had it brought near him to abash the commons and thanked the mayor warmly for what he had done. And when the commons saw that their leader, Wat Tyghler, was dead in such a manner, they fell to the ground among the wheat like men discomforted, crying to the king for mercy for their misdeeds. And the king benevolently granted them mercy and many of them took to flight; and the king ordered two knights to lead the rest of the Kentishmen through London and over London Bridge without doing them any harm, so that each of them could go in peace to his own home. Then the king ordered the mayor, William Walworth, to put on his head a helmet in anticipation of what was going to happen; the mayor asked why he was to do so and the king replied that he was greatly obliged to him and therefore was going to confer on him the order of knighthood. And the mayor answered that he was not worthy nor able to have or to keep up a knight's estate, for he was but a merchant and had to live by merchandise; but at last the king made him put on the helmet and took a sword in both his hands and dubbed him knight resolutely and with great goodwill. And the same day he made three other knights from among the citizens of London on that same spot, and these are their names—John Philipot [Philpott], Nicholas Brymber [Brember] and [blank in the MS.]; and the king gave Sir William Walworth £100 in land and each of the others £40 in land for themselves and their heirs; and afterwards the king took his way towards London to his wardrobe to ease himself after his great labours.

Meanwhile a party of the commons took their way towards Huntingdon to pass towards the north in their malice and evil will, to ravage the land and destroy honest men; but there they were repelled and could not cross the bridge of the said town, because William Wyghmane, spigurnel of the chancery, and Walter Rudham and other good folks of the town of Huntingdon and of the country round about met them at the said bridge and killed two or three of them. The rest of them were glad to flee and went to Ramsey to pass thereby and they took shelter in the town and sent to the abbey for victuals to refresh and strengthen themselves; and the abbot sent them bread, wine, ale, and other victuals in great abundance, for he dared not do otherwise. And they ate and drank until they could consume no more and then they went to bed and slept until late in the morning, to their destruction; for the men of Huntingdon arose and gathered to themselves other folk of the countryside and suddenly came upon the commons at Ramsey and killed twenty-four of them and put the others to flight without more ado; and many of them were slain as they fled through the countryside, and their heads were set on high trees as example to others.

At the same time the commons had risen in Suffolk in great numbers and had as their captain a Suffolk chaplain, Sir John Wraw by name, who brought more than 10,000 men; and they robbed many honest folk and cast their houses down to the ground and set them on fire and Sir John took the valuables of gold and silver for his own use. And they came to Cambridge and there did great damage by burning houses and then betook themselves to Bury and found in the town a justice, Sir John Cavendish, Chief Justice of the King's Bench, and brought him to the pillory and cut off his head and set it on the pillory. And afterwards they dragged to the pillory the prior of that abbey, a good and wise man and an excellent singer, and a certain monk with him, and cut off their heads, and set them on poles before the pillory, that all who passed along that street might see them. And Sir John, the leader, was afterwards taken as a traitor and brought to London, and condemned to death, and was drawn, hanged, disembowelled, and beheaded.

At the same time there were great levies in Norfolk and the rebels did great harm throughout the countryside; and therefore the Bishop of Norwich, Sir Henry Despenser, sent his letters to the commons to bid them cease their malice and go to their own homes, without perpetrating any more evil deeds. But they would not do so, and went throughout the countryside, destroying and despoiling many towns and houses of many folks. At this time they met a hardy and vigorous knight, Sir Robert Hall by name, but a great thief and brawler, and they cut off his head. Wherefore the said bishop, gathering to himself many men at arms and archers, assailed them at various places, wherever he could find them, and captured many of them; and the bishop first confessed them and then beheaded them for their evil deeds. And so the commons scattered through the countryside for default and mischief and for fear that they had of the king and the lords and took to flight like beasts that run to earth.

Afterwards the king sent out his messengers into various districts to take the evil doers and put them to death; and many were taken and hanged in London and other cities and towns in the south country. And finally, as God willed, the king saw that too many of his lieges would be undone and too much blood spilt, so he took pity in his heart, and discussed with his councillors. And it was ordained with their assent that the commons ought to have grace and pardon for their misdeeds, on condition that they should never rise again, on pain of loss of life and members, and that each of them should have a charter of pardon and pay to the king as fee for his seal twenty shillings, to make him rich. And so ended this wicked war.

Lecture in Theology at the Sorbonne

REINTEGRATION
AND INCLUSION

HEALING, HOPE, AND RENEWAL

A favorite literary device of the later Middle Ages was a rose or a jewel that represents all that is good and beautiful in the world, which in the face of distress, defeat, and death symbolizes—and activates—healing, hope, and renewal, which transcends unhappiness and pessimism. Thus it was with medieval civilization itself. After 1250 it went through 250 years of agonizing crises and disasters of one sort or another—political failures, devastating and protracted international wars, a very long economic depression, a biomedical holocaust, bitter class conflicts, and the collapse of the papacy as an effective governing institution of church discipline and reform. The failure of leadership, aristocratic and middle class alike, to counter impersonal, material forces of dark malevolence and the incapacity of long-standing institutions richly endowed in church and state to absorb and mediate these disasters was especially disappointing. Yet all through this time of stress and agony, so effectively captured on film by Ingmar Bergman in *The Seventh Seal,* powerful evocation of the finest medieval traditions, inspiring extensions and enrichments of these ideas, suggestive avenues of innovation were written down in brilliant discourse and remain for us today the rose or pearl that we can hold in our hands and enthusiastically study to represent the distillation of the medieval spirit.

The ultimate greatness of medieval civilization and ingenuity of its writers and artists was to withdraw from the pockmarked, churned-up battlefields of practical life in church and state; to turn away from pandemics and economic collapse to the sweet, reserved, peaceful realm of the imagination; to cultivate language at its finest edge; to enrich painting, sculpture, and the decorative arts with new layers of color and intricate design; and to improve the ambience of everyday life, its rhythms, and its tastes. The hyperimaginative and lyrically lovely world of medieval discovery and sensibility endures today through the great writings and art of those times and inspires us to perception and reflection as it did the denizens of a falling world five centuries ago.

THOMIST RATIONALISM

The Dominican Friar and Parisian professor Thomas Aquinas (d.1274) was well aware of the stresses and polarized conflicts in medieval culture and society. He was congenitally an optimist—a fat, happy, Neapolitan aristocrat, a man of serene disposition ("the Angelic Doctor") with the deepest faith that the power of human reason, even without the blessing of the additional truths learned from revelation, would provide the foundations of a happy life and a stable society. Human intellect would guide individuals and groups toward ethical consensus. There was no need for violence and hostility. It was possible to reason one's way to a harmony that would illuminate both belief and behavior. Here are two examples of Thomism at its best. In the first, Aquinas argues that the existence of God can be proved from rational scientific principles. In the second, he takes up the vexed issue of poverty that was noisily claimed by the radical wing of the Franciscan order as absolutely necessary for religious orders (and by some hyperradicals for the church as a whole) and calmly, sympathetically, yet firmly and succinctly considers what poverty ought to mean for Christian society. What distinguishes these remarks is learning, science, dialectal skill, experience, good humor, and common sense. These are not qualities in oversupply at any time anywhere.

Portrait of Thomas Aquinas

THE EXISTENCE OF GOD

God's existence can be proved in five ways. The first and clearest proof is the argument from motion. It is certain, and in accordance with sense experience, that some things in this world are moved. Now everything that is moved is moved by something else, since nothing is moved unless it is potentially that to which it is moved, whereas that which moves is actual. To move is nothing other than to bring something from potentiality to actuality, and a thing can be brought from potentiality to actuality only by something which is actual. Thus a fire, which is actually hot, makes wood, which is potentially hot, to be actually hot, so moving and altering it. Now it is impossible for the same thing to be both actual and potential in the same respect, although it may be so in different respects. What is actually hot cannot at the same time be potentially hot, although it is potentially cold. It is therefore impossible that, in the same respect and in the same way, anything should be both mover and moved, or that it should move itself. Whatever is moved must therefore be moved by something else. If, then, that by which it is moved is itself moved, this also must be moved by something else, and this in turn by something else again. But this cannot go on for ever, since there would then be no first mover, and consequently no other mover, because secondary movers cannot move unless moved by a first mover, as a staff cannot move unless it is moved by the hand. We are therefore bound to arrive at a first mover which is not moved by anything, and all men understand that this is God.

The second way is from the nature of an efficient cause. We find that there is a sequence of efficient causes in sensible things. But we do not find that anything is the efficient cause of itself. Nor is this possible, for the thing would then be prior to itself, which is impossible. But neither can the sequence of efficient causes be infinite, for in every sequence the first efficient cause is the cause of an intermediate cause, and an intermediate cause is the cause of the ultimate cause, whether the intermediate causes be many, or only one. Now if a cause is removed, its effect is removed. Hence if there were no first efficient cause, there would be no ultimate cause, and no intermediate cause. But if the regress of efficient causes were infinite, there would be no first efficient cause. There would consequently be no ultimate effect, and no intermediate causes. But this is plainly false. We are therefore bound to suppose that there is a first efficient cause. And all men call this God.

The third way is from the nature of possibility and necessity. There are some things which may either exist or not exist, since some things come to be and pass away, and may therefore be or not be. Now it is impossible that all of these should exist at all times, because there is at least some time when that which may possibly not exist does not exist. Hence if all things were such that they might not exist, at some time or other there would be nothing. But if this were true there would be nothing existing now, since what does not exist cannot begin to exist, unless through something which does exist. If there had been nothing existing, it would have been impossible for anything to begin to exist, and there would now be nothing at all. But this is plainly false, and hence not all existence is merely possible. Something in things must be necessary. Now everything which is necessary either derives its necessity from elsewhere, or does not. But we cannot go on to infinity with necessary things which have a cause of their necessity, any more than with efficient causes, as we proved. We are therefore bound to suppose something necessary in itself, which does not owe its necessity to anything else, but which is the cause of the necessity of other things. And all men call this God.

The fourth way is from the degrees that occur in things, which are found to be more and less good, true, noble, and so on. Things are said to be more and less because they approximate in different degrees to that which is greatest. A thing is the more hot the more it approximates to that which is hottest. There is therefore something which is the truest, the best, and the noblest, and which is consequently the greatest in being, since that which has the greatest truth is also greatest in being, as is said in 2 *Metaph.*, text 4. Now that which most thoroughly possesses the nature of any genus is the cause of all that the genus contains. Thus fire, which is most perfectly hot, is the cause of all hot things, as is said in the same passage. There is therefore something which is the cause of the being of all things that are, as well as of their goodness and their every perfection. This we call God.

The fifth way is from the governance of things. We see how some things, like natural bodies, work for an end even though they have no knowledge. The fact that they nearly always operate in the same way, and so as to achieve the maximum good, makes this obvious, and shows that they attain their end by design, not by chance. Now things which have no knowledge tend towards an end only through the agency of something which knows and also understands, as an arrow through an archer. There is therefore an intelligent being by whom all natural things are directed to their end. This we call God.

POVERTY

As we have said above, perfection does not consist essentially in poverty, but in following Christ. As Jerome says, "Because it is not enough to abandon everything Peter adds what is really perfect, namely, 'We have followed you.' " Poverty is a tool or a practice whereby we may come to perfection. . . .

The lack of all resources, or poverty, is a tool of perfection inasmuch as various obstacles to charity are removed by the absence of wealth. There are three important obstacles of this kind. The first is the anxiety which often accompanies wealth.

The first obstacle cannot be entirely divorced from riches, whether they are great or small, because people cannot help but be anxious in some way or another about obtaining or protecting external goods. But if such things are only sought or possessed in small quantities, enough for the sheer maintenance of life, then the anxiety that goes with them does not get in the way to any great extent. It does not therefore detract from the perfection of the Christian life, because the

Lord does not ban all anxiety, but only excessive and harmful anxiety. . . .

An abundant possession of wealth makes for a corresponding abundance of anxiety, and this does greatly distract and hinder people's minds from being totally given to God's service. And the other two obstacles, love of wealth and conceit or glorying in wealth, do not arise except in the case of abundant wealth.

It does make a difference, however, with regard to this whether wealth, be it abundant or modest, is possessed privately or in common. Anxiety over one's private wealth is part of the self-love with which people love themselves in a worldly way, but anxiety over common goods is part of charitable love, which "does not seek its own," but attends to the common interest. And since religious life is meant to serve the perfection of charity, which is made perfect by a love of God which goes so far as to make light of oneself, the possession of any private property is quite incompatible with the perfection of religious life. But anxiety over the goods of the community can be a part of charity, even though it may interfere with some higher act of charity, such as the contemplation of God or the instruction of one's neighbors.

This makes it clear that owning vast wealth in common, whether in the form of possessions or in the form of properties, is an obstacle to perfection, even if it does not absolutely prevent it. But owning external things in common, whether possessions or properties, enough to sustain one's life, does not interfere with the perfection of religious life, if poverty is considered in relationship to the common goal of all forms of religious life, namely the freedom to concentrate on God's service.

If we consider poverty in relationship with the specific purposes of different kinds of religious life, then, in view of their different goals, different degrees of poverty will be appropriate to them. And, from the point of view of poverty, each form of religious life will be more or less perfect depending on how well its poverty is adapted to its purpose.

It is clear that the outward, bodily works of

the active life call for a good supply of external goods, while few things are needed for contemplation. So the philosopher says that many things are needed for the accomplishment of deeds, and the greater and better the deed is, the more will be needed; but speculation needs none of these things for its functioning. All it needs are the essentials, and everything more will be a hindrance to it. So a religious order which is devoted to the bodily activities of the active life, like the military orders or the hospitallers, would obviously be imperfect if it lacked common wealth.

Religious orders devoted to the contemplative life, on the other hand, are more or less perfect depending on how free their poverty makes them from anxiety about temporal things. Any form of religious life is hindered by concern about temporal things in proportion to the degree of concern about spiritual things which is required for it. And it is obvious that a religious order founded for the purpose of contemplating and passing on to others what it has contemplated by teaching and preaching calls for a greater concern about spiritual things than one founded solely for contemplation. So that kind of religious order needs the kind of poverty which involves the least anxiety. And clearly what makes for the least anxiety is the practice of keeping the things that people need to use after obtaining them at some suitable time.

So three levels of poverty befit the three classes of religious order which we identified above. Orders devoted to the bodily works of the active life need to have plenty of wealth in common. Orders devoted to contemplation are best served by having modest possessions, unless they are also expected to offer hospitality and to help the poor, either personally or through their agents. But Orders devoted to passing on to others what they have contemplated need a way of life that is to the greatest extent possible unencumbered by external concerns, and this is achieved by keeping their few necessities of life after obtaining them at some suitable time. . . .

It is in line with the perfection that Christ taught by his example to keep money or anything else in common either for the support of the religious themselves or for the support of other poor people. . . .

It is not the strictness and austerity of its observances that makes a form of religious life particularly commendable. . . .

As it says in Isaiah 58:5, "Is this the fast I have chosen, to afflict your soul for a day?" Austerity is taken up by religious life as being necessary to mortify the flesh but, if it is practiced without discretion it carries with it the risk of faltering, as St. Anthony points out. So no religious life is superior just because it has more austere observances; what makes a form of religious life better is that its observances are more intelligently adapted to its purpose. For instance, self-control is more effectively served by mortifying the flesh by abstaining from food and drink, which is a matter of hunger and thirst, than by taking away people's clothes, which is a matter of cold and nakedness, or by bodily labor.

OCCAMIST ANTIRATIONALISM

Aquinas' great critic and opponent was a Franciscan friar of a slightly later generation, William of Occam, who taught at Oxford in the early years of the fourteenth century. Occam wanted to limit access to God to revelation and mystical experience. He believed that in Thomas' system human reason can get too close to God, e.g., by proving God's existence. Thereby, Occam felt, God was being limited by Thomism. God was being brought into a mechanical universe to which human reason had access. This was a big mistake. God was totally transcendent, intellectually untouchable, completely unto himself, beyond human reason. To arrive at this conclusion Occam set out to deconstruct Aquinas' rationalist assumption that the human mind, drawing up experience and exercising its dialectical power, can make general propositions ("universals") that allow the human intellect to reason about certain aspects of God, not His essence but His existence. Therefore Occam set about to show that universals only exist in the mind, like artistic images. Their being consists only in their being known. We cannot establish their independent, objective existence outside the mind, and these general propositions or universals therefore cannot be used to reason in any way about God. We are signifying no more by a general term like "angel" than we would by merely saying "angels." Quantity is not distinct from quality and substance. The schoolmen, the philosophers in the medieval universities, took up sides and argued furiously on this issue of the authority of human reason. The French philosophers supported Thomas, the German and English (for the most part), Occam; the Italians were split. This may seem like an abstruse and useless debate. But the questions of how and what we can know by reasoning and what terms signify are persistent central issues in philosophy, and the debate still goes on. Furthermore, the debate had practical implications for medieval thinkers. How can we say anything about God authentically, validly? In addition to revelation only what we gain from personal (mystical) experience (Occam) but also what we learn rationally (Thomas)? Some historians of science also see Occam preparing the way for modern science: If reason cannot discourse about God, then perhaps it can concentrate on a lower realm of nature. Whether Occam would have agreed with this proposition is debatable. He delivered a blow to Thomist theological rationalism; but it is uncertain whether he opened the intellectual way to modern science.

I

... Quantity is not a thing really distinct from substance and quality, but any quantity is really the same as substance, and any quantity is really the same as quality; ...

Only a diversity of modes of signification suffices to distinguish one concept from another; not that no thing may be signified absolutely through one, but that it may be signified by another. So also it is obvious from these two "homo" and "homines"; for it is impossible to grant any thing signified through one that may not be signified through the rest; yet it is false to say, "man is species." So the identity of significators through some species or genera obtains with the distinction of species and of genera; and, as was frequently proved, genera or species are not, unless concepts or names. ... And indeed there are no categories except certain predicables and signs of things and simple terms; from which are made

combinations true and false; but simple terms of this kind can be distinct to such a degree that the predication of one on another is impossible; although no thing through one is signified, but that the same thing may be signified by the rest; as no substantial or accidental thing is signified through this name "angelus" but that it may be signified through this name "angeli," and conversely; and indeed it is not inconsistent to posit that distinct predicables imply the same thing; notwithstanding, therefore, that substance, quality, and quantity may be distinct categories; yet every quantity could be a thing not really distinct from substance and quality ...

II

... A universal is not something real that exists in a subject [of inherence], either inside or outside the mind, but that it has being only as a thought-object in the mind. It is a kind of mental picture which as a thought-object has a being similar to that which the thing outside the mind has in its real existence. What I mean is this: The intellect, seeing a thing outside the mind, forms in the mind a picture resembling it, in such a way that if the mind had the power to produce as it has the power to picture, it would produce by this act a real outside thing which would be only numerically distinct from the former real thing. The case would be similar, analogously speaking, to the activity of an artist. For just as the artist who sees a house or building outside the mind first pictures in the mind a similar house and later produces a similar house in reality which is only numerically distinct from the first, so in our case the picture in the mind that we get from seeing something outside would act as a pattern. For just as the imagined house would be a pattern for the architect, if he who imagines it had the power to produce it in reality, so likewise the other picture would be a pattern for him who forms it. And this can be called a universal, because it is a pattern and relates indifferently to all the singular things outside the mind. Because of the similarity between its being as a thought-object and the being of like things outside the mind, it can stand for such things. And in this way a universal is not the result of generation, but of abstraction, which is only a kind of mental picturing.

RUNNING ON EMPTY: THE CLOUD OF UNKNOWING

Occamist antirationalism left open as the only ways to God the church's hierarchic authority and tradition and mystical experiences. The church's old institutions and personnel, subject to intense criticism, and the papacy discredited by a half-century schism when there were ridiculously two popes and at one point three, left mysticism as the attractive way to divinity. Occam himself had a falling out with the English bishops and the papacy and sought refuge in the court of the German emperor. He and his followers had little respect for hierarchic authority. The mystical way to God was their delight. The later Middle Ages were a time of outpouring of manuals and guides to mystical experience, at least two of them still much valued. The first of these was written in England in the late fourteenth century: *The Cloud of Unknowing*. In a manner close to the concept and practice of nirvana in oriental religion, *The Cloud* advocates not a reaching out to God, which is impossible, but an emptying out of all intellect, imagination, and feeling; a condition of total negativity and depersonalization that allows the inrushing of God's love and majesty.

Every single rational creature has two faculties: the power of knowledge and the power of love. God is always quite unable to be comprehended by the first faculty, that of intelligence, but he is totally and perfectly comprehensible by the second, the power of love. Every single creature, moreover, will know him differently. Thus each loving soul on its own can, through love, know him who is wholly and incomparably more than sufficient to fulfil all human souls or angels that could possibly exist. And this is the eternal and extraordinary miracle of love, because God will continue in this activity for ever, without ceasing. Dwell on this, if you have the grace to do so, because to experience this for oneself is everlasting joy, and the contrary is everlasting pain . . .

So for the love of God be careful and don't put any great strain on your mind or imagination. For I tell you truthfully, you cannot achieve it by any such strain, so leave your intellectual and your imaginative skills strictly alone.

And don't imagine that because I refer to a 'cloud' or 'darkness' that I am talking about a cloud of vapours that evaporates into thin air or a darkness you see in your house when your candle has been extinguished. That is the kind of darkness you can imagine with some degree of mental ingenuity on the brightest summer's day, just as on the darkest winter's night you can imagine a bright shining light. Do not waste your time with any of these false ideas. I didn't mean anything like that. When I use the word 'darkness' I mean an absence of knowledge, as when you say that the things you don't know or have forgotten are 'dark' to you because you cannot see them with your inner eye. And for the same reason, this 'cloud' is no cloud in the sky but a 'cloud of unknowing' between you and your God. . . .

If you want to stand fast in virtue and not fall prey to temptation, never let your intention fail. Beat constantly against the cloud of unknowing between you and your God with a piercing dart of longing love and be loath to let your mind wander on anything less than God. Don't give up for anything, because this is absolutely the only work that destroys the ground and root of sin. It doesn't matter how much you fast or keep long vigils, how early you get up, how hard your bed is or how painful your hair-shirt. Indeed, if it was lawful for you—as, of course, it isn't—to pluck out your eyes, cut your tongue from your mouth, stop your ears and nose, lop off your limbs and inflict all the pain that is possible or that you can imagine on your body, none of this would do you any good at all. The impulse and the temptation to sin would still be embedded in you.

What else can I tell you? However much you weep with remorse for your sins or sorrow for Christ's Passion or however firmly you fix your mind on the joys of heaven, what benefit would you derive? Certainly it would give you much good, much help, much profit, much grace. But compared with this blind yearning of love, it can do very little. . . . For if this loving impulse is properly rooted in the soul, it contains all the virtues, truly, perfectly and effectually, without in any way diluting the intention of the will towards God. Indeed, it doesn't matter how many virtues a man acquires, without this true love they are bound to be warped and thus imperfect.

This is because virtue is nothing else but a properly ordered and deliberate turning of the soul to God. Why? God as he is in himself is the one and only source of all the virtues, so much so that if anyone is inspired to acquire a single virtue with mixed motives, even if God is uppermost in his mind, that virtue is bound to be flawed. We shall understand this better if we concentrate on just one or two particular virtues, and these may as well be humility and love. For anyone who has acquired these two virtues doesn't need any more: he has got them all.

Set to work, therefore, with all possible speed: beat against this high cloud of unknowing—you can rest later! It is extremely hard work for the beginner, make no mistake about that, unless God makes it easier with a special grace or simply because after a while one gets used to it.

But in what sense exactly is it hard work? Certainly not in the devout and urgent motion of love that is always springing up in the will of a contemplative, because this is not produced mechanically but by the hand of almighty God, who is always ready to act in each eager soul who has done and continues to do everything in his power to prepare himself for this work.

So why is it so arduous? Obviously in the trampling on all memory of God's creatures and keeping them enveloped by that cloud of forgetting I mentioned earlier. This really is hard work because *we* have to do it, with God's help; the other aspect of the work, which I have just described—the urgent impulse of love—is entirely the work of God. So do your part and, I promise you, that he will not fail to do his.

Get to work as soon as possible, then. Let me see how you are bearing up. Can't you see that God is waiting for you? For shame! After just a short, hard period of effort you will find the immense difficulty of the work beginning to ease. It is true that it is hard and repressive at the start, when your devotion is weak, but later when you are more devout what once seemed extremely arduous has become much easier and you can begin to relax. You may only have to make a little effort—or even no effort at all, because sometimes God does everything himself. But this doesn't always happen and never for very long but whenever he chooses and as he chooses. But you will be more than happy then, so let him do what he likes.

Now you are going to ask me how you can destroy this stark awareness of yourself. You might be thinking that if you destroy this sense of yourself, you will destroy everything else too and you will be right. But I will answer this fear by telling you that without a very special grace from God and without a particular aptitude on your part, you will never be able to get rid of this naked sense of self. For your part, this aptitude consists in a robust and profound sorrow of spirit.

But it is essential that you exercise discretion in this matter. You mustn't put any excessive strain on your body or soul but should, as it were, sit quietly, almost as if you were asleep and en-

tirely saturated and immersed in sorrow. This is what true and complete sorrow is like and if you can achieve it you will find that it helps you. Everybody has a special reason for grief, but the person who has a deep experience of himself existing far apart from God feels the most acute sorrow. Any other grief seems trivial in comparison. Indeed, anybody who has never experienced this grief should be really sorry for himself because he has never felt perfect sorrow! Once we have acquired this sorrow it not only purifies our souls, but it takes away all the pain merited by sin and thus makes the soul capable of receiving that joy which takes from a man all sense of his own being. . . .

Everybody should know and experience this sorrowful weariness with self in some way or other. God promises to teach his spiritual disciples according to his good pleasure, but there must be a corresponding readiness in the disciple's own soul and body as he ascends the ladder of contemplation and cultivates the right disposition before he can be wholly united to God in perfect love—or as perfectly as possible in this world—if God wills.

THE BODY OF CHRIST: THOMAS À KEMPIS

Another approach to mysticism was in just the opposite direction from *The Cloud of Unknowing.* This was stress on the physical sacrament and its transubstantion into the Body of Christ. This was an active, practical mysticism, a commitment to frequent spiritual operation, not just in an abstract sense but through frequent communion. If the *Unknowing* seems similar to oriental nirvana, Thomas À Kempis' *The Imitation of Christ* is reminiscent of the mystery religions of the Roman Empire. It is a filling up, not an emptying out, that Kempis advocates; the eating of the Body of Christ in the Holy Wafer that sets up, stimulates, inspires, renews the transformation of the recipient. Obviously *Imitation* advocates a mystical regimen comprehensible and appealing to ordinary men and women. It is a particularly lower middle class and working class variant of mysticism. This kind of spirituality had profound impact. It helped to make the holy day of Corpus Christi one of the prime festivals of the church. It encouraged elaborate processions and the street theater. Its enduring influence in Mediterranean and Irish Christianity is still at work. It was hospitable to recognizing the need of women for active religious participation—they can't administer the sacrament but they can receive it, daily and often. Thomas À Kempis was a fifteenth-century representative of the Brethren of the Common Life, a quiet order popular in the Low Countries that prescribed middle class spiritual exercise involving thrift, hard work, postponed gratification, and frequent prayer. This regimen was called the *Modern Devotion.* It is what the sociologist Max Weber called "asceticism in the world." He regarded it as the foundation of the Protestant Reformation. *The Cloud of Unknowing* was an anal approach to religious experience, a holding back to the point of self-effacement. The *Imitation of Christ* was an oral approach, a cultivation of the physical, a full deployment of physical being and its sanctification. The latter approach was certain to be immensely more popular in medieval society, and today as well.

Jesus as guest at the Hospice of two Dominicans

ON THE BLESSED SACRAMENT

The Voice of Christ

'COME TO ME, ALL WHO LABOUR AND ARE HEAVY LADEN, AND I WILL REFRESH YOU,' SAYS THE LORD.

'THE BREAD THAT I WILL GIVE IS MY FLESH, FOR THE LIFE OF THE WORLD.'

'TAKE AND EAT; THIS IS MY BODY WHICH SHALL BE OFFERED FOR YOU; DO THIS IN COMMEMORATION OF ME.'

'WHOSOEVER EATS MY FLESH AND DRINKS MY BLOOD, DWELLS IN ME, AND I IN HIM.' 'THESE THINGS THAT I HAVE TOLD YOU ARE SPIRIT AND LIFE.'

On the Deep Reverence with Which Christ should be Received

THE DISCIPLE. O Christ, Eternal Truth, these are Your own words, although not spoken all at one time or in one place. And since they are Your words, and are true, I must accept them with gratitude and trust. They are Your words, and You have spoken them; they are also mine, since You have given them to me for my salvation. Gladly do I receive them from Your lips, that they may be the more deeply imprinted in my heart. Your words, so tender, so full of sweetness and love, give me courage; but my own sins appal me, and a stricken conscience restrains me from receiving so high a Sacrament.

You command me to approach You in faith if I wish to have part in You, and to receive the food of immortality if I desire life and glory. 'Come to Me,' You say, 'all who labour and are heavy laden, and I will refresh you.' O Lord my God! How sweet and loving in the ears of a sinner are these words, with which You invite the poor and needy to the Communion of Your most holy Body! But who am I, O Lord, that I should presume to approach You? The very Heaven of Heavens cannot contain You; and yet You say, 'Come you all to Me.'

What is the meaning of this kindly invitation? Unaware of any good in me on which I may presume, how shall I dare to come? How shall I invite You into my house, who have so often done evil in Your sight? The Angels and Archangels do You reverence; Saints and holy men stand in awe of You; yet You say, 'Come you all to Me'! Unless You Yourself had said it, who would believe it true? And who would dare approach, unless it were Your command?

Noah, a good man, is said to have worked a hundred years to build the ark, so that he and a few others might be saved. How, then, can I in one short hour prepare myself to receive with reverence the Creator of the world? Moses, Your great servant and especial friend, constructed an Ark of imperishable wood, and covered it with purest gold, in order to house the Tablets of the Law: and how shall I, a corruptible creature, dare so lightly to receive You, the Maker of the Law and Giver of life? Solomon, wisest of Israel's kings, spent seven years in building a splendid Temple in praise of Your name. For eight days he kept the Feast of its Dedication, and offered a thousand peace-offerings. To the sound of trumpets, he solemnly and joyfully bore the Ark of the Covenant to its appointed resting-place. How, then, shall I, unworthiest and poorest of men, welcome You into my house, when I can hardly spend half an hour devoutly? If only I could spend even half an hour as I ought!

O my God, how earnestly did all these strive to please You! And how little, alas, can I do! How short is the time that I employ in preparing myself

for Communion! Seldom am I entirely recollected, and very seldom free from all distraction. Yet in Your saving presence, O God, no unbecoming thought should enter my mind, for it is not an Angel, but the Lord of Angels who comes to be my guest.

How great a difference there is between the Ark of the Covenant and its relics, and Your most holy Body with its ineffable powers: between those sacrifices of the old Law which foreshadowed the Sacrifice to come, and the true Victim of Your Body, which fulfils all the ancient rites!

Alas, why does not my heart burn within me at Your adorable presence? Why do I not prepare myself to receive Holy Communion, when the Patriarchs and Prophets of old, Kings and Princes with all their people, showed so great a devotion in Your holy worship?

The holy King David danced before the Ark with all his might, recalling Your blessings to his fathers; he wrote psalms, and taught his people to sing with joy; inspired by the grace of the Holy Spirit, he often sang and played on the harp; he taught the people of Israel to praise God with the whole heart, and to bless Him every day. If all these performed such acts of praise and devotion before the Ark of the Covenant, how much greater devotion and reverence should I and all Christian people have in the presence of this Sacrament, and in receiving the most adorable Body of Christ?

Many make pilgrimages to various places to visit the relics of the Saints, wondering at the story of their lives and the splendour of their shrines; they view and venerate their bones, covered with silks and gold. But here on the Altar are You Yourself, my God, the Holy of Holies, Creator of men and Lord of Angels! When visiting such places, men are often moved by curiosity and the urge for sight-seeing, and one seldom hears that any amendment of life results, especially as their conversation is trivial and lacks true contrition. But here, in the Sacrament of the Altar, You are wholly present, my God, the Man Christ Jesus; here we freely partake the fruit of eternal salvation, as often as we receive You worthily and devoutly. No levity, curiosity, or sentimentality must draw us, but firm faith, devout hope, and sincere love.

O God, invisible Creator of the world, how wonderful are Your dealings with us! How sweetly and graciously You welcome Your chosen, to whom You give Yourself in this Sacrament! It passes all understanding; it kindles the love and draws the hearts of the faithful to Yourself. For Your faithful ones, who strive to amend their whole lives, receive in this most exalted Sacrament the grace of devotion and the love of virtue.

O wonderful and hidden grace of this Sacrament, known so well to Christ's faithful, but hidden from unbelievers and servants of sin! In this Sacrament, spiritual grace is conveyed, lost virtue restored to the soul, and its sin-ravaged beauty renewed. Such is the grace of this Sacrament, that from the fullness of devotion You afford greater powers not only to the mind, but to the frail body.

We cannot but regret and deplore our own carelessness and tepidity, which hinders us from receiving Christ with greater love, for in Him rests all our merit and hope of salvation. He is our Sanctification and Redemption: He is the comfort of pilgrims, and the everlasting joy of the Saints. How sad it is that so many have small regard for this saving Mystery, which is the delight of Heaven and preservative of the whole world. Alas, man is so blind, and his heart so hard, that he does not appreciate more fully this wonderful gift, and, from frequent use of it, grows even less reverent towards it!

If this most holy Sacrament were celebrated in one place only, and were offered by one priest only in the whole world, men would rush to this place and to the priest of God, to be present at the divine mysteries. But there are now many priests, and in many places Christ is offered, that the grace and love of God may be better known to men, the more widely Holy Communion is diffused through the world. O good Jesus, eternal Shepherd, we thank You that You deign to refresh us poor exiles with Your precious Body and Blood, and invite us to receive these Mysteries, saying, 'Come to Me, all who labour and are heavy laden, and I will refresh you.'

On the Great Goodness and Love of God in this Sacrament

THE DISCIPLE. Trusting wholly in Your goodness and great mercy, Lord, I come sick to my Saviour, hungry and thirsty to the Fount of Life, needy to the King of Heaven, a creature to its Creator, desolate to my loving Comforter. Yet whence is this favour, that You should come to me? What am I, that You should give me Your very Self? How dare a sinner appear before You? And how is it that You deign to visit a sinner? You know Your servant, and see that he possesses no good in himself that could merit this blessing. Thus do I confess my worthlessness; I acknowledge Your goodness, I praise Your kindness, and I offer my gratitude for Your boundless love. You do this of Your own will; not on account of my merits, but solely that Your goodness may be more evident to me, Your love more richly imparted to me, and that You may more perfectly commend humility to me. Therefore, since it is Your pleasure and You have thus commanded it, Your will is my delight; may no wickedness in me obstruct it.

O most kind and loving Jesus, what profound reverence, gratitude and eternal praise are Your due when we receive Your sacred Body; for none on earth can rightly extol Its majesty. What shall be my thoughts as I approach my Lord in Communion? I cannot pay Him the honour that is His due, and yet I desire to receive Him with devotion. What better or more salutary desire can I have than to humble myself completely before You, and to praise Your infinite goodness to me? Therefore, O my God, I offer You my praise, and will glorify You for ever, while in the depths of my insignificance I despise and abase myself in Your presence.

Lord, You are the Holy of Holies: I am the worst of sinners. Yet, O Lord, You stoop to me, who am not worthy even to raise my eyes towards You. Lord, You come to me, and desire to be with me; You invite me to Your Table; You wish to feed me with the Heavenly Food, the Bread of Angels.

This Food is none other than Yourself, The Living Bread, who came down from Heaven to give life to the world.

See, from whom this love proceeds! See the Source whence this high glory shines! How deep a gratitude, how high a praise are Your due for all these blessings! How greatly to our profit and salvation was Your counsel when You instituted this Sacrament! How sweet and delightful the Feast in which You give Yourself to be our food! How wonderful are Your ways, O Lord; how mighty Your power, how infallible Your truth! You spoke the word, and all things were made; You commanded, and it was done.

It is indeed wonderful to consider, worthy of faith, and transcending the mind of man, how You, my Lord and God, true God and true man, are wholly present under the simple forms of bread and wine, and are eaten without being consumed by whoso receives You. O Lord of all things, who stand in need of none, and who yet are pleased to dwell in us by means of this Sacrament; keep my heart and body spotless, that with a glad and pure conscience I may be enabled to celebrate Your holy Mysteries, and receive to my eternal salvation those things that You have hallowed and ordained to Your own especial honour and for Your perpetual memorial.

Be glad, my soul, and thank God for the noblest of all His gifts, for this unique comfort bestowed on you in this vale of tears. For as often as you consider this Mystery, and receive the Body of Christ, you set forward the work of your redemption, and become a sharer in all the merits of Christ. Therefore, continually dispose yourself to the renewal of your mind, and ponder deeply the great mystery of salvation. Whenever you celebrate or hear Mass, it should be as great, as fresh and as joyful to you as if on this very day Christ had come down for the first time into the womb of the Virgin, and was made man; or, hanging on the Cross, suffered and died for man's salvation.

On the Value of Frequent Communion

THE DISCIPLE. Lord, I come to You to receive the benefit of Your gift, and to enjoy the Feast that You have graciously prepared for the poor. In You I find all that I can or should desire; You are my Saviour and my Redeemer, my hopes and my strength, my honour and my glory. Therefore, Lord Jesus, gladden the soul of Your servant today, for to You I raise my soul. I desire to receive You with reverence and devotion: I long to invite You into my house, that, like Zaccheus, I may win Your blessing and be numbered among Your chosen. My soul longs to receive Your Body; my heart yearns to be united to You.

Give me Yourself, and it is enough; nothing but You can satisfy me. Without You I cannot exist; without Your visits I cannot live. Therefore I must often approach You, and receive You as the medicine of salvation, lest if I be deprived of this heavenly food, I faint by the way. For, O most merciful Jesus, it was Yourself who, when You had been preaching to the people and healing their many diseases, said, 'I will not send them away to their homes hungry, lest they faint on the way.' Deal in like manner with me now, since You remain in this Sacrament for the comfort of the faithful. You are the sweet refreshment of the soul, and whoever receives You worthily will be a partaker and heir of eternal glory. It is essential to me, who am so prone to frequent falls, and who so quickly grow lukewarm and careless, that I renew, cleanse, and enkindle myself by frequent prayer and confession, and by the holy reception of Your Body; if I neglect these for long, I may fall away from my holy purpose.

Man's senses are prone to evil from his youth up, and without the aid of this divine remedy he soon lapses into yet greater wickedness. Holy Communion both restrains a man from evil, and establishes him in goodness. For if I am so often careless and lukewarm now when I celebrate or communicate, what would become of me were I to neglect this remedy, or fail to seek this most powerful aid? And although I am neither fit nor rightly disposed to celebrate daily, yet I will endeavour at proper times to receive Your divine Mysteries, and present myself to receive this great grace. For this is the chief comfort of the faithful soul, as long as she dwells afar from You in this mortal body, that ever mindful of her God, she may often devoutly receive her Beloved.

O Lord God, Creator and Giver of life to all souls, how wonderful is Your kindness and mercy to us, that You should stoop to visit the poor and humble soul, and to satisfy her hunger with Your whole Divinity and Humanity! Happy the mind and blessed the soul that deserves to receive You with devotion, and in receiving You, to be filled with spiritual joy! How great a Lord does the soul receive! How beloved the Guest she welcomes! How delightful the Companion she invites to enter! How faithful the Friend she makes! How gracious and noble the Spouse she embraces—one to be loved and desired above all others! O dear and most beloved Lord, let Heaven and earth in all their beauty keep silence before You; for whatever of praise and beauty they possess comes from Your generous goodness. They cannot approach the beauty of Your Name, and Your Wisdom is infinite.

PETRARCH

SECULAR HUMANISM

The Italian humanist and scholar Petrarch, writing in the mid-fourteenth century, indicates a mind-set that is far removed from the scholastic philosophers and the mystics: the cultivation of the secular self. It owes much to classical models, particularly Cicero, whose Latin style Petrarch imitates. Petrarch likes books, travel, Rome, and friendship. It is a quiet egoism. His personal taste and individual feelings become the principle of valorization. Life-styles and learning require no justification beyond the personal gratification of the well-educated and affluent individual. What is also interesting is what is not said. The Christian framework is not denied, but it is eroded. A modern, sophisticated intellectual goes his own way. The modern idea of the free person, making his own choices, has emerged here.

I am still in the thrall of one insatiable desire, which hitherto I have been neither able nor willing to check. . . . I cannot get enough books. It may be that I have already more than I need, but it is with books as it is with other things: success in acquisition spurs the desire to get still more. Books, indeed, have a special charm. Gold, silver, gems, purple raiment, a house of marble, a well-tilled field, paintings, a steed with splendid trappings—things such as these give but a silent and superficial pleasure. Books delight us through and through, they talk with us, they give us good counsel, they enter into a living and intimate companionship with us.

. . . There is no place in the world that pleases me: wherever I turn my weary body I find only thorns and hardness. The time has come, it seems to me, when I should go hence to the other life, for here, I confess, I am ill content—whether the fault be in myself or in places or in men or in all alike. Amid my adversities I have by great effort and by persistent mental exercise achieved this one consolation: that wherever I am, even if I am badly off, even if I am very badly off indeed, I persuade myself—by deceiving myself and fancying myself not to be feeling what I am feeling— that I am well off.

If there is any region in the world in which I could find contentment, it is Italy. Nor is that surprising: for it is our fatherland, and it is such by its very nature that even foreigners and barbarians find delight in it. . . .

There is no place where I would rather dwell than in Rome, and that I would have dwelt there always had fortune permitted. No words can tell how highly I esteem the fragments of the glorious

Portrait of Francesco Petrarca (Petrarch)

queen of cities, her magnificent ruins, and the many impressive evidences of her virtues— evidences that offer light and point the way for those who enter on either the earthly or the heavenly road. And it is in that city—would that I could call it only half ruined!—that now even more than ever before I long to spend the little span of life that still remains for me. . . .

* * *

I live in indignation: for our fate,
Withholding us from birth until this age,
Ordains that we must live in evil years.
Better would it have been had we been born
Far earlier or far later. There was once,
And there may be again, a happier time.
This present age holds nought but sordidness:
All that is shameful, as you know full well,
Converges here and now, and holds us fast.
Wisdom and virtue and the love of glory
Have fled the world, where now dishonor rules,
With luxury and greed. Unless we rise
Again by mighty effort, soon for us
The end will come. We shall be cast on the rocks,
Or whirled away in a black raging stream.
Hard earth and a narrow tomb will cover o'er
Bodies and unremembered names; and soon
The fame we have so toiled to win will fade.
The urn that holds our ashes soon will fall,
And the wind will scatter them. The traveler,
Bending above the worn and broken marble,
Will scarce be able to spell out the name
That once was graven there. Time overwhelms
All things: would we resist, we must uplift
Our weary hopes from earth, and let no anchor
Fixed in the shifting sands hold back our voyage.
    Read then these hasty verses, O my friend,
Written for you in this my Helicon,
Amid the verdure, where the river runs
Murmuring from beneath the lonely cliff—
Written between two laurel trees that I
Had planted in your honor: tending them,
Often I bade them grow, sighing in hope
That some day you might come, and you and I
Might sit together 'neath their sacred shade.

FRANÇOIS VILLON

A POOR MAN'S FREEDOM

Writing around 1500 in Paris, François Villon on the margin of urban society claims for himself the freedom that Petrarch and the Italian humanists had asserted. This is the sensibility not of the upper middle class intellectual but of the urban proletariat and the criminal class in the streets of Paris. Villon at times feels free to do what he wants, but he realizes his absolutely lonely and defenseless condition, his bleak and desperate prospects, destined probably to end up on the gallows. He falls back on formal piety he doesn't much believe in. Villon probably captures the authentic voice of the proletarian and criminal classes in the slums of European cities. There were many thousands like him. He was different in being articulate.

I die of thirst beside the fountain
I'm hot as fire, I'm shaking tooth on tooth
In my own country I'm in a distant land
Beside the blaze I'm shivering in flames
Naked as a worm, dressed like a president
I laugh in tears and hope in despair
I cheer up in sad hopelessness
I'm joyful and no pleasure's anywhere
I'm powerful and lack all force and strength
Warmly welcomed, always turned away.

I'm sure of nothing but what is uncertain
Find nothing obscure but the obvious
Doubt nothing but the certainties
Knowledge to me is mere accident
I keep winning and remain the loser
At dawn I say "I bid you good night"
Lying down I'm afraid of falling
I'm so rich I haven't a penny
I await an inheritance and am no one's heir
Warmly welcomed, always turned away.

I never work and yet I labor
To acquire goods I don't even want
Kind words irritate me most
He who speaks true deceives me worst
A friend is someone who makes me think
A white swan is a black crow
The people who harm me think they help
Lies and truth today I see they're one

I remember everything, my mind's a blank
Warmly welcomed, always turned away.

Merciful Prince may it please you to know
I understand much and have no wit or learning
I'm biased against all laws impartially
What's next to do? Redeem my pawned goods
        again!
Warmly welcomed, always turned away.

Brother humans who live on after us
Don't let your hearts harden against us
For if you have pity on wretches like us
More likely God will show mercy to you
You see us five, six, hanging here
As for the flesh we loved too well
A while ago it was eaten and has rotted away
And we the bones turn to ashes and dust
Let no one make us the butt of jokes
But pray God that he absolve us all.

Don't be insulted that we call you
Brothers, even if it was by Justice
We were put to death, for you understand
Not every person has the same good sense
Speak up for us, since we can't ourselves
Before the son of the virgin Mary
That his mercy toward us shall keep flowing
Which is what keeps us from hellfire
We are dead, may no one taunt us
But pray God that he absolve us all.

The rain has rinsed and washed us
The sun dried us and turned us black
Magpies and ravens have pecked out our eyes
And plucked our beards and eyebrows
Never ever can we stand still
Now here, now there, as the wind shifts
At its whim it keeps swinging us
Pocked by birds worse than a sewing thimble

Therefore don't join in our brotherhood
But pray God that he absolve us all.

Prince Jesus, master over all
Don't let us fall into hell's dominion
We've nothing to do or settle down there
Men, there's nothing here to laugh at
But pray God that he absolve us all.

CHRISTINE DE PISAN

WOMEN ARE NOT FREE

The early-fifteenth-century Parisian journalist Christine de Pisan writes a specimen letter to a great lady from one of her own entourage warning against the dire consequences of pursuing a love affair. It is a very conservative message on its surface. This can be read as revealing in its subtext Christine's own rebellious feelings in the matter. Christine actually wants the noble lady to follow the dictates of her heart. She wants authentic behavior, not conformity to oppressive social regimens dictated by powerful men of the aristocracy. But the letter can be read another way: Christine does recognize with regret that the glory days of courtly love are over. Neoconservatism has taken over aristocratic life and imposed its rigidity on even great ladies, taking away their freedom. She recognizes the imposition of oppressive standards on women and there isn't anything they can do about it. Women are enmeshed in their family obligations and a code of behavior society imposes on them. The freedom of Petrarch or Villon is not possible for women who are victims of the double standard of sexual behavior. This condition endured until very recent decades.

Lady, I cannot speak to you as soon as I might like. I am bound to counsel you for your good as someone who has been in my tutelage from childhood until now, however unworthy I may have been. It seems to me that I would err in remaining silent about what I know might bring you grief if I didn't point it out to you. For that reason, dear Lady, I write you what follows in this letter, about which I implore you most humbly not to bear me ill will in any way, for you may be sure that very great love, and the desire ever to increase your noble renown and honor, move me to do this.

My Lady, I have heard rumors about your conduct such that I am saddened from the bottom of my heart, for I fear the ruin of your good reputation. And the rumors are of the ruinous kind, as it seems to me: it is right and reasonable for every

princess and high lady, as she is raised high in honor and status over others, to surpass all others in goodness, wisdom, manners, personal traits, and comportment, so that she may be the exemplar by which other ladies, and similarly all women, may govern themselves accordingly and as may be appropriate. Let her be pious toward God; and let her have an assured, quiet, and calm demeanor, and be moderate in her amusements and not noisy; may she laugh quietly and not without cause; may she have a noble manner, humble countenance, and stately bearing; may she respond kindly to everyone, and with an agreeable word; may her costume and ornaments be noble but not overdone; may she welcome foreigners in a dignified manner, speaking with restraint and not too familiarly; may she reflect

Noblewoman spinning with
her servants

thoughtfully upon matters and not be flighty; at no time should she appear harsh, cruel, or injurious, nor, in being served, too severe; may she be humane and kind and not too imperious toward her serving women and servants, and generous with gifts, within reason; let her know how to recognize those people who are the worthier for their goodness and uprightness, and the best among her servants, and let her draw them to her, men and women, and reward them according to their merits; let her neither believe nor trust flatterers, male or female, learning to recognize them instead and chasing them from her; let her not lightly believe things she is told; may she not be in the habit of taking counsel with stranger or friend in a secret or solitary place, especially not with any of her retainers or serving women, so that it may not be judged that one of them knows more of her private affairs than another; and let her never laugh and say in front of other people, to no matter what person, any veiled words not understood by all present, so that those within hearing may not suppose some foolish secret between her and that person; she must not keep herself in her chamber and too alone, nor must she be too much in sight, but let her at times withdraw and at other times appear in public. And though these qualities and all other manners suiting a high-ranking princess may have been yours in the past, you are at present completely changed, according to what people say. For you have become much livelier, more talkative, and gayer than you used to be, and commonly, that kind of conduct, when demeanor changes, makes other people judge that hearts have changed, too. Now you want to be alone and withdrawn from people, except for one or two of your women and some of your servants, with whom you hold counsel. And even in front of people, you laugh and utter innuendo, as if you all understood each other well, and as if only their company pleased you and the others could not serve you to your liking. Those things and the appearance they give are reason to move your other servants to envy and to cause others to judge that your heart has, somewhere, fallen in love.

Ah, my very sweet Lady! for God's sake, consider who you are and the high position to which God has elevated you, and do not consent to forgetting your soul and your honor for some foolish bit of pleasure. Do not place your confidence in those vain thoughts that many young women have who bring themselves to believe that there is no harm in loving in true love provided that it leads to no wrongful act (for I feel certain that you would not want to conceive of matters otherwise, on pain of death), and that one lives more happily because of it, and in doing this one makes a man become more valorous and renowned forevermore. Ah! my dear Lady, it is quite otherwise! For God's sake, do not deceive yourself on that score, and do not let yourself be deceived! Take a lesson from such great ladies as you've seen in your lifetime who, simply for having been suspected of such a love, without the truth of it ever having been ascertained or known, lost their honor and saw their lives ruined. There were such women; and I maintain, upon my soul, that they never sinned or acted in a basely culpable way; and you have seen their children reproached for it and less esteemed. Although for every woman, whether poor or rich, such foolish love is dishonorable, it is much more inappropriate and injurious in a princess and in a high-ranking lady, the more so as she is important. The reason for that is a good one, for the name of a princess is carried by everyone, and so, if there is any stain on her reputation, it is known throughout foreign countries, more than in the case of ordinary women. The reasoning is right, too, considering the children of princesses, who must rule lands and be princes of others, and so it is a great misfortune when there is any suspicion that they may not be the legitimate heirs, and many difficulties can come from that. For let us suppose that the body commits no misdeed: there are those who simply hear it said that such and such a lady is in love and they will not believe at all that there has been no wrongful act. And because of but a bit of unguarded foolishness, committed by chance out of youthfulness and without misstep, evil tongues will judge and will add things that never were thought or said. Thus

such talk goes from mouth to mouth, never diminishing, always increasing. So it is necessary for each great lady to be more careful in all her habits, demeanor, and words than other women. The reason is that when one comes into the presence of a great lady, each person looks at her and listens to hear what she will say, and attentively notes everything about her. Thus the lady cannot open an eye, utter a word, laugh, or give any appearance that will not be received, noted, and retained by many people and then reported in many a place. Do you not think, my dear Lady, that it might create a very bad appearance for a great lady—indeed, for any woman—when she becomes livelier and gayer than is her wont, and seeks to hear more talk of love, and then, because of something that happens, her heart changes and she suddenly becomes sullen, ungracious and quarrelsome, and no one can serve her in a manner that pleases her, and she does not care about her clothing or dress? People surely then say that she was in love and no longer is. My Lady, that is hardly the manner a lady ought to adopt, for she must take care, whatever her thoughts may be, that always her bearing and appearance prevent such judgments from being made about her. But it could well be difficult to maintain such composure when one is leading a life of love. For that reason, the surest way is to avoid that life and flee from it completely. So you can see, dear Lady, that every great princess—and, similarly, every woman—must be more eager to acquire a good reputation than any other treasure, for it makes her shine with honor and it remains forever with her and her children. Revered Lady, as I mentioned earlier, I can well imagine and envisage the reasons propelling a young lady to incline herself toward such a love: youth, ease of situation, and leisure make her think, "You are young, pleasure is all you need. You can well love without baseness. There is no evil in it when there is no sin. You will make a man valorous. No one will be the wiser. You will live more happily because of it and will have acquired a true servant and loyal friend." And so on. Ah! my Lady, for God's sake, take care that such foolish ideas do not deceive you! Because, as for pleasure, rest assured that in love there is a hundred thousand times more grief, searing pain, and perilous risk, especially on the ladies' side, than there is pleasure. For along with the fact that Love by itself delivers many different kinds of bitter moments, the fear of losing honor, and that it may all be known, remains in women's hearts continually and makes them pay dearly for such pleasure. And as for saying, "This will not be evil, since it will not be a sinful deed," alas! my Lady, no one, no woman, may be so sure of herself that she becomes certain, whatever firm resolve she may have, always to maintain moderation in such a love and that it will not be known. As I said above, that is certainly an impossibility, for there is no fire without smoke but there is often smoke without fire. And as for saying, "I will make a man valorous," indeed, I say that it is a very great folly to destroy oneself in order to enhance another, even if we suppose that he may thereby become valorous! She indeed destroys herself who, to refashion someone else, dishonors herself! And as for saying "I will have acquired a true friend and servant," Heavens! and how could such a friend be helpful to the lady? For if she had some troubling matter, he would not dare step in to help her under any circumstance for fear of her dishonor. Therefore, how can such a servant serve her who will not dare to apply himself for her good? Now, there are some who say that they serve their ladies whenever they do any number of things, be it with arms or in other ways. But I say that they serve themselves, since the honor and the profit remain with them and not at all with the lady! Still further, my Lady, if you or another wish to excuse yourselves in saying, "I have an inconstant husband who gives me little pleasure and loyalty, and for that reason I can, without committing a misdeed, take pleasure in another in order to forget my melancholy and pass the time"—surely, such an excuse, saving your grace and that of all other ladies who utter it, is worth nothing. For he who sets fire to his own house in order to burn his neighbor's commits too great a folly. But if she who has such a husband bears with him patiently and without damaging her reputation, so much the more will the merit of her soul, and her honor, increase in praiseworthiness. And as for pleasure, certainly a great lady—indeed, any woman, if she will—can, without such a love, find many permissible and correct pleasures to which she can give herself and pass the time without melancholy. For those who have children, what more gracious pleasure can one ask, nor more delight, than to see them often and take care that they are well-nourished and well-taught, as pertains to their high rank or station, and to see their daughters trained from childhood to acquire the rule of living properly and as befits them through the example of the right company. Alas! and if the mother did not conduct herself in an entirely prudent manner, what example would that be to the daughters? And for those who have no children, it is certainly honorable for every high-ranking lady, after she has said her prayers, to employ herself in doing some handiwork in order to avoid idleness, or to have fine linen made, marvelously worked, or silken sheets or other things that she can make use of; such occupations are worthwhile and prevent a person from thinking idle thoughts. I do not say that a noble young lady cannot amuse herself, laugh, and play in seemly fashion at the right time and place, even where there may be lords and gentlemen, nor that she must not honor foreign visitors as befits her high station, each according to his rank. But this must be done so soberly and with such fine deportment that there is not a single glance, nor a laugh, not a word that is not carefully weighed and governed by reason. And always, she must be on her guard that no one may perceive in her words, glance, or countenance anything unseemly or inappropriate.

Ah, Heavens! if every great lady—every woman, truly—really knew how attractive to her this fine bearing is, she would take greater pains to have it than any other finery, for there is no other precious jewel that can adorn her as much.

And further, my very dear Lady, it remains to talk of the perils and risks that are in such a love, which are without number. The first and greatest is that one angers God, after which, if the husband notices it, or the kinfolk, the woman is ruined or fallen into reproach, and never after has any respectability. Yet let us suppose that does not happen; let us talk in favor of lovers: although all may be loyal, discreet, and truthful (which they scarcely are: instead, it is well enough known that commonly they are deceitful, and in order to trick women they say what they do not intend or want to do)—it is nevertheless true that the ardor of such an affair does not last very long, even for the most loyal, and that is certain. Ah! dear Lady, when it happens that this love has subsided, can you conceive of how the lady who has been blinded by her envelopment in foolish pleasure bitterly repents when she realizes what she has done and reflects upon the follies and various perilous situations in which many a time she found herself? Can you conceive of how much she might wish it had never happened, no matter what the cost might have been, and that such a reproach could not be said of her? You certainly could not imagine the enormous feeling of repentance and the distasteful thoughts that remain in her heart. In addition to that, you and all ladies can see what folly it is to put one's self and one's honor at the mercy of tongues and in the hands of such servants—since they call themselves servants, but the result of their service is commonly such that, whatever they may have promised you and sworn to keep secret, they do not keep quiet at all. At the end of such love, moreover, people's blame and their talk remains with the ladies; at the very least, there is a fear and heartsick dread remaining that the very ones in whom they have placed their confidence may tell of it and boast, as might someone else who knows about it. Thus the ladies put themselves freely in bondage, and there you see the result of that love service! Can you conceive of what a great honor it seems to ladies' "servants" to be able to say and boast that they are loved, or have been, by a great lady or lady of renown? How then would they keep quiet about the truth? For God knows how they lie, and God be willing that, among you, ladies, you learn that well, for you would have cause to protect yourselves from it. Because I know that you like ballades and poems, my Lady, I send you one, composed on that subject by a good master, if you would please note it well. Now, as for the servants who know your secrets

and in whom you must trust—do you believe, by your faith, that they keep quiet about it, however much you may have them swear to do so? Indeed, the greatest part of them are the sort who would be very sad were it not known that they have a greater familiarity and boldness with you than the others; and if their mouths do not actually tell your secrets, they hint at them in various covert ways that they want others to notice. Ah! Heavens, what servitude for a lady and for every other woman in such a situation who will not dare to reprimand or blame her serving man or woman, in the event she sees them commit a great error, since she feels herself in their power. They will rise up against her so arrogantly that she will not dare say a word, rather having to suffer them to do and say things that she would not tolerate from any other. And what do you think those servingmen and -women say, who see this and note it? What they are thinking is only what really is, and be sure that they whisper about it a good deal. And should it happen that the lady becomes angry or dismisses her servants, God knows that everything is revealed and talked about in many places. Moreover, it often happens that servants are and have been the means and promoters through which this love is plotted, and it is something they have pursued willingly and assiduously in order to gain gifts, offices, or other emoluments. Very revered Lady, what can I say to you? You may be sure that one would as soon drain a great, yawning chasm than recount all the perilous evils that are in this life of love. Nor should you entertain the thought that it might be otherwise, because that is how it is. For that reason, very dear Lady, do not place yourself irretrievably in such peril. If you have given it some thought, for Heaven's sake, withdraw before a greater evil befalls you, for it is much better sooner than later, and later better than never. You can already see what words would be said if you continued your new ways, since they have already been noticed, and word of them is broadcast in many a place. I do not know what more to write you, except to beg you humbly, with all that is in my power, to bear me no ill will for this, but rather let it please you to take note of the good will that makes me say it. And besides, I should want to do my duty in loyally warning you, even should I incur your displeasure, than to counsel your destruction or keep quiet about it in order to remain in your favor. My Lady, please note my ballade, which I send you enclosed with this let-ter. Very revered Princess and my dear Lady, I pray God that He give you a good and long life, and Paradise. Written at La Tour, the 18th day of January.

Your humble creature
Sebile de Monthault, Dame de la Tour

MARSILIO OF PADUA

THE SOVEREIGN STATE

Petrarch and the Italian humanists developed a secular self-consciousness, a cultiva-tion of personal interests that amounted to an assertion of the freedom and dignity of the individual. Another Italian, Marsilio of Padua, in his political treatise *The Defender of the Peace* (1324), made a direct ideological onslaught on the medieval hierarchic tradition and specifically upon the papal rules. He denied the secular authority of the pope and all bishops. Social tranquility required that the state alone exercise sover-eignty over all groups and individuals within its territory, including churchmen. The papacy, while greatly declined from the zenity of medieval power, responded furiously and Marsilio—who had been a professor at the University of Paris—had to seek protection at the court of the German emperor, where he joined another radical thinker, William of Occam.

What Marsilio was advocating was nothing less than the repudiation of one of the three elements, at least on its political side, of the medieval order—all secular authority and social leadership on the part of the church. He had a vision of the postmedieval state, purely secular and sovereign. Within this state a system of popular sovereignty should operate, he believed. The ruler should not make laws arbitrarily, but only with the consent of a legislature representing the people. Here Marsilio reflected the experi-ence of the urban communes of northern Italy. Marsilio thus had a clear conception of the modern secular polity based on popular sovereignty and exercising full authortiy over all institutions and groups within its territory. This would be a revolutionary departure from the medieval political tradition of pluralist division of authority be-tween church and state and among kings, nobles, and various communities. The downside of Marsilio's doctrine was that he provided no practical way in which the authority of the ruler could be subjected to the legislative power of the people. His theoretical justification for the elimination of the political power of the church was a pragmatic one of public tranquility. But this criterion could be used by the ruler to justify any dictatorial measure, including repudiation of the legislative power of the people. If Thomas Aquinas' theory of law is the foundation of modern juristic liberal-ism, Marsilio is the forerunner of its opposite, the pragmatic or voluntarist theory of law—the state must have complete sovereignty to assure social peace through exer-cise of its will and there is no law above the sovereign power of the state. This argument leads, through Thomas Hobbes, to modern totalitarianism.

Tax Collectors

When the Roman bishop is permitted to have such general and unrestricted power to appoint officials and to distribute temporal goods and benefices, all kingdoms and polities are put in danger of destruction or violent turmoil, if such bishop seeks to subject secular governments to himself.

This bishop . . . is seeking, although wrongly, to have coercive . . . jurisdiction over all the rulers in the world; and by his distribution or donation of ecclesiastic temporal goods or benefices and tithes (of which an inestimable part have already come to belong to him, who has designs on all states), he can stir up great dissension, and has in fact done so hitherto and is still doing.

. . . The power to grant teaching licences should be revoked from the bishops. . . . In ancient times the legislator granted this power to the bishops because of their saintly lives and wide learning, as is quite clear from the science of civil acts. But at the present time the bishops, having the opposite qualities, subject to themselves colleges of learned men, taking them away from the secular rulers, and use them as no slight but rather very powerful instruments for perpetrating and defending their usurpations against the secular rulers. For since these learned men are unwilling to lose their professional titles, desiring the ease and glory resulting from possession of them, and believing that they have been obtained only by the authority of the Roman or other bishops, they carry out the bishops' wishes and oppose any persons, whether secular rulers or subjects, who contradict what they consider to be the authority of these bishops. But since such authority to bestow teaching licences belongs to the legislator or to the ruler by its authority, these alone should and lawfully can bestow, on their own authority, notary licences, professional titles, and the titles of other civil offices, in order that they may not lack but may rather acquire and preserve the favor of the learned and the wise, which favor must be considered to outweigh all other external aids for stabilizing and defending governments and constitutions.

Moreover, believing that they may do anything they like through the plenitude of power which they assert belongs to them, they have issued and are still issuing certain oligarchic ordinances called "decretals," wherein they command the observance of whatever measures they consider favorable to their own temporal welfare and to that of their clergymen as well as of certain laymen. . . . although these ordinances are very harmful to the rulers and other believers. Those who disobey them they punish with anathemization oral or written, as we have said above, and some of them have even broken out with such great insanity that they have issued decretals proclaiming that all the rulers and peoples in the world are subject to them in coercive jurisdiction, and that everyone must believe in the truth of this proposition in order to obtain eternal salvation.

And so the Roman bishops with their clerical coteries have the firm desire and determination to maintain and defend these outrages which, as we said, they have perpetrated against all rulers and peoples, although most extensively and flagrantly against the Italian peoples and the Roman rulers. But this is not their only aim, for with all their resourcefulness they are scheming to perpetrate similar or greater outrages upon the other states, taking every external step they dare for the realization of this aim. Nevertheless, they well know (although they pretend it is not so and strive both to obfuscate and to deny it with poetic, shadowy words) that to the human legislator belongs the authority to bestow all privileges and concessions, and to take them away when such removal is judged by it to be expedient; and hence the Roman bishops go to all vicious lengths to prevent the election and inauguration of the Roman ruler, conscious as they are of their own and their predecessors' ingratitude and viciousness, and fearing that their privileges and concessions will be forcibly revoked by the Roman ruler, and that they will have to suffer well-deserved punishment.

And again because of this fear and because the aforesaid privileges would only through chicanery offer them the means to seize the powers, jurisdictions, and possessions of other states, since some rulers perhaps claim exemption from the authority of the ruler of the Romans, the Roman bishops have sought to gain their ends through another crafty scheme. For they have assumed a title which they proclaim to be theirs and which they strive to make the instrument of these nefarious designs, the title of "plenitude of power," which they claim Christ gave to them in the person of St. Peter, inasmuch as they are the particular successors of this apostle. And by means of this execrable title and these equivocally sophistical statements which all believers everywhere and always must deny as being false in every sense, the Roman bishops have hitherto misreasoned, and are now misreasoning, and are striving to continue to misreason and to cast into servitude to themselves all the rulers, peoples, groups, and individuals in the world. For they assumed the title of plenitude of power first of all in that sense in which it seems to mean the universal cure of souls or a universal pastorate, and then in that sense in which it means the power to absolve all men from guilt and punishment under the guise of piety, charity, and mercy; but then, . . . they gradually and secretly effected a transfor-

mation, and finally claimed the title in that sense whereby they understand plenitude of power to mean the universal authority and supreme jurisdiction or coercive rulership over all rulers, peoples, and temporal things; this transformation and the resultant presumptuous claim being based, although wrongly, upon their metaphorical expositions of the texts.

That the deceptions of these bishops may no longer be hidden, I, as a herald of the truth, urgently proclaim and say to you, kings, princes, peoples, tribes, and men of all tongues, that by this written statement of theirs, which is most clearly false in its every sense, the Roman bishops with their coterie of clergymen or cardinals do the greatest harm to you all. For they are striving to cast you into subjection to them, and they will succeed if you allow this statement to go unchallenged, and especially if you allow it to have the force and validity of law. Note, thus, that if anyone has the primary authority to revoke the decree of any ruler or judge, then it necessarily follows that he has jurisdiction and coercive rulership over that ruler or judge, as well as the power to establish, disestablish, and depose his government. . . .

However, in order that the words or writings of the Roman bishops may no longer infect any person's mind, let us reiterate that although the gospel spoke truly in calling Christ "king of kings and lord of lords," and although it would still have been true to have added: "and of all creatures," nevertheless the person who asserted that any power of rulership or coercive jurisdiction, let alone plenary power, was given to the Roman or any other bishop in the person of St. Peter or of any other apostle, uttered a falsehood and an open lie which is contrary to the manifest doctrine of Christ. . . .

This plenitude of power, then, has in its past development been used by the Roman bishops continually for the worse, and it is still being so used, especially against the Roman ruler and government. For most fully upon the latter can these bishops perpetrate this vicious outrage of subjecting governments to themselves, because discord and strife both among the Roman subjects themselves and against their ruler have been stirred up in the past, and are still being stirred up and nourished, by these so-called "pastors" or "most holy fathers."

. . . Neither Peter nor any other apostle was greater than Paul, but rather they were all friends and equal. . . . in authority bestowed upon them immediately by Christ.

. . . The Roman bishop is not by God's immediate ordainment the particular successor of St. Peter or of any other apostle in such a way that superior authority over the other bishops belongs to him because of this. . . .

This treatise will be called *Defender of Peace,* because it discusses and explains the principal causes whereby civil peace or tranquillity exists and is preserved, and whereby the opposed strife arises and is checked and destroyed. For this treatise makes known the authority, the cause, and the concordance of divine and human laws and of all coercive governments, which are the standards of human acts, in whose proper unimpeded measure civil peace or tranquillity consists.

. . . The ruler will also learn that he must do nothing apart from the laws, especially on important matters, without the consent of the subject multitude or legislator, and that the multitude or legislator must not be provoked by injury, because in its expressed will consists the virtue and authority of government. . . .

. . . The subject multitude will also learn the extent to which it is possible to see to it that the ruler or any other part of the community does not assume for itself the arbitrary discretion to make judgments or to perform any other civil acts contrary to or apart from the laws.

For when these truths are comprehended, retained in mind, and diligently heeded and observed, the state or any other temperate civil community whatsoever will be preserved in peaceful or tranquil existence; through this, men who live a civil life attain a sufficiency of worldly life, while without it they are necessarily deprived of such sufficiency and are poorly disposed for eternal beatitude as well. That these are the ends and the best objects of human desire.

ERASMUS
UNIVERSAL PEACE

Desiderius Erasmus was a Dutch cleric at the end of the fifteenth century who combined Petrarch's neoclassical humanism with the earnestness of the Modern Devotion movement and Thomas Aquinas' sweet rationalism. Erasmus, a free-floating intellectual and a tireless self-promoter, gained a great reputation as a Biblical scholar and social commentator. He envisioned the dawn of a new era based on universal peace, social justice, and dissemination of Christian and classical learning. His plea for peace, published in 1517, while well received, did not have a practical outcome. Europe plunged into a century of international conflict. But Erasmus' *A Complaint of Peace* remains a memorial to the best intentions of the Christian, socially directed humanism he represented.

Portrait of Erasmus of Rotterdam

A COMPLAINT OF PEACE SPURNED AND REJECTED BY THE WHOLE WORLD

Peace speaks: If it were to their advantage for men to shun, spurn, and reject me, although I have done nothing to deserve it, I would only lament the wrong done me and their injustice; but since in rejecting me they deny themselves the source of all human happiness and bring on themselves a sea of disasters of every kind, I must shed tears rather for the misery they suffer than for any wrong they do me. I should have liked simply to be angry with them, but I am driven to feel pity and sorrow for their plight. To repel in any way one who loves you is cruel, to reject a benefactor is ungrateful, to distress your universal provider and guardian is wicked; but for men to deny themselves all the many remarkable benefits I bring with me, and deliberately to prefer instead a foul morass of manifold evils must surely look like the height of madness. Anger is the proper reaction to criminals, but for men thus hounded by the Furies what can we do but shed tears? They need our tears for no better reason than that they shed none for themselves; they have no greater unhappiness than in being unaware that they are unhappy, for the mere recognition of the gravity of a disease is a step towards recovery of health.

If then I am Peace, praised aloud by gods and men, the fount and source, the sustainer, amplifier, and preserver of all the good things of heaven or earth; if without me there can be no prosperity, no security, nothing sacred or undefiled, nothing pleasurable for men or acceptable to the gods; if on the other hand war is a kind of encircling ocean of all the evils in the world, if through its inherent wickedness prosperity immediately declines, increase dwindles, towers are undermined, sound foundations are destroyed, and sweetness is embittered; in short, if war is so unholy a thing that it is the greatest immediate destroyer of all piety and religion, if nothing is so unfortunate for men and hateful to the gods, in the name of immortal God I must say this: who would believe those beings to be human or possessed of any spark of sanity when they devote so much expenditure and application, such great effort and artifice, amid so many anxieties and dangers, to rid themselves of me—such as I am—while they are willing to pay the heavy price they do for such a burden of evils?

If I were rejected by wild animals in this way, I could bear it more easily and attribute their hostility towards me to nature, which endowed them with a savage disposition; if I were hateful to dumb cattle I would forgive their ignorance because they have been denied the intelligence which alone can discern my qualities. The shameful and monstrous truth is that Nature has produced only one animal gifted with reasoning power and possessed of divine insight, and created only one fitted for good will and concord, and yet you could put me amongst any wild beasts or dumb cattle and I should find a place there sooner than amongst men.

Even between the many celestial bodies, different as they are in motion and power, throughout so many centuries treaties have been established and maintained. The conflicting forces of the elements are evenly balanced so as to preserve unbroken peace, and despite their fundamental opposition they maintain concord by mutual consent and communication. In the bodies of living creatures we see how faithfully the limbs support each other and how ready they are to provide mutual assistance. And what can be so dissimilar as body and soul? Yet the closeness of the tie with which Nature has bound them together is indeed revealed when they are torn apart. Just as life is nothing other than the union of body and soul, so health is the harmony between all the parts of the body.

Animals, though they lack the faculty of reason, live together peacefully and harmoniously according to their different species; elephants, for example, live in herds, pigs and sheep graze together, cranes and rooks fly in flocks. Storks form their own communities and give us lessons in loyalty, dolphins protect each other with mutual services, and the harmony prevailing in colonies of ants and bees is well known. Shall I give further instances, where reason is lacking but not feeling? You can find friendliness in trees and plants. Some are barren unless they have a male nearby; the vine embraces the elm and the peach welcomes the vine. Even where things lack sense perception of the benefit of peace; though they have no power to perceive, yet they come very close to those having perception because they have life. Nothing could be so insensible as a stone, and yet you could say that stones too have a sense of peace and concord; thus the magnet draws iron to itself and holds it when attracted. Moreover, is there not some agreement between the fiercest of animals? Savage lions do not fight each other, nor does a boar threaten a fellow boar with his murderous tusks; there is peace amongst lynxes, no fighting between snakes, and the concord between wolves has won fame in proverbs. Furthermore, what is even more amazing, the evil spirits who first destroyed the harmony between heavenly beings and mortal men and continue to do so today can still observe a truce amongst themselves and maintain their tyranny by agreement, such as it is.

Only men, for whom concord was so fitting and who have the greatest need of it, are not reconciled to each other by Nature, so powerful and effective in other respects, or united by education; they can be neither bound together by the many advantages of agreement nor persuaded to love each other through their awareness and experience of many powerful evils. All men have the same shape and voice, whereas all other kinds of animal differ very widely in bodily shape; to man alone has been given the power of reason, which is common to all and shared with no other living creature. He is the only animal with the gift of speech, the chief promoter of friendly relationships; the seeds of learning and the virtues alike are implanted in him, along with a mild and gentle disposition which is inclined towards good will between him and his fellows, so that he delights in being loved for himself and takes pleasure in being of service to others—so long as he has not been corrupted by base desires, as if by Circe's potions, and degenerated from man to beast. Hence it is, I believe, that the word 'humane' is generally applied to anything to do with mutual good will. Man has also the capacity for tears, proof of a disposition which is readily persuaded, so that if some difference has arisen and a cloud has overcast the clear sky of friendship, a reconciliation can easily be achieved.

Now take a look at all the reasons Nature has provided for concord. She was not satisfied simply with the attractions of mutual good will; she wanted friendship to be not only enjoyable for man but also essential. So she shared out the gifts of mind and body in a way that would ensure that no one should be provided with everything and not need on occasion the assistance of the lowly; she gave men different and unequal capacities, so that their inequality could be evened out by mutual friendships. Different regions provided different products, the very advantage of which taught exchange between them. To all other creatures she assigned their own armour and weapons for self-protection, but man alone she made weak and unarmed and unable to find safety except in treaties and the need of one man for another. Need created cities, need taught the value of alliance between them, so that with combined forces they could repel the attacks of wild beasts or brigands.

Indeed, there is nothing in human affairs which can be self-sufficient. At the very start of life, the human race would have died out at once if it had not been propagated by conjugal harmony; for man would not be born at all, or would die immediately at birth and lose life as he entered it, if the tiny infant were not helped by the kind hand of the midwife and the kind care of his nurse. To meet the same need, Nature has implanted the glowing spark of family affection, so that parents can love the child they have not yet seen; and to this she has added the reciprocal love of children for their parents, so that in their turn they can relieve the helplessness of the old by their support; and we have what all alike find praiseworthy and the Greeks name so aptly 'mutual affection.' Then there are the ties of kinship and affinity, and similarity of disposition, interests, and appearance amongst several people which is certain to foster good will; many too possess a mysterious kind of spiritual perceptiveness and a marvellous propensity towards reciprocal love, something which the Ancients attributed in admiration to a man's godhead.

So Nature provided all these arguments for peace and concord, so many lures and inducements to draw us towards peace, so many means of coercion. But then what Fury appeared with such harmful powers, to scatter, demolish, and destroy them all and to sow an insatiable lust for fighting in the human heart? If custom did not blunt first our sense of amazement and then our awareness of evil, who would believe that there are men endowed with human reason who thus fight, brawl, and rage against each other in perpetual discord, strife, and war? Finally, they confound everything, sacred and profane, with pillaging, bloodshed, disaster, and destruction; no bond is sufficiently sacred to check them in their frenzy for mutual extinction. Were there nothing else, the common name of 'man' should be sufficient to ensure concord amongst men. But granted that Nature, who is such a powerful influence even on wild animals, can do nothing for men, has Christ no influence at all on Christians? And granted that Nature's teaching may well prove inadequate, although it is highly effective even where there is no perception, since the teaching of Christ is so far superior to Nature's, why does it not bring home to those who profess to follow it the importance of what is especially trying to promote, namely peace and mutual good will? Or at least dissuade men from the wickedness, savagery, and madness of waging war?

THE RISE OF PARLIAMENT

The English Parliament had begun in the thirteenth century as an instrument of royal power. Representatives of the gentry in the county courts and burgesses in the towns were added to special meetings of the king's council to help with administrative and legal matters and give consent to innovative forms of national taxation. But by the late fourteenth century Parliament had become an effective institution for limiting the legislative and tax powers of the monarchy and for exercising oversight on the king's ministers. At this time the lords and the commons had separated into distinct corporate bodies, the House of Lords and the House of Commons. The "Good Parliament" of 1376, dominated by opponents of John of Gaunt, Duke of Lancaster, marked an important advancement in the operations of the House of Commons. The Commons now elected their own Speaker, one Peter de la Mare, the steward or estate manager of the Earl of March, who was leading the anti-Lancastrian aristocrat faction. The Speaker's functions were to represent the Commons ("speak for" them) to the king, his ministers, and the lords, and to preside over debates in the House of Commons, which also in this Parilament asserted its right to impeach royal ministers for corrupt and illegal conduct. The following is the first extant record of a debate in the House of Commons. It was not an official record (that didn't come until 1800), but it is a full account by an eyewitness, doubtless one of the M.P.'s. What is important here is that as medieval government moved toward a protomodern secular, sovereign state such as Marsilio of Padua envisioned, the English had in Parliament the instrument for implementing the additional political goal that Marsilio advocated, namely popular sovereignty, the people's control over legislation and administration. Thereby, the rule of law over the will of the king that Bracton and Thomas Aquinas had advocated found an institutional means of long-term implementation. Many European counties had parliamentary estates in the Middle Ages, but only in England did parliamentary government endure and become one of the most important of medieval legacies.

. . . And on the said second day all the knights and commons aforesaid assembled and went into the chapter house and seated themselves about [the room] one next another. And they began to talk about their business, the matters before the parliament, saying that it would be well at the outset for them to be sworn to each other to keep counsel regarding what was spoken and decided among them, and loyally and without concealment to deliberate and ordain for the benefit of the kingdom. And to do this all unanimously agreed, and they took a good oath to be loyal to each other. Then one of them said that, if any of us knew of anything to say for the benefit of the king and the kingdom, it would be well for him to set forth among us what he knew and then, one after the other, [each of the rest could say] what lay next his heart.

Thereupon a knight of the south country rose and went to the reading desk in the centre of the chapter house so that all might hear and, pounding on the said desk, began to speak in this fashion: "*Jube domine benedicere, etc.*" [a Latin grace]. My lords, you have heard the grievous matters before the parliament—how our lord the king has asked of the clergy and the commons a tenth and a fifteenth and customs on wool and other merchandise for a year or two. And in my opinion it is much to grant, for the commons are so weakened and impoverished by the divers tallages and taxes which they have paid up to the present that they cannot sustain such a charge or at this time pay it. Besides, all we have given to the war for a long time we have lost because it has been badly wasted and falsely expended. And so it would be well to consider how our lord the king can live and govern his kingdom and maintain the war from his demesne property, and not hold to ransom his liegemen of the land. Also, as I have heard, there are divers people who, without his knowledge, have in their hands goods and treasure of our lord the king amounting to a great sum of gold and silver; and they have falsely concealed the said goods, which through guile and extortion they gained in many ways to the great damage of our lord the king and the kingdom. For the present I will say no more. *Tu autem domine meserere nostris.*" And he went back to his seat among his companions.

Thereupon another knight arose and went to the reading desk and said: "My lords, our companion has spoken to good purpose, and now, as God will give me grace, I will tell you one thing for the benefit of the kingdom. You have heard how it was ordained by common counsel in parliament that the staple of wool and other merchandise should be wholly at Calais, to the great advantage of our lord the king; and then the said town was governed and ruled by merchants of England, and they took nothing by way of payments to maintain the war or for the government of the said town. And afterwards the said staple was suddenly removed to divers cities and towns of England, and the merchants were ousted from

Calais, together with their wives and their households, without the knowledge or consent of parliament, but for the benefit of a few, illegally and against the statute thereupon made; so that the lord of Latimer and Richard Lyons of London and others could have advantages. And by concealment they took great sums of the maltote, which rightfully the king should have, because each year, to keep the town, the king spends sums amounting to £8000 of gold and silver, without getting anything there, where no expense used to be necessary. Wherefore it would be well to provide a remedy by advising that the staple should be restored to Calais." And he would say no more, but went back to his seat.

And the third man rose and went to the reading desk and said: "My lords, our companions have spoken very well and to good purpose. But it is my opinion that it would not be profitable or honourable for us to deliberate on such great affairs and such grievous matters for the benefit of the kingdom without the counsel and aid of those greater and wiser than we are, or to begin such procedure without the assent of the lords. Wherefore it would be well at the outset to pray our lord the king and his wise council in the parliament that they may grant and assign to us certain bishops and certain earls, barons, and bannerets, such as we may name, to counsel and aid us and to hear and witness what we shall say." And to this all agreed. Then two or three more arose in the same manner, one after the other, and spoke on various subjects. . . .

About the same time a knight from the march of Wales, who was steward to the earl of March and was named Sir Peter de la Mare, began to speak where the others had spoken, and he said: "My lords, you have well heard what our companions have had to say and what they have known and how they have expressed their views; and, in my opinion, they have spoken loyally and to good purpose." And he rehearsed, word for word, all the things that they had said, doing so very skilfully and in good form. And besides he advised them on many points and particulars, as will be more fully set forth below. And so they ended the second day.

Then on the third day all the knights and commons assembled in the said chapter house and day after day until the next Friday held discussion concerning various matters and [particularly] the extortions committed by divers persons, through treachery, as they were advised. During which discussion and counsel, because the said Sir Peter de la Mare had spoken so well and had so skilfully rehearsed the arguments and views of his companions, and had informed them of much that they did not know, they begged him on their part to assume the duty of expressing their will in the great parliament before the said lords, as to what they had decided to do and say according to their conscience. And the said Sir Peter, out of reverence to God and his good companions and for the benefit of the kingdom, assumed that duty [of speaker of the House of Commons]. . . .

And thereupon the following prelates and lords were assigned in parliament . . . to go to the said commons and be of aid to them, joining with them and discussing the said matters that had been declared to them, as aforesaid. . . .

Item, the commons, considering the sufferings of the land . . ., pray that the council of our lord the king may be afforced with lords of the land, prelates, and others, to remain constantly at the number of ten or twelve according to the king's will; so that no important business shall there pass or be determined without the advice and consent of all. . . . And our lord the king, believing the said request to be honourable and of good advantage to him and all his kingdom, has granted it. . . .

And afterwards the said commons came into parliament and made open protestation. . . . Then the said commons made complaint in parliament especially of the persons mentioned below, affirming that many deceits and other wrongs had been inflicted upon the king and his kingdom, as appears below. . . .

Hereafter follow the petitions presented in writing to the parliament by the commons, together with the responses made to those petitions in the same parliament. . . .

THE LEARNED PROFESSIONS

The requirements of what has been variously called the liberal democratic state and civil society involved not only secular sovereignty and parliamentary government but the operation of highly autonomous learned professions within the perimeter of the state. To the two traditional professions of the clergy and the military, medieval society added the legal and medical professions. Their operation imposed heavily on people's lives, as they do today. A hallmark of a civil society is your greater dependence upon the word of your doctor and lawyer than on government officials' communications. By this criterion England was a civil society by 1450. The fifteenth-century English medical profession was divided into three parts: physicians (internal medicine), surgeons, and apothecaries (pharmacists). Nursing did not become a learned profession until the late nineteenth century. The practice of surgery meant mostly amputation of limbs (this focus didn't change until the late nineteenth century). Here are the elaborate rules set down for the practice of surgery in mid-fourteenth-century London; the influence of craft guild regulations is evident. These medical rules are followed by a chief justice's description of the Inns of Court, the combined law schools and bar associations, in London about 1450. The four Inns of Court are still there in the same location in London, still providing the same services. In England, a lawyer still cannot be a barrister (litigator) in the high court unless he is a graduate of the Inns of Court. The postsecondary education of the sons of gentry in 1450 occurred more often in the Inns of Court than in the universities, unless they were destined for an ecclesiastical or academic career. It is still true that admission to the Inns of Court depends more heavily on social than on intellectual criteria. An early-sixteenth-century written bar exam has survived. It is easy.

RULES FOR SURGEONS

First, it behoves a surgeon who wishes to succeed in this craft always to put God first in all his doings, and always meekly to call with heart and mouth for his help, and sometimes give of his earnings to the poor, so that they by their prayers may gain him grace of the Holy Ghost. And he must not be found rash or boastful in his sayings or in his deeds; and he must abstain from much speech, especially among great men; and he must answer cautiously to all questions, so that he may not be trapped by his own words. For if his works are known to disagree often with his words and his promises, he will be held more unworthy, and he will tarnish his own good fame. . . . A surgeon should not laugh or joke too much; and as far as he can without harm, he should avoid the company of knaves and dishonest persons. He should be always occupied in things that belong to his craft, whether reading, studying, writing, or praying; the study of books is of great advantage to the surgeon, both by keeping him occupied and by making him wiser. Above all, it helps him much to be found always sober; for drunkenness destroys all wisdom and brings it to nought. In strange places he should be content with the meats and drinks which he finds there, using moderation in all things. . . . He must scorn no man. . . . If anyone talks to him about another surgeon, he must

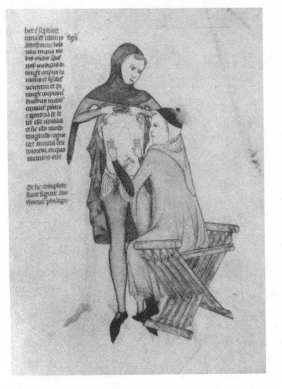

Anatomical examination

being able to undertake a case so that he does not hurt or anger some great man or friend, and does not interrupt some necessary work. Otherwise he could pretend to be hurt or ill or give some other likely excuse if he does not want to undertake a case. If he does undertake a case, he should make a clear agreement about payment and take the money in advance. But the surgeon should be sure not to make any definite pronouncement in any illness, unless he has first seen the sickness and the signs of it. When he has made an examination, even though he may think that the patient may be cured, he should warn the patient in his prognosis of the perils to come if treatment should be deferred. And if he sees that the patient is eager for the cure, then the surgeon must boldly adjust his fee to the man's status in life. But the surgeon should always beware of asking too little, for this is bad both for the market and the patient. Therefore for a case of fistula in ano, when it is curable, the surgeon may reasonably ask of a great man 100 marks or £40 with robes and fees to the value of 100 shillings each year for the rest of his life. From lesser men he may ask £40 or 40 marks without fees; but he must never take less than forty shillings. Never in my life have I taken less than 100 shillings for the cure of this disease; but of course every man must do what he thinks is right and most expedient. And if the patient or his friends and servants asks how long the cure will take, the surgeon had better always say twice as long as he really thinks; thus if a surgeon hopes to heal the patient in twenty weeks, which is the common period, let him add another twenty. For it is better to name a longer term for recovery than that the cure should drag on, a thing which might cause the patient to despair at the very time when confidence in the doctor is the greatest aid to recovery. For if the patient should later wonder or ask why the surgeon estimates so long for recovery when he was able to cure the patient in half the time, the surgeon should answer that it was because the patient had a strong heart and bore pain well and that he was of good complexion (that is, having such a combination of the four honours as would speed recovery) and that his flesh healed quickly; and he must think of other causes that would

neither set him at nought nor praise nor commend him too much, but he may answer courteously thus: "I have no real knowledge of him, but I have neither learnt nor heard anything of him but what is good and honest.". . . A surgeon should not look too boldly at the lady or the daughters or other fair women in great men's houses, nor offer to kiss them, nor to touch them secretly or openly . . . lest he arouses the indignation of the lord or one of his household. As far as possible, he should not annoy servants, but rather to try to gain their love and their good will. He must always abstain from harlotry in both word and deed, for if he practises harlotry in secret places, sometime he will be found out and publicly discredited for his evil practices. . . . If sick men or any of their friends come to the surgeon to ask help or advice, let him be neither too brusque nor too familiar, but adjust his manner according to the character of the person; to some respectful, to some friendly. . . . Also it is a help for him to have excuses ready for not please the patient, for by such words are patients made proud and glad. And a surgeon should always be soberly dressed, not likening himself in clothing or bearing to minstrels, but rather after the manner of a clerk; for any discreet man clad in clerk's dress may sit at a gentleman's table. A surgeon must also have clean hands and well shaped nails, free from all blackness and dirt. And he should be courteous at the lord's table, and not displease the guests sitting by either in word or deed; he should hear many things but speak only few. For a wise man says: "It is better to use ears than the tongue". . . . And when he does speak, his words should be brief, and, as far as possible, fair and reasonable without swearing. But he must beware that he never tell a lie; for if he be found truthful in his speech, few or none will lack confidence in his deeds. A young doctor should also learn good proverbs relating to his craft to comfort his patients. If patients complain that their medicines are bitter or sharp and so on, then the doctor shall say to the patient: "It is said in the last lesson of matins of the Nativity of Our Lord that Our Lord Jesus Christ came into the world for the health of mankind in the manner of a good and wise doctor." . . . Moreover, the surgeon should comfort his patient by admonishing him to be of great heart in pain; for a great heart will make a man hardy and strong to suffer sharp and grievous pain. He, indeed, who is faint-hearted is unlikely to be cured, for in all my life I have seen very few addicted to this failing who have been cured in any sickness. . . . It is also expedient for the surgeon to be able to tell good honest tales that may make the patient laugh, both from the Bible and from other great books; and also any other stories that are not too dubious which may make the patient more cheerful. A surgeon should never betray inadvertently the confidences of his patients, either men or women, nor belittle one to another, even if he should have cause . . . for if men see that you can keep other men's confidences, they will have more confidence in you.

THE INNS OF COURT

The laws of England are learned in three languages, namely, English, French, and Latin. . . .

Thus, since the laws of England are learned in these three languages, they could not be conveniently learned or studied in the Universities, where the Latin language alone is used. But those laws are taught and learned in a certain public academy, more convenient and suitable for their apprehension than any University. For this academy is situated near the king's courts, where these laws are pleaded and disputed from day to day, and judgements are rendered in accordance with them by the judges, who are grave men, mature, expert and trained in these laws. So those laws are read and taught in these courts as if in public schools, to which students of the law flock every day in term-time. That academy, also, is situated between the site of those courts and the City of London, which is the richest of all the cities and towns of that realm in all the necessaries of life. And that academy is not situated in the city, where the tumult of the crowd could disturb the student's quiet, but is a little isolated in a suburb of the city, and nearer to the aforesaid courts, so that the students are able to attend them daily at pleasure without the inconvenience of fatigue.

But, prince, in order that the form and arrangement of this academy may be clear to you, I will now describe it as far as I can. For there are in this academy ten lesser inns, and sometimes more, which are called Inns of Chancery. To each of them at least a hundred students belong, and to some of them a much greater number, though they do not always gather in them all at the same time. These students are, indeed, for the most part, young men, learning the originals and something of the elements of law, who, becoming proficient therein as they mature, are absorbed into the greater inns of the academy, which are called the Inns of Court. Of these greater inns there are four in number, and some two hundred students belong in the aforementioned form to the least of them. In these greater inns, no student could be maintained on less expense than £13 6s 8d a year, and if he had servants to himself alone, as the majority have, then he will by so much the more bear expenses. Because of this costliness, there are not many who learn the laws in the inns except the sons of nobles. For poor and common people cannot bear so much cost for the maintenance of their sons, and merchants rarely desire to reduce their stock by such annual burdens. Hence it comes about that there is scarcely a man learned in the laws to be found in the realm, who is not noble or sprung of noble lineage. So they care more for their nobility and for the preservation of their honour and reputation than others of like estate. In these greater inns, indeed, and also in the lesser, there is, beside as school of law, a kind of academy of all the manners that the nobles learn. There they learn to sing and to exercise themselves in every kind of harmonics. They are also taught there to practise dancing and all games proper for nobles, as those brought up in the king's household are accustomed to practise. In the vacations most of them apply themselves to the study of legal science, and at festivals to the reading, after the divine services, of Holy Scripture and of chronicles. This is indeed a cultivation of virtues and a banishment of all vice. So for the sake of the acquisition of virtue and the discouragement of vice, knights, barons, and also other magnates, and the nobles of the realm place their sons in these inns, although they do not desire

them to be trained in the science of the laws, nor to live by its practice, but only by their patrimonies. Scarcely any turbulence, quarrels, or disturbance ever occur there, but delinquents are punished with no other punishment than expulsion from communion with their society, which is a penalty they fear more than criminals elsewhere fear imprisonment and fetters. For a man once expelled from one of these societies is never received into the fellowship of any other of those societies. Hence the peace is unbroken and the conversation of all of them is as the friendship of united folk. It is not, forsooth, necessary to relate here the manner in which the laws are learned in these inns, for, prince, you are not to experience it. But be assured that it is pleasant, and in every way suited to the study of that law, and also worthy of every regard. But I want you to know one point—that neither in Orléans, where the canon as well as the civil laws are studied, and whither students resort from all parts, nor Angers, nor Caen, nor any other University of France, except only Paris, are so many students of mature age to be found as in this academy, though all the students there are of English birth alone.

EATING WELL IS THE BEST REVENGE

Another indicator of arrival at a condition of civil society is when the text of recipes is as well-articulated as the wording of prayers. These extracts from fifteenth-century English cookbooks indicate that England was fast approaching that point at the close of the Middle Ages. The only problem was that the English insisted on holding on to this cuisine well into the second half of the twentieth century.

FRUIT PUDDING

Take strawberries, and wash them, in season, in good red wine; then strain through a cloth, and put them in a pot with good almond milk; cover it with wheat flour or rice flour, and make it thick, and let it boil, and add currants, saffron, pepper, plenty of sugar, powdered ginger, cinnamon, galingale; make it acid with vinegar, and add a little

white grease; colour it with alkanet, and mix it together, sprinkle it with the grains of pomegranate, and then serve it up.

PORK PIE

Take fresh pork, cut it and grind it on a mortar, and put it into a fair vessel. Take the white and the yokes of eggs, and strain into a vessel through a strainer, and mix with the pork. Then take pines [seeds of fir or pepper pines], currants, and fry them in fresh grease, and add powdered pepper, ginger, cinnamon, sugar, saffron, and salt; and put all in a pie crust, and set on the crust lid above it, pines, cut dates, raisins, and small birds, or hard yokes of eggs; and if you use birds, fry them in a little grease, before you put them on the pie crust, and gild with yolks of eggs, and saffron. Bake the pie until it is done and then serve.

Take fair mutton that has been roasted or else capons or such other flesh, and mince it fair; put it into a little pot, or else between two silver dishes. Add fair parsley, and onions minced small; then add wine and a little vinegar or verjuice, powdered pepper, cinnamon, salt and saffron, and let it stew on the fair coals, and then serve. If you have no wine or vinegar, take ale, mustard, and a quantity of verjuice, and do this instead of wine or vinegar.

FRITTERS

Take the yolks of eggs, put them through a strainer, add fair flour, yeast, and ale; stir it together until it is thick. Take pared apples, cut them thick like sacramental wafers, lay them in butter; then put them into a frying pan, and fry them in fair grease or butter until they are golden brown. Then put them in dishes and strew sugar on them enough, and serve.

ROASTED PEACOCK

Take a peacock, break its neck, and cut its throat, and flay it, skin and feathers together, with the head still attached to the skin of the neck, and keep the skin and the feathers whole together. Draw the bird like a hen, and keep the bone to the neck whole, and roast it. And set the bone of the neck above the spit, as the bird was wont to sit when it was alive, and bend the legs to the body, as it was wont to sit when it was alive. And when it is roasted enough, take it off and let it cool, and then wind the skin with the feathers and the tail about the body, and serve as if the bird were still alive; or else pluck it clean and roast it and serve it as you do a hen.

FRUIT TART

Take figs, and boil them in wine, and grind them small, and put them in a vessel. And take powdered pepper, cinnamon, cloves, mace, powdered ginger, pines, raisins or currants, saffron, and salt, and add. And then make a fair low pie crust, and put the mixture in it, and put pines on top. And cut dates and fresh salmon in fair pieces or else fresh eels, and parboil them a little in wine, and place on top of the mixture in the pie. And cover the pie fair with the same pastry, and gild the crust outside with saffron and almond milk. Set it in the oven and let it bake.

JOACHIM OF FLORA

IMAGING THE END

Construction of a civil society and the theory to support it occurred in the context of persistent medieval apocalyptic and eschatalogical speculation—the envisioning of an early end of the world attendant upon the Second Coming. The most influential articulation of this vision of the imminent end of human time was propounded around 1200 by a southern Italian abbot, Joachim of Flora. The world is entering its final stage in which Babylon, Antichrist, the devil, appears to triumph, but a new era of peace and justice will then begin under the personal rule of Christ. What is important about Joachimism is not the theory of history. Anyone could develop it out of Christian doctrine and the more speculative writings in the Bible. What is important is the anxiety of imminence—the conviction that the termination of history and society is very near. Joachim also prophesied that a small band of holy brothers and sisters, the best kind of monk and nun, would raise the curtain on the final triumphant era of the neomessianic age. The radical wing of the Franciscan order espoused Joachimist doctrine as its special ideology—the last Babylon is the papacy and Antichrist sits on the Throne of Peter, but the little community of Spiritual Franciscans carries the light that turns back darkness. These kinds of eschatalogical speculations remained to the end of the Middle Ages one way of providing an integrative social and cultural vision and constituted the intellectual foundations of the more radical wing of the Protestant Reformation. Combining the idea of a sovereign state with Joachmist apocalyptic historicizing provides the intellectual ambience for modern communism and fascism. The medievals, however, never made this fatal association of the secular judicial and administrative state with an apocalyptic theory of history. The ingredients that comprised the explosive mixture of modern revolutionary totalitarianism are medieval in origin, but not their combustible union.

The Redeemer

It is almost evening. We have been brought to the sunset of this life. For an hour we must put up with weeping so that in the morning we may find joy (Ps. 29:5). Now is the time for the elect to weep over the imminent destruction of that youngest Babylon lest perchance we share in her sins and be forced to partake of her punishments, as if we did not have the letter Thau written on our foreheads (Ezech. 9:4–6; Apoc. 7:4) and were not able to avoid her threatening destruction. "Behold, the day of the Lord is coming; it is a cruel day, one full of shame, a day of wrath and fury that will make the earth waste and wipe out sinners" (Isa. 13:9). . . .

If only those who were born according to the flesh would stop persecuting those who want to walk according to the spirit! As if I had not told the brethren day and night how Joseph was sold into slavery and brought into Egypt by his owners! Those who seek to snuff out the spirit and who despise prophecy must exist, even in the present. Perhaps it is God's will that we cannot bring the mystery to completion soon. This provides no consolation. How many things distract me in many different ways and form a hindrance, with the result that he who is holy is still sanctified by faith and he who is filthy is still made unclean (Apoc. 22:11) until the hour of temptation suddenly arrives that is to come to prove those who dwell on earth. . . . Where there is faith and the desire for an explanation, let the whole Church realize that dangerous times approach in which her children will come to a situation in which there will be no power to produce anything. After the present temptation they will cry out at some time. Not too late Christians will be seen to come to the Lord and He will free them from the hand of the persecutor. When they have been freed they will once again take advantage of the peace that God has given to them.

The Lord will hand them over to their enemies so that they learn not to blaspheme (1 Tim. 1:20). But when the time of wrath and the hour of temptation will have been completed, the Lord will gaze upon his people. His heart will rejoice, and no man shall take his joy from them (John 16:22). There will be a little while when the humble will not see their king because the wicked will rule over the earth. And there will be another little while (Jo. 16:19). When this little while is finished they will begin to see a time of peace like nothing that has been since men began to exist on earth.

RETROMEDIEVALISM I: THE DIVINE COMEDY

Whatever the advancements toward civil society and secular humanism and science, challenged by fervent apocalyptic visions, the Middle Ages still remained at the core a culture rooted in the fusion of aristocratic heroism, hierarchic authority, and middle class sentimentality. While this world was moving powerfully toward a postmedieval secular and liberal culture on the one side, and eschatalogical nihilism on the other, two of the finest poets of the later medieval centuries held back from these extremes, refining once again the threefold elements of the authentic Middle Ages. The first of these remarkable works of retromedievalism was written in the early years of the fourteenth century by Dante in the Italian vernacular. Indeed, *The Divine Comedy* created the Italian language as literary vernacular. Dante came from an upper middle class family in Florence. Being on the losing side in a political quarrel, he was exiled from his beloved city on the Arno for the last two decades of his life. The yearning of the exile for his homeland combined with his Christian piety and motifs derived from the French romance to create a temperament engaged in perpetual yearning for renewal and return, for finding one's way from the dark wood of despair to the glorious sun-filled empyrean realms of joy and fulfillment. The myth of the eternal return is an architecture of the human mind. In Dante this structure is specifically reinforced by his Florentine homeward-bound imagining, by his Christian hierarchic thrust upward toward the godhead, and not least by a sublimated eroticism that finds erotic satisfaction in dreams of union with an entirely idealized lover whom he had made the theme of a previous book, *The New Life.* In developing these themes and combining them structurally in *The Divine Comedy,* Dante borrowed heavily from Thomist theology. Human reason, personified by Virgil, the Roman poet who was thought (erroneously) to have prophesied the birth of Christ, is Dante's guide through the Inferno and the entryway to Purgatory. There Beatrice—his chivalric, symbolic love—takes over. Beatrice is the beatific vision—the church and its sacraments, the institutional means of grace. She guides him partway up through the Paradise, to reach the highest circles of heaven and the ultimate experience of union with God. St. Bernard of Clairvaux, representing mysticism, assumes the role of Dante's guide. No English translation of *The Divine Comedy* has ever been highly successful. The following by C.H. Sisson is as good as there is. These selections comprise the more theoretical part of the work.

Dante Alighieri and scenes from his *Divine Comedy* outside the walls of the city of Florence

INFERNO

Canto I

Half way along the road we have to go,
I found myself obscured in a great forest,
Bewildered, and I knew I had lost the way.

It is hard to say just what the forest was like,
How wild and rough it was, how overpowering;
Even to remember it makes me afraid.

So bitter it is, death itself is hardly more so;
Yet there was good there, and to make it clear
I will speak of other things that I perceived.

I cannot tell exactly how I got there,
I was so full of sleep at that point of my journey
When, somehow, I left the proper way.

But when I had arrived at the foot of a hill
Which formed the far end of that menacing valley
Where fear had already entered into my heart,

I looked up, and saw the edges of its outline
Already glowing with the rays of the planet
Which shows us the right way on any road.

Then my fear was a little put at rest,
Although it had lain in the pool of my heart
    throughout
The night which I had passed in that pitiful state.

And, as a man who, practically winded,
Staggers out of the sea and up the beach,
Turns back to the dangerous water, and looks at
    it,

So my mind, which still felt as if it was in flight,
Turned back to take another look at the defile
No living person had ever passed before.

When I had rested my weary body a little,
I took up my journey again on that stretch of
    desert,
Walking so that my right foot was always the
    lower.

And, almost at the point where the slope began,
I saw a leopard, extremely light and active,
The skin of which was mottled.

And somehow it managed to stay in front of me
In such a manner that it blocked my way so much
That I was often forced to turn back the road I had
    come.

The time was the beginning of the morning;
And the sun was climbing in company with those
    stars
Which were with him when the divine love

First set those lovely things in motion; and this,
With the hour it was, and the delightful season,
Gave me reason to entertain good hope

Of that wild animal with the brilliant skin:
But not so that I found myself without fear
When a lion appeared before me, as it did.

When he came, he made his way towards me
With head high, and seemed ravenously hungry,
So that the air itself was frightened of him;

And a she-wolf, who seemed, in her thinness,
To have nothing but excessive appetites,
And she has already made many miserable.

She weighed down so heavily upon me
With that fear, which issued from her image,
That I lost hope of reaching the top of the hill.

And, like a man whose mind is on his winnings,
When the time comes for him to lose,
And all his thoughts turn into sorrow and tears:

So I was transformed by that restless animal
Who came against me, and gradually drove me
    down,
Back to the region where the sun is silent.

While I rushed headlong to the lower slopes,
Before my eyes a man offered himself,
One who, for long silence, seemed to be hoarse.

When I saw that fellow in the great desert,
I cried out to him: 'Have pity on me,
Whatever you are, shadow or definite man.'

And he replied: 'Not a man, though I was one,
And my parents were people of Lombardy,
Mantuans, both of them, they were born and bred
    there.

I was born *sub Julio,* although it was late
And I lived in Rome under the good Augustus
In the time of the gods who were false and told
    lies.

I was a poet, and I sang of the just
Son of Anchises, the man who came from Troy,
After the proud Ilion had been burnt down.

But you, why do you come back to such distur-
    bance?
Why do you not climb the delightful mountain
Which is the beginning and reason of all joy?'

'Are you indeed that Virgil, are you the spring
Which spreads abroad that wide water of
    speech?'
When I had spoken, I bowed my head for shame.

'You are the honour and light of other poets;
My long study and great love give me strength
Now, as they made me pore over your book.

You are my master, and indeed my author;
It is from you alone that I have taken
The exact style for which I have been honoured.

Look at the animal which made me turn back;
Help me to handle her, you are famous for wis-
    dom,
For she makes my veins and pulse shudder.'

'You will have to go another way than this,'
He answered, when he saw that I was weeping,
'If you want to get away from this wild place:

For that beast, which has made you so call out,
Does not allow others to pass her way,
But holds them up, and in the end destroys them;

And is by nature so wayward and perverted
That she never satisfies her wilful desires,
But, after a meal, is hungrier than before.

Many are the animals she makes herself a wife to,
And there will be more of them, until the Grey-
    hound
Comes, who will make her die a painful death.

He will not feed on land nor yet on money,
But upon wisdom, love, and upon courage;
His nation will be between Feltro and Feltro.

What he will save is that unassuming Italy
For which the girl Camilla died, Euryalus,
Turnus and Nisus, all of whom died of wounds;

He will pursue that wolf in every city
And put her back in Hell where she belongs,
And from which envy first let her out.

The course I think would be the best for you,
Is to follow me, and I will act as your guide,
And show a way out of here, by a place in eternity,

Where you will hear the shrieks of men without
    hope,
And will see the ancient spirits in such pain
That every one of them calls out for a second
    death;

And then you will see those who, though in the
    fire,
Are happy because they hope that they will
    come,
Whenever it may be, to join the blessed;

Among whom you may climb, but if you do,
It will be with a spirit more worthy than I am;
With her I will leave you, when I depart:

Because the Emperor, who reigns up there,
Since I was one of the rebels against his law,
Does not wish me to enter into his city.

He commands everywhere, and there he rules,
There is his city, there he has his throne:
Happy are those he chooses for that place!'

I said to him: 'Poet, now by that God,
Who is unknown to you, I ask your assistance:
Help me to escape both this evil, and worse;

Lead me now, as you have promised to do,
So that I come to see St Peter's Gate
And those whom you represent as being so sad.'

Then he moved forward, and I kept behind him.

Canto II

The day was going, and the brown evening
Was taking all the creatures of the earth
Away from toil: and I was the only one

Preparing himself to undergo the battle
Alike of the journey, and of that dutifulness,
Which the true memory will recollect.

O Muse! O profound inclination, help me!
O memory, which recorded what I saw,
Here will be shown what there is noble in you.

I began: 'Poet, you who are to be my guide,
Consider whether my strength is adequate
Before you trust me to make this terrible passage.

You tell me that the father of Sylvius,
While still in nature, went to eternity
And was there with the use of all his senses.

But, if the adversary of all evil
Was courteous to him—when one thinks of the
    great effects
Which followed from him, not only who, but
    what—

It does not seem unsuitable to a man of intellect:
Nor that he was chosen in empyreal heaven
To be the father of bountiful Rome and her em-
    pire;

The city and the power which, truth to tell,
Were there established for the holy place
Where the successor of great Peter sits.

By this journey, for which you praise him so,
He came to understand what were the reasons
Of his victory, and of the papal mantle.

And afterwards, the chosen vessel went there,
To bring back reassurance for that faith
Which is the beginning of the way to salvation.

But I, why should I go there? By whose permission?
I am not Aeneas, neither am I Paul;
Neither I nor others think that I deserve it.

Therefore, if I resign myself to going,
I fear my journey may be a foolish one;
You are wise, and understand more than I say.'

And just like somebody who shilly-shallies,
And thinks again about what he has decided,
So that he gives up everything he has started,

I found I was on that obscure hillside:
By thinking about it I spoiled the undertaking
I had been so quick to enter upon in the first place.

'If I have understood what you have said,'
The reply came from that shadow of generosity,
'Your spirit is touched by cowardice, which sometimes

Lies like a load on men, and makes them flag
So that they turn back from the fittest task,
Like an animal which mistakes what it looks at.

But, so that you may rid yourself from fears,
I will tell you why I came, and what I heard
At the point when first I became concerned for you.

I was among those who are in suspense;
And a lady called me, so blessed and beautiful
That I at once begged her to tell me what I should do.

The shining of her eyes was more than starlight;
And she began to speak, gently and quietly,
With the voice of an angel, but in her own language:

"O courteous spirit of that Mantuan
Whose fame endures still in the world, and will
Endure as long as the world itself shall last,

My friend, who is not also the friend of fortune,
On the desert hillside, is in such difficulty
Making his way, that he turns back for fear;

And I fear that already, he may be so far lost
That I have risen too late to be of help,
From all that I have heard of him in heaven.

Now leave this place, and with your apt speech,
And whatever may be necessary for his escape,
Help him, and so bring consolation to me.

I am Beatrice, and that is why I send you;
The place I come from I also wish to return to;
It is love which makes me speak to you as I do.

When I am back, standing before my master,
I shall often talk about you kindly to him."
So she was silent, and then I began:

"O lady of power, through whom, and through whom only,
The human race is better than all the rest
Under that heaven which bends closest to earth!

It pleases me so much to have your command
That if I had done it already, I should think myself slow;
There is no need to explain your wishes further.

But tell me why you do not hesitate
To come down here, into this central place,
From the ample heaven to which you burn to go back."

"Since you would like to be so far informed,
I will tell you briefly," so she replied to me,
"Why I am not afraid to come down here.

One has to fear only the things which have
The power of hurting others; for the rest,
They do not matter, they are not to be feared.

And I am made by God, I thank him, so
That all your suffering has no effect on me,
Nor am I touched by all these burning flames.

There is a gentle lady in heaven, who has pity
On this difficulty I am sending you to,
So that the sharp judgement of heaven is broken.

She called Lucy to her, and her request
Was this: 'Your devoted follower needs help;
I commend him to you, to do the best you can.'

Lucy, the enemy of all cruelty,
Stood up and came to the place where I was
And where I was sitting with the ancient Rachel.

She said: 'Beatrice, you who are a glory of God,
Why do you not help him who loved you so
    greatly
That for your sake he left the common crowd?

Do you not hear his pitiful complaint?
Do you not see the death he is struggling with
By that river over which the sea is powerless?'

Nobody on earth was ever more in haste
To seek an advantage or to avoid an evil
Than I, after such words as that had been spoken,

To come down here from my happy location,
Trusting you on account of your noble language
Which honours you and those who have listened
    to it."

When she had spoken to me in this manner,
Her eyes shining with tears, she turned away:
And that made me even more anxious to come.

And so I came to you, as she wished me to;
Took you away from that wild animal
Which stopped your short cut to the beautiful
    mountain.

What is it then? Why do you dawdle here?
Why do you let such cowardice sleep in your
    heart?
Why have you not more boldness and openness?

When three such ladies care for you in heaven,
Busying themselves about you in that court
And I report so promisingly to you?'

As little flowers, which in a frosty night
Droop and shut tight, when the sun shines on
    them
Stretch and look up, erect upon their stalks,

So I recovered from my failing strength,
My heart so filled with satisfying courage
That I began, like a man just released:

'How generous she was to give her assistance!
And how courteous you were, to obey her so
    quickly,
When she proffered her help and spoke the truth!

My heart is now so set in its desire
To come with you—and it is your words that have
    done this—
That I am back again with my first intention.

Now go, for a single will informs us both;
You are my guide, my master and my lord.'
So I spoke to him and, when he stirred from
    where he was,

I entered upon the deep and thorny way.

Canto III

'Through me you go into the city of weeping;
Through me you go into eternal pain;
Through me you go among the lost people.

Justice is what moved my exalted Maker;
I was the invention of the power of God,
Of his wisdom, and of his primal love.

Before me there was nothing that was created
Except eternal things; I am eternal:
No room for hope, when you enter this place.'

These words, in an uncertain colour,
Were written above a gate; and when I saw them,
I said: 'Master, it is hard to follow the meaning.'

He answered as a man who understood:
'Here you must leave all wariness behind;
All trace of cowardice must be extinguished.

We have come now to the place where, I have
    told you,
You will find the people for whom there is only
    grief:
Those who have lost the benefit of the intellect.'

With that, he put his hand on top of mine,
And looked glad, which made me feel more com-
    fortable,
And so he led me into that secret place.

Here, there were sighings and complaints and
    howlings,
Resounding in an air under no stars;
So that at first I found myself in tears.

A jumble of languages, deformities of speech,
Words which were pain, with intonations of anger,

Voices which were deep and hoarse, hands clapped together,

Made altogether a tumult, round and round,
Unceasingly in that air in which all was colourless,
Just as it might be in a perpetual sandstorm.

And I, who felt my head surrounded by horrors,
Said: 'Master, what then is it that I am hearing?
And what people are these, so crushed by pain?'

He answered: 'That is the manner of existence
Endured by the sad souls of those who live
Without occasion for infamy or praise.

They are mixed with that abject squadron of angels
Who did not think it worth their while to rebel
Or to be faithful to God, but were for themselves.

Heaven chased them out, so as not to become less beautiful,
And the depths of hell also rejected them,
Lest the evil might find occasion to glory over them.'

I said: 'Master, what is it lies so heavily
Upon them, that they call out as they do?'
He answered: 'I will tell you very briefly.

They are without even the hope of death;
Their blind existence is of such abjection
That they are envious of every other fate.

The world does not remember them at all;
Mercy and justice treat them with contempt:
Let us not talk about them. Look and pass on.'

And as I looked at them, I saw a flag
Flapping wildly as it was carried forward,
As if it was not fit to rest a moment;

Behind it came a huge torrent of people;
So many that I never should have thought
Death had been able to undo so many.

When I had recognised a few of them,
I saw and knew the shadow of that man
Who out of cowardice made the great refusal.

I understood at once beyond all doubt
That this was the miserable and useless gang

Of those who please neither God nor his enemies.

That calamitous crowd, who never were alive,
Were naked, and their skins blown with the bites
Of swarms of wasps and hornets following them.

Their faces ran with blood from these attacks
And, mixed with tears, it streamed down to their feet,
Where filthy creeping creatures swallowed it.

And when I cast my eyes a little further,
I saw people on the bank of a great river;
And so I said: 'Master, if you are willing, tell me:

Who are those people, and what is it determines
That they have such anxiety to cross,
Or so it seems to me in this faint light?'

He answered: 'These are things you will be told
When our steps come to a halt, as they will do,
On that sad strip of land beside Acheron.'

Then, with my eyes cast downward out of shame,
For fear that what I had said had given offence,
Until we reached the river I said nothing.

And then, there came towards us in a boat
An old man who was white with brittle hair,
Calling out: 'Woe to you, perverse spirits!

You need not hope that you will ever see heaven;
I have come to take you to the other side,
Into eternal darkness, fire and ice.

And you who are there, and still a living soul,
Keep well away from those there who are dead.'
But, when he saw that I had made no movement,

He said: 'There are other crossings, other ways
For you to reach the shore: do not pass here.
And you should travel in a lighter craft.'

My guide said: 'Charon, do not torment yourself:
It is willed there, where anything can be done
If it is willed: no need for further questions.'

There was no more movement of the bearded cheeks
Of that old pilot of the leaden marshes,
Around whose eyes there burned red rings of flame.

But those spirits, who were worn out and naked,
Changed colour and their teeth began to chatter;
Such was the effect of hearing those harsh words.

Then they blasphemed God and cursed their par-
    ents,
The human race, the place and time, the seed,
The land that it was sown in, and their birth.

And then they gathered, all of them together,
Weeping aloud, upon the evil shore
Which awaits every man who does not fear God.

The devil Charon, with his eyes like coals,
Points at them, and collects them all together;
Whoever dawdles gets a blow from his oar.

As leaves in autumn, one after the other,
Are blown away until the branch has given
All of its spoil back to the earth again,

So was it with the evil seed of Adam;
They threw themselves from that shore one by
    one,
As they were beckoned, like birds obeying a call.

And so they went away on the dark water;
And even before they had been disembarked,
Another flock had collected on this side.

My courteous master spoke to me: 'My son,
Those who have died under the wrath of God
Assemble here from every land on earth;

And they are ready enough to cross the stream,
For the divine justice digs its spurs in
So that their fear is turned into desire.

There is no crossing here for any good spirit;
Therefore, if Charon says he will not have you,
You know what sense you may give to his words.'

When he had finished, the murky countryside
Trembled so much, that even to think of it
Still leaves me terrified and bathed in sweat.

The melancholy land belched out a wind
From which there came a flash of carmine light
That left me utterly insensible;

And I fell, as a man who falls asleep.

Canto IV

There broke upon the deep sleep in my head
A solemn thunder, so that I started
Like someone who is wakened violently;

And so I cast my rested eyes around me,
And having stood up, I looked fixedly
To see what sort of place it was I was in.

The truth is, I was on the outer edge
Of the valley of the sorrowful abyss
Which echoes with infinite lamentations.

It was so dark, so deep, so filled with cloud,
That, when I fixed my eyes upon the bottom,
I could not there discern a single thing.

'Now let us go down into this blind world,'
Began the poet, and his face was pale:
'I will go first, you follow after me.'

And I, who had seen how his colour changed,
Said: 'How shall I come, if you are so afraid,
You who give comfort to me when I waver?'

He answered: 'It is the anguish of the people
Down there, which takes the colour from my
    face;
It is pity, although you take it for fear.

Let's go, it is a long way, we must not stop.'
So he moved forward, and made me follow him
Into that first circle round the abyss.

There, in so far as listening could tell me,
The only lamentations were the sighs,
Yet they made the eternal air tremble.

They came from the sadness, without any tor-
    ment,
Felt by the crowds—there were many of them,
    and huge—
Of infants and of women and of men.

The master said: 'Are you not going to ask
What spirits these are which you see in this place?
I think you should know, before you go on;

They have committed no sin, and if they have
    merits,
That is not enough, because they are not bap-
    tised,

Which all must be, to enter the faith which is
    yours.

And, if they lived before the Christian era,
They did not adore God as he should be adored:
And I am one of those in that position.

For these deficiencies, and no other fault,
We are lost; there is no other penalty
Than to live here without hope, but with desire.'

It grieved my heart when I heard him say that,
Because I knew there were people of high value
Who were in that limbo, as it were suspended.

'But, sir,' I said, 'will you explain to me,'
I asked because I wanted to be certain
About the faith which overcomes all error:

'Did anyone, either through his own merit,
Or through another's, ever get out of here
And achieve blessedness?' He understood

What I implied, and said: 'When I was new here,
I saw a powerful spirit come this way,
Crowned with the insignia of victory.

He took away the shade of our first parent,
With that of Abel and his son, the shade of Noah
And of Moses, the obedient law-giver,

With the patriarch Abraham, and David the king,
Israel with his father and his children,
And with Rachel, for whom he did so much;

And many others, and he made them blessed;
I think that you should know, that before these,
There were no human spirits who were saved.'

We did not stop walking while he spoke,
But went on through the forest none the less,
That forest, I say, which was so crowded with
    spirits.

We had not gone very far on our way
From the river of sleep, when I caught sight of a
    fire
Which carved for itself a hemisphere in the dark-
    ness.

We were still some little distance from the spot,
But not so far that I could not catch a glimpse
Of the honourable people who stood there.

'O you who honour sciences and arts,
Who then are these, who have so much honour,
    that
In this manner they are separated from the
    others?'

He answered me: 'The honoured reputation,
Which still re-echoes in your life up there,
Wins grace in heaven, which gives them this ad-
    vantage.'

Meanwhile, I heard a voice: 'Do honour,' it said,
'To the magnificent poet, for his shade,
Which had departed, is with us once again.'

And when the voice had stopped and all was
    quiet,
I saw four immense shadows come towards us:
They had no appearance either of grief or happi-
    ness.

The good master opened his mouth to speak:
'Observe the one who, sword in hand, comes
    first,
In front of the three others, as their chief.

That is Homer, there is no poet above him;
The next who comes is Horace, the satirist;
Ovid is third, then last of all comes Lucan.

Because they are all poets as I am,
It was our common name the voice called out;
They welcome me, and in that they do well.'

And so I saw together that excellent school
Of those who are masters of exalted song
Which, like an eagle, flies above the others.

When they had talked together a little while,
They turned towards me with signs of recogni-
    tion;
And my master smiled to see them do so.

And then, they did me a still greater honour;
They took me as a member of their company,
So that I was a sixth among those great intellects.

So we went on in the direction of the light,
Talking of things of which it is well to say nothing,
Although it was well to talk of them at the time.

We came then to the foot of a great castle,
Encircled seven times by lofty walls,
And around which there flowed a pleasant
   stream;

We went over the stream as on dry land;
And I entered seven gates with those wise men:
We came into a meadow where the grass was
   cool.

And there were people whose eyes were slow
   and serious,
Of great authority in their appearance:
They were not talkative and their voices were
   gentle.

We moved away a little to one side,
To an open place, well-lit, upon high ground,
So that I could see the whole group easily.

There, straight in front of me, on a green back-
   ground,
There were presented to me those great spirits,
Merely to have seen whom is an exaltation.

I saw Electra with many companions:
Amongst whom I knew Hector and Aeneas,
And the armed Caesar with the eyes of a hawk.

I saw Camilla there and Penthesilea
On the other side, and I saw the Latian king,
With his daughter Lavinia, sitting there.

I saw the Brutus who drove out the Tarquin,
Lucretia, Julia, Marcia and Cornelia;
And, standing by himself, I saw Saladin.

And, when I raised my eyes a little higher,
I saw the master of knowledge, Aristotle,
Sitting there with a company of philosophers.

All looked to him, and they all did him honour:
I saw there Socrates, as well as Plato,
The two who stood out and were nearest to him;

Democritus, who thought the world came by
   chance,
Diogenes, Anaxagoras and Thales;
Empedocles, Heraclitus and Zeno;

I saw the man who knew the virtue of herbs,
I mean Dioscorides; and I saw, too, Orpheus,
Cicero, Linus, and Seneca the moralist;

Euclid the geometrician, and Ptolemy;
Hippocrates, Galen and Avicenna;
Averrhoes, who wrote the great commentary.

I cannot give account of all of them,
For my main theme is such it hurries me on,
So that I often have to tell less than I saw.

The company of six was cut to two:
My skilful guide led me another way,
Out of the quiet, to where the air trembled:

And I came to a part where nothing is luminous.

Canto V

And so I went deeper down from the first circle
Into the second, smaller in circumference,
But greater in its cries, and stinging pain.

Minos was there, scowling and terrible,
Examining the faults of new arrivals;
He judges them, and sends each to his place.

I tell you, when the ill-born spirit comes
To him, there is nothing that is not confessed;
When he takes cognisance of any sin

He sees what place in hell is suited for it;
And whips his tail around himself as many
Times as the circles the sinner must go down.

A crowd of sinners always stands before him:
Each of them takes his turn to go to judgement;
They speak and listen; then they are swirled away.

'O you who come into this place of pain,'
Said Minos to me, when he saw me there,
And for a moment he paused from execution,

'Be careful how you enter and whom you trust:
Don't let yourself be tricked by the wide en-
   trance.'
My guide said to him: 'Why do you call out?

Do not impede him, for his going is fated:
It is willed where everything is possible
If it is willed: and ask no further questions.'

And now the painful notes began to fall
Upon my ears; for now I am come indeed
To where a great lamentation strikes me.

I have come to a place where every light is si-
   lenced,
Which roars just as the sea roars in a storm,
When it is beaten by conflicting winds,

The infernal gale, which blows and never pauses,
Directs the spirits which it carries before it:
Harassing them with turning and buffeting.

When they arrive at the threshold of this ruin,
There, there are cries, complaints and lamentations;
And there, they blaspheme against the divine
   power.

I understood it is to this torment
That are condemned those who sin in the flesh,
And let their reason give way to their wishes.

And, as starlings are carried on their wings
In the cold weather, in a vast wavering troop,
So that breath carries the unfortunate spirits:

It drives them here and there, now down, now
   up;
There is no hope ever to comfort them;
They cannot stop, or ever suffer less pain.

And as the cranes go, chanting as they fly,
Stretched out in a long ribbon in the air,
I saw the approaching shadows, uttering cries

As they were carried by the trouble I have spoken
   of;
And so I said: 'Master, who are those people,
Who are so punished by the black air?'

'The first of those about whom you are asking,'
He told me in reply, 'is that empress
Who ruled over so many lands and languages.

She was so at the mercy of sensuality,
That she made laws allowing what she liked
So that her own conduct could not be blamed.

That is Semiramis, of whom we are told
That she succeeded Ninus and was his wife;
She held the land which the Soldan now rules.

The other is she who killed herself for love,
And broke faith with the ashes of Sichaeus;
And there you see the lustful Cleopatra.

See Helen, who brought about such evil times,
Which lasted for so long; and great Achilles,
Who in the end was in combat with love.

See Paris, Tristram,' and then more than a thou-
   sand
Shadows he showed me, named and pointed out
Those whom love had separated from life.

When I had heard my instructor in this way
Naming the ladies and lovers of former times,
I felt pity, and was as if bewildered.

I began: 'Poet, I should like, if it were possible,
To speak to those two who are coming side by
   side
And seem to be so light upon the wind.'

He said to me: 'You will see them when they
   come
A little closer to us: you have only to ask them,
Invoking the love that brings them, and they will
   come.'

As soon as the wind blew them to where we were
   standing,
I raised my voice: 'O you two panting spirits,
Come now and speak to us, if it is not forbidden.'

And just as doves called home to their desire,
With stretched and steady wings, back to the
   nest,
Come through the air because they want to do so;

So, separating from the flock where Dido was,
They came towards us through the malignant air,
So strong was the affection of my cry.

'O kind and gracious living creature who
Go through the darkened air to visit us,
Although, when alive, we dyed the world with
   blood;

If only the king of the universe were our friend,
We would pray to him that you should have
   peace,
Because you pity our perversity.

Matters it pleases you to hear and speak of,
We will now hear and speak about to you,
While the wind is silent, as it is now.

The country I was born in lies along
The coast, just at the point the Po descends
To have some peace among its followers.

Love, which quickly fastens on gentle hearts,
Seized that wretch, and it was for the personal
        beauty
Which was taken from me; how it happened still
        offends me.

Love, which allows no one who is loved to es-
        cape,
Seized me so strongly with my pleasure in him,
That, as you see, it does not leave me now.

Love led us two to find a single death;
Caïna awaits him who brought us to this end.'
These were the words which came to us from
        them.

When I had heard those souls in their suffering,
I bowed my head, and kept it bowed so long
That at last the poet said: 'What are you thinking?'

When I replied, I started: 'Oh, alas,
That such sweet thoughts, desires that were so
        great,
Should lead them to the misery they are in.'

I turned to them again and spoke again,
Starting this time: 'Francesca, your great suffer-
        ings
Make me weep for you out of sadness and pity.

But tell me: in the time of those sweet sighs,
How and on what occasion did love allow
You to experience these uncertain desires?'

And she replied: 'There is no greater sorrow,
Than to think backwards to a happy time,
When one is miserable: your instructor knows
        this.

But if you have such a desire to know
The first root of our love, then I will tell you,
Although to do so, it will be as if I wept.

One day, when we were reading, for distraction,
How Lancelot was overcome by love—
We were alone, without any suspicion;

Several times, what we were reading forced
Our eyes to meet, and then we changed colour:
But one page only was more than we could bear.

When we read how that smile, so much desired,
Was kissed by such a lover, in the book,
He, who will never be divided from me,

Kissed my mouth, and the two of us were trem-
        bling.
The book, the writer played the part of Galahalt:
That day we got no further with our reading.'

While one of the spirits was speaking in this man-
        ner,
The other shed such tears that, out of pity,
I felt myself diminish, as if I were dying,

And fell down, as a dead body falls.

Canto VI
When consciousness returned, after the darken-
        ing
Caused by my pity for the two kinsfolk
Which made me so sad that I was stunned,

I saw then, all around me, fresh torments
And tormented spirits I had not seen before,
As I moved on, turning this way and that, and
        looking.

I was in the third circle, where it rains
Eternally, icily and implacably;
Weight and direction are invariable.

Great hailstones, muddy water, mixed with snow,
Fall through the darkened air without respite;
They rot the ground they fall on, and it stinks.

Cerberus, a cruel and outlandish beast,
Barks like a dog, from his three throats, at those
Who, under that downpour, are there sub-
        merged.

His eyes are red, his beard greasy and black,
His belly huge, and his fingers are clawed,
He scratches the spirits, skins them, pulls them to
        bits.

They howl like dogs, the rain so batters them;
With nothing to shelter one flank, but the other,
The irreligious twist in their misery.

When Cerberus, the great dragon, saw us,
He opened his mouths wide and showed his
     fangs;
He shivered, and no part of him was still.

PURGATORY

Canto I

To run on better water now, the boat
Of my invention hoists its sails and leaves
Away to stern that cruel stretch of sea;

And I will sing of this second kingdom
In which the human spirit cures itself
And becomes fit to leap up into heaven.

But here dead poetry rises again,
O holy Muses, since I am your own,
And here let Calliope rise a little,

Following my song with that sound from which
The pitiful Magpies felt so sharp a blow
That they despaired of ever being pardoned.

Sweet colour of oriental sapphire,
Which gathered in the clear face of the sky,
Right to the very edge of the first circle,

Restored to my eyes the touch of pleasure,
As soon as I issued from the dead air
Which had saddened my eyes and my heart.

The lovely planet which gives comfort in love
Was filling the whole eastern sky with laughter,
Hiding the Fish which followed in her train.

I turned towards the right, and fixed my mind
On the other pole, and there I saw four stars,
Never yet seen except by the first people.

The sky seemed to be glad in their sparkling:
O northern hemisphere, you are a widow
To be deprived of any sight of them!

When I had given up looking at those stars
And turned a little towards the other pole,
To where the Wain should have been, but it was
     gone;

I saw near me an old man, alone,
With looks deserving as much reverence
As ever any son owed to his father.

He wore his beard long and there were white
     strands
In it, like his hair which tumbled down
In two white bunches over his chest and shoul-
     ders;

The beams which came from those four holy
     lights
So played upon his face and lit it up
That I saw him as if he had been facing the sun.

'Who are you, who, going against the current
Of the blind stream, have escaped the eternal
     prison?'
He said, with a movement of his honoured
     plumage.

'Who was your guide? Whom did you have for
     lamp
To bring you out of the profound night
Which always darkens the infernal valley?

And are the laws of the abyss so broken?
Or has there been a change of plan in heaven,
So that, though damned, you come here to my
     rocks?'

My escort then took hold of me, and with
Words and touch and other indications
Made me bend knees and head in reverence.

Then he replied: 'It was not of myself
I came: a lady from heaven asked me
To help this man by bearing him company.

But since it is your will we should declare
More fully what our true condition is,
My will cannot be to say no to that.

This man has not yet seen his last evening;
But, through his madness, was so close to it
That there was hardly time to turn about.

As I have told you, I was sent to him
To rescue him; and there was no other way
Than this which I have set myself to follow.

I have shown him all the wicked people; now
I have in mind to show him all those spirits
Who cure themselves here under your care.

How I conducted him, would be a long story;
Virtue comes down from above and gives me help
In bringing him to see you and listen to you.

Now treat his coming as acceptable:
He looks for liberty, which is so loved,
As he knows who gives up his life for her.

You know this: that is why death was not bitter
To you in Utica, where you abandoned
That garment which will shine in the last day.

The eternal laws had no damage by us;
For this man is alive, I am not with Minos;
I am of the same circle as the chaste eyes

Of your Marcia, who is still to be seen praying,
O holy breast, that you will recognise her:
For her love, therefore, may you be inclined

To let us journey through your seven kingdoms:
I will convey your thanks to her, if you
Do not disdain to be mentioned in that place.'

'Marcia so pleased my eyes,' Cato replied,
'When I was still outside these present bounds,
That everything she asked of me, I did.

Now that she stays beyond the evil river,
She can move me no longer, by that law
Which was made when I issued from that place.

But if a lady from heaven moves and commands
        you,
As you assert, no need for flattery:
It is enough that you ask in her name.

Go therefore now, and put on him a girdle
Of simple rush, and wash his face, so that
Every trace of filth is removed from it;

For it would not do to go before
The first of the ministers of paradise
With the eyes dulled by any kind of mist.

All round about the base of this little island,
There where the waves are always beating on it,
Are rushes growing over the soft mud;

No other plant which puts out leaves and hardens
Itself, would ever live in such a place,
Because it would not give to the buffetings.

Afterwards do not come this way again;
The sun will show you, it is rising now,
A gentler way to take to climb the mountain.'

With that he disappeared; and I got up
Without a word, and went back to my escort
And turned my eyes entirely towards him.

He began: 'Follow my footsteps, let us turn
Back, for the plain slopes downwards here
Until it finishes at its lowest point.'

The dawn was conquering the morning hour
Which fled before it, so that far away
I recognised the trembling of the sea.

We went along over the lonely plain,
Like a man turning back to a road he has lost,
Who thinks he is wasting time until he finds it.

When we were at the point at which the dew
Resisted the sun, and, being on a stretch
Where there was shade, evaporated slowly,

My master gently stretched out both his hands
And touched the fine young grass; and when I saw
What his intention was, I proffered

My cheeks which were stained with tears, and
        there
He brought to light my natural complexion,
Which hell had hidden.

We came then to the deserted shore
Which never saw, sailing upon its waters,
Any who afterwards knew how to return.

Then he gave me the girdle another had willed for
        me;
And when he picked the plant of humility,
Miraculously it renewed itself at once,

Just in the very place from which he had taken it.

Canto II
Already the sun had reached the horizon
Of which the meridian circle, at its highest
Point, passes directly through Jerusalem;

And the night, which circles on the opposite side,
Issued out from the Ganges with the Scales
Which fall from her hand when she is sovereign;

So that from where I was the white and red
Of the lovely Aurora seemed to be
Turning to orange as if she were old.

We were wandering along the shore still,
Like people who are thinking about their route,
Advancing in mind, but in their bodies, halting.

And there as, at the approach of morning,
Through the close-gathered mists Mars glows
    deep red,
Down in the west, above the level sea,

So appeared to me—may it not be the last time—
A light coming over the sea so swiftly
That its motion was faster than any flight;

So that when I had withdrawn my gaze
A little, to make enquiry of my escort,
I saw it again already brighter and bigger.

Then on each side of it appeared to me
A little blob of white; and from underneath,
Bit by bit, another blob appeared.

My master still stood there without a word,
Until the first whiteness appeared as wings:
Then he easily recognised the pilot.

He cried: 'Quickly, quickly, bend your knees:
It is the angel of God: put your hands together:
From now on you will see such officers.

See how he scorns all human implements,
So that he does not wish to have other sail,
Between such distant shores, than his own wings.

See how he has them straight against the sky,
Striking the air with his eternal wings,
Which are not ruffled as mortal hair would be.'

Then, as little by little the divine bird
Advanced towards us, it appeared the brighter,
Until my eyes could not bear it so near,

And I lowered them: and he then came ashore
With a vessel so nimble and so light
That it did not displace any water.

At the stern there stood the celestial helmsman,
Whose blessedness was written all over him;
And more than a hundred spirits sat on board.

'In exitu Israel de Aegypto'
They sang together with a single voice,
With all that follows those words in the psalter.

Then over them, he made the sign of the cross;
And thereupon they threw themselves on the
    shore:
And he departed, as he had come, swiftly.

The crowd left there seemed to be shy of the
    place
And stared around them with the look of people
Who are familiarising themselves with novelties.

On every side the sun was showering day,
Having already with its single arrows
Driven Capricorn from the middle of the sky,

When the newcomers raised their faces towards
    us,
And spoke to us: 'If you know where the way is,
Show us how we should go to the mountain.'

And Virgil answered: 'You perhaps may think
That we are people familiar with this place:
But we in fact are strangers, as you are;

We came just now, only a little before you,
By another way, which is so rough and hard
That climbing now will seem like sport to us.'

The spirits who, by their attention to me,
From my breathing, saw that I was alive,
Wondered at the fact, and became pale.

And as, to the messenger who bears the olive,
People are drawn in order to hear the news
And nobody seems to worry about being stepped
    on,

So on my face those spirits, who one and all
Were fortunate, fastened their gaze, almost
Forgetting to go and make themselves fair.

I saw one of them pull out of the crowd
To embrace me, with such a show of feeling
As moved me to make a similar gesture.

O shadows empty of all but appearances!
Three times at his back I clasped my hands,
And each time brought them back to my chest.

With wonder, I think, I must have changed colour,
Because the shadow smiled, and drew back,
And I followed him and moved forward.

Gently he told me that I should be still:
Then I knew who he was, and begged him
That he would stop a moment to talk to me.

He answered me: 'Just as I loved you in
My mortal body, so I love you now I am free of it:
Therefore I stop; but why are you going this way?'

'Dear Casella, in order to come back
Where I now am, that's why I am making this
　　　journey,'
I said; 'but how have you lost so much time?'

And he to me: 'No one has done me wrong,
If he who takes when and whom he likes
Has several times refused me passage here;

For it is of a just will that his is made:
True enough that for three months he has taken
Whoever wished to enter, in all peace.

So I, who then had turned to the sea-shore
There where the water of the Tiber grows salt,
Was with benignity received by him.

To that estuary he now directs
His wings, because it is there that everyone
Is received, who is not to sink to Acheron.'

And I: 'If a new law has not taken from you
The memory or the use of that love-song
Which used to quieten my every desire,

Will you be kind enough to console my spirit
A little by that means, for it is very weary
Since I have come here in my own body.'

'Love which discourses with me in my mind,'
He began to sing, and so sweetly
That the sweetness still sounds inside me now.

My master and I and those people
Who were with him seemed to be so content
That no other thing could touch their minds.

We were all fixed and listening to his notes
When suddenly the good old man cried out:
'What are you doing, all you idle spirits?

What negligence, what dawdling is there here?
Run to the mountain and strip the outer skin
Which stops God being manifest to you.'

As when, having found corn or greenstuff, pi-
　　　geons
Are gathered in a flock at their feeding-ground,
Quietly and not showing their usual vanity,

If something appears which makes them afraid,
Suddenly they leave their feeding where it is
Because they are assailed by greater cares,

So I saw that band of newcomers
Abandon the song and go towards the hillside
Like people going without knowing where they
　　　will get to:

And our own departure was no less rapid.

PARADISE

Canto XXI

Already my eyes were fixed again on the face
Of my lady and, with them, my mind was fixed
And so removed from any other purpose.

And she did not smile; but, 'If I smiled,'
She began, 'you would become as was
Semele when she was turned to ashes;

For if my beauty, which lights up the more,
(As you have seen) the higher we ascend
Upon the stairs of the eternal palace,

If it were not tempered, it would so shine
That at its brilliance your mortal power
Would be a branch split by thunder.

We have risen up to the seventh splendour
Which, under the breast of the blazing lion,
Now sends its beams down mixed with his virtue.

Fix your mind on what your eyes see
And make them mirrors to the figure which will
Make its appearance to you in this mirror.'

Anyone who knew with what delectation
My sight was feeding upon her blessed appear-
　　　ance
When I was directed to other concerns,

Would know how pleasing it was to me
To do as my celestial escort told me,
Weighing the pleasure of looking against that of
    obedience.

Within the crystal which, circling round the
    world,
Carries the name of its beloved leader
Under whom every malice lies dead,
The colour of gold, with refulgent rays
I saw a ladder which was erected aloft
So far, my sight could not follow it.

I saw too, coming down the steps,
So many splendours, I thought all the stars
Which shine in heaven were pouring down there.

And as, in accordance with their natural habits,
The daws stir at the beginning of the day,
All together, to warm their cold feathers;

Then some go off and do not reappear,
While others return to where they started from,
And others stay wheeling in the air;

That is how that sparkling seemed to me
With those radiances which came all together
As soon as they touched upon a certain rung.

And that one which came to halt nearest us,
Became so bright, that I said to myself:
'I see the love of which you give such signs.

But she, from whom I take the how and when
Of speech and silence, is still; and therefore I,
Against my wishes, do well not to ask.'

So she, who perceived my silence
In the sight of him who sees everything,
Said to me: 'Let your warm desire have its way.'

And I began: 'My merit is not enough
To make me worthy of a reply from you
But, for the sake of her who lets me ask,

You blessed life, who remain hidden within
Your happiness, I beg you to inform me
What it is that has brought you so close?

And tell me why in this circle the sweet
Symphony of paradise is silent,

Though below in the others it sounds so fer-
    vently.'

'You have mortal hearing, as you have mortal
    sight,'
He answered me; 'so here is no singing
For the same reason that Beatrice has not smiled.

I came so far down the rungs of the ladder
Only in order to give you happiness
With what I say and with the light which cloaks
    me;

Nor did a greater love make me more willing;
For up there love as great as mine or greater
Burns, as the flames by their brightness show.

But the deep charity which makes us prompt
To serve the counsel which governs the world
Settles our places here as you observe.'

'I see well,' I said then, 'O sacred light,
How in this court an unrestrained love
Is all that is needed for following eternal provi-
    dence;

But this is what seems hard to understand:
Why it was you, of all your companions here,
Who alone was predestined to perform this of-
    fice?'

I did not come to the end of what I was saying
Before the light, making its mid-point the axis,
Whirled round and round like a quick millstone.

And then the love that was within replied:
'Divine light comes to a point upon me,
Penetrating what I am surrounded by,

The virtue of which, combined with my own
    sight,
Raises me so far above myself
That I see the supreme essence from which it is
    drawn.

Thence comes the happiness I am alight with;
For in proportion as my sight is clear,
So is the clarity of my flame.

But the most enlightened soul that is in heaven,
That seraph whose eye is most fixed on God,
Would not satisfy this demand of yours;

Because the thing you ask is so deep
Within the abyss of the eternal law
That it is cut off from all created sight.

And tell the mortal world, when you get back,
What I have told you, so that it does not presume
To move its steps towards so remote a goal.

The mind, which is light here, on earth is smoke;
Consider therefore how, below, it could achieve
What it could not do when heaven takes it up.'

His words set such limitations on me
That I gave up the question, and restricted
Myself to asking him humbly who he was.

'Between the two shores of Italy rise rocks
Not far distant from your own country,
So high, that thunder sounds much lower down,

And they make a hump which is called Catria,
Below which there was consecrated a retreat
Which used to be for prayer to God alone.'

So he began again the third discourse;
And then, continuing, said: 'In that place
I gave myself so solidly to God's service,

That with nothing but lenten foods I passed
Cheerfully through both hot and freezing
        weather,
Contented with contemplative thoughts.

That cloister yielded fruit to these heavens,
Richly indeed; and now it has become useless,
So much so that it must soon come to light.

In that place I was known as Peter Damian
And became Peter the Sinner in the house
Of Our Lady by the shore of the Adriatic.

Little mortal life remained to me
When I was put into one of those hats
Which seem always to have worse heads inside
        them.

Cephas came, and the great vessel of
The Holy Spirit, they were lean and barefoot,
Taking their food wherever they might get it.

Now the modern pastors have to be held up
On both sides, and to have someone to lead them,

They are so fat: and someone to push from behind.

They spread their cloaks over the backs of their
        horses
So that there are two beasts under one skin:
O patience, how great the load you have to bear!'

At these words I saw a number of little flames
Descend from rung to rung and spin round
And every turn made them look more lovely.

They surrounded the one that spoke, and came to
        a halt,
And uttered a cry which sounded so loud
That it resembled nothing upon earth:

Nor could I understand it; the roar flattened me.

Canto XXII

Crushed and amazed, I turned to my guide,
Just like a little child who runs to find
The person in whom he has most trust;

And she, like a mother who at once
Reassures her pale and gasping boy
By her voice, which soon puts him right,

Said to me: 'Don't you know you are in heaven?
And don't you know that heaven is all holy
And that all that happens here is done out of
        charity?

What effect that song had upon you,
And my smiling, you may now comprehend,
Since the cry made so great a disturbance;

For, if you had understood their prayers,
You would already be aware of the vengeance
Which you will certainly see before you die.

The sword which strikes from here will never
        strike
In haste or too late, though it appears so
To those who hanker after it, or fear it.

But turn to others now; and many and many
Illustrious spirits you will see before you
If you look in the direction I say.'

I turned my eyes as she wanted me to
And I saw a hundred little spheres together,
Beautiful in their own light and one another's.

I stood as one suppressing within himself
The itch of his desire, and does not dare
To ask, for fear that he may ask too much.

And the greatest and most luminous
Of those pearls came forward a little
To satisfy my wishes regarding him.

Then I heard inside him: 'If you were to see
As I do, the charity which burns in us,
What you have in mind would come out.

But so that you, by waiting, are not kept
From your high purpose, I will give an answer
To the mere thought which you hesitate to utter.

That hill upon whose slopes Cassino lies
Was formerly frequented, at the summit,
By deceived and ill-disposed people;

And it was I who first carried up there
The name of him who brought into the world
The truth which so elevates humankind;

And upon me there shone so much grace
That I converted all the country round
From the impious cult by which the world was
        seduced.

Those other flames were all contemplatives
Whose hearts were kindled with the heat
Which brings to birth holy flowers and fruit.

Here is Macarius, here is Romoaldus,
Here are my brothers who kept their feet
Inside the cloister and were sound of heart.'

And I to him: 'The love which you show
In speaking to me, and the benevolence
I see and mark in all your burnings,

Has opened out my confidence as the sun
Opens the rose, until it has become
As full as ever it has power to be.

Therefore I pray you, father, to satisfy me
As to whether I am to obtain so much grace
As to see your likeness without concealment.'

He then said: 'Brother, your exalted desire
Will be accomplished in the final sphere
Where all, including mine, will be so.

There is perfection, ripeness, wholeness
For every wish: for there and there alone
Every part is where it always was,

Because it is not in space, nor has it poles;
And our ladder stretches into it
So that it disappears from your sight

The patriarch Jacob saw the upper part
Stretching away up there, when it appeared to
        him
With the angels ascending and descending on it.

But no one now lifts his feet from the ground
To climb it, and the rule of my order
Is left there simply as so much waste parchment.

The walls which enclosed a house of prayer
Now make a den of thieves, and the monks'
        hoods
Are now sacks full of rotten flour.

But the worst usury is not taken
Against God's will more surely than that fruit
Which makes the heart of the monks so mad;

For whatever the Church has, belongs,
All of it, to those who ask in God's name;
Not to relatives or something uglier.

The flesh of mortals is so susceptible
That down there a good beginning does not last
From the oaks's first leaf to when it bears an
        acorn.

Peter began without gold and without silver,
And I with nothing but prayer and fasting,
And Francis humbly with his community.

And if you look at each of these beginnings
And then look again to see where they have got
        to,
You will see that the white has turned black.

But Jordan turning back to its source
Or the sea dividing, when God willed these things,
Were more marvellous than the relief needed now.'

He said that, and then at once rejoined
The company he came from, and they crowded
        closer;
Then, like a whirlwind, rose all together,

The gentle lady pushed me after them
With no more than a nod, up the ladder,
Her power so overcame my nature;

Never on earth, where movements up and down
Occur naturally, was ever movement so rapid
That it could be compared with my flight.

As I hope, reader, to return to that
Devout triumph on account of which I often
Weep for my sins and beat my breast,

You would not put your finger in a flame
And draw it out again, more speedily than I
Saw the sign after Taurus and found myself there.

O glorious stars, O light which is filled with
Immense power, from which I acknowledge
All my genius, whatever it may be,

Rising with you, and hiding myself with you,
Was he who is father of every mortal life,
When I first felt the air of Tuscany;

And then, when the grace was granted to me
To enter the high circle in which you turn,
It was in the quarter where you are.

My soul now sighs devotedly
To you that it may be given the power
For the hard passage which is now before it.

'You are so close to the ultimate salvation,'
Beatrice began, 'that your eyes should be
Able to see all clearly and sharply.

And so, before you go further in,
Look back below, and see how much of creation
I have already set under your feet;

So my heart presents itself as joyfully
As ever it may, to the triumphant crowd
Which comes in gladness through this circle of
    ether.'

I turned my eyes back through every one
Of the seven spheres and saw the globe which
    looked
Such a miserable thing that I smiled;

And I recognise that the best opinion about it
Is that which makes least of it; and the man whose
    thoughts
Are elsewhere can truly be called just.

I saw the daughter of Latona burning
Without that shadow which was the reason why
I once thought some parts less dense than others.

I there found that I could look upon the face
Of your son, Hyperion; and saw the movement
About and near him, Maia and Dione.

Next there appeared to me the tempering Jove,
Between father and son; and it was clear to me
In what manner they changed their positions.

And all the seven were displayed to me,
How big they are, and how fast they move,
And what are the intermediate distances.

The little plot which makes us so fierce
Appeared to me, with all its hills and outlets,
As I swept round with the eternal Gemini.

Then I turned back my eyes to the lovely eyes.

Canto XXIII

Like the bird which, within the beloved foliage,
Set on her nest with her sweet little ones,
At night, when things are hidden from us,

In order to see them looking up at her
And to find morsels she can feed them with,
A labour which she finds delightful to her,

Ahead of time, lights on an exposed twig,
Awaiting the sun in a blaze of love,
Fixedly gazing till the dawn appears;

So my lady stood erect and alert,
Turning to that quarter of the sky
Beneath which the sun shows least haste to ap-
    pear;

So that, seeing her full of expectancy,
I became as one who desires something
Other than what he has, and is content to hope.

It was but an instant between the moment when
I became attentive and the moment when I saw
The heavens growing brighter and brighter.

And Beatrice said: 'Look, there are the hosts
Of Christ's triumph, and there is all the harvest
Gathered from the circling of the spheres!'

Her whole face seemed to me to shine so,
And her eyes were so full of happiness
That I had better say nothing about it.

As in a cloudless sky at full moon,
Trivia smiles among the eternal nymphs
Who decorate all quarters of the heavens,

I saw, up above thousands of lamps,
A sun which lit up every one of them
As ours does what we see overhead;

And through the living light there shone through
The substance of light, which was so brilliant
To my eyes that they could not withstand it.

O Beatrice my sweet beloved guide!
She said to me: 'What overcomes you here
Is a power against which there is no defence.

Here is that wisdom and that power
Which opened the roads between heaven and
        earth,
For which there had been such longing so long.'

As fire bursts out of a cloud
Because it expands so that it will not hold
And, out of its element, rushes to the ground,

So my mind, among such feasts as these,
Grew greater and went out of itself,
And it cannot recall what happened to it.

'Open your eyes and see how I appear:
You have seen things which make it possible
Now, for you to sustain my smile.'

I was like one who still feels the effects
Of a forgotten vision, and tries in vain
To bring it back to his mind again,

When I heard this invitation, deserving
Of so much gratitude as never to be
Erased from the book which holds the past.

If now there were to sound all those tongues
Which Polyhymnia and her sisters made
Richest with the sweetest of their milk,

With these to aid me I should not arrive
At a thousandth part of the truth, as I sang
The holy smile and how clear the divine look
        made it.

And so, in presenting paradise,
The sacred poem has to make a jump
Like one who finds something in his way.

But anyone who thinks how weighty the theme is
And that the shoulders it is loaded on are mortal
Will not be disposed to blame them if they trem-
        ble.

It is no channel for a little boat,
That which my daring prow cuts as it goes,
Nor for a helmsman who is afraid of toil.

'Why does my face so fascinate you
That you do not turn to the beautiful garden
Which, under Christ's rays, bursts into flower?

Here is the rose in which the divine word
Was made flesh; here also are the lilies
The scent of which indicated the way.'

Thus Beatrice; and I, who readily followed
What she suggested, gave myself up again
To the battle my weak sight had undertaken.

As, by a brilliant sunbeam which poured down
Through broken cloud, my eyes, though in the
        shade,
Once saw a meadow full of flowers,

So I saw more than one crowd of brilliances
Struck by blazing beams from above
Without seeing where the blaze came from.

O benign power, setting your mark so on them:
You had raised yourself in order to give place
To eyes which were not able to behold you.

The name of the fair flower which I invoke
Morning and evening, compelled my whole mind
To fix my eyes upon the greatest flame.

And when both my eyes had painted for me
The nature and brightness of the living star
Which conquers up there as it did down here,

From within the heavens another light de-
        scended,
Formed in a circle, in the manner of a crown;
It settled around her and then moved about her.

The sweetest melody heard upon earth,
The most attractive to the listening soul,
Would be like a cloud split by thunder

In comparison with the sound of that lyre
With which the lovely sapphire was crowned,
Which filled the brightest heaven with sapphire.

'I am the angelic love which circles round
The exalted happiness which breathes from the
      womb
Which harboured once all we could wish;

And I will circle, lady of heaven, until
You follow your son, and make the supreme
      sphere
More divine because you enter it.'

So the melody which moved round and round
Came to a close, and all the other lights
Uttered aloud the name of Mary.

The royal mantle over all that enwraps
The universe, the mantle which burns brightest
And most lives in God's breath and his ways,

Had its inner border so far away
Above us that, from the place where I was,
How it looked did not yet appear:

Therefore my eyes did not have the strength
To follow as the flame with its crown
Lifted itself, as Mary rose to her son.

And as a child who holds out his arms
Towards his mother, when he has had his milk,
Having a mind which flames to what is beyond it;

So every one of these brilliances stretched up
With its flame, so that it was patent
How exalted was the love they bore to Mary.

Then they remained there in my sight,
Singing 'Regina coeli' so sweetly
That the delight of it has never left me.

O how great is the abundance which is con-
      tained,
In those rich granaries, of those who were
On earth the labourers of the good seed!

There they live and delight themselves with the
      wealth

Which was acquired weeping in Babylonian
Exile, when the gold was left untouched.

There, after his victory, there triumphs
Under the exalted son of God and Mary,
And with the company both old and new,

He who holds the keys of this glory.

Canto XXIV
'O fellowship called to the great supper
Of the blessed lamb, who so feeds you
That you always have all that you desire,

If, by the grace of God, this man has
A foretaste of what falls from your table
Before death prescribes the time for him,

Set your mind upon his immense affection;
Refresh him with your dew: for you drink
Always of the spring from which his thoughts
      flow.'

Thus Beatrice: and those joyful souls
Became spheres moving on fixed poles,
Flaming, as they circled, in the manner of comets.

And as the interdependent wheels in clocks
Turn so that, while the first may be observed
To be at rest, the last seems to fly;

So these groups of dancers, by the manner
Of their dancing, whether swift or slow
Enabled me to judge of their beatitude.

From the one I observed to be the most beautiful
I saw there emerged so exultant a flame
That none of the others there was more brilliant;

And it proceeded three times round Beatrice
With a song which was of such divinity
That my imagination cannot recall it.

So my pen takes a leap and I write nothing;
Because our speech, to say nothing of imagina-
      tion
Is too bright to show up anything brighter.

'O my holy sister, who so religiously
Asks, because of your burning love
I free myself from this lovely circle.'

Then, when it had stopped, the blessed flame
Which had spoken as I have recorded
Directed his breath to my lady.

And she: 'Eternal light of the great man
To whom our Lord delivered over the keys
Of these marvellous joys, which he had brought
down,

Examine him on easy or hard points,
As you please, regarding that faith
Which enabled you to walk upon the waters.

Whether he loves well, and hopes and believes
Is not hidden from you, because your sight
Is where everything is clearly seen;

But because this realm has admitted citizens
For the true faith, it is well for its glory
That he should have occasion to speak of it.'

As a student prepares himself and does not speak
Until the master has proposed the question,
To adduce the reason, not a definition,

So I prepared myself with all the reasons
While she was speaking, in order to be ready
For such an examiner and such a profession.

'Tell me, good Christian, make your position
clear:
What is faith?' Then I raised my head
Into that light from which the words were
breathed;

Then I turned to Beatrice, and she readily
Gave me an indication that I should pour out
The water which welled from my internal spring.

'The grace which permits me' — so I began —
'To make my confession to the old commander,
Enable me to make my ideas clear.'

I went on: 'Father, as was recorded
By the veracious pen of your dear brother
Who, with you, put Rome on the right track,

Faith is the substance of things hoped for
And the argument for what is not seen;
And that seems to me the quiddity of it.'

Then I heard: 'You have the matter right,
If you understand why he placed it

Among the substances and then among the arguments.'

And thereupon I: 'The profound matters
Which here vouchsafe their appearance to me
Are so hidden from the eyes there below,

That they exist there only in belief,
Upon which is founded the exalted hope,
And therefore they take on the nature of sub-
stance;

And from this belief we have to syllogise,
Without the intervention of sensible proof;
Therefore it partakes of the nature of argument.'

Then I heard: 'If all that is acquired below
As doctrine was understood in this manner
There would be no place for the inventions of
sophists.'

This was what that burning love breathed forth;
Then added: 'You have examined well
The value and the weight of that coin,

But tell me if you have any in your purse.'
So I: 'I have, yes; so shining and so round
That there is no doubt about the mint.'

Then there issued from the deep light
Which was blazing there: 'And this dear jewel
On which every virtue is founded.

Where did you get it from?' And I: 'The down-
pouring
Of the Holy Spirit which is diffused over
The pages of the old and new testaments,

Is a syllogism in which the conclusion
Is so convincing that, beside it
Every demonstration appears feeble.'

I heard then: 'The old proposition
And the new, from which you so conclude
— Why do you take it for the word of God?'

And I: 'The proof which reveals the truth to me
Is in the works which followed, for which nature
Did not heat the iron or strike the anvil.'

The reply I was given was: 'Tell me, who assured
you
That those works took place? The same scripture
That is to be proved, and no other, swears to it.'

'If the world turned to Christianity,'
I said, 'without miracles, it is itself so much
A miracle, that the others are nothing to it,

That you came, in poverty and hunger,
On to the field, to sow the good plant
Which was a vine and has become a thorn.'

That finished, the high court of heaven
Made 'We praise God' sound through the spheres
With the melody it is sung to up there.

And that great master whose examination
Had drawn me already from branch to branch
So that we were approaching the topmost leaves,

Began again: 'The grace which woos your mind
Has up to this point opened your mouth
In the manner in which it ought to open,

So that I approve what has come out:
But now you must say what you believe
And whence it is presented to your belief.'

'O holy father, you spirit who see
What you believe, as you went beyond
Younger feet into the sepulchre,'

I began: 'You desire me to make plain
The form of my ready belief, and ask
Me also what is the reason for it.'

And I replied: 'I believe in one God,
Sole and eternal, who moves all the heavens
With love and desire, and is himself unmoved.

And for this belief I have not only proofs,
Physical and metaphysical, but there is given me
Also the truth which is poured down on us

Through Moses, through the prophets, and the
     psalms,
Through the Evangelists and you who wrote
When the burning spirit had made you divine.

And I believe in three eternal persons, and these
I believe one essence, unity and trinity,
So that singular and plural are combined.

This mystery of the divine nature
I now speak of, is stamped in my mind
More than once by the doctrine of the gospel.

This is the beginning, this is the spark
Which spreads out into a living flame
And sparkles like a star in heaven.'

As a master who hears what pleases him
And so embraces his servant, to show his joy
At the news, the moment the man has finished;

So, giving me his blessing as he sang,
He circled me three times, when I was silent,
That apostolic light at whose command
I had spoken: so had what I said pleased him!

Canto XXV

If it ever happens that the sacred poem
To which both heaven and earth have set their
     hands,
So that it has made me thin for many a year,

Should overcome the cruelty which shuts me out
From that lovely fold where I slept, a lamb,
The enemy of wolves who war against it;

With a different voice now, and with different
     fleece,
I shall come back poet; and at the font
Of my baptism I shall put on my wreath;

Because it was there I entered into the faith
Which reckons souls for God, and afterwards
For its sake Peter circles round my head.

Then a light moved towards me, from that sphere
Whence there had issued the original
Of all the vicars Christ has left on earth;

And my lady, full of happiness,
Said to me: 'Look now, look, there is the master
For whose sake there are pilgrims in Galicia.'

As when a dove takes his place beside
His companion, and they manifest
Their affection to one another, circling and mur-
     muring,

So I saw the two great princes in glory
Received one by the other, both of them
Praising the food on which they feast up there.

But when the mutual greeting was completed,
They set themselves silently before me,
Alight so that I had to lower my eyes.

At that point, with a smile, Beatrice spoke:
'Illustrious spirit, through whom the liberality
Of our royal mansion was set on record,

Let the name of Hope resound through these
        heights:
You know, for you gave it shape as often
As Jesus showed more kindness to the three.'

'Raise your head and be more confident;
For what comes up here from the mortal world
Must be content to ripen in our rays.'

This comfort came to me from the second flame;
So I lifted my eyes to the hills
The weight of which had earlier bowed them
        down.

'Because through his grace our emperor
Wills that before your death you should meet the
        nobles
Face to face in his most sacred hall,

So that the verities seen in this court
May strengthen in you and in others
The hope which turns people to love below,

Say what it is, and how it is a garland
For your mind, and say where it comes to you
        from.'
That is how the second light continued.

And that compassionate lady who guided
My feathered wings in that exalted flight,
Gave the answer before I could do so myself:

'None of the sons of the church militant
Has more hope than this man, as it is written
In the sun which shines upon all our host:

Therefore it is permitted to him to come
From Egypt, to our Jerusalem,
Before the days of his soldiering are done.

The other two points—which are not put
To find out what he thinks, but so that he
May report how pleasing the virtue is to you—

I leave to him; for they will not be hard to him
Nor give occasion for boasting; let him reply
And may the grace of God allow him to.'

As a student who follows his teacher promptly
And willingly, when he knows the answer,
So that it may be seen how good he is,

I said: 'Hope is a certain expectation
Of future glory, and it is the product
Of divine grace and of precedent merits.

This light comes to me from many stars;
But he who first infused it in my heart
Was the supreme singer of the supreme head.

"They that know thy name," as he puts it
In his divine song, "will trust in thee":
And who does not know it, who has my faith?

Your dew lighted upon me, like his dew,
In your epistle; I am full of it
And overflow with your shower upon others.'

While I was speaking, there was a trembling flash
Inside the living heart of that fire;
It was sudden and repeated like lightning.

Then it breathed: 'The love with which I burn
Still towards the virtue which followed me
Right to the victory and my exit from the field,

Wills that I breathe on you who take delight
In it; and my pleasure is that you
Say what it is that hope promises you.'

And I: 'The new and old testaments
Set down the mark which points out to me
The souls of whom God has made his friends.

Isaiah says that every soul shall be
Dressed in a double garment, in his own land;
And "his own land" is this delightful life.

And your brother makes his revelation to us
With more particularity, when he talks
Of those who are "clothed with white robes." '

And then, as soon as these words were spoken,
'Sperent in te' was heard up above us;
To which all the dancing choirs replied.

Then from among them there flashed out a light
Such that, if Cancer had so bright a star,
Winter would have a month of complete daylight.

And as a happy girl gets on her feet
And joins the dance, simply to honour the bride
And not for any weakness of her own,

So I saw the splendour full of light
Come to the two who were circling with such
    notes
As were appropriate to their ardent love.

Then it joined their song and their circuit;
And my lady kept her gaze upon them,
Like a bride, silent and motionless.

'This is he who lay upon the breast
Of our pelican in the wilderness, and he
Who was chosen, from the cross, for the great
    office.'

So my lady; and her eyes did not stir
From the fixed look they had,
Either before or after speaking those words.

Like one who gazes and does all he can
To see the sun when it is in part eclipse
And, by looking, in the end ceases to see;

So did I with this last flame, until
I heard a voice: 'Why do you blind yourself
To see something which has no place here?

My body is earth in earth, and will be there
With all the others, until the day when
The number of the just shall be accomplished.

With two robes in this blessed cloister
There are only those two lights who rose:
And this you will report back in your world.'

At these words the flaming circle was still,
And with it the delightful intermingling
Which was made in the sound of the threefold
    voice,

As oars, which have been in and out of the water,
Suddenly, to rest or to avert danger,
All come to a stop at the sound of a whistle.

Ah what commotion there was in my mind
When I turned to see Beatrice
And did not see her, although I was near

To her, and in the world of the blessed.

Canto XXVI

While I was perturbed with the loss of my sight,
From the brilliant flame which had caused that
    loss
Breathed a voice which held my attention;

It said: 'While you are recovering
The sight which you burned up in me, it is well
That you should make up for it by talking.

Begin therefore; and say to what end
Your soul is directed, and be assured that
Your sight has lost its way but is not dead;

For the lady who is conducting you here,
Through this divine territory, has in her looks
The power Ananias had in his hand.'

I said: 'As she pleases, sooner or later,
May there be a cure for these eyes which were the
    gates
Through which she entered with the fire I still
    burn with.

The good which is the satisfaction here
Is Alpha and Omega of all the writings
Love reads to me in low tones or aloud.'

The same voice which had taken away the fear
I had felt at my sudden loss of sight,
Gave me another occasion for conversation,

And said: 'Certainly, but you must undergo
A further examination: for you must tell me
What it was that directed you to the target?'

And I: 'By philosophic arguments
And by authority which derives from here,
This love must be imprinted upon me.

For the good, so far as it is apprehended,
By its nature invites love, and does so the more
The more goodness there is contained in it.

Therefore it is to the Essence so superabundant
That every good which has an existence outside it
Is nothing more than a light from its radiance,

Rather than to any other object of love,
That must be moved the mind of everyone
Who sees the truth on which this proof is
    founded.

This truth is made plain to my intellect
By him who demonstrates to me the nature
Of the primal love of all eternal beings.

It is made plain by the voice of that veracious
Author, who said to Moses, speaking of himself:
"I will make all my goodness pass before thee."

It is made plain by you also, at the beginning
Of the great proclamation which cries on earth
The secrets of the place above all other edicts.'

And I heard: 'By human reasoning
And by authorities which accord with it,
The chief of your loves looks to God.

But tell me if you are aware of anything else
Drawing you to him, so that you let me hear
How many teeth love has to bite you with.'

The holy intention of the eagle of Christ
Was not obscure to me, I saw indeed
In what direction he was leading my declaration.

So again I began: 'Every one of those bites
Which are able to make the heart turn to God
Work together with my charity;

For the creation of the world and my own exis-
        tence,
The death which he sustained that I might live,
And what every believer hopes, as I do,

Together with the awareness I have spoken of,
Have dragged us out of the sea of perverted love
And put us on the shore of the love that is straight.

The leaves which make leafy the whole garden
Of the eternal gardener, I love according
As he has given them a share of good.'

When I stopped speaking a most sweet song
Resounded through the heavens, and my lady
Said with the others: 'Holy, holy, holy!'

And as a bright light which breaks on a sleeper
Because the power of sight runs through his
        membranes,
From one to another, to meet the brilliance,

And the waking man hates what he sees,
So undiscerning is the sudden awakening
Until reflection comes to his aid;

So from my eyes did Beatrice chase away
Every speck with the beams of her eyes
Which would shine from a thousand miles away!

So that I saw better than I had before;
And in a sort of stupefaction I asked
About a fourth light that I saw was with us.

And my lady: 'Within that radiance
The first soul that ever the first power
Created, gazes with longing upon his maker.'

As the top of a bough, which bends as the wind
        passes,
And then moves back into place once more
By its own energy which lifts it up,

So did I in the time that she was speaking,
Marvelling, and then I was reassured
By the desire to speak which flamed up in me.

And I began; 'Only apple that was ever produced
Ripe from the first, O you ancient father
For whom every bride is daughter and daughter-
        in-law,

Devoutly as I may I supplicate you:
Speak to me: you know what my wish is,
And to hear you the sooner I refrain from expres-
        sing it.'

Sometimes an animal under cover stirs
So that what he is after must appear
By the way the undergrowth follows his move-
        ments;

And so it was with the first of all souls;
He made it appear through the light that covered
        him,
How it delighted him to give me pleasure.

From it a breath: 'Although you do not utter it,
I can discern what you wish better
Than you can the things you see most clearly;

Because I see it in the true mirror
Which makes itself the image of other things
While nothing makes itself the image of him.

You want to hear how long it is since God put me
In that garden upon the mountain-top,
Where he prepared you for the long stairway.

And how long it delighted my eyes
And the exact reason for the great anger,
And the kind of language I used and indeed con-
    structed.

Now my son, the tasting of the tree
Was not in itself the reason for our exile,
But only the fact of going beyond the bounds.

From that place whence your lady brought Virgil,
I longed for this assembly while the sun
Revolved four thousand three hundred and two
    years;

And I saw it return to all the stars
On its pathway, nine hundred and thirty times
While I remained upon the earth below.

The language I spoke had fallen into disuse
Before the work that could not be completed
Was ever attempted by Nimrod's people;

For because human wishes are always changing,
Following the stars, never was any product
Of human reason made to last for ever.

That man should speak is a natural phenomenon;
But whether this way or that, nature allows
You to work out, as seems best to you.

Before I went down to the infernal anguish,
YAH was, on earth, the name of the highest good
From whom there comes the happiness which
    surrounds me;

And then he was called EL; which is as it should be,
For mortal usage is like a leaf on a bough;
One goes away and another comes in its place.

On the mountain which rises highest above the
    waves,
I was, counting my pure life and the other,
From the first hour until the hour which follows

The sixth hour, when the sun passes meridian.'

RETROMEDIEVALISM II: PEARL

Alongside Dante's prodigious and comprehensive effort at retromedievalism should be placed *Pearl,* which dates from late-fourteenth-century England. *Pearl* was written in an unfashionable local dialect, by an anonymous member of the gentry in the English midlands within a hundred miles north of Oxford. The two works are very different. *The Divine Comedy* is a four-hundred-page synthesis of theology, classical learning, medieval literary traditions, and Florentine politics. It has fused these multivaried sources so as to bring all of medieval culture to envelop the reader in a unique dramatization that Dante's imagination has solidified into a substratum of all the best that was thought in the Middle Ages. Both in his day and now, there is a widespread judgment that he succeeded. The *Comedy's* weakness, aside from a proclivity to excessive allusion to contemporary events and personalities, is its overassertiveness, a humanistic egoism that shows through at times. *Pearl* is some thirty pages long. It is an elegy for a dead child, a little girl, by someone who loves her dearly, presumably a parent or perhaps a sibling. It makes use, like Dante, of the traditional genre of a dream poem. The poet dreams he comes to a place where across the stream he can recognize his beloved lost one, who has been hypostatized into the precious pearl, again a common motif. He can communicate but cannot cross the river. Thus both *The Divine Comedy* and *Pearl* are formally dream reveries. But whereas *Comedy* is comprehensive and all-inclusive, *Pearl* closely articulates a narrow band of ideas and feelings. While *Comedy* provides an integrated encyclopedia, *Pearl* signals one person's emotions but within a formal and traditional genre. *Pearl* communicates a feeling of loss and at the same time exaltation in concentrated, tightly focused discourse. *Comedy* is like the medieval church, huge and amorphous, commanding every conceivable resource, and billowing out in all directions. *Pearl* is the evocation of a single moment of bittersweet illumination, very private and yet universal in its message. This combination of individualism and universalism is also characteristically medieval. *Comedy* reruns virtually the whole Middle Ages in speeded-up pace, pausing now and again for projection of a still frame. *Pearl* reminds at one moment what the spiritual intensity and cultural power of the Middle Ages were and may yet be again—in the "great symmetry," in the words of the *Pearl* poet, of this unique civilization. Here is the concluding section of *Pearl* in the splendid verse translation of Marie Borroff.

Beneath the moon so much amazed
No fleshly heart could bear to be
As by that city on which I gazed,
Its form so wondrous was to see.
As a quail that couches, dumb and dazed,
I stared on that great symmetry;
Nor rest nor travail my soul could taste,
Pure radiance so had ravished me.
For this I say with certainty:
Had a man in the body borne that boon,
No doctor's art, for fame or fee,
Had saved his life beneath the moon.

As the great moon begins to shine
While lingers still the light of day,
So in those ramparts crystalline
I saw a procession wend its way.
Without a summons, without a sign,
The city was full in vast array
Of maidens in such raiment fine
As my blissful one had worn that day.
As she was crowned, so crowned were they;
Adorned with pearls, in garments white;
And in like fashion, gleaming gay,
They bore the pearl of great delight.

With great delight, serene and slow,
They moved through every golden street;
Thousands on thousands, row on row,
All in one raiment shining sweet.
Who gladdest looked, was hard to know;
The Lamb led on at station meet,
Seven horns of gold upon his brow,
His robe like pearls with rays replete.
Soon they approached God's mighty seat;
Though thick in throng, unhurried quite;

As maidens at communion meet
They moved along with great delight.

Delight that at his coming grew
Was greater than my tongue can tell;
The elders when he came in view
Prostrate as one before him fell;
Hosts of angels in retinue
Cast incense forth of sweetest smell;
Then all in concert praised anew
That jewel with whom in joy they dwell.
The sound could pierce through the earth to hell
When the powers of heaven in song unite;
To share his praises in citadel
My heart indeed had great delight.

Delight and wonder filled me in flood
To hear all heaven the Lamb acclaim;
Gladdest he was, most kind and good
Of any that ever was known to fame.
His dress so white, so mild his mood,
His looks so gracious, himself the same;
But a wound there was, and wide it stood,
Thrust near his heart with deadly aim.
Down his white side the red blood came;
"O God," thought I, "who had such spite?
A breast should consume with sorrow and shame
Ere in such deeds it took delight."

The Lamb's delight was clearly seen,
Though a bitter wound he had to bear;
So glorious was his gaze serene,
It gladdened all who beheld him there.
I looked where that bright host had been,
How charged with life, how changed they were.
And then I saw my little queen

Moved by delight of sight and sound,
My maddened mind all fate defied.
I would follow her there, my newly found,
Beyond the river though she must bide.
I thought that nothing could turn me round,
Forestall me, or stop me in mid-stride,
And wade I would from the nearer ground
And breast the stream, though I sank and died.
But soon those thoughts were thrust aside;
As I made for the river incontinent
I was summoned away and my wish denied:
My Prince therewith was not content.

It contented him not that I, distraught,
Should dare the river that rimmed the glade;
Though reckless I was, and overwrought,
In a moment's space my steps were stayed.
For just as I started from the spot
I was reft of my dream and left dismayed;
I waked in that same garden-plot,
On that same mound my head was laid.
I stretched my hand where Pearl had strayed;
Great fear befell me, and wonderment;
And, sighing, to myself I said,
"Let all things be to his content."

I was ill content to be dispossessed
Of the sight of her that had no peer
Amid those scenes so bright and blessed;
Such longing seized me, I swooned, or near;
Then sorrow broke from my burning breast;
"O honored Pearl," I said, "how dear
Was your every word and wise behest
In this true vision vouchsafed me here.
If you in a garland never sere
Are set by that Prince all-provident,
Then happy am I in dungeon drear
That he with you is well content."

Had I but sought to content my Lord
And taken his gifts without regret,
And held my place and heeded the word
Of the noble Pearl so strangely met,
Drawn heavenward by divine accord
I had seen and heard more mysteries yet;
But always men would have and hoard
And gain the more, the more they get.
So banished I was, by cares beset,

Reliquary statue of St. Foy

That I thought but now I had stood so near.
Lord! how she laughed and made good cheer
Among her friends, who was so white!
To rush in the river then and there
I longed with love and great delight.

From realms eternal untimely sent;
How madly, Lord, they strive and fret
Whose acts accord not with your content!

To content that Prince and well agree,
Good Christians can with ease incline,
For day and night he has proved to be
A Lord, a God, a friend benign.
These words came over the mound to me

As I mourned my Pearl so flawless fine,
And to God committed her full and free,
With Christ's dear blessing bestowing mine,
As in the form of bread and wine
Is shown us daily in sacrament;
O may we serve him well, and shine
As precious pearls to his content.

Amen.

AUTHOR'S INDEX

COPYRIGHT ACKNOWLEDGMENTS

Garland Publishing Co., Inc.
Chretien de Troyes: Lancelot or, **The Knight of the Cart (Le Chevalier de la Charrete)** trans. by William W. Kibler, New York: Garland Publishing, Inc., 1981. Reprinted with permission.
The Dramas of Hrotsvit of Gandersheim, trans. by Katharina M. Wilson. Reprinted with permission from Katharina M. Wilson, **The Plays of Hrotsvit of Gandersheim** (New York: Garland Publishing, Inc. 1989).

HarperCollins Publishers
Sources of English Constitutional History, by Carl E. Stephenson and Frederick George Marcham. Copyright 1937 by Harper & Brothers, copyright renewed 1965 by Harper & Row Publishers, Inc. Reprinted by permission of HarperCollins Publishers, Inc.

Harvard University Press
The Steps of Humility, by Bernard, Abbot of Clairvaux, trans. by George Bosworth Burch, Cambridge Mass.: Harvard University Press, Copyright © 1940 by the President and Fellows of Harvard College.

Houghton Mifflin Company
The Poems of Francos Villon, trans by Galway Kinnell. Copyright © 1965, 1977 by Galway Kinnell. Reprinted by permission of Houghton Mifflin Co. All rights reserved.

Hodder & Stoughton
The Confessions of St. Augustine, trans. E.M. Blaiklock, 1983, by permission of the publisher and also of Thomas Nelson & Sons; Nashville, Tenn.

Kyle Cathie Limited
The English Mystics, trans. by Karen Armstrong, published by kind permission of the author and Kyle Cathie Ltd.

Labyrinth Press, and Robert Hanning
The Lais of Marie De France, trans by Robert Hanning and Joan Ferrante (1983). Durham, N.C., Labyrinth Press. Reprinted with permission of Labyrinth Press and Robert Hanning.

Longman Publishing Group and C.T. Allmand
Society at War, ed. by C.T. Allmand, reprinted with permissions of Longman Publishing Group, U.K. and C.T. Allmand.

Manchester University Press
The Poem of Cid, trans. by Rita Hamilton & Janet Perry Reprinted by permission of Manchester University Press.

Oxford University Press
Alcuin: The Bishops, Kings, and Saints of York, edited by Peter Godman (1982). Reprinted by permission of Oxford University Press'.
De Nugis Curalium: Courtiers' Trifles, by Walker Map, edited and translated by C.N.L. Brooke and R.A.B. Mynors (1983) Reprinted by permission of Oxford University Press.
The Ecclesiastical History of Orderic Vitalis, edited and trans. by Marjorie Chibnall, vol. IV (1973) Reprinted by permission of Oxford University Press.

The History of the Franks, by Gregory of Tours, translated by O.M. Dalton (1927). Reprinted by permission of Oxford University Press.

Paulist Press
Albert & Thomas: Selected Writings, Simon Tugwell, O.P., trans. and ed. © 1988 by Simon Tugwell, O.P. Used by permission of Paulist Press.
Apocalyptic Spirituality, trans. by Bernard McGinn. © 1979 by the Missionary Society of St. Paul the Apostle in the State of New York. Used by permission of Paulist Press.
Hildegard of Bingen, trans. by Mother Columba Hart and Jane Bishop. © 1990 by the Abbey of Regina Laudis: Benedictine Congregation Regina Laudis of the Strict Observance, Inc. Used by permission of Paulist Press.

Penguin Books Ltd.
The Book of Margery Kempe, trans. by BA Windeatt (Penguin Classics, 1985) copyright © BA Windeatt, 1985.
The Canterbury Tales, by Geoffrey Chaucer, trans. by Barbara Reynolds, (Penguin Classics 1951, Fourth revised edition 1977) copyright © Nevill Coghill, 1951, 1958, 1960, 1975, 1977.
Chronicles of The Crusades by Joinville and Villehardouin, trans. by MRB Shaw (Penguin Classics, 1963) copyright © M.R.B. Shaw, 1963.
The Decameron by Boccaccio, trans. by GH McWilliam (Penguin Classics, 1972) copyright © GH McWilliam, 1972
La Vita Nuova by Dante Alighieri, trans. by Barbara Reynolds (Penguin Classics, 1969) copyright © Barbara Reynolds, 1969.
Laxdaela Saga, trans. by Magnus Magnusson and Hermann Palsson (Penguin Classics, 1969) copyright © Magnus Magnusson and Hermann Palsson, 1969.
Le Morte D'Arthur, by Sir Thomas Malory, trans. by Keith Baines, translation copyright © 1962 by Keith Baines, renewed © 1990 by Francesca Evans. Introduction © 1962 by Robert Graves, renewed © 1990 by Beryl Graves. Used by permission of Dutton Signet, a division of Penguin Books USA Inc.
The Nibelunglied, trans. by A.T. Hatto (Penguin Classics, Revised ed. 1969)copyright © A.T. Hatto, 1965, 1969.
Parzival by Wolfram von Wschenbach, trans. by A.T. Hatto (Penguin Classics, 1980) copyright © A.T. Hatto, 1980.
The Quest of the Holy Grail, trans. by P.M. Matarasso (Penguin Classics, 1969) copyright © PM Matarasso
The Romance of the Rose, by Guillaume de Lorris and Jean de Meun, trans. by Harry W. Robbins, Translation copyright © 1962 by Florence L. Robbins, Introduction by Charles W. Dunn Copyright © 1962 by E.P. Dutton. Used by permission of Dutton Signet, a division of Penguin Books USA Inc.
Thomas A' Kempis. The Imitation of Christ, trans by. Leo Sherley-Price (Penguin Classics, 1952) copyright © Leo Sherley-Price, 1952.
The Treasure of the City of Ladies, by Christine de Pisan, trans. by Sarah Lawson (Penguin Classics, 1985) copyright © Sarah Lawson, 1985.

ILLUSTRATION CREDITS